THE INSTRUCTOR'S EDITION
CONTEMPORARY
READER

THIRD EDITION

THE INSTRUCTOR'S EDITION CONTEMPORARY READER

THIRD EDITION

Edited by
GARY GOSHGARIAN
Northeastern University

90

SCOTT, FORESMAN/LITTLE, BROWN HIGHER EDUCATION
A Division of Scott, Foresman and Company
Glenview, Illinois   London, England

Acknowledgments
Acknowledgments for the copyrighted materials not credited on
the page where they appear are listed in the Ackowledgments
section beginning on page 489. This section is to be considered a legal
extension of the copyright page.

Library of Congress Cataloging-in-Publication Data

The Contemporary reader / edited by Gary Goshgarian. — 3rd. ed.,
  instructor's ed.
        p.   cm.
  Rev. ed. of the The Contemporary reader from Little, Brown.
  ISBN 0-673-49885-9
    1. College readers.   2. English language—Rhetoric.
  I. Goshgarian, Gary.   II. Contemporary reader from Little, Brown.
  PE1417.C6523   1990
  808′.0427—dc20   89-10859
                                                                                       CIP

ISBN 0-673-52001-3, Student's Edition

The Instructor's Edition for *The Contemporary Reader,* Third Edition, contains
the same material covered in the Students' Edition along with an Instructor's
Manual beginning after the Student Edition.

THE INSTRUCTOR'S EDITION
CONTEMPORARY
READER

THIRD EDITION

This book is dedicated to my sons,
Nathan and David

▼ PREFACE

When the first edition of *The Contemporary Reader* came out in 1984, it was the only such reader on the college market. Dozens of freshman comp anthologies existed, full of bearded standards such as Jonathan Swift's "A Modest Proposal," George Orwell's "Shooting an Elephant" and Thucydides' "Corcyraen Revolution;" but there was not a single collection available that contained essays exclusively about contemporary experiences students could relate to—essays that were well written and that inspired students' enthusiasm.

Years of experience had revealed that students performed best when their own interests were addressed, and so the first edition of *The Contemporary Reader* was developed as an experiment to fill this obvious hole in the market. It was a collection containing essays specifically selected for their interest and accessibility to college students; essays on subjects students could relate to; essays that talked about the time and culture students were part of; and, of course, essays that inspired thought, stimulated class discussion, and served as writing models.

The enthusiastic response to the first edition made evident the experiment was a success. The even greater response to the second edition (1987) convinced us that we had started a good thing. This third edition reflects that enthusiasm.

▼ NEW TO THE THIRD EDITION

The Contemporary Reader must, by its very nature, be kept current. Therefore, I have made some major changes, several at the suggestions of instructors and students who used the second edition. Each of the thirteen areas has been updated and strengthened, and a fourteenth, "On Death and Dying," has been added. Dated material and readings that no longer seemed to meet the needs of students and instructors have been dropped, and new topics have been added—essays on the homeless in America, the AIDS epidemic, the rise of gang violence, women and the military, women and sports, the language of rock music, and religious faith. The Third Edition also includes pro-and-con views on euthanasia, capital punishment, gun control, and the legalization of drugs. In fact, there are thirty-one new essays in this edition, twenty-five of which have been written since the previous edition and are reprinted here for the first time.

The Contemporary Reader, Third Edition, contains eighty-seven selections, only a handful of which were written before 1980. Those few are classic pieces by prose masters, such as E.B. White, James Thurber, and Langston Hughes, and are as fresh today as they were when written.

▼ ABOUT THE ESSAYS

The third edition still reflects the wide range of student interests: television, advertising, the media, sports, the natural world, abortion, the nuclear threat, dating, sexual roles, the latest fads, jogging, gun control, weight control, drug control, capital punishment, teenage pregnancy, religious conversion, death and dying, and more. The writers are as diverse as their subjects: Maya Angelou, Jonathan Kozol, Loren Eiseley, Martin Luther King, Jr., Elizabeth Kübler-Ross, and Roger Angell, as well as familiar humorists such as Erma Bombeck, Dave Barry, Andy Rooney, Russell Baker, and Art Buchwald.

Many of the authors are well-known professional editors or columnists: Ellen Goodman, William F. Buckley, Jr., George F. Will, William Raspberry, Calvin Trillin, Diane White, Jeff Greenfield, Gwynne Dyer, Michael Kinsley, and Lance Morrow. Noted scientists and prize-winning authors are represented by Carl Sagan, Lewis Thomas, Stephen Jay Gould, and Dr. Benjamin Spock.

Also included are previously unanthologized essays by some of the most popular novelists writing today—Robert B. Parker, William F. Buckley, Jr., Garrison Keillor, Dan Wakefield, and Caryl Rivers.

The writing styles and techniques are equally diverse. Contained in this collection are examples of the "basic" essay as well as editorials, satirical narratives, letters, parodies, journal entries, parables, news reports, descriptive narratives, pointed arguments, commercial ads, and more. They vary in length from 500 words to 2000—a range most writing assignments fall within.

Debates

Essays on controversial topics are a special feature of *The Contemporary Reader,* Third Edition. As in the first two editions, many contemporary issues are examined from opposing points of view. Most of the fourteen sections contain debates. They might be indirect, as in Part 6, "On Television," where Jeff Greenfield's article "Don't Blame TV" argues against some of the preceding viewpoints on the dangers of television. Sometimes the arguments meet head-on, as do Edward Koch's and David Bruck's opposing views on capital punishment (in the "Conscience and Controversy" section). Sometimes writers make direct assaults on each other, as in Part 11, "War and Peace in the Nuclear Age," where Michael Kinsley in "Nuclear Holocaust in Perspective" attacks Jonathan Schell's stand in "The Effects of a Nuclear Explosion" as well as the nuclear freeze movement.

Debates can be found in non-issue sections as well. Part 7, "On Advertising," for example, contrasts some barbed attacks on TV commercials back-to-back with a cogent defense of familiar ads by professional advertiser Charles O'Neill.

Humor

There is no reason why the writing experience should not be fun, nor is there any reason why writing models cannot be entertaining. As you will discover, many of the selections in *The Contemporary Reader,* Third Edition, are funny and entertaining, and their humor has much to say. Nearly every section contains some humorous pieces. Even Part 11, "War and Peace in the Nuclear Age," concludes with Art Buchwald's satirical narrative, "Evacuating the Capital? No Need to Hurry Now."

Advertisements

Because of the strong response to the magazine ads in the section "On Advertising," the Third Edition includes a new sampling of recently run ads with specific questions to help students closely analyze how advertising works on us—and to spark some lively class discussions.

Apparatus

This book is not just a collection of interesting thoughts on contemporary experience. The selections offer varied but solid assistance to composition students trying to develop their own writing abilities. First, all of the essays were written by professionals, and so they serve as models of many different expository techniques and patterns. Second, each selection is preceded by a headnote containing thematic and biographic information, as well as clues to writing techniques and strategies. Third, each piece is followed by a series of review questions covering both thoughts and themes ("Topical Considerations") and compositional features ("Rhetorical Considerations"). These questions have been designed to help students think analytically about the content and form of the essays. Some writing assignments are also included to suggest ways students might relate the essays to other selections and to their own experiences. There is also a rhetorical table of contents in this edition, which groups the text's essays.

▼ ACKNOWLEDGMENTS

In producing this book, many people behind the scenes deserve thanks and acknowledgment. It would be impossible to thank all of them, but there are some for whose help I am particularly grateful. I would like to thank the following instructors who have rated the effectiveness of the essays and offered helpful comments and suggestions. They are Annette Adair, Yvonne J. Milspaw, Patricia L. Rottmund, Jon W. Tarrant, Carolyn L. Williams, and Gwen Yackee of Harrisburg Area Community College; Nancy Bent, Ithaca College; Michael Berberich, University of Nevada, Reno; Roberta Bothwell, Erie Community College; Cynthia Butos and Elizabeth Marafino, Tunxis Community College; Dorothy Cook, Wayne Cook, and Robert Spiegel, Central Connecticut State University; Terence A. Dalrymple and Kathleen Holcomb, Angelo State University; Patricia Harker and Bill Scarpaci, Rock Valley College; Bruce Hoffman, Rockland Community College; Marilyn Monaghan, Gwynedd-Mercy College; James Pictor, Saint Francis College; Charles Reinhart, Vincennes University; Roberta Simone, Grand Valley State College; and Nancy Sprehe, Kansas State University. I am also enormously grateful to all the instructors and students who used the first two editions of *The Contemporary Reader.*

A special thanks goes out to Professors David Vinopal of Paul Smith's College, Ann Taylor and Richard Elia of Salem State College, Michele Souda of Harvard University, and Mary Lee Donahue of Glassboro State College; also I must thank my colleagues Guy Rotella, Francis Blessington, Kathleen Kelley, and Marvin X. Lesser for their good suggestions of new material. Thanks also to Pamela B. Farrell for her continued support and encouragement.

Very special thanks also must be given to the people of Scott, Foresman/ Little Brown, particularly my editor Ted Simpson who cheerfully adopted me. Thanks.

Finally, to my wife Kathleen for her insight, her patience, and many hours of assistance—my loving appreciation.

GARY GOSHGARIAN

▼ CONTENTS

▼ RHETORICAL TABLE OF CONTENTS

PROCESS ANALYSIS: *Step-By-Step Explanation of How Something Operates*

COMPARISON AND CONTRAST: *Examining Similarities and Differences*

DIVISION AND CLASSIFICATION: *Sorting Things Out*

PERSUASION AND ARGUMENT: *Appealing to Reason and Emotions*

HUMOR AND SATIRE: *Making Us Laugh While We Think*

PERSONAL
DISCOVERIES

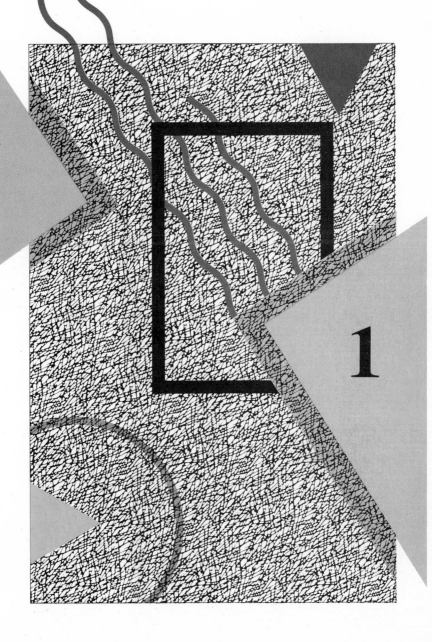

1

▼ SHAME
Dick Gregory

Dick Gregory is a well-known satirist, whose humor cuts below the surface of comedy. As a stand-up comic, he was a regular on a variety of television shows during the 1960s and 1970s. He continues to be active in the Civil Rights Movement. In recent years, Gregory has become a noted nutritionist, devoting his efforts to helping people suffering from obesity. The essay below is a sensitive narrative of a childhood experience that taught Gregory the meaning of shame. The selection comes from Gregory's 1964 autobiography, *nigger.*

I never learned hate at home, or shame. I had to go to school for that. I was about 1 seven years old when I got my first big lesson. I was in love with a little girl named Helene Tucker, a light-complexioned little girl with pigtails and nice manners. She was always clean and she was smart in school. I think I went to school then mostly to look at her. I brushed my hair and even got me a little old handkerchief. It was a lady's handkerchief, but I didn't want Helene to see me wipe my nose on my hand. The pipes were frozen again, there was no water in the house, but I washed my socks and shirt every night. I'd get a pot, and go over to Mister Ben's grocery store, and stick my pot down into his soda machine. Scoop out some chopped ice. By evening the ice melted to water for washing. I got sick a lot that winter because the fire would go out at night before the clothes were dry. In the morning I'd put them on, wet or dry, because they were the only clothes I had.

Everybody's got a Helene Tucker, a symbol of everything you want. I loved 2 her for her goodness, her cleanness, her popularity. She'd walk down my street and my brothers and sisters would yell, "Here comes Helene," and I'd rub my tennis sneakers on the back of my pants and wish my hair wasn't so nappy and the white folks' shirt fit me better. I'd run out on the street. If I knew my place and didn't come too close, she'd wink at me and say hello. That was a good feeling. Sometimes I'd follow her all the way home, and shovel the snow off her walk and try to make friends with her Momma and her aunts. I'd drop money on her stoop late at night on my way back from shining shoes in the taverns. And she had a Daddy, and he had a good job. He was a paper hanger.

I guess I would have gotten over Helene by summertime, but something 3 happened in that classroom that made her face hang in front of me for the next twenty-two years. When I played the drums in high school it was for Helene and when I broke track records in college it was for Helene and when I started standing behind microphones and heard applause I wished Helene could hear it, too. It wasn't until I was twenty-nine years old and married and making money that I finally got her out of my system. Helene was sitting in that classroom when I learned to be ashamed of myself.

It was on a Thursday. I was sitting in the back of the room, in a seat with a chalk circle drawn around it. The idiot's seat, the troublemaker's seat.   4

The teacher thought I was stupid. Couldn't spell, couldn't read, couldn't do arithmetic. Just stupid. Teachers were never interested in finding out that you couldn't concentrate because you were so hungry, because you hadn't had any breakfast. All you could think about was noontime, would it ever come? Maybe you could sneak into the cloakroom and steal a bite of some kid's lunch out of a coat pocket. A bite of something. Paste. You can't really make a meal of paste, or put it on bread for a sandwich, but sometimes I'd scoop a few spoonfuls out of the paste jar in the back of the room. Pregnant people get strange tastes. I was pregnant with poverty. Pregnant with dirt and pregnant with smells that made people turn away, pregnant with cold and pregnant with shoes that were never bought for me, pregnant with five other people in my bed and no Daddy in the next room, and pregnant with hunger. Paste doesn't taste too bad when you're hungry.   5

The teacher thought I was a troublemaker. All she saw from the front of the room was a little black boy who squirmed in his idiot's seat and made noises and poked the kids around him. I guess she couldn't see a kid who made noises because he wanted someone to know he was there.   6

It was on a Thursday, the day before the Negro payday. The eagle always flew on Friday. The teacher was asking each student how much his father would give to the Community Chest. On Friday night, each kid would get the money from his father, and on Monday he would bring it to the school. I decided I was going to buy me a Daddy right then. I had money in my pocket from shining shoes and selling papers, and whatever Helene Tucker pledged for her Daddy I was going to top it. And I'd hand the money right in. I wasn't going to wait until Monday to buy me a Daddy.   7

I was shaking, scared to death. The teacher opened her book and started calling out names alphabetically.   8

"Helene Tucker?"   9

"My daddy said he'd give two dollars and fifty cents."   10

"That's very nice, Helene. Very, very nice indeed."   11

That made me feel pretty good. It wouldn't take too much to top that. I had almost three dollars in dimes and quarters in my pocket. I stuck my hand in my pocket and held onto the money, waiting for her to call my name. But the teacher closed her book after she called everybody else in the class.   12

I stood up and raised my hand.   13

"What is it now?"   14

"You forgot me."   15

She turned toward the blackboard. "I don't have time to be playing with you, Richard."   16

"My Daddy said he'd ... "   17

"Sit down, Richard, you're disturbing the class."   18

"My Daddy said he'd give ... fifteen dollars."   19

She turned around and looked mad. "We are collecting this money for you   20 and your kind, Richard Gregory. If your Daddy can give fifteen dollars you have no business being on relief."

"I got it right now, I got it right now, my Daddy gave it to me to turn in today, my Daddy said . . . "   21

"And furthermore," she said, looking right at me, her nostrils getting big and her lips getting thin and her eyes opening wide, "we know you don't have a Daddy."   22

Helene Tucker turned around, her eyes full of tears. She felt sorry for me. Then I couldn't see her too well because I was crying, too.   23

"Sit down, Richard."   24

And I always thought the teacher kind of liked me. She always picked me to wash the blackboard on Friday, after school. That was a big thrill, it made me feel important. If I didn't wash it, come Monday the school might not function right.   25

"Where are you going, Richard?"   26

I walked out of school that day, and for a long time I didn't go back very often. There was shame there.   27

Now there was shame everywhere. It seemed like the whole world had been inside that classroom, everyone had heard what the teacher had said, everyone had turned around and felt sorry for me. There was shame in going to the Worthy Boys Annual Christmas Dinner for you and your kind, because everybody knew what a worthy boy was. Why couldn't they just call it the Boys Annual Dinner; why'd they have to give it a name? There was shame in wearing the brown and orange and white plaid mackinaw the welfare gave to three thousand boys. Why'd it have to be the same for everybody so when you walked down the street the people could see you were on relief? It was a nice warm mackinaw and it had a hood, and my Momma beat me and called me a little rat when she found out I stuffed it in the bottom of a pail full of garbage way over on Cottage Street. There was shame in running over to Mister Ben's at the end of the day and asking for his rotten peaches, there was shame in asking Mrs. Simmons for a spoonful of sugar, there was shame in running out to meet the relief truck. I hated that truck, full of food for you and your kind. I ran into the house and hid when it came. And then I started to sneak through alleys, to take the long way home so the people going into White's Eat Shop wouldn't see me. Yeah, the whole world heard the teacher that day, we all know you don't have a Daddy.   28

▼ TOPICAL CONSIDERATIONS

1. Gregory tried so hard to impress Helene Tucker that he often got sick from wearing wet clothes that couldn't dry because the fire had gone out in the night. When you were growing up, was there any one person for whom you went to such extremes to impress? What did you do? What was he or she like? Do you know any adults who would go (or have gone) to such extremes?

2. Helene Tucker seems to have been a success symbol for Gregory when he

was a child. He comments: "Everybody's got a Helene Tucker, a symbol of everything you want" (paragraph 2). What does Gregory's description of Helene tell you about what success meant to him? What influenced his view? Describe a person who represents success to you. What influences have shaped this view?

3. What do you think of the way Gregory handled himself in school the day the teacher embarrassed him? Would you have responded in the same way? Was his refusal to go to school after this incident the only way he could deal with his shame? What would have been your answer?

4. Is shame caused by outward circumstances or by what an individual has done himself? Which should it be? What does shame mean to Gregory? What does it mean to you?

5. Why did the memory of Helene Tucker's presence the day he was shamed in class motivate Gregory to excel as a teenager? Do you think this is a useful motivational device? What other incentives can be effective?

6. Gregory remarks that he wasn't able to get Helene Tucker out of his system for twenty-two years. Why was he finally able to forget her? Do you think that if he were confronted with the same kind of experience now, he would respond in the same way? Why? Is there anything about Gregory's experience that you can relate to your own life?

7. How sensitive was the teacher? How else might she have responded to Gregory?

8. Do you think most welfare recipients are like Gregory and do not want to be on welfare? Give reasons for your answer.

▼ RHETORICAL CONSIDERATIONS

1. Where does Gregory state his thesis? Is this the best place for it? Explain.

2. What adjectives does Gregory use in his description of Helene Tucker in the first paragraph? Does he use too many? Not enough? Are they essential to the development of his thesis? Why or why not?

3. What is the primary rhetorical pattern Gregory uses in this essay? Are others used as well? Cite sample passages.

4. Does Gregory *tell* or *show* his reader how he feels about Helene Tucker? What rhetorical patterns does he use to accomplish this?

5. What can you say about Gregory's conclusion? Does it tie in with his thesis? Is it an effective ending? Why or why not?

▼ WRITING ASSIGNMENTS

1. Have you ever had an experience that caused you to feel shame? Write an essay describing the incident. Include concrete details, illustrations, and dialogue (as Gregory does) that will show your reader exactly what happened.

2. What does success mean to you? In an essay, analyze your own answer to this question. Discuss the influences that have shaped your view.
3. Write an essay describing someone you idealize and would like to impress. Narrate some of the things you would do or have done to gain this person's esteem.

▼ BLACK MEN AND PUBLIC SPACE

Brent Staples

Brent Staples, born in Chester, Pennsylvania in 1951, is first assistant metropolitan editor of the *New York Times*. In the piece below, Staples tells of a shocking realization he had at the age of twenty-two: that because he was a black male, he could "alter public space in ugly ways." Forever a suspect, Staples describes the alienation and danger he suffers from such a perception—a perception he has learned to deal with. This essay appeared in *Harper*'s in December 1987.

My first victim was a woman—white, well dressed, probably in her early twenties. I came upon her late one evening on a deserted street in Hyde Park, a relatively affluent neighborhood in an otherwise mean, impoverished section of Chicago. As I swung onto the avenue behind her, there seemed to be a discreet, uninflammatory distance between us. Not so. She cast back a worried glance. To her, the youngish black man—a broad six feet two inches with a beard and billowing hair, both hands shoved into the pockets of a bulky military jacket—seemed menacingly close. After a few more quick glimpses, she picked up her pace and was soon running in earnest. Within seconds she disappeared into a cross street. 1

That was more than a decade ago, I was twenty-two years old, a graduate student newly arrived at the University of Chicago. It was in the echo of that terrified woman's footfalls that I first began to know the unwieldy inheritance I'd come into—the ability to alter public space in ugly ways. It was clear that she thought herself the quarry of a mugger, a rapist, or worse. Suffering a bout of insomnia, however, I was stalking sleep, not defenseless wayfarers. As a softy who is scarcely able to take a knife to a raw chicken—let alone hold one to a person's throat—I was surprised, embarrassed, and dismayed all at once. Her flight made me feel like an accomplice in tyranny. It also made it clear that I was indistinguishable from the muggers who occasionally seeped into the area from the surrounding ghetto. That first encounter, and those that followed, signified that a vast, unnerving gulf lay between nighttime pedestrians—particularly women—and me. And I soon gathered that being perceived as dangerous is a hazard in itself. I only needed to turn a corner into a dicey situation, or crowd some frightened, armed person in a foyer somewhere, or make an errant move after being pulled over by a policeman. Where fear and weapons meet—and they often do in urban America—there is always the possibility of death. 2

In that first year, my first away from my hometown, I was to become thoroughly familiar with the language of fear. At dark, shadowy intersections, I could 3 cross in front of a car stopped at a traffic light and elicit the *thunk, thunk, thunk, thunk* of the driver—black, white, male, or female—hammering down the door locks. On less traveled streets after dark, I grew accustomed to but never comfortable with people crossing to the other side of the street rather than pass me. Then there were the standard unpleasantries with policemen, doormen, bouncers, cabdrivers, and others whose business it is to screen out troublesome individuals *before* there is any nastiness.

I moved to New York nearly two years ago and I have remained an avid night   4
walker. In central Manhattan, the near-constant crowd cover minimizes tense one-on-one street encounters. Elsewhere—in SoHo, for example, where sidewalks are narrow and tightly spaced buildings shut out the sky—things can get very taut indeed.

After dark, on the warrenlike streets of Brooklyn where I live, I often see   5
women who fear the worst from me. They seem to have set their faces on neutral, and with their purse straps strung across their chests bandolier-style, they forge ahead as though bracing themselves against being tackled. I understand, of course, that the danger they perceive is not a hallucination. Women are particularly vulnerable to street violence, and young black males are drastically over-represented among the perpetrators of that violence. Yet these truths are no solace against the kind of alienation that comes of being ever the suspect, a fearsome entity with whom pedestrians avoid making eye contact.

It is not altogether clear to me how I reached the ripe old age of twenty-two   6
without being conscious of the lethality nighttime pedestrians attributed to me. Perhaps it was because in Chester, Pennsylvania, the small, angry industrial town where I came of age in the 1960s, I was scarcely noticeable against a backdrop of gang warfare, street knifings, and murders. I grew up one of the good boys, had perhaps a half-dozen fistfights. In retrospect, my shyness of combat has clear sources.

As a boy, I saw countless tough guys locked away; I have since buried several,   7
too. They were babies, really—a teenage cousin, a brother of twenty-two, a childhood friend in his mid-twenties—all gone down in episodes of bravado played out in the streets. I came to doubt the virtues of intimidation early on. I chose, perhaps unconsciously, to remain a shadow—timid, but a survivor.

The fearsomeness mistakenly attributed to me in public places often has a   8
perilous flavor. The most frightening of these confusions occurred in the late 1970s and early 1980s, when I worked as a journalist in Chicago. One day, rushing into the office of a magazine I was writing for with a deadline story in hand, I was mistaken for a burglar. The office manager called security and, with an ad hoc posse, pursued me through the labyrinthine halls, nearly to my editor's door. I had no way of proving who I was. I could only move briskly toward the company of someone who knew me.

Another time I was on assignment for a local paper and killing time before an   9
interview. I entered a jewelry store on the city's affluent Near North Side. The proprietor excused herself and returned with an enormous red Doberman pinscher straining at the end of a leash. She stood, the dog extended toward me, silent to my questions, her eyes bulging nearly out of her head. I took a cursory look around, nodded, and bade her good night.

Relatively speaking, however, I never fared as badly as another black male 10 journalist. He went to nearby Waukegan, Illinois, a couple of summers ago to work on a story about a murderer who was born there. Mistaking the reporter for the killer, police officers hauled him from his car at gunpoint and but for his press credentials would probably have tried to book him. Such episodes are not uncommon. Black men trade tales like this all the time.

Over the years, I learned to smother the rage I felt at so often being taken for a 11 criminal. Not to do so would surely have led to madness. I now take precautions to make myself less threatening. I move about with care, particularly late in the evening. I give a wide berth to nervous people on subway platforms during the wee hours, particularly when I have exchanged business clothes for jeans. If I happen to be entering a building behind some people who appear skittish, I may walk by, letting them clear the lobby before I return, so as not to seem to be following them. I have been calm and extremely congenial on those rare occasions when I've been pulled over by the police.

And on late-evening constitutionals I employ what has proved to be an 12 excellent tension-reducing measure: I whistle melodies from Beethoven and Vivaldi and the more popular classical composers. Even steely New Yorkers hunching toward nighttime destinations seem to relax, and occasionally they even join in the tune. Virtually everybody seems to sense that a mugger wouldn't be warbling bright, sunny selections from Vivaldi's *Four Seasons.* It is my equivalent of the cowbell that hikers wear when they know they are in bear country.

▼ TOPICAL CONSIDERATIONS

1. What did Staples' episode with the fleeing woman in Hyde Park make him realize? How did it make him feel?
2. Staples learns that his being a black male is perceived as a danger to others. How could this perception be a hazard to him? How has this perception actually been hazardous to him?
3. How does Staples' personal background explain his unawareness of the threat he posed to nighttime pedestrians?
4. How does Staples explain the submergence of his rage at being "taken for a criminal"?
5. What are some of the ways Staples has tried to mitigate the threat he poses to other night pedestrians? If you were Staples, would you resort to these strategies or not bother at all?
6. Does Staples describe attitudes and fears to which you can relate?

▼ RHETORICAL CONSIDERATIONS

1. Comment on the effectiveness of the opening sentence of this essay. Why does Staples use the word "victim"? What is the woman a victim of?

2. Why does Staples choose to describe himself in the first paragraph?
3. Do you find any examples of humor in the essay? If so, do you think this humor adds to or detracts from the seriousness of the subject?

▼ WRITING ASSIGNMENTS

1. Have you ever felt threatened by a person or persons on a street at night? Write a paper in which you describe the experience and the threat you felt.
2. Have you ever been aware of the threat you might have posed to strangers in public places? If so, describe how you might have been perceived in such circumstances.
3. If you were Staples, how would you feel knowing that you were perceived as dangerous? Could you imagine yourself going through the measures he does, just to make those around you feel at ease? Write out your thoughts in an essay.

▼ THE AMBIVALENCE OF ABORTION

Linda Bird Francke

Abortion is one of the most controversial issues in our society. At the heart of all the moral, political, legal, and religious debates is the very definition of life itself. Does it begin at conception, or not? Does a fetus have human status and rights, or not? Science and the courts have not yet resolved these questions, and the issue is further complicated by the demands for a woman's right not to give birth to unwanted children. The author of the piece below powerfully dramatizes this fundamental conflict—a conflict between heart and mind. Francke tells how her strong pro-choice convictions suddenly came into question with her own conscience, when faced with her own unwanted pregnancy. Francke, who is a journalist and biographer, collaborated with Rosalynn Carter on *First Lady from Plains* (1984) and with Geraldine Ferraro on her autobiography, *Ferraro* (1986). Her latest collaboration is a work on Madame Jihan Sidat. Francke is also the author of *Growing up Divorced: Children of the Eighties* (1983). This article first appeared in the *New York Times* in 1976.

1   We were sitting in a bar on Lexington Avenue when I told my husband I was pregnant. It is not a memory I like to dwell on. Instead of the champagne and hope which had heralded the impending births of the first, second and third child, the news of this one was greeted with shocked silence and Scotch. "Jesus," my husband kept saying to himself, stirring the ice cubes around and around, "Oh, Jesus."

2   Oh, how we tried to rationalize it that night as the starting time for the movie came and went. My husband talked about his plans for a career change in the next year, to stem the staleness that fourteen years with the same investment-banking firm had brought him. A new baby would preclude that option.

3   The timing wasn't right for me either. Having juggled pregnancies and child care with what freelance jobs I could fit in between feedings, I had just taken on a full-time job. A new baby would put me right back in the nursery just when our youngest child was finally school age. It was time for *us,* we tried to rationalize. There just wasn't room in our lives now for another baby. We both agreed. And agreed. And agreed.

4   How very considerate they are at the Women's Services, known formally as the Center for Reproductive and Sexual Health. Yes, indeed, I could have an abortion that very Saturday morning and be out in time to drive to the country that afternoon. Bring a first morning urine specimen, a sanitary belt and napkins, a money order or $125 cash—and a friend.

My friend turned out to be my husband, standing awkwardly and ill at ease as   5
men always do in places that are exclusively for women, as I checked in at nine
A.M. Other men hovered around just as anxiously, knowing they had to be there,
wishing they weren't. No one spoke to each other. When I would be cycled out of
there four hours later, the same men would be slumped in their same seats, locked
downcast in their cells of embarrassment.

The Saturday morning women's group was more dispirited than the men in   6
the waiting room. There were around fifteen of us, a mixture of races, ages and
backgrounds. Three didn't speak English at all and a fourth, a pregnant Puerto
Rican girl around eighteen, translated for them.

There were six black women and a hodgepodge of whites, among them a   7
T-shirted teenager who kept leaving the room to throw up and a puzzled middle-
aged woman from Queens with three grown children.

"What form of birth control were you using?" the volunteer asked each one of   8
us. The answer was inevitably "none." She then went on to describe the various
forms of birth control available at the clinic, and offered them to each of us.

The youngest Puerto Rican girl was asked through the interpreter which she'd   9
like to use: the loop, diaphragm, or pill. She shook her head "no" three times.
"You don't want to come back here again, do you?" the volunteer pressed. The
girl's head was so low her chin rested on her breastbone. *"Si,"* she whispered.

We had been there two hours by that time, filling out endless forms, giving   10
blood and urine, receiving lectures. But unlike any other group of women I've
been in, we didn't talk. Our common denominator, the one which usually floods
across language and economic barriers into familiarity, today was one of shame.
We were losing life that day, not giving it.

The group kept getting cut back to smaller, more workable units, and finally I   11
was put in a small waiting room with just two other women. We changed into
paper bathrobes and paper slippers, and we rustled whenever we moved. One of
the women in my room was shivering and an aide brought her a blanket.

"What's the matter?" the aide asked her. "I'm scared," the woman said. "How   12
much will it hurt?" The aide smiled. "Oh, nothing worse than a couple of bad
cramps," she said. "This afternoon you'll be dancing a jig."

I began to panic. Suddenly the rhetoric, the abortion marches I'd walked in,   13
the telegrams sent to Albany to counteract the Friends of the Fetus, the Zero
Population Growth buttons I'd worn, peeled away, and I was all alone with my
microscopic baby. There were just the two of us there, and soon, because it was
more convenient for me and my husband, there would be one again.

How could it be that I, who am so neurotic about life that I step over bugs   14
rather than on them, who spend hours planting flowers and vegetables in the
spring even though we rent out the house and never see them, who make sure the
children are vaccinated and inoculated and filled with vitamin C, could so arbitrar-
ily decide that this life shouldn't be?

"It's not a life," my husband had argued, more to convince himself than me.   15
"It's a bunch of cells smaller than my fingernail."

But any woman who has had children knows that certain feeling in her taut,   16 swollen breasts, and the slight but constant ache in her uterus that signals the arrival of a life. Though I would march myself into blisters for a woman's right to exercise the option of motherhood, I discovered there in the waiting room that I was not the modern woman I thought I was.

When my name was called, my body felt so heavy the nurse had to help me   17
into the examining room. I waited for my husband to burst through the door and yell "stop," but of course he didn't. I concentrated on three black spots in the acoustic ceiling until they grew in size to the shape of saucers, while the doctor swabbed my insides with antiseptic.

"You're going to feel a burning sensation now," he said, injecting Novocain   18
into the neck of the womb. The pain was swift and severe, and I twisted to get away from him. He was hurting my baby, I reasoned, and the black saucers quivered in the air. "Stop," I cried. "Please stop." He shook his head, busy with his equipment. "It's too late to stop now," he said. "It'll just take a few more seconds."

What good sports we women are. And how obedient. Physically the pain   19
passed even before the hum of the machine signaled that the vacuuming of my uterus was completed, my baby sucked up like ashes after a cocktail party. Ten minutes start to finish. And I was back on the arm of the nurse.

There were twelve beds in the recovery room. Each one had a gaily flowered   20
draw sheet and a soft green or blue thermal blanket. It was all very feminine. Lying on these beds for an hour or more were the shocked victims of their sex, their full wombs now stripped clean, their futures less encumbered.

It was very quiet in that room. The only voice was that of the nurse, locating   21
the new women who had just come in so she could monitor their blood pressure, and checking out the recovered women who were free to leave.

Juice was being passed about, and I found myself sipping a Dixie cup of   22
Hawaiian Punch. An older woman with tightly curled bleached hair was just getting up from the next bed. "That was no goddamn snap," she said, resting before putting on her miniskirt and high white boots. Other women came and went, some walking out as dazed as they had entered, others with a bounce that signaled they were going right back to Bloomingdale's.

Finally then, it was time for me to leave. I checked out, making an appoint-   23
ment to return in two weeks for an IUD insertion. My husband was slumped in the waiting room, clutching a single yellow rose wrapped in a wet paper towel and stuffed into a Baggie.

We didn't talk the whole way home, but just held hands very tightly. At home   24
there were more yellow roses and a tray in bed for me and the children's curiosity to divert.

It had certainly been a successful operation. I didn't bleed at all for two days   25
just as they had predicted, and then I bled only moderately for another four days. Within a week my breasts had subsided and the tenderness vanished, and my body felt mine again instead of the eggshell it becomes when it's protecting someone else.

My husband and I are back to planning our summer vacation and his career   26
switch.

And it certainly does make more sense not to be having a baby right now—we   27
say that to each other all the time. But I have this ghost now. A very little ghost
that only appears when I'm seeing something beautiful, like the full moon on the
ocean last weekend. And the baby waves at me. And I wave at the baby. "Of
course, we have room," I cry to the ghost. "Of course, we do."

▼ TOPICAL CONSIDERATIONS

1. What are the reasons the author and her husband do not want another
   child?
2. How does Francke describe the state of the men in the waiting room of the
   abortion clinic? What feelings do they seem to share?
3. According to Francke, what "common denominator" links the women at
   the clinic?
4. In paragraph 13, Francke says she suddenly panicked. Why did she?
5. What had been Francke's political stand on the abortion issue before her
   visit to the clinic? Do you think she has had a change of heart since?
   Explain your reasons for your answer.
6. In paragraph 16, Francke admits that she "was not the modern woman" she
   had thought she was. What does she mean by this statement? Why the term
   "modern woman"?
7. In paragraph 17, Francke says that she .waited for her husband to burst
   through the door of the operating room and yell "stop." What does this say
   about what was going on in Francke's mind? What does it say about her
   own strength of will? Do you think this is another confession that she is not
   the "modern woman" she thought she was but, rather, one who hopes to be
   rescued from a bad situation by a man? Or is this a momentary fantasy that
   goes beyond sex roles?
8. Francke says that the physical pain of the operation was "swift and severe."
   But the mental pain, though also severe, is not so swift in passing. What
   evidence is there in the essay that Francke's mental anguish persisted after
   the operation?

▼ RHETORICAL CONSIDERATIONS

1. What does *ambivalence* mean? How does the author demonstrate ambivalence in the first paragraph? Where in the essay does she actually discuss
   her ambivalence rather than simply dramatizing it?
2. Explain the rhetorical effect of the repetition in paragraph 3: "We both
   agreed. And agreed. And agreed." Where else do you find such repetition?
   Explain its effect, too.
3. This is a highly emotional and moving essay. Does the author convey her
   emotional trauma by becoming overly emotional or sentimental in the

piece? If you think so, cite examples. If you think not, how does she avoid being sentimental?

4. What is the effect of telling us that the Women's Services is formally known as the Center for Reproductive and Sexual Health? What does the name difference suggest about the clinic's self-perception? About the clinic's relationship to the community?

5. Discuss the matter-of-fact tone of paragraph 4. How is Francke's own emotional anxiety sustained by the seemingly neutral tone? Is her tone ironic? Explain your answers.

6. Francke says that the women at the abortion clinic were a mixture of ages, races, and social strata. How would you describe Francke's attitude toward these other women? What is her feeling toward the youngest girl?

7. At the end of paragraph 12, the aide with a smile tells one scared woman, "This afternoon you'll be dancing a jig." What is the effect of the observation of the aide's manner and words? How does it contrast with what is going on inside the author?

8. Discuss the effect of the first two lines of paragraph 19: "What good sports we women are. And how obedient."

9. Why would Francke mention the seemingly minor detail of her husband "clutching a single yellow rose wrapped in a wet paper towel and stuffed into a Baggie" (paragraph 23)? Does this detail have a higher, symbolic function in the essay?

10. Throughout the essay, Francke writes in the past tense. Why did she switch to the present tense in the last two paragraphs? To what effect?

▼ WRITING ASSIGNMENTS

1. Abortion is one of our society's most controversial issues, because what is being debated hinges on the definition of life itself—whether life begins at conception or at birth. Write an essay stating your own feelings about when life begins and about the abortion issue. In your essay, also discuss whether modern science has helped or complicated the problem of determining when life occurs.

2. Write a political speech defending a woman's right to have a legal abortion.

3. Write a political speech against the legalization of abortion.

4. Linda Bird Francke's essay is about her ambivalence on a particularly sensitive social issue. Write a paper in which you face your own ambivalence about some social issue. Like Francke, consider both sides and explain your ambivalence. You might want to consider some of the other social issues talked about in this book—capital punishment, legalization of drugs, gun control, etc.

5. None of the women at Francke's abortion clinic had used any birth control measures. Write an essay in which you argue for or against compulsory sex

education programs in elementary schools. In your essay, be sure to state your stand clearly and give your reasons behind it.

6. Francke's essay is a powerful piece, not just because the issue is highly controversial but because she was caught up in an emotional tug-of-war between strong political convictions and an intense personal experience. If you have ever been caught up in such a conflict between ideals and real experience, write a first-person account describing it, and explore any ambivalence or change of heart you might have experienced as a result. (If you have been a victim of a crime, for example, you might want to consider your attitudes toward criminals and punishment before and after the event.)

▼ GRADUATION

Maya Angelou

One of the most important events in a young person's life is graduation day. This selection, a vivid recollection of one such day and the events leading up to it, is by the famous black author, Maya Angelou. Born Marguerita Johnson in 1928, Angelou survived some terrible childhood experiences—a broken home, being raped at the age of eight, becoming an unwed mother at sixteen. As an adult, she involved herself in theatre, television, and journalism. She also served as a coordinator of Martin Luther King's Southern Christian Leadership Conference. She is perhaps best known for her autobiographical books, including *I Know Why the Caged Bird Sings* (1970), from which this piece was taken, and *The Heart of a Woman* (1981), a recent memoir.

The children in Stamps trembled visibly with anticipation. Some adults were 1 excited too, but to be certain the whole young population had come down with graduation epidemic. Large classes were graduating from both the grammar school and the high school. Even those who were years removed from their own day of glorious release were anxious to help with preparations as a kind of dry run. The junior students who were moving into the vacating classes' chairs were tradition-bound to show their talents for leadership and management. They strutted through the school and around the campus exerting pressure on the lower grades. Their authority was so new that occasionally if they pressed a little too hard it had to be overlooked. After all, next term was coming, and it never hurt a sixth grader to have a play sister in the eighth grade, or a tenth-year student to be able to call a twelfth grader Bubba. So all was endured in a spirit of shared understanding. But the graduating classes themselves were the nobility. Like travelers with exotic destinations on their minds, the graduates were remarkably forgetful. They came to school without their books, or tablets, or even pencils. Volunteers fell over themselves to secure replacements for the missing equipment. When accepted, the willing workers might or might not be thanked, and it was of no importance to the pregraduation rites. Even teachers were respectful of the now quiet and aging seniors, and tended to speak to them, if not as equals, as beings only slightly lower than themselves. After tests were returned and grades given, the student body, which acted like an extended family, knew who did well, who excelled, and what piteous ones had failed.

Unlike the white high school, Lafayette County Training School distinguished 2 itself by having neither lawn, nor hedges, nor tennis court, nor climbing ivy. Its two buildings (main classrooms, the grade school and home economics) were set on a dirt hill with no fence to limit either its boundaries or those of bordering farms. There was a large expanse to the left of the school which was used alternately as a baseball diamond or a basketball court. Rusty hoops on the swaying poles represented the permanent recreational equipment, although bats and balls could be borrowed from the P.E. teacher if the borrower was qualified and if the diamond wasn't occupied.

Over this rocky area relieved by a few shady tall persimmon trees the graduating class walked. The girls often held hands and no longer bothered to speak to the lower students. There was a sadness about them, as if this old world was not their home and they were bound for higher ground. The boys, on the other hand, had become more friendly, more outgoing. A decided change from the closed attitude they projected while studying for finals. Now they seemed not ready to give up the old school, the familiar paths and classrooms. Only a small percentage would be continuing on to college—one of the South's A & M (agricultural and mechanical) schools, which trained Negro youths to be carpenters, farmers, handymen, masons, maids, cooks, and baby nurses. Their future rode heavily on their shoulders, and blinded them to the collective joy that had pervaded the lives of the boys and girls in the grammar school graduating class.

Parents who could afford it had ordered new shoes and ready-made clothes for themselves from Sears and Roebuck or Montgomery Ward. They also engaged the best seamstresses to make the floating graduating dresses and to cut down second-hand pants which would be pressed to a military slickness for the important event.

Oh, it was important, all right. Whitefolks would attend the ceremony, and two or three would speak of God and home, and the Southern way of life, and Mrs. Parsons, the principal's wife, would play the graduation march while the lower-grade graduates paraded down the aisles and took their seats below the platform. The high school seniors would wait in empty classrooms to make their dramatic entrance.

In the Store I was the person of the moment. The birthday girl. The center. Bailey* had graduated the year before, although to do so he had had to forfeit all pleasures to make up for his time lost in Baton Rouge.

My class was wearing butter-yellow piqué dresses, and Momma launched out on mine. She smocked the yoke into tiny crisscrossing puckers, then shirred the rest of the bodice. Her dark fingers ducked in and out of the lemony cloth as she embroidered raised daisies around the hem. Before she considered herself finished she had added a crocheted cuff on the puff sleeves, and a pointy crocheted collar.

I was going to be lovely. A walking model of all the various styles of fine hand sewing and it didn't worry me that I was only twelve years old and merely graduating from the eighth grade. Besides, many teachers in Arkansas Negro schools had only that diploma and were licensed to impart wisdom.

The days had become longer and more noticeable. The faded beige of former times had been replaced with strong and sure colors. I began to see my classmates'

*Angelou's brother.—Ed.

clothes, their skin tones, and the dust that waved off pussy willows. Clouds that lazed across the sky were objects of great concern to me. Their shiftier shapes might have held a message that in my new happiness and with a little bit of time I'd soon decipher. During that period I looked at the arch of heaven so religiously my neck kept a steady ache. I had taken to smiling more often, and my jaws hurt from the unaccustomed activity. Between the two physical sore spots, I suppose I could have been uncomfortable, but that was not the case. As a member of the winning team (the graduating class of 1940) I had outdistanced unpleasant sensations by miles. I was headed for the freedom of open fields.

Youth and social approval allied themselves with me and we trammeled   10
memories of slights and insults. The wind of our swift passage remodeled my features. Lost tears were pounded to mud and then to dust. Years of withdrawal were brushed aside and left behind, as hanging ropes of parasitic moss.

My work alone had awarded me a top place and I was going to be one   11
of the first called in the graduating ceremonies. On the classroom blackboard, as well as on the bulletin board in the auditorium, there were blue stars and white stars and red stars. No absences, no tardinesses, and my academic work was among the best of the year. I could say the preamble to the Constitution even faster than Bailey. We timed ourselves often: "WethepeopleoftheUnited-Statesinordertoformamoreperfectunion . . . " I had memorized the Presidents of the United States from Washington to Roosevelt in chronological as well as alphabetical order.

My hair pleased me too. Gradually the black mass had lengthened and   12
thickened, so that it kept at last to its braided pattern, and I didn't have to yank my scalp off when I tried to comb it.

Louise and I had rehearsed the exercises until we tired out ourselves. Henry   13
Reed was class valedictorian. He was a small, very black boy with hooded eyes, a long, broad nose and an oddly shaped head. I had admired him for years because each term he and I vied for the best grades in our class. Most often he bested me, but instead of being disappointed I was pleased that we shared top places between us. Like many Southern Black children, he lived with his grandmother, who was as strict as Momma and as kind as she knew how to be. He was courteous, respectful, and soft-spoken to elders, but on the playground he chose to play the roughest games. I admired him. Anyone, I reckoned, sufficiently afraid or sufficiently dull could be polite. But to be able to operate at a top level with both adults and children was admirable.

His valedictory speech was entitled "To Be or Not to Be." The rigid tenth-   14
grade teacher had helped him to write it. He'd been working on the dramatic stresses for months.

The weeks until graduation were filled with heady activities. A group of small   15
children were to be presented in a play about buttercups and daisies and bunny rabbits. They could be heard throughout the building practicing their hops and their little songs that sounded like silver bells. The older girls (non-graduates, of course) were assigned the task of making refreshments for the night's festivities. A tangy scent of ginger, cinnamon, nutmeg, and chocolate wafted around the home

economics building as the budding cooks made samples for themselves and their teachers.

In every corner of the workshop, axes and saws split fresh timber as the 16
woodshop boys made sets and stage scenery. Only the graduates were left out of the general bustle. We were free to sit in the library at the back of the building or look in quite detachedly, naturally, on the measures being taken for our event.

Even the minister preached on graduation the Sunday before. His subject was, 17
"Let your light so shine that men will see your good works and praise your Father, Who is in Heaven." Although the sermon was purported to be addressed to us, he used the occasion to speak to backsliders, gamblers, and general ne'er-do-wells. But since he had called our names at the beginning of the service we were mollified.

Among Negroes the tradition was to give presents to children going only from 18
one grade to another. How much more important this was when the person was graduating at the top of the class. Uncle Willie and Momma had sent away for a Mickey Mouse watch like Bailey's. Louise gave me four embroidered handkerchiefs. (I gave her three crocheted doilies.) Mrs. Sneed, the minister's wife, made me an underskirt to wear for graduation, and nearly every customer gave me a nickel or maybe even a dime with the instruction "Keep on moving to higher ground," or some such encouragement.

Amazingly the great day finally dawned and I was out of bed before I knew it. 19
I threw open the back door to see it more clearly, but Momma said, "Sister, come away from that door and put your robe on."

I hoped the memory of that morning would never leave me. Sunlight was itself 20
still young, and the day had none of the insistence maturity would bring it in a few hours. In my robe and barefoot in the backyard, under cover of going to see about my new beans, I gave myself up to the gentle warmth and thanked God that no matter what evil I had done in my life He had allowed me to live to see this day. Somewhere in my fatalism I had expected to die, accidentally, and never have the chance to walk up the stairs in the auditorium and gracefully receive my hard-earned diploma. Out of God's merciful bosom I had won reprieve.

Bailey came out in his robe and gave me a box wrapped in Christmas paper. 21
He said he had saved his money for months to pay for it. It felt like a box of chocolates, but I knew Bailey wouldn't save money to buy candy when we had all we could want under our noses.

He was as proud of the gift as I. It was a soft-leather-bound copy of a 22
collection of poems by Edgar Allan Poe, or, as Bailey and I called him, "Eap." I turned to "Annabel Lee" and we walked up and down the garden rows, the cool dirt between our toes, reciting the beautifully sad lines.

Momma made a Sunday breakfast although it was only Friday. After we 23
finished the blessing, I opened my eyes to find the watch on my plate. It was a dream of a day. Everything went smoothly and to my credit. I didn't have to be reminded or scolded for anything. Near evening I was too jittery to attend to chores, so Bailey volunteered to do all before his bath.

Days before, we had made a sign for the Store and as we turned out the 24 lights Momma hung the cardboard over the doorknob. It read clearly: CLOSED. GRADUATION.

My dress fitted perfectly and everyone said that I looked like a sunbeam in it. 25 On the hill, going toward the school, Bailey walked behind with Uncle Willie, who muttered, "Go on, Ju." He wanted him to walk ahead with us because it embarrassed him to have to walk so slowly. Bailey said he'd let the ladies walk together, and the men would bring up the rear. We all laughed, nicely.

Little children dashed by out of the dark like fireflies. Their crepepaper 26 dresses and butterfly wings were not made for running and we heard more than one rip, dryly, and the regretful "uh uh" that followed.

The school blazed without gaiety. The windows seemed cold and unfriendly 27 from the lower hill. A sense of ill-fated timing crept over me, and if Momma hadn't reached for my hand I would have drifted back to Bailey and Uncle Willie, and possibly beyond. She made a few slow jokes about my feet getting cold, and tugged me along to the now-strange building.

Around the front steps, assurance came back. There were my fellow "greats," 28 the graduating class. Hair brushed back, legs oiled, new dresses and pressed pleats, fresh pocket handkerchiefs and little handbags, all homesewn. Oh, we were up to snuff, all right. I joined my comrades and didn't even see my family go in to find seats in the crowded auditorium.

The school band struck up a march and all classes filed in as had been rehearsed. 29 We stood in front of our seats, as assigned, and on a signal from the choir director, we sat. No sooner had this been accomplished than the band started to play the national anthem. We rose again and sang the song, after which we recited the pledge of allegiance. We remained standing for a brief minute before the choir director and the principal signaled to us, rather desperately I thought, to take our seats. The command was so unusual that our carefully rehearsed and smooth-running machine was thrown off. For a full minute we fumbled for our chairs and bumped into each other awkwardly. Habits change or solidify under pressure, so in our state of nervous tension we had been ready to follow our usual assembly pattern: the American National Anthem, then the pledge of allegiance, then the song every Black person I knew called the Negro National Anthem. All done in the same key, with the same passion and most often standing on the same foot.

Finding my seat at last, I was overcome with a presentiment of worse things to 30 come. Something unrehearsed, unplanned, was going to happen, and we were going to be made to look bad. I distinctly remember being explicit in the choice of pronoun. It was "we," the graduating class, the unit, that concerned me then.

The principal welcomed "parents and friends" and asked the Baptist minister 31 to lead us in prayer. His invocation was brief and punchy, and for a second I thought we were getting back on the high road to right action. When the principal came back to the dais, however, his voice had changed. Sounds always affected me profoundly and the principal's voice was one of my favorites. During assembly it melted and lowed weakly into the audience. It had not been in my plan to listen to him, but my curiosity was piqued and I straightened up to give him my attention.

He was talking about Booker T. Washington, our "late great leader," who said   32
we can be as close as the fingers on the hand, etc. . . . Then he said a few vague
things about friendship and the friendship of kindly people to those less fortunate
than themselves. With that his voice nearly faded, thin, away. Like a river diminishing to a stream and then to a trickle. But he cleared his throat and said, "Our
speaker tonight, who is also our friend, came from Texarkana to deliver the
commencement address, but due to the irregularity of the train schedule, he's
going to, as they say, 'speak and run.' " He said that we understood and wanted the
man to know that we were most grateful for the time he was able to give us and
then something about how we were willing always to adjust to another's program,
and without more ado—"I give you Mr. Edward Donleavy."

Not one but two white men came through the door offstage. The shorter one   33
walked to the speaker's platform, and the tall one moved over to the center seat
and sat down. But that was our principal's seat, and already occupied. The
dislodged gentleman bounced around for a long breath or two before the Baptist
minister gave him his chair, then with more dignity than the situation deserved,
the minister walked off the stage.

Donleavy looked at the audience once (on reflection, I'm sure that he wanted   34
only to reassure himself that we were really there), adjusted his glasses, and began
to read from a sheaf of papers.

He was glad "to be here and to see the work going on just as it was in the other   35
schools."

At the first "Amen" from the audience I willed the offender to immediate   36
death by choking on the word. But Amens and Yes, sir's began to fall around the
room like rain through a ragged umbrella.

He told us of the wonderful changes we children in Stamps had in store. The   37
Central School (naturally, the white school was Central) had already been granted
improvements that would be in use in the fall. A well-known artist was coming
from Little Rock to teach art to them. They were going to have the newest
microscopes and chemistry equipment for their laboratory. Mr. Donleavy didn't
leave us long in the dark over who made these improvements available to Central
High. Nor were we to be ignored in the general betterment scheme he had in
mind.

He said that he had pointed out to people at a very high level that one of the   38
first-line football tacklers at Arkansas Agricultural and Mechanical College had
graduated from good old Lafayette County Training School. Here fewer Amen's
were heard. Those few that did break through lay dully in the air with the
heaviness of habit.

He went on to praise us. He went on to say how he had bragged that "one of   39
the best basketball players at Fisk sank his first ball right here at Lafayette County
Training School."

The white kids were going to have a chance to become Galileos and Madame   40
Curies and Edisons and Gauguins, and our boys (the girls weren't even in on it)
would try to be Jesse Owenses and Joe Louises.

Owens and the Brown Bomber were great heroes in our world, but what   41 school official in the white-goddom of Little Rock had the right to decide that those two men must be our only heroes? Who decided that for Henry Reed to become a scientist he had to work like George Washington Carver, as a bootblack, to buy a lousy microscope? Bailey was obviously always going to be too small to be an athlete, so which concrete angel glued to what country seat had decided that if my brother wanted to become a lawyer he had to first pay penance for his skin by picking cotton and hoeing corn and studying correspondence books at night for twenty years?

The man's dead words fell like bricks around the auditorium and too many   42
settled in my belly. Constrained by hard-learned manners I couldn't look behind me, but to my left and right the proud graduating class of 1940 had dropped their heads. Every girl in my row had found something new to do with her handkerchief. Some folded the tiny squares into love knots, some into triangles, but most were wadding them, then pressing them flat on their yellow laps.

On the dais, the ancient tragedy was being replayed. Professor Parsons sat, a   43
sculptor's reject, rigid. His large, heavy body seemed devoid of will or willingness, and his eyes said he was no longer with us. The other teachers examined the flag (which was draped stage right) or their notes, or the windows which opened on our now-famous playing diamond.

Graduation, the hush-hush magic time of frills and gifts and congratulations   44
and diplomas, was finished for me before my name was called. The accomplishment was nothing. The meticulous maps, drawn in three colors of ink, learning and spelling decasyllabic words, memorizing the whole of *The Rape of Lucrece* — it was nothing. Donleavy had exposed us.

We were maids and farmers, handymen and washerwomen, and anything   45
higher that we aspired to was farcical and presumptuous. Then I wished that Gabriel Prosser and Nat Turner had killed all whitefolks in their beds and that Abraham Lincoln had been assassinated before the signing of the Emancipation Proclamation, and that Harriet Tubman had been killed by that blow on her head and Christopher Columbus had drowned in the *Santa Maria.*

It was awful to be Negro and have no control over my life. It was brutal to be   46
young and already trained to sit quietly and listen to charges brought against my color with no chance of defense. We should all be dead. I thought I should like to see us all dead, one on top of the other. A pyramid of flesh with the whitefolks on the bottom, as the broad base, then the Indians with their silly tomahawks and teepees and wigwams and treaties, the Negroes with their mops and recipes and cotton sacks and spirituals sticking out of their mouths. The Dutch children should all stumble in their wooden shoes and break their necks. The French should choke to death on the Louisiana Purchase (1803) while silkworms ate all the Chinese with their stupid pigtails. As a species, we were an abomination. All of us.

Donleavy was running for election, and assured our parents that if he won we   47
could count on having the only colored paved playing field in that part of Arkansas. Also — he never looked up to acknowledge the grunts of acceptance — also, we were bound to get some new equipment for the home economics building and the workshop.

He finished, and since there was no need to give any more than the most   48
perfunctory thank-you's, he nodded to the men on the stage, and the tall white
man who was never introduced joined him at the door. They left with the attitude
that now they were off to something really important. (The graduation ceremonies
at Lafayette County Training School had been a mere preliminary.)

The ugliness they left was palpable. An uninvited guest who wouldn't leave.   49
The choir was summoned and sang a modern arrangement of "Onward, Christian
Soldiers," with new words pertaining to graduates seeking their place in the world.
But it didn't work. Elouise, the daughter of the Baptist minister, recited "Invictus,"
and I could have cried at the impertinence of "I am the master of my fate, I am the
captain of my soul."

My name had lost its ring of familiarity and I had to be nudged to go and   50
receive my diploma. All my preparations had fled. I neither marched up to the
stage like a conquering Amazon, nor did I look in the audience for Bailey's nod of
approval. Marguerite Johnson, I heard the name again, my honors were read,
there were noises in the audience of appreciation, and I took my place on the
stage as rehearsed.

I thought about colors I hated: ecru, puce, lavender, beige, and black.   51

There was shuffling and rustling around me, then Henry Reed was giving his   52
valedictory address, "To Be or Not to Be." Hadn't he heard the whitefolks? We
couldn't *be,* so the question was a waste of time. Henry's voice came out clear and
strong. I feared to look at him. Hadn't he got the message? There was no "nobler
in the mind" for Negroes because the world didn't think we had minds, and they
let us know it. "Outrageous fortune"? Now, that was a joke. When the ceremony
was over I had to tell Henry Reed some things. That is, if I still cared. Not "rub,"
Henry, "erase." "Ah, there's the erase." Us.

Henry had been a good student in elocution. His voice rose on tides   53
of promise and fell on waves of warnings. The English teacher had helped
him to create a sermon winging through Hamlet's soliloquy. To be a man,
a doer, a builder, a leader, or to be a tool, an unfunny joke, a crusher of funky
toadstools. I marveled that Henry could go through with the speech as if we had
a choice.

I had been listening and silently rebutting each sentence with my eyes closed;   54
then there was a hush, which in an audience warns that something unplanned is
happening. I looked up and saw Henry Reed, the conservative, the proper, the A
student, turn his back to the audience and turn to us (the proud graduating class of
1940) and sing, nearly speaking,

> Lift ev'ry voice and sing
> Till earth and heaven ring
> Ring with the harmonies of Liberty . . .

It was the poem written by James Weldon Johnson. It was the music composed by
J. Rosamond Johnson. It was the Negro National Anthem. Out of habit we were
singing it.

Our mothers and fathers stood in the dark hall and joined the hymn of   55 encouragement. A kindergarten teacher led the small children onto the stage and the buttercups and daisies and bunny rabbits marked time and tried to follow:

> Stoney the road we trod
> Bitter the chastening rod
> Felt in the days when hope, unborn, had died.
> Yet with a steady beat
> Have not our weary feet
> Come to the place for which our fathers sighed?

Every child I knew had learned that song with his ABC's and along with "Jesus Loves Me This I Know." But I personally had never heard it before. Never heard the words, despite the thousands of times I had sung them. Never thought they had anything to do with me.   56

On the other hand, the words of Patrick Henry had made such an impression on me that I had been able to stretch myself tall and trembling and say, "I know not what course others may take, but as for me, give me liberty or give me death."   57

And now I heard, really for the first time: 58

> We have come over a way that with tears has been watered,
> We have come, treading our path through the blood of the slaughtered.

While echoes of the song shivered in the air, Henry Reed bowed his head, said "Thank you," and returned to his place in the line. The tears that slipped down many faces were not wiped away in shame.   59

We were on top again. As always, again. We survived. The depths had been icy and dark, but now a bright sun spoke to our souls. I was no longer simply a member of the proud graduating class of 1940; I was a proud member of the wonderful, beautiful Negro race.   60

Oh, Black known and unknown poets, how often have your auctioned pains sustained us? Who will compute the lonely nights made less lonely by your songs, or the empty pots made less tragic by your tales?   61

If we were a people much given to revealing secrets, we might raise monuments and sacrifice to the memories of our poets, but slavery cured us of that weakness. It may be enough, however, to have it said that we survive in exact relationship to the dedication of our poets (include preachers, musicians, and blues singers).   62

▼ TOPICAL CONSIDERATIONS

1. What signs does Angelou give that reveal graduation to be an important occasion for the children in Stamps? Why do you think it was so important, not only to the children and parents but also to the community?
2. Is there any particular reason why the principal should allude to Booker T. Washington just prior to Mr. Donleavy's speech? How does the audience's response to his speech reflect the black leader's own feelings about how blacks should act toward white people?

3. Angelou appears to have been particularly sensitive to what was happening during the graduation ceremony. What first prompted her to suspect that something was amiss? How does the atmosphere change as Mr. Donleavy's speech progresses? What specifically does he say to cause the change?
4. What does Angelou resent most about Donleavy's remarks? Are his assumptions about the future aspirations of the Lafayette County Training School graduates justified? What clues do we have about the quality of education at Angelou's school that might suggest otherwise? Note Angelou's frequent historical and literary allusions.
5. The Negro National Anthem was not sung at the usual place in the program. Why does its postponement turn out to be a blessing? What effect does it have on Angelou?
6. If Dick Gregory had been attending Angelou's graduation as an adult, he no doubt would have been singing as loudly as the next person. Why? How might graduation have been different if he had been the guest speaker instead of Mr. Donleavy? What might Gregory have said?
7. How is this graduation a "commencement" for Angelou?

▼ RHETORICAL CONSIDERATIONS

1. Look closely at Angelou's first paragraph. What specific word choices does she use to suggest how important graduation is for children and teachers? How do these words contribute to the development of the essay?
2. How would you describe Angelou's point of view? Does she exaggerate the importance of this event? Or do you think her account is fairly accurate? How might the narrative have been different if told by Bailey (Angelou's older brother)? By the minister? By Mr. Donleavy?
3. In paragraph 36, Angelou remarks that "Amens and Yes, sir's began to fall around the room like rain through a ragged umbrella." What does this suggest about the atmosphere in the room during Mr. Donleavy's speech? What other figurative language does Angelou use?
4. Writers strive to make their material interesting by using specific, concrete details. How successful is Angelou in doing this? Cite specific examples to prove your point.

▼ WRITING ASSIGNMENTS

1. If Maya Angelou were asked to be a guest speaker at Lafayette County Training School today, what do you think she would say? Write her speech. Imitate her frequent allusions to important historical events and literary works.
2. In an essay, describe the graduation ceremonies at Lafayette County Train-

ing School from the minister's point of view, from Bailey's, and from Mr. Donleavy's.

3. Write an essay about your own graduation. Describe how you, your classmates, the school, and the community prepared for the event. Use figurative language and other vivid word pictures to recreate the atmosphere of the graduation hall during the ceremony.

▼ A FEW WORDS ABOUT BREASTS

Nora Ephron

Nora Ephron is a novelist (*Heartburn,* 1983) and a widely published freelance writer, with articles appearing in *The New Yorker, McCall's, Cosmopolitan, Esquire,* and *Rolling Stone.* Her essays, which have been collected in several books, including *Crazy Salad* (1975) and *Scribble, Scribble* (1978), display a characteristically wry sense of humor. One of her constant subject matters is the roles of men and women in our society. This essay, from *Crazy Salad,* is a rather frank though wry complaint about how growing up in the fifties—an era that embraced rigid sexual stereotypes—created in her lasting psychological hang-ups about her breast size.

"Do you want to marry my son?" the woman asked me.   1

"Yes," I said.   2

I was nineteen years old, a virgin, going with this woman's son, this big strange   3
woman who was married to a Lutheran minister in New Hampshire and pretended she was gentile and had this son, by her first husband, this total fool of a son who ran the hero-sandwich concession at Harvard Business School and whom for one moment one December in New Hampshire I said—as much out of politeness as anything else—that I wanted to marry.

"Fine," she said. "Now, here's what you do. Always make sure you're on top of   4
him so you won't seem so small. My bust is very large, you see, so I always lie on my back to make it look smaller, but you'll have to be on top most of the time."

I nodded. "Thank you," I said.   5

"I have a book for you to read," she went on. "Take it with you when you   6
leave. Keep it." She went to the bookshelf, found it, and gave it to me. It was a book on frigidity.

"Thank you," I said.   7

That is a true story. Everything in this article is a true story, but I feel I have to   8
point out that that story in particular is true. It happened on December 30, 1960. I think about it often. When it first happened, I naturally assumed that the woman's son, my boyfriend, was responsible. I invented a scenario where he had had a little heart-to-heart with his mother and had confessed that his only objection to me was that my breasts were small; his mother then took it upon herself to help out. Now I think I was wrong about the incident. The mother was acting on her own, I think: that was her way of being cruel and competitive under the guise of being helpful and maternal. You have small breasts, she was saying; therefore you will never

29

make him as happy as I have. Or you have small breasts; therefore you will doubtless have sexual problems. Or you have small breasts; therefore you are less woman than I am. She was, as it happens, only the first of what seems to me to be a never-ending string of women who have made competitive remarks to me about breast size. "I would love to wear a dress like that," my friend Emily says to me, "but my bust is too big." Like that. Why do women say these things to me? Do I attract these remarks the way other women attract married men or alcoholics or homosexuals? This summer, for example. I am at a party in East Hampton and I am introduced to a woman from Washington. She is a minor celebrity, very pretty and Southern and blond and outspoken, and I am flattered because she has read something I have written. We are talking animatedly, we have been talking no more than five minutes, when a man comes up to join us. "Look at the two of us," the woman says to the man, indicating me and her. "The two of us together couldn't fill an A cup." Why does she say that? It isn't even true, dammit, so why? Is she even more addled than I am on this subject? Does she honestly believe there is something wrong with her size breasts, which, it seems to me, now that I look hard at them, are just right? Do I unconsciously bring out competitiveness in women? In that form? What did I do to deserve it?

As for men. 9

There were men who minded and let me know they minded. There were men 10
who did not mind. In any case, *I* always minded.

And even now that I have been countlessly reassured that my figure is 11
a good one, now that I am grown up enough to understand that most of my feelings have very little to do with the reality of my shape, I am nonetheless obsessed by breasts. I cannot help it. I grew up in the terrible fifties—with rigid stereotypical sex roles, the insistence that men be men and dress like men and women be women and dress like women, the intolerance of androgyny—and I cannot shake it, cannot shake my feelings of inadequacy. Well, that time is gone, right? All those exaggerated examples of breast worship are gone, right? Those women were freaks, right? I know all that. And yet here I am, stuck with the psychological remains of it all, stuck with my own peculiar version of breast worship. You probably think I am crazy to go on like this: here I have set out to write a confession that is meant to hit you with the shock of recognition and instead you are sitting there thinking I am thoroughly warped. Well, what can I tell you? If I had had them, I would have been a completely different person. I honestly believe that.

After I went into therapy, a process that made it possible for me to tell total 12
strangers at cocktail parties that breasts were the hang-up of my life, I was often told that I was insane to have been bothered by my condition. I was also frequently told, by close friends, that I was extremely boring on the subject. And my girl friends, the ones with nice big breasts, would go on endlessly about how their lives had been far more miserable than mine. Their bra straps were snapped in class. They couldn't sleep on their stomachs. They were stared at whenever the word "mountain" cropped up in geography. And *Evangeline,* good God what they went through every time someone had to stand up and recite the Prologue to

Longfellow's *Evangeline:* "... stand like druids of eld .../With beards that rest on their bosoms." It was much worse for them, they tell me. They had a terrible time of it, they assure me. I don't know how lucky I was, they say.

I have thought about their remarks, tried to put myself in their place, considered their point of view. I think they are full of shit.   13

▼ TOPICAL CONSIDERATIONS

1. Ephron writes: "I have set out to write a confession that is meant to hit you with the shock of recognition and instead you are sitting there thinking I am thoroughly warped" (paragraph 11). Do you feel Ephron's experience is one for which many women would feel a "shock of recognition," or would most women fail to identify with it?
2. What do you see as some of the causes of Ephron's "obsession" or "hang-up"? What obsessions or hang-ups about physical appearance are typical of teenagers or even of adults? Do you have any?
3. Was Ephron more concerned about her breast size when she was nineteen than when she was older? Why or why not? Are people more or less likely to be concerned about their physical appearance when they are teenagers than when they are adults? Explain.
4. What were the "rigid stereotypical sex roles" of the fifties? Are these roles still rigid? What current social trends might have caused the change (if any)?
5. Who were some of the motion picture sex symbols of the fifties? Who are some of today's television and motion picture idols? Have our views of what makes a woman beautiful or a man handsome changed?
6. What do you think of the conversation among Ephron, the minor celebrity from Washington, and the man who joins them? Was the celebrity's remark about breast size surprisingly candid or typical? Would you be likely to overhear such remarks at a college fraternity party?

▼ RHETORICAL CONSIDERATIONS

1. How would you characterize the tone of this essay? Is it thoughtful? Serious? Scholarly? Flippant? Angry? Do you see any similarities or differences in tone between this essay and others you have read in this section?
2. What can you say about Ephron's style, especially her sentence structure? How does it contribute to the tone of the essay?
3. Is the title attention-getting? Why or why not?
4. How and where does Ephron establish the thesis for her essay?
5. Do you note any one-sentence or unusually short paragraphs? How do they compare with others in the essay? What might be the writer's intent in keeping them so short? Are they adequately developed?
6. What effect does Ephron's ending have? How does she achieve this? Does it

tie the essay together and give it completeness? Does it leave the essay dangling? Explain.

▼ WRITING ASSIGNMENTS

1. Write an essay in which you discuss an obsession or hang-up regarding physical appearance that you experienced while growing up. Imitate Ephron's use of narrative and dialogue to show how sensitive you were on the subject.
2. In an essay, compare and contrast the sex roles of the fifties with those of the eighties. Have they changed? If so, how have they changed and what have been some of the causes?

▼ SALVATION

Langston Hughes

> Langston Hughes (1902–67) was a remarkably prolific and cele-
> brated writer. In addition to his autobiography, *The Big Sea* (1940),
> Hughes published seventeen books of poetry, two novels, seven
> short story collections, and twenty-six plays. He also wrote a column
> for the *New York Post.* Much of his life was devoted to the promotion
> of black art, music, and history. In the essay below, Hughes looks
> back to a dramatic event that took place when he was twelve—an
> event that would forever leave its mark on him. The essay, taken from
> his autobiography, is a fine example of how a writer's control of
> language and detail can recreate the point of view of a child.

I was saved from sin when I was going on thirteen. But not really saved. It 1
happened like this. There was a big revival at my Auntie Reed's church. Every
night for weeks there had been much preaching, singing, praying, and shouting,
and some very hardened sinners had been brought to Christ, and the membership
of the church had grown by leaps and bounds. Then just before the revival ended,
they held a special meeting for children, "to bring the young lambs to the fold."
My aunt spoke of it for days ahead. That night I was escorted to the front row and
placed on the mourners' bench with all the other young sinners, who had not yet
been brought to Jesus.

My aunt told me that when you were saved you saw a light, and something 2
happened to you inside! And Jesus came into your life! And God was with you
from then on! She said you could see and hear and feel Jesus in your soul. I
believed her. I have heard a great many old people say the same thing and it
seemed to me they ought to know. So I sat there calmly in the hot, crowded
church, waiting for Jesus to come to me.

The preacher preached a wonderful rhythmical sermon, all moans and shouts 3
and lonely cries and dire pictures of hell, and then he sang a song about the ninety
and nine safe in the fold, but one little lamb was left out in the cold. Then he said:
"Won't you come? Won't you come to Jesus? Young lambs, won't you come?" And
he held out his arms to all us young sinners there on the mourners' bench. And the
little girls cried. And some of them jumped up and went to Jesus right away. But
most of us just sat there.

A great many old people came and knelt around us and prayed, old women 4
with jet-black faces and braided hair, old men with work-gnarled hands. And the
church sang a song about the lower lights are burning, some poor sinners to be
saved. And the whole building rocked with prayer and song.

Still I kept waiting to *see* Jesus.   5

Finally all the young people had gone to the altar and were saved, but one boy   6
and me. He was a rounder's son named Westley. Westley and I were surrounded by
sisters and deacons praying. It was very hot in the church, and getting late now.
Finally Westley said to me in a whisper: "God damn! I'm tired o' sitting here. Let's
get up and be saved." So he got up and was saved.

Then I was left all alone on the mourners' bench. My aunt came and knelt at   7
my knees and cried, while prayers and songs swirled all around me in the little
church. The whole congregation prayed for me alone, in a mighty wail of moans
and voices. And I kept waiting serenely for Jesus, waiting, waiting—but he didn't
come. I wanted to see him, but nothing happened to me. Nothing! I wanted
something to happen to me, but nothing happened.

I heard the songs and the minister saying: "Why don't you come? My dear   8
child, why don't you come to Jesus? Jesus is waiting for you. He wants you. Why
don't you come? Sister Reed, what is this child's name?"

"Langston," my aunt sobbed.   9

"Langston, why don't you come? Why don't you come and be saved? Oh,   10
Lamb of God! Why don't you come?"

Now it was really getting late. I began to be ashamed of myself, holding   11
everything up so long. I began to wonder what God thought about Westley, who
certainly hadn't seen Jesus either, but who was now sitting proudly on the platform,
swinging his knickerbockered legs and grinning down at me, surrounded by
deacons and old women on their knees praying. God had not struck Westley dead
for taking his name in vain or for lying in the temple. So I decided that maybe to
save further trouble, I'd better lie, too, and say that Jesus had come, and get up
and be saved.

So I got up.   12

Suddenly the whole room broke into a sea of shouting, as they saw me rise.   13
Waves of rejoicing swept the place. Women leaped in the air. My aunt threw her
arms around me. The minister took me by the hand and led me to the platform.

When things quieted down, in a hushed silence, punctuated by a few ecstatic   14
"Amens," all the new young lambs were blessed in the name of God. Then joyous
singing filled the room.

That night, for the last time in my life but one—for I was a big boy   15
twelve years old—I cried. I cried, in bed alone, and couldn't stop. I buried
my head under the quilts, but my aunt heard me. She woke up and told my uncle
I was crying because the Holy Ghost had come into my life, and because I had
seen Jesus. But I was really crying because I couldn't bear to tell her that
I had lied, that I had deceived everybody in the church, that I hadn't seen Jesus,
and that now I didn't believe there was a Jesus any more, since he didn't come to
help me.

▼ TOPICAL CONSIDERATIONS

1. Why does Hughes say in the first sentence that he was "saved from sin" then, in the second sentence, "But not really saved"?
2. Young Hughes does not get up until the very end. What finally moves him to rise up and be saved? How do his motives compare or contrast with those of Westley's?
3. What reasons does Hughes offer for his crying at the end? How does it compare with his aunt's explanation? What has young Hughes learned from his experience?
4. If you were Hughes's aunt or uncle and were aware of his plight, how might you have comforted young Langston? What words of consolation or explanation would you have offered him?
5. How does Hughes's experience underscore the problems inherent in some people's expectations of religion?

▼ RHETORICAL CONSIDERATIONS

1. Hughes chose to recreate the scene of his actual "salvation" like a short story, rather than simply tell what happened in an expository format. Why do you think he chose this format? How effective do you think his efforts were to recapture the episode?
2. Comment on how effective Hughes was in recreating the scene in the church. Consider his use of descriptive details.
3. Hughes recalls the story of his "salvation" as an adult. How does Hughes's language help create a twelve-year-old's point of view? Find passages where the adult author's attitude toward the experience comes through. How would you describe that attitude?

▼ WRITING ASSIGNMENTS

1. Have you ever had a religious experience? If so, try to describe the circumstances and the experience as best you can.
2. Have you ever been compelled by group pressure to do something you didn't believe in? If so, describe the experience.
3. Write a paper in which you explore your own religious beliefs. Do you believe in a supreme being and find evidence of such in the natural world? Do you not believe in a supreme being? In either case, state the reasons behind your stand.

▼ RETURNING TO CHURCH

Dan Wakefield

> He was sitting in a bar one night before Christmas when he got the sud-
> den and unexpected urge to go to church. It was out of character. As
> a best-selling novelist and screenwriter, he had been living in the fast
> lane, where salvation was sought through alcohol, drugs, and promis-
> cuity. But his life was troubled. As Dan Wakefield explains in this
> inspiring personal narrative, returning to church did not solve his
> problems, but it provided his life with a greater context and significance.
> This piece was taken from Wakefield's autobiographical odyssey,
> *Returning: A Spiritual Journey* (1988). He is also the author of *Starting
> Over* (1972), a national best seller that became a hit movie. His other
> novels include, *Going All the Way* (1970) and *Selling Out* (1986).

Just before Christmas of 1980, I was sitting in the Sevens, a neighborhood bar on   1
Beacon Hill (don't all these stories of revelation begin in bars?), when a housepainter
named Tony remarked out of the blue that he wanted to find a place to go to mass
on Christmas Eve. I didn't say anything, but a thought came into my mind, as swift
and unexpected as it was unfamiliar: *I'd like to do that, too.*

I had not gone to church since leaving my boyhood Protestant faith as a   2
rebellious Columbia College intellectual more than a quarter-century before, yet I
found myself that Christmas Eve in King's Chapel, which I finally selected from
the ads on The Boston Globe religion page because it seemed least threatening. It
was Unitarian, I knew the minister slightly as a neighbor, and I assumed "Candlelight
Service" meant nothing more religiously challenging than carol singing.

As it happened, the Rev. Carl Scovel gave a sermon about "the latecomers" to   3
the church on a text from an Evelyn Waugh novel called "Helena." I slunk down in
my pew, literally beginning to shiver from what I thought was only embarrassment
at feeling singled out for personal attention, and discomfort at being in alien
surroundings. It turned out that I had a temperature of 102 that kept me in bed for
three days with a violent case of the flu and a fearful suspicion that church was a
very dangerous place, at least if you weren't used to it.

Perhaps my flesh was rebelling against this unaccustomed intrusion of spirit.   4
Certainly going to church was out of character for me. My chosen public image
was the jacket photo of "Starting Over," my novel about a divorced man seeking
salvation through drugs, alcohol and promiscuity. I proudly posed for the picture
in 1973 at my new living room bar, flanked by bottles of favorite vodkas, bourbons
and burgundies. It did not look like the picture of a man who was headed to church.

In the year that led to my going to the Christmas Eve service, I felt I was   5 headed for the edge of a cliff. I could have scored at the top of those magazine tests that list the greatest stresses of life, for that year saw the dissolution of a seven-year relationship with the woman I had fully expected to live with the rest of my life, I ran out of money, left the work I was doing, the house I owned, and the city I was living in, and attended the funeral of my father in May and my mother in November.

In the midst of this chaos, I one day grabbed an old Bible from among my 6 books, and with a desperate instinct turned to the 23rd Psalm. It brought a sense of relief, and sometimes I recited it in my mind in the months that followed, but it did not give me any sense that I suddenly believed in God. It simply seemed an isolated source of solace and calm, such as any great poem might be. It certainly did not give rise to the notion of anything as radical as going to church.

After my Christmas Eve experience at King's Chapel, I didn't get up the nerve 7 to go back again until Easter. I did not have any attacks of shivering or chills in the spring sunshine of that service, so it seemed that even as a "latecomer" and former avowed atheist, I could safely enter a place regarded as a house of God. Still, the prospect was discomforting. My two initial trips of return had been on major holidays, occasions when "regular" people went to church, simply in observance of tradition. To go back again meant crossing the Boston Common on a non-holiday Sunday morning wearing a suit and tie, a giveaway sign of churchgoing. I did it furtively, as if I were engaged in something that would not be approved of by my peers. I hoped they would all be home doing brunch and the Sunday papers, so I would not be "caught in the act." I recalled the remark of William F. Buckley Jr. in a television interview that if you mention God more than once at New York dinner parties, you aren't invited back.

To my surprise, I recognized neighbors and even some people I considered 8 friends at church, on a "regular" Sunday. I had simply assumed I did not know people who went to church, yet here they were, with intellects intact, worshiping God. Once inside the church myself, I understood the appeal. No doubt my friends and neighbors found, as I did, relief and refreshment in connecting with age-old rituals, reciting psalms and singing hymns. There was a calm reassurance in the stately language of the litanies and chants of the Book of Common Prayer. (King's Chapel is "Unitarian in theology, Anglican in worship, and congregational in governance," a historical Boston amalgam that will be three centuries old next June.) I was grateful for the sense of shared reverence, of reaching beyond one's flimsy physical presence, while praying with a whole congregation.

I began to appreciate what was meant by the church as "sanctuary." The word 9 itself took on new resonance for me; when I later heard of the "sanctuary" movement of New England churches offering shelter to Central American political refugees, I thought of the kind of private refuge that fortunate citizens like myself find in church from the daily assaults of business and personal pressures and worries, the psychic guerrilla warfare of everyday life.

Caught in an escalation of that kind of battle in my own professional cam- 10 paigns (more painful because so clearly brought on by my own blundering), I joined the church in May 1982, not wanting to wait until the second Christmas Eve anniversary of my entry, as I had planned. I wanted the immediate sense of safety and refuge implied in belonging, being a member—perhaps like getting a passport and fleeing to a powerful embassy in the midst of some chaotic revolution.

Going to church, even belonging to it, did not solve life's problems—if anything, they seemed to intensify around this time—but it gave me a sense of living in a larger context, of being part of something greater than what I could see through the tunnel vision of my personal concerns. I now looked forward to Sunday because it *meant* going to church; what once was strange now felt not only natural but essential. Even more remarkably, the practice of regular attendance at Sunday services, which such a short time ago seemed religiously "excessive," no longer seemed enough. Whatever it was I was getting from church on Sunday morning, I wanted—needed, it felt like—more of it.

I experienced what is a common phenomenon for people who in some way or other begin a journey of the kind I so unexpectedly found myself on—a feeling simply and best described as a "thirst" for spiritual understanding and contact; to put it bluntly, I guess, *for God.* I noticed in the church bulletin an announcement of a Bible-study class in the parish house, and I went one stormy autumn evening to find myself with only the church's young seminarian on hand and one other parishioner. Rather than being disappointed by the tiny turnout, as I ordinarily would have been, I thought of the words "Where two or three are gathered together in My name, there am I in the midst of them," and I felt an interior glow that the pouring rain outside and occasional claps of thunder only made seem more vital and precious. I don't remember what text we studied that evening, but I can still smell the rain and the coffee and feel the aura of light and warmth.

Later in the season, I attended a Bible-study session the minister led for a gathering of about 20 people on the story of Abraham and Isaac, and I came away with a sense of the awesomeness and power of faith, a quality that loomed above me as tremendous and hard and challenging and tangibly real as mountains. The Bible-study classes, which I later, with other parishioners, learned to lead on occasion myself, became a source of power, like tapping into a rich vein.

Bible study was not like examining history, but holding up a mirror to my own life, a mirror in which I sometimes saw things I was trying to keep hidden, even from myself. The first scripture passage I was assigned to lead was from Luke, about the man who cleans his house of demons, and seven worse ones come. I did not have any trouble relating this to "contemporary life." It sounded unnervingly like an allegory about a man who had stopped drinking and so was enjoying much better health, but took up smoking marijuana to "relax," all the while feeling good and even self-righteous about giving up the booze. It was my own story. I realized, with a shock, how I'd been deceiving myself, how much more "housecleaning" I had to do.

I was not only going to church and devoting time to Bible study and prayer during this period, I was actively engaged in purely secular programs of physical and mental therapy and "personal growth" to try to pull myself out of the pit I found myself in when I fled home to Boston in the spring of 1980. I got into an

Exercycle and diet program that in six months cut my pulse rate from a dangerously stress-induced 120 to a healthy 60, and shed 20 pounds. I gave up the alcohol that I had used as regularly and purposely as daily medicine for 25 years, then gave up the marijuana that replaced it, and even threw away the faithful briar pipe I had clenched and puffed for a quarter of a century.

I used to worry about which of these addictions I kicked through "church" and which through secular programs, as if I had to assign proper "credit," and as if it were possible to compartmentalize and isolate the influence of God, like some kind of vitamin. The one thing I know about the deepest feeling connected with all my assortment of life-numbing addictions is that at some point or other they felt as if they were "lifted," taken away, and instead of having to exercise iron control to resist them, it simply felt better not to have to do them anymore. The only concept I know to describe such experience is that of "grace," and the accompanying adjective "amazing" comes to mind along with it. [16]

I do not for a moment suggest that giving up booze or even drugs, or losing weight or reducing the heart rate is necessarily — or even desirably — a byproduct of religious experience. For many people, such effects may not have anything to do with religion. Each person's quest is his own, with its own imperatives and directions. [17]

I became fascinated by other people's spiritual experiences and, 30 years after it was first recommended to me, I read Thomas Merton's "The Seven Storey Mountain." I had avoided it even when the late poet Mark Van Doren, my favorite professor and Merton's former mentor at Columbia, had spoken of it with high regard, but now I devoured it, and went on to read everything else of Merton's I could get my hands on, from the sociopolitical "Conjectures of a Guilty Bystander" to the mystical "The Ascent to Truth." Most meaningful of all was a slim "meditation" by Merton, called "He Is Risen," which I found by chance in a New York bookstore; it says in matter-of-fact prose that Christ "is in history with us, walking ahead of us to where we are going. . . . " [18]

I thought of these words walking the brick sidewalks of Beacon Hill, thinking for the first time of my life as a "journey" rather than a battle I was winning or losing that moment, on whose immediate crashing outcome the fate of the universe (i.e., the turbulent one in my own head) depended. I remembered years ago reading Dorothy Day's column in The Catholic Worker when I lived in Greenwich Village, and I appreciated now for the first time the sense of the title: "On Pilgrimage." [19]

I cannot pinpoint any particular time when I suddenly believed in God again while all this was going on. I only know that such belief seemed as natural as for 25 or more years before it had been inconceivable. I realized this while looking at fish. [20]

I had gone with my girlfriend of the last several years to the New England Aquarium, and as we gazed at the astonishingly brilliant colors of some of the small tropical fish — reds and yellows and oranges and blues that seemed to be splashed on by some innovative artistic genius — and watched the amazing lights of [21] the flashlight fish that blinked on like the beacons of some creature of a sci-fi epic, I wondered how anyone could think that all this was the result of some chain of accidental explosions! Yet I realized in frustration that to try to convince me otherwise five years before would have been hopeless. Was this what they called "conversion?"

The term bothered me because it suggested being "born again," and like many 22 of my contemporaries, I have been put off by what seems the melodramatic nature of that label, as well as the current political beliefs that seem to go along with it. Besides, I don't *feel* "reborn." No voice came out of the sky nor did a thunderclap strike me on the path through the Boston Common on the way to King's Chapel. I was relieved when our minister explained that the literal translation of "conversion" in both the Hebrew and Greek is not "rebirth" but "turning." That's what this has felt like — as if I were walking in one direction and then, in response to some inner pull, I turned — not even all the way around, but only at what seemed a slightly different angle.

I wish I could say that this turning has put me on a straight, solid path with 23 blue skies above and a warm, benevolent sun shining down. I certainly enjoy better health than when I began to "turn" five years ago, but the path I am on now seems often as dangerous and difficult as the one I was following before. Sometimes it doesn't even seem like a path at all. Sometimes I feel like a hapless passenger in the sort of small airplane they used to show in black and white movies of the 1930's, caught in a thunderstorm, bobbing through the night sky over jagged mountains without a compass.

I find strength in the hard wisdom of those who have delved much deeper into 24 the spiritual realm than I, like Henri Nouwen, the Dutch Roman Catholic theologian who wrote in a book our minister recommended, called "Reaching Out," that " . . . it would be just another illusion to believe that reaching out to God will free us from pain and suffering. Often, indeed, it will take us where we rather would not go. But we know that without going there we will not find our life."

I was thrilled to meet Nouwen at lunch a few years ago, through the con- 25 sideration of my friend and neighbor James Carroll, the former priest, now novelist. I told Father Nouwen I had read and appreciated his work, but that it dismayed me to read of his anguish in "Cry for Mercy: Prayers From the Genessee"; it made me wonder with discouragement what chance a neophyte had in pursuit of the spiritual, when someone as advanced as Father Nouwen experienced anguish and confusion in his relation to God (I was neglecting numerous other, even more powerful examples, such as Jesus Christ calling out from the cross). Father Nouwen answered sharply that contrary to what many people may think, "Christianity is not for getting your life together!"

About a year ago, I felt as if finally, with God's help, I was on the right track in 26 my own journey. Then I had an experience that was like running head-on into a wall. First, shock, then a kind of psychic pain as unrelenting as a dentist's drill. And in the torment I prayed, and there was no relief, and twice I turned back to my old way of dealing with things, by trying to numb the pain with drugs. Throughout all this, I never lost faith in God, never imagined He was not there, but only that His presence was obscured. Then the storm broke, like a fever, and I felt in touch again, and in the light. I was grateful, but I also knew such storms would come again, perhaps even more violently.

I learned that belief in God does not depend on how well things are going,   27 that faith and prayer and good works do not necessarily have any correlation to earthly reward or even tranquility, no matter how much we wish they would and think they should. I believe in God because the gift of faith (if not the gift of understanding) has been given to me, and I go to church and pray and meditate to try to be closer to His presence, and, most difficult of all, to discern His will. I know, as it says in the Book of Common Prayer, that His "service is perfect freedom," and my great frustration and anxiety is in the constant choices of how best to serve, with the particular gifts as well as limitations I've been given.

A month or so ago, I went to Glastonbury Abbey, a Benedictine monastery in   28 Hingham, only 40 minutes or so from Boston, to spend a day and night in private retreat. I went with about 17 questions in my head about following God or the path He wills us to take. In the chapel bookstore, I saw a thin paperback volume, "Abandonment to Divine Providence," which I picked up, took to my room and devoured. It was written by an 18th-century Jesuit named Jean-Pierre de Caussade, and it sounds (at least in this new translation) as if it had been written yesterday, specifically to answer my questions. I continue to read in it almost every day, and I always find some new passage that seems to speak to the urgency of that moment. This is what I read today, when I felt again jarred and confused about what to choose and where to turn:

"So we follow our wandering paths, and the very darkness acts as our guide   29 and our doubts serve to reassure us. The more puzzled Isaac was at not finding a lamb for the sacrifice, the more confidently did Abraham leave all to providence."

▼ TOPICAL CONSIDERATIONS

1. What prompted Wakefield to attend church?
2. What kinds of stress was Wakefield dealing with before his return to church? How was the Twenty-Third Psalm a comfort to him then?
3. What is the appeal of attending church on a "regular" Sunday for Wakefield?
4. Explain what the author means when he says Bible study was like "holding up a mirror to my own life." Have you ever had a similarly strong reaction to a particular biblical passage? If so, explain the experience.
5. How does Wakefield explain his success in giving up addictions such as alcohol, marijuana, and pipe tobacco?
6. Why is Wakefield uncomfortable with the term "conversion"? What term does he prefer? Why?
7. What do you think Father Nouwen meant when he said to Wakefield, "Christianity is not for getting your life together"? Do you agree or disagree with this statement?

▼ RHETORICAL CONSIDERATIONS

1. Wakefield's essay begins in a bar and ends in a Benedictine monastery. How do these locations suggest the changes that have occurred in the author's life?
2. Wakefield's initial self-consciousness about returning to church is expressed in several comic remarks such as that in the first paragraph: "don't all these stories of revelation begin in bars?" Find other examples of this self-conscious humor. What is the effect of this humor? How does it add to the essay?
3. For Wakefield, a novelist, words are his profession, and he used them carefully and precisely. Consider the use of the word "sanctuary" in paragraph 9. How does he use the term here? What metaphors in paragraphs 9 and 10 rely on the concept of sanctuary?
4. To illustrate the impact of Bible study, Wakefield describes three meetings. Why do you think he chose these three? What distinct insight does he gain from each meeting?

▼ WRITING ASSIGNMENTS

1. Wakefield cannot pinpoint the moment he believed in God again. However, he realized he did, in fact, believe in God while gazing at fish. Write an essay describing the experience you had when you realized that you did or did not believe in God.
2. Wakefield writes of his conversion: "I wish I could say that this turning has put me on a straight, solid path with blue skies above and a warm, benevolent sun shining down. . . . but the path I am on now seems often as dangerous and difficult as the one I was following before." Write an essay explaining how Wakefield's faith offers him joy as well as pain. How does Wakefield's experience compare with your own?
3. What attitudes do you and your friends hold regarding the values of faith in today's world? Write a paper in which you talk about your attitudes toward religion.

FAMILY
MATTERS

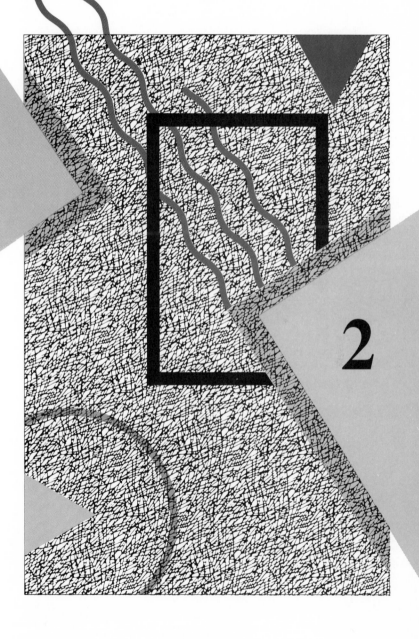

2

▼ IT'S IN THE GENES

Dave Barry

Most middle-class families have the wherewithal to turn their homes into neat, tasteful environments. Then there are the Barrys, who lack not the money for decent furniture but the special "glands" for interior decorating. Dave Barry has been described as "America's most preposterous newspaper columnist," a man "incapable of not being funny." He is the author of eight books and a Pulitzer-Prize-winning *Miami Herald* columnist syndicated in more than 200 publications. With his characteristic deadpan wit he exposes not just his own family's neuroses, but some lunatic habits we all can identify with. Barry is the author of *Babies and Other Hazards of Sex* (1984), *Bad Habits* (1987), from which this article came, and *Dave Barry's Greatest Hits* (1989).

1 My wife and I were both born without whatever brain part it is that enables people to decorate their homes. If we had lived in the Neanderthal era, ours would be the only cave without little drawings of elk on the walls.

2 When we moved into our house eight years ago, there was this lighting fixture in the dining room that obviously had been installed by vandals. Simply removing this fixture would be too good for it; this is the kind of fixture that needs to be taken out in the backyard and shot. When people came over to visit, back when we first moved in, we'd gesture toward the fixture derisively and say "Of course *that's* got to go."

3 Of course we still have it. We have no way of deciding what to replace it with. What we *have* done is get an electrician to come in and move the fixture to another part of the dining room, because, after years of thinking about it with our defective brains, we thought this might be a good decorative idea. To move the fixture, the electrician had to punch holes, some of them big enough to put your fist through, in the wall and ceiling. I have taped plastic sandwich bags over these holes, to keep the air from rushing in and out.

4 So now, after eight years, we have the original vandal fixture, *plus* we have holes with plastic bags over them. We eat in the kitchen. We will always eat in the kitchen, and our dining room will always look like the South Bronx. We have learned that anything we try to do to improve it will just make it worse, because of these missing brain parts.

5 We do a lot of work with plastic bags. We made curtains for several rooms by taping up dark plastic garbage bags. My wife feels guilty about this, because she believes women are supposed to have this Betty Crocker gland somewhere that secretes a hormone that enables them to sew curtains. God knows she has tried.

She reads articles, she takes measurements, she even goes to the fabric store, but because of what she perceives to be a deficiency of her Betty Crocker gland, she never actually produces any curtains. Which is fine, because I have a deficiency of my Mr. Goodwrench gland and would never put them up.

So we use plastic garbage bags. They work fine, but I have noticed that most of our friends, now that we're all grown-ups, have switched over to actual cloth curtains. Also they have tasteful Danish furniture. They just went out and got it somehow, as if it were no big deal, and now everything matches, like those photographs in snotty interior design magazines featuring homes owned by wealthy people who eat out and keep their children in Switzerland. We have this green armchair we got at an auction for twenty-five cents. This is not one of those chairs that are sold for a song but turn out to be tasteful antiques worth thousands of dollars. This chair, at twenty-five cents, was clearly overpriced. It looks, from a distance, like a wad of mucus, and it could not possibly match any other furniture because any furniture that looked like it would have been burned years ago.

Accompanying this chair is a sofa that some people we know tried to throw away six years ago, which we have covered with a blanket to prevent guests from looking directly at it and being blinded or driven insane. Such is the tastelessness of this sofa. And these are two of our better pieces. The only really nice furniture we own is manufactured by the Fisher-Price toy company for my son's little Fisher-Price people, although I certainly don't begrudge them that, inasmuch as they have no arms or legs.

I imagine you're going to suggest that we go out and buy a nice piece of furniture, and then, when we can afford it, another one, and so on until we have a regular grown-up neat and tasteful home. This would never work. If we were to put a nice piece of furniture in our living room, all the other furniture would wait until we'd gone to bed, then ridicule and deride the new furniture, and emit all kinds of shabbiness germs into the living room atmosphere, and by morning the new furniture would be old and stained and hideous. I also firmly believe that if we were to leave our chair in one of our friends' tasteful living rooms for several days, it would become sleek and Danish.

This interior decorating problem extends to cars. None of my friends, for example, have plaster models of their teeth in their cars. I have two in my car. My dentist gives them to me from time to time, sort of like a treat, and I'm afraid to throw them away for fear he'll get angry and make me come in for an appointment. I keep them in my car because God knows the house is already bad enough, but I know they are not tasteful. I can't put them under the seat, because my car, like all the cars we've ever owned, has developed Car Leprosy, which causes all the nonessential parts such as window cranks to gradually fall off and collect under the seat and merge with French fries from the drive-thru window at the Burger King. I'm not about to put my teeth down *there.* So they sit in plain view, grinning at me as I drive and snickering at my lack of taste.

My wife and I are learning to accept all this. We realize that if the present trends continue, we will not be able to admit people into our house without blindfolds. I can live with that. What I worry about is that we will get in trouble with the bank or the government or something. One day there will be a violent pounding on the door, and we will be subjected to a surprise inspection by the Committee of Normal Grown-ups, headed by my wife's home economics teacher and my shop teacher. They'll take one look at our curtains, and they'll take away our house and cars and put us in a special institution where the inmates are roused at 4:30 A.M., chained together, and forced to install wallpaper all day. Nancy Reagan would be the warden.

▼ TOPICAL CONSIDERATIONS

1. After eight years, what have the Barrys done about the light fixture?
2. What excuse does Barry offer for not going out and buying new furniture?
3. In contrast to the Barrys, how have their friends "grown up"?
4. Why can't Barry part with the plastic models of his teeth, which he keeps in his car? How does this relate to his greater problem with the furniture?
5. Can you identify with the Barry's decorating "deficiency"? Do you know anyone who suffers the same syndrome?

▼ RHETORICAL CONSIDERATIONS

1. Writers employ several strategies for creating the various humorous effects. Try to find humorous passages whose effects are created by allusion, surprise, satire, irony, understatement, overstatement, a deliberate pretense to ignorance, and absurd analogy. Can you find any other comic devices?
2. Where does Barry make his thesis statement in this piece? Is it stated directly, or is it implied?
3. How effective is Barry's opening paragraph in establishing his tone and theme? Consider his word choice as well as what he says.
4. What is the point in Barry's barb in paragraph 6 about "wealthy people who eat out and keep their children in Switzerland"?

▼ WRITING ASSIGNMENTS

1. The major thrust of Barry's humor here is self-deprecation, that is, making fun of himself. Try writing some self-deprecating humor of your own by describing some of your own "deficiencies." As does Barry, use exaggeration, irony, overstatement, understatement, and other humorous strategies.
2. Have you ever held onto something that you objectively knew was ugly and useless? If so, what was (or is) it, and how do you explain your attachment to it?

▼ MY GRANDMOTHER, THE BAG LADY

Patsy Neal

What follows is a touching portrait of an elderly woman, the author's grandmother, whose world has shrunken away to the contents of a paper bag. Not one of the pathetic homeless who roam big-city streets, this "bag lady" lives comfortably in a nursing home with around-the-clock attendance and a family who cares and visits her regularly. Yet she shares with the homeless the loss of possessions, place, and independence. Neal teaches physical education and is the volleyball coach at Montreat-Anderson College in North Carolina. This article first appeared in the "My Turn" column in *Newsweek* in 1985.

1 Almost all of us have seen pictures of old, homeless ladies, moving about the streets of big cities with everything they own stuffed into a bag or a paper sack.

2 My grandmother is 89 years old, and a few weeks ago I realized with a jolt that she, too, had become one of them. Before I go any further, I had best explain that I did not see my grandmother's picture on TV. I discovered her plight during a face-to-face visit at my mother's house—in a beautiful, comfortable, safe, middle-class environment with good china on the table and turkey and chicken on the stove.

3 My grandmother's condition saddened me beyond words, for an 89-year-old should not have to carry around everything she owns in a bag. It's enough to be 89, without the added burden of packing the last fragments of your existence into a space big enough to accommodate only the minutest of treasures.

4 Becoming a bag lady was not something that happened to her overnight. My grandmother has been in a nursing home these last several years; at first going back to her own home for short visits, then less frequently as she became older and less mobile.

5 No matter how short these visits were, her greatest pleasure came from walking slowly around her home, touching every item lovingly and spending hours browsing through drawers and closets. Then, I did not understand her need to search out all her belongings.

6 As she spent longer days and months at the nursing home, I could not help noticing other things. She began to hide her possessions under the mattress, in her closet, under the cushion of her chair, in every conceivable, reachable space. And she began to think that people were "stealing" from her.

7 **Unsteady:** When a walker became necessary, my mother took the time to make a bag that could be attached to it, so that my grandmother could carry things around while keeping her hands on the walker. I had not paid much

attention to this bag until we went to the nursing home to take her home with us for our traditional Christmas Eve sharing of gifts.

As we left, my grandmother took her long, unsteady walk down the hallway, balancing herself with her walker, laboriously moving it ahead, one step at a time, until finally we were at the car outside. Once she was safely seated, I picked up her walker to put it in the back. I could barely lift it. Then I noticed that the bag attached to it was bulging. Something clicked, but it still wasn't complete enough to grasp.   8

At home in my mother's house, I was asked to get some photographs from my grandmother's purse. Lifting her pocketbook, I was surprised again at the weight and bulk. I watched as my mother pulled out an alarm clock, a flashlight, a small radio, thread, needles, pieces of sewing, a book and other items that seemed to have no reason for being in a pocketbook.   9

I looked at my grandmother, sitting bent over in her chair, rummaging through the bag on the walker, slowly pulling out one item and then another, and lovingly putting it back. I looked down at her purse with all its disconnected contents and remembered her visits to her home, rummaging through drawers and through closets.   10

"Oh, Lord," I thought with sudden insight. "That walker and that purse are her home now."   11

I began to understand that over the years my grandmother's space for living had diminished like melting butter—from endless fields and miles of freedom as a child and young mother to, with age, the constrictions of a house, then a small room in a nursing home and finally to the tightly clutched handbag and the bag on her walker.   12

When the family sent her to a nursing home, it was the toughest decision it had ever had to make. We all thought she would be secure there; we would no longer have to worry about whether she had taken her medicine, or left her stove on, or was alone at night.   13

But we hadn't fully understood her needs. Security for my grandmother was not in the warm room at the nursing home, with 24-hour attendants to keep her safe and well fed, nor in the family who visited and took her to visit in their homes. In her mind her security was tied to those things she could call her own—and over the years those possessions had dwindled away like sand dropping through an hourglass: first her car, sold when her eyes became bad and she couldn't drive; then some furnishings she didn't really need. Later it was the dogs she had trouble taking care of. And finally it would be her home when it became evident that she could never leave the nursing home again. But as her space and mobility dwindled, so did her control over her life.   14

Dignity: I looked at my grandmother again, sitting so alone before me, hair totally gray, limbs and joints swollen by arthritis, at the hearing aid that could no longer help her hear, and the glasses too thick but so inadequate in helping her to see . . . and yet there was such dignity about her. A dignity I could not understand.   15

The next day, after my grandmother had been taken back to the nursing home   16 and my mother was picking up in her room, she found a small scrap of paper my grandmother had scribbled these words on:

"It is 1:30 tonight and I had to get up and go to the bathroom. I cannot go back to sleep. But I looked in on Margaret and she is sleeping *so* good, and Patsy is sleeping too." 17

With that note, I finally understood, and my 89-year-old bag-lady grandmother changed from an almost helpless invalid to a courageous, caring individual still very much in control of her environment. 18

What intense loneliness she must have felt as she scribbled that small note on that small piece of paper with the small bag on her walker and her small purse next to her. Yet she chose to experience it alone rather than wake either of us from much-needed sleep. Out of her own great need, she chose to meet our needs. 19

As I held that tiny note, and cried inside, I wondered if she dreamed of younger years and more treasured possessions and a bigger world when she went back to sleep that night. I certainly hoped so. 20

▼ TOPICAL CONSIDERATIONS

1. Describe how Neal's eighty-nine-year-old grandmother became a bag lady.
2. The grandmother's family sent her to a nursing home to provide security. How did the family's definition of security differ from the grandmother's? How, paradoxically, did the nursing home erode the woman's sense of security?
3. What does the grandmother's note reveal to the author?
4. Although she is feeble and infirm, control is still a major issue for Neal's grandmother. In what ways does she manifest control over her life?

▼ RHETORICAL CONSIDERATIONS

1. How does the labeling of a grandmother as a bag lady capture the reader's attention?
2. What similes does the author use to describe the gradual diminishing of her grandmother's world and possessions? Are they effective? Are they original? Try to supply some of your own, if you can.
3. Did you find the concluding paragraph of the essay sentimental, that is, a deliberate ploy of the author to evoke emotion from the reader?

▼ WRITING ASSIGNMENTS

1. In this essay, seemingly minor events give great insight into the grandmother's character. Write a brief character sketch, in which a seemingly insignificant event (or events) lends insight into the character of someone you know.

2. Write a portrait of someone in your neighborhood, community, or school, who for whatever reasons, does not seem to adjust. Use specific details about the person's behavior and dialogue to capture the individual.

▼ RACHEL AND HER CHILDREN

Jonathan Kozol

> Most people associate the word "home" with an environment of comfort and security, of love and family care—a refuge where private joys and sorrows are shared. It is a place assumed essential for every human being. In America, however, more than 2 million people are homeless, and many more will be soon. Not just individuals, the new class of homeless includes whole families who were housed in apartments or in homes they once could afford. The prime cause of homelessness in America, it has been shown, is simply the lack of housing that poor people can afford. Although some families have been placed in "temporary" shelters, these "welfare hotels" are grim substitutes for homes. The piece that follows has been taken from Jonathan Kozol's book of the same title. The intent of the book, published in 1988, was not just to expose this national shame but to reveal what it means to be homeless. And, as in the excerpt below, Kozol lets the homeless speak for themselves. "Rachel and Her Children" is a portrait of a mother with no hope and children with no future. Kozol is the author of the National Book Award-winning *Death at an Early Age* (1967) and *Illiterate America* (1985).

Mr. Allesandro is too shaken to attempt to hide his frailties from me. He tells me: "When you're running scared you do some things you'd rather not...." He does not regard himself as saint or martyr. There are virtues, feelings and commitments he has forfeited during this long ordeal. Love is not one of them. His desperation for his son and daughters and his adoration of his mother are as solid and authentic as the marble pillars of the Martinique Hotel. The authenticity of love deserves some mention in discussion of the homeless. 1

Houses can be built without a number of ingredients that other ages viewed as indispensable. Acrylics, plastics and aluminum may substitute for every substance known to nature. Parental love cannot be synthesized. Even the most earnest and methodical foster care demonstrates the limits of synthetic tenderness and surrogate emotion. So it seems of keen importance to consider any ways, and *every* way, by which a family, splintered, jolted and imperiled though it be by loss of home and subsequent detention in a building like the Martinique, may nonetheless be given every possible incentive to remain together. 2

The inclination to judge harshly the behavior of a parent under formidable stress seems to be much stronger than the willingness to castigate the policies that undermine the competence and ingenuity of many of these people in the first place. 3

"Men can be unequal in their needs, in their honor, in their possessions," 4 writes historian Michael Ignatieff, "but also in their rights to judge others." The king's ultimate inequality, he says, "is that he is never judged." An entire industry of scholarship and public policy exists to judge the failing or defective parent; if we listen to some of these parents carefully we may be no less concerned by their impaired abilities, but we may be less judgmental or, if we remain compelled to judge, we may redirect our energies in more appropriate directions.

New Year's Eve. 5

She stalks into the room. Her eyes are reddened and her clothes in disarray. 6 She wears a wrinkled and translucent nightgown. On her feet: red woolen stockings. At her throat: a crucifix. Over her shoulders is a dark and heavy robe. Nothing I have learned in the past week prepares me for this apparition.

She cries. She weeps. She paces left and right and back and forth. Pivoting 7 and turning suddenly to face me. Glaring straight into my eyes. A sudden halt. She looks up toward the cracked and yellowish ceiling of the room. Her children stand around her in a circle. Two little girls. A frightened boy. They stare at her, as I do, as her arms reach out—for what? They snap like snakes and coil back. Her hair is gray—a stiff and brushlike Afro.

Angelina is twelve years old, Stephen is eleven, Erica is nine. The youngest 8 child, eleven months, is sitting on the floor. A neighbor's child, six years old, sits in my lap and leans her head against my chest; she holds her arms around my neck. Her name or nickname (I do not know which) is Raisin. When she likes she puts her fingers on my mouth and interrupts the conversation with a tremolo of rapid words. There are two rooms. Rachel disappears into the second room, then returns and stands, uneasy, by the door.

Angie: "Ever since August we been livin' here. The room is either very hot or 9 freezin' cold. When it be hot outside it's hot in here. When it be cold outside we have no heat. We used to live with my aunt but then it got too crowded there so we moved out. We went to welfare and they sent us to the shelter. Then they shipped us to Manhattan. I'm scared of the elevators. 'Fraid they be stuck. I take the stairs."

Raisin: "Elevator might fall down and you would die." 10

Rachel: "It's unfair for them to be here in this room. They be yellin'. Lots of 11 times I'm goin' to walk out. Walk out on the street and give it up. No, I don't do it. BCW [Bureau of Child Welfare] come to take the children. So I make them stay inside. Once they walk outside that door they are in danger."

Angie: "I had a friend Yoki. They was tryin' to beat her. I said: 'Leave her.' 12 They began to chase me. We was runnin' to the door. So we was runnin'. I get to the door. The door was stuck. I hit my eye and it began to bleed. So I came home and washed the blood. Me and my friends sat up all night and prayed. Prayin' for me. 'Dear Lord, can you please help me with my eye? If you do I promise to behave.' I was askin' God why did this happen. I wish someone in New York could help us. Put all of the money that we have together and we buy a building. Two or three rooms for every family. Everybody have a kitchen. Way it is, you frightened all the time. I think this world is coming to the end."

Stephen: "This city is rich." 13

Angie: "Surely is!" 14

Erica: "City and welfare, they got something goin'. Pay $3,000 every month to 15
stay in these here rooms . . . "

Rachel: "I believe the City Hall got something goin' here. Gettin' a cut. They 16
got to be. My children, they be treated like chess pieces. Send all of that money off
to Africa? You hear that song? They're not thinking about people starvin' here in
the United States. I was thinkin': Get my kids and all the other children here to
sing, 'We are the world. We live here too.' How come do you care so much for
people you can't see? Ain't we the world? Ain't we a piece of it? We are so close
they be afraid to see. Give us a shot at something. We are something! Ain't we
something? I'm depressed. But we are *something!* People in America don't want
to see."

Angie: "Christmas is sad for everyone. We have our toys. That's not the 17
reason why. They givin' you toys and that do help. I would rather that we have a
place to be."

Erica: "I wrote a letter to Santa Claus. Santa say that he don't have the 18
change."

Raisin: "I saw Santa on the street. Then I saw Santa on another street. I pulled 19
his beard and he said something nasty."

Angie: "There's one thing I ask: a home to be in with my mother. That was 20
my only wish for Christmas. But it could not be."

Raisin: "I saw Mr. Water Bug under my mother's bed. Mr. Rat be livin' with us 21
too."

Angie: "It's so cold right now you got to use the hot plate. Plug it in so you be 22
warm. You need to have a hot plate. Are you goin' to live on cold bologna all your
life?"

Raisin: "Mr. Rat came in my baby sister's crib and bit her. Nobody felt sorry 23
for my sister. Then I couldn't go to sleep. I started crying. All of a sudden I pray
and went to sleep and then I woke up in the mornin', make my bed, and took a
bath, and ate, and went to school. So I came back and did my homework. And all
of a sudden there was something *irritatin'* at my hand. I looked out the window
and the moon was goin' up. And then—I had a dream. I went to sleep and I was
dreamin' and I dreamed about a witch that bit me. I felt *dead.* When I woke back
up I had a headache."

Angie: "School is bad for me. I feel ashamed. They know we're not the same. 24
My teacher do not treat us all the same. They know which children live in the
hotel."

Erica: "My teacher isn't like that. She treats all of us the same. We all get 25
smacked. We all get punished the same way."

Stephen: "I'm in sixth grade. When I am a grown-up I be a computer." 26

Erica: "You're in the fifth. You lie." 27

Raisin: "When I grow up I want to be multiplication and subtraction and 28
division."

Angie: "Last week a drug addict tried to stab me. With an ice pick. Tried to 29
stab my mother too. Older girls was botherin' us. They try to make us fight. We

don't fight. We don't start fires. They just pickin' on us. We ran home and got our mother. They ran home and got their mother."

Raisin: "Those girls upstairs on the ninth floor, they be bad. They sellin' crack." 30

Erica: "Upstairs, ninth floor, nine-o-five, they sellin' crack." 31

Raisin: "A man was selling something on the street. He had some reefers on him and the po-lice caught him and they took him to the jail. You know where the junkies put the crack? Put the crack inside the pipe. Smoke it like that. They take a torch and burn the pipe and put it in their mouth. They go like this." [Puffs.] 32

I ask: "Why do they do it?" 33

Erica: "Feel good! Hey! Make you feel fine!" 34

Angie: "This girl I know lives in a room where they sell drugs. One day she asks us do we want a puff. So we said: 'No. My mother doesn't let us do it.' One day I was walkin' in the hall. This man asked me do I want some stuff. He said: 'Do you want some?' I said no and I ran home." 35

Raisin: "One day my brother found these two big plastic bags inside his teddy bear. Po-lice came up to my room and took that teddy bear." She's interrupted. "I ain't finished! And they took it. One day we was by my uncle's car and this man came and he said: 'Do you want some?' We said no. We told my uncle and he went and found the man and he ran to the bar and went into the women's bathroom in the bar. And so we left." 36

Angie: "I think this world is ending. Yes. Ending. Everybody in this city killin' on each other. Countries killin' on each other. Why can't people learn to stick together? It's no use to fightin'. Fightin' over nothin'. What they fightin' for? A flag! I don't know what we are fightin' for. President Reagan wants to put the rockets on the moon. What's he doin' messin' with the moon? If God wanted man and woman on the moon He would of put us there. They should send a camera to the moon and feed the people here on earth. Don't go messin' there with human beings. Use that money to build houses. Grow food! Buy seeds! Weave cloth! Give it to the people in America!" 37

Erica: "When we hungry and don't have no food we borrow from each other. Her mother [Raisin's] give us food. Or else we go to Crisis. In the mornin' when we wake up we have a banana or a cookie. If the bus ain't late we have our breakfast in the school. What I say to President Reagan: Give someone a chance! I believe he be a selfish man. Can't imagine how long he been president." 38

Raisin: "Be too long." 39

Angie: "Teacher tell us this be a democracy. I don't know. I doubt it. Rich people, couldn't they at least give us a refund?" 40

Raisin: "This man say his son be gettin' on his nerves. He beat his little son 'bout two years old. A wooden bat. He beat him half to death. They took him to the hospital and at five-thirty he was dead. A little boy. [Interrupted.] Let me talk!" 41

Erica: "The little boy. He locked himself into the bathroom. He was scared. After he died police came and his father went to jail. His mother, she went to the store." 42

Raisin, in a tiny voice: "People fight in here and I don't like it. Why do they do it? 'Cause they're sad. They fight over the world. I ain't finished!" 43

Erica: "One time they was two cops in the hall. One cop pulled his gun   44
and he was goin' shoot me. He said did I live there? I said no. So I came
home."

Raisin: "I was in this lady room. She be cryin' because her baby died. He had   45
[mispronounced] pneumonia. He was unconscious and he died." Soft voice:
"Tomorrow is my birthday."

The children are tended by a friend. In the other bedroom, Rachel, who is   46
quieter now, paces about and finally sits down.

"Do you know why there's no carpet in the hall? If there was a carpet it would   47
be on fire. Desperate people don't have no control. You have to sleep with one eye
open. Tell the truth, I do not sleep at night.

"Before we lived here we were at the Forbell shelter [barracks shelter on   48
Forbell Street in Brooklyn]. People sleep together in one room. You sleep across.
You have to dress in front of everybody. Men and women. When you wake, some
man lookin' at you puttin' on your clothes. Lookin' at your children too. Angelina,
she be only twelve years old . . .

"There's one thing. My children still are pure. They have a concept of life.   49
Respect for life. But if you don't get 'em out of here they won't have anything for
long. If you get 'em out right now. But if you don't . . . My girls are innocent still.
They are unspoiled. Will they be that way for long? Try to keep 'em in the room.
But you can't lock 'em up for long.

"When we moved here I was forced to sign a paper. Everybody has to do it.   50
It's a promise that you will not cook inside your room. So we lived on cold
bologna. Can you feed a child on that? God forgive me but nobody shouldn't have
to live like this. I can't even go downstairs and get back on the elevator. Half the
time it doesn't work. Since I came into this place my kids begun to get away from
me."

There's a crucifix on the wall. I ask her: "Do you pray?"   51

"I don't pray! Pray for what? I been prayin' all my life and I'm still here. When   52
I came to this hotel I still believed in God. I said: 'Maybe God can help us to
survive.' I lost my faith. My hopes. And everything. Ain't nobody—no God, no
Jesus—gonna help us in no way.

"God forgive me. I'm emotional. I'm black. I'm in a blackness. Blackness is   53
around me. In the night I'm scared to sleep. In the mornin' I'm worn out. I don't
eat no breakfast. I don't drink no coffee. If I eat, I eat one meal a day. My stomach
won't allow me. I have ulcers. I stay in this room. I hide. This room is safe to me. I
am afraid to go outside.

"If I go out, what do I do? People drink. Why do they drink? A person gets   54
worn out. They usin' drugs. Why they use drugs? They say: 'Well, I won't think
about it now.' Why not? You ain't got nothin' else to do, no place to go. 'Where I'm
gonna be tomorrow or the next day?' They don't know. All they know is that they
don't have nothin'. So they drink. And some of them would rather not wake up.
Rather be dead. That's right.

"Most of us are black. Some Puerto Rican. Some be white. They suffer too.   55

Can you get the government to know that we exist? I know that my children have potential. They're intelligent. They're smart. They need a chance. There's nothin' wrong with them for now. But not for long. My daughter watches junkies usin' needles. People smokin' crack in front a them. Screwin' in front a them. They see it all. They see it everywhere. What is a man and woman gonna do when they are all in the same room?

"I met a girl the other day. She's twelve years old. Lives on the fourteenth floor. She got a baby the same age as mine. Her mother got five children of her own. I don't want my daughter havin' any baby. She's a child. Innocent. Innocent. No violence. She isn't bitter. But she's scared. You understand? This is America. These children growin' up too fast. We have no hope. And you know why? Because we all feel just the same way deep down in our hearts. Nowhere to go . . . I'm not a killer. My kids ain't no killers. But if they don't learn to kill they know they're goin' to die.

"They didn't go to school last week. They didn't have clean clothes. Why? Because the welfare messed my check. It's supposed to come a week ago. It didn't come. I get my check today. I want my kids to go to school. They shouldn't miss a day. How they gonna go to school if they don't got some clothes? I couldn't wash. I didn't have the money to buy food.

"Twice the welfare closed my case. When they do it you are s'posed to go for a fair hearing. Take some papers, birth certificates. So I went out there in the snow. Welfare worker wasn't there. They told me to come back. Mister, it ain't easy to be beggin'. I went to the Crisis. And I asked her, I said, 'Give me somethin' for the kids to eat. Give me *somethin'!* Don't turn me away when I am sittin' here in front of you and askin' for your help!' She said she had nothin'. So my kids went out into the street. That's right! Whole night long they was in Herald Square panhandlin'. Made five dollars. So we bought bologna. My kids is good to me. We had bread and bologna.

"Welfare, they are not polite. They're personal. 'Did you do this? Did you do that? Where your husband at?' Understand me? 'Cause they sittin' on the other side of this here desk, they think we're stupid and we do not understand when we're insulted. 'Oh, you had another baby?' Yeah! I had another baby! What about it? Are you goin' to kill that baby? I don't say it, but that's what I feel like sayin'. You learn to be humble.

"I'm here five miserable months. So I wonder: Where I'm goin'? Can't the mayor give us a house? A part-time job? I am capable of doin' *somethin'.*

"You go in the store with food stamps. You need Pampers. You're not s'posed to use the stamps for Pampers. Stores will accept them. They don't care about the law. What they do is make you pay a little extra. They know you don't have no choice. So they let you buy the Pampers for two dollars extra.

"Plenty of children livin' here on nothin' but bread and bologna. Peanut butter. Jelly. Drinkin' water. You buy milk. I bought one gallon yesterday. Got *this* much left. They drink it fast. Orange juice, they drink it fast. End up drinkin' Kool Aid.

"Children that are poor are used like cattle. Cattle or horses. They are owned by welfare. They know they are bein' used—for what? Don't *use* them! Give 'em somethin'!

"In this bedroom I'm not sleepin' on a bed. They won't give me one. You can 64 see I'm sleepin' on a box spring. I said to the manager: 'I need a bed instead of sleepin' on a spring.' Maid give me some blankets. Try to make it softer."

The Bible by her bed is opened to the Twenty-third Psalm. 65

"I do believe. God forgive me. I believe He's there. But when He sees us like 66 this, I am wonderin' where is He? I am askin': Where the hell He gone?

"Before they shipped us here we lived for five years in a basement. Five years 67 in a basement with no bathroom. One small room. You had to go upstairs two floors to use the toilet. No kitchen. It was fifteen people in five rooms. Sewer kept backing up into the place we slept. Every time it flooded I would have to pay one hundred dollars just to get the thing unstuck. There were all my children sleepin' in the sewage. So you try to get them out and try to get them somethin' better. But it didn't get no better. I came from one bad place into another. But the difference is this is a place where I cannot get out.

"If I can't get out of here I'll give them up. I have asked them: 'Do you want to 68 go away?' I love my kids and, if I did that, they would feel betrayed. They love me. They don't want to go. If I did it, I would only do it to protect them. They'll live anywhere with me. They're innocent. Their minds are clean. They ain't corrupt. They have a heart. All my kids love people. They love life. If they got a dime, a piece of bread, they'll share it. Letting them panhandle made me cry. I had been to welfare, told the lady that my baby ain't got Pampers, ain't got nothin' left to eat. I got rude and noisy and it's not my style to do that but you learn that patience and politeness get you nowhere.

"When they went out on the street I cried. I said: 'I'm scared. What's gonna 69 happen to them?' But if they're hungry they are goin' to do *something*. They are gonna find their food from somewhere. Where I came from I was fightin' for my children. In this place here I am fightin' for my children. I am tired of fightin'. I don't want to fight. I want my kids to live in peace.

"I was thinkin' about this. If there was a place where you could sell part of 70 your body, where they buy an arm or somethin' for a thousand dollars, I would do it. I would do it for my children. I would give my life if I could get a thousand dollars. What would I lose? I lived my life. I want to see my children grow up to live theirs.

"A lot of women do not want to sell their bodies. This is something that good 71 women do not want to do. I will sell mine. I *will*. I will solicit. I will prostitute if it will feed them."

I ask: "Would you do it?" 72

"Ain't no 'would I?' I would do it." Long pause . . . "Yes. I *did*. 73

"I had to do it when the check ain't come. Wasn't no one gonna buy my arm 74 for any thousand dollars. But they's plenty gonna pay me twenty dollars for my body. What was my choice? Leave them out there on the street, a child like Angelina, to panhandle? I would take my life if someone found her dead somewhere. I would go crazy. After she did it that one time I was ashamed. I cried that night.

All night I cried and cried. So I decided I had one thing left. In the mornin' I got up out of this bed. I told them I was goin' out. Out in the street. Stand by the curb. It was a cold day. Freezin'! And my chest is bad. I'm thirty-eight years old. Cop come by. He see me there. I'm standin' out there cryin'. Tells me I should go inside. Gives me three dollars. 'It's too cold to be outside.' Ain't many cops like that. Not many people either . . .

"After he's gone a man come by. Get in his car. Go with him where he want. Takin' a chance he crazy and he kill me. Wishin' somehow that he would.   75

"So he stop his car. And I get in. I say a price. That's it. Go to a room. It's some hotel. He had a lot of money so he rented a deluxe. Asked me would I stay with him all night. I tell him no I can't 'cause I have kids. So, after he done . . . whatever he did . . . I told him that I had to leave. Took out a knife at me and held it at my face. He made me stay. When I woke up next day I was depressed. Feel so guilty what I did. I feel real scared. I can understand why prostitutes shoot drugs. They take the drugs so they don't be afraid.   76

"When he put that knife up to my throat, I'm thinkin' this: What is there left to lose? I'm not goin' to do any better in this life. If I be dead at least my kids won't ever have to say that I betrayed them. I don't like to think like that. But when things pile up on you, you do. 'I'm better if I'm dead.'   77

"So I got me twenty dollars and I go and buy the Pampers for the baby and three dollars of bologna and a loaf of bread and everyone is fed.   78

"That cross of Jesus on the wall I had for seven years. I don't know if I believe or not. Bible say that Jesus was God's son. He died for us to live here on this earth. See, I believe—Jesus was innocent. But, when He died, what was it for? He died for nothin'. Died in vain. He should a let us die like we be doin'—we be dyin' all the time. We dyin' every day.   79

"God forgive me. I don't mean the things I say. God had one son and He gave His son. He gave him up. I couldn't do it. I got four. I could not give any one of them. I couldn't do it. God could do it. Is it wrong to say it? I don't know if Jesus died in vain."   80

She holds the Bible in her hands. Crying softly. Sitting on the box spring in her tangled robe.   81

"They laid him in a manger. Right? Listen to me. I didn't say that God forsaken us. I am confused about religion. I'm just sayin' evil overrules the good. So many bad things goin' on. Lot of bad things right here in this buildin'. It's not easy to believe. I don't read the Bible no more 'cause I don't find no more hope in it. I don't believe. But yet and still . . . I know these words." She reads aloud: " 'Lie down in green pastures . . . leadeth me beside still waters . . . restores my soul . . . I shall not want.'   82

"All that I want is somethin' that's my own. I got four kids. I need four plates, four glasses, and four spoons. Is that a lot? I know I'm poor. Don't have no bank account, no money, or no job. Don't have no nothin'. No foundation. Then and yet my children have a shot in life. They're innocent. They're pure. They have a chance." She reads: " 'I shall not fear . . . ' I fear! A long, long time ago I didn't fear. Didn't fear for nothin'. I said God's protectin' me and would protect my children. Did He do it?   83

"Yeah. I'm walkin'. I am walkin' in the wilderness. That's what it is. I'm   84
walkin'. Did I tell you that I am an ex-drug addict? Yeah. My children know it.
They know and they understand. I'm walkin'. Yeah!"

The room is like a chilled cathedral in which people who do not believe in   85
God ask God's forgiveness. "How I picture God is like an old man who speaks
different languages. His beard is white and He has angels and the instruments they
play are white and everything around is white and there is no more sickness, no
more hunger for nobody. No panhandlin'. No prostitutes. No drugs. I had a dream
like that.

"There's no beauty in my life except two things. My children and"—she   86
hesitates—"I write these poems. How come, when I write it down, it don't come
out my pencil like I feel? I don't know. I got no dictionary. Every time I read it over
I am finding these mistakes.

Deep down in my heart
I do not mean these things I said.
Forgive me. Try to understand me.
I love all of you the same.
Help me to be a better mother.

"When I cry I let 'em know. I tell 'em I was a drug addict. They know and they   87
try to help me to hold on. They helpin' me. My children is what's holdin' me
together. I'm not makin' it. I'm reachin'. And they see me reachin' out. Angelina take
my hand. They come around. They ask me what is wrong. I do let them know when
I am scared. But certain things I keep inside. I try to solve it. If it's my department,
I don't want them to be sad. If it be too bad, if I be scared of gettin' back on drugs,
I'll go to the clinic. They have sessions every other night.

"Hardest time for me is night. Nightmares. Somethin's grabbin' at me. Like a   88
hand. Some spirit's after me. It's somethin' that I don't forget. I wake up in a sweat.
I'm wonderin' why I dream these dreams. So I get up, turn on the light. I don't go
back to sleep until the day is breakin'. I look up an' I be sayin': 'Sun is up. Now I
can go to sleep.'

"After the kids are up and they are dressed and go to school, then I lay down. I   89
go to sleep. But I can't sleep at night. After the sun go down makes me depressed.
I want to turn the light on, move around.

"Know that song—'Those Monday Blues'? I had that album once."   90
I say the title: " 'Monday Blues'?"   91
"I got 'em every day. Lots of times, when I'm in pain, I think I'm goin'   92
to die. That's why I take a drink sometimes. I'm 'fraid to die. I'm wonderin': Am
I dying?"

▼ TOPICAL CONSIDERATIONS

1. What is behind Rachel's complaint about sending "all that money off to
   Africa"?

2. Child psychologists point out that the "work" of childhood is to play. How does this apply to Rachel's children? What is the "work" of their childhood?
3. Kozol writes, "The authenticity of love deserves some mention in discussion of the homeless." How does Rachel embody "the authenticity of love"? What sacrifices does she make to provide for her children?
4. Kozol quotes historian Michael Ignatieff: "Men can be unequal in their needs, in their honor, in their possessions, but also in their rights to judge others." Has this essay changed the way you judge the homeless and the poor? Why or why not? Does understanding the homeless help to curb the urge to judge harshly?
5. Rachel's greatest fear is that her children will lose their innocence. "My children are still pure. They have a concept of life. But if you don't get em out of here they won't have anything for long." Do you feel that her children can maintain their innocence? Will their environment destroy their innocence? What are the consequences for such children and for society, if their innocence is lost too soon?
6. What role does religious faith play in the lives of Rachel and her children? How do their experiences shape their image of God?

▼ RHETORICAL CONSIDERATIONS

1. Kozol directly quotes Rachel and her children. What are the advantages of presenting their story in their own words, instead of straight exposition?
2. Can you find instances where Kozol injects comments meant to influence the reader?
3. How effective is the inclusion of Rachel's poem at the conclusion of the essay?

▼ WRITING ASSIGNMENTS

1. Write a paper in which you speculate on what the future holds for Rachel's children.
2. Write a paper in which you speculate on the future of Rachel.
3. Rachel points to a condition from which many people on welfare suffer: being made to feel demeaned or humiliated by those dispensing the aid. Write a paper in which you try to examine why this is. Do you think welfare recipients need to suffer shame for having to seek public aid?
4. Write an essay in which you record your feelings about Rachel as a woman and a mother. Do you feel sorry for her? Do you feel sorry for her children? Explain why, or why not.

▼ A SON ON HIS OWN

George Fasel

No other male ancestor in the Fasel family line had ever served in the military. But shortly before graduating from high school, the author's son announced that he had signed up for the Navy. A long family tradition is broken and so are the dreams of the author, who had expected his son to head off to college, and not boot camp. In what follows, a father tries to determine why exactly his son's decision troubles him so. George Fasel is a public relations executive for a New York City bank. This essay first appeared in the *New York Times Magazine* in 1987.

Shortly after graduating from high school next June, my son will join the Navy. He announced this decision—which I don't much like—by telephone, just before arriving for one of his holiday visits from the Middle West, where he lives with his mother. 1

I knew he had been toying with the idea, but I assumed this was largely symbolic—a gesture of independence, a kind of bluff in the game of family politics. I had planned to use his visit to engage in some shrewdly tactful but persuasive discouragement. But this kid has learned something about shrewdness himself, and he signed up before coming to see Dad the Discourager. 2

We talk about it as we drive upstate to Cooperstown, to see the Baseball Hall of Fame. I had originally figured he would pump me for anecdotes about players he was too young to have seen—Musial and Mays, Koufax and Gibson, Yaz in '67, the '72 A's—and in the interstices of the conversation I would subtly plant the seeds of doubt. Instead, I am pumping him for information about what he has done, what he's going to do. 3

—How long are you in for? 4
—Four years. 5
—Isn't that a big chunk of your life? 6
—It might be a big chunk out of your life, but it's not much at my age. 7
—Where will you be? 8
—Great Lakes, then Memphis, then who knows where? 9
—What will you do? 10
—They're going to train me to be an air-traffic controller. 11

The next question forms itself: Do you realize that air-traffic controllers are expected to function under a phenomenal amount of stress? But there's no point in asking it, his answer won't change his plans. 12

The signs announce towns like Davenport and West Davenport and Davenport Center, but I don't really see them. Why does my son's decision bother me so 13 much? I'm worried that he'll end up in the Persian Gulf, or whatever corner of the world is rendered dangerous by men who don't have sons in the service, but that's not really it. Maybe I'm upset because what he has decided is so different from what I decided for myself.

When I was his age, in the mid-1950's, I saw no reason whatsoever to give over   14
two years of my life to being yelled at, crawling on my stomach while live ammunition was fired over my head, or performing push-ups because of some marginal imperfection.

In those years, the draft was there to deal with recalcitrants like me. Therefore,   15
10 years before the young men who did not wish to visit Vietnam, and completely without any ideological motive, I became intimately conversant with the deferment lore of the Selective Service System. I knew better than to register, at age 18, in the small town where I attended college, and chose, instead, my hometown big city, where the draft pool was much larger. I started preparing for graduate school in my junior year. I knew that I could ignore my first order to turn up for a physical, which arrived just before graduation.

But how much does this difference really bother me? And haven't things   16
changed in the meantime? Thirty years ago, a dreaded "Greetings!" letter could send me straight into the clutches of some sociopathic drill instructor. Today, an enlistee signs a contract that guarantees him pay, schooling, assignments, and even sets the maximum physical goals he must achieve in boot camp. You can probably negotiate the push-ups. When my son goes into the Navy, he will have certain rights, some control over his future.

Maybe I'm upset because I fear he'll try to get by without college. The   17
education is important for its own sake, but let's face it, we're probably also talking about an issue of social class. In any case, college is a big deal in our family: I went through eight years of it, his mother has a couple of degrees, Big Sister is a junior now, Bigger Sister an honors graduate. For his part, my son has always loved school, except for the part about courses.

We stroll through the Hall of Fame, with its collection of plaques.   18
—So what about school? Is this it?   19
—I doubt it. I'll get two years of college credit from my service classes, and   20
the Navy will pay for two more years later. The worst that can happen is I'll hate the service and be out at 22, with college paid for and money in the bank.

—Hey, look at this. Ted Williams. Check out those numbers. Imagine what he   21
would have done if he hadn't spent five years flying for the Marines.

—I don't know, Dad. Five-hundred-twenty-one homers is pretty good, anyway.   22
The bottle is half empty, the bottle is half full.   23
The Hall of Fame celebrates tradition, and I think of our family. No direct   24
male ancestor of my son's, on either side of the family, has ever served in the military. We're not especially political, but we're not military either. Indeed, his paternal great-great-grandfather, heir to a Prussian noble title and army commission, renounced them to pursue an artist's career in this country: the creative spirit triumphant over the destructive impulse. On the other hand, he ended up illustrating trashy romantic novels. I decide to forgo the argument from family tradition.

We return from Cooperstown, talking Clemente and Paige and the next .400   25
hitter. The car radio announces a series of football scores, including a victory by
the Naval Academy. Silently, my son raises his fist in triumph. He drives very
well—actually, a little fast at times, but, by and large, responsibly. I tell him so, and
he loves it; his sisters close their eyes in the car with him. But he's old enough to
drive a car well and, for that matter, to make good decisions—this might be one of
them—about his own life. That, it finally occurs to me, is what's bothering me.

My son is ready—so quickly, it now seems—to make his own choices, by   26
himself, on his own, and to take the consequences for them. He loves me, he even
likes me, but he doesn't need me to tell him what might be best and how to hedge
against the worst. He knows he'll make mistakes—this might be one of them—and
there'll be times he'll want advice. But the fact is that he can manage, and he's
saying so for the first time, unforgettably. His sisters have made this same transition,
but slowly, almost imperceptibly. Not him. I say to myself: It's all right, I'm still his
father, aren't I?

Aren't I?   27

▼ TOPICAL CONSIDERATIONS

1. Compare the opportunities military service offers the son with those offered
   to his father thirty years ago. How would you describe the differences? Do
   you think the military today is an attractive option for young men and
   women? Would you consider military service?
2. Why is the father bothered by his son's decision to join the Navy? What
   does he discover lies at the heart of his concern?
3. In paragraph 23 Fasel writes, "The bottle is half empty, the bottle is
   half full." How does this statement typify the father's and son's attitudes?
4. How would you answer the father's last question: "It's all right, I'm still his
   father, aren't I? . . . Aren't I?"
5. Describe a situation in which a close friend or relative made a decision you
   did not approve of. What were your objections? Can you separate the real
   from the imagined objections?

▼ RHETORICAL CONSIDERATIONS

1. Why is the Baseball Hall of Fame so effective a setting for this essay? How
   is it ironic?
2. How does the brief exchange about Ted Williams's batting average illustrate a fundamental difference in attitudes between father and son?
3. Consider the effectiveness of the dialogue throughout the essay. What does
   it reveal about the father-son relationship?

▼ WRITING ASSIGNMENTS

1. Compose a letter that Fasel's son might write to his father following their trip to Cooperstown. In it, try to capture how the young man might view his decision and his father's reaction to it.
2. Think of a situation in which your parents disagreed with an important decision made by you. Write an essay from your parents' point of view, analyzing their feelings about your decision.
3. At the end of the essay, Fasel says that he had to come to terms with his son being on his own. Write an essay in which you reflect on the necessary separation between parent and child. In other words, discuss how parents must let go of the decision-making powers over their children, for the benefit of each.

▼ HOMOSEXUALITY: ONE FAMILY'S AFFAIR

Michael Reese and Pamela Abramson

The Chronisters lived an ideal American life until their son, Kelly, told them he was gay. It was a moment of dashed expectations for Joan and Paul. That moment was soon followed by anger and anguish, but they gradually began to accept their only son's homosexuality. The report below is the story of the Chronister family's struggle to accept and understand. It is also Kelly's story, the sharing of his pained loneliness and guilt, his depression and fears, and his courage. Thoughtfully and sensitively written, this essay served as a cover story for *Newsweek* in January 1986.

1   It was the hardest question she'd ever had to ask. "Are you gay?" Joan Chronister finally blurted out to her son, Kelly, who was fidgeting at the other end of the sofa. When he begrudgingly, almost bitterly, replied yes, Joan immediately felt her tears and disgust dissolve into detachment. After 22 years of nursing him through mumps and measles, tending his cuts and bruises and applauding his football feats and straight-A report cards, Joan suddenly saw her son as a stranger. *He's my child,* she thought as he walked out the door. *And I don't even know him.*

2   That afternoon Joan sat and sobbed, unsure whether she was crying for Kelly or the family's dashed expectations. He had been named after K. O. Kelly, Brenda Starr's rough-and-tough comic-strip boyfriend, because his father wanted him to be "tough as hell." But expectations die hard, and if Paul Chronister was disappointed that Kelly hadn't always been his idea of tough, it was nothing compared with the betrayal he felt when he learned that his son was homosexual. It was, he says bitterly, like "the son I knew had died, and a new one was born." Four years have passed, and the Chronisters are still trying to cope with that jarring midlife adjustment. It's been both an individual and a family struggle—and has coincided with the nation's heightened awareness of homosexuality because of the AIDS health crisis. What the Chronisters have learned is that there is no easy way for an American family to confront homosexuality. Joan has taped a saying to her refrigerator door to remind herself of that. "Be into acceptance," it says. "Not understanding."

3   The Chronisters' entire notion of homosexuality had been shaped by stereotypes: effeminate men with limp wrists. But Kelly wasn't like that. His preppy good looks, athletic prowess and All-America demeanor never foretold that today, at 26, he would be living with his lover, Randy Ponce, in a fashionable brownstone in a gay enclave of northwestern Portland, Ore. It's just 15 miles south of his parents' tidy ranch house in Vancouver, Wash., but it might as well be a foreign country.

Though Joan was raised in a tolerant rural Canadian family and Paul broke early from his own Pentecostal upbringing, they have remained conservative in their social values—clinging to tenets that took them from being penniless newlyweds to life as owners of three successful pizza franchises in Washington state.

Paul was proud of his own aggressive instincts in business but thought them lacking in his son. "If we could just get him to be a little meaner," Paul would say, "he could go as far as he wanted to go." That wasn't Kelly. He could be competitive, playing a hard game of street hockey or starring as first-string tackle on his high-school football team. But he was always hardest on himself, a perfectionist who still remembers a B in seventh-grade science as a crushing defeat. Even at home Kelly was almost *too* good, always eager to fix dinners and do the laundry. "Odd that a teen-age boy wants to help his mom," Joan remembers thinking. Both she and Paul came to regard Kelly's perfectionism as his greatest fault. "Everyone is looking for the perfect kid," sighs Paul. "Then you have one and you wish they'd be a little bit ornery." 4

ON THE FRINGE

Kelly saw his perfectionism as a way of hiding from himself and from others. By always being the teacher's pet, by being a hustler in football practice and by being the fringe member of many social groups but the leader of none, Kelly managed to mask his insecurities. Despite his achievements, he had long felt himself an outsider, separate from his peers. He remembers vague sexual feelings as early as the age of seven, when he would linger in the boys' showers after swimming lessons. When his feelings blossomed in his early teens, Kelly had no point of reference and no one he felt comfortable talking to. The only person he even suspected might be gay was a coach whom all the other boys laughed at when they caught him eyeing them in the showers. And though Kelly knew he was only looking for guys when he peeked at his father's girlie magazines, it confused him when he once saw a pornographic picture of a man putting on nylons. "That isn't me," he thought. 5

It was easier for Kelly to know what he wasn't. He wasn't comfortable when his football buddies told faggot jokes; he knew he might betray himself by not laughing, so he even told a few himself. He wasn't able to join in their postgame drinking and picking-up-girls sprees: he was afraid that if he got drunk the truth might slip out. Most of all, he wasn't interested in girls. He came up with lame excuses for those bold enough to ask him out. When that failed, he made up an imaginary girlfriend who lived out of town and to whom he loudly professed he would always remain loyal. 6

At home, Kelly's cover-ups were just as elaborate. He refused to ask his parents to buy him a coat and tie for his senior yearbook photo session because he was afraid they would expect him to wear the new clothes to a dance or on a date. Then, when his father inevitably asked why he wasn't going to the senior prom, Kelly could shrug and say he had nothing to wear. The ruse seemed to work. His parents never suspected that their son might be homosexual. That was something 7 entirely beyond their realm of experience; Kelly, they assured each other, was simply shy and would "come out of his shell" in college. But Kelly knew all along that he was postponing the crisis. He saw college as his only escape.

After a few months at Eastern Washington University near Spokane, Kelly began to feel despair. There was no one on campus he even remotely thought might be gay. Then one fall day Kelly found himself on the athletic field staring at another student; the young man returned Kelly's stare, came over and struck up a conversation. That night Kelly agonized over the overture: *Maybe he's gay. Maybe it'll finally happen.* But Kelly still wasn't sure, even when they met again the next day on the athletic field and exchanged an awkward touch. Finally, a few weeks later, they moved into a private music room, where Kelly listened for hours while his friend played the piano. There Kelly had his first sexual experience with another man.

It left him scared, happy but even more confused than before. "What's going to happen to me? What kind of a life will I have?" he kept asking himself between encounters with his friend that continued sporadically for the next four years. "Why do I feel this way?" There were few places to turn for answers. At that time the gay community at Eastern Washington was virtually invisible. There was not—as there is now—a Gay Students' Union nor places that openly offered counseling to gay students. His sexual contact throughout college was restricted to that single relationship. Kelly channeled his energy into his business studies and long, lonely bicycle rides along the wheat fields near campus. He sometimes rode a hundred miles a day, as if just by pedaling hard enough and fast enough he could push away his feelings.

Knowing what he now knew about himself, Kelly couldn't face long family visits or summers working for his father at the pizza parlor. Instead, he moved from the dorms into an apartment of his own, immersed himself in classes and timidly continued his sexual education. He went to the campus bookstore, furtively browsing through gay psychology texts he was too afraid to buy. Through the mail he ordered a "gay guide" of Spokane but couldn't work up the nerve to go into the three gay bars that were listed. Finally, one Thanksgiving, he imploded. After fixing himself Cornish game hen, mashed potatoes, gravy and pumpkin pie, he went for a long walk in the snow. *I know what I am,* he thought, *but why me? Why was I dealt this?* He began to cry. *I'm alone,* he sobbed, *and it's because I'm gay that I'm alone.*

Kelly's fear of rejection meant he could share his secret with no one, especially not his family. When his parents called and teased him about girls, he always responded with a curt "Leave me alone." That's just Kelly's way, they told themselves, glad that at least he seemed to be doing well in school. And when he graduated with high honors in business management, they proudly drove the six hours to Spokane thinking their son's future was made—that surely a wife and grandchildren would soon follow. But Paul never made it to the ceremonies. After suffering chest pains, he was rushed by air ambulance back to Portland for open-heart surgery. Kelly, who had made no firm postgraduation plans, suddenly found himself back in Vancouver watching TV and helping to run the pizza parlors.

He could stand it only for so long. Soon he was back on his bicycle—speeding   12
across the river to Portland, a gay-bar guide tucked in his back pocket. Still too
scared to go inside, Kelly usually ended up alone in some shopping-mall restaurant,
drinking coffee. That's where he met David, whom Kelly, despite his apprehension,
accompanied to his first gay bar, The Rafters. It was not at all what he had
imagined. Instead of being dark and ominous, it was bright and friendly; instead
of aging drag queens and tough guys in leather, the bar was filled with good-
looking young men dancing and having a good time. *They're just average Joes!*
Kelly thought. *Guys just like me.*

Kelly didn't feel that way about David, who was loud, flamboyant and sissified   13
in his dress—not at all the sort Kelly wanted his parents to meet. Or did he? To this
day, Kelly isn't sure whether he wasn't trying to make a statement the one time he
brought David home—or whether he really wanted to slip him out before Joan,
eager to meet the first friend Kelly had brought home in years, confronted them at
the front door. Joan took one look and went pale. "Oh, my God," she said to Paul
after they had left. "That boy with Kelly is queer."

A SECRET SEARCH

She tried to make sense of it. She looked back on Kelly's mood swings, his long,   14
unexplained bike rides into Portland and his almost giddy excitement about going
to a Halloween party; that wasn't like Kelly, especially staying out all night with
the excuse he'd had too much to drink. But Joan needed proof. Shaking with guilt
and apprehension, she steamed open a letter and searched through his dresser
drawers, where she found a scrap of paper. Written on it was the title of a book:
"Young, Gay and Proud." "He's queer! He's queer!" she screamed, running hysteri-
cally into the arms of her husband, who held her and tried to tell her it was going
to be OK.

When Joan confronted Kelly the next day, Paul decided to get "the hell out of   15
the house." Unable to face Kelly or more of Joan's tears, Paul beat a hasty
overnight retreat to one of his pizza parlors; he felt he needed to be alone with his
anger, sadness and confusion. He tried not to place blame, but the thoughts came
anyway: "Jesus, Joan was more domineering than I was." He felt anger toward
Kelly: "He can't cope with the ladies. He's taking the easy way out." He wondered
whether they should send him to a psychiatrist: "You have a flat tire, you fix it."
Finally, alone in a motel room, Paul broke down and cried, an uncharacteristic
release for a man who always held everything inside. But it didn't help: that night
Paul suffered a mild heart attack.

With Paul sick and uneager to talk about Kelly, Joan had no one to share her   16
own quandary. Finally she looked in the Yellow Pages under "H" for homosexuals
and then under "G," where she found a listing for a gay-crisis hot line. She was
trembling when she picked up the phone, and her voice cracked when she first
heard herself say the words out loud: "My son is gay." The hot line put her in
touch with another mother, who listened to Joan's story and promised to send her

a pamphlet about a support group for friends and parents of gay people. She invited Joan to a Gay Men's Chorus Christmas performance. Joan, accompanied by Kelly's older sister, Rhonda, was overwhelmed to see hundreds of gay men, so many of them just like Kelly. She asked them questions: "Where do you work?" "Where do you live?" "Do your parents accept you?" But most of all she kept asking, "Are you happy?"

ICY STARES

Joan realized she'd been closed off from Kelly's world, and she wanted to make up for lost time. But she had to do it on her own. Paul was in retreat, refusing to talk about it or even to acknowledge Kelly when he came home to pick up some of his possessions; he had moved in with a man in Portland. Kelly continued to keep his mother at arm's length; their phone calls and visits consisted of monosyllables and icy stares. Finally, while Paul slumped silently in his chair in the family room, Joan attended a monthly support-group meeting. It took her months to choke out the words: "I'm Joan Chronister and I have a gay son." 17

She listened and learned, quickly realizing that Kelly was not going to change and that no one was to blame. She started manning the hot line and joining excursions to Portland's gay bars. She talked with all kinds of people—from drag queens and lesbians to other parents of gays—and if she couldn't completely understand, at least she was beginning to accept. One June day she attended Portland's Gay Pride Day parade. As she watched the curious crowd go by, Joan noticed a lone man holding a sign, "Parents and Friends of Lesbians and Gay Men." Overcome with emotion, she stepped out into the street and joined him. 18

Paul never marched or went to a support-group meeting. Instead, he stayed at home and hoped time would work its wonders. For a while he thought Kelly might come home lisping and limp-wristed; when he didn't, Paul breathed a sigh of relief and decided it was enough to accept what he'd accepted that first night in his motel room: that as much as he hated Kelly's homosexuality, he could never close the door on his only son. He still doesn't want to know what Kelly's gay life and friends are like, or to imagine what he does inside his bedroom. Joan's transformation into self-proclaimed gay-rights activist sometimes creates a strain. "I don't want to hash it over all the time," says Paul. "But she has the need, an exceptional need." 19

STABLE RELATIONSHIP

It's also hard on Kelly, who is still trying to find a comfortable way to express his sexuality. He's come a long way since he and a boyfriend showed up at Rhonda's wedding wearing identical blazers and pink shirts. Now Kelly tries to make a softer statement by inviting his parents to dinner and letting his relationship with Randy speak for itself. They met more than two years ago through a mutual friend; they 20 found they shared a distaste for the bar scene and a desire for a stable relationship. Since then they've exchanged identical gold rings, furnished a home together and worked side by side at a suburban Portland video store; with their joint savings account, they now plan to go back to college and maybe start a business. And if Paul still can't bring himself to refer to Randy as his son's "lover," Kelly understands. He knows by the way his father teases and firmly shakes Randy's hand that Paul is, in his own way, making an effort to accept them both.

It is problematic whether the fractures Kelly's homosexuality have opened in the Chronister family will ever completely heal. Paul continues to struggle with his inner anguish and could not bring himself to accompany his wife to the Portland Gay Pride Day parade, where she spoke last June ("My name is Joan Chronister and I'm proud my child is homosexual"). Joan for her part blames her husband for not being more understanding. Both are trying to reach some sort of common ground between themselves. 21

And for Kelly there remains detachment from his parents and uncertainty about the future. He was all of 10 when the gay-rights movement was born with the 1969 Stonewall Inn riot. And though he has never been inside a bathhouse or slipped into the boozy world of obsessive sex, he knows that AIDS—not cries of liberation—is the historical force shaping his generation of gay men. He hears evangelists call the epidemic divine retribution for crimes against nature and he fears the political backlash that might come. But he has no illusions about changing society—or changing himself. Says Kelly, "It's part of my being." 22

▼ TOPICAL CONSIDERATIONS

1. How was Kelly's "perfectionism . . . a way of hiding from himself and from others"?
2. When did Kelly first realize that he was gay? How did he deal with that realization?
3. How did Kelly cover up his homosexuality at home?
4. The article says that Kelly anticipated college life "as his only escape" from his crisis. What escape, if any, did campus life afford him?
5. How did Kelly announce to his parents that he was gay?
6. How did Kelly's parents blame themselves for his being gay?
7. How have Joan and Paul Chronister adjusted to Kelly's homosexuality?

▼ RHETORICAL CONSIDERATIONS

1. Where exactly do the authors give their thesis statement?
2. As the title suggests, the article looks at the struggle of the entire family. Did the authors give equal time to the struggles of each of the three Chronisters?
3. From the tone of the essay, did you feel that the authors were judgmental of any of the Chronisters? If so, explain where.

4. Consider the audience for which this article was written. Would you say that it was addressed to the "enlightened" reader, one who would accept and understand the issues of a gay man coming out? Or would you say the reader addressed is someone who might experience extreme discomfort at the discovery of a gay family member?

▼ WRITING ASSIGNMENTS

1. What are your own feelings regarding homosexuality? Are you tolerant toward gays, or not? Write a paper in which you explore what prejudices you have against gays, if any. You might even talk about how this article affected your attitude toward gays, if it did.
2. How would your parents react if you told them that you were gay? Do you think the news would have an impact like that on Joan and Paul Chronister in the article? Write a paper in which you speculate on how your parents might react to your announcement.

▼ DADDY TUCKED THE BLANKET

Randall Williams

> In this autobiographical account of a young man who grew up in poverty, Randall Williams illustrates the physical and emotional conditions of growing up poor. He also shows how the environment of poverty—the deprivation and humiliation—can destroy a family. Williams is a journalist living in Alabama. This article first appeared in the *New York Times* in 1975.

About the time I turned 16, my folks began to wonder why I didn't stay home any more. I always had an excuse for them, but what I didn't say was that I had found my freedom and I was getting out. 1

I went through four years of high school in semirural Alabama and became active in clubs and sports; I made a lot of friends and became a regular guy, if you know what I mean. But one thing was irregular about me: I managed those four years without ever having a friend visit at my house. 2

I was ashamed of where I lived. I had been ashamed for as long as I had been conscious of class. 3

We had a big family. There were several of us sleeping in one room, but that's not so bad if you get along, and we always did. As you get older, though, it gets worse. 4

Being poor is a humiliating experience for a young person trying hard to be accepted. Even now—several years removed—it is hard to talk about. And I resent the weakness of these words to make you feel what it was really like. 5

We lived in a lot of old houses. We moved a lot because we were always looking for something just a little better than what we had. You have to understand that my folks worked harder than most people. My mother was always at home, but for her that was a full-time job—and no fun, either. But my father worked his head off from the time I can remember in construction and shops. It was hard, physical work. 6

I tell you this to show that we weren't shiftless. No matter how much money Daddy made, we never made much progress up the social ladder. I got out thanks to a college scholarship and because I was a little more articulate than the average. 7

I have seen my Daddy wrap copper wire through the soles of his boots to keep them together in the wintertime. He couldn't buy new boots because he had used the money for food and shoes for us. We lived like hell, but we went to school well-clothed and with a full stomach. 8

It really is hell to live in a house that was in bad shape 10 years before you 9

73

moved in. And a big family puts a lot of wear and tear on a new house, too, so you can imagine how one goes downhill if it is teetering when you move in. But we lived in houses that were sweltering in summer and freezing in winter. I woke up every morning for a year and a half with plaster on my face where it had fallen out of the ceiling during the night.

X   This wasn't during the Depression; this was in the late 60's and early 70's.   10

When we boys got old enough to learn trades in school, we would try to fix up   11 the old houses we lived in. But have you ever tried to paint a wall that crumbled when the roller went across it? And bright paint emphasized the holes in the wall. You end up more frustrated than when you began, especially when you know that at best you might come up with only enough money to improve one of the six rooms in the house. And we might move out soon after, anyway.

The same goes for keeping a house like that clean. If you have a house full of   12 kids and the house is deteriorating, you'll never keep it clean. Daddy used to yell at Mama about that, but she couldn't do anything. I think Daddy knew it inside, but he had to have an outlet for his rage somewhere, and at least yelling isn't as bad as hitting, which they never did to each other.

But you have a kitchen which has no counter space and no hot water, and you   13 will have dirty dishes stacked up. That sounds like an excuse, but try it. You'll go mad from the sheer sense of futility. It's the same thing in a house with no closets. You can't keep clothes clean and rooms in order if they have to be stacked up with things.

Living in a bad house is generally worse on girls. For one thing, they traditionally   14 help their mother with the housework. We boys could get outside and work in the field or cut wood or even play ball and forget about living conditions. The sky was still pretty.

But the girls got the pressure, and as they got older it became worse. Would   15 they accept dates knowing they had to "receive" the young man in a dirty hallway with broken windows, peeling wallpaper and a cracked ceiling? You have to live it to understand it, but it creates a shame which drives the soul of a young person inward.

I'm thankful none of us ever blamed our parents for this, because it would   16 have crippled our relationships. As it worked out, only the relationship between our parents was damaged. And I think the harshness which they expressed to each other was just an outlet to get rid of their anger at the trap their lives were in. It ruined their marriage because they had no one to yell at but each other. I knew other families where the kids got the abuse, but we were too much loved for that.

Once I was about 16 and Mama and Daddy had had a particularly violent   17 argument about the washing machine, which had broken down. Daddy was on the back porch—that's where the only water faucet was—trying to fix it and Mama had a washtub out there washing school clothes for the next day and they were screaming at each other.

Later that night everyone was in bed and I heard Daddy get up from the couch   18 where he was reading. I looked out from my bed across the hall into their room. He was standing right over Mama and she was already asleep. He pulled the blanket up and tucked it around her shoulders and just stood there and tears were dropping off his cheeks and I thought I could faintly hear them splashing against the linoleum rug.

Now they're divorced.   19

I had courses in college where housing was discussed, but the sociologists   20
never put enough emphasis on the impact living in substandard housing has on a person's psyche. Especially children's.

Small children have a hard time understanding poverty. They want the same   21
things children from more affluent families have. They want the same things they see advertised on television, and they don't understand why they can't have them.

Other children can be incredibly cruel. I was in elementary school in Georgia—   22
and this is interesting because it is the only thing I remember about that particular school—when I was about eight or nine.

After Christmas vacation had ended, my teacher made each student describe   23
all his or her Christmas presents. I became more and more uncomfortable as the privilege passed around the room toward me. Other children were reciting the names of the dolls they had been given, the kinds of bicycles and the grandeur of their games and toys. Some had lists which seemed to go on and on for hours.

It took me only a few seconds to tell the class that I had gotten for Christmas a   24
belt and a pair of gloves. And then I was laughed at—because I cried—by a roomful of children and a teacher. I never forgave them, and that night I made my mother cry when I told her about it.

In retrospect, I am grateful for that moment, but I remember wanting to die at   25
the time.

▼ TOPICAL CONSIDERATIONS

1. Why, after he had turned sixteen, did Williams not stay home any more?
2. What were some of the conditions of the houses Williams and his family lived in? Why was it so hard to keep those houses neat and clean?
3. How does he characterize his parents? Why, according to the author, did the Williams family never make much "progress up the social ladder"?
4. According to Williams, what was the main reason his parents' marriage fell apart?
5. How do you interpret the last sentence in the essay? Why would Williams be "grateful for that moment"?

▼ RHETORICAL CONSIDERATIONS

1. Where exactly does Williams make his thesis statement?
2. How does the author illustrate the impoverished conditions of his family life?
3. How does Williams illustrate how poverty helped ruin his parents' marriage?

4. Cite some descriptive details Williams employs. Do you think he could have used more?
5. The author's style of writing is quite direct and simple. How is this style created? Consider his sentence length and structure, his vocabulary and expressions, and the length of most of his paragraphs.
6. Why do you think Williams chose the title he did for this essay? Where in the essay does it have particular meaning?
7. Did you find this essay sentimental in places? If so, where? Did you think there were places where Williams consciously avoided being overly emotional or sentimental?

▼ WRITING ASSIGNMENTS

1. We have all seen evidence of poverty; many of us have lived in poverty. Write an essay in which you show through specific illustrations poverty as you have experienced or seen it in your neighborhood or city or state, or some place you have visited.
2. Williams talks about how poverty adversely affected his parents. Write an essay in which you describe through illustration how certain conditions affected your parents' relationship. You might choose to talk about how the economic status of your family affected them. Or you might focus on sickness in the family, education, religion, love, children, etc.
3. Williams selects from his past a few key instances that characterize the relationship between his mother and father. Write an essay in which you recall a few telling moments that help characterize the relationship between your parents.

▼ "IN MY DAY . . ."

Russell Baker

> Russell Baker is the Pulitzer Prize-winning columnist of the *New York Times.* Since 1962, he has written his "Observer" column, famous for its humorous, sometimes biting criticisms of social issues, American politics, and current jargon. The selection that appears here shows a somewhat different voice of the famous humorist. Taken from his enchanting memoir, *Growing Up* (1982), this essay is a quiet yet moving protest about the passage of time that separates the boy from the man and the child from the parent. Baker is the author of eleven books, including *The Good Times* (1989), his most recent memoirs.

At the age of eighty my mother had her last bad fall, and after that her mind wandered free through time. Some days she went to weddings and funerals that had taken place half a century earlier. On others she presided over family dinners cooked on Sunday afternoons for children who were now gray with age. Through all this she lay in bed but moved across time, traveling among the dead decades with a speed and ease beyond the gift of physical science.   1

"Where's Russell?" she asked one day when I came to visit at the nursing home.   2

"I'm Russell," I said.   3

She gazed at this improbably overgrown figure out of an inconceivable future and promptly dismissed it.   4

"Russell's only this big," she said, holding her hand, palm down, two feet from the floor. That day she was a young country wife with chickens in the backyard and a view of hazy blue Virginia mountains behind the apple orchard, and I was a stranger old enough to be her father.   5

Early one morning she phoned me in New York. "Are you coming to my funeral today?" she asked.   6

It was an awkward question with which to be awakened. "What are you talking about, for God's sake?" was the best reply I could manage.   7

"I'm being buried today," she declared briskly, as though announcing an important social event.   8

"I'll phone you back," I said and hung up, and when I did phone back she was all right, although she wasn't all right, of course, and we all knew she wasn't.   9

She had always been a small woman—short, light-boned, delicately structured—but now, under the white hospital sheet, she was becoming tiny. I thought of a doll with huge, fierce eyes. There had always been a fierceness in her. It showed in that angry, challenging thrust of the chin when she issued an opinion, and a great one she had always been for issuing opinions.   10

"I tell people exactly what's on my mind," she had been fond of boasting. "I tell   11 them what I think, whether they like it or not." Often they had not liked it. She could be sarcastic to people in whom she detected evidence of the ignoramus or the fool.

"It's not always good policy to tell people exactly what's on your mind," I used to caution her. 12

"If they don't like it, that's too bad," was her customary reply, "because that's the way I am." 13

And so she was. A formidable woman. Determined to speak her mind, determined to have her way, determined to bend those who opposed her. In that time when I had known her best, my mother had hurled herself at life with chin thrust forward, eyes blazing, and an energy that made her seem always on the run. 14

She ran after squawking chickens, an axe in her hand, determined on a beheading that would put dinner in the pot. She ran when she made the beds, ran when she set the table. One Thanksgiving she burned herself badly when, running up from the cellar oven with the ceremonial turkey, she tripped on the stairs and tumbled back down, ending at the bottom in the debris of giblets, hot gravy, and battered turkey. Life was combat, and victory was not to the lazy, the timid, the slugabed, the drugstore cowboy, the libertine, the mushmouth afraid to tell people exactly what was on his mind whether people liked it or not. She ran. 15

But now the running was over. For a time I could not accept the inevitable. As I sat by her bed, my impulse was to argue her back to reality. On my first visit to the hospital in Baltimore, she asked who I was. 16

"Russell," I said. 17

"Russell's way out west," she advised me. 18

"No, I'm right here." 19

"Guess where I came from today?" was her response. 20

"Where?" 21

"All the way from New Jersey." 22

"When?" 23

"Tonight." 24

"No. You've been in the hospital for three days," I insisted. 25

"I suggest the thing to do is calm down a little bit," she replied. "Go over to the house and shut the door." 26

Now she was years deep into the past, living in the neighborhood where she had settled forty years earlier, and she had just been talking with Mrs. Hoffman, a neighbor across the street. 27

"It's like Mrs. Hoffman said today: The children always wander back to where they come from," she remarked. 28

"Mrs. Hoffman has been dead for fifteen years." 29

"Russ got married today," she replied. 30

"I got married in 1950," I said, which was the fact. 31

"The house is unlocked," she said. 32

So it went until a doctor came by to give one of those oral quizzes that medical men apply in such cases. She failed catastrophically, giving wrong answers or none at all to "What day is this?" "Do you know where you are?" "How old are you?" and so on. Then, a surprise. 33

"When is your birthday?" he asked. 34

"November 5, 1897," she said. Correct. Absolutely correct. 35

"How do you remember that?" the doctor asked. 36

"Because I was born on Guy Fawkes Day," she said. 37

"Guy Fawkes?" asked the doctor. "Who is Guy Fawkes?" 38

She replied with a rhyme I had heard her recite time and again over the years 39
when the subject of her birth date arose:

"Please to remember the Fifth of November,
Gunpowder treason and plot.
I see no reason why gunpowder treason
Should ever be forgot."

Then she glared at this young doctor so ill informed about Guy Fawkes' failed scheme to blow King James off his throne with barrels of gunpowder in 1605. She had been a schoolteacher, after all, and knew how to glare at a dolt. "You may know a lot about medicine, but you obviously don't know any history," she said. Having told him exactly what was on her mind, she left us again.

The doctors diagnosed a hopeless senility. Not unusual, they said. "Hardening 40
of the arteries" was the explanation for laymen. I thought it was more complicated than that. For ten years or more the ferocity with which she had once attacked life had been turning to a rage against the weakness, the boredom, and the absence of love that too much age had brought her. Now, after the last bad fall, she seemed to have broken chains that imprisoned her in a life she had come to hate and to return to a time inhabited by people who loved her, a time in which she was needed. Gradually I understood. It was the first time in years I had seen her happy.

She had written a letter three years earlier which explained more than "hardening 41
of the arteries." I had gone down from New York to Baltimore, where she lived, for one of my infrequent visits and, afterwards, had written her with some banal advice to look for the silver lining, to count her blessings instead of burdening others with her miseries. I suppose what it really amounted to was a threat that if she was not more cheerful during my visits I would not come to see her very often. Sons are capable of such letters. This one was written out of a childish faith in the eternal strength of parents, a naive belief that age and wear could be overcome by an effort of will, that all she needed was a good pep talk to recharge a flagging spirit. It was such a foolish, innocent idea, but one thinks of parents differently from other people. Other people can become frail and break, but not parents.

She wrote back in an unusually cheery vein intended to demonstrate, I 42
suppose, that she was mending her ways. She was never a woman to apologize, but for one moment with the pen in her hand she came very close. Referring to my visit, she wrote: "If I seemed unhappy to you at times—" Here she drew back, reconsidered, and said something quite different:

"If I seemed unhappy to you at times, I am, but there's really nothing anyone 43
can do about it, because I'm just so very tired and lonely that I'll just go to sleep and forget it." She was then seventy-eight.

Now, three years later, after the last bad fall, she had managed to for- 44
get the fatigue and loneliness and, in these free-wheeling excursions back
through time, to recapture happiness. I soon stopped trying to wrest her back to
what I considered the real world and tried to travel along with her on those
fantastic swoops into the past. One day when I arrived at her bedside she was
radiant.

"Feeling good today," I said. 45

"Why shouldn't I feel good?" she asked. "Papa's going to take me up to 46
Baltimore on the boat today."

At that moment she was a young girl standing on a wharf at Merry Point, 47
Virginia, waiting for the Chesapeake Bay steamer with her father, who had been
dead sixty-one years. William Howard Taft was in the White House, Europe still
drowsed in the dusk of the great century of peace, America was a young country,
and the future stretched before it in beams of crystal sunlight. "The greatest
country on God's green earth," her father might have said, if I had been able to
step into my mother's time machine and join him on the wharf with the satchels
packed for Baltimore.

I could imagine her there quite clearly. She was wearing a blue dress with big 48
puffy sleeves and long black stockings. There was a ribbon in her hair and a big
bow tied on the side of her head. There had been a childhood photograph in her
bedroom which showed all this, although the colors of course had been added
years later by a restorer who tinted the picture.

About her father, my grandfather, I could only guess, and indeed, about the 49
girl on the wharf with the bow in her hair, I was merely sentimentalizing. Of my
mother's childhood and her people, of their time and place, I knew very little. A
world had lived and died, and though it was part of my blood and bone I knew
little more about it than I knew of the world of the pharaohs. It was useless now to
ask for help from my mother. The orbits of her mind rarely touched present
interrogators for more than a moment.

Sitting at her bedside, forever out of touch with her, I wondered about my 50
own children, and their children, and children in general, and about the disconnec-
tions between children and parents that prevent them from knowing each other.
Children rarely want to know what their parents were before they were parents,
and when age finally stirs their curiosity there is no parent left to tell them. If a
parent does lift the curtain a bit, it is often only to stun the young with some
exemplary tale of how much harder life was in the old days.

I had been guilty of this when my children were small in the early 1960s and 51
living the affluent life. It galled me that their childhoods should be, as I thought,
so easy when my own had been, as I thought, so hard. I had developed the habit,
when they complained about the steak being overcooked or the television being
cut off, of lecturing them on the harshness of life in my day.

"In my day all we got for dinner was macaroni and cheese, and we were glad 52
to get it."

"In my day we didn't have any television." 53

"In my day . . . " 54

"In my day . . ."   55

At dinner one evening a son had offended me with an inadequate report card,   56
and as I leaned back and cleared my throat to lecture, he gazed at me with
an expression of unutterable resignation and said, "Tell me how it was in your
days, Dad."

I was angry with him for that, but angrier with myself for having become one   57
of those ancient bores whose highly selective memories of the past become
transparently dishonest even to small children. I tried to break the habit, but must
have failed. A few years later my son was referring to me when I was out of earshot
as "the old-timer." Between us there was a dispute about time. He looked upon the
time that had been my future in a disturbing way. My future was his past, and
being young, he was indifferent to the past.

As I hovered over my mother's bed listening for muffled signals from her   58
childhood, I realized that this same dispute had existed between her and me.
When she was young, with life ahead of her, I had been her future and resented
it. Instinctively, I wanted to break free, cease being a creature defined by
her time, consign her future to the past, and create my own. Well, I had finally
done that, and then with my own children I had seen my exciting future become
their boring past.

These hopeless end-of-the-line visits with my mother made me wish I had not   59
thrown off my own past so carelessly. We all come from the past, and children
ought to know what it was that went into their making, to know that life is a
braided cord of humanity stretching up from time long gone, and that it cannot be
defined by the span of a single journey from diaper to shroud.

I thought that someday my own children would understand that. I thought   60
that, when I am beyond explaining, they would want to know what the world was
like when my mother was young and I was younger, and we two relics passed
together through strange times. I thought I should try to tell them how it was to be
young in the time before jet planes, superhighways, H-bombs, and the global
village of television. I realized I would have to start with my mother and her
passion for improving the male of the species, which in my case took the form of
forcing me to "make something of myself."

Lord, how I hated those words. . . .   61

▼ TOPICAL CONSIDERATIONS

1. What do Baker's visits with his mother cause him to yearn for most? Why?
2. What has Baker learned that he would someday like to share with his
   children? When he does talk to them, how do you think they will respond?
   Do you think they will feel that what he has to say is important? What kinds
   of experiences might help them hear what he has to say?
3. Baker's mother dwells in the past. Much of her conversation includes
   stories from her childhood or young womanhood. Is this typical of any
   older people you know? Are the causes similar?

4. Why does Baker stop "trying to wrest [his mother] back to . . . the real world" (paragraph 44)? Do you agree with his reasons?

▼ RHETORICAL CONSIDERATIONS

1. Do you like Baker's opening? If so, what do you like about it? If not, why not?
2. Is Baker's use of dialogue effective? Give reasons for your answer.
3. Find passages that you think give a particularly vivid portrayal of Baker's mother. Why are they vivid? Does Baker use figurative language? Does he use narrative? How does his physical description of her convey her personality?
4. What are some of the verbs Baker uses to describe the way his mother faced life as a young woman? How do these word choices reflect her personality?

▼ WRITING ASSIGNMENTS

1. Baker discovered late in his life that his mother was not as invulnerable as he had always believed. In paragraph 41, he remarks: "It was such a foolish, innocent idea, but one thinks of parents differently from other people. Other people can become frail and break, but not parents." How do you feel about this? Do you see your parents as different from other people? Are they invulnerable? Write an essay in which you discuss your answers to these questions. Include specific illustrations to prove your point.
2. Visit with an older member of your family—perhaps your grandfather or grandmother. Ask him or her to tell you what the world was like when your parents were growing up. Write a personal history spanning those years. Include references to significant political events, inventions, and social trends.

CHANGING
TIMES

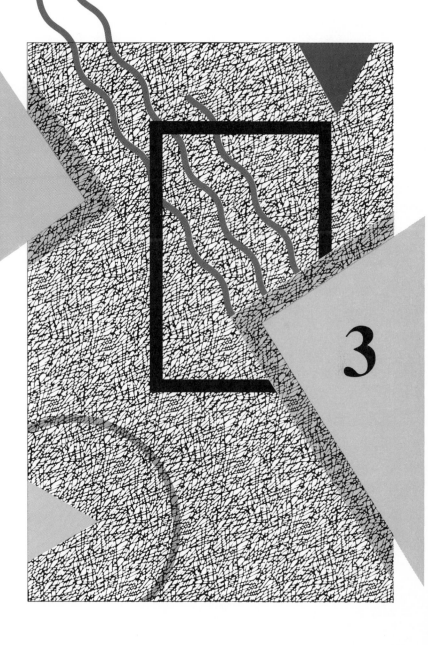

3

▼ TECHNOLOGY'S COMING...
TECHNOLOGY'S COMING

Erma Bombeck

Ours is an age of transitions, of near-dizzying social and cultural changes that are the direct results of technological progress. With every innovation and invention, the future is redefined. Some look upon this revolution as the new Golden Age. Others wonder if we will survive our own technology, if, in fact, we might in our headlong rush into tomorrow render humankind obsolete. This section begins with an amusing SOS from one mother who comes face-to-face with the latest electronic convenience. Erma Bombeck, celebrated for her wit and wisdom, is the author of eight books including the bestselling *Motherhood: The Second Oldest Profession* (1985) and *Family: The Ties that Bind . . . and Gag!* (1987), from which this essay comes. Her thrice-weekly humor column, "At Wit's End," appears in 900 newspapers throughout the world. She is the mother of three children.

The younger son made his move first. He jumped up from the table and said, "I've 1 gotta get my laundry started or I can't go out. What time is it?"

I looked at my watch. "It's 6 A.M. in Hamburg, Germany, if that helps." 2

"Why do you know the time in Hamburg, Mom?" 3

"Because that is where the watch was made and set and the directions for 4 resetting it are written in German."

"The clock on the oven says it's 11." 5

"That's wrong," said my husband. "Your mother can't see what she's twirling 6 half the time without her glasses and sometimes when she sets the timer, she resets the clock."

"And the one on the VCR?" he asked. 7

" . . . is always 12 and blinking," I said, "because your father screwed up 8 between steps two and five when the power went out."

"God, Mom, you and Dad are out of it. It's like the *Twilight Zone.* How do 9 you two function around here? I'd be lost without technology. This little beeper," he said, patting his shirt pocket, "keeps me in touch with the world."

"He's right, Mom," said our daughter, "you oughta have one of those signals 10 attached to your car keys and your glasses. Think of the time you could save."

It was a subject I hated. 11

"Maybe we should have tranquilized you with a dart and fitted you with a 12 beeper to track your migratory habits when you were seventeen and we'd have all slept better," I snapped.

"Mom, why do you resist the twenty-first century? You don't even have a   13
home computer."

"I don't need a home computer. What would I do with it?"   14

"A lot of things. You could store all your personal documents in one   15
place . . . your marriage license, your insurance policies, your warranties. Just
think, you and Dad could punch up your insurance policies in seconds."

"We could die from the excitement," I said.   16

"You could even use a copier around here," piped in her brother, "to dupli-   17
cate all of our medical records and your dental bills, not to mention a Christmas
newsletter."

"We need a copier like the Osmonds need a cavity fighter," I said.   18

"She's hopeless," they shrugged.   19

I sat there alone, toying with my coffee. They had told me what I didn't want   20
to hear. Their father and I were casualties in the war of automation. Why did we
resist it? Maybe because there was a time when there weren't enough hours in the
day to fulfill all the skills of my job description. I was chauffeur, cook, nurse,
decorator, financier, psychologist, and social director. I was important. All the
slick magazines said so.

Slowly but steadily I was replaced by beeps, switches, flashing lights, elec-   21
tronic devices, and monotone voices.

In the beginning, I taught my children how to tie their shoes and button and   22
zip their clothing. Then along came Velcro tabs on their shoes and on their clothes
where buttons and zippers used to be.

I used to tell them how to place an emergency call to Grandma if they needed   23
her. Now it was a matter of pushing a button on a memory phone and it was done
for them.

I used to enlighten them about the stove. I showed them how to turn it on and   24
off so they wouldn't get burned. They don't have stoves anymore. They have
microwave ovens that have little buttons to push and are cool to the touch.

At one time I pulled them on my lap and together we traced our fingers across   25
the printed page as I read to them. I don't read anymore. All they have to do is
insert book cassettes into their stereos and hear them read by professionals.

I have been replaced by ouchless adhesive bandages, typewriters that correct   26
their spelling, color-coded wardrobes, and computers that praise them when they
get the right answers. The future is here.

The kids are wrong. It isn't that we don't give technology a chance. We   27
use the VCR. True, it was in our home for a full six months before we turned
it on.

From time to time my husband would leaf through the manual with an   28
intensity usually reserved for a nervous flier reading about the evacuation proce-
dures on an aircraft. Then one day he said, "Since we are going out to dinner, I am
going to tape 'Dallas' so we can watch it later."

I put my hand over his. "I want you to know that whatever happens, I think   29
you're the bravest man I have ever met."

Looking back, that was the beginning of our march against time.   30

There are 24 hours in every day. I used to watch television 6 hours and 44 **31**
minutes a day, leaving me with 17 hours and 16 minutes.

After I scheduled 7 hours and 5 minutes to sleep and 2 hours and 15 minutes **32**
to eat, it only left me with 7 hours and 56 minutes to do my job.

Then we got cable television and what with the news channel, first-run **33**
movies, MTV, country western, spiritual, entertainment, and sports, my viewing
cut into my workday. The VCR was supposed to solve our problem.

But when do you watch the shows you've taped? **34**

I took time away from my 2 hours and 15 minutes eating time by eating in **35**
front of the TV set. Naturally, we began to buy cassettes to fit the VCR. I bought
Jane Fonda so I could get my body into shape. However, I had to take time away
from my 7 hours and 5 minutes of sleeping to do it.

On my birthday, a son rented two movies as a present. I panicked. They had to **36**
be viewed by 10 A.M. the next morning. Already I had a stack of shows that had
been taped that I hadn't had time to view. I put the movies ahead of the tapes,
rescheduled Jane Fonda for 4 A.M., and watched *Terms of Endearment* and *Easy
Money* at 5 and 7 A.M. It was close but I made it.

Other scheduling problems were not so easily solved. Before dinner one night, **37**
I approached the VCR with my Julia Child cassette. My husband was watching
Dan Rather. When I asked him to watch Dan in the bedroom, he said it wouldn't
do any good as he was taping a *M*A*S*H* rerun on the other channel. I went into
the kitchen, turned on another set, and watched *Wheel of Fortune,* and we didn't
eat until 9:30 in front of *Magnum P.I.*

As the weeks go on, I feel the pressure more and more. With the VCR taping **38**
shows day and night, with my husband running from room to room, channel-
searching to see what we're missing, the new cassettes on everything from how to
repair your plumbing to how to be more assertive, the new films and video music,
we're falling behind.

Already we're beginning to cut corners. We've got *60 Minutes* down to 30, **39**
20/20 to 10/10, and anything on World War II we fast-forward because we know
the ending.

But the cassettes are winning. We both know that. It's only a matter of time. **40**

Our son returned to the kitchen with his father's running watch in his hand. "I **41**
don't believe you, Dad. You've been telling time by your memory/recall lap 4,
total time. Here, let me show you how it works. You've got a multimode chrono-
graph and multimode countdown timer with one-tenth second accuracy."

I watched the two of them hunched over the watch as my son patiently **42**
explained the mechanism.

Had it been twenty-some years since they had huddled over the kitchen table **43**
together and my husband brought forth the brand-new watch for his son and
taught him how to tell time? They had "walked through" all the parts when they
got down to the basics. When the big hand pointed toward the refrigerator and the
small hand was toward the stove, it was 6 o'clock and time to eat. When the big
hand was toward the mixer and the little hand was pointed toward the portable
television set, it was time to go to bed.

If the kid went into a home or building where the furniture was not positioned   44
in the same spot as our kitchen, he was to go to the nearest person and ask, "What
time is it?"

With deft fingers, our son twisted dials and adjusted minute screws on the   45
watch. My husband watched with admiration and awe. He had come a long way
since that day twenty years ago at the kitchen table.

Minutes later, "Mr. Technology" yelled from the utility room, "Mom, how do   46
you turn the washer on?"

Maybe not.   47

▼ TOPICAL CONSIDERATIONS

1. What specific "technologies" are encroaching upon Bombeck's life? What
   kinds of difficulties has she had with such devices?
2. Bombeck, a casualty in the "war of automation," says that she resists
   modern technology. What reasons does she offer? How does she demonstrate her resistance? Can you identify with her plight? Do you know
   anyone from an older generation, like your parents or grandparents, who
   are also casualties of modern technology?
3. How has the modern electronic world "slowly but steadily replaced" Bombeck
   in her different roles as mother?
4. The author says that she used to watch television "6 hours and 44 minutes a
   day." Doesn't that sound like a lot of television to view? What might
   Bombeck's message be here?
5. Erma Bombeck is a humorist whose satire makes fun of things—in this
   case, our high-tech world, her family, and herself. Lurking beneath the
   satirist's ridicule is always a serious lament. What complaints is Bombeck
   making about our contemporary society? What complaints does she make
   about her family life? What complaints does she make about herself?
6. Much of the humorous tension in this story has to do with the conflict
   between the past and the present. How does Bombeck portray life in the
   past? How is contemporary life different?
7. Bombeck's children suggest that the author and her husband could use
   time-saving machines. Do you think life is easier with such technologies?
   Do you think that the quality of life is better?

▼ RHETORICAL CONSIDERATIONS

1. In personal narratives, a writer will often adopt a *persona,* that is, a role or
   presence in the work. Distinguished from the author, the persona can be
   identified by the tone of the piece as well as some of the assumptions,
   prejudices, preferences, concerns, and doubts. Try to characterize the
   persona Bombeck adopts in this essay. How does the tone—degree of

formality or informality, irony, sarcasm, and humor—create this persona? Point out words or passages to support your conclusions.

2. Explain the choice of titles for this essay. How is it appropriate? (Do you recognize any movie allusion here?)

3. Rather than simply telling the reader about the coming of technology and the threat it poses, Bombeck attempts to dramatize matters in words. She recreates a family scene. How effective is her strategy? How is it better than just telling us about her adjustment to the high-tech world?

4. Did you find this piece funny? If so, cite specific lines and try to explain what amused you.

5. Explain the irony of the final two paragraphs. How does the final paragraph strike a note of hope for the author?

▼ WRITING ASSIGNMENTS

1. Do you identify more with Bombeck or with her children? Write a paper in which you explain your sympathies.

2. What do you think of all the time-saving devices on the market today? Do you think life is easier with them? Do you think the quality of life is better with them? Consider some of the modern electronic devices such as VCRs, food processors, pocket calculators, PCs, memory phones, answering machines, digital watches, and microwave ovens.

3. Bombeck brings up an interesting question: Do people who own time-saving machines necessarily enjoy greater leisure time? Are they spending the time saved doing more work? What are your own observations on this question?

▼ STRIPPING DOWN TO BARE HAPPINESS

Linda Weltner

Here's a story of two people whose rebellion against the onslaught of the modern world went all the way. As Linda Weltner reports, Sara and Michael decided that the world was too much with them, that they could live much happier lives without all electronic conveniences and the "gee-whiz" gadgets they once thought were essential. Without depriving themselves, they simply reduced the clutter, expense, and waste of modern living. In many ways, theirs is a story of the way life used to be—free of the myths of consumerism and the throwaway mentality. One wonders just how many of us could make such a drastic change in our lifestyle. Weltner is a columnist for the *Boston Globe* and the author of children's books. This article first appeared in her column, "Ever So Humble," in 1982.

"What we're talking about is simplification, not deprivation," explains a friend of 1
mine. "It isn't that you can't do all the things you like, but you change. You don't like them anymore. Some of the old habits seem so wasteful and unsatisfying, you really lose your taste for them. So you still have everything you want—only on less money."

When I first met them, Sara and Michael were a two-career couple with a 2
home of their own, and a large boat bought with a large loan. What interested them in a concept called voluntary simplicity was the birth of their daughter and a powerful desire to raise her themselves. Neither one of them, it turned out, was willing to restrict what they considered their "real life" into the brief time before work and the tired hours afterward.

"A lot of people think that as they have children and things get more expensive, 3
the only answer is to work harder in order to earn more money. It's not the only answer," insists Michael.

The couple's decision was to trade two full-time careers for two half-time 4
careers, and to curtail consumption. They decided to spend their money only on things that contributed to their major goal, the construction of a world where family and friendship, work and play, were all of a piece, a world, moreover, which did not make wasteful use of the earth's resources.

Today, they live in the same suburban community in a handsome, energy- 5
efficient home they designed themselves. Small by most standards, it is easy to clean, furnish, maintain and heat. The first floor, one large room, has a kitchen area along one wall, a birch table and chairs for dining, a living area defined by a

comfortable couch and a wood stove, and a corner work area. Upstairs is a child's bedroom, topped by a loft which is the master bedroom, an office that serves them both, and a bathroom. It is bright and light and in harmony with its surroundings. Soon there will be a solar greenhouse outside the front door.

How can a couple with two part-time freelance jobs afford to build their own   6
home, own a car, and share a small boat with another couple—all without a loan? How can they maintain a high standard of living that provides "everything" they want? What is it they have given up that they do not miss?

Expensive clutter, for one thing—medicine cabinets full of cosmetics and   7
over-the-counter drugs they will never use, kitchen cabinets crowded with items they would eventually throw away. The one clothes closet Sara shares with Michael easily contains the basic items in their wardrobes, many of them well-made classic styles from L. L. Bean. "I'm constantly giving things away," Sara explains. By sifting and discarding, by keeping track of what they have, Sara and Michael have a clear idea of what they really need.

They do not have a dishwasher. The number of hand-thrown pottery dishes   8
they own would not fill one. They do not own a clothes dryer; the wet clothes, drying indoors in winter, eliminate the need for a humidifier. Sara's dark hair is short. She does not need a hairdryer, electric curlers, or a curling iron. Their front yard is wooded. They do not need a power mower, grass spreader, or electric clippers. They do not own a TV, and so they and their child are not constantly saturated with images of new toys, new things, and new temptations.

They have exchanged the expenses of work in a commuter age—the extra car,   9
the cost of gasoline, professional wardrobes, lunches and frequent dinners out, and babysitting fees—for the time to pay attention to the quality of their lives. They have given up paper products, processed foods, expensive hobbies, first-run movies, restaurants, and paying for the services of others in return for home cooking, mid-week family picnics, library books, participation in community arts programs, thrift shops, an active YMCA membership, and do-it-yourself projects.

"That yearning feeling that's so much a part of this culture goes on forever,"   10
says Sara. "But it doesn't matter if you're making $15,000 or $50,000. There'll always be things you wish you could afford. Money really wasn't the reason we changed. We did it for our own personal satisfaction, and for anyone thinking of simplifying life, there's only one basic rule: 'If it isn't satisfying, don't do it.'"

Sara and Michael lent me their copy of "99 Ways to a Simple Lifestyle," an   11
Anchor Press/Doubleday paperback compiled by the Center for Science in the Public Interest, a handbook of practical suggestions that can be applied to anyone's living situation. I read it carefully, giving myself high marks in some areas, surprised at my socially sanctioned irrational behavior in others.

That night, accompanying my daughter on a shopping trip, I came across an   12
inexpensive hand towel that matched our kitchen wallpaper, and a pair of "bargain" sandals too handsome to resist. When I stood in the parking lot, $11 poorer, no happier on leaving the store than I had been entering it, I felt like a child, helpless in the face of my own impulses.

It is a world of illusion, this shopping merry-go-round we ride, but with all the   13 action and excitement, it is sometimes hard to find the resolve and the courage to dismount.

▼ TOPICAL CONSIDERATIONS

1. Why exactly did Sara and Michael decide to "strip down" their lives? Do you know people who, from a similar philosophical stand, "stripped down" their lives to bare happiness? Could you do that and still be happy?
2. Do you get the impression that Sara and Michael made some major sacrifices when they turned their lifestyle around? Would such a stripping down result in major sacrifices for your parents? For your friends? For yourself?
3. What does this essay say about the way Americans have become accustomed to certain material possessions? What does it say about the values projected by our consumer economy? How has television aided in our conditioning?
4. If you are familiar with apparel sold by L. L. Bean, try to characterize its style. Why would L. L. Bean products make up much of Sara and Michael's wardrobes? Do you find anything ironic in the fact that their "stripping down" stopped at wardrobes with L. L. Bean labels?
5. Sara and Michael do not own a dishwasher or a clothes dryer. (In fact, most people in the world don't own these appliances.) Does their adjustment suggest that the American consumer can shake the habit of dependence on such modern conveniences? What does this say about consumer conditioning versus consumer need?
6. Sara and Michael now live without television. What benefit have they found from such an adjustment? Could you live without television? Do you agree that there would be some real benefits in not having it? What disadvantages would there be in a life without television?

▼ RHETORICAL CONSIDERATIONS

1. What is the rhetorical advantage of beginning this piece with a quotation from the author's friends rather than with a little of their background?
2. In paragraph 6, Weltner asks three questions. Are these rhetorical questions or real ones that she then answers?
3. Weltner begins the essay with a quotation from Sara and ends with some self-reflection of her own after a shopping trip. How effective is this conclusion? How does it dramatize the point of the essay?
4. What do you make of the fact that the paragraphs in this essay are quite short? Could some of them be combined? Do you think the short paragraphs reflect Weltner's journalistic style? (She writes for *The Boston Globe.*)

▼ WRITING ASSIGNMENTS

1. Write an essay in which you describe how you bought something you did not really need. Try to explore your impulses. Did they arise out of "socially sanctioned irrational behavior"? Did you buy out of some deeper need for security?

2. Do you think you could live the rest of your life without television and still be happy? Write an essay in which you explore that possibility. Examine whether you think your life would be changed for better or for worse.

3. Try to imagine yourself making a drastic change in lifestyles—stripping down to bare essentials. Do you think you could live happily, like Sara and Michael, without all the modern conveniences and consumer commodities to which you have grown accustomed?

▼ STRANGER THAN FICTION

Roderick Anscombe

> The electronic media have made us the most knowledgeable and worldly audience in history, yet, at what expense? In this essay, Roderick Anscombe wonders how writers of books, movie scripts, and television shows can possibly intrigue or shock a public that has already seen it all on the news. "We need secrets . . . and taboos," argues the author, a psychiatrist who teaches at Harvard Medical School. His article first appeared in *Newsweek* in 1987.

Something is happening to our stories. Not so many years ago, the plots of TV   1
shows and movies contained some element of patriotism, chivalry, loyalty or special endeavor. Today, matters to be dealt with are more likely to be a suitcase full of cocaine or the body of a dead lover in the trunk of a car. I would have no trouble involving myself with these stirring topics, if only greed and jealousy were not the sole motives on the menu. But there doesn't seem to be a whole lot else that stories *can* be about these days. I believe the reason has less to do with writers' lack of creativity and more to do with changes in the world: reality is putting fiction out of business.

The idea that the head of the KGB would become a leader of the Soviet   2
Union seems like a clumsy caricature of the Soviet political system. That a college basketball star would be struck dead by cocaine on the very evening he was celebrating the promise of a brilliant professional career seems more like the ploy of a writer trying too hard for dramatic effect. That a president of the United States secretly bargained with the very terrorists whom he said we must stand firm against would have been too cynical for a spy thriller in the 1970s. Who wrote this script, anyway? Plotting that would have seemed heavy-handed even for a made-for-TV drama is served up with impeccable credibility: it really happened.

Stories answer the wish "If only . . . " and to serve that purpose they must be   3
removed—just a little—from fact. Yet the middle ground between news and amusement is shrinking. The rise of the docu-drama reflects the change: real life is becoming fantastical to the point that it is pre-empting fiction. Fact and fantasy are drawing closer in many ominous ways. Like fiction, psychiatry explores the gap between reality and what is imagined. But increasingly in my practice, I find that what used to be just imagined is now actually being done.

In the privacy of the home, parents abuse their children in ways I wish were   4
beyond the realm of possibility. No cruelty is so extreme that it is beyond human perpetration. Incest has lost its capacity to shock; studies suggest that one girl in 22 is sexually abused by her father or stepfather before she reaches the age of 18.

A much higher proportion are abused by other relatives. Runaways are prostituted even before they become teenagers. Who are the customers of these children? They cannot be isolated "sickos"—there are too many of them. Some of them must commute in station wagons from the suburbs to inner-city vice areas.

SATED AUDIENCE

No sexual coupling is unbelievable anymore—fathers, daughters, brothers, babies, sea gulls, nothing is off the map, nothing is so bizarre that it could never really happen. Perhaps it has always been this way and the change is that we know about it. But I believe that *we* are also changing. People are now doing what they had previously thought of doing for one guilty moment before they rejected the possibility of doing it. The exposure given to the molestation of children and the violence against women in the home has turned these private abuses into a public reality. Once it is known that these horrors are not unique, that they are not isolated curiosities from a psychiatry textbook but widespread practices among us, then the behavior ceases to be extraordinary and becomes part of everyday life. 5

When the boundary between what a person does and what he simply imagines breaks down, fiction becomes pointless. How do scriptwriters go about entertaining people who live in a world in which almost anything can happen and who still demand to be surprised? What can writers possibly invent that their public has not already tried or been subjected to? In increasing desperation, movies and television series compete with each other to scare, shock or intrigue a sated audience that has already seen it on the news. They can touch up reality, as in the docu-drama, by making the characters prettier, wittier and simpler than the real people ever were—or reverse it, as in special effects, to make the abdominal contents clutched by the movie maniac far more moist and lurid than anything I remember from the operating room. They can also try to beat reality at its own game. If the trend is to break down barriers, to loosen the restraints that hold social relations together, why not beat events to the punch by showing what has only been whispered about? 6

But the strategy of taboo busting is self-defeating. A secret can be revealed only once. And at the dead end of the process of revealing all, when everything else has been used up and worn out, there is pornography. The ultimate docu-drama, pornography pretends to be a story, but it stages real events. Just as real people died in Roman coliseums when gladiators battled for the pleasure of cheering crowds, real orgasms are shown on the screen for convenient viewing by the public. The audience is a monster that fiction can no longer satisfy, it demands reality. It is hungry for stimulation, and like a drug addict who is running out of veins, it needs to inject heavier doses into stranger and stranger places to get the same intense feeling of being entertained. 7

But nerve endings no longer tingle when they are stimulated repeatedly. As an audience, we are not only becoming worldly and knowledgeable but also jaded 8 and unshockable. We are becoming less and less capable of being curious or intrigued. Tear the wrappings off a mystery and what have you got? We need secrets, inner sanctums and taboos—otherwise we will be left with nothing but reality.

▼ TOPICAL CONSIDERATIONS

1. According to the author, how do today's television shows differ from shows of the past? To what does he ascribe the change?
2. How does the author explain the rise of the docu-drama? Can you think of any recent docu-dramas that substantiate Anscombe's point?
3. In paragraph 5, Anscombe says he believes "that we are changing" as a result of our exposure to the horrors of the world. Do you agree with him? Do you think people have lost their capacity to be shocked? Are you shocked by some of the horrors Anscombe mentions—that is, incest, preteen prostitution, child abuse, violence against women in the home, and pornography?
4. Anscombe says that the general television audience is "sated" on real horrors and, therefore, "demand[s] to be surprised" (paragraph 6). Do you agree that the viewing audience is "a monster that . . . is hungry for stimulation"? Do you think such is the perception of scriptwriters and television producers?
5. How has today's reality-sated audience presented a special challenge for scriptwriters? Can you think of any current shows or television movies that substantiate this observation? Any shows or movies that contradict it?
6. What measures do moviemakers resort to even in docu-dramas, and why?
7. Anscombe says that "the strategy of taboo busting is self-defeating." What does he mean by this?
8. "The ultimate docu-drama is pornography," says the author. How does he mean this? How is this "taboo" "self-defeating"?

▼ RHETORICAL CONSIDERATIONS

1. Anscombe says that today's movies and television shows must compete with reality to keep their audiences entertained. Do you think he could have strengthened his argument by naming current films and shows? Do you think there was no need to name the shows?
2. If Anscombe did not say he was a psychiatrist, could you have guessed from the essay?
3. Describe the effect the last sentence in this essay had on you. How did you respond? Did it have impact?

▼ WRITING ASSIGNMENTS

1. In paragraph 1, Anscombe says that "greed and jealousy . . . [are] the sole motives on the menu" of most television shows and movies. How accurate a statement is this? Referring to specific movies and television shows, write a paper in which you analyze the dominant motivations of character. Do greed and jealousy appear to be the most common? Do you find any other motivations? How about "patriotism, chivalry, loyalty or special endeavor"?

2. In paragraph 7, Anscombe declares that "the strategy of taboo busting is self-defeating." Write an essay in which you argue this point by analyzing certain shows or movies, or both.

3. Write an essay in which you discuss the effects of taboo-busting movies or television on yourself or someone you know.

4. Write an essay in which you discuss the effects of the news on you or someone you know. Do you think that the news media have had desensitizing effects?

5. Write an essay in which you argue our need for "secrets, inner sanctums and taboos."

▼ THEY ALSO WAIT WHO STAND AND SERVE THEMSELVES

Andrew Ward

One of the most familiar institutions in modern America is the corner gas station. Like the corner grocery store and movie house, however, it is rapidly being replaced by the slick, efficient, and impersonal. Andrew Ward, contributing editor to *The Atlantic Monthly* and the author of *Bits and Pieces* (1980) and *The Blood Seed* (1985), describes in vivid, humorous detail his local gas station and what, in the name of progress, happens to it—and by extension to the quality of American life. This article first appeared in the *Atlantic Monthly* in 1979.

Anyone interested in the future of American commerce should take a drive 1
sometime to my neighborhood gas station. Not that it is or ever was much of a
place to visit. Even when I first moved here, five years ago, it was shabby and
forlorn: not at all like the garden spots they used to feature in the commercials,
where trim, manicured men with cultivated voices tipped their visors at your
window and asked what they could do for you.

Sal, the owner, was a stocky man who wore undersized, popped-button shirts, 2
sagging trousers, and oil-spattered work shoes with broken laces. "Gas stinks" was
his motto, and every gallon he pumped into his customers' cars seemed to take
something out of him. "Pumping gas is for morons," he liked to say, leaning
indelibly against my rear window and watching the digits fly on the pump register.
"One of these days I'm gonna dump this place on a Puerto Rican, move to Florida,
and get into something nice, like hero sandwiches."

He had a nameless, walleyed assistant who wore a studded denim jacket and, 3
with his rag and squeegee, left a milky film on my windshield as my tank was
filling. There was a fume-crazed, patchy German shepherd, which Sal kept chained
to the air pump, and if you followed Sal into his cluttered, overheated office next
to the service bays, you ran a gantlet of hangers-on, many of them Sal's brothers
and nephews, who spent their time debating the merits of the driving directions he
gave the bewildered travelers who turned into his station for help.

"I don't know," one of them would say, pulling a bag of potato chips off the 4
snack rack, "I think I would have put 'em onto 91, gotten 'em off at Willow, and
then—bango!—straight through to Hamden."

Sal guarded the rest room key jealously and handed it out with reluctance, as 5
if something in your request had betrayed some dismal aberration. The rest room

was accessible only through a little closet littered with tires, fan belts, and cases of oil cans. Inside, the bulb was busted and there were never any towels, so you had to dry your hands on toilet paper—if Sal wasn't out of toilet paper, too.

The soda machine never worked for anyone except Sal, who, when complaints were lodged, would give it a contemptuous kick as he trudged by, dislodging warm cans of grape soda which, when their pop-tops were flipped, gave off a fine purple spray. There was, besides the snack rack in the office, a machine that dispensed peanuts on behalf of the Sons of Garibaldi. The metal shelves along the cinderblock wall were sparsely stocked with cans of cooling system cleaner, windshield de-icer, antifreeze, and boxed head lamps and oil filters. Over the battered yellow wiper case, below the Coca Cola clock, and half hidden by a calendar from a janitorial supply concern, hung a little brass plaque from the oil company, awarded in recognition of Salvatore A. Castallano's ten-year business association. 6

I wish for the sake of nostalgia that I could say Sal was a craftsman, but I can't. I'm not even sure he was an honest man. I suspect that when business was slow he may have cheated me, but I never knew for sure because I don't know anything about cars. If I brought my Volvo in because it was behaving strangely, I knew that as far as Sal was concerned it could never be a simple matter of tightening a bolt or re-attaching a hose. "Jesus," he'd wearily exclaim after a look under the hood. "Mr. Ward, we got problems." I usually let it go at that and simply asked him when he thought he could have it repaired, because if I pressed him for details he would get all worked up. "Look, if you don't want to take my word for it, you can go someplace else. I mean, it's a free country, you know? You got spalding on your caps, which means your dexadrometer isn't charging, and pretty soon you're gonna have hairlines in your flushing drums. You get hairlines in your flushing drums and you might as well forget it. You're driving junk." 7

I don't know what Sal's relationship was with the oil company. I suppose it was pretty distant. He was never what they call a "participating dealer." He never gave away steak knives or NFL tumblers or stuffed animals with his fill-ups, and never got around to taping company posters on his windows. The map rack was always empty, and the company emblem, which was supposed to rotate thirty feet above the station, had broken down long before I first laid eyes on it, and had frozen at an angle that made it hard to read from the highway. 8

If, outside of television, there was ever such a thing as an oil company service station inspector, he must have been appalled by the grudging service, the mad dog, the sepulchral john. When there was supposed to have been an oil shortage a few years ago, Sal's was one of the first stations to run out of gas. And several months ago, during the holiday season, the company squeezed him out for good. 9

I don't know whether Sal is now happily sprinkling olive oil over salami subs somewhere along the Sun Belt. I only know that one bleak January afternoon I turned into his station to find him gone. At first, as I idled by the no-lead pump, I thought the station had been shut down completely. Plywood had been nailed over the service bays, Sal's name had been painted out above the office door, and all that was left of his dog was a length of chain dangling from the air-pump's vacant mast. 10

But when I got out of the car I spotted someone sitting in the office with his   11
boots up on the counter, and at last caught sight of the "Self-Service Only" signs
posted by the pumps. Now, I've always striven for a degree of self-sufficiency. I fix
my own leaky faucets and I never let the bellboy carry my bags. But I discovered
as I squinted at the instructional sticker by the nozzle that there are limits to my
desire for independence. Perhaps it was the bewilderment with which I approach
anything having to do with the internal combustion engine; perhaps it was my
conviction that fossil fuels are hazardous; perhaps it was the expectation of
service, the sense of helplessness, that twenty years of oil company advertising
had engendered, but I didn't want to pump my own gas.

A mongrel rain began to fall upon the oil-slicked tarmac as I followed the   12
directions spelled out next to the nozzle. But somehow I got them wrong. When I
pulled the trigger on the nozzle, no gas gushed into my fuel tank, no digits flew on
the gauge.

"Hey, buddy," a voice sounded out of a bell-shaped speaker overhead. "Flick   13
the switch."

I turned toward the office and saw someone with Wild Bill Hickok hair   14
leaning over a microphone.

"Right. Thanks," I answered, and turned to find the switch. There wasn't one.   15
There was a bolt that looked a little like a switch, but it wouldn't flick.

"The switch," the voice crackled in the rain. "Flick the switch."   16

I waved back as if I'd finally understood, but I still couldn't figure out what he   17
was talking about. In desperation, I stuck the nozzle back into my fuel tank and
pulled the trigger. Nothing.

In the office I could see that the man was now angrily pulling on a slicker.   18
"What the hell's the matter with you?" he asked, storming by me. "All you gotta do
is flick the switch."

"I couldn't find the switch," I told him.   19

"Well, what do you call this?" he wanted to know, pointing to a little lever near   20
the pump register.

"A lever," I told him.   21

"Christ," he muttered, flicking the little lever. The digits on the register   22
suddenly formed neat rows of zeros. "All right, it's set. Now you can serve
yourself," the long-haired man said, ducking back to the office.

As the gas gushed into my fuel tank and the fumes rose to my nostrils, I   23
thought for a moment about my last visit to Sal's. It hadn't been any picnic: Sal
claimed to have found something wrong with my punting brackets, the German
shepherd snapped at my heels as I walked by, and nobody had change for my ten.
But the transaction had dimension to it: I picked up some tips about color
antennas, entered into the geographical debate in the office, and bought a can of
windshield wiper solvent (to fill the gap in my change). Sal's station had been a
dime a dozen, but it occurred to me, as the nozzle began to balk and shudder in
my hand, that gas stations of its kind were going the way of the village smithy and
the corner grocer.

I got a glob of grease on my glove as I hung the nozzle back on the pump, and   24 it took more than a minute to satisfy myself that I had replaced the gas cap properly. I tried to whip up a feeling of accomplishment as I headed for the office, but I could not forget Sal's dictum: Pumping gas is for morons.

The door to the office was locked, but a sign directed me to a stainless steel   25
teller's drawer which had been installed in the plate glass of the front window. I stood waiting for a while with my money in hand, but the long-haired man sat inside with his back to me, so at last I reached up and hesitantly knocked on the glass with my glove.

The man didn't hear me or had decided, in retaliation for our semantic   26
disagreement, to ignore me for a while. I reached up to knock again, but noticed that my glove had left a greasy smear on the window. Ever my mother's son, I reflexively reached into my pocket for my handkerchief and was about to wipe the grease away when it hit me: at last the oil industry had me where it wanted me—standing in the rain and washing its windshield.

▼ TOPICAL CONSIDERATIONS

1. In this short piece, Ward gives us a clear sense of Sal's gas station and the men associated with it. Cite some examples of succinct descriptions. How typical of gas stations is Sal's place? Does familiarity with gas stations help us visualize the place?
2. A writer's attitude toward his subject is determined not just by what he says about it but by the details he selects to describe it. What would you say Ward's attitude is toward Sal and his station? What select details reflect that attitude?
3. How does Ward feel toward what replaces Sal's station? How does Ward convey that attitude (or attitudes)?
4. In paragraph 7, Ward brings up the topic of nostalgia. How does this essay transcend a simple nostalgic reflection on a neighborhood gas station? In other words, what is Ward talking about on a higher level?
5. In paragraph 23, the author says that, even though his last visit to Sal's "hadn't been any picnic . . . the transaction had dimension to it." What does Ward mean by this statement? How did the transaction with the man with the "Wild Bill Hickok hair" lack dimension?
6. How does the scene in the last paragraph dramatize Ward's major complaint in this essay?

▼ RHETORICAL CONSIDERATIONS

1. Cite examples of descriptions in this essay that typify gas stations we know. Do any descriptions here strike you as unique to Sal's place?
2. Cite descriptions that help create humor. Does our familiarity with gas stations help carry the humor?

3. What is the effect of Sal's award of recognition coming where it does in paragraph 6?

4. Diagnosing the problems with Ward's Volvo, Sal says "You got spalding on your caps, . . . your dexadrometer isn't charging, and pretty soon you're gonna have hairlines in your flushing drums" (paragraph 7). Are these real car problems, or is Sal trying to pull a fast one on Ward? Is this the author's way of admitting his ignorance of auto repair talk?

5. Why does Ward call the rain "mongrel" in paragraph 12? What does the word connote, and how does it characterize the rain?

6. This essay contains several examples of irony. Cite some and describe how the irony works and its effects.

▼ WRITING ASSIGNMENTS

1. Good writing uses details and specifics. Inferior writing is just the opposite; it lacks sharp details and is riddled with vague generalities. Paragraph 6 is a good example of Ward's use of sharp details and specifics. First make note of them all, and then rewrite the paragraph, substituting vague generalities for the details and specifics.

2. Write an essay in which you describe how some familiar and traditional element of American society is "going the way of the village smithy and the corner grocer." You consider the plight of the corner grocer, the proprietor of a general store, the family doctor who once made house calls, a human bank teller.

3. Write an essay in which you describe an experience you've had with depersonalizing institutions.

4. Take the opposite stand from that in Assignment 3—that is, write an essay arguing that you prefer the added efficiency of the modern supermarket, for example, to the personal touch of the corner grocer. You might discuss the virtues of the computerized, twenty-four-hour bank teller versus a human one, or an automatic highway toll gate versus a human toll collector.

▼ ONCE MORE TO THE LAKE

E. B. White

Elwyn Brooks White, who died in 1985 at the age of eighty-six, was considered one of the finest essayists in America. He had written in a wide variety of forms—editorials, essays, columns (for *The New Yorker*), and children's books, including the classic *Charlotte's Web* (1952). He was also coauthor of the well-known guide for writers, *The Elements of Style* (1959). White's style is characterized by remarkably fresh and vivid descriptions and observations that are at once simple and profound. In this classic essay, White, with his son, returns to a beloved boyhood scene, where his father had taken him. But the quiet, nostalgic experience by the lakeside suddenly brings on a shocking realization of the passing of generations. This essay first appeared in *Essays of E. B. White* (1941).

One summer, along about 1904, my father rented a camp on a lake in Maine and   1
took us all there for the month of August. We all got ringworm from some kittens and had to rub Pond's Extract on our arms and legs night and morning, and my father rolled over in a canoe with all his clothes on; but outside of that the vacation was a success and from then on none of us ever thought there was any place in the world like that lake in Maine. We returned summer after summer— always on August 1 for one month. I have since become a salt-water man, but sometimes in summer there are days when the restlessness of the tides and the fearful cold of the sea water and the incessant wind that blows across the afternoon and into the evening make me wish for the placidity of a lake in the woods. A few weeks ago this feeling got so strong I bought myself a couple of bass hooks and a spinner and returned to the lake where we used to go, for a week's fishing and to revisit old haunts.

I took along my son, who had never had any fresh water up his nose and who   2
had seen lily pads only from train windows. On the journey over to the lake I began to wonder what it would be like. I wondered how time would have marred this unique, this holy spot—the coves and streams, the hills that the sun set behind, the camps and the paths behind the camps. I was sure that the tarred road would have found it out, and I wondered in what other ways it would be desolated. It is strange how much you can remember about places like that once you allow your mind to return into the grooves that lead back. You remember one thing, and that suddenly reminds you of another thing. I guess I remembered clearest of all the early mornings, when the lake was cool and motionless, remembered how the bedroom smelled of the lumber it was made of and of the wet woods whose scent

entered through the screen. The partitions in the camp were thin and did not extend clear to the top of the rooms, and as I was always the first up I would dress softly so as not to wake the others, and sneak out into the sweet outdoors and start out in the canoe, keeping close along the shore in the long shadows of the pines. I remembered being very careful never to rub my paddle against the gunwale for fear of disturbing the stillness of the cathedral.

The lake had never been what you would call a wild lake. There were cottages 3 sprinkled around the shores, and it was in farming country although the shores of the lake were quite heavily wooded. Some of the cottages were owned by nearby farmers, and you would live at the shore and eat your meals at the farmhouse. That's what our family did. But although it wasn't wild, it was a fairly large and undisturbed lake and there were places in it that, to a child at least, seemed infinitely remote and primeval.

I was right about the tar: it led to within half a mile of the shore. But when I 4 got back there, with my boy, and we settled into a camp near a farmhouse and into the kind of summertime I had known, I could tell that it was going to be pretty much the same as it had been before—I knew it, lying in bed the first morning, smelling the bedroom and hearing the boy sneak quietly out and go off along the shore in a boat. I began to sustain the illusion that he was I, and therefore, by simple transposition, that I was my father. This sensation persisted, kept cropping up all the time we were there. It was not an entirely new feeling, but in this setting it grew much stronger. I seemed to be living a dual existence. I would be in the middle of some simple act, I would be picking up a bait box or laying down a table fork, or I would be saying something, and suddenly it would be not I but my father who was saying the words or making the gesture. It gave me a creepy sensation.

We went fishing the first morning. I felt the same damp moss covering the 5 worms in the bait can, and saw the dragonfly alight on the tip of my rod as it hovered a few inches from the surface of the water. It was the arrival of this fly that convinced me beyond any doubt that everything was as it always had been, that the years were a mirage and that there had been no years. The small waves were the same, chucking the rowboat under the chine as we fished at anchor, and the boat was the same boat, the same color green and the ribs broken in the same places, and under the floorboards the same fresh-water leavings and debris—the dead helgramite, the wisps of moss, the rusty discarded fishhook, the dried blood from yesterday's catch. We stared silently at the tips of our rods, at the dragonflies that came and went. I lowered the tip of mine into the water, tentatively, pensively dislodging the fly, which darted two feet away, poised, darted two feet back, and came to rest again a little farther up the rod. There had been no years between the ducking of this dragonfly and the other one—the one that was part of memory. I looked at the boy, who was silently watching his fly, and it was my hands that held his rod, my eyes watching. I felt dizzy and didn't know which rod I was at the end of.

We caught two bass, hauling them in briskly as though they were mackerel, 6 pulling them over the side of the boat in a businesslike manner without any landing net, and stunning them with a blow on the back of the head. When we got back for a swim before lunch, the lake was exactly where we had left it, the same number of inches from the dock, and there was only the merest suggestion of a breeze. This seemed an utterly enchanted sea, this lake you could leave to its own devices for a few hours and come back to, and find that it had not stirred, this constant and trustworthy body of water. In the shallows, the dark, water-soaked sticks and twigs, smooth and old, were undulating in clusters on the bottom against the clean ribbed sand, and the track of the mussel was plain. A school of minnows swam by, each minnow with its small individual shadow, doubling the attendance, so clear and sharp in the sunlight. Some of the other campers were in swimming, along the shore, one of them with a cake of soap, and the water felt thin and clear and unsubstantial. Over the years there had been this person with the cake of soap, this cultist, and here he was. There had been no years.

Up to the farmhouse to dinner through the teeming, dusty field, the road 7
under our sneakers was only a two-track road. The middle track was missing, the one with the marks of the hooves and the splotches of dried, flaky manure. There had always been three tracks to choose from in choosing which track to walk in; now the choice was narrowed down to two. For a moment I missed terribly the middle alternative. But the way led past the tennis court, and something about the way it lay there in the sun reassured me; the tape had loosened along the backline, the alleys were green with plantains and other weeds, and the net (installed in June and removed in September) sagged in the dry noon, and the whole place steamed with midday heat and hunger and emptiness. There was a choice of pie for dessert, and one was blueberry and one was apple, and the waitresses were the same country girls, there having been no passage of time, only the illusion of it was in a dropped curtain—the waitresses were still fifteen; their hair had been washed, that was the only difference—they had been to the movies and seen the pretty girls with the clean hair.

Summertime, oh, summertime, pattern of life indelible, the fadeproof lake, 8
the woods unshatterable, the pasture with the sweetfern and the juniper forever and ever, summer without end; this was the background, and the life along the shore was the design, the cottagers with their innocent and tranquil design, their tiny docks with the flagpole and the American flag floating against the white clouds in the blue sky, the little paths over the roots of the trees leading from camp to camp and the paths leading back to the outhouses and the can of lime for sprinkling, and at the souvenir counters at the store the miniature birch-bark canoes and the postcards that showed things looking a little better than they looked. This was the American family at play, escaping the city heat, wondering whether the newcomers in the camp at the head of the cove were "common" or "nice," wondering whether it was true that the people who drove up for Sunday dinner at the farmhouse were turned away because there wasn't enough chicken.

It seemed to me, as I kept remembering all this, that those times and those 9
summers had been infinitely precious and worth saving. There had been jollity and peace and goodness. The arriving (at the beginning of August) had been so big a business in itself, at the railway station the farm wagon drawn up, the first smell of the pine-laden air, the first glimpse of the smiling farmer, and the great

importance of the trunks and your father's enormous authority in such matters, and the feel of the wagon under you for the long ten-mile haul, and at the top of the last long hill catching the first view of the lake after eleven months of not seeing this cherished body of water. The shouts and cries of the other campers when they saw you, and the trunks to be unpacked, to give up their rich burden. (Arriving was less exciting nowadays, when you sneaked up in your car and parked it under a tree near the camp and took out the bags and in five minutes it was all over, no fuss, no loud wonderful fuss about trunks.)

Peace and goodness and jollity. The only thing that was wrong now, really, was   10
the sound of the place, an unfamiliar nervous sound of the outboard motors. This was the note that jarred, the one thing that would sometimes break the illusion and set the years moving. In those other summertimes all motors were inboard; and when they were at a little distance, the noise they made was a sedative, an ingredient of summer sleep. They were one-cylinder and two-cylinder engines, and some were make-and-break and some were jump-spark, but they all made a sleepy sound across the lake. The one-lungers throbbed and fluttered, and the twin-cylinder ones purred and purred, and that was a quiet sound, too. But now the campers all had outboards. In the daytime, in the hot mornings, these motors made a petulant, irritable sound; at night, in the still evening when the afterglow lit the water, they whined about one's ears like mosquitoes. My boy loved our rented outboard, and his great desire was to achieve single-handed mastery over it, and authority, and he soon learned the trick of choking it a little (but not too much), and the adjustment of the needle valve. Watching him I would remember the things you could do with the old one-cylinder engine with the heavy flywheel, how you could have it eating out of your hand if you got really close to it spiritually. Motorboats in those days didn't have clutches, and you would make a landing by shutting off the motor at the proper time and coasting in with a dead rudder. But there was a way of reversing them, if you learned the trick, by cutting the switch and putting it on again exactly on the final dying revolution of the flywheel, so that it would kick back against compression and begin reversing. Approaching a dock in a strong following breeze, it was difficult to slow up sufficiently by the ordinary coasting method, and if a boy felt he had complete mastery over his motor, he was tempted to keep it running beyond its time and then reverse it a few feet from the dock. It took a cool nerve, because if you threw the switch a twentieth of a second too soon you would catch the flywheel when it still had speed enough to go up past center, and the boat would leap ahead, charging bull-fashion at the dock.

We had a good week at the camp. The bass were biting well and the sun shone   11
endlessly, day after day. We would be tired at night and lie down in the accumu-lated heat of the little bedrooms after the long hot day and the breeze would stir almost imperceptibly outside and the smell of the swamp drift in through the rusty screens. Sleep would come easily and in the morning the red squirrel would be on the roof, tapping out his gay routine. I kept remembering everything, lying in bed in the mornings—the small steamboat that had a long rounded stern like the lip of a Ubangi, and how quietly she ran on the moonlight sails, when the older boys

played their mandolins and the girls sang and we ate doughnuts dipped in sugar, and how sweet the music was on the water in the shining night, and what it had felt like to think about girls then. After breakfast we would go up to the store and the things were in the same place—the minnows in a bottle, the plugs and spinners disarranged and pawed over by the youngsters from the boys' camp, the Fig Newtons and the Beeman's gum. Outside, the road was tarred and cars stood in front of the store. Inside, all was just as it had always been, except there was more Coca-Cola and not so much Moxie and root beer and birch beer and sarsaparilla. We would walk out with a bottle of pop apiece and sometimes the pop would backfire up our noses and hurt. We explored the streams, quietly, where the turtles slid off the sunny logs and dug their way into the soft bottom; and we lay on the town wharf and fed worms to the tame bass. Everywhere we went I had trouble making out which was I, the one walking at my side, the one walking in my pants.

One afternoon while we were there at that lake a thunderstorm came up. It 12 was like the revival of an old melodrama that I had seen long ago with childish awe. The second-act climax of the drama of the electrical disturbance over a lake in America had not changed in any important respect. This was the big scene, still the big scene. The whole thing was so familiar, the first feeling of oppression and heat and a general air around camp of not wanting to go very far away. In mid-afternoon (it was all the same) a curious darkening of the sky, and a lull in everything that had made life tick; and then the way the boats suddenly swung the other way at their moorings with the coming of a breeze out of the new quarter, and the premonitory rumble. Then the kettle drum, then the snare, then the bass drum and cymbals, then crackling light against the dark, and the gods grinning and licking their chops in the hills. Afterward the calm, the rain steadily rustling in the calm lake, the return of light and hope and spirits, and the campers running out in joy and relief to go swimming in the rain, their bright cries perpetuating the deathless joke about how they were getting simply drenched, and the children screaming with delight at the new sensation of bathing in the rain, and the joke about getting drenched linking the generations in a strong indestructible chain. And the comedian who waded in carrying an umbrella.

When the others went swimming, my son said he was going in, too. He pulled 13 his dripping trunks from the line where they had hung all through the shower and wrung them out. Languidly, and with no thought of going in, I watched him, his hard little body, skinny and bare, saw him wince slightly as he pulled up around his vitals the small, soggy, icy garment. As he buckled the swollen belt, suddenly my groin felt the chill of death.

▼ TOPICAL CONSIDERATIONS

1. Returning with his son to the lake of his childhood, White wonders "how time would have marred this unique, this holy spot" (paragraph 2). What changes has time brought? What things have not changed?

2. In paragraph 4, White makes some observations that give him "a creepy

sensation." What are these observations, and why do they make him feel creepy?

3. In paragraph 7, White writes that "the middle track was missing" from the old road to the farmhouse. Why "for a moment" does he miss that middle track? What about that track suggests that its loss is greater than just losing another path? In other words, what higher meaning does White give to that brief observation—a meaning consistent with the rest of the essay?

4. In paragraph 6, the author describes his beloved lake as "this constant and trustworthy body of water." In what ways does he attempt to create a sense of the lake's eternal, changeless nature?

5. In paragraph 10 there is a discussion of outboard and inboard motors. What do these have to do with this essay's attention to change?

6. Throughout the essay, the author is aware of his own mortality. Find examples of images or details that underscore this awareness.

▼ RHETORICAL CONSIDERATIONS

1. Discuss the appropriateness of "cathedral," the last word in paragraph 2. Why does White use this religious term? For what is it a metaphor? How appropriate is it? Are there any other religious metaphors or images in the essay?

2. In paragraph 5, White records his observations of dragonflies. These are more than just casual observations, however. How do the dragonflies function rhetorically? How do they function to further the idea of time past overlapping with time present?

3. This essay is divided between remembrance of things past and an awareness of the present ebbing away. Where exactly is the turning point in the essay? What does White use as a pivot? How appropriate is it?

4. "A school of minnows swam by, each minnow with its small individual shadow, doubling the attendance, so clear and sharp in the sunlight" (paragraph 6). So writes White, giving us another example of his fine eye for detail. Again, however, the brilliant simplicity is deceptive. What about the double image? How is it consistent with the rest of the essay, both in style (doubling) and in meaning?

5. Discuss the appropriateness of the metaphors of musical instruments in paragraph 12.

6. Discuss the impact of the last line of the essay.

▼ WRITING ASSIGNMENTS

1. Write an essay in which you describe a place you loved to visit as a child. Try to give details that appeal not just to your reader's senses of sight and sound, but to all senses, as White does.

2. Write an essay about your experience in returning to a favorite place from your childhood. Attempt, as White does, to create a sense of nostalgia and to capture the experience of change, from the past you remember to the present.

GENDER ROLES

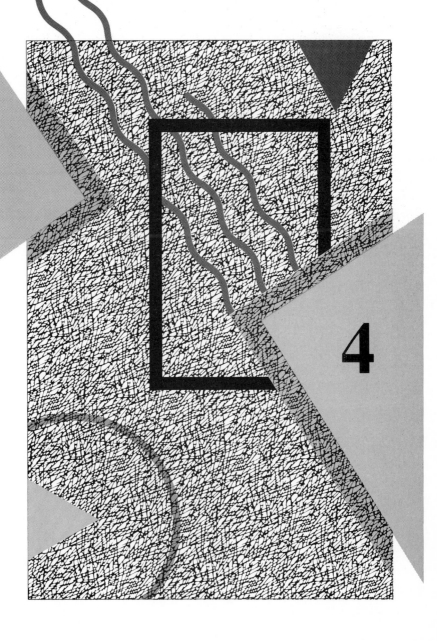

4

▼ COURTSHIP THROUGH THE AGES

James Thurber

We open this section, "Gender Roles," with an entertaining piece about courting by one of America's most famous humorists. Born in 1894, Thurber was on the staff of *The New Yorker* as a writer, cartoonist, and social commentator. He was the author of several plays and books, including *Men, Women and Dogs, My Life and Hard Times* (1933), *Is Sex Necessary?* (1929), and, with E. B. White, *My World and Welcome to It* (1942), which included his famous story "The Secret Life of Walter Mitty." This essay, first published in *The New Yorker* in 1942 humorously surveys some of the problems the males of all species have to face in wooing potential mates.

Surely nothing in the astonishing scheme of life can have nonplussed Nature so much as the fact that none of the females of any of the species she created really cared very much for the male, as such. For the past ten million years Nature has been busily inventing ways to make the male attractive to the female, but the whole business of courtship, from the marine annelids up to man, still lumbers heavily along, like a complicated musical comedy. I have been reading the sad and absorbing story in Volume 6 (Cole to Dama) of the *Encyclopaedia Britannica.* In this volume you can learn all about cricket, cotton, costume designing, crocodiles, crown jewels, and Coleridge, but none of these subjects is so interesting as the Courtship of Animals, which recounts the sorrowful lengths to which all males must go to arouse the interest of a lady.

We all know, I think, that Nature gave man whiskers and a mustache with the quaint idea in mind that these would prove attractive to the female. We all know that, far from attracting her, whiskers and mustaches only made her nervous and gloomy, so that man had to go in for somersaults, tilting with lances, and performing feats of parlor magic to win her attention; he also had to bring her candy, flowers, and the furs of animals. It is common knowledge that in spite of all these "love displays" the male is constantly being turned down, insulted, or thrown out of the house. It is rather comforting, then, to discover that the peacock, for all his gorgeous plumage, does not have a particularly easy time in courtship; none of the males in the world do. The first peahen, it turned out, was only faintly stirred by her suitor's beautiful train. She would often go quietly to sleep while he was whisking it around. The *Britannica* tells us that the peacock actually had to learn a certain little trick to wake her up and revive her interest: he had to learn to vibrate his quills so as to make a rustling sound. In ancient times man himself,

113

observing the ways of the peacock, probably tried vibrating his whiskers to make a rustling sound; if so, it didn't get him anywhere. He had to go in for something else; so, among other things, he went in for gifts. It is not unlikely that he got this idea from certain flies and birds who were making no headway at all with rustling sounds.

One of the flies of the family Empidae, who had tried everything, finally hit on 3 something pretty special. He contrived to make a glistening transparent balloon which was even larger than himself. Into this he would put sweetmeats and tidbits and he would carry the whole elaborate envelope through the air to the lady of his choice. This amused her for a time, but she finally got bored with it. She demanded silly little colorful presents, something that you couldn't eat but that would look nice around the house. So the male Empis had to go around gathering flower petals and pieces of bright paper to put into his balloon. On a courtship flight a male Empis cuts quite a figure now, but he can hardly be said to be happy. He never knows how soon the female will demand heavier presents, such as Roman coins and gold collar buttons. It seems probable that one day the court-ship of the Empidae will fall down, as man's occasionally does, of its own weight.

The bowerbird is another creature that spends so much time courting the 4 female that he never gets any work done. If all the male bowerbirds became nervous wrecks within the next ten or fifteen years, it would not surprise me. The female bowerbird insists that a playground be built for her with a specially constructed bower at the entrance. This bower is much more elaborate than an ordinary nest and is harder to build; it costs a lot more, too. The female will not come to the playground until the male has filled it up with a great many gifts: silvery leaves, red leaves, rose petals, shells, beads, berries, bones, dice, buttons, cigar bands, Christmas seals, and the Lord knows what else. When the female finally condescends to visit the playground, she is in a coy and silly mood and has to be chased in and out of the bower and up and down the playground before she will quit giggling and stand still long enough even to shake hands. The male bird is, of course, pretty well done in before the chase starts, because he has worn himself out hunting for eyeglass lenses and begonia blossoms. I imagine that many a bower bird, after chasing a female for two or three hours, says the hell with it and goes home to bed. Next day, of course, he telephones someone else and the same trying ritual is gone through with again. A male bowerbird is as exhausted as a night-club habitué before he is out of his twenties.

The male fiddler crab has a somewhat easier time, but it can hardly be said 5 that he is sitting pretty. He has one enormously large and powerful claw, usually brilliantly colored, and you might suppose that all he had to do was reach out and grab some passing cutie. The very earliest fiddler crabs may have tried this, but, if so, they got slapped for their pains. A female fiddler crab will not tolerate any caveman stuff; she never has and she doesn't intend to start now. To attract a female, a fiddler crab has to stand on tiptoe and brandish his claw in the air. If any female in the neighborhood is interested—and you'd be surprised how many are not—she comes over and engages him in light badinage, for which he is not in the mood. As many as a hundred females may pass the time of day with him and go on about their business. By nightfall of an average courting day, a fiddler crab who has been standing on tiptoe for eight or ten hours waving a heavy claw in the air is in pretty sad shape. As in the case of the males of all species, however, he gets out of bed next morning, dashes some water on his face, and tries again.

The next time you encounter a male web-spinning spider, stop and reflect that   6 he is too busy worrying about his love life to have any desire to bite you. Male web-spinning spiders have a tougher life than any other males in the animal kingdom. This is because the female web-spinning spiders have very poor eyesight. If a male lands on a female's web, she kills him before he has time to lay down his cane and gloves, mistaking him for a fly or a bumblebee who has tumbled into her trap. Before the species figured out what to do about this, millions of males were murdered by ladies they called on. It is the nature of spiders to perform a little dance in front of the female, but before a male spinner could get near enough for the female to see who he was and what he was up to, she would lash out at him with a flat-iron or a pair of garden shears. One night, nobody knows when, a very bright male spinner lay awake worrying about calling on a lady who had been killing suitors right and left. It came to him that this business of dancing as a love display wasn't getting anybody anywhere except the grave. He decided to go in for web-twitching, or strand-vibrating. The next day he tried it on one of the near-sighted girls. Instead of dropping in on her suddenly, he stayed outside the web and began monkeying with one of its strands. He twitched it up and down and in and out with such a lilting rhythm that the female was charmed. The serenade worked beautifully; the female let him live. The *Britannica*'s spider-watchers, however, report that this system is not always successful. Once in a while, even now, a female will fire three bullets into a suitor or run him through with a kitchen knife. She keeps threatening him from the moment he strikes the first low notes on the outside strings, but usually by the time he has got up to the high notes played around the center of the web, he is going to town and she spares his life.

Even the butterfly, as handsome a fellow as he is, can't always win a mate   7 merely by fluttering around and showing off. Many butterflies have to have scent scales on their wings. Hepialus carries a powder puff in a perfumed pouch. He throws perfume at the ladies when they pass. The male tree cricket, Oecanthus, goes Hepialus one better by carrying a tiny bottle of wine with him and giving drinks to such doxies as he has designs on. One of the male snails throws darts to entertain the girls. So it goes, through the long list of animals, from the bristle worm and his rudimentary dance steps to man and his gift of diamonds and sapphires. The golden-eye drake raises a jet of water with his feet as he flies over a lake; Hepialus has his powder puff, Oecanthus his wine bottle, man his etchings. It is a bright and melancholy story, the age-old desire of the male for the female, the age-old desire of the female to be amused and entertained. Of all the creatures on earth, the only males who could be figured as putting any irony into their courtship are the grebes and certain other diving birds. Every now and then a courting grebe slips quietly down to the bottom of a lake and then, with a mighty "Whoosh!," pops out suddenly a few feet from his girl friend, splashing water all over her. She seems to be persuaded that this is a purely loving display, but I like to think that the grebe always has a faint hope of drowning her or scaring her to death.

I will close this investigation into the mournful burdens of the male with the *Britannica*'s story about a certain Argus pheasant. It appears that the Argus displays himself in front of a female who stands perfectly still without moving a feather. . . . The male Argus the *Britannica* tells about was confined in a cage with a female of another species, a female who kept moving around, emptying ashtrays and fussing with lampshades all the time the male was showing off his talents. Finally, in disgust, he stalked away and began displaying in front of his water trough. He reminds me of a certain male (Homo sapiens) of my acquaintance who one night after dinner asked his wife to put down her detective magazine so that he could read a poem of which he was very fond. She sat quietly enough until he was well into the middle of the thing, intoning with great ardor and intensity. Then suddenly there came a sharp, disconcerting *slap!* It turned out that all during the male's display, the female had been intent on a circling mosquito and had finally trapped it between the palms of her hands. The male in this case did not stalk away and display in front of a water trough; he went over to Tim's and had a flock of drinks and recited the poem to the fellas. I am sure they all told bitter stories of their own about how their displays had been interrupted by females. I am also sure that they all ended up singing "Honey, Honey, Bless Your Heart."

8

▼ TOPICAL CONSIDERATIONS

1. Thurber compares the courtship of animals to a "complicated musical comedy" that "lumbers heavily along." What are some examples Thurber gives to illustrate his point? How do these examples relate to the courtship habits of male *Homo sapiens?* What do Thurber's examples imply about the trials that the male encounters in his courtship of the female? Do you agree? Does the male really have as difficult a time as Thurber suggests?

2. In his opening sentence, Thurber suggests what he feels is the chief reason why the male courtship of the female has such trouble getting off the ground and why, as he comments later, it often falls by its own weight. What is the reason? What does Thurber's remark suggest about the typical attitude a female takes in the courtship ritual? Is there any hint of truth in what he is saying? Does the female really care so little for the male? Or is she just pretending?

3. What is a "love display"? What are some of the love displays that Thurber describes in his essay? Are they typical? Can you think of others? Are the ones that Thurber mentions as unsuccessful as he suggests?

4. In Thurber's treatment of the subject of courtship, he describes men as playing the dominant role. Is this always necessarily the case? Does the woman sometimes take the initiative? If so, is her approach the same? Or does she have her own typical love displays and methods of courting? Explain.

5. Are men's and women's attitudes toward courtship the same as they were a generation ago? What is your attitude toward courtship? Who do you think should take the initiative? How should a courtship be conducted?

▼ RHETORICAL CONSIDERATIONS

1. What is Thurber's aim in this essay? Is he simply being absurd and funny, or does he make a serious point? Explain.
2. In the first paragraph, what does Thurber mean literally when he comments that "the whole business of courtship . . . lumbers heavily along, like a complicated musical comedy"? What is he suggesting figuratively about the ritual of courtship? Why is *lumber* a good word choice? How does this figure of speech relate to Thurber's thesis? Are there any other figures of speech in this paragraph?
3. Thurber also uses gloomy words and phrases in his first paragraph: The story of the courtship of animals is "*sad* and absorbing." Males go to "*sorrowful* lengths" to arouse a lady's interest. What is Thurber's purpose in choosing these words? Find similar phrases throughout the essay. How do these phrases reinforce the figure of speech introduced in the beginning?
4. Discuss the organization of this essay. Is it well-structured? Does one part flow naturally from another? Does Thurber follow through on the ideas he introduces in the beginning? How does he achieve transition? Is his conclusion consistent with the attitude he establishes in the beginning?

▼ WRITING ASSIGNMENTS

1. Did you detect a bias in Thurber's discussion of the courtship patterns of men and women? Is his treatment of the subject objective and balanced? Write an essay in which you defend or criticize Thurber's impression of courtship. Give examples to prove your points.
2. Write an essay in which you give examples of what you feel are typical "love displays" that men use when they seek to arouse a woman's interest. Discuss what you consider to be typical methods that women use to interest men.

▼ MASCULINE/FEMININE

Prudence Mackintosh

> Prudence Mackintosh, a free-lance writer, is the author of a very
> funny book, *Thundering Sneakers* (1981) from which this essay was
> taken. She is also the mother of three boys, whom she intended to
> raise free of sex-role differences and cultural stereotyping. She gave
> them dolls to play with rather than guns and taught them that mom
> and dad shared household chores. As she has sadly learned, however,
> there is "more to this sex-role learning than the home environment
> can handle," including powerful forces of culture and, perhaps, nature.

I had every intention to raise liberated, nonviolent sons whose aggressive tenden- 1
cies would be mollified by a sensitivity and compassion that psychologists claim
were denied their father's generation.

I did not buy guns or war toys (although Grandmother did). My boys even had 2
a secondhand baby doll until the garage sale last summer. I did buy Marlo
Thomas' *Free to Be You and Me* record, a collection of nonsexist songs, stories,
and poems, and I told them time and time again that it was okay to cry and be
scared sometimes. I overruled their father and insisted that first grade was much
too early for organized competitive soccer leagues. They know that moms *and*
dads do dishes and diapers. And although they use it primarily for the convenient
bathroom between the alley and the sandpile, my boys know that the storeroom is
now mother's office. In such an environment, surely they would grow up free of
sex-role stereotypes. At the very least wouldn't they pick up their own socks?

My friends with daughters were even more zealous. They named their daugh- 3
ters strong, cool unisex names like Blakeney, Brett, Brook, Lindsay, and Blair,
names that lent themselves to corporate letterheads, not Tupperware party
invitations. These moms looked on Barbie with disdain and bought trucks and
science kits. They shunned frilly dresses for overalls. They subscribed to Feminist
Press and read stories called "My Mother the Mail Carrier" instead of "Sleeping
Beauty." At the swimming pool one afternoon, I watched a particularly fervent
young mother, ironically clad in a string bikini, encourage her daughter. "You're
so strong, Blake! Kick hard, so you'll be the strongest kid in this pool." When my
boys splashed water in Blakeney's eyes and she ran whimpering to her mother, this
mom exhorted, "You go back in that pool and shake your fist like this and say,
'You do that again and I'll bust your lights out.'" A new generation of little girls,
assertive and ambitious, taking a backseat to no one?

It's a little early to assess the results of our efforts, but when my seven-year-old 4
son, Jack, comes home singing—to the tune of *"Frère Jacques"*—"Farrah Fawcett,

Farrah Fawcett, I love you" and five minutes later asks Drew, his five-year-old brother, if he'd like his nose to be a blood fountain, either we're backsliding or there's more to this sex-role learning than the home environment can handle.

I'm hearing similar laments from mothers of daughters. "She used to tell   5
everyone that she was going to grow up to be a lawyer just like Daddy," said one, "but she's hedging on that ambition ever since she learned that no one wears a blue fairy tutu in the courtroom." Another mother with two sons, a daughter, and a very successful career notes that, with no special encouragement, only her daughter keeps her room neat and loves to set the table and ceremoniously seat her parents. At a Little League game during the summer, fearful that this same young daughter might be absorbing the stereotype "boys play while girls watch," her parents readily assured her that she too could participate when she was eight years old. "Oh," she exclaimed with obvious delight, "I didn't know they had cheerleaders."

How does it happen? I have my own theories, but decided to do a little   6
reading to see if any of the "experts" agreed with me. I was also curious to find out what remedies they recommended. The books I read propose that sex roles are culturally induced. In simplistic terms, rid the schools, their friends, and the television of sexism, and your daughters will dump their dolls and head straight for the boardroom while your sons contemplate nursing careers. *Undoing Sex Stereotypes* by Marcia Guttentag and Helen Bray is an interesting study of efforts to overcome sexism in the classroom. After reading it, I visited my son's very traditional school and found it guilty of unabashedly perpetrating the myths that feminists abhor. Remember separate water fountains? And how, even if the line was shorter, no boy would be caught dead drinking from the girls' fountain and vice versa? That still happens. "You wouldn't want me to get cooties, would you, Mom?" my son says, defending the practice. What did I expect in a school where the principal still addresses his faculty, who range in age from 23 to 75, as "girls"?

Nevertheless, having been a schoolteacher myself, I am skeptical of neatly   7
programmed nonsexist curriculum packets like Guttentag and Bray's. But if you can wade through the jargon ("people of the opposite sex hereafter referred to as POTOS"), some of the observations and exercises are certainly thought-provoking and revealing. In one exercise fifth-grade students were asked to list adjectives appropriate to describe women. The struggle some of the children had in shifting their attitudes about traditional male roles is illustrated in this paragraph written by a fifth-grade girl who was asked to write a story about a man using the adjectives she had listed to describe women:

Once there was a boy who all his life was very *gentle.* He never hit anyone or started a fight and when some of his friends were not feeling well, he was *loving* and *kind* to them. When he got older he never changed. People started not liking him because he was *weak, petite,* and he wasn't like any of the other men—not strong or tough. Most of his life he sat alone thinking about why no one liked him. Then one day he went out and tried to act like the other men. He joined a baseball team, but he was no good, he always got out. Then he decided to join the hockey team. He couldn't play good. He kept on breaking all the rules. So he quit the team and joined the soccer team. These men were *understanding* to him. He was really good at soccer, and was the best on the team. That year they won the championship and the rest of his life he was happy.*

After reading this paragraph it occurred to me that this little girl's self-esteem and subsequent role in life would be enhanced by a teacher who spent less time on "nonsexist intervention projects" and more time on writing skills. But that, of course, is not what the study was meant to reveal. 8

The junior high curriculum suggested by *Undoing Sex Stereotypes* has some laudable consciousness-raising goals. For example, in teaching units called "Women's Roles in American History" and "The Socialization of Women and the Image of Women in the Media" teenagers are encouraged to critically examine television commercials, soap operas, and comic books. But am I a traitor to the cause if I object when the authors in another unit use *Romeo and Juliet* as a study of the status of women? Something is rotten in Verona when we have to consider Juliet's career possibilities and her problems with self-actualization. The conclusions of this project were lost on me; I quit reading when the author began to talk about ninth-graders who were "cognitively at a formal operational level." I don't even know what my "external sociopsychological situation" is. However, I think I did understand some of the conclusions reached by the kids: 9

"Girls are smart."
"If a woman ran a forklift where my father works, there would be a walkout."
"Men cannot be pom-pom girls."

Eminently more readable, considering that both authors are educators of educators, is *How to Raise Independent and Professionally Successful Daughters,* by Drs. Rita and Kenneth Dunn. The underlying and, I think, questionable assumption in this book is that little boys have been reared correctly all along. Without direct parental intervention, according to the Dunns, daughters tend to absorb and reflect society's values. The Dunns paint a dark picture indeed for the parents who fail to channel their daughters toward professional success. The woman who remains at home with children while her husband is involved in the "real world" with an "absorbing and demanding day-to-day commitment that brings him into contact with new ideas, jobs, and people (attractive self-actualized females)" is sure to experience lowered IQ, according to the Dunns. They go on to predict the husband's inevitable affair and the subsequent divorce, which leaves the wife emotionally depressed and probably financially dependent on her parents. 10

Now I'm all for women developing competency and self-reliance, but the Dunns' glorification of the professional is excessive. Anyone who has worked longer than a year knows that eventually any job loses most of its glamour. And 11

*From *Undoing Sex Stereotypes* by Marcia Guttentag and Helen Bray © 1976 McGraw-Hill, Inc. Used with permission of McGraw-Hill Book Co.

the world is no less "real" at home. For that matter, mothers at home may be more "real" than bankers or lawyers. How is a corporate tax problem more real than my counseling with the maid whose boyfriend shot her in the leg? How can reading a balance sheet compare with comforting a five-year-old who holds his limp cat and wants to know why we have to lose the things we love? And on the contrary, it is my husband, the professional, who complains of lowered IQ. Though we wooed to Faulkner, my former ace English major turned trial lawyer now has time for only an occasional *Falconer* or Peter Benchley thriller. Certainly there is value in raising daughters to be financially self-supporting, but there is not much wisdom in teaching a daughter that she must achieve professional success or her marriage probably won't last.

In a chapter called "What to Do from Birth to Two," the authors instruct 12 parents to introduce dolls only if they represent adult figures or groups of figures. "Try not to give her her own 'baby.' A baby doll is acceptable only for dramatizing the familiar episodes she has actually experienced, like a visit to the doctor." If some unthinking person should give your daughter a baby doll, and she likes it, the Dunns recommend that you permit her to keep it without exhibiting any negative feelings, "but do not lapse into cuddling it or encouraging her to do so. Treat it as any other object and direct attention to other more beneficial toys." I wonder if the Dunns read an article by Anne Roiphe called "Can You Have Everything and Still Want Babies?" which appeared in *Vogue* a couple of years ago. Ms. Roiphe was deploring the extremes to which our liberation has brought us. "It is nice to have beautiful feet, it may be desirable to have small feet, but it is painful and abusive to bind feet. It is also a good thing for women to have independence, freedom and choice, movement, and opportunity; but I'm not so sure that the current push against mothering will not be another kind of binding of the soul. . . . As women we have thought so little of ourselves that when the troops came to liberate us we rushed into the streets leaving our most valuable attributes behind as if they belonged to the enemy."

The Dunns' book is thorough, taking parents step-by-step through the elementary 13 years and on to high school. Had I been raising daughters, however, I think I would have flunked out in the chapter "What to Do from Age Two to Five." In discussing development of vocabulary, the Doctors Dunn prohibit the use of nonsensical words for bodily functions. I'm sorry, Doctors, but I've experimented with this precise terminology and discovered that the child who yells "I have to defecate, Mom" across four grocery aisles is likely to be left in the store. A family without a few poo-poo jokes is no family at all.

These educators don't help me much in my efforts to liberate my sons. And 14 although I think little girls are getting a better deal with better athletic training and broader options, I believe we're kidding ourselves if we think we can raise our sons and daughters alike. Certain inborn traits seem to be immune to parental and cultural tampering. How can I explain why a little girl baby sits on a quilt in the park thoughtfully examining a blade of grass, while my baby William uproots grass by handfuls and eats it? Why does a mother of very bright and active daughters confide that until she went camping with another family of boys, she feared that my sons had a hyperactivity problem? I'm sure there are plenty of rowdy, noisy little girls, but I'm not just talking about rowdiness and noise. I'm talking about some sort of primal physicalness that causes the walls of my house to pulsate on rainy days. I'm talking about something inexplicable that makes my sons fall into a mad, scrambling, pull-your-ears-off-kick-your-teeth-in heap just before bedtime, when they're not even mad at each other. I mean something that causes them to climb the doorjamb with honey and peanut butter on their hands while giving me a synopsis of *Star Wars* that contains only five intelligible words: "And this this guy, he 'pssshhhhhhh.' And then this thing went 'vronggggggg.' But this little guy said, 'Nong-neee-nonh-nee.' " When Jack and Drew are not kicking a soccer ball or each other, they are kicking the chair legs, the cat, the baby's silver rattle, and, inadvertently, Baby William himself, whom they have affectionately dubbed "Tough Eddy." Staying put in a chair for the duration of a one-course meal is torturous for these boys. They compensate by never quite putting both feet under the table. They sit with one leg doubled under them while the other leg extends to one side. The upper half of the body appears committed to the task at hand—eating—but the lower extremities are poised to lunge should a more compelling distraction present itself. From this position, I have observed, one brother can trip a haughty dessert-eating sibling who is flaunting the fact he ate all his "sweaty little peas." Although we have civilized them to the point that they dutifully mumble, "May I be excused, please?" their abrupt departure from the table invariably overturns at least one chair or whatever milk remains. This sort of constant motion just doesn't lend itself to lessons in thoughtfulness and gentleness.

Despite my encouragement, my sons refuse to invite little girls to play anymore. 15 Occasionally friends leave their small daughters with us while they run errands. I am always curious to see what these females will find of interest in my sons' roomful of Tonka trucks and soccer balls. One morning the boys suggested that the girls join them in playing Emergency with the big red fire trucks and ambulance. The girls were delighted and immediately designated the ambulance as theirs. The point of Emergency, as I have seen it played countless times with a gang of little boys, is to make as much noise with the siren as possible and to crash the trucks into each other or into the leg of a living-room chair before you reach your destination.

The girls had other ideas. I realized why they had selected the ambulance. It 16 contained three dolls: a driver, a nurse, and sick man on the stretcher. My boys have used that ambulance many times, but the dolls were always secondary to the death-defying race with the fire trucks; they were usually just thrown in the back of the van as an afterthought. The girls took the dolls out, stripped and re-dressed them tenderly, and made sure that they were seated in their appropriate places for the first rescue. Once the fire truck had been lifted off the man's leg, the girls required a box of Band-Aids and spent the next half hour making a bed for the patient and reassuring him that he was going to be all right. These little girls and my sons had seen the same NBC *Emergency* series, but the girls had apparently picked up on the show's nurturing aspects, while Jack and Drew were interested only in the equipment, the fast driving, and the sirens. . . .

Of course, I want my sons to grow up knowing that what's inside a woman's 17
head is more important than her appearance, but I'm sure they're getting mixed
signals when I delay our departure for the swimming pool to put on lipstick. I also
wonder what they make of their father, whose favorite aphorism is "beautiful
women rule the world." I suppose what we want for these sons and the women
they may marry someday is a sensitivity that enables them to be both flexible and
at ease with their respective roles, so that marriage contracts are unnecessary.
When my sons bring me the heads of two purple irises from the neighbor's yard
and ask, "Are you really the most beautiful mama in the whole world like Daddy
says, and did everyone want to marry you?" do you blame me if I keep on waffling?

▼ TOPICAL CONSIDERATIONS

1. Mackintosh discusses what raising a family has taught her about the differences in the way boys and girls behave. She includes a number of amusing
   illustrations. What are some of these examples? Do the scenes she describes
   sound like any you've experienced in your own home?
2. Reread Mackintosh's description of how her sons and their little girl
   visitors played *Emergency*. What is significant about this illustration? Do
   you think its implications are always true? For example, do nurturing
   qualities belong exclusively to girls? Is aggressiveness typical only of boys?
   Give examples to support your answer.
3. What do you think of the efforts Mackintosh and her friends have made to
   keep their children from assuming stereotypical sex roles? Would you raise
   your children the same way or differently? Explain your answer.
4. Mackintosh's essay encourages a healthy acceptance of the fact that boys
   and girls act differently when they are growing up and that these differences are inherent. Can you also think of some qualities or traits that boys
   and girls have in common? Or some that could be expressed by either?
5. Mackintosh implies that boys don't need to be encouraged to be nurses,
   just to avoid stereotypical sex roles. Is it necessarily true, though, that
   a man wouldn't want to be a nurse? Or a secretary? Or a kindergarten
   teacher? Or that he wouldn't have a natural aptitude for these careers?
   Is Mackintosh implying that a woman naturally wouldn't want to be a
   lawyer? Would you agree if this were the assumption? Give reasons for
   your answer.

▼ RHETORICAL CONSIDERATIONS

1. Where does Mackintosh state her thesis? Is it implicit or explicit?
2. What is the primary rhetorical strategy Mackintosh uses to develop her
   essay? Cite individual passages to substantiate your answer.
3. Find five sentences that demonstrate Mackintosh's use of concrete detail.

Revise the sentences by replacing these specifics with generalities. Read the two versions aloud. What is the difference in effect?

4. Examine Mackintosh's first and last paragraphs. Explain how the last paragraph ties in with the first to unify the essay and bring it to a conclusive finish.

▼ WRITING ASSIGNMENTS

1. What was it like growing up in your home? Were you encouraged to assume a stereotypical sex role? Or did your parents try to avoid this? In an essay, discuss these questions.

2. Identify a career that tends to be either male-oriented or female-oriented. Write an essay in which you discuss why this is true. Analyze whether you think it should or will continue to be this way.

▼ AN OFFICER AND A FEMINIST

James M. Dubik

James Dubik grew up believing that women were supposed to be passive and noncompetitive. Life in the army—"the last bastion of male chauvinism"—sustained the stereotypes of female behavior until two things happened. First was his assignment to teach philosophy at West Point. Second was his daughters growing up. What he learned first hand was that aggressiveness, ambition, and the competitive spirit are not just male virtues. In what follows, Dubik celebrates "today's women" and his own "liberation." This article first appeared in *Newsweek,* in April, 1987.

I'm a member of a last bastion of male chauvinism. I'm an infantry officer, and there are no women in the infantry. I'm a Ranger and no women go to Ranger School. I'm a member of America's special-operation forces—and there, although women are involved in intelligence, planning and clerical work, only men can be operators, or "shooters." Women can become paratroopers and jump out of airplanes alongside me—yet not many do. All this is as it should be, according to what I learned while growing up.

Not many of the women I knew in high school and college in the '60s and early '70s pushed themselves to their physical or mental limits or had serious career dreams of their own. If they did, few talked about them. So I concluded they were exceptions to the rule. Then two things happened. First, I was assigned to West Point, where I became a philosophy instructor. Second, my two daughters grew up.

I arrived at the Academy with a master's degree from Johns Hopkins University in Baltimore and a graduation certificate from the U.S. Army Command and General Staff College at Fort Leavenworth. I was ready to teach, but instead, I was the one who got an education.

The women cadets, in the classroom and out, did not fit my stereotype of female behavior. They took themselves and their futures seriously. They persevered in a very competitive environment. Often they took charge and seized control of a situation. They gave orders; they were punctual and organized. They played sports hard. They survived, even thrived, under real pressure. During field exercises, women cadets were calm and unemotional even when they were dirty, cold, wet, tired and hungry. They didn't fold or give up.

Most important, such conduct seemed natural to them. From my perspective all this was extraordinary; to them it was ordinary. While I had read a good bit of "feminist literature" and, intellectually, accepted many of the arguments against stereotyping, this was the first time my real-life experience supported such ideas. And seeing is believing.

Enter two daughters: Kerith, 12; Katie, 10.   6

Kerith and Katie read a lot, and they write, too—poems, stories, paragraphs   7
and answers to "thought questions" in school. In what they read and in what they
write, I can see their adventurousness, their inquisitiveness and their ambition.
They discover clues and solve mysteries. They take risks, brave dangers, fight
villains—and prevail. Their schoolwork reveals their pride in themselves. Their
taste for reading is boundless; they're interested in everything. "Why?" is forever
on their lips. Their eyes are set on personal goals that they, as individuals, aspire to
achieve: Olympic gold, owning their own business, public office.

ROUGH PLAY AND RISK

Both play sports. I've witnessed a wholesome, aggressive, competitive spirit born   8
in Kerith. She played her first basketball season last year, and when she started,
she was too polite to bump anyone, too nice to steal anything, especially if some
other girl already had the ball. By the end of the season, however, Kerith was
taking bumps and dishing them out. She plays softball with the intensity of a
Baltimore Oriole. She rides and jumps her horse in competitive shows. Now she
"can't imagine" not playing a sport, especially one that didn't have a little rough
play and risk.

In Katie's face, I've seen Olympic intensity as she passed a runner in the last   9
50 yards of a mile relay. Gasping for air, knees shaking, lungs bursting, she dipped
into her well of courage and "gutted out" a final kick. Her comment after the race:
"I kept thinking I was Mary Decker beating the Russians." For the first time she
experienced the thrill of pushing herself to the limit. She rides and jumps, too.
And her basketball team was a tournament champion. The joy and excitement
and pride that shone in the eyes of each member of the team was equal to that in
any NCAA winner's locker room. To each sport Katie brings her dedication to
doing her best, her drive to excel and her desire to win.

Both girls are learning lessons that, when my wife and I were their age, were   10
encouraged only in boys. Fame, aggressiveness, achievement, self-confidence—
these were territories into which very few women (the exception, not the rule)
dared enter. Kerith and Katie, most of their friends, many of their generation
and the generations to come are redefining the social game. Their lives contradict
the stereotypes with which I grew up. Many of the characteristics I thought
were "male" are, in fact, "human." Given a chance, anyone can, and will,
acquire them.

My daughters and the girls of their generation are lucky. They receive a lot of   11
institutional support not available to women of past generations: from women
executives, women athletes, women authors, women politicians, women adventurers,
women Olympians. Old categories, old stereotypes and old territories don't fit the
current generation of young women; and they won't fit the next generation, either.
As Kerith said, "I can't even imagine not being allowed to do something or be
something just because I am a girl."

All this does not negate what I knew to be true during my own high-school and college years. But what I've learned from both the women cadets at West Point and from my daughters supports a different conclusion about today's women and the women of tomorrow from the beliefs I was raised with. Ultimately we will be compelled to align our social and political institutions with what is already becoming a fact of American life. Or more precisely, whenever biological difference is used to segregate a person from an area of human endeavor, we will be required to demonstrate that biological difference is relevant to the issue at hand.

▼ TOPICAL CONSIDERATIONS

1. Given what you've read here, how would Dubik define "male chauvinism"? How might he define a "feminist"?
2. How did Dubik's assignment as instructor at West Point change his perceptions of women?
3. How did the growing up of his daughters change his perceptions of women?
4. From his perspective, Dubik finds the change in women "extraordinary" (paragraph 5). How does he explain this? What changes in women does he remark upon? What standards for measuring women does he use?
5. In paragraph 10, Dubik says that "Fame, aggressiveness, achievement, self-confidence . . . were territories into which very few women . . . dared enter" in the past. Does this assessment describe any women you know from Dubik's generation? Does this describe any of the women of today's generation? In other words, from your own observations have women changed much since Dubik was young?
6. According to the author, how are women of today's generation "lucky" compared to women of past generations? Do you agree?
7. Dubik no doubt takes great pride in his daughters' achievements and ambitions. How might he regard his daughters were they not physical and aggressive? How might his views be altered?
8. Dubik says that over the years as an instructor, he "was the one who got an education" regarding women. Would you say Dubik is a reformed male chauvinist? Does he still measure women against male yardsticks?

▼ RHETORICAL CONSIDERATIONS

1. How does the first paragraph forecast the attitudes and discussion development that follows?
2. What does Dubik imply when he informs us that his daughters "read a lot" and write poems, too?
3. In paragraph 10, Dubik says that his daughters' generation and the generations to come "are redefining the social game." Why does he use the word

"game"? What are the connotations? How does his choice of terms affect the seriousness of what he is remarking about?

4. In paragraph 5, Dubik says he's familiar with "feminist literature." Why the use of quotation marks? What is their message?

5. Explain the meaning of the concluding sentence. How does it reflect upon the opening sentences?

▼ WRITING ASSIGNMENTS

1. Write a paper in which you express your own observations of how women have successfully competed along side with men in sports, the business world, and the military.

2. Do you think that Dubik's evaluation of women's capabilities is too male-biased? If so, write a response to his arguments.

3. Dubik says in paragraph 1 that there are no women in the infantry, special-operation forces, and field intelligence operations. What are your own feelings about this "last bastion of male chauvinism"? In other words, do you think women should be allowed to be "shooters"?

▼ HOMEMAKING

William Raspberry

Homemaking is akin to an executive enterprise—complex and very important, says William Raspberry, a distinguished syndicated columnist for the *Washington Post*. He has written articles on a wide range of subjects, from Washington politics to black education. What he writes about here is a discovery he made one weekend while his wife was away—a discovery about the nature of homemaking. Cleaning the house and taking care of his children taught him that homemaking was more than a series of chores. Raspberry's article is as much a defense of homemaking, however, as it is a defense of homemakers, whose careers have long been undervalued by both men and women. This article first appeared in his column in 1977.

1 Since my wife was out of town last weekend—leaving me to look after our children and the house—I suppose I could make the case that I now have a better appreciation of what homemaking is about.

2 Well, if I do, it isn't because of what I had to do in her absence but because of what I didn't have to do. I had to cook and make sure that the little ones were warmly clothed, that they spent some time playing outside, that they got baths, picked up after themselves, and so on. In short, I took over a series of chores, many of which I would have performed even if my wife had been home.

3 But I didn't have to plan anything, schedule anything, or fit anything into an overall design. I didn't have to see to my children's overall nutrition; I only had to see that they weren't too bored and didn't tear the house down. What I did was episodic, a combination of housework and babysitting. What my wife does is part of an ongoing enterprise: homemaking. Hers is an executive role, though neither she nor I had ever thought to describe it as such.

4 I strongly suspect that the failure to make the distinction between homemaking and chores is one of the chief reasons why homemaking has fallen into such disrepute of late. As Jinx Melia, founder and director of the Martha Movement,* observed in a recent interview, "ethnic" homemakers, as a rule, have managed to retain a higher sense of respect for their calling, partly, she suspects, because their husbands may be somewhat more likely to work at blue-collar jobs that hold no attraction for their wives.

5 A larger part, though, may be that "traditional" husbands—whatever jobs they work at—are likelier to be ignorant (perhaps deliberately so) of homemaking skills. Homemaking may involve as much a sense of mystique for these husbands as outside

*A movement to give voice to housewives and homemakers in the United States.—Ed.

work holds for their wives. Men of all classes are increasingly likely these days to help out with the chores, or even take over for a spell, as I did last weekend. And if we aren't careful, we come to believe that we can do easily everything our wives do—if we can only survive the boredom of it. The result is that we lose respect for what they do. Think of homemaking as a series of more or less unpleasant chores and the disrespect is virtually automatic.

Well, most jobs are a series of more or less unpleasant chores. But it doesn't   6 follow that that's all they are. Looking up cases and precedents, trying to draw information out of a client who doesn't quite understand what you need to know, keeping records, writing "boiler-plate" contracts—all these things are routine, and a bright high school graduate could quickly learn to do them all. The chores are a drag; but lawyering is a fascinating career. Reducing a career to a series of chores creates this additional problem of perspective: Any time not spent on one or another of the chores is viewed as time wasted.

As Melia also pointed out, the men who work at professions spend an   7 enormous amount of time doing the mirror image of what their noncareer wives may be chided or even openly criticized for doing. They talk on the phone a lot (perhaps about business, but they often aren't doing business). They hold staff meetings or unit meetings that are hardly different from coffee klatches. A business lunch with a client you've already sold (or for whom you have no specific proposal at the moment) is not vastly different from a gathering of homemakers in somebody's kitchenette.

The main difference is that a man gets to call all these things "work." One   8 reason for the difference is that the details of homemaking are far more visible (to the spouse) than the details of work done outside. As a result, husbands often not only devalue their wives' work but also feel perfectly free to question the wisdom of what they do as part of that work. Wives generally know too little about their husbands' work to question any aspect of it. They are more likely to magnify its importance.

None of this should be taken as a proposal that women be kept out of   9 the labor market. There are women whose talents are so far removed from home and hearth that it would be criminal to encourage them to become homemakers. There are women who need to earn income, for reasons ranging from fiscal to psychic. Women who choose careers outside the home, or who have no choice but to pursue careers, ought to be free to do so without any discrimination of any sort.

But there are also women who seek outside work primarily because they   10 know their homemaking role is undervalued, by their husbands and by themselves. There is nothing intrinsic about producing income, on the one hand, or nurturing children and managing a household, on the other, that would lead to a natural conclusion that income-production is of greater value. The opposite conclusion would appear likelier, as in the distinction between worker and queen bees, for instance. But worker bees don't claim sole ownership and discretion over what they produce; they work for the hive. It would go a long way toward changing the onerous working conditions of homemakers if we could learn to think of family income as belonging to the family, not primarily to the person who happens to bring it home.

Maybe there is a logical reason why the marriage partner who doesn't produce income should be the fiscal dependent of the one who does. Off hand, I can't think what it might be.

11

▼ TOPICAL CONSIDERATIONS

1. What does Raspberry see as the major reasons that homemaking fails to receive the respect it deserves? What analogy does he use to prove his point? Is he convincing? Is his analogy appropriate? Give reasons for your answers.
2. Raspberry comments that he came to appreciate better what homemaking was all about not because of what he did in his wife's absence but because of what he didn't do. What does he mean? What are some of the things he didn't do? Who does these things in your home? Do you think these skills are as important as Raspberry implies? Explain.
3. Describe the audience that you think would best appreciate what Raspberry is saying. Who might fail to appreciate it? Do you think it might encourage a wife who is a homemaker to live her life any differently? How? Would it produce any changes in her husband's attitude?
4. Traditionally, the wife is the homemaker and the husband earns the salary and pays the bills. Is this always the case? Can you describe marriages in which the roles are reversed? Should they be reversed? Who should assume responsibility for the home when both partners in the marriage work?
5. What are Raspberry's views about who in the family should manage the money? How does his analogy of the worker bees in a beehive reveal his attitudes? Do you agree or disagree with him?
6. What is Raspberry's attitude toward wives who choose to work outside the home? What are some reasons he gives for his opinion? How does this fit with the thesis of his essay? Does he make a valid point?
7. What specific conclusions is Raspberry drawing about women's place in the work force? What general conclusions is he drawing about attitudes toward work?
8. How does Raspberry's view of women agree with or differ from Thurber's, in "Courtship Through the Ages?" Do you think the typical female that Thurber describes would live up to Raspberry's expectations of an executive homemaker? How might Raspberry's homemaker conduct herself in a courtship?

▼ RHETORICAL CONSIDERATIONS

1. What is Raspberry's purpose in this essay? Where does he state it?

2. What can you say about Raspberry's treatment of his subject? Is it objective and balanced? Do you detect a bias?
3. How does Raspberry attract the reader's attention in the opening paragraph? Is this an effective way to begin? Why, or why not?
4. What kind of essay has Raspberry written? Is it primarily narrative, descriptive, expository, or persuasive?

▼ WRITING ASSIGNMENTS

1. Homemaking is not the only kind of work that people mistakenly consider routine and uninteresting. Write an essay in which you describe another career that people view in this way. Persuade your readers to appreciate that career more fully.
2. Raspberry unequivocally states his attitude toward wives who choose to work outside the home. In an essay, defend or criticize his stand. Give reasons and examples to substantiate your arguments.
3. Write an essay comparing and contrasting Raspberry's view of women with Thurber's. Discuss how each one's version of a woman would be likely to conduct herself in a courtship or in the home.

▼ I WANT A WIFE

Judy Syfers

> Having assumed a housewife's perspective for a weekend, William Raspberry came to the conclusion that the duties of a homemaker have long been devalued—seen simply as endlessly boring chores and services instead of as a complex and important "executive" enterprise. Taking a husband's perspective, Judy Syfers here gives us a far less ennobling look at homemaking, based on years of being a housewife and mother. "Who wouldn't want a wife?" she asks. Syfers gives a host of reasons for wanting a wife and, in the process, raises some fundamental questions about gender roles and the American family. This classic feminist piece first appeared in *Ms.* in May 1971.

1   I belong to that classification of people known as wives. I am A Wife. And, not altogether incidentally, I am a mother.

2   Not too long ago a male friend of mine appeared on the scene fresh from a recent divorce. He had one child, who is, of course, with his ex-wife. He is obviously looking for another wife. As I thought about him while I was ironing one evening, it suddenly occurred to me that I, too, would like to have a wife. Why do I want a wife?

3   I would like to go back to school so that I can become economically independent, support myself, and, if need be, support those dependent upon me. I want a wife who will work and send me to school. And while I am going to school I want a wife to take care of my children. I want a wife to keep track of the children's doctor and dentist appointments. And to keep track of mine, too. I want a wife to make sure my children eat properly and are kept clean. I want a wife who will wash the children's clothes and keep them mended. I want a wife who is a good nurturant attendant to my children, who arranges for their schooling, makes sure that they have an adequate social life with their peers, takes them to the park, the zoo, etc. I want a wife who takes care of the children when they are sick, a wife who arranges to be around when the children need special care, because, of course, I cannot miss classes at school. My wife must arrange to lose time at work and not lose the job. It may mean a small cut in my wife's income from time to time, but I guess I can tolerate that. Needless to say, my wife will arrange and pay for the care of the children while my wife is working.

4   I want a wife who will take care of *my* physical needs. I want a wife who will keep my house clean. A wife who will pick up after me. I want a wife who will keep my clothes clean, ironed, mended, replaced when need be, and who will see

to it that my personal things are kept in their proper place so that I can find what I need the minute I need it. I want a wife who cooks the meals, a wife who is a *good* cook. I want a wife who will plan the menus, do the necessary grocery shopping, prepare the meals, serve them pleasantly, and then do the cleaning up while I do my studying. I want a wife who will care for me when I am sick and sympathize with my pain and loss of time from school. I want a wife to go along when our family takes a vacation so that someone can continue to care for me and my children when I need a rest and change of scene.

I want a wife who will not bother me with rambling complaints about a wife's 5 duties. But I want a wife who will listen to me when I feel the need to explain a rather difficult point I have come across in my course of studies. And I want a wife who will type my papers for me when I have written them.

I want a wife who will take care of the details of my social life. When my wife 6 and I are invited out by my friends, I want a wife who will take care of the babysitting arrangements. When I meet people at school that I like and want to entertain, I want a wife who will have the house clean, will prepare a special meal, serve it to me and my friends, and not interrupt when I talk about the things that interest me and my friends. I want a wife who will have arranged that the children are fed and ready for bed before my guests arrive so that the children do not bother us. I want a wife who takes care of the needs of my guests so that they feel comfortable, who makes sure that they have an ashtray, that they are passed the hors d'oeuvres, that they are offered a second helping of the food, that their wine glasses are replenished when necessary, that their coffee is served to them as they like it. And I want a wife who knows that sometimes I need a night out by myself.

I want a wife who is sensitive to my sexual needs, a wife who makes love 7 passionately and eagerly when I feel like it, a wife who makes sure that I am satisfied. And, of course, I want a wife who will not demand sexual attention when I am not in the mood for it. I want a wife who assumes the complete responsibility for birth control, because I do not want more children. I want a wife who will remain sexually faithful to me so that I do not have to clutter up my intellectual life with jealousies. And I want a wife who understands that *my* sexual needs may entail more than strict adherence to monogamy. I must, after all, be able to relate to people as fully as possible.

If, by chance, I find another person more suitable as a wife than the wife I 8 already have, I want the liberty to replace my present wife with another one. Naturally, I will expect a fresh, new life; my wife will take the children and be solely responsible for them so that I am left free.

When I am through with school and have a job, I want my wife to quit working 9 and remain at home so that my wife can more fully and completely take care of a wife's duties.

My God, who *wouldn't* want a wife? 10

▼ TOPICAL CONSIDERATIONS

1. Why *does* Syfers want a wife? What would she like a wife to do for her?
2. Syfers is speaking rather eloquently for women's liberation. Why would today's feminist applaud her article? What opinions is she suggesting about a wife's role that are not explicitly stated? Consider, for example, her comment: "He had one child, who is, of course, with his ex-wife" (paragraph 2). Why "of course"? Find other examples.
3. What is the "husband" in Syfers's essay like? Do you like him? What do you think of his expectations and demands? Do you know anyone who expects what he does from his wife or girlfriend?
4. Does the wife that Syfers describes have an identity of her own? Does she lack identity? Where in the essay do you see evidence for your answer?
5. Would you say that Syfers's picture of the wife's role is exaggerated and distorted? Is it a fair and accurate representation of reality? Point out specific details to prove your point.
6. How is Raspberry's "executive" homemaker similar to or different from the wife Syfer would like to have? Is either of the wives they describe like anyone you know?

▼ RHETORICAL CONSIDERATIONS

1. What is Syfers's thesis? Where is it stated in the essay? Is it explicitly stated? Explain.
2. Discuss the irony in Syfers's statement: "I want a wife." What other evidence of irony do you find in the essay?
3. Compare and contrast Syfers's point of view with Thurber's in "Courtship Through the Ages" and Raspberry's in "Homemaking."
4. How would you characterize the tone of this essay? Is it friendly and persuasive? Exasperated and critical? Absurd and humorous? Serious and thoughtful? Compare the tone of this essay with others in this section. Cite specific passages to substantiate your answer.
5. Note how many times (after paragraph 2) Syfers begins a sentence with "I want." How does this affect the essay? Does Syfers have a reason for doing this, or is this a weakness in the essay? Explain.

▼ WRITING ASSIGNMENTS

1. Write an essay entitled "I Want a Husband." Imitate Syfers's tone. What are some of the expectations women have about the role a husband should play that are as unreasonable and thoughtless as the expectations of the husband Syfers portrays?

2. In an essay, compare and contrast Raspberry's "executive" homemaker with the wife Syfers would like to have.

3. Suppose that you have just read Syfers's recently published essay, "I Want a Wife," in *Ms.* magazine. Write a letter to the editor in which you express your opinion of the essay.

▼ THE ANDROGYNOUS MALE

Noel Perrin

Consider the traditional all-American, all-male, he-man stereotype: a guy who is attracted to physical power, dominance, and football. A man who can fix his car and who wouldn't be caught dead kissing a cat. But what about the rest of us—who are, say, only 50 to 75 percent red-blooded? Are we a limited, barely male minority? No, just the opposite, says Noel Perrin. In fact, there is a large class of androgynous men and women who are a lot freer than macho-men and feminismo-women. Noel Perrin teaches American literature at Dartmouth College and raises beef cattle in Vermont. His books include *Vermont in All Weathers* (1973), *First Person Rural* (1978), and *Second Person Rural* (1980). This essay first appeared in the "On Men" column in the *New York Times Magazine* in February 1984.

The summer I was 16, I took a train from New York to Steamboat Springs, Colo.,   1
where I was going to be assistant horse wrangler at a camp. The trip took three days, and since I was much too shy to talk to strangers, I had quite a lot of time for reading. I read all of "Gone With the Wind." I read all the interesting articles in a couple of magazines I had, and then I went back and read all the dull stuff. I also took all the quizzes, a thing of which magazines were even fuller then than now.

The one that held my undivided attention was called "How Masculine/Feminine   2
Are You?" It consisted of a large number of inkblots. The reader was supposed to decide which of four objects each blot most resembled. The choices might be a cloud, a steam engine, a caterpillar and a sofa.

When I finished the test, I was shocked to find that I was barely masculine at   3
all. On a scale of 1 to 10, I was about 1.2. Me, the horse wrangler? (And not just wrangler, either. That summer, I had to skin a couple of horses that died—the camp owner wanted the hides.)

The results of that test were so terrifying to me that for the first time in my life   4
I did a piece of original analysis. Having unlimited time on the train, I looked at the "masculine" answers over and over, trying to find what it was that distinguished real men from people like me—and eventually I discovered two very simple patterns. It was "masculine" to think the blots looked like man-made objects, and "feminine" to think they looked like natural objects. It was masculine to think they looked like things capable of causing harm, and feminine to think of innocent things.

Even at 16, I had the sense to see that the compilers of the test were   5
using rather limited criteria—maleness and femaleness are both more complicated

137

than *that*—and I breathed a huge sigh of relief. I wasn't necessarily a wimp, after all.

That the test did reveal something other than the superficiality of its makers I 6 realized only many years later. What it revealed was that there is a large class of men and women both, to which I belong, who are essentially androgynous. That doesn't mean we're gay, or low in the appropriate hormones, or uncomfortable performing the jobs traditionally assigned our sexes. (A few years after that summer, I was leading troops in combat and, unfashionable as it now is to admit this, having a very good time. War is exciting. What a pity the 20th century went and spoiled it with high-tech weapons.)

What it does mean to be spiritually androgynous is a kind of freedom. Men 7 who are all-male, or he-man, or 100 percent red-blooded Americans, have a little biological set that causes them to be attracted to physical power, and probably also to dominance. Maybe even to watching football. I don't say this to criticize them. Completely masculine men are quite often wonderful people: good husbands, good (though sometimes overwhelming) fathers, good members of society. Furthermore, they are often so unself-consciously at ease in the world that other men seek to imitate them. They just aren't as free as us androgynes. They pretty nearly have to be what they are; we have a range of choices open.

The sad part is that many of us never discover that. Men who are not 100 8 percent red-blooded Americans—say, those who are only 75 percent red-blooded— often fail to notice their freedom. They are too busy trying to copy the he-men ever to realize that men, like women, come in a wide variety of acceptable types. Why this frantic imitation? My answer is mere speculation, but not casual. I have speculated on this for a long time.

Partly they're just envious of the he-man's unconscious ease. Mostly they're 9 terrified of finding that there may be something wrong with them deep down, some weakness at the heart. To avoid discovering that, they spend their lives acting out the role that the he-man naturally lives. Sad.

One thing that men owe to the women's movement is that this kind of failure is 10 less common than it used to be. In releasing themselves from the single ideal of the dependent woman, women have more or less incidentally released a lot of men from the single ideal of the dominant male. The one mistake the feminists have made, I think, is in supposing that *all* men need this release, or that the world would be a better place if all men achieved it. It wouldn't. It would just be duller.

So far I have been pretty vague about just what the freedom of the androgynous 11 man is. Obviously it varies with the case. In the case I know best, my own, I can be quite specific. It has freed me most as a parent. I am, among other things, a fairly good natural mother. I like the nurturing role. It makes me feel good to see a child eat—and it turns me to mush to see a 4-year-old holding a glass with both small hands, in order to drink. I even enjoyed sewing patches on the knees of my daughter Amy's Dr. Dentons when she was at the crawling stage. All that pleasure I would have lost if I had made myself stick to the notion of the paternal role that I started with.

Or take a smaller and rather ridiculous example. I feel free to kiss cats. Until 12 recently it never occurred to me that I would want to, though my daughters have been doing it all their lives. But my elder daughter is now 22, and in London. Of course, I get to look after her cat while she is gone. He's a big, handsome farm cat named Petrushka, very unsentimental, though used from kittenhood to being kissed on the top of the head by Elizabeth. I've gotten very fond of him (he's the adventurous kind of cat who likes to climb hills with you), and one night I simply felt like kissing him on the top of the head, and did. Why did no one tell me sooner how silky cat fur is?

Then there's my relation to cars. I am completely unembarrassed by my inability to diagnose even minor problems in whatever object I happen to be driving, and don't have to make some insider's remark to mechanics to try to establish that I, too, am a "Man With His Machine." 13

The same ease extends to household maintenance. I do it, of course. Service people are expensive. But for the last decade my house has functioned better than it used to because I've had the aid of a volume called "Home Repairs Any Woman Can Do," which is pitched just right for people at my technical level. As a youth, I'd as soon have touched such a book as I would have become a transvestite. Even though common sense says there is really nothing sexual whatsoever about fixing sinks. 14

Or take public emotion. All my life I have easily been moved by certain kinds of voices. The actress Siobhan McKenna's, to take a notable case. Give her an emotional scene in a play, and within 10 words my eyes are full of tears. In boyhood, my great dread was that someone might notice. I struggled manfully, you might say, to suppress this weakness. Now, of course, I don't see it as a weakness at all, but as a kind of fulfillment. I even suspect that the true he-men feel the same way, or one kind of them does, at least, and it's only the poor imitators who have to struggle to repress themselves. 15

Let me come back to the inkblots, with their assumption that masculine equates with machinery and science, and feminine with art and nature. I have no idea whether the right pronoun for God is He, She or It. But this I'm pretty sure of. If God could somehow be induced to take that test, God would not come out macho, and not feminismo, either, but right in the middle. Fellow androgynes, it's a nice thought. 16

▼ TOPICAL CONSIDERATIONS

1. What were the test-makers' criteria for determining "masculine/feminine"? Why was Perrin critical of the criteria?
2. What does Perrin mean when, in paragraph 7, he says that "to be spiritually androgynous is a kind of freedom"?
3. How has being androgynous freed Perrin as a family man?
4. How has the women's movement helped the "androgynes' movement"?
5. Perrin talks a bit about the androgynous man. By extension, how would you describe an androgynous woman?
6. Do you consider yourself an androgynous man or woman? Do you feel a

kind of liberation from restrictive biological or spiritual roles as Perrin does? Do you ever feel self-conscious because you act in ways that are contrary to the way men or women are supposed to act?

▼ RHETORICAL CONSIDERATIONS

1. Why do you suppose Perrin chose to begin his essay with a personal anecdote about taking a magazine's masculine/feminine test when he was a boy?
2. Where does Perrin write his thesis statement?
3. How convincing are Perrin's examples of his androgynous freedom?
4. Consider the final paragraph. How does it unify the essay? How effective is the speculation about the results of God taking the masculine/feminine test? Explain the impact of the final sentence.

▼ WRITING ASSIGNMENTS

1. Do you consider yourself an androgynous man or woman? Write a paper in which you examine your own degrees of androgyny as Perrin does. While growing up, did you feel any pressure to conform to traditional sexual roles? Did you ever feel that something was wrong with you? Did you feel the kind of spiritual freedom Perrin describes?
2. Perrin says that he is not critical of "100 percent red-blooded" American he-men; he also says the world would be a duller place without them. Expanding upon the latter, write an essay in which you argue how we need our "red-blooded all-American" he-men.
3. Perrin writes about the androgynous man. Write a paper in which you describe the androgynous woman. You might describe yourself or a woman you know. Is your androgynous woman "liberated" from the demands of traditional sexual roles?

FADS AND FANCIES

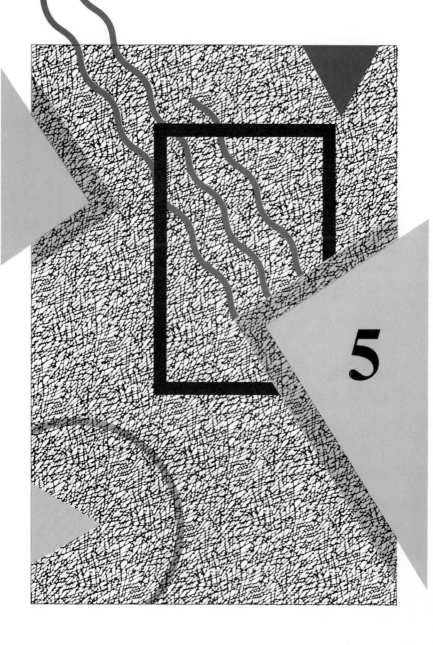

5

▼ SUCCESS

Calvin Trillin

It has been said that ours is a culture that celebrates the rich and puts a premium on what you own, not what you are. What follows is a brief parable of the American Dream, of having it all—fortune and fame—and of the price paid. Calvin Trillin's "Uncivil Liberties" column has been appearing in newspapers across the country since 1978. Collections of his columns have been published as *Uncivil Liberties* (1982) and *With All Disrespect* (1986). Called "a classic American humorist," Trillin writes regularly for *The New Yorker.* This essay was taken from his latest collection *If You Can't Say Something Nice* (1987).

A young man of humble origins came to New York from the Midwest to seek his   1
fortune. He dreamed, in the American way, of becoming a millionaire. He tried his luck on Wall Street. He was diligent and shrewd and, when he had to be, devious. He put together the National Worldwide Universal deal and he did some things with an electronics acquisition that wouldn't bear explaining. He succeeded even beyond his dream: he made twelve million dollars.

At first the young man assumed that everything was working out splendidly.   2
"Isn't it grand?" he said to his wife, once it was apparent that he had made twelve million dollars.

"No, it isn't," his wife said. "You're a nobody."   3

"But that's impossible," the young man said. "I'm a rich person. We live   4
in an era that celebrates rich people. Rich people are shown in the newspapers in the company of movie stars and famous novelists and distinguished dress designers. The names of the richest corporate raiders are known to every schoolboy. There are rich real estate sharks whose faces appear on the covers of glossy magazines."

"Yours won't," his wife said. "You're a nobody."   5

"But I have twelve million dollars," the young man said.   6

"So do a lot of people," his wife said. "They're nobodies, too."   7

"I could buy our way onto the committees of important charity balls," the   8
young man said. "Then we'd be mentioned in the columns."

"Don't kid yourself," his wife said. "The important committees are already   9
filled up with people who are really rich. People like us would end up working on something like a dinner-dance to benefit the American Psoriasis Foundation."

"But I own a co-op apartment on Fifth Avenue that's worth two million   10
dollars," the young man said.

"Two-million-dollar co-ops are a dime a dozen," his wife said. "So to speak."   11

"I have a stretch limousine," the young man said. "It's twenty-one and a half 12
feet long."

"Nobody famous has ever ridden in it," his wife said. "Henry Kissinger and 13
Calvin Klein have never heard of you. You're a nobody."

The young man was silent for a while. "Are you disappointed in me?" he 14
finally said to his wife.

"Of course I'm disappointed in you," she said. "When you asked me to marry 15
you, you said you would surely amount to something. How was I to know that
you'd turn out to be a nobody?"

For a moment the young man looked defeated. Then he squared his shoulders 16
and cleared his throat. "I'll make them pay attention," he said. "I'll buy a professional football team and argue a lot with the coach in public. Celebrities will join
me to watch big games from the owner's box."

"You can't buy a professional football team for twelve million dollars," his wife 17
said. "Professional football teams cost big bucks."

"Then I'll buy a magazine and appoint myself chief columnist," the young 18
man said. "A tiny but exceedingly flattering picture of me will run next to my
column every week. The owners of professional football teams will invite me to
watch big games from the owner's box."

"You might be able to buy one of those weekly-shopper throwaways for twelve 19
million dollars, but not a real magazine," his wife said. "You can't buy a real
magazine for chicken feed."

"Is that what you call what we have?" the young man asked. "Is twelve million 20
dollars chicken feed?"

"It's not big bucks," his wife said. "What can I tell you?" 21

"But that's not fair," the young man said. "I'm a young man of humble origins 22
who made twelve million dollars. I succeeded even beyond my dream."

"Some of those things you did with the electronics acquisition probably 23
weren't fair either," his wife said. "Fair isn't being measured these days. What they
measure is money."

"Then I'll get more money," the young man said. "I'm going to go back to Wall 24
Street and make fifty million dollars."

But before the young man could make fifty million dollars a man from the 25
Securities and Exchange Commission came and arrested him for having committed insider-trading violations in the electronics acquisition.

The young man was taken away from his office in handcuffs. A picture on the 26
front page of the afternoon paper showed him leaving his arraignment, trying to
hide his face behind an $850 Italian overcoat. A long article in the morning paper
used him as an example of a new breed of Wall Street traders who were the victims
of their own greed, probably because of their humble origins. His friends and
associates avoided him.

Only his wife stuck by him. She tried to see the bright side. "For someone with 27
only twelve million dollars," she said to the young man, "you're getting to be
pretty well known."

▼ TOPICAL CONSIDERATIONS

1. What does the expression "American Dream" mean to you? How is Calvin Trillin satirizing it here?
2. Can you think of any current events Trillin is basing his satire on? Can you think of any particular individual(s) Trillin might have modeled the young man after?
3. How do the characters of the husband and wife differ with regards to "success"? Consider how only the wife sticks by the young man at the end.
4. What would you say "success" means to you? What kind of life or lifestyle would be a success to you?

▼ RHETORICAL CONSIDERATIONS

1. This piece reads more like a short story than an essay. What particular elements define it as fiction rather than expository prose?
2. One of the features of satire is exaggeration. What exaggerations of reality can you find here? How well do these exaggerations work to make their point? Another feature of satirical humor is irony. What examples of irony can you find?
3. Evaluate the wife's last words. How are they consistent with the wife's character? How do they function to complete the story? Did they strike you as funny?

▼ WRITING ASSIGNMENTS

1. By its very nature, satire distorts something for the sake of making fun of it. Yet, beneath the distortions and humor is a moral message. What would you say is Trillin's moral message?
2. Write an essay in which you explore what the meaning of "success" is to you. Is fame and fortune part of that definition? How does your definition differ from that of the people represented in this little story?
3. Write a profile of someone you know who is successful. Is material wealth a major feature of that person's success? What about fame? A sense of well-being? Pride? A clear conscience?
4. Write an essay in which you attempt to define the "American Dream" as it exists in today's culture. What was the original meaning of the concept? How, if at all, has it changed over the years?
5. Try to write a little satirical parable of your own. You might consider doing a follow up of Trillin's piece, perhaps a story about what happens when the young man is released from prison. You might want to satirize some other contemporary issues using your own characters.

▼ FINDING THE FURY

Bill Boggs

> The essay below is the story of an obsession that lasted for thirty years. It is told by a man who as a boy fell in love with a car that he could neither afford nor drive—a car that over the decades haunted him like a restless ghost. But more than that, it is a moving statement about growing up and looking back. Bill Boggs is a television personality and producer. This essay first appeared in the *New York Times Magazine* in 1987.

There were 10 minutes to kill before I had to leave for the Police Athletic League   1
baseball game. I sat on the side of my bed to look through Popular Mechanics magazine. When I reached the article on the new 1956 Plymouth Fury, my heart started to pound. It would be years before I defined the experience as a *coup de foudre;* later on, I would meet a woman and fall in love at first sight. But that day in Philadelphia I was 14 years old, and the object of my passion was a car.

I'd never seen a car with something that looked like a lightning bolt shooting   2
along its side. Actually, the eggshell-white Fury sported a unique anodized gold aluminum trim on each side, giving the design a thrilling sense of motion. It was the most beautiful car I'd ever seen.

It cost $2,800. I had a measly $235 saved up from neighborhood jobs and   3
Christmas gifts. Buying the Fury was as out of reach as playing with the Phillies. Besides, I didn't even have a driver's license. But someday, I vowed, I would get a '56 Fury.

I pedaled my bicycle to Plymouth showrooms all over Philadelphia. My Uncle   4
John drove me to far-away dealerships in the suburbs. But we never found a Fury. It was a special production model, and only 4,485 were manufactured. Rich people with $2,800 had ordered them all.

A year would pass before I even saw one. My father and I were out   5
driving, and coming toward us was a '56 Fury. Could the Lone Ranger have been more thrilled on seeing the great horse Silver for the first time? "That's it, Dad!" I yelled. My father glanced at the gleaming car and let out a loud "Hmmm" of admiration. In the 30 years since, I have seen a '56 Fury only three other times.

During my freshman year at the University of Pennsylvania, I bought a used   6
1956 Plymouth Belvedere convertible. It was as close as I could get to the Fury. Two more owner's cards passed through my wallet before I bought the car I still drive today, a 1968 Mercury Parklane convertible. The Merc has taken me 148,000 miles over nearly 20 years. It has driven Hubert Humphrey to the airport, whisked

me away on two honeymoons, raced my dying dog to the vet and endured years of living outside that people said would kill it.

But I could never find a '56 Fury. For 15 years, I have checked the antique and 7 classic car ads. In the early 1980's, I placed ads myself. No callers. I've told everyone from gas station attendants to strangers on airplanes what I was looking for. Once, interviewing the race car driver Richard Petty on television, I blurted out that I craved a '56 Fury. Surely that will do it, I thought. During my years as a television host, viewers have sent me unsolicited items that ranged from handknitted cat costumes to a 100-year-old corncob stripper, but this time there was no response.

Then, finally, in Hemmings Motor News, I saw the words: "Plymouth: 1956 8 Fury, superb condition, all original and complete."

I was working in Los Angeles, but I made an immediate call to the advertiser 9 in Seattle. A voice on the telephone assured me that the car had been restored to perfect condition.

Would a small deposit hold it for two weeks, when I'd have a break in my 10 schedule and could go see it?

No. A buyer from Kansas was seriously interested. 11

I hung up. If I don't get this Fury, I rationalized, I'll find another one some 12 other time.

Then I laughed out loud at myself. 13

How easy it has been for me to postpone important decisions. I've delayed 14 making commitments to good relationships until I ruined them and waited far too long to get out of bad ones. I've put off having a child for years, always thinking I wasn't ready, only to discover that fatherhood is my greatest source of joy. I've postponed buying a home and taking vacations as if there were some guarantee there will always be enough time, as if I expected to live two lives instead of one.

I canceled everything I had scheduled for the next 48 hours and flew to 15 Seattle. When the garage door swung open and I saw the Fury, I let out a long "Hmmmm" and remembered that day with my father.

"I like to take old beat-up things and make them beautiful again," said 16 Bob Dally, the owner, who had been working on the car for seven years. He had succeeded. Under a full moon in the clear Seattle sky, the Fury seemed to glow in the dark. "Let's go for a ride," he said. I slid the car into first gear, slowly released the clutch and depressed the accelerator. We roared into the darkness.

"It's still fast," I thought. When we pulled into a gas station, we were quickly 17 surrounded by teen-agers looking at us as if we'd just driven off the set of "Back to the Future."

Less than an hour later, we were back at Bob's house. I had piloted the Fury 18 through the quiet streets, and it had performed perfectly. But when I turned off the engine, I had a feeling I would never have anticipated. My fantasy seemed fulfilled; I didn't have to buy the car. I was like a man who pursues a woman, finally makes love to her and then doesn't want to take the responsibility of seeing her again. Finding the car had been wonderful, but I was afraid to commit to ownership. Bob Dally seemed surprised when I told him I had to do some thinking and wanted to walk around the block.

Could I handle the responsibility of realizing my childhood fantasy? Adult experience told me that owning this car was totally impractical. To start with, where would I put it? I travel back and forth between New York and Los Angeles, and I have no garage in either place.   19

I have no mechanical ability and would have to depend on others to track down out-of-stock parts and fix the car. The Fury is perfect now. Would each inevitable scratch drive me into a rage? Would a stolen hubcap turn me into a bounty hunter?   20

It all boiled down to asking myself this: did I really need to own the Fury to enjoy it any more than I already had? A younger voice inside me said, "Yes."   21

"But," I argued with myself, "is this really the best time to get it? Maybe I should wait."   22

The 14-year-old voice said, "Today is the someday."   23

I bought the Fury. I drove it from Seattle down the Pacific Coast Highway to Los Angeles. I took my time along Big Sur. I'd planned all my life to make that trip.   24

▼ TOPICAL CONSIDERATIONS

1. How did Boggs first discover the Fury? What was so special about this particular model?
2. Why do you suppose Boggs still drives his twenty-year-old Mercury Parklane? What does this say about the man?
3. What kind of measures did the author go through trying to locate a Fury? How did he actually find the one he bought?
4. When Boggs learns that a buyer from Kansas was "seriously interested" in the Fury, he rationalizes that since he can't find the time to fly off to Seattle, he'd have to "find another one some other time." What realization about himself finally convinces him to drop everything and act?
5. How does Boggs almost talk himself out of buying the car? What practical reasons does he come up with?
6. What ultimately moves Bill Boggs to buy his Fury?

▼ RHETORICAL CONSIDERATIONS

1. Comment on the appropriateness of the title of Boggs' essay. What different meanings might it have?
2. When Boggs at last lays eyes on the dream Fury, he lets out a long "Hmmmm" the way his father did years ago. Why would the author include this little detail? How is it appropriate? What effect does it create?
3. When he drives the Fury into a gas station, Boggs says that the car was

"quickly surrounded by teenagers looking at us as if we'd just driven off the set of *Back to the Future.*" Discuss the appropriateness of this little detail.

4. Toward the end of the essay Boggs resorts to quoting the voices in his head. Why does he do this instead of just summarizing his thoughts? What do the direct quotations add to the overall effect of the essay?

5. What effect did the essay's last line have on you?

6. How well did Boggs maintain the element of suspense in this essay? In other words, did he have you guessing right to the end as to whether or not he'd actually buy his dream car?

▼ WRITING ASSIGNMENTS

1. Write Bill Boggs a letter congratulating him on buying the Fury and in it, specify your reasons.

2. The 1956 Plymouth Fury was the object of young Bill Boggs' passion. Describe an object of your passion—some material thing that once took hold of you, something that you someday would like to own, or now do own. Describe the object and your obsession. Describe the fulfillment you've derived or hope to derive from it.

▼ THE JEANING OF AMERICA—AND THE WORLD

Carin C. Quinn

Perhaps no article of clothing is more synonymous with America than blue jeans. And no blue jean label is more recognized than Levi-Strauss. Levi's have spanned all ages, all social classes, and all continents—and a hundred and forty years. In this article, Carin C. Quinn narrates the development of this all-American symbol now gone worldwide. She also gives some of the reasons Levi's have become so popular. Quinn's essay first appeared in *American Heritage* in 1984.

This is the story of a sturdy American symbol which has now spread throughout 1 most of the world. The symbol is not the dollar. It is not even Coca-Cola. It is a simple pair of pants called blue jeans, and what the pants symbolize is what Alexis de Tocqueville called "a manly and legitimate passion for equality. . . . " Blue jeans are favored equally by bureaucrats and cowboys; bankers and deadbeats; fashion designers and beer drinkers. They draw no distinctions and recognize no classes; they are merely American. Yet they are sought after almost everywhere in the world—including Russia, where authorities recently broke up a teen-aged gang that was selling them on the black market for two hundred dollars a pair. They have been around for a long time, and it seems likely that they will outlive even the necktie.

This ubiquitous American symbol was the invention of a Bavarian-born Jew. 2 His name was Levi Strauss.

He was born in Bad Ocheim, Germany, in 1829, and during the European 3 political turmoil of 1848 decided to take his chances in New York, to which his two brothers already had emigrated. Upon arrival, Levi soon found that his two brothers had exaggerated their tales of an easy life in the land of the main chance. They were landowners, they had told him; instead, he found them pushing needles, thread, pots, pans, ribbons, yarn, scissors, and buttons to housewives. For two years he was a lowly peddler, hauling some 180 pounds of sundries door-to-door to eke out a marginal living. When a married sister in San Francisco offered to pay his way West in 1850, he jumped at the opportunity, taking with him bolts of canvas he hoped to sell for tenting.

It was the wrong kind of canvas for that purpose, but while talking with a 4 miner down from the mother lode, he learned that pants—sturdy pants that would stand up to the rigors of the digging—were almost impossible to find. Opportunity beckoned. On the spot, Strauss measured the man's girth and inseam with a piece of string and, for six dollars in gold dust, had [the canvas] tailored into a pair of stiff but rugged pants. The miner was delighted with the result, word got around about "those pants of Levi's," and Strauss was in business. The company has been in business ever since.

When Strauss ran out of canvas, he wrote his two brothers to send more. He received instead a tough, brown cotton cloth made in Nîmes, France—called *serge de Nîmes* and swiftly shortened to "denim" (the word "jeans" derives from *Gênes,* the French word for Genoa, where a similar cloth was produced). Almost from the first, Strauss had his cloth dyed the distinctive indigo that gave blue jeans their name, but it was not until the 1870s that he added the copper rivets which have long since become a company trademark. The rivets were the idea of a Virginia City, Nevada, tailor, Jacob W. Davis, who added them to pacify a mean-tempered miner called Alkali Ike. Alkali, the story goes, complained that the pockets of his jeans always tore when he stuffed them with ore samples and demanded that Davis do something about it. As a kind of joke, Davis took the pants to a blacksmith and had the pockets riveted; once again, the idea worked so well that word got around; in 1873 Strauss appropriated and patented the gimmick—and hired Davis as a regional manager.

By this time, Strauss had taken both his brothers and two brothers-in-law into the company and was ready for his third San Francisco store. Over the ensuing years the company prospered locally, and by the time of his death in 1902, Strauss had become a man of prominence in California. For three decades thereafter the business remained profitable though small, with sales largely confined to the working people of the West—cowboys, lumberjacks, railroad workers, and the like. Levi's jeans were first introduced to the East, apparently, during the dude-ranch craze of the 1930s, when vacationing Easterners returned and spread the word about the wonderful pants with rivets. Another boost came in World War II, when blue jeans were declared an essential commodity and were sold only to people engaged in defense work. From a company with fifteen salespeople, two plants, and almost no business east of the Mississippi in 1946, the organization grew in thirty years to include a sales force of more than twenty-two thousand, with fifty plants and offices in thirty-five countries. Each year, more than 250,000,000 items of Levi's clothing are sold—including more than 83,000,000 pairs of riveted blue jeans. They have become, through marketing, word of mouth, and demonstrable reliability, the common pants of America. They can be purchased pre-washed, pre-faded, and pre-shrunk for the suitably proletarian look. They adapt themselves to any sort of idiosyncratic use; women slit them at the inseams and convert them into long skirts, men chop them off above the knees and turn them into something to be worn while challenging the surf. Decorations and ornamentations abound.

The pants have become a tradition, and along the way have acquired a history of their own—so much so that the company has opened a museum in San Francisco. There was, for example, the turn-of-the-century trainman who replaced a faulty coupling with a pair of jeans; the Wyoming man who used his jeans as a towrope to haul his car out of a ditch; the Californian who found several pairs in an abandoned mine, wore them, then discovered they were sixty-three years old and still as good as new and turned them over to the Smithsonian as a tribute to their toughness. And then there is the particularly terrifying story of the careless construction worker who dangled fifty-two stories above the street until rescued, his sole support the Levi's belt loop through which his rope was hooked.

▼ TOPICAL CONSIDERATIONS

1. Why are jeans so popular today? Are they popular now for the same reasons they were originally?
2. How does Strauss's success story reflect the popular myth that America is the land of opportunity?
3. Was Strauss's success purely the result of luck? Could it have happened to anyone, or was he an unusually astute businessman with an eye for what sells? Cite specific incidents in his story to prove your answer.
4. Quinn points out that the sale of jeans became a booming business through "marketing, word of mouth, and demonstrable reliability" (paragraph 6). Is this true of today's products? Which of these three factors do you think is most effective in securing the success of a product today? Why?
5. Quinn refers to jeans as a "sturdy American symbol." How do jeans represent America and Americans? Can you name other American symbols that Quinn does not mention?

▼ RHETORICAL CONSIDERATIONS

1. Does this essay have a beginning, a middle, and an end? How would you divide it? What rhetorical pattern does Quinn use to develop each section?
2. Rewrite Quinn's first paragraph so that no specific details, quotations, or illustrations are used. Substitute a general word or phrase when necessary to preserve the meaning. Read your version aloud. Which version is more interesting?
3. What is Quinn's attitude toward jeans? Cite specific adjectives, quotations, and illustrations that reveal how she feels.
4. How does Quinn's ending tie the essay together?

▼ WRITING ASSIGNMENTS

1. Do you know of anyone (perhaps yourself) who has been given an opportunity to accomplish something worthwhile and has been successful? Write an essay about it.
2. Identify an American symbol that Quinn doesn't mention. Write about it. Consider the following questions: Why is it a symbol? What does it say

about America and Americans? Use a variety of rhetorical strategies to develop your essay: definition, description, narration, analogy.

3. If you wear jeans, write a paper in which you consider exactly why. Is it tradition? Identity? Comfort? Prestige? Peer pressure? A little of each? If you have a favorite label, try to explain why you prefer it.

▼ THAT LEAN AND HUNGRY LOOK

Suzanne Britt

Not everybody thinks thin—particularly not author Suzanne Britt Jordan. As she says in the following essay, she has made a hobby of observing thin people and has decided that she doesn't like what she sees. It might be said that Ms. Jordan thinks fat. In fact, her essay is a humorous look at the thin world through the eyes of a "chubby." But there is more here than just fat-thin joking. Jordan makes some interesting statements about people, personalities, and stereotypes. This essay first appeared in *Newsweek* and was later expanded into her book *Skinny People Are Dull and Crunchy Like Carrots* (1982).

1   Caesar was right. Thin people need watching. I've been watching them for most of my adult life, and I don't like what I see. When these narrow fellows spring at me, I quiver to my toes. Thin people come in all personalities, most of them menacing. You've got your "together" thin person, your mechanical thin person, your condescending thin person, your tsk-tsk thin person, your efficiency-expert thin person. All of them are dangerous.

2   In the first place, thin people aren't fun. They don't know how to goof off, at least in the best, fat sense of the word. They've always got to be adoing. Give them a coffee break, and they'll jog around the block. Supply them with a quiet evening at home, and they'll fix the screen door and lick S&H green stamps. They say things like "there aren't enough hours in the day." Fat people never say that. Fat people think the day is too damn long already.

3   Thin people make me tired. They've got speedy little metabolisms that cause them to bustle briskly. They're forever rubbing their bony hands together and eyeing new problems to "tackle." I like to surround myself with sluggish, inert, easygoing fat people, the kind who believe that if you clean it up today, it'll just get dirty again tomorrow.

4   Some people say the business about the jolly fat person is a myth, that all of us chubbies are neurotic, sick, sad people. I disagree. Fat people may not be chortling all day long, but they're a hell of a lot *nicer* than the wizened and shriveled. Thin people turn surly, mean, and hard at a young age because they never learn the value of a hot-fudge sundae for easing tension. Thin people don't like gooey soft things because they themselves are neither gooey nor soft. They are crunchy and dull, like carrots. They go straight to the heart of the matter while fat people let things stay all blurry and hazy and vague, the way things actually are. Thin people want to face the truth. Fat people know there is no truth. One of my

thin friends is always staring at complex, unsolvable problems and saying, "The key thing is. . . ." Fat people never say that. They know there isn't any such thing as the key thing about anything.

Thin people believe in logic. Fat people see all sides. The sides fat people see are rounded blobs, usually gray, always nebulous and truly not worth worrying about. But the thin person persists. "If you consume more calories than you burn," says one of my thin friends, "you will gain weight. It's that simple." Fat people always grin when they hear statements like that. They know better. 5

Fat people realize that life is illogical and unfair. They know very well that God is not in his heaven and all is not right with the world. If God was up there, fat people could have two doughnuts and a big orange drink anytime they wanted it. 6

Thin people have a long list of logical things they are always spouting off to me. They hold up one finger at a time as they reel off these things, so I won't lose track. They speak slowly as if to a young child. The list is long and full of holes. It contains tidbits like "get a grip on yourself," "cigarettes kill," "cholesterol clogs," "fit as a fiddle," "ducks in a row," "organize," and "sound fiscal management." Phrases like that. 7

They think these 2,000-point plans lead to happiness. Fat people know happiness is elusive at best and even if they could get the kind thin people talk about, they wouldn't want it. Wisely, fat people see that such programs are too dull, too hard, too off the mark. They are never better than a whole cheesecake. 8

Fat people know all about the mystery of life. They are the ones acquainted with the night, with luck, with fate, with playing it by ear. One thin person I know once suggested that we arrange all the parts of a jigsaw puzzle into groups according to size, shape, and color. He figured this would cut the time needed to complete the puzzle by at least 50 percent. I said I wouldn't do it. One, I like to muddle through. Two, what good would it do to finish early? Three, the jigsaw puzzle isn't the important thing. The important thing is the fun of four people (one thin person included) sitting around a card table, working a jigsaw puzzle. My thin friend had no use for my list. Instead of joining us, he went outside and mulched the boxwoods. The three remaining fat people finished the puzzle and made chocolate, double-fudged brownies to celebrate. 9

The main problem with thin people is they oppress. Their good intentions, bony torsos, tight ships, neat corners, cerebral machinations, and pat solutions loom like dark clouds over the loose, comfortable, spreadout, soft world of the fat. Long after fat people have removed their coats and shoes and put their feet up on the coffee table, thin people are still sitting on the edge of the sofa, looking neat as a pin, discussing rutabagas. Fat people are heavily into fits of laughter, slapping their thighs and whooping it up, while thin people are still politely waiting for the punch line. 10

Thin people are downers. They like math and morality and reasoned evaluation of the limitations of human beings. They have their skinny little acts together. They expound, prognose, probe, and prick. 11

Fat people are convivial. They will like you even if you're irregular and have acne. They will come up with a good reason why you never wrote the great 12

American novel. They will cry in your beer with you. They will put your name in the pot. They will let you off the hook. Fat people will gab, giggle, guffaw, gallumph, gyrate, and gossip. They are generous, giving, and gallant. They are gluttonous and goodly and great. What you want when you're down is soft and jiggly, not muscled and stable. Fat people know this. Fat people have plenty of room. Fat people will take you in.

▼ TOPICAL CONSIDERATIONS

1. Why do you think Jordan wrote this essay—to be entertaining? To be serious and persuasive? A little of both? Explain your answer.
2. In paragraph 6, Jordan remarks: "They know very well that God is not in his heaven and all is not right with the world." What is the literary allusion in this line? What other allusions do you see? Note, for example, the title and the opening line.
3. Do you agree with Jordan's generalities about fat and thin people? On what points do you agree? Disagree?
4. Does Jordan's characterization of thin people remind you of anyone you know? Describe specific incidents to show how such an individual fits Jordan's description.
5. Identify some of the comments that Jordan makes in defense of fat people. How might a thin person reverse these so that they are an attack instead of a defense of fatness? Consider, for example: "Fat people think the day is too damn long already" (paragraph 2) or "If God was up there, fat people could have two doughnuts and a big orange drink anytime they wanted it" (paragraph 6).

▼ RHETORICAL CONSIDERATIONS

1. How does Jordan order her comparison and contrast of thin people and fat people? Analyze her essay paragraph by paragraph to explain your answer.
2. Point out some of the adjectives Jordan uses to show the contrast between thin people and fat people.
3. What connotations does the word *rutabagas* have that make it a good word choice in paragraph 10? What does Jordan seek to achieve by using this word? Cite other apt word choices.
4. Jordan uses alliteration extensively in her concluding paragraph. Why? How does it contribute to the total effect she seeks to achieve?
5. Discuss Jordan's use of clichés. How do they contribute to the humor in her essay?
6. Jordan often opens a paragraph with a short declarative sentence. Why is this effective? How does it compare with the length of other sentences in any given paragraph?

▼ WRITING ASSIGNMENTS

1. Adopt the point of view of one of Jordan's thin people. Write a rebuttal essay in which you turn Jordan's remarks into a criticism of fat people. Think of an appropriate title similar to Jordan's.
2. Assume that you have just read Jordan's essay in a magazine. Write a letter to the editor expressing your response to it. You may either defend or attack the essay.

▼ FAREWELL TO FITNESS

Mike Royko

Mike Royko is just one of those millions of us who got caught up in "thinking thin." Like Suzanne Britt Jordan, he rejected it; but it wasn't skinny people who turned him off. It was all the dieting, the workouts, and the sacrifices. In this very witty and funny piece, Royko takes some swipes at America's obsession with getting in shape. He is a well-known columnist for the *Chicago Tribune* and the author of *Boss* (1971), a biography of Chicago's late mayor, Richard Daley. The latest collection of Royko's columns is *Like I Was Sayin'...* (1984). This piece first appeared in his column in 1980.

At least once a week, the office jock will stop me in the hall, bounce on the balls of his feet, plant his hands on his hips, flex his pectoral muscles and say: "How about it? I'll reserve a racquetball court. You can start working off some of that...." And he'll jab a finger deep into my midsection. 1

It's been going on for months, but I've always had an excuse: "Next week, I've got a cold." "Next week, my back is sore." "Next week, I've got a pulled hamstring." "Next week, after the holidays." 2

But this is it. No more excuses. I made one New Year's resolution, which is that I will tell him the truth. And the truth is that I don't want to play racquetball or handball or tennis, or jog, or pump Nautilus machines, or do push-ups or sit-ups or isometrics, or ride a stationary bicycle, or pull on a rowing machine, or hit a softball, or run up a flight of steps, or engage in any other form of exercise more strenuous than rolling out of bed. 3

This may be unpatriotic, and it is surely out of step with our muscle-flexing times, but I am renouncing the physical-fitness craze. 4

Oh, I was part of it. Maybe not as fanatically as some. But about 15 years ago, when I was 32, someone talked me into taking up handball, the most punishing court game there is. 5

From then on it was four or five times a week—up at 6 A.M., on the handball court at 7, run, grunt, sweat, pant until 8:30, then in the office at 9. And I'd go around bouncing on the balls of my feet, flexing my pectoral muscles, poking friends in their soft guts, saying: "How about working some of that off? I'll reserve a court," and being obnoxious. 6

This went on for years. And for what? I'll tell you what it led to: I stopped eating pork shanks, that's what. It was inevitable. When you join the physical-fitness craze, you have to stop eating wonderful things like pork shanks because they are full of cholesterol. And you have to give up eggs benedict, smoked 7

158

liverwurst, Italian sausage, butter-pecan ice cream, Polish sausage, goose-liver pate, Sara Lee cheesecake, Twinkies, potato chips, salami-and-Swiss-cheese sandwiches, double cheeseburgers with fries, Christian Brothers brandy with a Beck's chaser, and everything else that tastes good.

Instead, I ate broiled skinless chicken, broiled whitefish, grapefruit, steamed broccoli, steamed spinach, unbuttered toast, yogurt, eggplant, an apple for dessert and Perrier water to wash it down. Blahhhhh! 8

You do this for years, and what is your reward for panting and sweating around a handball-racquetball court, and eating yogurt and the skinned flesh of a dead chicken? 9

— You can take your pulse and find that it is slow. So what? Am I a clock? 10

— You buy pants with a narrower waistline. Big deal. The pants don't cost less than the ones with a big waistline. 11

— You get to admire yourself in the bathroom mirror for about 10 seconds a day after taking a shower. It takes five seconds to look at your flat stomach from the front, and five more seconds to look at your flat stomach from the side. If you're a real creep of a narcissist, you can add another 10 seconds for looking at your small behind with a mirror. 12

That's it. 13

Wait, I forgot something. You will live longer. I know that because my doctor told me so every time I took a physical. My fitness-conscious doctor was very slender—especially the last time I saw him, which was at his wake. 14

But I still believe him. Running around a handball court or jogging five miles a day, eating yogurt and guzzling Perrier will make you live longer. 15

So you live longer. Have you been in a typical nursing home lately? Have you walked around the low-rent neighborhoods where the geezers try to survive on Social Security? 16

If you think living longer is rough now, wait until the 1990s, when today's Me Generation potheads and coke sniffers begin taking care of the elderly (today's middle-aged joggers). It'll be: "Just take this little happy pill, gramps, and you'll wake up in heaven." 17

It's not worth giving up pork shanks and Sara Lee cheesecake. 18

Nor is it the way to age gracefully. Look around at all those middle-aged jogging chicken-eaters. Half of them tape hairpieces to their heads. That's what comes from having a flat stomach. You start thinking that you should also have hair. And after that comes a facelift. And that leads to jumping around a disco floor, pinching an airline stewardess and other bizarre behavior. 19

I prefer to age gracefully, the way men did when I was a boy. The only time a man over 40 ran was when the cops caught him burglarizing a warehouse. The idea of exercise was to walk to and from the corner tavern, mostly to. A well-rounded health-food diet included pork shanks, dumplings, Jim Beam and a beer chaser. 20

Anyone who was skinny was suspected of having TB or an ulcer. A fine figure of a man was one who could look down and not see his knees, his feet or anything else in that vicinity. What do you have to look for, anyway? You ought to know if anything is missing. 21

A few years ago I was in Bavaria, and I went to a German beer hall. It was a 22 beautiful sight. Everybody was popping sausages and pork shanks and draining quart-sized steins of thick beer. Every so often they'd thump their magnificent bellies and smile happily at the booming sound that they made.

Compare that to the finish line of a marathon, with all those emaciated 23 runners sprawled on the grass, tongues hanging out, wheezing, moaning, writhing, throwing up.

If that is the way to happiness and a long life, pass me the cheesecake. 24

May you get a hernia, Arnold Schwarzenegger. And here's to you, Orson 25 Welles.

▼ TOPICAL CONSIDERATIONS

1. Why does Royko mention pork shanks so often in his essay? Why is broiled skinless chicken an anathema to him?
2. It seems obvious that Royko would be sure to fail miserably with a strict diet plan. What does he say to suggest this?
3. How do you feel about some of the conclusions Royko reaches about keeping fit? Are you ready to give up your regimen of a daily run and yogurt for lunch? Why or why not?
4. Royko ridicules the office jock who bounces around flexing his muscles. Is there any truth in his observations? Are there other people that Royko makes fun of?
5. How does Royko plan to "age gracefully"? What does he believe is an "ungraceful" way to grow old? Why? What do you think? Give reasons for your answer.

▼ RHETORICAL CONSIDERATIONS

1. Where does Royko state his thesis? What rhetorical strategy does he use to introduce it? Is it attention-getting? Why?
2. Reread paragraph 7. What do you note about the length of the sentences? How does this affect the reading of the paragraph? Find another similar paragraph.
3. How would you characterize the tone of this essay? Cite specific passages that prove your point.
4. Royko achieves humor by exaggerating points of contrast. Find examples of this in the essay.

▼ WRITING ASSIGNMENTS

1. Write an essay about the importance of keeping fit from the point of view of the office jock Royko satirizes in his essay. Imitate Royko's use of satire, this time ridiculing flabby fat people.
2. Americans today seem to be obsessed with the need to keep fit. In an essay, argue for or against the current fitness craze.

▼ THE BACKPACKER

Patrick F. McManus

> In the old days before backpacking became fashionable, you'd hoof your way up a mountain with a plywood-and-canvas pack that was your own weight plus that of the kitchen range. Your sleeping bag was a rolled-up mattress full of "sawdust, horsehair, and No. 6 bird shot." Today, with the sport refined by high technology, the packs come in almost weightless magnesium; the sleeping bags are filled with "the down of unborn goose"; and the tents are made of "waterproof smoke." So writes Patrick F. McManus in this hilarious look at a current craze. For years, McManus has been regaling readers of such magazines as *Field & Stream, Reader's Digest,* and *Sports Illustrated* with his witty exposes of the "pleasures and rewards" of the Great Outdoors. This essay comes from his popular collection *A Fine and Pleasant Misery* (1981).

1 Strange, the things that suddenly become fashionable. Take backpacking for instance.

2 I know people who five years ago had never climbed anything higher than a tall barstool. Now you can scarcely name a mountain within three hundred miles they haven't hoofed up in their Swiss-made waffle-stompers.

3 They used to complain about the price of sirloin steak. Now they complain about the price of beef jerky (which is about three times that of Maine lobster in Idaho).

4 Their backpacking is a refined sport, noted for lightness. The gear consists of such things as silk packs, magnesium frames, dainty camp stoves. Their sleeping bags are filled with the down of unborn goose, their tents are made of waterproof smoke. They carry two little packets from which they can spread out a nine-course meal. One packet contains the food and the other a freeze-dried French chef.

5 Well, it wasn't like that back in the old days, before backpacking became fashionable. These latecomers don't know what real backpacking was like.

6 The rule of thumb for the old backpacking was that the weight of your pack should equal the weight of yourself and the kitchen range combined. Just a casual glance at a full pack sitting on the floor could give you a double hernia and fuse four vertebrae. After carrying the pack all day, you had to remember to tie one leg to a tree before you dropped it. Otherwise, you would float off into space. The pack eliminated the need for any special kind of ground-gripping shoes, because your feet would sink a foot and a half into hard-packed earth, two inches into solid rock. Some of the new breed of backpackers occasionally wonder what caused a

swath of fallen trees on the side of a mountain. That is where one of the old backpackers slipped off a trail with a full pack.

My packboard alone met the minimum weight requirement. It was a canvas and plywood model, surplus from the Second World War. These packboards apparently were designed with the idea that a number of them could be hooked together to make an emergency bridge for Sherman tanks. The first time you picked one up you thought maybe someone had forgotten to remove his tank. 7

My sleeping bag looked like a rolled-up mattress salvaged from a fire in a skid row hotel. Its filling was sawdust, horsehair, and No. 6 bird shot. Some of today's backpackers tell me their sleeping bags are so light they scarcely know they're there. The only time I scarcely knew my sleeping bag was there was when I was in it at 2 A.M. on a cold night. It was freckled from one end to the other with spark holes, a result of my efforts to stay close enough to the fire to keep warm. The only time I was halfway comfortable was when it was ablaze. It was the only sleeping bag I ever heard of which you could climb into in the evening with scarcely a mark on you and wake up in the morning bruised from head to toe. That was because two or three times a night my companions would take it upon themselves to jump up and stomp out my sleeping-bag fires—in their haste neglecting to first evacuate the occupant. Since I was the camp cook, I never knew whether they were attempting to save me from immolation or getting in a few last licks for what they thought might be terminal indigestion. 8

Our provisions were not distinguished by variety. Dehydrated foods were considered effeminate. A man could ruin his reputation for life by getting caught on a pack trip with a dried apple. If you wanted apples, brother, you carried them with the water still in them. No one could afford such delicacies as commercial beef jerky. What you carried was a huge slab of bacon. It was so big that if the butcher had left on the legs, it could have walked behind you on a leash. 9

A typical meal consisted of fried bacon, potatoes and onions fried in bacon grease, a pan of beans heated in bacon grease, bacon grease gravy, some bread fried in bacon grease, and cowboy coffee (made by boiling an old cowboy in bacon grease). After meals, indigestion went through our camp like a sow grizzly with a toothache. During the night coyotes sat in nervous silence on surrounding hills and listened to the mournful wailing from our camp. 10

There were a few bad things, too, about backpacking in the old style, but I loved all of it. I probably would never have thought of quitting if it hadn't been for all those geophysical changes that took place in the Western Hemisphere a few years ago. 11

The first thing I noticed was a distinct hardening of the earth. This occurred wherever I happened to spread out my sleeping bag, so I knew that the condition was widespread. (Interestingly enough, my children, lacking their father's scientific training, were unable to detect the phenomenon.) 12

A short while later it became apparent to me that the nights in the mountains had become much colder than any I could remember in the past. The chill would sink its fangs into my bones in the pre-dawn hours and hang on like a terrier until the sun was high. I thought possibly that the drop in temperature was heralding a new ice age. 13

Well, I could put up with the hard and the cold but then the air started getting   14
thinner. The only way you could get sufficient oxygen to lug a pack the size of an
adolescent pachyderm was by gasping and wheezing. (Some of my wheezes were
sufficient to strip small pine trees bare of their needles.) My trail speed became so
slow it posed a dangerous threat to my person. If we were in fact at the onset of a
new ice age, there was a good chance I might be overtaken and crushed by a
glacier.

The final straw was the discovery that a trail I had traveled easily and often in   15
my youth had undergone a remarkable transformation. In the intervening years
since I had last hiked it, the damn thing had nearly doubled in length. I must admit
that I was puzzled, since I didn't know that trails could stretch or grow. The fact
that it now took me twice as long to hike it, however, simply did not allow for any
other explanation. I asked a couple of older friends about it, and they said that
they had seen the same thing happen. They said probably the earth shifted on its
axis every once in a while and caused trails to stretch. I suggested that maybe that
was also the cause for the ground getting harder, the nights colder, and the air
thinner. They said that sounded like a plausible theory to them. (My wife had
another theory, but it was so wild and farfetched that I won't embarrass her by
mentioning it here.)

Anyway, one day last fall while I was sitting at home fretting about the   16
environment, a couple of friends telephoned and invited me along on a pack trip
they were taking into the Cascades. Both of them are of the new school of
backpacking, and I thought I owed it to them to go along. They could profit
considerably by watching an old trail hand in action.

When I saw the packs R.B. and Charley showed up with I almost had   17
to laugh. Neither pack was large enough to carry much more than a cheese
sandwich. I carried more bicarbonate of soda than they had food. I didn't know
what they planned to sleep in, but it certainly couldn't be in those tidy little tote
bags they had perched on top of their packs. Anyway, I didn't say anything. I just
smiled and got out my winch and they each got a pry pole and before you knew it
we had my pack out of the car and on my shoulders. As we headed up the trail
I knew it was going to be a rough trip. Already a few flakes of snow had fallen on
my eyeballs.

The environment on that trip was even harsher than I had remembered.   18
The trails were steeper, the air thinner, the ground harder, the nights colder.
Even my trail speed was slower. Several porcupines shot past me like I was
standing still.

R.B. and Charley showed obvious signs of relief when I made it into camp that   19
first night.

"You probably thought I wouldn't make it with all the food," I chided them.   20

"No," R.B. said. "It was just that for a moment there we didn't recognize you.   21
We thought we were being attacked by a giant snail."

I explained to them that we old-time backpackers made a practice of traveling   22
the last mile or so on our hands and knees in order to give our feet a rest.

It was disgusting to see them sitting there so relaxed and cheerful after a hard   23 day's hike. They didn't seem to have any notion at all what backpacking was about. I could hardly stand it when they whipped out a little stove and boiled up some dried chunks of leather and sponge for supper. It probably would have hurt their feelings if I had got out the slab of bacon, so I didn't mention it. I just smiled and ate their food—four helpings in fact, just to make my act convincing. I never told them, but the Roast Baron of Beef was not quite rare enough for my taste and they had forgotten the cream sauce for the asparagus tips. And I have certainly tasted better Baked Alaska in my day, too.

Well, they can have their fashionable new-school backpacking if they want it.   24 I'm sticking with the old way. Oh, I'm making a few concessions to a harsher environment, but that's all. When I got back from that trip, I did order a new pack frame. It was designed by nine aeronautical engineers, three metallurgists, and a witch doctor, and weighs slightly less than the down of a small thistle. My new sleeping bag weighs nine ounces, including the thermostatic controls. If I want to sleep in, my new cook kit gets up and puts on the coffee. Then I bought a few boxes of that dried leather and sponge. But that's all. I'm certainly not going to be swept along on the tides of fashion.

▼ TOPICAL CONSIDERATIONS

1. What contrasts between the backpacking of the "old days" and today does McManus point out?
2. Why did the author resist the new backpacking gear and defend the old?
3. In a tongue-in-cheek manner, McManus cites several "geo-physical changes that took place in the Western Hemisphere a few years ago." What are these changes? What transformation in McManus do they explain?
4. What concessions to the harsher environment does McManus finally make?

▼ RHETORICAL CONSIDERATIONS

1. Much humor in this piece depends upon exaggeration. Examine paragraph 6 and cite some examples of the author's exaggeration.
2. Find an example of humor through repetition.

▼ WRITING ASSIGNMENTS

1. Select a sport or pastime you enjoy and write a tongue-in-cheek defense of it in a style similar to the author's here. For humorous effects, try to employ irony, exaggeration, repetition, and other devices.
2. Write an essay describing someone you know who prefers to do something "the old-fashioned way"—someone who rejects the latest conveniences and efficiencies.

3. Write an essay explaining the values of doing something "the old-fashioned way"—for instance, using a manual typewriter instead of a word processor, a traditional oven instead of a microwave, or an adding machine instead of a calculator.

TELEVISION

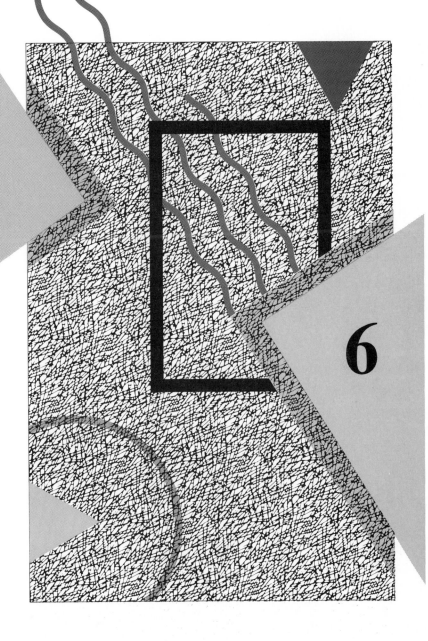

6

▼ WHAT DID KIDS DO BEFORE TELEVISION WAS INVENTED?

Peter C. Kratcoski

Television is the primary source of entertainment for Americans. It is also the prime target of many psychologists and sociologists who see television as dangerous to health. The lead piece in this section reflects one major criticism—that television threatens the creative activity of children. Peter C. Kratcoski is an editor for *USA Today* and a professor of sociology and criminal justice at Kent State University. His criticism here is not leveled at the quality of television, as is the criticism of others in this section, but at the passive nature of the experience. His essay also gives a glimpse of how kids filled their time before television. This first appeared in *USA Today* in 1981.

When adults who grew up in the 1940's or early 1950's describe the days of their 1
youth to their children, they paint a Norman Rockwell-style portrait of life. Hats went off as the flag passed by; days were filled with fishing, swimming, playing ball, or chatting with kindly adults; and parents' dreams for their children could be attained within the town limits—a good report card, a date for the prom, a romance with the boy next door. No matter how rosy the picture is painted, however, the question inevitably comes back: "Yes, but what did you do without television?" With television currently taking a good deal of criticism for its violence, suggestiveness, and debunking of authority figures in children's lives, it seems appropriate to recall the sorts of pastimes in which children of a small-town background engaged in the pre-television era.

One of our particular favorite activities was playing in the cemetery. Although 2
children seen roaming unsupervised in a cemetery today would probably be viewed suspiciously as potential vandals, we spent quite a few hours walking among the markers, commenting on the age and life status of the deceased and speculating on the character of those whose stones were particularly ornate. The children buried in the cemetery were most intriguing to us. We would talk about what dread disease might have finished them off and how old they would be today if they had lived; they even were sometimes included as imaginary playmates in our games.

This rather ghoulish preoccupation with the other-worldly also extended to 3
our favorite holiday, Halloween. "Trick or treat," rather than being a one-night affair, extended for two or more weeks before the haunting day. A group of children disguised as hobos, ghosts, scarecrows, or gypsies might descend on a household at any time, and the hauntee had to be ready with treats or face the

penalty of having his or her windows "soaped" (coated over with swirls and squiggles of bar soap). A code of "soaping" ethics existed—"nice" kids used bar soap, never pieces of wax, which had to be scraped from the window with a razor blade. The climax of the Halloween season came with the town parade, in which every kid who could walk or be carried participated. Many adults also joined in the fun, and prizes were awarded. One of the oddities of our particular area was the custom of fashioning costumes from suits of long underwear and then stuffing pillows into every possible inch of the material to produce droopy, horrendous-looking, fatty creatures. *Buying* a costume was unthinkable. Some mothers took this as the yearly opportunity to show off their sewing skills and fashioned elaborate crepe-paper costumes for their pretty, curly haired daughters. Those of us not so blessed uttered secret prayers for rain during the parade, in the hope that these strutting beauties would be reduced to dripping, runny nothings. Hours were spent talking about what this year's costume would be, pretending we were going to dress another way to keep others from stealing our prize-winning idea, and spying on friends to find out what they were *really* going to wear.

© The *Boston Globe* 1988. L.A. Times Syndicate.

Some of our pastimes centered about the church and the parochial school,   4
but were not necessarily inspirational in intent. Holy Saturday was a day of great
rejoicing, because at noon on that day Lent ended and we could again eat candy,
read comic books, drink pop, or return to whatever other vice our parents had
helped us promise to give up for the past 40 days. We would gravely prepare the
forbidden fruit and wait for the signal of the church bell tolling at noon before
gleefully digging in. Another important day was Aug. 15, the Feast of the Assumption,
when the nuns who taught in the school received their assignments for the
following year. It was a clear case of fate intervening in our lives. A word from the
Mother Superior on that day would send a particularly feared presence from
among us, never to be seen again, or would commit us to another year of toeing
the line. The 8 A.M. Mass was crowded, rumors flew, and we would intently study
the faces of the nuns for any sign that a packed suitcase was waiting in the
convent. When the news came out, it would spread like wildfire, and then a period
of relief or resignation followed.

It seemed that we did a good deal more reading than children do today, but   5
the adventure themes we favored were not unlike those of television escapism.
Nancy Drew was frowned upon by the town librarian, a fact which made her even
more appealing to the girls. The older boys' interest ran to novels smuggled from
their parents' collections or paperbacks purchased at the drugstore. All of the
"juicy" parts were marked for rereading and discussion.

These few examples seem to suggest that, even without television, we were   6
preoccupied in our early lives with the same themes of violence, rather ghoulish
aspects of the supernatural, testing and disrespect for authority, vandalism, a
desire to shock adults, and references to things considered "taboo" which we now
object to in television fare available to children. The apparent difference is the
level and visibility of these themes. A good deal of the rebellious or aberrant
activity of the past occurred only in the imaginations of the youths of that time, in
contrast to the graphic visual presentation of these themes on television. In
addition, a good deal of the testing of limits or rebelliousness was expressed in
activities of which adults were unaware. In contrast to television programming—
which is prepared, produced, and projected by adults—the testing activities
engaged in years ago had an element of social control by the children themselves.
Parents were not seen as friends or buddies, and the kids' world was closed to
them. Adults seemed comfortable with this idea and kept a hands-off attitude
unless behavior became blatantly rebellious, disruptive, or destructive. One possible answer, then, to the question, "What did kids do before television was
invented?" seems to be that they acted out their fantasies themselves, rather than
depending on film characters to do it for them.

▼ TOPICAL CONSIDERATIONS

1. What are the implications in the question asked of adults: "But what did
   you do without television?"

2. According to Kratcoski, how did his childhood activities differ from those of kids today?
3. Did your own Halloween experiences differ much from those of the author? In what ways? In general, how have Halloween activities changed since the days of Kratcoski's childhood?
4. How does the author answer the question in the title?

▼ RHETORICAL CONSIDERATIONS

1. Explain the allusion in paragraph 1 to "a Norman Rockwell-style portrait of life." How does the author characterize such a portrait?
2. Comment on the tone of Kratcoski's word choice, "finished them off," when he refers to the children buried in the cemetery (paragraph 2).
3. Does this essay have an organizing scheme? Outline it according to paragraphs.
4. Where is the thesis statement in this piece? What is the rhetorical strategy of placing it where it is? How well does Kratcoski support that statement in the essay?

▼ WRITING ASSIGNMENTS

1. Kratcoski's complaint is aimed not at the quality of television but at the nature of the experience itself, which he says is passive. Before television, kids used to act out their own fantasies, but today they depend on programs produced by adults to do it for them. Do you agree with Kratcoski? Write a paper evaluating his claim, and use your own childhood memories as evidence. Did you have a free and active fantasy life?
2. One of the arguments people make against television is that children read less because of it. Evaluate the effects television has had on your own reading experience. Did you like to read as a child? What did you read? Did you prefer television to books?
3. Part of Kratcoski's essay centers on his pretelevision activities, such as his memories of Halloween. Write your own recollection of Halloweens past. What kinds of preparations did you make? Did you design and create your own costumes, or did you buy them? What trick-or-treat experiences did you have? In a narrative, try to capture some of the things you did.

▼ THE PLUG-IN DRUG

Marie Winn

For years, the harmful effects of television, particularly on children, have been the professional interest of social commentator and writer Marie Winn. She is author of *The Plug-In Drug: TV* (1977), from which this essay has been adapted, and *Children Without Childhood* (1983). She says that home and family life have changed considerably—and in ways we may not care to imagine—since the invention of television. She makes a strong case against television, accusing it of being a prime force in the warping of children and in the disintegration of the American family.

A quarter of a century after the introduction of television into American society, a period that has seen the medium become so deeply ingrained in American life that in at least one state the television set has attained the rank of a legal necessity, safe from repossession in case of debt along with clothes, cooking utensils, and the like, television viewing has become an inevitable and ordinary part of daily life. Only in the early years of television did writers and commentators have sufficient perspective to separate the activity of watching television from the actual content it offers the viewer. In those early days writers frequently discussed the effects of television on family life. However, a curious myopia afflicted those early observers: almost without exception they regarded television as a favorable, beneficial, indeed, wondrous influence upon the family. 1

"Television is going to be a real asset in every home where there are children," predicts a writer in 1949. 2

"Television will take over your way of living and change your children's habits, but this change can be a wonderful improvement," claims another commentator. 3

"No survey's needed, of course, to establish that television has brought the family together in one room," writes *The New York Times* television critic in 1949. 4

Each of the early articles about television is invariably accompanied by a photograph or illustration showing a family cozily sitting together before the television set, Sis on Mom's lap, Buddy perched on the arm of Dad's chair, Dad with his arm around Mom's shoulder. Who could have guessed that twenty or so years later Mom would be watching a drama in the kitchen, the kids would be looking at cartoons in their room, while Dad would be taking in the ball game in the living room? 5

Of course television sets were enormously expensive in those early days. The idea that by 1975 more than 60 percent of American families would own two or 6 more sets was preposterous. The splintering of the multiple-set family was something the early writers could not foresee. Nor did anyone imagine the number of hours children would eventually devote to television, the common use of television by parents as a child pacifier, the changes television would effect upon child-rearing methods, the increasing domination of family schedules by children's viewing requirements—in short, the *power* of the new medium to dominate family life.

After the first years, as children's consumption of the new medium increased, together with parental concern about the possible effects of so much television viewing, a steady refrain helped to soothe and reassure anxious parents. "Television always enters a pattern of influences that already exist: the home, the peer group, the school, the church and culture generally," write the authors of an early and influential study of television's effects on children. In other words, if the child's home life is all right, parents need not worry about the effects of all that television watching.

But television does not merely influence the child; it deeply influences that "pattern of influences" that is meant to ameliorate its effects. Home and family life have changed in important ways since the advent of television. The peer group has become television-oriented, and much of the time children spend together is occupied by television viewing. Culture generally has been transformed by television. Therefore it is improper to assign to television the subsidiary role its many apologists (too often members of the television industry) insist it plays. Television is not merely one of a number of important influences upon today's child. Through the changes it has made in family life, television emerges as *the* important influence in children's lives today.

THE QUALITY OF FAMILY LIFE

Television's contribution to family life has been an equivocal one. For while it has, indeed, kept the members of the family from dispersing, it has not served to bring them together. By its domination of the time families spend together, it destroys the special quality that distinguishes one family from another, a quality that depends to a great extent on what a family *does,* what special rituals, games, recurrent jokes, familiar songs, and shared activities it accumulates.

"Like the sorcerer of old," writes Urie Bronfenbrenner, "the television set casts its magic spell, freezing speech and action, turning the living into silent statues so long as the enchantment lasts. The primary danger of the television screen lies not so much in the behavior it produces—although there is danger there—as in the behavior it prevents: the talks, the games, the family festivities and arguments through which much of the child's learning takes place and through which his character is formed. Turning on the television set can turn off the process that transforms children into people."

Yet parents have accepted a television-dominated family life so completely that they cannot see how the medium is involved in whatever problems they might be having. A first-grade teacher reports:

"I have one child in the group who's an only child. I wanted to find out more   12
about her family life because this little girl was quite isolated from the group,
didn't make friends, so I talked to her mother. Well, they don't have time to do
anything in the evening, the mother said. The parents come home after picking up
the child at the baby-sitter's. Then the mother fixes dinner while the child watches
TV. Then they have dinner and the child goes to bed. I said to this mother, 'Well,
couldn't she help you fix dinner? That would be a nice time for the two of you to
talk,' and the mother said, 'Oh, but I'd hate to have her miss "Zoom." It's such a
good program!' "

Even when families make efforts to control television, too often its very   13
presence counterbalances the positive features of family life. A writer and mother
of two boys aged 3 and 7 described her family's television schedule in an article in
the *New York Times:*

> We were in the midst of a full-scale War. Every day was a new battle and
> every program was a major skirmish. We agreed it was a bad scene all
> around and were ready to enter diplomatic negotiations. . . . In principle
> we have agreed on 2½ hours of TV a day, "Sesame Street," "Electric
> Company" (with dinner gobbled up in between) and two half-hour shows
> between 7 and 8:30 which enables the grown-ups to eat in peace and
> prevents the two boys from destroying one another. Their pre-bedtime
> choice is dreadful, because, as Josh recently admitted, "There's nothing
> much on I really like." So . . . it's "What's My Line" or "To Tell the
> Truth." . . . Clearly there is a need for first-rate children's shows at this
> time. . . .

Consider the "family life" described here: Presumably the father comes home   14
from work during the "Sesame Street"–"Electric Company" stint. The children are
either watching television, gobbling their dinner, or both. While the parents eat
their dinner in peaceful privacy, the children watch another hour of television.
Then there is only a half-hour left before bedtime, just enough time for baths,
getting pajamas on, brushing teeth, and so on. The children's evening is regimented
with an almost military precision. They watch their favorite programs, and when
there is "nothing much on I really like," they watch whatever else is on—because
watching is the important thing. Their mother does not see anything amiss with
watching programs just for the sake of watching; she only wishes there were some
first-rate children's shows on at those times.

Without conjuring up memories of the Victorian era with family games and   15
long, leisurely meals, and large families, the question arises: isn't there a better
family life available than this dismal, mechanized arrangement of children watching
television for however long is allowed them, evening after evening?

Of course, families today still do *special* things together at times: go camping   16
in the summer, go to the zoo on a nice Sunday, take various trips and expeditions.
But their *ordinary* daily life together is diminished—that sitting around at the
dinner table, that spontaneous taking up of an activity, those little games invented
by children on the spur of the moment when there is nothing else to do, the

scribbling, the chatting, and even the quarreling, all the things that form the fabric of a family, that define a childhood. Instead, the children have their regular schedule of television programs and bedtime, and the parents have their peaceful dinner together.

The author of the article in the *Times* notes that "keeping a family sane means mediating between the needs of both children and adults." But surely the needs of adults are being better met than the needs of the children, who are effectively shunted away and rendered untroublesome, while their parents enjoy a life as undemanding as that of any childless couple. In reality, it is those very demands that young children make upon a family that lead to growth, and it is the way parents accede to those demands that builds the relationships upon which the future of the family depends. If the family does not accumulate its backlog of shared experiences, shared *everyday* experiences that occur and recur and change and develop, then it is not likely to survive as anything other than a caretaking institution.   17

FAMILY RITUALS

Ritual is defined by sociologists as "that part of family life that the family likes about itself, is proud of and wants formally to continue." Another text notes that "the development of a ritual by a family is an index of the common interest of its members in the family as a group."   18

What has happened to family rituals, those regular, dependable, recurrent happenings that gave members of a family a feeling of *belonging* to a home rather than living in it merely for the sake of convenience, those experiences that act as the adhesive of family unity far more than any material advantages?   19

Mealtime rituals, going-to-bed rituals, illness rituals, holiday rituals, how many of these have survived the inroads of the television set?   20

A young woman who grew up near Chicago reminisces about her childhood and gives an idea of the effects of television upon family rituals: 21

"As a child I had millions of relatives around—my parents both come from relatively large families. My father had nine brothers and sisters. And so every holiday there was this great swoop-down of aunts, uncles, and millions of cousins. I just remember how wonderful it used to be. These thousands of cousins would come and everyone would play and ultimately, after dinner, all the women would be in the front of the house, drinking coffee and talking, all the men would be in the back of the house, drinking and smoking, and all the kids would be all over the place, playing hide and seek. Christmas time was particularly nice because everyone always brought all their toys and games. Our house had a couple of rooms with go-through closets, so there were always kids running in a great circle route. I remember it was just wonderful.   22

"And then all of a sudden one year I remember becoming suddenly aware of how different everything had become. The kids were no longer playing Monopoly or Clue or the other games we used to play together. It was because we had a   23 television set which had been turned on for a football game. All of that socializing that had gone on previously had ended. Now everyone was sitting in front of the television set, on a holiday, at a family party! I remember being stunned by how awful that was. Somehow the television had become more attractive."

As families have come to spend more and more of their time together engaged in the single activity of television watching, those rituals and pastimes that once gave family life its special quality have become more and more uncommon. Not since prehistoric times when cave families hunted, gathered, ate, and slept, with little time remaining to accumulate a culture of any significance, have families been reduced to such a sameness. 24

REAL PEOPLE

It is not only the activities that a family might engage in together that are diminished by the powerful presence of television in the home. The relationships of the family members to each other are also affected, in both obvious and subtle ways. The hours that the young child spends in a one-way relationship with television people, an involvement that allows for no communication or interaction, surely affect his relationships with real-life people. 25

Studies show the importance of eye-to-eye contact, for instance, in real-life relationships, and indicate that the nature of a person's eye-contact patterns, whether he looks another squarely in the eye or looks to the side or shifts his gaze from side to side, may play a significant role in his success or failure in human relationships. But no eye contact is possible in the child-television relationship, although in certain children's programs people purport to speak directly to the child and the camera fosters this illusion by focusing directly upon the person being filmed. (Mr. Rogers is an example, telling the child "I like you, you're special," etc.) How might such a distortion of real-life relationships affect a child's development of trust, of openness, of an ability to relate well to other *real* people? 26

Bruno Bettelheim writes: 27

> Children who have been taught, or conditioned, to listen passively most of the day to the warm verbal communications coming from the TV screen, to the deep emotional appeal of the so-called TV personality, are often unable to respond to real persons because they arouse so much less feeling than the skilled actor. Worse, they lose the ability to learn from reality because life experiences are much more complicated than the ones they see on the screen. . . .

A teacher makes a similar observation about her personal viewing experiences: 28
"I have trouble mobilizing myself and dealing with real people after watching a few hours of television. It's just hard to make that transition from watching television to a real relationship. I suppose it's because there was no effort necessary while I was watching, and dealing with real people always requires a bit of 29

effort. Imagine, then, how much harder it might be to do the same thing for a small child, particularly one who watches a lot of television every day."

But more obviously damaging to family relationships is the elimination of   30
opportunities to talk, and perhaps more important, to argue, to air grievances, between parents and children and brothers and sisters. Families frequently use television to avoid confronting their problems, problems that will not go away if they are ignored but will only fester and become less easily resolvable as time goes on.

A mother reports: 31

"I find myself, with three children, wanting to turn on the TV set when they're   32
fighting. I really have to struggle not to do it because I feel that's telling them this is the solution to the quarrel—but it's so tempting that I often do it."

A family therapist discusses the use of television as an avoidance mechanism: 33

"In a family I know the father comes home from work and turns on the   34
television set. The children come and watch with him and the wife serves them their meal in front of the set. He then goes and takes a shower, or works on the car or something. She then goes and has her own dinner in front of the television set. It's a symptom of a deeper-rooted problem, sure. But it would help them all to get rid of the set. It would be far easier to work on what the symptom really means without the television. The television simply encourages a double avoidance of each other. They'd find out more quickly what was going on if they weren't able to hide behind the TV. Things wouldn't necessarily be better, of course, but they wouldn't be anesthetized."

The decreased opportunities for simple conversation between parents and   35
children in the television-centered home may help explain an observation made by an emergency room nurse at a Boston hospital. She reports that parents just seem to sit there these days when they come in with a sick or seriously injured child, although talking to the child would distract and comfort him. "They don't seem to know *how* to talk to their own children at any length," the nurse observes. Similarly, a television critic writes in *The New York Times:* "I had just a day ago taken my son to the emergency ward of a hospital for stitches above his left eye, and the occasion seemed no more real to me than Maalot or 54th Street, south-central Los Angeles. There was distance and numbness and an inability to turn off the total institution. I didn't behave at all; I just watched. . . . "

A number of research studies substantiate the assumption that television   36
interferes with family activities and the formation of family relationships. One survey shows that 78 percent of the respondents indicated no conversation taking place during viewing except at specified times such as commercials. The study notes: "The television atmosphere in most households is one of quiet absorption on the part of family members who are present. The nature of the family social life during a program could be described as 'parallel' rather than interactive, and the set does seem to dominate family life when it is on." Thirty-six percent of the respondents in another study indicated that television viewing was the only family activity participated in during the week.

In a summary of research findings on television's effect on family interactions,   37

James Gabardino states: "The early findings suggest that television had a disruptive effect upon interaction and thus presumably human development. . . . It is not unreasonable to ask: 'Is the fact that the average American family during the 1950's came to include two parents, two children and a television set somehow related to the psychosocial characteristics of the young adults of the 1970's?' "

UNDERMINING THE FAMILY

In its effect on family relationships, in its facilitation of parental withdrawal from 38 an active role in the socialization of their children, and in its replacement of family rituals and special events, television has played an important role in the disintegration of the American family. But of course it has not been the only contributing factor, perhaps not even the most important one. The steadily rising divorce rate, the increase in the number of working mothers, the decline of the extended family, the breakdown of neighborhoods and communities, the growing isolation of the nuclear family—all have seriously affected the family.

As Urie Bronfenbrenner suggests, the sources of family breakdown do not 39 come from the family itself, but from the circumstances in which the family finds itself and the way of life imposed upon it by those circumstances. "When those circumstances and the way of life they generate undermine relationships of trust and emotional security between family members, when they make it difficult for parents to care for, educate and enjoy their children, when there is no support or recognition from the outside world for one's role as a parent and when time spent with one's family means frustration of career, personal fulfillment and peace of mind, then the development of the child is adversely affected," he writes.

But while the roots of alienation go deep into the fabric of American social 40 history, television's presence in the home fertilizes them, encourages their wild and unchecked growth. Perhaps it is true that America's commitment to the television experience masks a spiritual vacuum, an empty and barren way of life, a desert of materialism. But it is television's dominant role in the family that anesthetizes the family into accepting its unhappy state and prevents it from struggling to better its condition, to improve its relationships, and to regain some of the richness it once possessed.

Others have noted the role of mass media in perpetuating an unsatisfactory 41 *status quo.* Leisure-time activity, writes Irving Howe, "must provide relief from work monotony without making the return to work too unbearable; it must provide amusement without insight and pleasure without disturbance—as distinct from art which gives pleasure through disturbance. Mass culture is thus oriented towards a central aspect of industrial society: the depersonalization of the individual." Similarly, Jacques Ellul rejects the idea that television is a legitimate means of educating the citizen: "Education . . . takes place only incidentally. The clouding of his consciousness is paramount. . . . "

And so the American family muddles on, dimly aware that something is amiss 42 but distracted from an understanding of its plight by an endless stream of television images. As family ties grow weaker and vaguer, as children's lives become more separate from their parents', as parents' educational role in their children's lives is taken over by television and schools, family life becomes increasingly more unsatisfying for both parents and children. All that seems to be left is Love, an abstraction that family members *know* is necessary but find great difficulty giving each other because the traditional opportunities for expressing love within the family have been reduced or destroyed.

For contemporary parents, love toward each other has increasingly come to mean successful sexual relations, as witnessed by the proliferation of sex manuals and sex therapists. The opportunities for manifesting other forms of love through mutual support, understanding, nurturing, even, to use an unpopular word, *serving* each other, are less and less available as mothers and fathers seek their independent destinies outside the family.   43

As for love of children, this love is increasingly expressed through supplying material comforts, amusements, and educational opportunities. Parents show their love for their children by sending them to good schools and camps, by providing them with good food and good doctors, by buying them toys, books, games, and a television set of their very own. Parents will even go further and express their love by attending PTA meetings to improve their children's schools, or by joining groups that are acting to improve the quality of their children's television programs.   44

But this is love at a remove, and is rarely understood by children. The more direct forms of parental love require time and patience, steady, dependable, ungrudgingly given time actually spent *with* a child, reading to him, comforting him, playing, joking, and working with him. But even if a parent were eager and willing to demonstrate that sort of direct love to his children today, the opportunities are diminished. What with school and Little League and piano lessons and, of course, the inevitable television programs, a day seems to offer just enough time for a good-night kiss.   45

▼ TOPICAL CONSIDERATIONS

1. According to Winn, in what specific ways does television destroy "the special quality that distinguishes one family from another" (paragraph 9)? What family behavior is dangerously "prevented"?
2. How does television threaten family unity and closeness, according to the author?
3. What does Winn say about the quality of television programs?
4. In what specific ways does television affect children's play and creativity?
5. What evidence does Winn present to support her claim that TV has endangered family rituals?
6. How can television adversely affect the way people—including children—relate to one another?
7. In paragraph 41, Irving Howe is quoted as saying that the mass media,

including television, "must provide amusement without insight and pleasure without disturbance." Do you think this is a fair assessment of the nature of network television? Do you think this is what the general American public wants? What it needs? What about public television? How would Howe assess PBS programs?

▼ RHETORICAL CONSIDERATIONS

1. In what ways is television a "plug-in drug"? Is this a fair metaphor?
2. Winn says that people today are so dominated by the television set "that they cannot see how the medium is involved in whatever problems they might be having" (paragraph 11). How well does she illustrate that claim?
3. What would you say Winn's attitude is toward the American television public? Cite some passages in her essay to support your statement.
4. In paragraph 44, Winn speaks of love of children, stating that its expression has been reduced to material display. Do you think she oversimplifies? Does she offer much evidence? Need she?
5. Evaluate the kind and amount of evidence Winn summons to support her thesis in the essay. Is some of it excessive? Is it lacking in other places?

▼ WRITING ASSIGNMENTS

1. Did television play a prominent role in your home? Did you and your family watch it regularly as you were growing up? If so, try to evaluate any negative effects television had on your family and your upbringing. Consider how it might have functioned as a babysitter for you and how it affected communication between family members, rituals, and creativity.
2. Winn calls television a "plug-in drug." The use of a drug often leads to some effort to shake the habit. Write a paper in which you explore the difficulties some people you know would have in adjusting to life without television. Consider the rigid patterns that might have evolved over the years with television.
3. Imagine what life might be like twenty years from now, given the rapid development and spread of television across America. Consider that television might someday have hundreds of channels broadcasting twenty-four hours a day. Create a scenario of the total-television family of the future, extrapolating from some of Winn's observations.
4. In paragraph 13, Winn refers to the plight of a mother who tries to "control television" in her home. Write this woman a letter in which you suggest how she can creatively reorganize her family's day around activities other than television and still get things accomplished.

▼ THE VIOLENCE IS FAKE, THE IMPACT IS REAL

Ellen Goodman

Perhaps the most common concern among critics of television is the effect of violence on children. Many studies by private institutions and by the government conclude that children do, in fact, learn aggressive behavior from what they see on the screen, despite the disclaimers of broadcasters. The issue Ellen Goodman raises here is what television violence fails to teach kids about the consequences of real violence. Ellen Goodman is a widely syndicated, Pulitzer Prize-winning columnist for the *Boston Globe*. Collections of her columns have been published in *Close to Home* (1981), *At Large* (1983), and *Keeping in Touch* (1985). This article first appeared in 1977 in the *Boston Globe*.

I don't usually think of television executives as being modest, shy and retiring. But 1 for a decade or two, the same souls who have bragged about their success in selling products have been positively humble about their success in selling messages.

Yes indeed, they would tell advertisers, children see, children do . . . do buy 2 candy bars and cereals and toys. But no, no, they would tell parents, children see, but children don't . . . imitate mangling and mayhem.

But now the government has released another study on TV and violence. The 3 predictable conclusion is that "violence on television does lead to aggressive behavior by children and teenagers who watch the programs." After analyzing 2500 studies and publications since 1970, the "overwhelming" scientific evidence is that "excessive" violence on the screen produces violence off the screen.

Somehow or other, I feel like I have been here before. By now, the protesta- 4 tions of the networks sound like those of the cigarette manufacturers who will deny the link between cigarettes and lung disease to their (and our) last breath. By now, studies come and go, but the problem remains.

Today the average kid sits in front of the tube for 26 hours a week. The kids 5 don't begin with a love of violence. Even today, one runaway favorite in the Saturday morning line-up is about the benign "Smurfs." But eventually they learn from grown-ups.

In the incredible shrinking world of kidvid, there is no regularly scheduled 6 program for kids on any of the three networks between the hours of 7 A.M. and 6 P.M. A full 80 percent of the programs kids watch are adult television. For those who choose adventures, the broadcasters offer endless sagas of terror, chase, murder, rescue.

As Peggy Charren, who has watched this scene for a long time as head of Action for Children's Television, puts it: "Broadcasters believe that the more violent the problems, the more attractive the adventure to audiences in terms of sitting there and not turning it off. The ultimate adventure is doing away with someone's life. The ultimate excitement is death." 7

The government, in its report, listed some theories about why there is this link between violence on TV and violence in kids' behavior. One theory was that TV is a how-to lesson in aggression. Children learn "how to" hit and hurt from watching the way they learn how to count and read. Another theory is that kids who see a world full of violence accept it as normal behavior. 8

But I wonder whether violence isn't accepted because it is normalized—sanitized and packaged. We don't see violence on television in terms of pain and suffering, but in terms of excitement. In cartoons, characters are smashed with boulders, and dropped from airplanes only to get up unscathed. In adventure shows, people are killed all the time, but they are rarely "hurt." 9

As Charren put it, "There is no feeling badly about violence on television." We don't bear witness to the pain of a single gunshot wound. We don't see the broken hand and teeth that come from one blow to the jaw. We don't share the blood or the guilt, the anguish or the mourning. We don't see the labor of rebuilding a car, a window, a family. 10

Our television stars brush themselves off and return same time, same station, next week without a single bruise. Cars are replaced. The dead are carted off and forgotten. 11

In Japan, I am told there is an unwritten rule that if you show violence on television, you show the result of that violence. Such a program is, I am sure, much more disturbing. But maybe it should be. Maybe that's what's missing. 12

In the real world, people repress aggression because they know the consequences. But on television, there are no consequences. In the end kids may be less affected by the presence of violence than by the absence of pain. They learn that violence is okay. That nobody gets hurt. 13

So, if the broadcasters refuse to curb their profitable adventures in hurting, their national contribution to violence, then let them add something to the mix: equal time for truth and consequences. 14

▼ TOPICAL CONSIDERATIONS

1. What is Goodman's major criticism of television broadcasters? How are they like cigarette manufacturers?
2. What are some of the problems with network television for children?
3. What is Goodman's central complaint about the way violence is portrayed on television? Is it just that it is too graphic?
4. How does the Japanese treatment of television violence differ from the American treatment?

5. What suggestions does Ellen Goodman make about portrayal of violence on television? Would you make the same suggestions?

▼ RHETORICAL CONSIDERATIONS

1. Where is the thesis statement in this essay? Would you have placed it elsewhere? Explain your answer.
2. Explain Goodman's use of the word "sanitized" in describing television violence in paragraph 9. What does the word mean, and how good a choice is it?
3. What is the rhetorical effect of the parallel sentence structures in paragraph 10?
4. How does paragraph 12 fit Goodman's thesis?

▼ WRITING ASSIGNMENTS

1. Do you agree with Goodman's claim that pain and suffering are missing from television's treatment of violence? Using your own knowledge of television, write a paper in which you answer this question. You may want to watch a few shows in which violence and its consequences are dramatized.
2. Watch a typical Saturday morning cartoon show and make note of the way violence is handled. Then write a paper in which you analyze just how violence is depicted and how it might be interpreted by children. Does cartoon violence seem normal? Are people hurt? Are children left feeling that violence is okay?
3. Have you ever seen a television program or a made-for-TV movie in which both the "truth and consequences" of violence were fairly portrayed? If so, write a paper in which you defend the accuracy of the portrayal of the pain and suffering that follow violence.

▼ PACKAGED NEWS

Brendan Boyd

And now for the news—or, more exactly, the non-news. Have you ever wondered how television newscasters always manage to fill their half-hour slots on days when nothing newsworthy has happened? Have you ever noticed how the same kinds of stories—the same news *packages*—are aired on all the networks? Sure you have, and so has professional writer Brendan Boyd, who gives us some very funny insights into the seven o'clock news. Boyd has written comic strips, rock music reviews, and two books—*The Great American Baseball Card* (1973) and *And a Player to Be Named Later* (1982). He is currently a book editor and the author of the syndicated column "Investor's Notebook."

1   Good evening, ladies and gentlemen. Welcome to *The Seven o'Clock News.*
Nothing happened today.
Goodnight.

That's the way television *should* handle the four out of seven days every week when current events go into suspended animation. But don't hang by your rabbit ears waiting for it to happen. Because the television news, contrary to FCC disclaimers, is not really the news at all. It's just another way for the networks to sell Efferdent, and for corporate America to unwind after its collective tough day at the office.

2   Thus, on those not-so-infrequent days when the Pope has not been shot, Afghanistan has not been invaded, and no member of the British Royal Family has needlessly disgraced himself, the networks still carry out their contractual obligation, if not necessarily their duty, to report the news, even though there's no news to report. They dust off their file of canned headlines, change a few names, and settle in to perpetuate the requisite delusion that something really did happen today.

3   Of course, the day will come when absolutely nothing happens. And on that day we'll all be subjected to the ultimate in televised monotony: *The Seven o'Clock News with Absolutely Nothing New About It Whatsoever.* As always, the events of this numbingly uneventful day will be sorted into the usual predictable categories.

185

WORLD UPDATE

This first class of story is intended to make viewers feel that because an event 4 has limitless scale it also has limitless importance. Television newscasters like to distract us from the vacuousness of their stories by impressing us with the amount of ground these stories cover.

Soviet Leader Mikhail Gorbachev Ill. This is the perfect lead item for a slow 5 news day. It's both potentially earthshaking and completely irrefutable. It replaces that perennial favorite, *Mao Rumored Dead,* which passed into blessed obsolescence several years back when the Chinese leader actually died. If Gorbachev has not been looking particularly well lately, some other Iron Curtain bureaucrat's name may safely be substituted. And in a pinch, a more generalized notion about totalitarians will suffice—say, *Kremlin Shake-up Hinted.*

846 Perish in Indian Train Mishap. Or *267 Killed as Mexican Bus Plunges off* 6 *Mountain.* Or *536 Die in Burmese Ferry Crash.* In all Third World disasters the volume of the victimization is meant to compensate for our physical and emotional distance from the event. But no matter how many Africans starve to death in any given famine, television doesn't really consider it news unless Frank Sinatra didn't punch a photographer that day. The New York tabloids are rumored to use a formula in determining space allocations for such stories. *800 Dead in Bolivian Earthquake,* for example, is said to equal *6 Felled by Ptomaine at Staten Island Clambake.*

Troops Mass Along Nepalese Border. Troops are always massing somewhere. 7 That's what troops do. And their massing is always supposed to mean something ominous, although usually it doesn't. Notice that we never see a follow-up story about troops *disbanding* along the Nepalese border.

SALT Talks Winding Down. For ten years the only thing we knew about 8 the SALT talks was that they were about to reopen. Now that we've finally figured out what the SALT talks are supposed to be, they seem always to be winding down. To establish the proper tedious mood, this story should be followed by one of the following diplomatic grace notes: *NATO Maneuvers Begin. Rumblings in SEATO.* Or *Bilateral Trade Agreements Signal New Era in U.S.–New Zealand Friendship.*

Christian Democrats Score Gains in Belgium. There are 627 political parties 9 in Europe. All but nine have the word Christian or Democrat in their names. And they're always scoring gains.

U.N. General Assembly Convenes. This is a portentous occurrence which 10 everyone in the world thinks he or she should care about, but which nobody actually does.

U.S.–Cuba Thaw Seen Possible. This is the obligatory hopeful note in East- 11 West relations. It alternates with pictorial essays of visiting American plumbers teaching mainland Chinese apprentices how to steam-clean a grease trap.

Cyprus After Makarios. Another in the always popular series, "Incredibly 12 Shallow Profiles of Enigmatic Dictators." A personal favorite has always been *Souvanna Phouma, Cambodia's Neutralist Playboy,* although I must admit a lingering fondness for the now obsolete *Ethiopian Ruler Haile Selassie Marks 87th Birthday by Buying New Summerweight Uniform.*

Pope Urges World Leaders to Seek Peace. But notice he never says exactly *how.* 13

NATIONAL UPDATE

The second class of story is intended to make viewers feel that because something 14
is happening *near* them it is somehow relevant *to* them. And let's face it, there is something more compelling about even the most banal range of events if the boredom they engender has a distinctly local flavor.

Former Senator Eugene McCarthy Mulling Third Party Try. Ah, the sixties. 15
They provide the networks with an endless source of thirty-second filmclips on how Joan Baez has mellowed, Jane Fonda hasn't, and Dick Gregory remains the world's skinniest nudge.

Conspiracy Theorists Hint New Oswald Evidence. Mention of President 16
Kennedy's assassin is frequently linked in a two-cushion shot with news that there are *Fresh Indications James Earl Ray Acted Alone in King Killing.*

47 Percent Favor Easing of Marijuana Laws. And the other 53 percent are too 17
stoned to care. Polls are a favorite ploy for slow news days. Who, after all, can fail to attach at least marginal significance to a finding such as "72 percent of Americans believe that asparagus turns urine green, whereas a surprising 38 percent feel that getting in an eight-item supermarket express line with nine items should be punishable by death"?

Kennedy Family Marks Anniversary of First Congressional Victory. Every day 18
of the year is some sort of anniversary for the Kennedys. No anchorman worth his capped teeth would let one slide by without paying perfunctory homage to "three decades of heartbreak."

Switch to Metric System Poses Problems. Or, "Is Celsius a Communist plot to 19
bore us to death?"

Ex-Nixon Crony Robert Vesco Linked to New Illegalities. Just as every corpo- 20
ration in the United States is destined to be bought by ITT, every white-collar crime committed in the free world during the past fifteen years will eventually be linked to Robert Vesco.

Parents Unite to Fight Pornography in School Libraries. No doubt they're up 21
in arms against *Huckleberry Finn,* the underwear section of the Sears catalog, and the Manhattan Yellow Pages.

BUSINESS AND FINANCE

The third class of story is meant to appeal to *the* primal interest of every potential 22
viewer—money. Economics is the ultimate mystery. And television broadcasters do nothing to allay our bewilderment with their nightly recalculations of our shrinking worth.

Housing Starts Decline 23 Percent. Housing starts, domestic car sales, and 23
American exports have declined every month for the past twenty years. How far
down, pray tell, is down?

Prime Rate Rises ¼ Percent. All together now, class, what is the prime rate? 24
That's right. It's the rate the nation's banks charge their most credit-worthy
customers. And why did the Dow Jones Industrial Average go down yesterday?
That's right. Profit taking. And why is it going up today? That's right. Bargain
hunting. One of the more comforting characteristics of television news is that,
having told us any salient fact about a given situation, it can safely be counted on
to tell us that fact, and only that fact, over and over again.

HUMAN INTEREST, HUMAN HORROR

Television newscasters have always depended on the misfortune of strangers. 25
These stories are meant to appeal to the kind of people who slow down on the
highway to get a good look at a car wreck. That is to say—all of us.

Cancer Linked to Banana Daiquiris. This one comes from television news's 26
extensive "Life Causes Death" file.

Detroit Man Goes Berserk, Turns Rifle on Crowd. He was unquestionably a 27
quiet, neat, well-mannered man whom neighbors say would be the last person
you'd ever expect to do such a thing.

National Guard, Boy Scouts Scour Woods for Missing Toddler. Aside to 28
Gloria Steinem: Why aren't the Girl Scouts ever called out on such occasions?

SIDELIGHTS

Plus, if time permits (and unfortunately it always seems to) we can count on a 29
quick hopscotching of headlines drawn from all of the preceding categories.
These stories are too important sounding to ignore but too familiar to devote more
than thirty seconds to.

G.M. Recalls Every Car It Made Last Year
New Bomber Hits Cost Overruns
Guam Accelerates Drive for Statehood
Teamster Insurgents Press Leadership for Reforms
All-Volunteer Army Seen Foundering
Recluse Found Starved to Death With $3 Million Stuffed in Mattress
Postal Service to Seek Rate Increases
First Thompsons Gazelle in 27 Years Born in Captivity
Seven Tie for First-Round Lead in Greater Greensboro Open

PARTING INSPIRATIONAL FEATURE

This final story is meant to send the now ossified viewers away either laughing, shaking their heads, or feeling grateful that none of the awful things that happened that day happened to them. [30]

Nation's Oldest Living Man Observes 116th Birthday. Every slow news day can use an uplifting senior citizen feature to top it off. There are only three possibilities here. The first involves either a visit to a rest home by a third-tier celebrity like Corbett Monica or Deborah Raffin, or a mass golden-ager outing to some heinously inappropriate setting (*150 Elders Enjoy Day at New Jersey Drag Speedway*). The second is a courage-in-the-face-of-adversity story such as *Despite Beatings, Blindness, Bankruptcy, Widowed Iron Lung Inhabitant Counts Blessings.* (I demand a recount.) The third, and most popular alternative, chronicles a birthday party for a senior citizen who, having achieved a particularly ill-advised longevity, is then required to state his prescription for long life. This recipe usually consists of equal parts smoking, drinking, and womanizing. But it makes no mention whatsoever of watching the seven o'clock news. [31]

▼ TOPICAL CONSIDERATIONS

1. Boyd's opening paragraph says that "television news, contrary to FCC disclaimers, is not really news at all." How does Boyd mean such a claim? What do network news programs report instead of news?
2. According to Boyd, in what specific ways do news programs give more entertainment than news? In what ways are network news shows "packaged"?
3. In paragraph 7, Boyd says that we always hear about somebody's troops massing on somebody else's border, but "we never see a follow-up story about troops *disbanding.*" What exactly is Boyd's point here? Is he saying that we are rarely told the good news of the day? Or that ominous news reporting is a subtle way of keeping us tuned in day after day? Or that news programs don't have in their files "canned headlines" about troops disbanding?
4. Beneath almost all of Boyd's satirical jabs, he is making some serious, critical statements about news broadcasting. Select a few of his headlines, and determine his more serious criticisms.
5. How does television news try to appeal to the viewer's "primal interest" in money? To the viewer's taste for horror?

▼ RHETORICAL CONSIDERATIONS

1. How accurate are Boyd's news story categories? How well do they organize his essay?
2. Evaluate the satirical effect of paragraph 6. What is the brunt of Boyd's humor here?

3. What is the message in Boyd's final sentence, and how does it summarize his overall thesis?

▼ WRITING ASSIGNMENTS

1. Do you think network news programs are "no-news" packages? Write a paper in which you express your own views about television news programs. (Do you think matters would be different if network news shows were expanded to a full hour each night?)
2. Watch the news for the next several nights and test Boyd's package of news categories. How well do they conform to the organization of the programs?
3. Local news can be considered packaged as well. Write a parody—in the spirit of Brendan Boyd—of local news programs, giving categories such as world update, national update, state and local news, sports, weather, human interest, the daily crime log, and so on. Structure your paper according to these categories and provide canned headlines.
4. If you frequently or exclusively watch one network news program, try to assess your preference. Does it have anything to do with the way the news is packaged, or with the personalities of the newscasters? Just how important is the personality factor in network news competition?
5. Attempt to write a script for a typical news program. Make up typical headlines and stories and attempt to capture the reporting styles you see on nightly news programs. (Try to do a parody of television broadcast news, if possible.)

▼ MTV'S MESSAGE
Newsweek

> We have now read several warnings about the dangerous power of
> television—how it holds and molds an audience, stifles creativity, and
> adversely affects the behavior of the young. What about television's
> latest innovation—rock video? With its dazzling imagery, deft chore-
> ography, brilliant flickering colors, and slick special effects, music
> video has been touted as the newest art form. Cable TV, VCRs, and
> video discs have brought music videos into the home, and many
> parents are worried about the sex and violence in the videos. Are
> videos really bad for kids? The following report—a December 1985
> *Newsweek* cover story—examines the phenomenon of music video
> and its potential impact on our kids.

It's violent and riddled with sexual innuendo. Most of it is tasteless and witless. It   1
frequently celebrates the drug culture and crime. The culprit is prime-time
network television, of course, and parents, educators and other social critics have
worried about its effects on the young for years. Now they have something new to
worry about, something that seems to distill all the worst elements of television
into one potent package: music video.

With its striking imagery, deft choreography, bright colors and quick cuts,   2
music video has attracted a huge audience. It's also caused an angry stir, albeit a
confused one: assessments of its impact are highly subjective, with anecdotes
available to support any point of view. And it may simply be impossible to sort out
the effects of music videos from network programming, not to mention other
social phenomena. So take your choice: "Children are being bombarded with
messages of violence and sexuality that are very confusing and suggest easy ways
out of complex problems," says Dr. Eli Newberger, director of family-development
study at Children's Hospital in Boston. "For any kids who are reasonably put
together, it doesn't drive them into anything," counters David Elkind, a professor
of child study at Tufts University. "Nobody knows exactly what MTV is doing to
us," suggests Robert Jay Lifton, the author of numerous studies on violence, who
is now a professor at John Jay College of Criminal Justice in New York. "If
anybody says he or she knows, I don't believe it. It's too new."

In part, the controversy isn't new at all. Ever since it began, rock and roll   3
has had two themes: rebellion and sex. Before it, rhythm and blues celebrated
raunch. The Hootchy-Cootchy Man wasn't describing his skill as a tickler of
babies, after all. But video is simply far more explicit. A song you listen to may
haunt your reveries; watch it on television, and it can have the impact of

a nightmare. "Listening to 'Let's Spend the Night Together' didn't get any girl to hop into bed with me or anyone else," says Dr. Victor Strasburger, director of adolescent medicine at Bridgeport (Conn.) Hospital and a member of the American Academy of Pediatrics' Task Force on TV and Children. "But seeing a sexy video can teach you that if you're not sexually active, there's something wrong with you. Once you've depicted the song, you've magnified the effect a hundredfold."

Like most other observers, Strasburger, who is a rock fan, readily concedes that he has no hard data to back him up. But testaments to the power of MTV's message abound. Two years ago New Yorker Marilee Stayr's youngest child began having nightmares. "After a while I realized he was describing Michael Jackson's 'Thriller' and a couple of other weird videos where things exploded," she says. "Right then I said no more MTV for him and less for the other kids." The effects of the ban were salutary. Stayr noticed that her 13-year-old daughter started reading a book a week, and her 11-year-old son invited friends to the house more often.

4

BLACK LACE

Mary Fuchs's encounter with the power of video came after Madonna began overexposing herself on the tube. "I looked up and my 14-year-old daughter was coming out of her room dressed in a black lace bra and a miniskirt, and very little else," says Fuchs, 46, a Manhattan secretary. "I was so shocked I couldn't speak; I thought surely she'd be too embarrassed to go out like that. But she did."

5

One potentially insidious aspect of music videos is that they can reach a very young audience. John Wright, director of the Center for Research on the Influence of Television on Children at the University of Kansas, says videos are "well suited to the attention spans of little bitty kids." At the Daybridge Learning Center in Overland Park, Kans., this year, MTV stole Halloween; children came in wearing Madonna, Cyndi Lauper and Michael Jackson costumes. Daybridge kindergarten teacher Susan Albers says she has seen preschoolers cry when listening to "Thriller" because they had been frightened by the ghoulish video. And one second-grade boy has talked about undressing Madonna and marrying her as soon as her husband dies.

6

As others see it, the very young may be protected by their very youth. Marcia Davidson, a former day-care worker who now coordinates training programs for Head Start, says preschoolers "are fascinated by the bright colors and the movement." But they understand little of what they see. "They are more into pretending to be Skeletor and comic-cartoon characters," she says. Watching "Sesame Street," for example, they will often talk back to the screen. "When Big Bird says, 'Where's my tennis shoe?' the three-year-old says, 'It's right over there, Big Bird.' I've never seen them get that engrossed in music videos." And as for prompting antisocial behavior, Albers, for one, is far more concerned about cartoon shows. "We see some real aggressive physical behavior, a lot of martial arts, kung fu and karate," she says.

7

"They see more of that through what they're watching on Saturday morning—He-Man [and the] Masters of the Universe."

As far as the record industry is concerned, all considerations of taste and decorum are beside the point. "When you ask are we supposed to be moral, are we supposed to be humanistic, are we supposed to titillate . . . we're *supposed* to be none of those things," says Ken Walz, who has produced videos for Lauper, The Oak Ridge Boys, Sister Sledge and Huey Lewis. "What we are supposed to do is . . . sell records, concert tickets and artists." 8

To sell records, though, the video must get wide exposure, and that means MTV must play it. MTV has written guidelines on sex and violence, but they are the kind of civic-minded pieties that permit unlimited flexibility. "Videos containing gratuitous violence are unacceptable . . . Exceptional care must be taken in instances where women and children are victims of, or are threatened by, acts of violence." 9

VIOLENT ACTS

Barry Sherman, assistant professor of telecommunications at the University of Georgia, evaluated 366 videos aired during the spring of 1984 on MTV and elsewhere. More than half were performance footage. In the rest, Sherman found a "predominantly white, male world." Fifty percent of the women were provocatively clothed; 10 percent of the men. Sixty percent of the music videos showed violence; men accounted for three-fourths of all aggressors and a slightly larger percentage of victims. About 10 percent of the violence resulted in visible incapacity or injury. Only three out of every 100 violent acts resulted in a death. Most of the videos with violence also included sexual imagery, "most of it preening and looking and suggestive stares," says Sherman. Bondage and transvestism were rare. "It was very tame, tamer than we expected," he says. 10

In a follow-up study, Sherman discerned no harmful effects on kids who watched MTV—a result that surprised him. His graduate students interviewed 500 junior-high-school students in Danielsville, a small town northeast of Atlanta. "We didn't find negative effects, either in perceiving the world as more violent or more sexist than it really is." The adolescents who watched the most MTV "tended to be better students . . . they usually played in bands or belonged to the music society. They were more involved in clubs." Sherman believes those results may be due to the economic status of their parents, who must be able to afford cable to get MTV. Children from prosperous homes generally outperform others in school. 11

Even in the mental-health community, MTV has its defenders. Some of the videos have positive messages about racial harmony, for example. Dr. Jack Snyder, a child psychiatrist on the staff of the New York Medical College, believes Billy Joel's clip about teen suicide, "You're Only Human (Second Wind)," is useful because it helps children to come to grips with a painful subject. To Lifton, MTV represents a rebirth of the "protean style" he celebrated in the '60s—the healthy willingness to entertain new ways of looking at the world and adopt new values. 12

"It's at least a resurgence of experimentation," he says. "I'd want to investigate with an open mind the impact of MTV on the imagination."

STYLE SHIFT

The problem, such as it is, seems to be abating: most observers agree that MTV is getting tamer. According to MTV president Robert Pittman, that isn't the result of outside pressure; it simply represents a shift in musical styles. "Every year has its trend," he says. "Nineteen eighty-two was the year of New Wave, 1983 was the year of R&B, 1984 was the year of heavy metal, and 1985 has been the year of the superstars of the past dominating the channel." Pittman's explanation doesn't explain why superstars of the past make milder videos, however.   13

Music video stands as one more tribute to the power of television: TV has gobbled up entertainment, sports, news, and now music. For all the worry over television's impact, little has been done to alter its content. "There have been more than 3,000 studies linking violent programs with aggressive behavior, and all that work, all that energy hasn't made a damn bit of difference," says Strasburger. He thinks there is perhaps a more disturbing aspect of the MTV controversy: the willingness of parents to surrender their children to the tube. Parents applauded when "Sesame Street" used flashy images and razzle-dazzle techniques to enchant children; when those same techniques produce an MTV or "Miami Vice," they are appalled. But they don't want to take their kids away from the set.   14

Appalled or merely concerned, parents would do well to heed the advice of musician Frank Zappa, who told a Senate hearing on obscenity in rock lyrics: "I would say that a buzz-saw blade between the guy's legs on the album cover is a good indication that it's not for little Johnny." Parental supervision may be the sanest answer to any threat posed by music video. "Parents need to watch it with their children and not use it too much as a babysitter," says educator Davidson, who is the mother of an 11-year-old MTV fan. "At least have an ear out so you know what's going on." Television makes an easy scapegoat for the problems of adolescence or the failure of the family. But unlike many other potentially destructive influences, television sits right in the home; it is one of the few social scourges that parents can control directly. Ultimately, those who don't like what it's doing to their kids can resort to the most radical solution of all: turn it off.   15

▼ TOPICAL CONSIDERATIONS

1. According to this article, what are some of the specific differences between MTV and general television programming?
2. How is MTV potentially detrimental to child viewers, according to some critics?
3. What were some of the results of the studies on videos and their effects on

junior high viewers? How did economic factors possibly affect the results of the studies?

4. As far as the record industry is concerned, what is the purpose of MTV?
5. How does the article implicate parents in the MTV controversy?
6. What are your own feelings about MTV's messages? Do you think music videos are too violent and too sexually explicit? Do you think the effects are detrimental to young people? Have you felt any effects on you?

▼ RHETORICAL CONSIDERATIONS

1. Where is the thesis statement of this article?
2. A number of parents, specialists, and professionals have differing views on the effects of MTV on children. Does the article present a balance of views? Is there a consensus on the issue?
3. In the final paragraph, television is referred to as "an easy scapegoat." What is meant by this term? What, as stated in the article, is the relationship between MTV and television? How does the suggested "radical solution" reflect the opening paragraph and thus unify the essay?

▼ WRITING ASSIGNMENTS

1. Does MTV play a role in your life? Do you enjoy watching it? In an essay, give your opinions of MTV. Consider any effects it has had on you.
2. Write an essay in which you discuss the effects MTV might have on a susceptible viewer. Consider the influence on dress and behavior.
3. If you have access to MTV or other music video channels, write an analysis of a particular video and try to determine some of its "messages." Was it violent? Was there a sexual message? What were the roles of the males and females in it?

▼ WHY I QUIT WATCHING TELEVISION

P. J. O'Rourke

"Well, I was nuzzling her ear, making little kissy noises . . . Then, all of a sudden, I experienced one of those devastating realizations: She was watching a *Star Trek* rerun over my shoulder." So laments P. J. O'Rourke, recalling when he decided that he had had it with television. Television was dumb. It was a waste of time. It kept him from more worthwhile activities. But as the author discovered in this humorous little essay, the lack of a television has severe aftereffects. P. J. O'Rourke was the editor of the *National Lampoon* during the late 1970s. His work has since appeared in a variety of magazines. Currently, he is "investigative humorist" for *Rolling Stone.* The most recent collection of his essays is *Republican Party Reptile* (1987). This article first appeared in *Parade* magazine in December 1985.

I remember the exact moment I quit watching television. It was 10 years ago. I had   1
a girlfriend who was a compulsive viewer. We were at her apartment on a Sunday afternoon, sitting on the couch, and I was . . . Well, I was nuzzling her ear, making little kissy noises, and generally acting like a boyfriend. Then, all of a sudden, I experienced one of those devastating realizations: She was watching a *Star Trek* rerun over my shoulder.

We had a big fight. I'm still wondering where our relationship went wrong.   2
She's still wondering if Captain Kirk got beamed up in time to escape from the Klingons.

I was tired of watching television anyway. TV was too dumb. And TV was too   3
much trouble. Not too much trouble to watch, of course, but there was too much trouble on the screen. Every show seemed to be about murder, theft, car chases or adultery. I was living in Manhattan at the time, and if I wanted to see those things, I could look out my window. Even comedy shows like *M*A*S*H* were about people getting blown apart. I figured there was enough real tragedy every day. Why get four more hours of it on TV every night? I gave my television set away.

TV is such a waste of time, I thought. I never considered how else I'd fill my   4
evenings and weekends. It turns out there are worse things to do with time than waste it; more expensive things, anyway.

In my newfound leisure hours, I fixed up my apartment. This cost $12,000—$600   5
for the do-it-yourself remodeling and $11,400 for the carpenters, painters and plasterers to repair the damage I'd done. I also took up downhill skiing and paid $1500 for equipment when I probably could have gotten somebody to break my

leg for free. And I began to read. This sounds worthwhile, but anyone who worries about the lewdness and mayhem on TV ought to peek into *The Satyricon* by Petronius or *Gargantua and Pantagruel* by Rabelais or some Shakespeare plays or even the Old Testament. Most of my reading, though, wasn't quite so brainy. I read paperbacks like *Murder for Brunch.* It's hard to call these more intellectual than *The Gong Show.*

Without a TV set (and with a new girlfriend), I had time for conversation. But 6
a lot of conversations, if they go on long enough, turn into arguments. What's dumber—watching *Family Feud* or arguing about whether to get a TV so we *could* watch *Family Feud?*

Not having a TV is supposed to bring families closer together. I didn't have a 7
family, so this didn't help me.

Not having a TV turns out to be more strange than virtuous. I don't see any 8
trend-setting shows like *Miami Vice,* so I don't know what to wear. I still dress like John Cameron Swayze. Without TV advertising, I don't understand new consumer products. Styling mousse, for instance—is it edible? And since, as a spectator, I'm limited to home teams, I've lost interest in most professional sports. I'm honestly not sure what the Seattle Seagulls are. They may be a girls' field hockey team, for all I know. (Editor's note: They're the Sea*hawks* —a football team.)

People magazine, newspaper gossip columns and friends' conversations 9
are filled with names that mean nothing to me—"Prince," "Sting," "Peewee," "Appollonia." Sounds like a litter of puppies. And the celebrities I do recognize are mystifying. Imagine Mr. T completely out of *The A-Team* context: What kind of character could he possibly play?

Lack of a television set has more severe effects too. No TV means no VCR. 10
That is, I actually paid to see *Flashdance* and couldn't even fast-forward through the parts where Jennifer Beals has all her clothes on. Furthermore, I'm getting fat. When you don't have to wait for a commercial to get up and get a sandwich and a beer, you can get up and get a lot more beer and sandwiches.

So maybe television isn't so bad for us as it's supposed to be. To research this 11
story, I borrowed my next-door neighbor's TV—or, rather, I borrowed his whole TV room, since televisions are connected to cables now, so you can get 100 silly channels instead of five or six. I watched some shows at the start of the new season: *Hell Town, Hometown, Crazy Like a Fox, Stir Crazy,* etc. There were a few surprises. On MTV, I saw the video of a song I thought was a tender love ballad. It turns out to be sung by guys in leather underwear chasing a girl through a sewer.

But, mostly, television was just the same. It was kind of comforting to see 12
Johnny Carson again, a little grayer but with the same slack gags. Most of the shows are still violent, but I live in New Hampshire these days, and we don't have as much murder, theft or car-chasing (and not even as much adultery) as some might like. The shows are still dumb, but I'm 10 years older, and I've forgotten how perfect everything is in the television world. The people are all pretty. The pay phones all work. And all the endings are hopeful. That's not so bad. Most of us real people are a bit homely, and lots of our endings are hopeless. TV's perfect

world was a relief. So I was sitting, comfortable as a pig, in my neighbor's armchair, punching remote-control buttons with my snout.

But I didn't enjoy it. No, sir. Not me. I've spent a whole decade acting superior   13
to everybody because I don't watch television. I'm not about to back down and start liking it now. (Though I might drop in next door about 8 tonight. That's when *Amazing Stories* comes on.)

▼ TOPICAL CONSIDERATIONS

1. Why did O'Rourke quit watching television?
2. The author complains that after giving up television what he did to fill his time turned out to be worse. What were some of those things, and why were they worse than watching television?
3. According to O'Rourke, what are some of the drawbacks of not having a television?
4. What changes in television does the author discover after a ten-year hiatus? What has stayed the same? Why does he say the "shows are still dumb"?
5. This essay is satirical, of course. What is O'Rourke mainly satirizing here? What does he actually suggest is wrong with television?
6. In paragraph 12, O'Rourke mentions "how perfect everything is in the television world." Then, he adds "That's not so bad." How does television create an illusion of a perfect world? Do you agree that such an illusion is "not so bad"? Can that illusion of a perfect world create problems for viewers?

▼ RHETORICAL CONSIDERATIONS

1. One means of creating a humorous effect is irony. Find some examples of irony in this essay.
2. Consider the structure of this essay. Can you find a clear beginning, middle, and end? Where would you make the cuts, and why?
3. How well does the final paragraph illustrate the central point of this essay?

▼ WRITING ASSIGNMENTS

1. Could you ever stop watching television? Write an essay in which you explore this possibility. Could you live without it? What might you miss? What could you afford to miss? What would you do to fill your leisure time (be realistic)?
2. O'Rourke humorously suggests that his girlfriend's addiction to television helped break up their relationship. Write a paper in which you describe how people's lives are governed by television schedules and how television intrudes on relationships.

3. "No TV means no VCR." So says the author who complains that he actually had to pay to see the movie *Flashdance.* From your own perspective, what are the advantages and disadvantages of watching movies on VCRs instead of in movie houses? Do you think VCRs will be the death of movie houses?

4. O'Rourke says that coming back to TV after ten years he still finds the shows "dumb." Write a paper in which you talk about what's "dumb" about television. You might consider analyzing a particular show—its characters and situations, its treatment of the real world and real people, and its messages, both subtle and obvious.

5. O'Rourke also says, "Most of the shows are still violent." Write a paper about television violence, analyzing a particular show or series. Is the violence realistic? Is it overdone? Do you think the violence is damaging to viewers? Do you agree with Ellen Goodman's claim (see "The Violence Is Fake, the Impact Is Real" in this reader) that pain and suffering are missing from television violence?

▼ DON'T BLAME TV

Jeff Greenfield

Television has been indicted for nearly all our social ills—the rise in crime, increased divorce rate, lower voter turnout, falling SAT scores, the rise in sexual promiscuity, the collapse of family life. Indeed, television has been cited as the cause of the decline of Western Civilization. Now a word from the defense: Jeff Greenfield, a correspondent for ABC's "Nightline" and "Evening News" and a syndicated columnist. What follows is some criticism of the critics of television— or, more exactly, an attack on their knee-jerk assumptions that every American social and political ill can be blamed on television. This article first appeared in *TV Guide* in January 1986.

1   One of the enduring pieces of folk wisdom was uttered by the 19th-century humorist Artemus Ward, who warned his readers: "It ain't what you don't know that hurts you; it's what you know that just ain't so."

2   There's good advice in that warning to some of television's most vociferous critics, who are certain that every significant change in American social and political life can be traced, more or less directly, to the pervasive influence of TV.

3   It has been blamed for the decline of scores on scholastic achievement tests, for the rise in crime, for the decline in voter turnout, for the growth of premarital and extramarital sex, for the supposed collapse of family life and the increase in the divorce rate.

4   This is an understandable attitude. For one thing, television is the most visible, ubiquitous device to have entered our lives in the last 40 years. It is a medium in almost every American home, it is on in the average household some seven hours a day, and it is accessible by every kind of citizen from the most desperate of the poor to the wealthiest and most powerful among us.

5   If so pervasive a medium has come into our society in the last four decades, and if our society has changed in drastic ways in that same time, why not assume that TV is the reason why American life looks so different?

6   Well, as any philosopher can tell you, one good reason for skepticism is that you can't make assumptions about causes. They even have an impressive Latin phrase for that fallacy: *post hoc, ergo propter hoc.* For instance, if I do a rain dance at 5 P.M. and it rains at 6 P.M., did my dance bring down the rains? Probably not. But it's that kind of thinking, in my view, that characterizes much of the argument about how television influences our values.

7   It's perfectly clear, of course, that TV *does* influence some kinds of behavior. For example, back in 1954, *Disneyland* launched a series of episodes on the life of

Davy Crockett, the legendary Tennessee frontiersman. A song based on that series swept the hit parade, and by that summer every kid in America was wearing a coonskin cap.

The same phenomenon has happened whenever a character on a prime-time 8 television show suddenly strikes a chord in the country. Countless women tried to capture the Farrah Fawcett look a decade ago when *Charlie's Angels* first took flight. Schoolyards from Maine to California picked up—instantly, it seemed—on such catch phrases as "Up your nose with a rubber hose!" (*Welcome Back, Kotter*), "Kiss my grits!" (*Alice*) and "Nanu-nanu!" (*Mork & Mindy*). Today, every singles bar in the land is packed with young men in expensive white sports jackets and T-shirts, trying to emulate the macho looks of *Miami Vice's* Don Johnson.

These fads clearly show television's ability to influence matters that do not 9 matter very much. Yet, when we turn to genuinely important things, television's impact becomes a lot less clear.

Take, for example, the decline in academic excellence, measured by the 10 steady decline in Scholastic Aptitude Test scores from 1964 to 1982. It seemed perfectly logical to assume that a younger generation spending hours in front of the TV set every day with Fred Flintstone and Batman must have been suffering from brain atrophy. Yet, as writer David Owen noted in a recent book on educational testing, other equally impassioned explanations for the drop in scores included nuclear fallout, junk food, cigarette smoking by pregnant women, cold weather, declining church attendance, the draft, the assassination of President Kennedy and fluoridated water.

More significant, SAT scores stopped declining in 1982; they have been rising 11 since then. Is TV use declining in the typical American home? On the contrary, it is increasing. If we really believed that our societal values are determined by new media, we might conclude that the birth of MTV in 1981 somehow caused the test scores to rise.

Or consider the frequently heard charge that the increase in TV violence is 12 somehow responsible for the surge in crime. In fact, the crime rate nationally has been dropping for three straight years. It would be ludicrous to "credit" television for this; explanations are more likely to be found in the shift of population away from a "youth bulge" (where more crimes are committed) and improved tracking of career criminals in many big cities.

But why, then, ignore the demographic factors that saw in America an 13 enormous jump in teen-agers and young adults in the 1960s and 1970s? Why *assume* that television, with its inevitable "crime-does-not-pay" morality, some-how turned our young into hoodlums? The same kind of problem bedevils those who argue that TV has triggered a wave of sexually permissive behavior. In the first place, television was the most sexually conservative of all media through the first quarter-century of its existence. While Playboy began making a clean breast of things in the mid-1950s, when book censorship was all but abolished in the "Lady Chatterly's Lover" decision of 1958, when movies began showing it all in the 1960s, television remained an oasis—or desert—of twin beds, flannel nightgowns and squeaky-clean dialogue and characters.

In fact, as late as 1970, CBS refused to let Mary Tyler Moore's Mary Richards   14
character be a divorcee. The audience, they argued, would never accept it.
Instead, she was presented as the survivor of a broken relationship.

Why, then, do we see so many broken families and divorces on television   15
today? Because the networks are trying to denigrate the value of the nuclear
family? Hardly. As *The Cosby Show* and its imitators show, network TV is only
too happy to offer a benign view of loving husbands, wives and children.

The explanation, instead, lies in what was happening to the very fabric of   16
American life. In 1950, at the dawn of television, the divorce rate was 2.6 per 1000
Americans. By 1983, it had jumped to five per thousand; nearly half of all
marriages were ending in divorce. The reasons range from the increasing mobility
of the population to the undermining of settled patterns of work, family, and
neighborhood.

What's important to notice, however, is that it was not television that made   17
divorce more acceptable in American society; it was changes in American society
that made divorce more acceptable on television. (Which is why, in her new
sitcom, Mary Tyler Moore can finally play a divorced woman.) In the mid 1980s,
divorce has simply lost the power to shock.

That same argument, I think, undermines much of the fear that television has   18
caused our young to become sexually precocious. From my increasingly dimming
memory of youthful lust, I have my doubts about whether young lovers really need
the impetus of *Dallas* or *The Young and the Restless* to start thinking about sex.
The more serious answer, however, is that the spread of readily available birth
control was a lot more persuasive a force in encouraging premarital sex than the
words and images on TV.

We can measure this relative impotence of television in a different way. All   19
through the 1950s and early 1960s, the images of women on TV were what
feminists would call "negative"; they were portrayed as half-woman, half-child,
incapable of holding a job or balancing a checkbook or even running a social
evening. (How many times did Lucy burn the roast?) Yet the generation of women
who grew up on television was the first to reject forcefully the wife-and-homemaker
limitations that such images ought to have encouraged. These were the women
who marched into law schools, medical schools and the halls of Congress.

The same was true of the images of black Americans, as TV borrowed the   20
movie stereotypes of shiftless handymen and relentlessly cheerful maids. We
didn't begin to see TV blacks as the equal of whites until Bill Cosby showed up in
I Spy in 1966. Did the generation weaned on such fare turn out to be indifferent to
the cause of black freedom in America? Hardly. This was the generation that
organized and supported the civil-rights sit-ins and freedom rides in the South.
Somehow, the reality of second-class citizenship was far more powerful than the
imagery of dozens of television shows.

I have no argument with the idea that television contains many messages that   21
need close attention; I hold no brief for shows that pander to the appetite for
violence or smarmy sexuality or stereotyping. My point is that these evils ought to
be fought on grounds of taste and common decency. We ought not to try and

prove more than the facts will bear. Television, powerful as it is, has shown precious little power over the most fundamental values of Americans. Given most of what's on TV, that's probably a good thing. But it also suggests that the cries of alarm may be misplaced.

▼ TOPICAL CONSIDERATIONS

1. What are some of the social ills television has been blamed for, according to the author? Why?
2. What does Greenfield say is wrong with the thinking of those critical of television?
3. How does Greenfield counter the argument that television was the main cause of the decline in SAT scores from 1964 to 1982?
4. How does Greenfield answer the charges that television violence is responsible for the rise in crime rates?
5. How does Greenfield seek to refute the claim that television is to blame for the rise in sexual promiscuity?
6. How does Greenfield answer the charge that television is responsible for the increased divorce rate?
7. According to Greenfield, how has television affected the image of women and black Americans?

▼ RHETORICAL CONSIDERATIONS

1. How well does the Artemus Ward quotation in the opening paragraph establish Greenfield's line of argument?
2. Which of Greenfield's arguments seems the strongest and most convincing? Which seems the weakest and least convincing?
3. Paragraph 13 consists of two rhetorical questions. How effective are these questions in making Greenfield's point? Would straight statements have been more effective, given his argument?

▼ WRITING ASSIGNMENTS

1. Do you agree with Greenfield that television gets too much of the blame for our social problems? Using your own knowledge of television, write a paper in which you answer this question.
2. Do you disagree with any of Greenfield's views here? In other words, do you feel that television contributes to social problems such as violence, sexual promiscuity, the divorce rate, and the collapse of family life? Write a paper in which you explain your feelings.
3. At the end of his essay, Greenfield admits that "television contains many

messages that need close attention"—messages that "pander to the appetite for violence or smarmy sexuality or stereotyping." What problems of "taste and common decency" do you find with television? Specify by singling out certain shows.

ADVERTISING

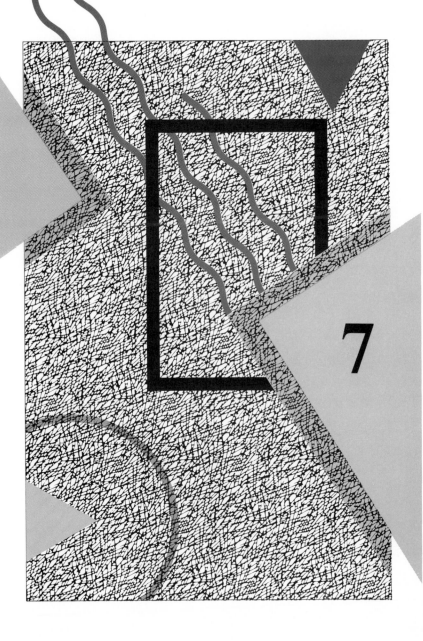

7

▼ IS EVERYBODY HAPPY?

John Ciardi

Advertising is the prime mover in our consumer society. It is also the creator and reflector—sometimes a distorted one—of the images and myths of ourselves. In this section, we will examine various aspects of advertising and some current magazine ads. We begin with an overview of how the forces of advertising manipulate not just our buying habits but our sense of values. Just open any magazine, suggests John Ciardi, and the message is as clear as the four-color spreads: happiness means possessing products whether we need them or not. Born in 1916, John Ciardi taught literature and writing at Harvard and Rutgers. He distinguished himself as a poet and essayist and for years served as poetry editor of *Saturday Review* magazine, writing a column for that magazine under the title "Manner of Speaking." His many publications include translations of Dante, collections of poems for both children and adults, and books on language and literature, including the classic *How Does a Poem Mean?* This article first appeared in "Manner of Speaking" in March 1964. Although individual ads may have changed over the years, the basic strategy and appeal of advertising remain unchanged.

1   The right to pursue happiness is issued to Americans with their birth certificates, but no one seems quite sure which way it ran. It may be we are issued a hunting license but offered no game. Jonathan Swift seemed to think so when he attacked the idea of happiness as "the possession of being well-deceived," the felicity of being "a fool among knaves." For Swift saw society as Vanity Fair, the land of false goals.

2   It is, of course, un-American to think in terms of fools and knaves. We do, however, seem to be dedicated to the idea of buying our way to happiness. We shall all have made it to Heaven when we possess enough.

3   And at the same time the forces of American commercialism are hugely dedicated to making us deliberately unhappy. Advertising is one of our major industries, and advertising exists not to satisfy desires but to create them— and to create them faster than any man's budget can satisfy them. For that matter, our whole economy is based on a dedicated insatiability. We are taught that to possess is to be happy, and then we are made to want. We are even told it is our duty to want. It was only a few years ago, to cite a single example, that car dealers across the country were flying banners that read "You Auto Buy Now." They were calling upon Americans, as an act approaching patriotism, to buy at once with money they did not have, automobiles they did not

really need, and which they would be required to grow tired of by the time the next year's models were released.

Or look at any of the women's magazines. There, as Bernard DeVoto once 4 pointed out, advertising begins as poetry in the front pages and ends as pharmacopoeia and therapy in the back pages. The poetry of the front matter is the dream of perfect beauty. This is the baby skin that must be hers. These, the flawless teeth. This, the perfumed breath she must exhale. This, the sixteen-year-old figure she must display at forty, at fifty, at sixty, and forever.

Once past the vaguely uplifting fiction and feature articles, the reader finds 5 the other face of the dream in the back matter. This is the harness into which Mother must strap herself in order to display that perfect figure. These, the chin straps she must sleep in. This is the salve that restores all, this is her laxative, these are the tablets that melt away fat, these are the hormones of perpetual youth, these are the stockings that hide varicose veins.

Obviously no half-sane person can be completely persuaded either by such 6 poetry or by such pharmacopoeia and orthopedics. Yet someone is obviously trying to buy the dream as offered and spending billions every year in the attempt. Clearly the happiness market is not running out of customers, but what are we trying to buy?

The idea "happiness," to be sure, will not sit still for easy definition: the best 7 one can do is to try to set some extremes to the idea and then work in toward the middle. To think of happiness as acquisitive and competitive will do to set the materialistic extreme. To think of it as the idea one senses in, say, a holy man of India will do to set the spiritual extreme. That holy man's ideal of happiness is in needing nothing from outside himself. In wanting nothing, he lacks nothing. He sits immobile, rapt in contemplation, free even of his own body. Or nearly free of it. If devout admirers bring him food he eats it; if not, he starves indifferently. Why be concerned? What is physical is an illusion to him. Contemplation is his joy and he achieves it through a fantastically demanding discipline, the accomplishment of which is itself a joy within him.

Is he a happy man? Perhaps his happiness is only another sort of illusion. But 8 who can take it from him? And who will dare say it is more illusory than happiness on the installment plan?

But, perhaps because I am Western, I doubt such catatonic happiness, as I 9 doubt the dreams of the happiness market. What is certain is that his way of happiness would be torture to almost any Western man. Yet these extremes will still serve to frame the area within which all of us must find some sort of balance. Thoreau—a creature of both Eastern and Western thought—had his own firm sense of that balance. His aim was to save on the low levels in order to spend on the high.

Possession for its own sake or in competition with the rest of the neighbor- 10 hood would have been Thoreau's idea of the low levels. The active discipline of heightening one's perception of what is enduring in nature would have been his idea of the high. What he saved from the low was time and effort he could spend on the high. Thoreau certainly disapproved of starvation, but he would put into feeding himself only as much effort as would keep him functioning for more important efforts.

Effort is the gist of it. There is no happiness except as we take on life-engaging 11 difficulties. Short of the impossible, as Yeats put it, the satisfactions we get from a lifetime depend on how high we choose our difficulties. Robert Frost was thinking in something like the same terms when he spoke of "the pleasure of taking pains." The mortal flaw in the advertised version of happiness is in the fact that it purports to be effortless.

We demand difficulty even in our games. We demand it because without 12 difficulty there can be no game. A game is a way of making something hard for the fun of it. The rules of the game are an arbitrary imposition of difficulty. When the spoilsport ruins the fun, he always does so by refusing to play by the rules. It is easier to win at chess if you are free, at your pleasure, to change the wholly arbitrary rules, but the fun is in winning within the rules. No difficulty, no fun.

The buyers and sellers at the happiness market seem too often to have lost 13 their sense of the pleasure of difficulty. Heaven knows what they are playing but it seems a dull game. The Indian holy man seems dull to us, I suppose, because he seems to be refusing to play anything at all. The Western weakness may be in the illustration that happiness can be bought. Perhaps the Eastern weakness is in the idea that there is such a thing as perfect (and therefore static) happiness.

Happiness is never more than partial. There are no pure states of mankind. 14 Whatever else happiness may be, it is neither in having nor in being, but in becoming. What the Founding Fathers declared for us as an inherent right, we should do well to remember, was not happiness but the *pursuit* of happiness. What they might have underlined, could they have foreseen the happiness market, is the cardinal fact that happiness is in the pursuit itself, in the meaningful pursuit of what is life-engaging and life-revealing, which is to say, in the idea of *becoming*. A nation is not measured by what it possesses or wants to possess, but by what it wants to become.

By all means let the happiness market sell us minor satisfactions and even 15 minor follies so long as we keep them in scale and buy them out of spiritual change. I am no customer for either puritanism or asceticism. But drop any real spiritual capital at those bazaars, and what you come home to will be your own poorhouse.

▼ TOPICAL CONSIDERATIONS

1. In paragraph 2, Ciardi says that we Americans "seem to be dedicated to the idea of buying our way to happiness." What does he mean by this claim? Do you agree with him?
2. How does the advertising industry deliberately try to make the consumer feel "unhappy"?
3. What, according to the author, is the organizational strategy of advertising in women's magazines? Can you document this strategy with current issues

of women's magazines? Do you see similar strategies of "happiness" regarding the advertising arrangement in men's magazines?

4. What point is Ciardi making in his reference to the Indian holy man in paragraph 7?

5. Ciardi says that "effort is the gist of" happiness. What does he mean by this? Can you think of any examples of "effort" making you happy? What "effort" does advertising pose to the consumer?

6. What is Ciardi's definition of "happiness"?

▼ RHETORICAL CONSIDERATIONS

1. "Is Everybody Happy?" is the title of this essay throughout which Ciardi offers an extended definition. What is the strategy of building up to a definition of "happiness"? Where exactly does he offer a definition of happiness?

2. Ciardi opens up his discussion with a reminder of the declared rights of our Founding Fathers. How effective is this as an opener and how does he build upon the idea in the essay?

▼ WRITING ASSIGNMENTS

1. Ciardi takes an abstract notion such as "happiness" and defines it by citing familiar experiences from daily life. Do the same with another abstract concept. Consider, for instance, the idea of "frustration" in our fast-paced world. Consider some other abstract concepts such as: "manners," "self-satisfaction," "friendship," or "relaxation."

2. Select a women's magazine and analyze it according to the way its advertising presents the dreams of happiness. Consider the particular ads at the beginning, middle, and end. Do you see the pattern to which Ciardi remarks?

3. Do the same as above, but with a men's magazine.

4. Select a particular "poetry" ad or "pharmacopoeia and orthopedics" ad from a magazine and analyze it. To what fantasies and promises, fears and distress do they appeal? What specific devices—language, images, "guarantees," etc.—are employed to compel the reader to buy the product?

4. Consider the effects of advertising on you. Select a particular commercial or magazine ad. Does the presentation make you want to have the product? Why and how? What "happiness" is promised here? Do you feel the threat of unhappiness at not owning the product? Do you feel the threat of unhappiness at not being able to afford it?

5. Do you know anybody who is addicted to buying? Describe that person and his or her need to find happiness in commercial consumption.

6. "A nation is not measured by what it possesses or wants to possess, but by what it wants to become." So writes John Ciardi at the end of paragraph 14. This statement can also be applied to individuals. Write an essay in which you discuss the measurement of a person not by what he or she possesses, but by what he or she wants to become.

▼ ADVERTISING

Andy Rooney

Here is a wry and reasonable complaint about one basic fact about advertising: it's everywhere. Not just where it's suppose to be, such as in magazines and on billboards, but on license plates, luggage, and underpants! This piece is written with the dry, rueful humor and down-home common sense that is characteristic of Andy Rooney. Since 1978, he has delighted millions of people with his observations of everyday life on CBS–TV's *60 Minutes.* In addition to his television work, Rooney writes a syndicated column three days a week. The following is from one of his several collections of essays, *A Few Minutes with Andy Rooney* (1982).

1 My grandfather told me when I was a small boy that if a product was any good, they shouldn't have to advertise it.

2 I believed my grandfather at the time, but then years later my mother said that when *she* was a little girl he had told her that they'd never be able to build an automobile that would go up a hill. So I never knew whether to believe my grandfather or not.

3 Like so many things, I've really never made up my mind about advertising. I know all the arguments for it and against it, but the one thing I'm sure of is that there ought to be some sanctuaries, some places we're safe from being advertised at. There ought to be some open space left in the world without any advertising on it, some pieces of paper, some painted surfaces that aren't covered with entreaties for us to buy something.

4 Advertising doesn't belong on license plates, for instance. Of the fifty states, twenty-seven of them have slogans trying to sell themselves to the rest of us. It's offensive and wrong. The license plate has an important function and it's a cheap trick to tack something else on it. Most of the legends the states put on aren't true anyway.

5 Rhode Island, for instance, says it's the "Ocean State." There are fifteen states with more ocean than Rhode Island has. If they want to say something on their plate, why don't they explain why they call Rhode an island when it isn't one?

6 Florida says it's the "Sunshine State." I like Florida, but why don't they also say that Miami has more rain than any city in the whole United States except for Mobile, Alabama?

7 North Carolina says it's "First in Freedom." It doesn't say anywhere on the license plate who they think is *second* in freedom. South Carolina? Michigan?

8 Connecticut says it's the "Constitution State." I called the license bureau in

Connecticut and no one there could tell me why they call it the Constitution State. Connecticut is not the Constitution state, of course. *Pennsylvania* is the Constitution state. And Pennsylvania calls itself the "Keystone State." Does anyone really care?

Maine says it's "Vacationland." How would you like to drive a garbage truck   9
for eight hours in Augusta with a sign hanging on the back that says "Vacationland"?

New Hampshire plates carry the pretentious legend "Live Free or Die." Some   10
religious organization that apparently wasn't willing to die if they couldn't be free objected and taped over those words on all their license plates. The state said this was illegal and the case went to the Supreme Court. The Court ruled that the religious order did have the right to block out those words. New Hampshire would have saved us all a lot of time and money if they'd never put them on in the first place.

New Mexico calls itself "Land of Enchantment." This is not the kind of slogan   11
that gets the work of the world done.

Hawaii says it's the "Aloha State." Hawaii ought to get over its palm-tree   12
mentality and removing "Aloha" from its plates would be a good start. What sensible state would want to conjure up a picture of dancing girls draping flower ropes over the necks of visitors every time anyone thought about it?

Wisconsin "America's Dairyland"? Never mind that, Wisconsin, if you're   13
dairyland why don't you tell us on your license plates what ever happened to heavy cream? That's the kind of stuff we'd like to read about when we're driving along behind a car from your state.

And then Idaho. How would you like to work hard, save your money and   14
decide, when the kids were educated and the house paid for, to buy yourself a Mercedes-Benz. You plunk down your $28,000, the dealer screws on the license plate and there you are with your dream car; you drive away, and affixed to the bumper is the sign that says "Famous Potatoes."

"If a state is any good," I imagine my grandfather would have said, "it   15
shouldn't have to advertise."

License-plate advertising is a small part of what we're faced with when we're   16
driving. On the highways, trucks are turned into rolling billboards. The companies that own them look on it as easy advertising, too cheap to pass up. On major highways the commercials come along more often than on a late-night television movie.

On city streets, the billboards on Coca-Cola and Pepsi trucks are often   17
double-parked while the driver makes deliveries. In most cities now, taxis and buses carry advertising. When you're paying a buck and a half a mile, you shouldn't have to carry a sign pushing cigarettes.

In California there's a company called Beetleboards. What Beetleboards will   18
do for you is paint your Volkswagen, apply a commercial motif from a sponsor who is paying them and pay you twenty dollars a month to drive around in it.

And if you can understand businesses advertising their products on our roads,   19
how do you account for the private citizens who use the back end of their cars to tell us about themselves or about some private campaign of theirs? A typical car

or van in a parking lot outside a tourist attraction in Washington, D.C., will announce, through the decals attached to it somewhere, that the owner is insured by Allstate, boosts the Northern Virginia Ramparts—a team of some sort, I guess—is against forest fires because he has a little Smokey the Bear stuck to his car, gives to the International Convention of Police Chiefs and believes in God because his bumper sticker tells us so.

If someone has to take pride in having people know what insurance company gets his money, he's in trouble for things to be proud of. 20

A third of the cars on the road have reading matter stuck to them somewhere trying to sell the rest of us a place, an opinion or a way of life. Sometimes it looks as though half the cars in the United States have been to a roadside stand in South Carolina called South of the Border, and for some reason the entrepreneurs who have made tourist attractions out of caves love to slap "Visit Secret Caverns" on visitors' bumpers. 21

One of the most incredible commercial coups of the century has been pulled off by the designers who have conned women into thinking it's chic to wear a piece of apparel on which the maker's name is imprinted as part of the design. 22

The French luggage maker Louis Vuitton may have started the trend when he made the brown LV the only design on his product, but the women's fashion designers have taken it over. Bill Blass makes towels with his name all over them. Why would anyone want to take a shower and buff themselves dry on a piece of cloth bearing Bill Blass's name? Why would a woman go around with the name "Bloomies" on the seat of her underpants? Is there something I don't understand here? 23

Why would I or anyone else want to lay me down to sleep with my head on a pillowcase embossed with the signature of Yves Saint Laurent? 24

The first time I remember seeing a designer's name on something, the name was Pucci. It seemed amusing enough but now they're all doing it. Halston, Calvin Klein and Diane Von Furstenberg must all be wonderfully famous and talented, but if I buy anything of theirs I'd prefer to have it anonymous. If I got a scarf with Diane Von Furstenberg's name on it, which is unlikely, my first inclination would be to send it out to the cleaners to have them try to get it out. 25

The advertisers are coming at us from all directions all the time. If we were deer, a closed season would be declared on us to protect an endangered species. It just seems wrong to me that we're spending more time and money trying to sell some things than we are making them in the first place. I'm an all-American consumer but there are just certain times and places I don't want to be sold anything. 26

▼ TOPICAL CONSIDERATIONS

1. According to Andy Rooney, in what ways do license plates falsely advertise their states? In what ways are they silly advertisements? Do you think Rooney is making a lot out of nothing? Is he just being humorous, or is he making some valid points?

2. What are your views about advertising on license plates?
3. How does Rooney feel about people who put bumper stickers and decals on their cars?
4. Why is Rooney most offended by designer towels and clothes that display the designers' names? Would you buy an Yves Saint Laurent pillowcase? Why, or why not?
5. Summarize Rooney's stand in this essay.

▼ RHETORICAL CONSIDERATIONS

1. How does Rooney use his grandfather's wisdom at the beginning of this piece? How does it work throughout?
2. What is the thesis statement of this essay? Where is it? Does the author stick to this thesis throughout?
3. Which of Rooney's complaints are more tongue-in-cheek than serious? Identify the serious criticisms against advertising?
4. How effective is Rooney's metaphor of the "endangered species" in his last paragraph?

▼ WRITING ASSIGNMENTS

1. Rooney mentions that a third of the cars on the roads have some form of reading matter on them—decals, bumperstickers, ads. The next time you're on the road, make note of the kinds of reading material on particular cars. Try to classify the kinds of material and slogans; then attempt to draw up a portrait of the person or persons in the cars, based on what they advertise about themselves. What kinds of self-images do they want to portray?
2. Do you agree with Andy Rooney that there is just too much advertising in our lives? If so, write your own response to advertising. Do you find it nearly impossible to avoid ads and commercials?

▼ THE LANGUAGE OF ADVERTISING

Charles A. O'Neill

The language of advertising is very special. Charming and seductive, it is a language calculated to separate consumers from their money. Charles O'Neill has been a professional advertising writer for many years. In this essay, he explains just what advertising language does and how it does it. He examines some familiar television commercials and magazine ads and explains their continued prominence in these media. While admitting to some of the craftiness of his profession, O'Neill defends advertising language against critics who see it as a distorter of language and reality. This essay, which first appeared in *Exploring Language* (1977) by Gary Goshgarian, has been updated for this edition of this text.

One night in 1964, a copywriter named Shirley Polykoff was pacing around her 1
office, thinking about Clairol's new hair coloring, Nice 'n Easy. The interesting,
"saleable" thing about Nice 'n Easy—important to Clairol, to the advertising
agency, and (at least potentially) to the hair color-using public—was its basic
difference from other hair colorings. Until the day Clairol put Nice 'n Easy
on the market, a woman who wanted to dye her hair had to put the dye onto every
strand. Coloring the older, longer hairs sometimes meant missing the roots.
The result was an interesting, but somewhat less than fashionable, horizontal-
striped look. New Nice 'n Easy, however, could be shampooed right through
the hair, producing what Miss Polykoff calls that "beautiful, even, natural-
looking color."

But that night, Shirley Polykoff's problem was to translate the product feature 2
into a benefit consumers could feel; she had to translate the idea of even coloring
into a memorable, potent and attractive advertisement. As she remembers it, this
is what happened:

> My mind wandered back to those early days when George and I used to
> meet each other after work and I'd spend the afternoon anticipating the
> rush of joy when I'd first glimpse him coming down the block. We'd be
> flying toward each other, but, compared to our eagerness to bridge the
> distance, it was like wading through molasses.
>
> Though the street was crowded, we were alone, the people in our
> path merely obstacles to cut around. On about the fourth time we met this
> way, he lifted me off my feet with a hug of sheer happiness. We were both

a little breathless and as we stood there grinning at each other he said, "You know, you look pretty good from afar."

"And from near?"

"Even better."*

To anyone but Shirley Polykoff, that brief romantic reverie would probably 3 have been nothing more than a pleasant distraction, but way back in her mind, she was still thinking about Nice 'n Easy.

As I sat there recalling those delicious days, the campaign for Nice 'n Easy shampoo-in hair color unfolded like a dream. And, as if in a dream, the man and woman in the commercial would float toward each other in slow motion across fields or through crowds with arms outstretched in anticipation. Though the message would have to express to the consumer that the color results would be even enough to pass closest inspection, it would have to capture the romance of the visual. And that is how I hit on the line, *The closer he gets . . . the better you look! With Nice 'n Easy, it's hair color so natural, the closer he gets the better you look?*†

Clairol found the concept appealing, and Nice 'n Easy sales proved that Polykoff 4 had indeed touched something deep in the psyche of the public. The campaign had immediate, lasting impact: across America, women who had feared that telltale, horizontal-striped, less than convincing look changed their minds and bought Nice 'n Easy. In the media-advertising business, as elsewhere, imitation is the sincerest form of flattery. Suddenly, everybody who made television commercials wanted to show slim, long-haired women running in slow motion across sunlit fields.

Through a carefully chosen combination of visual images and spoken words, 5 one small group of human beings had caused a larger group to take a specific, desired course of action. When Polykoff conceived "The closer he gets . . . the better you look!" she set in motion a sequence of events that changed the buying habits of millions of people. Those who had previously bought other brands of hair-color products now switched to Nice 'n Easy; others who had never thought much about coloring their hair now felt an impulse to do so. Creating the impulse to *buy* is the reason for advertising. The final test of any advertising program (whether for hair color, automobiles, detergents, cereals, life insurance, or pantyhose) is simply the degree to which it creates that impulse.

What creates the impulse? The strategy may call for ads in magazines, 6 30-second spots on national television, newspaper inserts, T-shirts, town criers or music videos. Whatever the strategy, advertisements derive their power from a purposeful, directed combination of images. Images can take several forms: words—spoken or written—or visuals; or, most powerfully, a combination of the two. The precise formula is determined by the creative concept and the medium chosen. The combination is the language of advertising.

*Shirley Polykoff, *Does She . . . or Doesn't She?* (Garden City, New York: Doubleday, 1975), pp. 98–99.

†Ibid., p. 99.

Every member of our society soon learns that advertising language is different   7
from other languages. Most children would be unable to explain how "With Nice
'n Easy, it's color so natural, the closer he gets the better you look!" differed from
ordinary language; but they *would* be able to tell you, "It sounds like an ad."
Advertising language is different from most of the other languages we use in our
everyday lives. Its differences exist because when Polykoff sits down to write an
ad, she is attempting to change our behavior, to motivate us, to sell us something.

Over the years, the texture of advertising language has frequently changed.   8
Styles and creative concepts come and go. But there are at least four distinct
general characteristics of the language of advertising that make it different from
other languages.

1. The language of advertising is edited and purposeful.
2. The language of advertising is rich and arresting; it is specifically intended to
   attract and hold our attention.
3. The language of advertising involves us; in effect, *we* complete the message.
4 The language of advertising holds no secrets from us; it is a simple language.

EDITED AND PURPOSEFUL

One easy way to develop a feeling for basic differences between advertising   9
language and other languages is to transcribe a television talk show.* An examination of such a transcript will show the conversation skipping from one topic to
another, even though the guest and the host may attempt to stick to a specific
subject. The conversation also is rife with repetition. After all, informal, conversational language transactions are not ordinarily intended to meet specific objectives.
Advertising language cannot afford to be so desultory. It *does* have a specific
purpose—to sell us something.

In *Future Shock,* Alvin Toffler draws a distinction between normal "coded"   10
messages and "engineered" messages. As an example of an uncoded message,
Toffler writes about a random, unstructured experience:

> A man walks along a street and notices a leaf whipped along a sidewalk by
> the wind. He perceives this event through his sensory apparatus. He hears
> a rustling sound. He sees movement and greenness. He feels the wind.
> From these sensory perceptions he somehow forms a mental image. We
> can refer to these sensory signals as a message. But the message is not, in
> any ordinary sense of [the] term, man-made. It is not designed by anyone
> to communicate anything, and the man's understanding of it does not
> depend directly on a social code—a set of agreed-upon signs and
> definitions.†

---

*The dialogue on a television talk show provides a good example of free-form, unstructured speech.
An even better example is a casual conversation about an innocuous topic like the weather.
†Alvin Toffler, *Future Shock* (New York: Random House, 1970), p. 146.

The talk show conversation, however, is coded; the guests' ability to exchange   11
information with their host, and our ability to understand it, depend, as Toffler
puts it, upon social conventions.

Beyond coded and uncoded messages there is another kind—the engineered   12
message—a variation of the coded message. The language of advertising is a
language of finely engineered, ruthlessly purposeful messages. By Toffler's
calculation,* the average adult American is assaulted by at least 560 advertising
messages a day. Not one of these messages would reach us, to attract and hold our
attention, if it were uncoded or completely unstructured. Similarly, even if they
happened to attract us for a fleeting moment, coded but unengineered messages
(for example, the conversation of talk show guests chatting about Nice 'n Easy)
would quickly lose our attention. But when a woman runs through the field in slow
motion and a voice says, "The closer he gets,... the better you look!" viewers
who are looking for a hair color product pay attention, because the message has
been carefully engineered, carefully compressed. Advertising messages have a
clear purpose; they are intended to trigger a specific response.

RICH AND ARRESTING

Advertisements—no matter how carefully "engineered" and packed with informa-   13
tion—cannot succeed unless they capture our attention in the first place. Of the
hundreds of advertising messages in store for us each day, very few (Toffler
estimates seventy-six) will actually obtain our conscious attention.† The rest are
screened out. The people who design and write ads know about this screening
process; they anticipate and accept it as a basic premise of their business. They
expend a great deal of energy to guarantee that their ads will make it past the
defenses and distractions that surround us. The classic, all-time favorite device used
to penetrate the barrier is sex. The archetypal sex ad is simply headlined "SEX"
with the text running something like this: "Now that we've got your attention...."
Whether it takes this approach or another, every successful advertisement contains
a "hook." The hook can take the form of strong visuals (photos or illustrations with
emotional value) or a disarming, unexpected—even incongruous —set of words:

"My chickens eat better than you do."	(Perdue Chickens)
"Introducing the ultimate concept in air freight. Men that fly."	(Emery Air Freight)
"Look deep into our ryes."	(Wigler's bakery products)
"Me. 4 U."	(The State of Maine)
"If gas pains persist, try Volkswagen."	(Volkswagen)

Even if the text contains no incongruity and does not rely on a pun for its   14
impact, every effective ad needs a creative strategy based on some striking concept

*Ibid., p. 149.
†Ibid.

or idea. In fact, the concept and execution are often so good that many successful ads entertain while they sell.

For examples of ads where salesmanship and good ideas combine to achieve memorable results, consider the campaigns created by Ally and Gargano for Federal Express. By 1982, the company's initial campaign ("When it absolutely, positively has to get there overnight") was five years old. Other competitors had entered the market, and a new twist was developed to position Federal Express as the company that would deliver packages, not just "overnight," but "by 10:30 A.M." the next day. The plight of the junior executive in "Presentation," one ad in the new campaign, is stretched for dramatic purposes, but it is, nonetheless, all too real: the young executive, who is presumably trying to climb his way up the corporate ladder, is shown calling another parcel delivery service and all but begging for assurance that he will have his slides in hand by 10:30 the next morning. "No slides, no presentation," he pleads. Only a viewer with a heart of stone can watch without feeling sympathetic, as the next morning our junior executive struggles to make his presentation *sans* slides. He is so lost without them that he is reduced to using his hands to perform imitations of birds and animals in shadows on the movie screen. What does the junior executive *viewer* think when he or she sees this ad? 15

1. Federal Express guarantees to deliver packages "absolutely, positively overnight."
2. Federal Express packages arrive early in the day.
3. What happened to that fellow in the commercial will absolutely not happen to me, now that I know what package delivery service to call.

A sound creative strategy, well executed, sells the service offered by Federal Express.

Soft drink and fast food companies often take another common approach. "Slice of life" ads (so-called because they purport to provide glimpses of people in "real life" situations), replete with beautiful babies frolicking at family picnics or Fourth of July parades, seduce us into thinking that if we drink the right beverage or eat the right hamburger, we'll fulfill our deep yearning for a world where old folks and young folks live together in perfect suburban bliss. Such ads are often deliberately designed to bring a lump to the viewer's throat. 16

Lifestyle—and the natural affiliation of a particular lifestyle with a product— has also been used effectively as an advertising strategy for other types of merchandise. This TV spot for Levi's Corduroys was produced by Foote, Cone & Belding (1985): 17

Music up. (Open on quick shot of saxophone player.
Cut to man at sink drying his face with a towel.
   Reflection seen in mirror.)
Male singer: Gotta be there at eight. Gotta luminate.
(Cut to two women at a table in a 24-hour diner. A man tries to coax
   them.)
Male singer: Got to be lookin' much better than great.

(Cut to man and woman walking down the street.)

Male singer: Grab a flash of color, add a little more style . . .

(Cut to shot of two different women at a table. Man does a quick turn landing on a chair. He laughs. The women get up to leave.)

Male singer: . . . Looks like Levi's Corduroy night.

(Cut to shot of large neon sign "Levi's Cords Tonite.")

Male Singer with Group Singers: Levi's Corduroy night.

(Cut back to last man on chair. He shrugs.)

Male Singer: Lookin' good . . .

(Quick cut to neon sign. Camera pulls back.)

Male Singer with Group Singers: It's a Levi's Corduroy night.

(Cut to two women at phone booth. One is talking on phone, other waits impatiently.)

Male Singer: Looks like it's gonna be another Levi's Corduroy night/ Levi's . . .

(Cut back to first man at the mirror. He taps the mirror and walks away.)

Group Singers: Corduroy night.

Super: Levi's batwing. Quality never goes out of style.

Music fade out.

This ad doesn't appeal to everyone, and that's just the point. It *will* appeal to 18
the young people identified by Levi's marketing research as the prime target market for the product. The ad encourages the viewer to make a connection: "I'm a flexible, luminous, streetwise kind of guy, just like the man at the mirror. Levi's Corduroys are o.k. Better buy some soon."

The prominence of ads containing puns or cleverly constructed headlines 19
would seem to suggest that ads emerge, like Botticelli's Venus from the sea, flawless and full grown. Usually they do not. The idea that becomes the platform for an effective creative strategy is most often developed only after exhaustive research. The product is examined for its potential, and the prospective buyers are examined for their habits, characteristics and preferences.

"Who will be interested in our product? How old are they? Where do 20
they live? How much money do they earn? What problem will our product solve?" Once an advertising writer has a sense of the answers to these questions, information from other sources can be drawn on to develop the creative strategy.

The creative people in the advertising business are well aware that consumers 21
do not watch television or read magazines in order to see ads. Ads have to earn the right to be seen, read and heard. Jerry Della Femina, a man who earns a good living in the advertising business, sums up the problem:

There are a lot of copywriters who get mixed up and think they're Faulkner or Hemingway. They sit there and they mold and they play and when it's over they've written something that's absolutely beautiful but they forgot one thing. It's within the confines of a page. . . . What kills most copywriters is that people don't buy *Life* magazine to read their ads. People don't buy *Gourmet* to read their ad for Bombay Gin. People are buying *Gourmet* to read the recipes, and the ads are just an intrusion on people's time. That is why our job is to get more attention than anything else.*

INVOLVING

We have seen that the language of advertising is carefully engineered; we have seen that it uses various devices to get our attention. Clairol has us watching the young woman running across a field in slow motion. Frank Perdue has us looking at a photo of his chickens at a dinner table. Now that they have our attention, advertisers present information intended to show us that the product they are offering for sale fills a need and, in filling this need, differs from the competition. The process is called "product positioning." On the night she developed the central idea of the Nice 'n Easy campaign, Polykoff's problem was to express the differences between the Clairol product and its competitors. Nice 'n Easy *was* different. Its feature was that it could be shampooed through the hair. To the consumer, the benefit was that it did not cause telltale streaks. Once our attention has been captured, it is the copywriter's responsibility to express such product differences and to exploit and intensify them.   22

What happens when product differences do not exist? Then the writer must glamorize the superficial differences (for example, differences of color, packaging, or other qualities without direct bearing on the product's basic function) or else *create* differences. It is at this stage that we, the consumers, are brought most directly into the process. As long as the ad is trying to get our attention, the "action" is mostly in the ad itself, in the words and visual images. But as we read an ad or watch it on television, we become more deeply involved. The action starts to take place in *us.* Our imagination is set in motion, and our individual fears and aspirations, our little quirks and insecurities, superimpose themselves on that tightly engineered, attractively packaged message. Polykoff did not create the consumers' need to feel attractive "up close." The drive to feel attractive was already there; she merely exploited and intensified it.   23

So the language of advertising is different from other languages because it holds up a brightly lit mirror. Once we have been brought into an ad we become participants.   24

This process is especially significant in ads for products that do not differ significantly from their competitors. The running battle among the low-calorie soft drinks, for example, has spawned many "look-alike" advertisements, because the product features and consumer benefits are generic, applying to all products in the category. Substitute one product name for another, and the messages are   25

*Jerry Della Femina, *From Those Wonderful Folks Who Brought You Pearl Harbor* (New York: Simon and Schuster, 1970), p. 118.

often identical, right down to the way the cans are photographed in the closing sequence. Such commercials may sell a particular product, but they don't always lead to lasting results. As with all advertising, the challenge to marketers of low-calorie soft drinks is to find or create differences which set their product apart from its competitors. BBDO's solution for Diet Pepsi relied on crisp, striking visuals and well-paced music with lyrics that do not disguise what the product is for—it's for people who want to have lean, perfect bodies.

> Singers: *Now you see it*
> *Now you don't*
> *Here you have it*
> *Here you won't*
> *Oh Diet Pepsi*
> *One small calorie*
> *Now you see it*
> *Now you don't.*
> *That great Pepsi taste*
> *Diet Pepsi*
> *Won't go to your waist*
> *So now you see it*
> *Now you don't.*
> *Oh Diet Pepsi one small calorie*
> *Now you see it*
> *Now you don't.*

Quick cuts show a man and woman in poses intended to display their bodies (what else?) to best advantage. The commercial is designed to build in our minds an association between the people and the product. Even if we make a conscious effort to reject that association, we will remember the Diet Pepsi woman and the Diet Pepsi man, and the Diet Pepsi messages we see in the future will trigger the memory.

Symbols have become important elements in the language of advertising, not   26 so much because they carry meanings of their own but because we bring a meaning to them: we charge them with significance. Symbols are efficient, compact vehicles for the communication of an advertising message. As Toffler says:

> Today, advertising men, in a deliberate attempt to cram more messages into the individual's mind within a given moment of time, make increasing use of the symbolic techniques of the arts. Consider the "tiger" that is allegedly put into one's tank. Here a single word transmits to the audience a distinct visual image that has been associated since childhood with power, speed, and force.*

Federal Trade Commission regulations are making it increasingly difficult for   27 oil companies to say they put anything into the tank but fuel. But symbolism is, nonetheless, pervasive and powerful.

*Toffler, *Future Shock,* p. 149.

One example of a particularly effective use of symbolism is the campaign 28
begun in 1978 by Somerset Importers for Johnnie Walker Red Scotch. Sales of
Johnnie Walker Red had been trailing sales of Johnnie Walker Black, and Somerset Importers needed to position Red as a fine product in its own right. The
Smith/Greenland Agency produced ads which made heavy use of the color red.
One ad, often printed as a two-page spread, is dominated by a close-up photo of
red autumn leaves. At lower right, the copy reads, "When their work is done, even
the leaves turn to red." Another ad—also suitably dominated by a photograph in
the appropriate color—reads: "When it's time to quiet down at the end of the day,
even a fire turns to Red." *Red.* Warm. Experienced. Bright. A perfect symbol to
use in a liquor advertisement; all the more for the fact that it offers great
possibilities for graphic design and copywriting: more fuel for the advertiser's
creative art.

The reference to the tiger in the tank and the use of the color red are 29
variations on the same theme. The tiger and the color are tangible; the advertiser
makes no effort to disguise them as symbols. They appear on the surface.

From time to time a more abstract form of symbolism is also used—the 30
"hidden message" symbol. Take a close, hard look at liquor ads and occasionally
you will see, reflected in the photograph of a glass of spirits, peculiar, demon-like
shapes. Are these shapes merely the product of one consumer's imagination or an
accident of photography? Or were they deliberately superimposed onto the product photograph by the careful application of ink and airbrush?

The art of advertising contains many such ambiguities. Some are charged, like 31
this one, with multiple shades of meaning. The demons may be taken to represent
the problems and cares which one can presumably chase away through consumption of the advertised product. Or they can, just as easily, be taken as representa-
tions of the playful spirits which will be unleashed once the product has been
consumed. What *did* the advertising director have in mind?

Not all the symbols of advertising are innocent. Examples abound. Demonic 32
shapes look positively innocent compared to some of the images commonly
used in advertising. Magazine ads appearing in 1985-1986 to promote Georges
Marciano clothing (copyright Guess?, Inc.) are, in a peculiar way, "lifestyle" ads in
the sense that they associate the product with a particular, presumably desired
way of life.

A two-page spread run in *New York* magazine (January 20, 1986) is typical. On 33
the left-hand side, a man walks down a paved road; draped over his shoulder—and
clinging to his shirt and the back pocket of his trousers—is a young woman in
jeans. On the right-hand page the young lady appears to be climbing out of the
back seat of a car. She is wearing a wrinkled, unbuttoned blouse and a slip. She is
expressionless. The man, whose face is not visible, clutches her. Why is she being
carried off? Why is she clinging to the man? What are the characters depicted
feeling—ecstacy? Joy? Fear? Longing? Warmth? Comfort? Terror? We haven't a
clue. Within both photos there is an unmistakable tension, bordering on violence.
Viewed this way, the ad is disturbing, but viewed as an example of the advertiser's
art—and as a reflection of our times—it does not fall short of the mark. The

reader is involved, given a chance to learn what this clothing is all about—a certain lifestyle, a certain detached way of viewing the world. Isn't *that* what the 80s are all about?

Another human desire advertising writers did not invent (although they liberally   34 exploit it) is to associate with successful people. All of us tend to admire people— and even storybook characters—who are widely known for their achievements. We are therefore already primed for the common advertising device of the testimonial or personality ad. Once we have seen a famous person in an advertisement, we associate the product with the person. "I like Mr. X. Mr. X likes (endorses) this product. I like this product, too." The logic is faulty, but we fall for it just the same. That is how Joe DiMaggio sold Mr. Coffee. Although cartoon characters are not admired per se, they too are easily recognized; that's why Pac-Man sold vitamins and Bugs Bunny sold Post Raisin Bran. The people who write testimonial ads did not create our trust in famous personalities. They merely recognize our inclinations and exploit them.

The language of advertising is different from other languages because we   35 participate in it; in fact, we—not the words we read on the magazine page or the pictures unreeling before us on the television screen—charge the ads with most of their power.

SIMPLE

Clip a typical story from the publication you read most frequently. Calculate the   36 number of words in an average sentence. Count the number of words of three or more syllables in a typical 100-word passage, omitting words that are capitalized, combinations of two simple words, or verb forms made into three-syllable words by the addition of -ed or -es. Add the two figures (the average number of words per sentence and the number of three-syllable words per 100 words), then multiply the result by .4. According to Robert Gunning, if the resulting number is seven, there is a good chance that you are reading *True Confessions.** He developed this equation, the "Fog Index," to determine the comparative ease with which any given piece of written communication can be read. With this equation, the first paragraphs of this essay measure somewhere between *Reader's Digest* and *Time.*

Now consider the complete text of a typical cigarette advertisement: 37

I demand two things from my cigarette. I want a cigarette with low tar and nicotine. But, I also want taste. That's why I smoke Winston Lights. I get a lighter cigarette, but I still get a real taste. And real pleasure. Only one cigarette gives me that: Winston Lights.

The average sentence in this ad runs seven words. *Cigarette* and *nicotine* are   38 three-syllable words, with *cigarette* appearing four times; *nicotine,* once. Consid-

*Curtis D. MacDougall, *Interpretive Reporting* (New York: Macmillan, 1968), p. 94.

ering *that's* as two words, the ad is exactly fifty words long, so the average number of three-syllable words per 100 is ten.

$$7 \text{ words per sentence}$$
$$+ \ 10 \text{ three-syllable words/100}$$
$$\overline{17}$$
$$\times \ .4$$
$$\overline{6.8 \text{ Fog Index}}$$

According to Gunning's scale, this particular ad is written at about the seventh grade level, comparable to most of the ads found in mass circulation magazines.* It's about as sophisticated as *True Confessions,* harder to read than a comic book, but easier than *Ladies Home Journal.*

Of course, the Fog Index cannot evaluate the visual aspect of an ad. The headline, "I demand two things from my cigarette," works with the picture (that of an attractive woman) to arouse consumer interest. The text reinforces the image. It is unlikely that many consumers actually take the trouble to read the entire text, but it is not necessary for them to do so in order for the ad to work.

Since three-syllable words are harder to read than one- or two-syllable words, and since simple ideas are more easily transferred from one human being to another than complex ideas, advertising copy tends to use even simpler language all the time. Toffler speculates:

> If the [English] language had the same number of words in Shakespeare's time as it does today, at least 200,000 words—perhaps several times that many—have dropped out and been replaced in the intervening four centuries. . . . The high turnover rate reflects changes in things, processes, and qualities in the environment from the world of consumer products and technology.†

It is no accident that the first terms Toffler uses to illustrate his point ("fast-back," "wash-and-wear," and "flashcube") were invented not by engineers, journalists, or marketing managers, but by advertising copywriters.

Advertising language is simple language; in the engineering process, difficult words and images (which could be used in other forms of communication to lend color or fine shades of meaning) are edited out and replaced by simple words or images not open to misinterpretation.

Some critics view the entire advertising business as a cranky, unplanned child of the free enterprise system, a noisy, whining, brash kid who must somehow be kept in line, but can't just yet be thrown out of the house. Because advertising mirrors the fears, quirks, and aspirations of the society that creates it (and is, in turn, sold by it), it is wide open to parody and ridicule.

Perhaps the strongest, most authoritative critic of advertising language in

*Ibid., p. 95.
†Toffler, *Future Shock,* p. 151.

recent years is journalist Edwin Newman. In his book *Strictly Speaking,* he poses the question, "Will America be the death of English?" Newman's "mature, well thought out judgment" is that it will. As evidence, he cites a number of examples of fuzzy thinking and careless use of the language, not just by advertisers, but by many people in public life, including politicians and journalists:

> The federal government has adopted the comic strip character Snoopy as a symbol and showed us Snoopy on top of his doghouse, flat on his back, with a balloon coming out of his mouth, containing the words, "I believe in conserving energy," while below there was this exhortation: savEnergy.
>
> savEnergy. An entire letter e at the end was savd. In addition, an entire space was savd. Perhaps the government should say onlYou can prevent forest fires. . . . Spelling has been assaulted by Duz, E-Z Off, Fantastik, Kool, Kleen . . . and by products that make you briter, so that you will not be left hi and dri at a parti, but made welkom. . . . Under this pressure, adjectives become adverbs; nouns become adjectives; prepositions disappear; compounds abound.*

In this passage, Newman presents three of the charges most often levied against advertising:

1. Advertising debases English.
2. Advertising downgrades the intelligence of the public.
3. Advertising warps our vision of reality, implanting in us groundless fears and insecurities. (He cites, as examples of these groundless fears, "tattletale grey," "denture breath," "morning mouth," "unsightly bulge," and "ring around the collar.")

Other charges have been made from time to time. They include: 45

1. Advertising sells daydreams; distracting, purposeless visions of lifestyles beyond the reach of most of the people who are most exposed to advertising.
2. Advertising feeds on human weaknesses and exaggerates the importance of material things, encouraging "impure" emotions and vanities.
3. Advertising encourages bad, even unhealthy habits like smoking.
4. Advertising perpetuates racial and sexual stereotypes.

What can be said in advertising's defense? Advertising is only a reflection of 46
society; slaying the messenger (and just one of the messengers, at that) would not alter the fact—if it is a fact—that "America will be the death of English." A case can be made for the concept that advertising language is an acceptable stimulus for the natural evolution of the language. (At the very least, advertising may stimulate debate about what current trends in language are "good" and "bad.") Another point: *is* "proper English" the language we actually speak and write, or is it the language we are told we should speak and write, the language of *The Elements of Style* and *The Oxford English Dictionary?*

*Edwin Newman, *Strictly Speaking* (Indianapolis: Bobbs-Merrill, 1974), p. 13.

In a letter to the editor of *Advertising Age* (December 19, 1985), Alan Dittrich, 47
president of the Cahill Dittrich advertising agency, summarized this view very well:

"English is a mongrel language," Dittrich wrote, "—germanic, latinate, Asian, 48
with an agglomeration of vocabulary from scores of other languages. To attempt to
mold it exactly is as futile as trying to judge a mongrel dog by the criteria for whippets.

"What few hard and fast rules we have all spring from the admirable goal of 49
making communication sensible to reasonable people. All other putative rules are
merely someone's interpretations, or recommendations for convenience.

"English grows every day. It changes fast. We can wrap ourselves in the mantle 50
of 'authorities' and stand still; or we can move with it, using our wits and creativity
to evoke the fullest power of the language, making clarity and resonance our
goals, sometimes at the expense of minute pedantry."

What about the charge that advertising debases the intelligence of the public? 51
Those who support this particular criticism would do well to ask themselves
another question: Exactly how intelligent is the public? How many people know
the difference between adverbs and adjectives? How many people *want* to know?

The fact is that advertisements are effective, not because agencies say they 52
are effective, but because they sell products.

Advertising attempts to convince us to buy products; we are not forced to buy 53
something because it is heavily advertised. Who, for example, is to be blamed for
the success, in the mid-70s, of a nonsensical, nonfunctional product—Pet Rocks?
The people who designed the packaging, the people who created the idea of
selling ordinary rocks as pets, or those who bought the product?

Perhaps much of the fault lies with the public, for accepting advertising so 54
readily. S. I. Hayakawa finds "the uncritical response to the incantations of
advertising . . . a serious symptom of widespread evaluational disorder." He does
not find it "beyond the bounds of possibility" that "today's suckers for national
advertising will be tomorrow's suckers for the master political propagandist who
will, by playing up the 'Jewish menace,' in the same way as national advertisers
play up the 'pink toothbrush menace,' and by promising us national glory and
prosperity, sell fascism in America."*

Fascism in America is fortunately a far cry from Pet Rocks, but the point is 55
well taken. The intelligent consumer is the good advertiser's best friend. Emerson
observed: "Nothing astonishes men so much as common sense and plain dealing."
Consumers should apply common sense, and they should expect advertisers to
practice the art of plain dealing.

Do advertisements sell distracting, purposeless visions? Occasionally. But 56
perhaps such visions are necessary components of the process through which our
society changes and improves.

Other arguments may be made in support of advertising as it is practiced 57
today. Advertising stimulates product development, thus helping people lead
more comfortable lives. The information presented in ads helps people make
more intelligent purchasing decisions.

*S. I. Hayakawa, *Language in Action* (New York: Harcourt, Brace, 1941), p. 235.

We have the right to evaluate both sides of the various questions advertising— and the language of advertising—present to us. But we should recognize that advertising is likely to continue to influence our behavior, regardless of what we think of the process. 58

Business enterprises of all kinds spend vast sums of money to drive their messages home to us, and they are spending more every year: advertising expenditures in the United States alone have grown from about three billion dollars in 1944 to well over $100 billion by 1987. 59

Advertisers are also aided in their efforts by a continuing stream of technological developments. Beyond the development of the printing press and the advent of widespread literacy, radio and television have perhaps been most responsible for unleashing the advertiser's power. Print advertising appeals to only one of our senses—the visual—and in so doing, presents a static image. Radio added the auditory dimension, enabling advertisers to drive us crazy with jingles. Television combines the visual stimulation of print advertising with the auditory stimulation of radio and to these adds motion. But technology never sleeps: 60

- Thanks to devices called speech compressors, producers can increase the speed of an audiotaped message without introducing distortion. Listeners notice the difference; they pay more attention to the message, but they don't know why.
- The use of computers to drive and control systems of cameras and to create images combining animation with photos of real people and objects enables producers to take best advantage of both film and video techniques. As this technology becomes more routinely accessible, television commercials will become more visually appealing than the programs they interrupt. Indeed, this is already beginning to happen.

  Such production techniques are already routinely used in a relatively new medium that itself is a form of advertising disguised as pure entertainment: music videos.
- As integrated circuits, the building blocks of computing power, shrink in size and cost, we are likely to witness the birth of a yet another revolutionary new advertising medium: the "ad in a chip," embedded in the page or binding of a book, magazine, or newspaper. IBM has already created such an ad, planted in the pages of a French news magazine. When the reader turned the page, a tiny electric current, generated by chemicals, triggered a message on a wafer-thin screen. At some point in the future, ads in magazines may literally scream to demand our attention.
- The now commonplace presence of videotape recording equipment in the homes of consumers. People who own home video equipment use it mostly to record programs they wish to see again. Although the equipment can be put in stop or pause positions to prevent the recording of commercials while the viewer is present, it is not yet "smart" enough to discriminate between commercials and ordinary programs on its own. As a result, by recording programs off the air, people who own this equipment are giving the commercials an extended

shelf life, and are, in effect, almost guaranteeing that they will be viewed again after the initial broadcast. Properly maintained, there is virtually no limit to the life of a video cassette.

Whatever we think of these developments—whether we view them with alarm for their power to shape our perception of the world around us, or greet them as new tools for communication and understanding—whatever we think of advertising itself, it is clear that advertising will continue to exert a profound influence on our lives. 61

Advertising is a mirror. It is not perfect; sometimes it distorts. When we view ourselves in it, we're not always pleased with what we see. But perhaps, all things considered, that's the way it should be. 62

▼ TOPICAL CONSIDERATIONS

1. The author uses the phrases "advertising language" and "other languages." What assumptions about language is he making? Are they valid? Why or why not?
2. O'Neill describes several ways in which the language of advertising differs from other kinds of language. Briefly list the different ways he mentions. Can you think of any other characteristics of advertising language that set it apart?
3. In his last section, O'Neill presents several of the most frequent charges levied against advertising language. What are they? What does he say in defense of advertising? Which set of arguments seems the stronger?
4. "Symbols are efficient, compact vehicles for the communication of an advertising message" (paragraph 26). What symbols from the advertising world do you associate with your own life? Are they effective symbols for selling?

▼ RHETORICAL CONSIDERATIONS

1. O'Neill's essay is constructed around a story about copywriter Shirley Polykoff. How does this construction contribute to the essay?
2. O'Neill is an advertising professional. Does his writing style reflect the advertising techniques he describes? Cite examples to support your answer.
3. Describe the author's point of view about advertising. Does he ever tell us how he feels? Does his style indicate his attitude?

▼ WRITING ASSIGNMENTS

1. The author believes that advertising language mirrors the fears, quirks, and aspirations of the society that creates it. Do you agree or disagree with this statement? Explain in a brief essay.

2. Choose a brand-name product you use regularly and one of its competitors—one whose differences are negligible, if they exist at all. Examine some advertisements for each brand. Write a short paper explaining what really makes you prefer your brand.

3. Write a description of a common object in "formal standard English." Now write an advertisement for the same object. Analyze what has happened to the language in your writing.

4. Write a paper on sexism or racism in advertising. Use specific examples from current ads and commercials.

5. In paragraph 32, O'Neill talks about some disturbing "lifestyle" ads such as those for Georges Marciano. Have you ever been disturbed by an ad? Has any ad ever created tension in you, or seemed to convey to you a suggestion of violence? See if you can find such a "lifestyle" ad in a current magazine. In an essay, attempt to point out the disturbing undercurrents. What do you make of the "creative strategy" of the makers of the ad?

▼ PRINTED NOISE

George F. Will

Most of us are so accustomed to the incessant roar of commerce that we hear it without listening. If we stopped and thought about some of the names advertisers have given their products, we might recognize a peculiarly American form of language pollution. In this amusing essay, George Will takes a look at some of the fanciful and familiar names given to menu items such as "Egg McMuffin," "Fishamigig," and "Hot Fudge Nutty Buddy." He concludes that all the asphyxiating cuteness amounts to a lot of verbal litter. Will, a former philosophy professor, is a nationally syndicated Pulitzer Prize-winning columnist for the *Washington Post* and *Newsweek.* He is also a television news commentator for the American Broadcasting Corporation. This essay first appeared in Will's column in 1977.

The flavor list at the local Baskin-Robbins ice cream shop is an anarchy of names 1
like "Peanut Butter 'N Chocolate" and "Strawberry Rhubarb Sherbert." These are not the names of things that reasonable people consider consuming, but the names are admirably businesslike, briskly descriptive.

Unfortunately, my favorite delight (chocolate-coated vanilla flecked with nuts) 2
bears the unutterable name "Hot Fudge Nutty Buddy," an example of the plague of cuteness in commerce. There are some things a gentleman simply will not do, and one is announce in public a desire for a "Nutty Buddy." So I usually settle for a plain vanilla cone.

I am not the only person suffering for immutable standards of propriety. The 3
May issue of *Atlantic* contains an absorbing tale of lonely heroism at a Burger King. A gentleman requested a ham and cheese sandwich that the Burger King calls a Yumbo. The girl taking orders was bewildered.

"Oh," she eventually exclaimed, "you mean a Yumbo." 4

Gentleman: "The ham and cheese. Yes." 5

Girl, nettled: "It's called a Yumbo. Now, do you want a Yumbo or not?" 6

Gentleman, teeth clenched: "Yes, thank you, the ham and cheese." 7

Girl: "Look, I've got to have an order here. You're holding up the line. You 8
want a Yumbo, don't you? You want a Yumbo!"

Whereupon the gentleman chose the straight and narrow path of virtue. He 9
walked out rather than call a ham and cheese a Yumbo. His principles are anachronisms but his prejudices are impeccable, and he is on my short list of civilization's friends.

That list includes the Cambridge don who would not appear outdoors without 10 a top hat, not even when routed by fire at 3 A.M., and who refused to read another line of Tennyson after he saw the poet put water in fine port. The list includes another don who, although devoutly Tory, voted Liberal during Gladstone's day because the duties of prime minister kept Gladstone too busy to declaim on Holy Scripture. And high on the list is the grammarian whose last words were: "I am about to—or I am going to—die: either expression is correct."

Gentle reader, can you imagine any of these magnificent persons asking a 11
teenage girl for a "Yumbo"? Or uttering "Fishamagig" or "Egg McMuffin" or "Fribble" (that's a milk shake, sort of)?

At one point in the evolution of American taste, restaurants that were relentlessly 12
fun, fun, fun were built to look like lemons or bananas. I am told that in Los Angeles there was the Toed Inn, a strange spelling for a strange place shaped like a giant toad. Customers entered through the mouth, like flies being swallowed.

But the mature nation has put away such childish things in favor of menus that 13
are fun, fun, fun. Seafood is "From Neptune's Pantry" or "Denizens of the Briny Deep." And "Surf 'N Turf," which you might think is fish and horsemeat, actually is lobster and beef.

To be fair, there are practical considerations behind the asphyxiatingly cute 14
names given hamburgers. Many hamburgers are made from portions of the cow that the cow had no reason to boast about. So sellers invent distracting names to give hamburgers cachet. Hence "Whoppers" and "Heroburgers."

But there is no excuse for Howard Johnson's menu. In a just society it would 15
be a flogging offense to speak of "steerburgers," clams "fried to order" (which probably means they don't fry clams for you unless you order fried clams), a "natural cut" (what is an "unnatural" cut?) of sirloin, "oven-baked" meat loaf, chicken pot pie with "flaky crust," "golden croquettes," "grilled-in-butter Frankforts [sic]," "liver with smothered onions" (smothered by onions?), and a "hearty" Reuben sandwich.

America is marred by scores of Dew Drop Inns serving "crispy green" salads, 16
"garden fresh" vegetables, "succulent" lamb, "savory" pork, "sizzling" steaks, and "creamy" or "tangy" coleslaw. I've nothing against Homeric adjectives ("wine-dark sea," "wing-footed Achilles") but isn't coleslaw just coleslaw? Americans hear the incessant roar of commerce without listening to it, and read the written roar without really noticing it. Who would notice if a menu proclaimed "creamy" steaks and "sizzling" coleslaw? Such verbal litter is to language as Muzak is to music. As advertising blather becomes the nation's normal idiom, language becomes printed noise.

▼ TOPICAL CONSIDERATIONS

1. What is George F. Will's major assertion here regarding the language of American menus? Is he concerned that some items have been given fanciful names to disguise inferior food? Is he more concerned with the way advertising hype reduces language?

2. Are you so used to fast food menu names such as "Fishamagig," "Egg McMuffin," or "Yumbo" that you never questioned them? Have they ever seemed silly or offensive to you? Can you think of some other similar names for fast foods?
3. In paragraph 15, Will attacks the language of Howard Johnson menus. What is wrong with "steerburgers"? "Oven-baked" meat loaf? Clams "fried to order"? "Liver with smothered onions"? And what's wrong with a "hearty" Reuben sandwich?
4. Will makes the point in the last paragraph that menus make us adjective-blind (or deaf). But just how effective would a menu be if it were stripped of all the empty adjectives? Is a "crispy green" salad more attractive than "salad"? Is "sizzling" steak more tantalizing than just plain "steak," or "tangy" coleslaw more appetizing than "coleslaw"? Are we so accustomed to the adjectives that we need the assurance they give?

▼ RHETORICAL CONSIDERATIONS

1. How does Will use examples here? In other words, does he use examples to convince us of his position, or just to inform us?
2. How effective is the example of the *Atlantic* anecdote about the gentleman ordering a Yumbo? Did you find that example funny? Did it sufficiently dramatize Will's point?
3. How would you characterize Will's sense of humor? In what ways does he establish it? What humorous word choices can you find?
4. In the last paragraph, Will makes an analogy: "Such verbal litter is to language as Muzak is to music." What is Muzak, and how effective is the comparison?

▼ WRITING ASSIGNMENTS

1. Write your own essay on printed noise. Go through newspapers and magazines and find examples of advertisers' names for products to use in your essay.
2. Construct a menu of your own, using some of the advertising principles Will attacks here. Use silly, childish names, overblown adjectives, and euphemisms to make ordinary fast food sound tantalizing.

▼ RESISTING THOSE AWFUL COMMERCIALS

Diane White

Have you ever seen a television commercial you found so offensive that you refused to buy the product? According to a poll of consumers, a majority of people will not purchase products whose commercials they don't like. But there are some people, such as *Boston Globe* columnist Diane White, who out of some unexplained perverse impulse will buy a product whose ads they actually hate. The following is White's humorous confession—a confession, perhaps, appropriate for many of us torn between dark urgings to buy and to resist. This article first appeared in her *Boston Globe* column in 1982.

A story in *New York* magazine reports that companies called "monitoring services" 1
are trying to pin down our tastes in TV advertising.

They've been sending pollsters out to shopping malls to stop people at 2
random and ask them which television commercials they hate most. One of the
things they've found is that people have trouble remembering the commercials
they don't like.

I was kind of surprised by this because, if somebody were to walk up and ask 3
me which commercials I really despise, I could bore them for hours singing awful
jingles and describing hateful ads in detail.

After reading the *New York* magazine story, I realized something curious: 4
Sometimes, when I find an ad particularly offensive, I deliberately run right out
and buy the product.

For example, one of my least favorite television commercials pushes a product 5
called Murphy's Oil Soap.

You may have seen the ad. It features a man, a woman and a little girl hopping 6
around and singing, to the tune of "Turkey in the Straw," a jingle that goes, in part,
like this:

> I've been using Murphy's Oil Soap
> On this wood floor of mine
> Now the dirt is finished
> But the finish is fine!

I can't even begin to tell you how much I hate this ad. I hate the jingle. I hate 7
the three people who sing it. I hate the grinning mom and dad. I especially hate
the obnoxious little girl. I hate this ad so much I went out and bought a bottle of
Murphy's Oil Soap.

I don't know why I bought it. Maybe because I couldn't get that stupid jingle   8
out of my head. Maybe because some part of my subconscious needs to be
dominated by lousy advertising. Maybe because I felt guilty for hating that family
so much. After all, what have they ever done to me? Maybe because I was curious
to find out if the product could be as bad as the commercial.

Anyway, I went out and bought it. And, as much as I don't like to admit it, the   9
stuff really works. I don't know anything about the sales figures, but I bet they'd
triple overnight if the company had a decent advertising campaign.

Unless, of course, there are lots of other people out there who respond to   10
offensive advertising the way I do.

However, according to the polling companies featured in the *New York*   11
magazine story, they don't. There's no evidence, they say, that annoying commercials increase sales or brand-name recall. In fact, one company found that 55
percent of the people they interviewed had vowed not to buy certain products
whose commercials they didn't like.

Not me. Just the other day I bought some Close-Up Toothpaste because I hate   12
the ads for it.

I don't know when I've ever seen a commercial quite as nauseating as the   13
Close-Up commercial featuring a young couple called Desiree and Rob. These
two are so in love that their eyes glaze over when they moon about each other,
which they do in public, on television.

What, you may ask, does their passion have to do with toothpaste? Well, it   14
seems that the reason Desiree loves Rob is that his teeth are so white. And the
reason Rob loves Desiree is that her breath smells like new-mown hay. Or maybe
it's the other way around. Anyway, they owe it all to Close-Up toothpaste, and I
say they deserve just what they get.

I could go on listing other awful commercials that have moved me to buy the   15
products. The Papa Gino's Pizza ad with the horrible adolescent who sings
"Gimme that thick pan pizza, Papa . . . " and then sinks her teeth into a big slice of
the stuff. Donny and Marie's Hawaiian Punch ads. The No Nonsense Pantyhose
commercials featuring that woman who talks like Betty Boop.

There are some items I have actually had to restrain myself from buying   16
because, even though I may hate the ads, I have no use for the products.
Arthritis Pain Formula is one. That woman who picks up the frying pan drives
me crazy. Preparation H is another. I practically froth at the mouth when
that man hops on his bicycle and starts pedaling like mad to show how well
the stuff works.

Obnoxious advertising must work on some level, on some people. It's possible,   17
on the other hand, that there are some who don't find these ads as awful as I do.
But I don't like to think about that.

What kind of perversity is at work here? I'm not sure. I only know I'll never   18
buy Carvel Ice Cream or Uncle Ben's Rice. And I'll never consult a Bache broker.
Even I have my limits.

▼ TOPICAL CONSIDERATIONS

1. Why was Diane White surprised at the findings of the advertising pollsters?
2. What theories does White offer to explain why she went out and bought Murphy's Oil Soap even though she hated the commercial? Do any of her hypotheses seem more valid than others? Have you ever had similar reactions—that is, have you bought a product because you hated the commercial for it? What were your reasons?
3. What is there about the Close-Up commercial that makes White hate it so?
4. White reports that 55 percent of those interviewed by pollsters said they would never buy products whose commercials they didn't like. Are you such a person? Have you gone out of your way to avoid a product because a television commercial for it offended you? If so, which product? What was there about the commercial that you disliked?

▼ RHETORICAL CONSIDERATIONS

1. Is there something significant in White's claim that she can't understand why she buys products whose commercials she hates? Do you think her not knowing is part of her rhetorical strategy—part of her message about the way commercials work on us? If she did know, would her point be blunted?
2. Does White ever tell us exactly why she hates any of the commercials she cites? Where is she the most analytical? The least?
3. Comment on White's writing style. Is she formal? Informal? Conversational? Friendly? Do you find her humorous in places? If so, try to evaluate her humorous effects.

▼ WRITING ASSIGNMENTS

1. Are there television commercials that you just can't stand? If so, which ones in particular? Why do you hate them? Write a paper in which you try to analyze why these particular commercials are obnoxious to you. Would you still buy the products advertised? Would you go out of your way to buy a competitive product?
2. Do you think the commercials that draw the most attention are the most successful, or the other way around? Analyze some television commercials that do and do not draw attention to themselves. Which seem the most successful?

▼ SAMPLE ADS AND STUDY QUESTIONS

Here we reproduced ten recently published magazine ads—familiar pitches for perfume, cereal, condoms, photographic film, liquor, jeans, photocopiers, and the National Rifle Association. The ads are as diversified in their products as in their selling strategies. Some are nearly all graphics with no hard-sell copy, while others are informative, even chatty. To demonstrate the wide variety in advertising strategies and styles, we have included three different ads for the same product—whiskey. Following each ad is a set of questions to assist you in analyzing how the ads work their appeal on us—how they subtly and not so subtly try to convince us that the product is worth our money.

Courtesy of Revlon Inc.

▼ "HOW TO BUILD A FIRE BY JOAN COLLINS"

1. Other than by scenting the paper the ad appears on, the only way an advertiser can make a perfume or cologne appealing to the reader is in the presentation of images. Describe the image of Joan Collins and discuss why she is an appropriate model for the selling of a perfume called "Scoundrel."

2. Reread John Ciardi's essay "Is Everybody Happy?" How does this ad illustrate the major points Ciardi makes about the appeal of advertising? What promises of happiness does this ad make? What anxieties does it prey on?

3. Why would a manufacturer (Revlon) name a perfume "Scoundrel"? Doesn't that word have negative connotations? How does that name fit the image of Joan Collins?

4. How do the following reinforce the image Joan Collins projects: her hair, makeup, earrings, dress, pose, and expression?

5. Why do you think a book title/author format was used for the ad copy?

6. In step 5 of her instructions on "How to Build a Fire," Joan Collins says Scoundrel is "sophisticated," "elegant," and "sexy." How do the other instructions suggest these qualities of the perfume?

7. Why is the actual bottle of Scoundrel shown in the lower right corner? How does the style of the bottle fit the image projected for the contents?

Courtesy Kellogg's

▼ "THEY'RE IN A HURRY."

1. What would you say is the main appeal of this ad's visuals? Try to explain how that appeal works.
2. The statement of this ad is "They're in a hurry." What different messages does this convey? How do these messages appeal to our emotions? How do these messages help promote Kellogg's cereals?
3. How would the impact of the ad be affected were the children not smiling? What would be the impact if the girl was taller than the boy? What if their clothes were less stylish or formal? What if their postures and hand positions were different?
4. Why do you suppose the advertisers chose not to include a particular box of Kellogg's cereal in the ad?
5. Does this ad make you want to purchase Kellogg's cereal? Why, or why not?

Twelve months a year, Steve Wade and
Ernest Paine punch, brand and drive
2200 head of cattle across 500,000 acres
of land. Without a discouraging word.
So they each received a bottle of V.O.

The reward.

Reprinted courtesy of Seagram Distillers Company

▼ "SEAGRAM'S V.O. THE REWARD."

1. According to the ad, why do Steve Wade and Ernest Paine deserve "the reward" of Seagram's V.O.?
2. What image of men does the ad project? Consider the men's clothes, physical condition, expressions, age, and the locale. Do they look like the kinds of men who fit the copy? Do they strike you as extraordinary looking? Ordinary looking? Would the male model in the Polo ad be right for this ad? Why or why not?
3. How would the ad be affected if the two men were holding glasses of Seagram's V.O. in their hands? How would the ad be affected if the men were smiling with their arms around each other's shoulders?
4. Consider the setting of the ad. How do the distant rugged mountains add to the appeal and message of the ad? What about the flat plains and the animals grazing behind the fence?
5. What is the strategy of laying the bottle of Seagram's V.O. on it's side? What about the way the bottle divides the copy?

Courtesy the Buckingham Wile Company

▼ "WHEN YOU LIVE A CUTTY ABOVE."

1. In his essay, "The Language of Advertising," Charles O'Neill made the point that much of an ad's appeal depends upon the consumer's identification with the image projected. Consider the two models in this Cutty Sark ad. What image is projected by the following: their clothing? their hair? the setting? their ages? the expressions on their faces? their general appearances? How do these images help sell the product?

2. Judging from the setting and the men's apparel, what might be the occasion of the photograph? How does this help support the statement in the ad's brief copy, "When you live a Cutty above"?

3. Consider the line, "When you live a Cutty above." Why was it positioned where it is in the ad? Do you find the line catchy? Do you think the pun is intended to stick in one's mind? Is it likely to become a familiar phrase such as other commercial slogans?

4. How do the visual images coordinate with the copy: "When you live a Cutty above"? How do the visual images coordinate with the copy: "Uncommon Quality"? How do the visuals help sell Cutty Sark?

5. Consider the attitude of the two men. What kind of exchange might be going on between them? Is it clear which man made the remark they are laughing about? What is the "message" of their laughing and how does it relate to the product? How would the ad be affected if the two men were looking seriously at each other?

6. Consider the "body messages" of the two models. What do their poses say about their relationship? How would the message be altered were their poses reversed—that is, were the older man's head bowed and his arm resting on the younger man's shoulder? Now consider the message in the positions of the men's glasses.

7. How old would you say the two models are? Why do you suppose the advertisers chose an older and younger man rather than two of the same generation?

8. Do you find this ad appealing? If so, why? If not, why?

Courtesy Schenley Imports Company

▼ "DEWAR'S PROFILE: HENRY THREADGILL"

1. For years Dewar's has run "profiles" featuring men and women of differing age, profession, race, income bracket, and life style. Which segments of the alcohol-drinking population are being targeted in this profile? Which segments are being excluded? Is this an effective approach to selling Dewar's in your estimation?

2. Henry Threadgill chose as his "quote" the following: "Tradition is a background of ingredients; in itself it's nothing. If you can't make something out of it, the world can do without it." What do these words mean? What do they say about the kind of man Henry Threadgill is? How might this philosophy have determined his being chosen for the ad?

3. At first glance, what is the most arresting aspect of this ad? In other words, what grabbed your attention, and why?

4. Compare and contrast the images of men projected in this ad and that for Cutty Sark and Seagram's Which is more appealing to you and why?

5. Setting is very important in ads because it helps make associations and project images. What about the setting here—or lack of it? How would this ad be altered were it shot "on location"—as was the Cutty Sark—instead of in a studio?

6. Draw up a Dewar's profile of yourself. In it list some of your latest accomplishments, the last book read, your hobbies, a choice quotation of yours, and why you do what you do. Do you think your profile would sell "White Label"? Why, or why not?

"Someone I respect has been urging me to use condoms. He's the Surgeon General."

"I've heard what the Surgeon General is saying about condoms. And believe me, I'm listening."

The makers of Trojan latex condoms would like you to know that there are really only two ways to be absolutely sure of safety regarding sex.

One is a faithful marriage to a healthy person.

And the other is abstinence.

In all other cases, as the Surgeon General of the United States says, "An individual must be warned to use the protection of a condom."

Trojan latex condoms, America's most widely used and trusted brand, help reduce the risk of spreading many sexually transmitted diseases.

We urge you to use them in any situation where there is any possibility of sexually transmitted disease.

Look at it this way. You have nothing to lose. And what you stand to save is your life.

TROJAN

BRAND LATEX CONDOMS

For all the right reasons.

© 1987 Carter-Wallace, Inc.

Courtesy of Carter-Wallace, Inc.

▼ "TROJAN BRAND LATEX CONDOMS: FOR ALL THE RIGHT REASONS"

1. What first caught your attention about this ad? Was it the photographs of the models? Was it the ad copy? Was it the large-type Trojan name at the bottom?

2. The makers of Trojan brand latex condoms want to associate their product with particular values and images. Consider the two models in this ad. What images are projected by the man and the woman? Consider their ages, appearances, clothes, hair styles, expressions, attractiveness, the positions of their heads, and the way they are looking at the camera. Do they seem to be the kind of people who would listen to the Surgeon General? Would they practice "safety regarding sex"?

3. What kind of audience does this ad appeal to?

4. How would the impact, message, images, and values be altered if the ad had just the male model speaking? How would these things be altered with just the female model speaking?

5. Consider the phrase "safety regarding sex." Why do you think this particular wording was chosen? What kind of "safety" do the manufacturers want you to think about? What other kind of "safety" is implied, but intentionally avoided in the ad? Why?

6. National magazines began running ads for condoms in the mid-1980s. Why do you suppose they had not been run before then? Why are they being run today? How has the authority of the Surgeon General been enlisted here to sell condoms?

7. Consider the first guarantee of safe sex claimed by the makers of Trojan brand latex condoms: "a faithful marriage to a healthy person." How would the message be altered were it worded: "marriage to a healthy person"? or, "a faithful relationship with a healthy person"? or, "a relationship with a healthy person"? or, "relationships with healthy persons"?

8. What do you make of the second "guarantee"—"abstinence"? What is the message here?

9. Consider the next paragraph: "In all other cases, as the Surgeon General of the United States says, 'An individual must be warned to use the protection of a condom.'" What might "all other cases" cover? Would sex in marriage be one of the cases? What about premarital sex? What about extramarital sex? What about sex between gays? Does the direct quote from the Surgeon General imply that he is endorsing the use of condoms as opposed to other means of "protection"?

10. How might the Catholic Church react to this ad?

Courtesy Canon U.S.A., Inc.

▼ "CANON: 'GOOD THING CANON DOESN'T THINK LIKE YOU'"

1. Most ads are aimed at making people feel good about themselves and their decisions. How does this ad differ? What specific anxieties does this ad prey on?
2. What particular audience is this ad aimed at? Consider the style of the men's clothing, their ages, their general demeanor. Consider also the copy.
3. Besides the quoted exchange, how is the sense of confrontation made apparent? Is it clear which man says which line? What is the strategy behind this? How is the Canon copier promoted in the brief exchange?
5. Consider the lighting—or lack of it—in this ad. What mood is created by it? How does the lighting help create the emotional impact of the ad?
6. In "The Language of Advertising," Charles A. O'Neill argued that advertising "holds up a . . . mirror" to our society. How does this ad for Canon copiers mirror the economic and political state of our society?
7. Examine the copy for this ad. What specific corporate threats are named? How does Canon promise to triumph in spite of these threats?
8. Examine the specific language of the copy. What jargonistic terms and phrases do you find? Which expressions are the "language" of the audience targeted by the ad? Which are more technical and, thus, meant to impress.

Reprinted courtesy of Eastman Kodak Company

▼ "HE JUST SLAYED HIS LAST DRAGON."

1. Many ads appeal to our desires. How does this ad for Kodak film appeal to our emotions? Consider the appearance of the little boy, his clothes, what he has in his hands, what he seems to be doing, the setting (a field of green grass), the backdrop (dark green woods), etc.

2. Although most of this ad consists of a photograph, there is some copy, set in three different sizes of print. What is the strategy behind heading the copy with a line in the largest type reading, "He just slayed his last dragon"? What is the first message this line conveys to you? Do you sense a subtle, more ominous message in the wording? Do you find any ominous message elsewhere in the ad copy? In the visuals?

3. The middle-sized print is at the bottom: "Kodak film. Because time goes by." What is the strategy of placing it at the bottom and in the next largest size type? What is the subtle strategy of printing it in the same style of type as the first line, "He just slayed his last dragon"?

4. Consider how the wording in the smallest print continues to work on an emotional level. What particular emotions are subtly addressed in this block of copy?

5. How does the actual layout of the ad suggest the way Kodak can help stop time?

© 1986 PFI Photograph by permission of Polo/Ralph Lauren.
Photograph by Bruce Weber.

▼ "POLO RALPH LAUREN"

1. As Charles O'Neill pointed out in his essay, image is everything. Much of an ad's appeal depends upon the consumer's identification with the image projected. Consider these Polo models. What image is projected by the following: the models' facial expressions? their body poses? their ages? their general appearances?

2. What image is projected by the man's outfit—in particular, the tweed top coat over a denim jacket? What about the scarf and shoestring tie and buckle?

3. What image is projected by the woman's outfit—in particular, the suede jacket over an open blouse? What about the leather gloves?

4. How would the effect of the ad be altered if the man were alone or if the woman were alone? If the woman were not holding the man by his jacket front? If the man's hand were on the woman's jacket?

5. What kind of people would identify with the images of these models? Explain your answer.

6. Both Seagram's and Polo use male models to sell their products. Compare the different images of men that are projected. Would the same man attracted to the Seagram's ad be attracted to the Polo ad?

7. Do you find this ad appealing? If so, why? If not, why?

8. The only copy in this ad is the label: "Polo Ralph Lauren." What products are actually being advertised here? Men's clothing, women's clothing, or both? Do you suppose all of the items have the Polo label? How important is label recognition?

CASEY STEENBURGEN: 4th Grader, Hunter, Graduate
of Hunter Safety Course,
Member of the National Rifle Association.

"I'm nine years old. I was seven when I started
hunting with my dad and grandpa. I got a shotgun about a year
ago, but it just sat in the closet until I passed
my state's Hunter Safety Course. We spent a lot of time in
classes, then took a test. I got a 98 score.

"My dad and brother and I like to hunt together. We went dove
hunting for my first real hunt. It was a lot of fun. I also
like to hunt squirrels, rabbits and ducks. When ducks fly over I can
hear them coming, even when I'm in class at school.

"I joined the NRA right after I passed the safety
course. My dad signed me up. I like the NRA because they
make sure you can keep your guns and hunt.

"I like football, baseball and soccer, but
hunting is my favorite. It's more exciting."  **I'm the NRA.**

Each year NRA-certified instructors teach hundreds of thousands of young people
safe gun handling and basic marksmanship skills. If you would like to join the NRA or want
more information about our programs and benefits, write Harlon Carter,
Executive Vice President, P.O. Box 37484, Dept. CS-13, Washington, D.C. 20013.
Paid for by the members of the National Rifle Association of America Copyright 1985

Reprinted courtesy of the National Rifle Association

▼ "I'M THE NRA"

1. For several years the National Rifle Association has been running "I'm the NRA" in national magazines and newspapers. Most often the ad subjects are adults, but on occasion children are used. Do you find the photo of Casey Steenburgen holding a shotgun particularly provocative? Why, or why not? Why do you think the NRA used a nine-year-old boy?
2. How does the ad want you to perceive the NRA? Explain your answer from specifics in the ad.
3. Why do you think the NRA chose to use Casey Steenburgen's own words in describing his feelings about hunting rather than paraphrase them?
4. How would you describe the image Casey Steenburgen projects? Does he appear to be the kind of boy responsible enough to own a shot gun? To be a member of the NRA? Consider his position, the way he holds his shotgun, the expression on his face, his attire, etc. In general, what kind of image does the NRA ad want to project of the young hunter?
5. How is the theme of safe gun handling variously emphasized in the ad?
6. Gun control has been a controversial issue in America for years. How does this ad express the position of the NRA in different ways?
7. The copy mentions Casey's father and grandfather. Why did the advertiser want to mention them? What is the message here?
8. If you are someone who has never had much interest in guns, does this ad provoke your interest in them at all? In gun owners or hunters? Did it alter your attitude toward the NRA? Did it make you consider the possibility of joining someday? Explain your answer.

▼ MORE SUGGESTED WRITING ASSIGNMENTS

1. Look over the ten ads in our collection. Try to determine which ad you thought was the most effective and which was the least effective. Explain your choices as fully as you can.
2. Select one of the ads and revise its copy and/or visuals so that it appeals to a completely different audience. For example, try to redo the Seagrams V.O. ad so that it appeals to the swinging yuppie set.
3. Using the ads printed here and others you have seen for illustration, write a paper in which you discuss some of the ways advertisers project images of women. Do you find any of these images offensive?
4. Do the same as the previous question, but for men.

ON
VIOLENCE
IN AMERICA

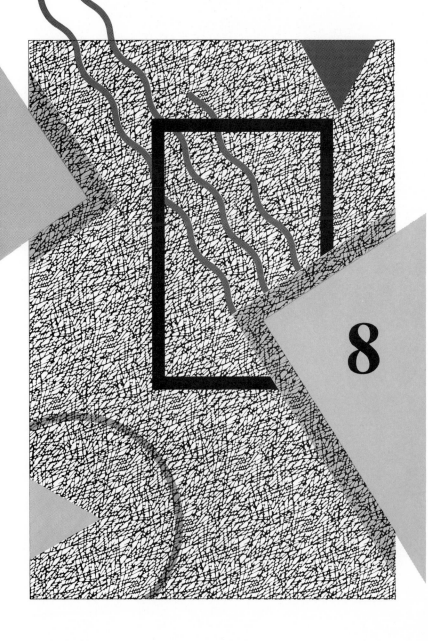

8

▼ PILGRIMAGE TO NONVIOLENCE

Martin Luther King, Jr.

Violence in America has become the number one issue of our contemporary society. Each day, newspapers and television news chronicle the latest murders, rapes, and muggings. While violence threatens the very nature of American life, debates rage over the issues of criminal justice and gun control. We open this section with an essay by one of America's most prominent and charismatic opponents to violence, Dr. Martin Luther King, Jr. Written at a time when American blacks were suffering racial injustice, sometimes violently, this essay served as a call for social change through peaceful means. King was a clergyman and a prominent civil rights leader. In 1957, he organized the Southern Christian Leadership Conference to extend his nonviolent efforts toward equality and justice for his people. In 1964, he was awarded the Nobel Peace Prize. Four years later, while supporting striking sanitation workers in Memphis, King was shot and killed. The following statement comes from his *Stride Toward Freedom* (1958).

When I went to Montgomery as a pastor, I had not the slightest idea that I would 1 later become involved in a crisis in which nonviolent resistance would be applicable. I neither started the protest nor suggested it. I simply responded to the call of the people for a spokesman. When the protest began, my mind, consciously or unconsciously, was driven back to the Sermon on the Mount, with its sublime teachings on love, and the Gandhian method of nonviolent resistance. As the days unfolded, I came to see the power of nonviolence more and more. Living through the actual experience of the protest, nonviolence became more than a method to which I gave intellectual assent; it became a commitment to a way of life. Many of the things that I had not cleared up intellectually concerning nonviolence were now solved in the sphere of practical action.

Since the philosophy of nonviolence played such a positive role in the 2 Montgomery Movement, it may be wise to turn to a brief discussion of some basic aspects of this philosophy.

First, it must be emphasized that nonviolent resistance is not a method for 3 cowards; it does resist. If one uses this method because he is afraid or merely because he lacks the instruments of violence, he is not truly nonviolent. This is why Gandhi often said that if cowardice is the only alternative to violence, it is better to fight. He made this statement conscious of the fact that there is always another alternative: no individual or group need submit to any wrong, nor need they use violence to right the wrong; there is the way of nonviolent resistance. This is ultimately the way of the strong man. It is not a method of stagnant passivity. The phrase "passive resistance" often gives the false impression that this is a sort of "do-nothing method" in which the resister quietly and passively accepts evil. But nothing is further from the truth. For while the nonviolent resister is passive in the sense that he is not physically aggressive toward his opponent, his mind and emotions are always active, constantly seeking to persuade his opponent that he is wrong. The method is passive physically, but strongly active spiritually. It is not passive nonresistance to evil, it is active nonviolent resistance to evil.

A second basic fact that characterizes nonviolence is that it does not seek to   4
defeat or humiliate the opponent, but to win his friendship and understanding. The nonviolent resister must often express his protest through noncooperation or boycotts, but he realizes that these are not ends themselves; they are merely means to awaken a sense of moral shame in the opponent. The end is redemption and reconciliation. The aftermath of nonviolence is the creation of the beloved community, while the aftermath of violence is tragic bitterness.

A third characteristic of this method is that the attack is directed against   5
forces of evil rather than against persons who happen to be doing the evil. It is evil that the nonviolent resister seeks to defeat, not the persons victimized by evil. If he is opposing racial injustice, the nonviolent resister has the vision to say that the basic tension is not between races. As I like to say to the people in Montgomery: "The tension in this city is not between white people and Negro people. The tension is, at bottom, between justice and injustice, between the forces of light and the forces of darkness. And if there is a victory, it will be a victory not merely for fifty thousand Negroes, but a victory for justice and the forces of light. We are out to defeat injustice and not white persons who may be unjust."

A fourth point that characterizes nonviolent resistance is a willingness to   6
accept suffering without retaliation, to accept blows from the opponent without striking back. "Rivers of blood may have to flow before we gain our freedom, but it must be our blood," Gandhi said to his countrymen. The nonviolent resister is willing to accept violence if necessary, but never to inflict it. He does not seek to dodge jail. If going to jail is necessary, he enters it "as a bridegroom enters the bride's chamber."

One may well ask: "What is the nonviolent resister's justification for this   7
ordeal to which he invites men, for this mass political application of the ancient doctrine of turning the other cheek?" The answer is found in the realization that unearned suffering is redemptive. Suffering, the nonviolent resister realizes, has tremendous educational and transforming possibilities. "Things of fundamental importance to people are not secured by reason alone, but have to be purchased with their suffering," said Gandhi. He continues: "Suffering is infinitely more powerful than the law of the jungle for converting the opponent and opening his ears which are otherwise shut to the voice of reason."

A fifth point concerning nonviolent resistance is that it avoids not only   8
external physical violence but also internal violence of spirit. The nonviolent

resister not only refuses to shoot his opponent but he also refuses to hate him. At the center of nonviolence stands the principle of love. The nonviolent resister would contend that in the struggle for human dignity, the oppressed people of the world must not succumb to the temptation of becoming bitter or indulging in hate campaigns. To retaliate in kind would do nothing but intensify the existence of hate in the universe. Along the way of life, someone must have sense enough and morality enough to cut off the chain of hate. This can only be done by projecting the ethic of love to the center of our lives.

In speaking of love at this point, we are not referring to some sentimental or affectionate emotion. It would be nonsense to urge men to love their oppressors in an affectionate sense. Love in this connection means understanding, redemptive good will. Here the Greek language comes to our aid. There are three words for love in the Greek New Testament. First, there is *eros.* In Platonic philosophy *eros* meant the yearning of the soul for the realm of the divine. It has come now to mean a sort of aesthetic or romantic love. Second, there is *philia,* which means intimate affection between personal friends. *Philia* denotes a sort of reciprocal love; the person loves because he is loved. When we speak of loving those who oppose us, we refer to neither *eros* nor *philia;* we speak of a love which is expressed in the Greek word *agape. Agape* means understanding, redeeming good will for all men. It is an overflowing love which is purely spontaneous, unmotivated, groundless, and creative. It is not set in motion by any quality or function of its object. It is the love of God operating in the human heart.

Agape is disinterested love. It is a love in which the individual seeks not his own good, but the good of his neighbor (I Cor. 10:24). *Agape* does not begin by discriminating between worthy and unworthy people, or any qualities people possess. It begins by loving others *for their sakes.* It is entirely "neighbor-regarding concern for others," which discovers the neighbor in every man it meets. There, *agape* makes no distinction between friend and enemy; it is directed toward both. If one loves an individual merely on account of friendliness, he loves him for the sake of the benefits to be gained from the friendship, rather than for the friend's own sake. Consequently, the best way to assure oneself that Love is disinterested is to have love for the enemy-neighbor from whom you can expect no good in return, but only hostility and persecution.

Another basic point about *agape* is that it springs from the *need* of the other person—his need for belonging to the best in the human family. The Samaritan who helped the Jew on the Jericho Road was "good" because he responded to the human need that he was presented with. God's love is eternal and fails not because man needs his love. St. Paul assures us that the loving act of redemption was done "while we were yet sinners"—that is, at the point of our greatest need for love. Since the white man's personality is greatly distorted by segregation, and his soul is greatly scarred, he needs the love of the Negro. The Negro must love the white man, because the white man needs his love to remove his tensions, insecurities, and fears.

Agape is not a weak, passive love. It is love in action. *Agape* is love seeking to preserve and create community. It is insistence on community even when one seeks to break it. *Agape* is a willingness to sacrifice in the interest of mutuality.

Agape is a willingness to go to any length to restore community. It doesn't stop at the first mile, but it goes the second mile to restore community. It is a willingness to forgive, not seven times, but seventy times seven to restore community. The cross is the eternal expression of the length to which God will go in order to restore broken community. The resurrection is a symbol of God's triumph over all the forces that seek to block community. The Holy Spirit is the continuing community creating reality that moves through history. He who works against community is working against the whole of creation. Therefore, if I respond to hate with a reciprocal hate I do nothing but intensify cleavage in broken community. I can only close the gap in broken community by meeting hate with love. If I meet hate with hate, I become depersonalized, because creation is so designed that my personality can only be fulfilled in the context of community. Booker T. Washington was right: "Let no man pull you so low as to make you hate him." When he pulls you that low he brings you to the point of working against community; he drags you to the point of defying creation, and thereby becoming depersonalized.

In the final analysis, *agape* means a recognition of the fact that all life is   13
interrelated. All humanity is involved in a single process, and all men are brothers. To the degree that I harm my brother, no matter what he is doing to me, to that extent I am harming myself. For example, white men often refuse federal aid to education in order to avoid giving the Negro his rights; but because all men are brothers they cannot deny Negro children without harming their own. They end, all efforts to the contrary, by hurting themselves. Why is this? Because men are brothers. If you harm me, you harm yourself.

Love, *agape,* is the only cement that can hold this broken community together.   14
When I am commanded to love, I am commanded to restore community, to resist injustice, and to meet the needs of my brothers.

A sixth basic fact about nonviolent resistance is that it is based on the   15
conviction that the universe is on the side of justice. Consequently, the believer in nonviolence has deep faith in the future. This faith is another reason why the nonviolent resister can accept suffering without retaliation. For he knows that in his struggle for justice he has cosmic companionship. It is true that there are devout believers in nonviolence who find it difficult to believe in a personal God. But even these persons believe in the existence of some creative force that works for universal wholeness. Whether we call it an unconscious process, an impersonal Brahman, or a Personal Being of matchless power and infinite love, there is a creative force in this universe that works to bring the disconnected aspects of reality into a harmonious whole.

▼ TOPICAL CONSIDERATIONS

1. From reading King's essay, what kind of education would you say King had as a young man? How is this training reflected in the essay?
2. King was strongly influenced by Mahatma Gandhi, political activist and

leader of the Indian people in the first half of this century. What do you know about Gandhi and his civil disobedience movement?

3. During the Vietnam War, thousands of young men fled to Canada and Europe to avoid being drafted. Would you call them nonviolent resisters? Consider the motives and aims of both types of protestors. Are conscientious objectors the same as nonviolent resisters, as described by Dr. King?

4. King refers to the Sermon on the Mount. What similarities do you see between its teachings and King's definition of nonviolent resistance? What differences do you see?

5. Is King's philosophy practical in today's world, in which there is so much terrorism and violence? Give reasons for your answer.

6. When King defines *agape,* he discusses how it promotes community responsibility. Identify citizen groups in your community or on your campus that demonstrate the kind of love King defines here. What other evidence of *agape* do you find in our society?

7. Do you agree with King's philosophy? Could you practice it? Describe a situation in which you might find yourself wanting to resist. Explain how you would deal with the crisis. How would it be the same or different from King's approach?

8. King was a charismatic figure of the early sixties. Is there anything about this essay that would suggest why this was true?

▼ RHETORICAL CONSIDERATIONS

1. Did King's opening capture your interest immediately? Was it an effective way to introduce his subject matter? Explain your reactions.

2. What is King's thesis? Is it stated explicitly or implicitly?

3. What primary rhetorical strategy does King use in developing his essay?

4. What transitional devices does King use when moving from one idea to another? How does he achieve variety so that he is not repeating the same words and phrases too often?

5. What do you think of King's conclusion? Does he need to summarize the points he made in his essay? Or has he successfully brought the essay to a close without the need for this? How would you have ended it?

▼ WRITING ASSIGNMENTS

1. In paragraph 1, King remarks: "Many of the things I had not cleared up intellectually concerning nonviolence were now solved in the sphere of practical action." King's practical experiences molded his philosophy. In an essay, write about an experience you have had that taught you something about your own standards of behavior in society.

2. Were the young men who fled to Canada and Europe during the Vietnam

War nonviolent resisters? In an essay, compare and contrast this type of resistance with the type King describes.

3. Identify a community action group in your community or on your campus that is involved in demonstrating *agape*. Write an essay describing the goals and actions of the group. Explain how the group demonstrates the kind of community responsibility King discusses in his essay.

▼ 38 WHO SAW MURDER DIDN'T CALL THE POLICE

Martin Gansberg

Martin Gansberg has been a reporter and editor for the *New York Times* since 1942. The article reprinted here was written in 1964, just a few days after Kitty Genovese was murdered in full view of dozens of people. The incident shocked the nation and became a springboard for countless editorials and articles—even a television movie— about public indifference and fear. This article won Gansberg several awards for best feature and news story of the year.

For more than half an hour 38 respectable, law-abiding citizens in Queens watched 1 a killer stalk and stab a woman in three separate attacks in Kew Gardens.

Twice their chatter and the sudden glow of their bedroom lights interrupted 2 him and frightened him off. Each time he returned, sought her out, and stabbed her again. Not one person telephoned the police during the assault; one witness called after the woman was dead.

That was two weeks ago today. 3

Still shocked is Assistant Chief Inspector Frederick M. Lussen, in charge of 4 the borough's detectives and a veteran of 25 years of homicide investigations. He can give a matter-of-fact recitation on many murders. But the Kew Gardens slaying baffles him—not because it is a murder, but because the "good people" failed to call the police.

"As we have reconstructed the crime," he said, "the assailant had three 5 chances to kill this woman during a 35-minute period. He returned twice to complete the job. If we had been called when he first attacked, the woman might not be dead now."

This is what the police say happened beginning at 3:20 A.M. in the staid, 6 middle-class, tree-lined Austin Street area:

Twenty-eight-year-old Catherine Genovese, who was called Kitty by almost 7 everyone in the neighborhood, was returning home from her job as manager of a bar in Hollis. She parked her red Fiat in a lot adjacent to the Kew Gardens Long Island Rail Road Station, facing Mowbray Place. Like many residents of the neighborhood, she had parked there day after day since her arrival from Connecticut a year ago, although the railroad frowns on the practice.

She turned off the lights of her car, locked the door, and started to walk the 8 100 feet to the entrance of her apartment at 82-70 Austin Street, which is in a Tudor building, with stores in the first floor and apartments on the second.

The entrance to the apartment is in the rear of the building because the front 9 is rented to retail stores. At night the quiet neighborhood is shrouded in the slumbering darkness that marks most residential areas.

Miss Genovese noticed a man at the far end of the lot, near a seven-story apartment house at 82-40 Austin Street. She halted. Then, nervously, she headed up Austin Street toward Lefferts Boulevard, where there is a call box to the 102nd Police Precinct in nearby Richmond Hill.   10

She got as far as a street light in front of a bookstore before the man grabbed her. She screamed. Lights went on in the 10-story apartment house at 82-67 Austin Street, which faces the bookstore. Windows slid open and voices punctuated the early-morning stillness.   11

Miss Genovese screamed: "Oh, my God, he stabbed me! Please help me! Please help me!"   12

From one of the upper windows in the apartment house, a man called down: "Let that girl alone!"   13

The assailant looked up at him, shrugged, and walked down Austin Street toward a white sedan parked a short distance away. Miss Genovese struggled to her feet.   14

Lights went out. The killer returned to Miss Genovese, now trying to make her way around the side of the building by the parking lot to get to her apartment. The assailant stabbed her again.   15

"I'm dying!" she shrieked. "I'm dying!"   16

Windows were opened again, and lights went on in many apartments. The assailant got into his car and drove away. Miss Genovese staggered to her feet. A city bus, O-10, the Lefferts Boulevard line to Kennedy International Airport, passed. It was 3:35 A.M.   17

The assailant returned. By then, Miss Genovese had crawled to the back of the building, where the freshly painted brown doors to the apartment house held out hope for safety. The killer tried the first door; she wasn't there. At the second door, 82-62 Austin Street, he saw her slumped on the floor at the foot of the stairs. He stabbed her a third time—fatally.   18

It was 3:50 by the time the police received their first call, from a man who was a neighbor of Miss Genovese. In two minutes they were at the scene. The neighbor, a 70-year-old woman, and another woman were the only persons on the street. Nobody else came forward.   19

The man explained that he had called the police after much deliberation. He had phoned a friend in Nassau County for advice and then he had crossed the roof of the building to the apartment of the elderly woman to get her to make the call.   20

"I didn't want to get involved," he sheepishly told the police.   21

Six days later, the police arrested Winston Moseley, a 29-year-old business-machine operator, and charged him with homicide. Moseley had no previous record. He is married, has two children and owns a home at 133-19 Sutter Avenue, South Ozone Park, Queens. On Wednesday, a court committed him to Kings County Hospital for psychiatric observation.   22

When questioned by the police, Moseley also said that he had slain Mrs. Annie May Johnson, 24, of 146-12 133d Avenue, Jamaica, on Feb. 29 and Barbara   23

Kralik, 15, of 174-17 140th Avenue, Springfield Gardens, last July. In the Kralik case, the police are holding Alvin L. Mitchell, who is said to have confessed that slaying.

The police stressed how simple it would have been to have gotten in touch   24
with them. "A phone call," said one of the detectives, "would have done it." The police may be reached by dialing "O" for operator or SPring 7-3100.

Today witnesses from the neighborhood, which is made up of one-family   25
homes in the $35,000 to $60,000 range with the exception of the two apartment houses near the railroad station, find it difficult to explain why they didn't call the police.

A housewife, knowingly if quite casually, said, "We thought it was a lovers'   26
quarrel." A husband and wife both said, "Frankly, we were afraid." They seemed aware of the fact that events might have been different. A distraught woman, wiping her hands in her apron, said, "I didn't want my husband to get involved."

One couple, now willing to talk about that night, said they heard the first   27
screams. The husband looked thoughtfully at the bookstore where the killer first grabbed Miss Genovese.

"We went to the window to see what was happening," he said, "but the light   28
from our bedroom made it difficult to see the street." The wife, still apprehensive, added: "I put out the light and we were able to see better."

Asked why they hadn't called the police, she shrugged and replied: "I don't   29
know."

A man peeked out from a slight opening in the doorway to his apartment and   30
rattled off an account of the killer's second attack. Why hadn't he called the police at the time? "I was tired," he said without emotion. "I went back to bed."

It was 4:25 A.M when the ambulance arrived to take the body of Miss   31
Genovese. It drove off. "Then," a solemn police detective said, "the people came out."

▼ TOPICAL CONSIDERATIONS

1. Suppose you had been one of the 38 witnesses who heard Kitty Genovese scream. What would you have done?
2. What do you think of the reasons the witnesses gave for not calling the police? Are any of the reasons justifiable?
3. What does the article reveal about Kitty Genovese's neighborhood? Is there anything about it that would suggest that it is particularly crime-prone? Is it surprising that such a crime would happen in it?
4. How would you have felt if the victim had been your best friend? Your sister? Your girlfriend? How would you have felt toward her neighbors?
5. What impact do you think this article had when it was first published in 1964? What impact did it have on you?

▼ RHETORICAL CONSIDERATIONS

1. Gansberg gives specific times, addresses, and ages in his article. He even lists the phone number for the police department. Why does he do this? How would the article be affected if he didn't include these specifics?
2. What is Gansberg's aim in writing this article? What impact do you think he intended to have on his audience? Do you think he was successful?
3. Although this article is written in an objective, journalistic style, Gansberg's own bias often reveals itself. For example, why does he describe the Austin Street area as "staid" and "middle-class"? Why does he point out that it is a neighborhood of "one-family homes in the $35,000 to $60,000 range"? What does this tell you about his point of view? What other revealing clues do you see?
4. How effective is Gansberg's use of dialogue? Would the article have a greater impact without it? Give reasons for your answers.
5. Does Gansberg's conclusion tie in with his thesis? Is it an effective conclusion? Why or why not? What does it reveal about the author's point of view?

▼ WRITING ASSIGNMENTS

1. Have you ever been a victim of a crime? If so, write a narrative account of what happened to you. Include a description of how witnesses to the crime came or failed to come to your aid.
2. How do you think a newscaster would have reported the Kitty Genovese crime? Write a brief news blurb that could be used on a nightly TV news program. Include many of the details Gansberg provides in his article.
3. Gansberg's article is written from the point of view of the victim. Adopt another point of view—that of a witness, the murderer, a bus driver, a police officer—and write two brief papers. In the first, describe your own response to what happened the night of the crime. In the second, describe how you felt two weeks later, when Gansberg's article was published.

▼ A WEST COAST STORY

George F. Will

Over the last few years we have seen an enormous rise in violence and mayhem on the streets of major cities, much of it the result of urban gangs. Far from the alienated youth romanticized in *West Side Story,* today's urban tribes are armed with Uzis and trafficking in drugs. Here, *Newsweek* columnist George F. Will assesses the ugly phenomenon in an interview with one "gang banger." This piece first appeared in Will's column in March 1988.

Across his nearly expressionless face flicker mingled traces of boredom and lightly 1
sleeping menace. Sam (not his real name), wearing blue prisoner's garb at the Los
Angeles County Jail, is sitting out his latest sentence, for a drug offense, in one of
the two wings reserved for the 700 or so strictly segregated members of two
warring gangs, the Bloods and the Crips. Only because I have prompted him, Sam
is thinking, as much as he ever does, about tomorrow. He has been a mugger,
armed robber, car thief, drug dealer—is he, I ask, running out of career moves?
"Naw, the world is too big to run out."

Sam's sabbatical ends soon and he will be out and about, being what he has 2
been since he was expelled from the 10th grade for constant fighting. He is what is
known here as a "gang banger."

He cannot count the number of times he has been shot, but he still has in him 3
two of the nine slugs from the first time, which he survived because "the Lord was
with me." The Lord would have saved the LAPD a lot of trouble by being
elsewhere. Sam is 35, weighs 250 pounds and is the ugly new face of an old
phenomenon, urban gangs. Time was when they were part of a rite of passage, a
subculture that inner-city adolescence outgrew. But in this drug-swamped decade,
gang banging is a career.

Call this the gentrification of juvenile delinquency. The juveniles are staying 4
on, juvenile no more, and acquiring Uzis, Soviet AK-47s and other automatic
weapons. "Delinquency," which suggests sporadic naughtiness, does not describe
the new epidemic of viciousness, both random and purposive. The violence
expresses both the tribalism of small primitive groups and the big business of
cocaine and other drugs. What the life often lacks in longevity it makes up for in
intensity. Overhearing a detective talking on a telephone, Sam recognizes the
name of a murder victim and says, with only slight interest and no surprise, that it
is the second of his cousins killed in 10 days. Fifteen-year-olds drive BMW's and
make bail from pocket cash. Young teenagers have been arrested with $10,000 in
their jeans. No wonder young dealers wear phone beepers in school.

Every ethnic group in this seething city of unmelted blocs contributes to the   5
many hundreds of gangs that have perhaps 70,000 members. But the black
community is bleeding most, because of the Bloods and the Crips. The jail world
of steel and concrete echoes to the clinking shuffle of lines of men manacled at
the ankles, protected from other lines of manacled and color-coded criminals. In
this jail, as in the neighborhoods, Crips, who wear blue accessories, would
slaughter on sight Bloods wearing any of their trademark red. Why? No reason is
required. Atavism often is a sufficient explanation for the random "drive by"
shootings that are a favorite mode of self-expression. There is, of course, the
traditional territorial imperative, the gangs' struggle for "turf." What is new is the
killing for commerce, for market shares in the cocaine and crack business. Also
new is an unsentimental view of gangs.

Thirty years ago on Broadway a musical was in its first year of a long run. It   6
was "Romeo and Juliet" set among Manhattan's fighting gangs. "West Side Story"
was a facet of the romantic interpretation of gangs. Intellectuals who found the
'50s—peace, prosperity, Eisenhower: yuck—boringly bourgeois found "alienation"
fascinating. They were reading too much Camus and were too much taken with
the idea of "existential assertion" through spontaneous violence, such as the
murder by Meursault, Camus's "Stranger" (or the murder by Belmondo in the
movie "Breathless"). If academic interpreters, pursuing alienation and tenure
simultaneously, could not sit in Paris cafés wearing black turtlenecks and sipping
black coffee and thinking black thoughts, they could at least sympathize with
juvenile delinquents as rebels against the anonymity, anomie or whatever of
modern life. Those "kids" did after all (sorry, James Dean) have a "cause." They
were avoiding the suffocation of life as "the organization man" (remember that
book?). A boy in a "black leather jacket and motorcycle boots" (remember that
song? remember Brando as "The Wild One"?) was preferable to "The Man in the
Gray Flannel Suit" (remember that novel?).

REBUKES TO SOCIETY

Viewed through the lenses of the social sciences, juvenile gangs were seen as   7
rebukes to society by society's young victims who were condemned to "Growing
Up Absurd" (remember Paul Goodman's polemic?) in industrial societies composed of a "dust of individuals" (Durkheim's phrase). Gangs also were considered
"protest masculinity" on the part of young men lacking role models. Or, in a less
exotic theory, gangs were regarded as a rational response to society's inadequate
"opportunity structure."

Three decades and intellectual light-years separate "West Side Story" from   8
"The Bonfire of the Vanities," Tom Wolfe's mesmerizing novel about the urban
sense of pervasive menace: "It was that deep worry that lives in the base of the
skull of every resident of Park Avenue south of 96th Street—a black youth, tall,
rangy, wearing white sneakers." No one will make a musical from "Bonfire."

The cost to the black community, and America, is incalculable. It is caused by   9 people like Sam. And of course virtually all victims of black violence are blacks struggling to rise past the savagery of large, lazy, brutal men-children like Sam. His speech is barely semiliterate but, such is the downward seepage of the social sciences, it includes a smattering of jargon for allocating blame to "peer pressure" and "the media" (they give gangs a bad "image") and "society." But whatever made him what he is, he, like thousands like him, now is an "institutional man." He is an unreformable recidivist, unfit for society. He is an example of a rapidly expanding class of semisociopaths, utterly indifferent to social norms or any notion of right and wrong, and with the time horizon of a child. He sheds his lethargy and becomes slightly indignant when it is suggested that his future is not in doubt and that he will be back in jail soon and often. He protests, "I am patient. I might get a job." (Pause.) "For six or seven months." But, he adds, "If I can't get what I want, I'll quit." What does he want? "A thousand dollars a day." Really? Really. "It's out there." Indeed it is. And the huge demand for drugs produces a terrifying supply of Sams.

▼ TOPICAL CONSIDERATIONS

1. Why, according to Will, does the old term "juvenile delinquency" not describe today's urban gang activities? Why does he call the current problem the "gentrification of juvenile delinquency"?

2. What is Sam's reaction to the overheard telephone conversation of the detective? What does his reaction suggest?

3. How does Will explain the romanticization of juvenile gangs during the 1950s?

4. Having read the article, where do you think Will stands on the issue of capital punishment? Substantiate your answer with evidence from his piece.

5. Will refers to gang bangers as "unreformable recidivists," "semisociopaths," and individuals "unfit for society." Do you think that his assessment is fair? Do you think that he neglects to take into account the link between environment and what it breeds?

6. In paragraph 3, Will says that "the Lord would have saved the LAPD a lot of trouble by being elsewhere" when Sam was shot. Do you agree? In other words, do you think people like Sam are better off dead? Do you think that even Sam's life should be granted the same respect as other's?

7. This essay stirred up many outraged responses in the form of letters to *Newsweek*. Some people accused Will of unfair representation of the black community. Do you think Will does a disservice to black Americans here? Do you think he encourages racist attitudes?

▼ RHETORICAL CONSIDERATIONS

1. Explain Will's choice of title for this essay. What is the reference and what effect is created by it?
2. What is Will's purpose in using terms such as "career moves" and "sabbatical" in paragraphs 1 and 2? What effects do these terms create and how do they help convey Will's attitude toward Sam? Can you find other "euphemistic" terms in the essay?
3. Will says that "atavism" is a "sufficient explanation for the random 'drive by' shootings" by gang bangers. What does "atavism" mean and how does it help underscore Will's sizing up of gang bangers?
4. How, from this article, would you politically characterize George Will? Defend your answer with specific statements from the essay.

▼ WRITING ASSIGNMENTS

1. Write a letter to George F. Will telling him what you think of his essay. In your letter comment on specific statements and ideas.
2. Will characterizes Sam as a "large, lazy, brutal" man-child, a "semiliterate . . . unreformable recidivist, unfit for society . . . [and] indifferent to social norms or any notion of right and wrong." Do you think people like Sam are better off dead? Do you think that victims of environment should be shown more respect than the author does here?

▼ WHY I BOUGHT A GUN

Gail Buchalter

Why would an intelligent, sensitive, liberal woman purchase a handgun? That was the question posed to writer Gail Buchalter, who after years of resistance bought a gun. Her article that follows is not intended to argue for or against any particular gun-control legislation, or even to debate whether anyone should purchase a handgun. Rather, it is an attempt to understand why a person might feel the need to own a pistol and to explore the root causes of such a profound decision. Buchalter, who lives with her young son in a middle-class section of Los Angeles, is one of more than 12 million women in the United States who own guns. This essay was first published in *Parade* magazine in February 1988.

1   I was raised to wear black and cultured pearls in one of Manhattan's more desirable neighborhoods. My upper-middle-class background never involved guns. If my parents felt threatened, they simply put another lock on the door.

2   By high school, I had traded in my cashmere sweaters for a black arm band. I marched for Civil Rights, shunned Civil Defense drills and protested the Vietnam war. It was easy being 18 and a peacenik. I wasn't raising an 11-year-old child then.

3   Today, I am typical of the women whom gun manufacturers have been aiming at as potential buyers—and one of the millions who have succumbed: Between 1983 and 1986, there was a 53 percent increase in female gun-owners in the U.S.—from 7.9 million to 12.1 million, according to a Gallup Poll paid for by Smith & Wesson, the gun manufacturer.

4   Gun enthusiasts have created ad campaigns with such snappy slogans as "You Can't Rape a .38" or "Should You Shoot a Rapist Before He Cuts Your Throat?" While I was trying to come to a rational decision, I disliked these manipulative scare tactics. They only inflamed an issue that I never even dreamed would touch me.

5   I began questioning my beliefs one Halloween night in Phoenix, where I had moved when I married. I was almost home when another car nearly hit mine head-on. With the speed of a New York cabbie, I rolled down my window and screamed curses as the driver passed me. He instantly made a U-turn, almost climbing on my back bumper. By now, he and his two friends were hanging out of the car windows, yelling that they were going to rape, cut and kill me.

6   I already had turned into our driveway when I realized my husband wasn't home. I was trapped. The car had pulled in behind me. I drove up to the back

porch and got into the kitchen, where our dogs stood waiting for me. The three men spilled out of their car and into our yard.

My adrenaline was pumping faster than Edwin Moses' legs clearing a hurdle. I grabbed the collars of Jack, our 200-pound Irish wolfhound, and his 140-pound malamute buddy, Slush. Then I kicked open the back door—I was so scared that I became aggressive—and actually dared the three creeps to keep coming. With the dogs, the odds had changed in my favor, and the men ran back to the safety of their car, yelling that they'd be back the next day to blow me away. Fortunately, they never returned. 7

A few years and one divorce later, I headed for Los Angeles with my 3-year-old son, Jordan (the dogs had since departed). When I put him in preschool a few weeks later, the headmistress noted that I was a single parent and immediately warned me that there was a rapist in my new neighborhood. 8

I called the police, who confirmed this fact. The rapist had no *modus operandi.* Sometimes he would be waiting in his victim's house; other times he would break in while the person was asleep. Although it was summer, I would carefully lock my windows at night and then lie there and sweat in fear. Thankfully, the rapist was caught, but not before he had attacked two more women. 9

Courtesy of S. Kelley and Copley News Service.

Over some time, at first imperceptibly, my suburban neighborhood became   10
less secure. A street gang took over the apartment building across from my house,
and flowers and compact cars gave way to graffiti and low-riders.

Daytime was quiet, but these gang members crawled out like cockroaches   11
after dark. Several nights in a row they woke me up. It was one of the most
terrifying times in my life. I could hear them talking and laughing as they leaned
against our fence, tossing their empty beer cans into our front yard. I knew that
they were drinking, but were they also using violence-inducing drugs such as PCP
and crack? And if they broke in, could I get to the police before they got to me?

I found myself, to my surprise, wishing that I had a loaded pistol under my   12
pillow. In the clear light of day, I found this reaction shocking and simply decided
to move to a safer neighborhood, although it cost thousands of dollars more.
Luckily, I was able to afford it.

Soon the papers were telling yet another tale of senseless horror. Richard   13
Ramirez, who became known as "The Walk-In Killer," spent months crippling and
killing before he was caught. His alleged crimes were so brutal and bizarre, his
desire to inflict pain so intense, that I began to question my beliefs about the
sanctity of human life—his, in particular. The thought of taking a human life is
repugnant to me, but the idea of being someone's victim is worse. And how, I
began to ask myself, do you talk pacifism to a murderer or a rapist?

Finally, I decided that I would defend myself, even if it meant killing another   14
person. I realized that the one-sided pacifism I once so strongly had advocated
could backfire on me and, worse, on my son. Reluctantly, I concluded that I had
to insure the best option for our survival. My choices: to count on a cop or to own
a pistol.

But still I didn't go out and buy a gun. Everything about guns is threatening.   15
My only exposure to them had been in movies; owning one, I feared, would bring
all that violence off of the screen and into my home.

So, instead, I called up my girlfriend (who has begged to remain nameless)   16
and told her I had decided to buy a gun. We were both surprised that I didn't know
she already had one. She was held up at gunpoint several years ago and bought
what she said was a .37. We figured out it must be either a .38 or a .357. I was
horrified when she admitted that not only had she no idea what type of gun she
owned, but she also had never even shot it. It remains in her drawer, loaded and
unused.

Upset, I hung up and called another friend. He was going to the National Rifle   17
Association convention that was being held in Reno and suggested I tag along. My
son's godmother lives there, so I figured I could visit her and kill two birds with
one stone.

My first night in Reno, I attended the Handgun Hunters' Awards dinner and   18
sat next to a contributing editor for one of the gun magazines. He bitterly
complained that killing elephants had been outlawed, although there were thousands still running around Africa. Their legs, he explained, made wonderful trash
baskets. I felt like Thumper on opening day of the hunting season, and my foot
kept twitching under the table.

The next day at the convention center, I saw a sign announcing a seminar for   19
women on handguns and safety. I met pistol-packing grandmas, kids who were
into competitive shooting and law-enforcement agents. I listened to a few of them
speak and then watched a video, "A Woman's Guide to Firearms." It explained
everything from how guns worked to an individual's responsibilities as a gun
owner.

It was my kind of movie, since everything about guns scares me—especially   20
owning one. Statistics on children who are victims of their parents' handguns are
overwhelming: About 300 children a year—almost a child a day—are killed by
guns in this country, according to Handgun Control, Inc., which bases its numbers
on data from the National Safety Council. Most of these killings are accidental.

As soon as I returned to Los Angeles, I called a man I had met a while ago   21
who, I remembered, owned several guns. He told me he had a Smith & Wesson .38
Special for sale and recommended it, since it was small enough for me to handle
yet had the necessary stopping power.

I bought the gun. That same day, I got six rounds of special ammunition with   22
plastic tips that explode on impact. These are not for target practice; these are for
protection.

For about $50, I also picked up the metal safety box that I had learned about   23
in the video. Its push-button lock opens with a touch if you know the proper
combination, possibly taking only a second or two longer than it does to reach
into a night-table drawer. Now I knew that my son, Jordan, couldn't get his hands
on it while I still could.

When I brought the gun home, Jordan was fascinated by it. He kept picking it   24
up, while I nervously watched. But knowledge, I believe, is still our greatest
defense. And since I'm in favor of education for sex, AIDS and learning to drive, I
couldn't draw the line at teaching my son about guns.

Next, I took the pistol and my son to the target range. I rented a .22 caliber   25
pistol for Jordan. (A .38 was too much gun for him to handle.) I was relieved when
he put it down after 10 minutes—he didn't like the feel of it.

But that didn't prevent him from asking me if he should use the gun if   26
someone broke into our house while I wasn't home. I shrieked "no!" so loud, we
both jumped. I explained that, if someone ever broke in, he's young and agile
enough to leap out the window and run for his life.

Today he couldn't care less about the gun. Every so often, when we're   27
watching television in my room, I practice opening the safety box, and Jordan
times me. I'm down to three seconds. I'll ask him what's the first thing you do
when you handle a gun, and he looks at me like I'm a moron, saying for the
umpteenth time: "Make sure it's unloaded. But I know I'm not to touch it or tell
my friends about it." Jordan's already bored with it all.

I, on the other hand, look forward to Mondays—"Ladies' Night" at the target   28
range—when I get to shoot for free. I buy a box of bullets and some targets from
the guy behind the counter, put on the protective eye and ear coverings and walk
through the double doors to the firing lines.

Once there, I load my gun, look down the sights of the barrel and adjust my   29 aim. I fire six rounds into the chest of a life-sized target hanging 25 feet away. As each bullet rips a hole through the figure drawn there, I realize I'm getting used to owning a gun and no longer feeling faint when I pick it up. The weight of it has become comfortable in my hand. And I am keeping my promise to practice. Too many people are killed by their own guns because they don't know how to use them.

It took me years to decide to buy a gun, and then weeks before I could load it. 30 It gave me nightmares.

One night I dreamed I woke up when someone broke into our house. I 31 grabbed my gun and sat waiting at the foot of my bed. Finally, I saw him turn the corner as he headed toward me. He was big and filled the hallway—an impossible target to miss. I aimed the gun and froze, visualizing the bullet blowing a hole through his chest and spraying his flesh all over the walls and floor. I didn't want to shoot, but I knew my survival was on the line. I wrapped my finger around the trigger and finally squeezed it, simultaneously accepting the intruder's death at my own hand and the relief of not being a victim. I woke up as soon as I decided to shoot.

I was tearfully relieved that it had only been a dream. 32

I never have weighed the consequences of an act as strongly as I have that of 33 buying a gun—but, then again, I never have done anything with such deadly repercussions. Most of my friends refuse even to discuss it with me. They believe that violence begets violence.

They're probably right. 34

▼ TOPICAL CONSIDERATIONS

1. How does Buchalter's decision to purchase a handgun contradict her upbringing and attitudes as a young woman?
2. What was the turning point for the author's attitude regarding handguns? What event or events made her question her pacifist beliefs? What finally convinced Buchalter to buy a gun?
3. Why had Buchalter's nameless woman friend purchased her handgun?
4. What does Buchalter learn at the National Rifle Association? How did her experience there make it easier for her to buy her own gun?
5. What reason does Buchalter give for teaching her young son about guns?
6. Do you sympathize with Buchalter's decision to purchase a gun? Would you have bought one if you were she?

▼ RHETORICAL CONSIDERATIONS

1. Where does Buchalter state the thesis of her essay?
2. At the Handgun Hunters' Award dinner, Buchalter sits next to a man who complains about elephant-hunting laws. What is the function of this little

detail? How does it comment on the change taking place in her? Explain her comment about feeling like "Thumper on opening day of the hunting season."

3. Comment on the effect of the concluding line of the article. What's the author's strategy behind making it a one-line paragraph? How do you interpret the meaning of this final comment?

▼ WRITING ASSIGNMENTS

1. Do you or anyone you know own a handgun? If so, write a paper explaining how you feel about owning a handgun or how your friend feels about owning one.
2. Write a letter to Gail Buchalter in which you express your support for her decision to purchase a handgun.
3. Write a letter to Gail Buchalter in which you express your disappointment that she broke down and bought a handgun.
4. This essay brings up the question of gun control. What are your feelings on this issue? Do you think that there should be stronger gun control laws?

CONSCIENCE
AND
CONTROVERSY

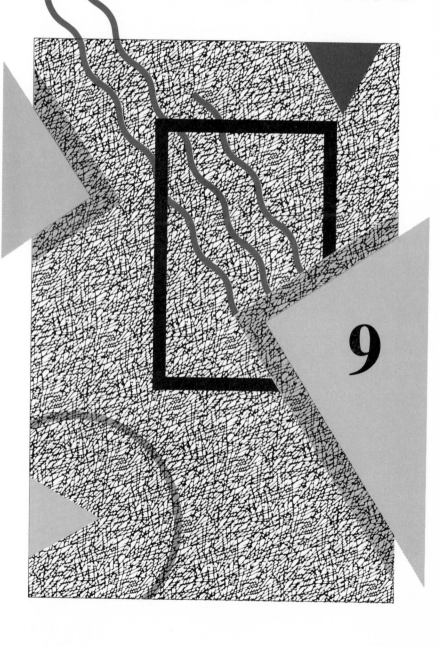

9

▼ IT'S TIME TO BAN HANDGUNS

Lance Morrow

While the crime rate in America climbs, one of the debates that continues to rage is what to do about handguns. Some people cry for stronger gun control—even a ban—while others argue that gun control will not reduce the crime, claiming that criminals will always find a means to kill, but that gun control would deny law-abiding citizens their constitutional right to bear arms. The essay reprinted below was written by Lance Morrow, a senior writer for *Time.* It appeared a few days after March 31, 1981, when then-President Ronald Reagan was shot and wounded in an assassination attempt in the nation's capital.

By a curiosity of evolution, every human skull harbors a prehistoric vestige: a reptilian brain. This atavism, like a hand grenade cushioned in the more civilized surrounding cortex, is the dark hive where many of mankind's primitive impulses originate. To go partners with that throwback, Americans have carried out of their own history another curiosity that evolution forgot to discard as the country changed from a sparsely populated, underpoliced agrarian society to a modern industrial civilization. That vestige is the gun—most notoriously the handgun, an anachronistic tool still much in use. Since 1963 guns have finished off more Americans (400,000) than World War II did. 1

After one more handgun made it into American history last week (another nastily poignant little "Saturday night" .22 that lay like an orphan in a Dallas pawnshop until another of those clammy losers took it back to his rented room to dream on), a lôt of Americans said to themselves, "Well, maybe *this* will finally persuade them to do something about those damned guns." Nobody would lay a dime on it. The National Rifle Association battened down its hatches for a siege of rough editorial weather, but calculated that the antigun indignation would presently subside, just as it always does. After Kennedy. After King. After Kennedy. After Wallace. After Lennon. After Reagan. After . . . the nation will be left twitching and flinching as before to the pops of its 55 million pistols and the highest rate of murder by guns in the world. 2

The rest of the planet is both appalled and puzzled by the spectacle of a superpower so politically stable and internally violent. Countries like Britain and Japan, which have low murder rates and virtual prohibitions on handguns, are astonished by the over-the-counter ease with which Americans can buy firearms. 3

Americans themselves are profoundly discouraged by the handguns that seem to breed uncontrollably among them like roaches. For years the majority of them have favored restrictions on handguns. In 1938 a Gallup poll discovered that 84% wanted gun controls. The latest Gallup finds that 62% want stricter laws governing 4 handgun sales. Yet Americans go on buying handguns at the rate of one every 13 seconds. The murder rate keeps rising. It is both a cause and an effect of gun sales. And every few years—or months—some charismatic public character takes a slug from an itinerant mental case caressing a bizarre fantasy in his brain and the sick, secret weight of a pistol in his pocket.

Why do the bloody years keep rolling by without guns becoming subject to the   5 kind of regulation we calmly apply to drugs, cars, boat trailers, CB radios and dogs? The answer is only partly that the National Rifle Association is, by some Senators' estimate, the most effective lobbying organization in Washington and the deadliest at targeting its congressional enemies at election time. The nation now has laws, all right—a patchwork of some 25,000 gun regulations, federal, state and local, that are so scattered and inconsistent as to be preposterously ineffectual.

Firearms have achieved in the U.S. a strange sort of inevitability—the nation's   6 gun-ridden frontier heritage getting smokily mingled now with a terror of accelerating criminal violence and a sense that as the social contract tatters, the good guys must have their guns to defend themselves against the rising tribes of bad guys. It is very hard to persuade the good guys that all those guns in their hands wind up doing more lethal harm to their own kind than to the animals they fear; that good guys sometimes get drunk and shoot other good guys in a rage, or blow their own heads off (by design or accident) or hit their own children by mistake. Most murders are done on impulse, and handguns are perfectly responsive to the purpose: a blind red rage flashes in the brain and fires a signal through the nerves to the trigger finger—BLAM! Guns do not require much work. You do not have to get your hands bloody, as you would with a knife, or make the strenuous and intimately dangerous effort required to kill with bare hands. The space between gun and victim somehow purifies the relationship—at least for the person at the trigger—and makes it so much easier to perform the deed. The bullet goes invisibly across space to flesh. An essential disconnection, almost an abstraction, is maintained. That's why it is so easy—convenient, really—to kill with one of the things.

The post-assassination sermon, an earnest lamentation about the "sickness   7 of American society," has become a notably fatuous genre that blames everyone and then, after 15 minutes of earnestly empty regret, absolves everyone. It is true that there is a good deal of evil in the American air; television and the sheer repetitiousness of violence have made a lot of the country morally weary and dull and difficult to shock. Much of the violence, however, results not from the sickness of the society but the stupidity and inadequacy of its laws. The nation needs new laws to put at least some guns out of business. Mandatory additional punishments for anyone using a gun in a crime—the approach that Ronald Reagan favors—would help. But a great deal more is necessary. Because of the mobility of guns, only federal laws can have any effect upon them. Rifles and shotguns—long guns—are not the problem; they make the best weapons for defending the house anyway, and they are hard for criminals to conceal. Most handguns are made to fire at people, not at targets or game. Such guns should be banned. The freedoms of an American individualism bristling with small arms must yield to the larger communal claim to sanity and safety—the "pursuit of happiness."

That would, of course, still leave millions of handguns illegally in circulation; the penalties for possessing such weapons, and especially for using them in crime, would have to be severe. Even at that, it would take years to start cleansing the nation of handguns. Whatever its content, no substantive program for controlling guns probably stands any chance of getting through Congress unless Ronald Reagan supports it. He ought to do so, not because he has been shot in the chest but because it should be done. 8

The indiscriminate mass consumption of guns has finally come to disgrace Americans abroad and depress them at home. It has been almost 90 years since the historian Frederick Jackson Turner propounded his famous thesis about the end of the American frontier. But the worst part of the frontier never did vanish. Its violence, once tolerable in the vast spaces, has simply backed up into modern America, where it goes on blazing away. 9

▼ TOPICAL CONSIDERATIONS

1. Does anyone you know own a gun? What are his or her reasons? How do you feel about this?
2. What argument does Morrow introduce in his opening and carry through the entire essay? Do you agree with him?
3. Morrow recalls a number of assassinations that have resulted from the use of handguns. What is your response to this? Should these assassinations necessarily impel us to take a firmer stand against handguns? Why or why not?
4. According to Morrow, both Britain and Japan prohibit handguns and have low murder rates. If you were debating the issue of gun control with Morrow, what could you say in rebuttal?
5. What are some of the statistics Morrow cites to win support for his arguments? Are they convincing?
6. Morrow points out that the National Rifle Association is part of the reason our country has no effective national gun control legislation. Why is this? What is your opinion of this lobbying organization? Why do you think it has so much influence?
7. Although he is critical of its opposition, Morrow apparently does not feel that the National Rifle Association is the primary cause of the problem. What does he identify as the real cause? Do you agree with him? Give reasons for your answer.
8. Given his views on nonviolent resistance and *agape,* what do you think Martin Luther King's response would have been to Morrow's statement in paragraph 7: "The freedoms of an American individualism bristling with small arms must yield to the larger communal claim to sanity and safety— the 'pursuit of happiness' "?

▼ RHETORICAL CONSIDERATIONS

1. In his opening, Morrow suggests that the use of handguns without regulation is a potentially explosive situation. How does he communicate this idea?
2. What is Morrow's thesis? Is it stated implicitly or explicitly? Explain.
3. Throughout the essay, Morrow paints a graphic picture of the violent, bloody effect that the absence of handgun regulation has on our nation. What figures of speech does he use to achieve this aim? How effective are they?
4. How would you characterize the tone of this essay—reasoned and objective? Emotional and flag-waving? Angry and bitter? Resigned and frustrated? Is it similar to or different from the tone of Gansberg's article? King's essay? Explain.
5. What do you think of Morrow's conclusion? Is his mention of Frederick Jackson Turner's thesis about the American frontier consistent with the rest of the essay? Explain.

▼ WRITING ASSIGNMENTS

1. Write an essay in which you offer a rebuttal to Morrow's argument in favor of gun control.
2. Do you own a gun? If so, and if you do not use it for hunting or target-shooting, explain why you own it.
3. If you are not a gun owner, do you think you ever could be? Can you imagine circumstances in which you might feel compelled to purchase one?

▼ WHY GUN CONTROL LAWS DON'T WORK

Barry Goldwater

A voice that has long represented the other side of the gun control issue is that of the conservative Republican and ex-senator from Arizona, Barry Goldwater. Here he says that if he believed gun control legislation would reduce violent crime, he would not hesitate to support it. He argues, however, that no matter what kinds of laws are enacted—registration or even outright banning—criminals would still be able to get weapons. He claims that America has a crime problem, not a gun problem, and on that premise he argues for stronger punishment for gun-related crimes. This article first appeared in *Reader's Digest* in 1975.

Let me say immediately that if I thought more gun-control laws would help   1
diminish the tragic incidence of robberies, muggings, rapes and murders in the
United States, I would be the first to vote for them. But I am convinced that
making more such laws approaches the problem from the wrong direction.

It is clear, I think, that gun legislation simply doesn't work. There are already   2
some 20,000 state and local gun laws on the books, and they are no more effective
than was the prohibition of alcoholic beverages in the 1920s. Our most recent
attempt at federal gun legislation was the Gun Control Act of 1968, intended to
control the interstate sale and transportation of firearms and the importation of
uncertified firearms; it has done nothing to check the availability of weapons. It
has been bolstered in every nook and cranny of the nation by local gun-control
laws, yet the number of shooting homicides per year has climbed steadily since its
enactment, while armed robberies have increased 60 percent.

Some people, even some law-enforcement officials, contend that "crimes of   3
passion" occur because a gun just happens to be present at the scene. I don't buy
that. I can't equate guns with the murder rate, because if a person is angry enough
to kill, he will kill with the first thing that comes to hand—a gun, a knife, an ice
pick, a baseball bat.

I believe our *only* hope of reducing crime in this country is to control not the   4
weapon but the user. We must reverse the trend toward leniency and permissiveness
in our courts—the plea bargaining, the pardons, the suspended sentences and
unwarranted paroles—and make the lawbreaker pay for what he has done by

spending time in jail. We have plenty of statutes against killing and maiming and threatening people with weapons. These can be made effective by strong enforcement and firm decisions from the bench. When a man knows that if he uses a potentially deadly object to rob or do harm to another person he is letting himself in for a mandatory, unparolable stretch behind bars, he will think twice about it.

Of course, no matter what gun-control laws are enacted—including national registration—the dedicated crook can always get a weapon. So, some people ask, even if national registration of guns isn't completely airtight, isn't it worth trying? Sure, it would cause a little inconvenience to law-abiding gun owners. And it certainly wouldn't stop all criminals from obtaining guns. But it might stop a few, maybe quite a few. What's wrong with that?   5

There are several answers. The first concerns enforcement. How are we going to persuade the bank robber or the street-corner stickup artist to register his means of criminal livelihood? Then there is the matter of expense. A study conducted eight years ago showed a cost to New York City of $72.87 to investigate and process one application for a pistol license. In mid-1970 dollars, the same procedure probably costs over $100. By extrapolation to the national scale, the cost to American taxpayers of investigating and registering the 40 to 50 million handguns might reach $4 billion or $5 billion. On top of that, keeping the process in operation year after year would require taxpayer financing of another sizable federal bureau. We ought to have far better prospects of success before we hobble ourselves with such appalling expenditures.   6

Finally, there are legal aspects based on the much-discussed Second Amendment to the Bill of Rights, which proclaims that "A well regulated Militia, being necessary to the security of a free State, the right of the people to keep and bear Arms, shall not be infringed." The anti-gun faction argues that this right made sense in the days of British oppression but that it has no application today. I contend, on the other hand, that the Founding Fathers conceived of an armed citizenry as a necessary hedge against tyranny from within as well as from without, that they saw the right to keep and bear arms as basic and perpetual, the one thing that could spell the difference between freedom and servitude. Thus I deem most forms of gun control unconstitutional in intent.   7

Well, then, I'm often asked, what kind of gun laws *are* you for? I reply that I am for laws of common sense. I am for laws that prohibit citizen access to machine guns, bazookas and other military devices. I am for laws that are educational in nature. I believe that before a person is permitted to buy a weapon he should be required to take a course that will teach him how to use it, to handle it safely and keep it safely about the house.   8

Gun education, in fact, can actually reduce lawlessness in a community, as was demonstrated in an experiment conducted in Highland Park, Mich. City police launched a program to instruct merchants in the use of handguns. The idea was to help them protect themselves and their businesses from robbers, and it was given wide publicity. The store-robbery rate dropped from an average of 1.5 a day to none in four months.   9

Where do we go from here? My answer to this is based on the firm belief that   10 we have a crime problem in this country, not a gun problem, and that we must meet the enemy on his own terms. We must start by making crime as unprofitable for him as we can. And we have to do this, I believe, by getting tough in the courts and corrections systems.

A recent news story in Washington, D.C., reports that, of 184 persons convicted   11 of gun possession in a six-month period, only 14 received a jail sentence. Forty-six other cases involved persons who had previously been convicted of a felony or possession of a gun. Although the maximum penalty for such repeaters in the District of Columbia is ten years in prison, half of these were not jailed at all. A study last year revealed that in New York City, which has about the most prohibitive gun legislation in the country, only one out of six people convicted of crimes involving weapons went to jail.

This sorry state of affairs exists because too many judges and magistrates   12 either don't know the law or are unwilling to apply it with appropriate vigor. It's time to demand either that they crack down on these criminals or be removed from office. It may even be time to review the whole system of judicial appointments, to stop weakening the cause of justice by putting men on the bench who may happen to be golfing partners of Congressmen and too often lack the brains and ability for the job. In Arizona today we elect our judges, and the system is working well, in part because we ask the American and local bar associations to consider candidates and make recommendations. In this way, over the last few years, we have replaced many weaklings with good jurists.

We have long had all the criminal statutes we need to turn the tide against the   13 crime wave. There is, however, one piece of proposed legislation that I am watching with particular interest. Introduced by Sen. James McClure (R., Idaho), it requires that any person convicted of a federal crime in which a gun is used serve five to ten years in jail automatically on top of whatever penalty he receives for the crime itself. A second conviction would result in an extra ten-year-to-life sentence. These sentences would be mandatory and could not be suspended. It is, in short, a "tough" bill. I think that this bill would serve as an excellent model for state legislation.

And so it has in California which, last September, signed into law a similar bill   14 requiring a mandatory jail sentence for any gun-related felony.

Finally, it's important to remember that this is an area of great confusion; an   15 area in which statistics can be juggled and distorted to support legislation that is liable to be expensive, counterproductive or useless. The issue touches upon the freedom and safety of all of us, whether we own firearms or not. The debate over gun control is an adjunct to the war against crime, and that war must be fought with all the intelligence and tenacity we can bring to it.

▼ TOPICAL CONSIDERATIONS

1. Goldwater argues that new gun control legislation can't be expected to be effective since existing laws are not. What would Morrow reply to this argument?

2. Supporters of gun control argue that guns encourage "crimes of passion" and contribute directly to an increased murder rate. Goldwater disagrees. What is his reasoning on this? How do his views differ from Morrow's?

3. Goldwater supports stronger enforcement of criminal sentences as a more effective deterrent for preventing crimes of passion. In defense of this, he reasons that such enforcement will cause a man to think twice before using any deadly weapon, including a gun. Do you see any contradiction between this and his reasoning about crimes of passion?

4. Why does Goldwater believe gun control is unconstitutional? Does he make a valid point?

5. What does Goldwater mean when he says that "we have a crime problem in this country, not a gun problem" (paragraph 10)? How is this different from Morrow's approach? What solutions does Goldwater suggest?

6. If you were judging a debate between Goldwater and Morrow, who would you decide had won? Consider how well each of them addresses the issues and whether either one successfully argues a point that the other fails to note.

▼ RHETORICAL CONSIDERATIONS

1. Compare Goldwater's opening to Morrow's. Which did you find more interesting? Why?

2. How is Goldwater's writing style different from Morrow's? Which one seems more literary? Which essay would work well as a political speech? Give reasons for your answers.

3. In a well-balanced argumentative essay, the writer considers the opposing arguments and offers a rebuttal. Does Goldwater do this? If so, how does he order his pro and con arguments?

4. Does Goldwater offer sufficient specific facts, details, and illustrations to support his arguments? Are there any points that need more development?

5. Do Goldwater's ideas flow logically from one to another? Point out some of the ways he achieves transition.

6. At several points, Goldwater asks questions of his reader. How effective is this technique? Why?

▼ WRITING ASSIGNMENTS

1. Suppose that you have just heard Barry Goldwater giving a political speech that argues along the same lines as this essay. Decide whether or not you are convinced of his stand. Write a letter telling him what you thought of his speech.

2. Write a newspaper editorial favoring or opposing gun control. Use the arguments you find in either Goldwater's essay or Morrow's that you believe are most convincing.

3. Have you ever witnessed a gun-related crime? If so, write a narrative description of the incident. Comment on how it influenced your views (if at all) on gun control.
4. Does anyone you know own a handgun? Write a paper in which you express how you feel about this.

▼ IT'S OVER, DEBBIE

Anonymous

The Journal of the American Medical Association is not known as a hotbed of controversy. Most of its articles are highly technical; and any debates found on its pages are cool exchanges in arcane language between medical specialists. Nevertheless, in 1988 the editors of JAMA created an uproar by publishing an article by an unidentified doctor describing how he had ended the life of a young woman dying painfully of cancer. According to the author, a resident physician, the only words from the woman were "Let's get this over with." A few minutes later the doctor gave the woman a lethal dose of morphine. The story of "Debbie" touched off widespread debate on the ethics of euthanasia. It also brought down considerable criticism of the Journal for not publishing the author's name (withheld by request) and for not including a clear statement of the AMA's opposition to mercy killing. Some of the hundreds of letters to the editors defended the doctor's action, courage, and compassion; but more expressed outrage. Reprinted here is It's over, Debbie as it originally appeared in JAMA in January 1988. On the following pages are three of the several letters subsequently published.

The call came in the middle of the night. As a gynecology resident rotating through a large, private hospital, I had come to detest telephone calls, because invariably I would be up for several hours and would not feel good the next day. However, duty called, so I answered the phone. A nurse informed me that a patient was having difficulty getting rest, could I please see her. She was on 3 North. That was the gynecologic-oncology unit, not my usual duty station. As I trudged along, bumping sleepily against walls and corners and not believing I was up again, I tried to imagine what I might find at the end of my walk. Maybe an elderly woman with an anxiety reaction, or perhaps something particularly horrible. 1

I grabbed the chart from the nurses station on my way to the patient's room, and the nurse gave me some hurried details: a 20-year-old girl named Debbie was dying of ovarian cancer. She was having unrelenting vomiting apparently as the result of an alcohol drip administered for sedation. Hmmm, I thought. Very sad. As I approached the room I could hear loud, labored breathing. I entered and saw an emaciated, dark-haired woman who appeared much older than 20. She was receiving nasal oxygen, had an IV, and was sitting in bed suffering from what was obviously severe air hunger. The chart noted her weight at 80 pounds. A second woman, also dark-haired but of middle age, stood at her right, holding her hand. Both looked up as I entered. The room seemed filled with the patient's desperate 2 effort to survive. Her eyes were hollow, and she had suprasternal and intercostal retractions with her rapid inspirations. She had not eaten or slept in two days. She had not responded to chemotherapy and was being given supportive care only. It was a gallows scene, a cruel mockery of her youth and unfulfilled potential. Her only words to me were, "Let's get this over with."

I retreated with my thoughts to the nurses station. The patient was tired and needed rest. I could not give her health, but I could give her rest. I asked the nurse to draw 20 mg of morphine sulfate into a syringe. Enough, I thought, to do the job. I took the syringe into the room and told the two women I was going to give Debbie something that would let her rest and to say good-bye. Debbie looked at the syringe, then laid her head on the pillow with her eyes open, watching what was left of the world. I injected the morphine intravenously and watched to see if my calculations on its effects would be correct. Within seconds her breathing slowed to a normal rate, her eyes closed, and her features softened as she seemed restful at last. The older woman stroked the hair of the now-sleeping patient. I waited for the inevitable next effect of depressing the respiratory drive. With clocklike certainty, within four minutes the breathing rate slowed even more, then became irregular, then ceased. The dark-haired woman stood erect and seemed relieved.   3

It's over, Debbie.   4

Name Withheld by Request

▼ TOPICAL CONSIDERATIONS

1. In your opinion, which description best fits the doctor's reaction to Debbie's plight—aggravation or sympathy?
2. While in the nurse's station the doctor comes to the following conclusion: "The patient was tired and needed rest. I could not give her health, but I could give her rest." Do you think this represents an adequate analysis of the situation? What factors does the doctor consider? What factors does the doctor ignore?
3. According to the doctor, Debbie's only words were "Let's get this over with." How did the doctor interpret her remark? What other possible interpretations could have been made from her remark?
4. What details suggest that Debbie and her companion knew and approved of what the doctor was doing? Do you find them convincing?
5. If you were the doctor, what would you have done for Debbie?

▼ RHETORICAL CONSIDERATIONS

1. What do you think the doctor's purpose was in the first paragraph? How does it enhance or detract from our opinion of the doctor and the actions taken?

2. How does the doctor's statement, "It was a gallows scene, a cruel mockery of her youth and unfulfilled potential," encapsulate the doctor's point of view and interpretation of the situation?
3. In the style or tone of this letter, is there any clue as to the gender of the doctor? Do you think the doctor was a man or a woman? Explain your reasoning.

▼ WRITING ASSIGNMENTS

1. Write your own letter to the editors of *JAMA* responding to the doctor's story.
2. Try to imagine how Debbie might have felt in the last moments of her life. In an essay, attempt to create from her point of view her encounter with the doctor.
3. Why do you think the doctor chose to write about the death of Debbie anonymously? Does this suggest a fear of possible repercussions or, perhaps, the doctor's own doubts about the propriety of the action? Write a paper in which you explore the doctor's choice of anonymity.
4. In a paper, write your own feelings about mercy killing. What specific conditions would you say have to be met for euthanasia to be practiced?

▼ RESPONSE TO *IT'S OVER, DEBBIE*

The extraordinary response to the publication of *It's Over, Debbie* showed a clear split between the medical profession and the public. While doctors were concerned with the preservation of life, the public was more interested in dying with minimal suffering and pain. At the heart of the debate is a question of ethics: What is more humane, prolonging the misery of a terminally-ill patient or ending it with a lethal injection? The letter from Susan D. Wilson to the editor of *JAMA* represents one of the several responses from lay people who defended the physician's decision to end Debbie's suffering.

To the Editor. —I read with a great deal of interest the article entitled "It's Over, Debbie." 1

My father, age 85 years, has been in a nursing home for more than a year. He is 2 incontinent, has lost his memory and ability to comprehend and reason, and is hospitalized periodically for pneumonia, urinary tract infection, dehydration, and so on.

He has now lost his ability to swallow, and since Christmas he has been fed 3 through a tube inserted in his nose. Because he tries to remove the tube, his hands are tied at all times to the bed rails. He is not comatose but he does not recognize his family and. he has no understanding of why he is being forced to lie in bed under these circumstances. I believe that if I were asked to make a list of ways in which to torture people, this would have to be placed somewhere near the top.

I am fully aware that a physician's duty is to treat and heal, but when healing is 4 clearly not possible, should not mercy killing be allowed? Humaneness is also a definitive part of the medical profession, and it seems that something should be done to prevent so many people from existing for sustained periods of time in a living hell. The technology we have today is wonderful, but it cannot and should not be used in every instance.

Susan D. Wilson
Glen Ellyn, Ill

▼ TOPICAL CONSIDERATIONS

1. Susan D. Wilson describes her aged father's condition and concludes, "The technology we have today is wonderful, but it cannot and should not be used in every instance." Do you agree that it should not be used in her father's case? Why, or why not?

2. How might the physician who terminated Debbie's life react to this letter from Susan D. Wilson? Do you think the physician would be willing to end the man's suffering?
3. If you were a doctor treating Wilson's father, how would you react to her appeal?

▼ RHETORICAL CONSIDERATION

1. Do you consider Susan Wilson's letter too emotional an appeal? Why, or why not?

▼ WRITING ASSIGNMENT

1. Suppose there was a movement in your state to put on the ballot a measure allowing a terminally-ill patient the right to request a lethal injection from a physician. Write an editorial supporting or condemning this movement.

▼ RESPONSE TO *IT'S OVER, DEBBIE*

> The following two letters to the editors of *JAMA* condemn the action taken by the anonymous physician to end Debbie's life. The first letter is from a member of the medical community, Harold Y. Vanderpool, who raises some troubling questions about professional ethics. The second letter, from Don C. Shaw, expresses the disapproval from the Hemlock Society, which advocates legalized doctor-assisted death only in conformation with specific requirements.

To the Editor. — The story entitled "It's Over, Debbie" raises profoundly troubling ethical issues — the more so because its sentimental surface masks a dark and worrisome underside. 1

On the surface of the story, a hassled but resolutely caring resident physician ends the hollow-eyed suffering of a young woman named Debbie by putting a stop to the cruel, "gallows"-like technology that mocks her youth and former vitality. 2

Just beneath the surface of these heartwarming themes lies the real point of the story — that in cases like this it is ethical for physicians to kill patients. Unfortunately, "It's Over, Debbie" only disguises and distorts the debate and clarification that are necessary for a moral assessment of mercy killing. First, the story's rhetoric (which is equated with the way the physician thinks) masks the act of killing Debbie with such euphemisms as doing one's "job," giving Debbie the "rest" she needs, and enabling her "to say goodbye." Second, the physician's premeditated manslaughter is associated only with such positive themes as hero-ically resisting a blind technological imperative within medicine or displaying unique empathy for this cancer patient's plight. Debbie's physician never struggles with opposing moral issues, such as whether this action could be generalized or whether killing constitutes a betrayal of one's promises to self and peers or what would happen if the term "physician" is also associated with putting persons to death. In fact, the resident kills Debbie with no moral qualms whatsoever. 3

Even more problematic than the morality of premeditated manslaughter per se, however, are the terribly murky grounds for killing in this instance. The physician's database on this new patient was gathered entirely while walking toward the patient's room (when the chart was scanned and as the nurse was talking), followed by a single visit to the patient. The one sentence uttered by the patient at the time, "Let's get this over with," was taken to be a firm request for a painless death from a fully competent adult. There are no consultations, no further conversations with anyone, no sophistication regarding pain relief as a beginning point, and no worries that Debbie's intentions may well have been 4 misread and that the physician may be committing murder in the second degree. The story ends with the physician observing that the "older woman" standing next to the patient the whole time "seemed relieved" when the morphine overdose (quickly supplied by the nurse) ends Debbie's life. Anything but relieved, I believe "It's Over, Debbie" needs a sequel entitled "It's Not Over, Doctor."

Harold Y. Vanderpool, PhD
Institute for the Medical Humanities
University of Texas Medical Branch
Galveston

To the Editor. —Hemlock of Illinois is grateful to *JAMA* for publishing "It's Over,   1 Debbie." In so doing, *JAMA* has contributed substantially to the dialogue on the important and unresolved issue of physician aid-in-dying.

    The Debbie story is the opposite of what the Hemlock Society espouses. It is   2 also the perfect story for what those supporting the right to life perceive as the dangers of legalizing physician aid-in-dying.

    We condemn the Debbie case as both illegal and unethical, both by present   3 law and ethics and by the law we hope to achieve in the near future. The Hemlock Society firmly believes in legalized physician aid-in-dying only when it confirms to the following requirements:

1. There must be adequate legal documentation that the euthanasia was requested by the patient well in advance of its occurring.
2. The physician who aids the patient in dying must have known the patient and must have been fully aware of his/her medical history and desire for aid-in-dying in the event of terminal illness.
3. The physician must have a second opinion from another qualified physician that affirms that the patient's condition is indeed terminal.
4. The rights of physicians who cannot in good conscience perform aid-in-dying are to be fully respected, providing they in no way obstruct the practice of physicians who in good conscience give such aid.

    There is indeed danger of abuse in euthanasia, just as there is in everything from   4 issuing drivers' licenses to selling alcohol and over-the-counter medications and, indeed, as there is in keeping "brain dead" comatose patients alive for long periods of time by the dogmatic use of modern technology. In the case of Debbie, there was simply the illegal and unethical killing of a patient by a resident physician.

Don C. Shaw
Hemlock of Illinois
Chicago

▼ TOPICAL CONSIDERATIONS

1. How, according to Vanderpool, does the physician use language to paint the lethal injection as "heroic" action? What terms does Vanderpool use to describe the physician's action? How does the language used by each writer influence the readers' responses?
2. Are you convinced by Vanderpool that the decision to end Debbie's life was done on "terribly murky grounds"?
3. How do the guidelines set down by the Hemlock Society for "aid-in-dying" guard against abuse by euthanasia?
4. Don C. Shaw warns of the "dangers of abuse in euthanasia." What are some possible dangers you might imagine?

▼ RHETORICAL CONSIDERATIONS

1. Harold Vanderpool ends his letter with the statement, "Anything but relieved, I believe 'It's Over, Debbie,' needs a sequel entitled 'It's Not Over, Doctor.'" What attitude does this statement convey about the doctor? What are the implications of "It's Not Over, Doctor"?
2. Don C. Shaw says that there is "danger of abuse in euthanasia" likening it to dangers in issuing drivers' licenses and selling alcohol and over-the-counter drugs. Is his analogy accurate and effective?

▼ WRITING ASSIGNMENT

1. One of the hundreds of letters received by the editors of *JAMA* in response to *It's Over, Debbie* described the physician in question as "jury, judge, and executioner of this young patient." Another called the doctor "a brave, caring, and progressive member" of the medical profession. Write an essay explaining which view you take of the doctor.

▼ IT ISN'T WORKING

William F. Buckley, Jr.

Should drugs be legal? The very notion seems unthinkable, however, the idea has gained a surprising amount of support from politicians, pundits, and drug experts. Logical and well-meaning proponents argue that the war on drugs is unwinnable and enormously costly in terms of dollars and potential infringement on civil liberties. One such voice for legalization is editor and columnist William F. Buckley, Jr., a man with impeccably conservative credentials. Buckley is editor of the periodical *National Review* and host of TV's long-running *Firing Line*. He is also the author of several books of nonfiction including *Overdrive* (1983) and *Up from Liberalism* (1984), and such best-selling novels as *See You Later, Alligator* (1985) and *High Jinx* (1986). Buckley's essay first appeared in his "On the Right" column in 1985.

1 We are with reason angry at the Mexican officials who ho-hummed their way through an investigation of the torture and killing of a U.S. drug agent who did what in Mexico is intolerable, namely stand in the way of graft. In Mexico, to do this is on the order of standing in the way of sex. Sex will prevail, graft will prevail.

2 It is true that a few years ago the government of Mexico cooperated in a program designed to spray the marijuana crop, but it proved temporary. Somewhat like wage and price controls. If for a season the marijuana crop from Mexico declines, then marijuana from elsewhere—Hawaii, for instance—will increase. If there is less marijuana being smoked today than 10 years ago, it is a reflection not of law enforcement but of creeping social perception. It has gradually transpired that the stuff is more harmful than originally thought, and a culture that spends billions of dollars on health foods and barbells is taking a longer, critical look at marijuana.

3 We read about cocaine. In a vivid image, someone recently said that the big radars along the 2,000-mile border between Mexico and the United States begin, night after night, to track what looks like a swarm of locusts headed our way. Private planes, carrying coke to the American market.

4 So we bag a large number of them today, and they show up on the television news. That plane over there was carrying $10 million (or was it $100 million?) worth of coke, hurray for the Drug Enforcement Agency. But then the sober evaluation comes through. Last year—a splendid year for drug apprehension—resulted in interdicting, oh, maybe 10 percent, 20 percent of the stuff coming in.

And of course the measure of success in the drug business, like that in the business of robbing banks, is, what are your chances of getting through? Answer: terrific. The odds will always be high, when you consider that the amount of coke you can stuff into a single pocket of a man's jacket can fetch $200,000, and that the cost of the stuff where picked up can be as low as $1,000. A profit of 2,000 percent (modest in the business) is a powerful engine to attempt to try to stop in a free society. In other societies the answer is as simple as executing anybody caught smuggling or using dope, exit the dope problem.

So what are we going to do about it? My resourceful brother William Safire has a hot bundle of ideas aimed at catching the people who launder the profits from drugs. These ideas include changing the color of our currency, so that the boys with big sacksful of green under their mattresses will be forced to bring them out, revealing their scarlet letters. Maybe we should breed 50 million drug-trained dogs to sniff at everyone getting off a boat or an airplane, what a great idea!

No, we are face to face with the rawest datum of them all, which is that the problem would not exist, except that in the United States there is a market for the stuff, and that the stuff is priced very high. If we cannot effectively prevent its insinuating its way into the country, what is it that we can prevent? The answer, of course, is its price. The one thing that could be done, overnight, is to legalize the stuff. Exit crime, and the profits from vice.

It is hardly a novel suggestion to legalize dope. Shrewd observers of the scene have recommended it for years. I am on record as having opposed it in the matter of heroin. The accumulated evidence draws me away from my own opposition, on the purely empirical grounds that what we have now is a drug problem plus a crime problem plus a problem of a huge export of capital to the dope-producing countries.

Congress should study the dramatic alternative, which is legalization followed by a dramatic educational effort in which the services of all civic-minded, and some less than civic-minded, resources are mobilized. Television, for instance. Let the Federal Communications Commission make it a part of the overhead of a TV license to broadcast 30 minutes a week, prime time, what dope does to you.

Ours is a free society in which oodles of people kill themselves with tobacco and booze. Some will do so with coke and heroin. But we should count in the lives saved by having the deadly stuff available at the same price as rat poison.

▼ TOPICAL CONSIDERATIONS

1. According to Buckley, why is marijuana being smoked less today than 10 years ago? According to your own observations and readings, does his explanation ring true?
2. Why does Buckley conclude that the cocaine business in America seems to be unstoppable by conventional law enforcement? What specific reasons does he offer?

3. Buckley refers to other societies where people caught smuggling or using dope are executed. Do you think Buckley would be in favor of employing the death penalty for drug users, drug smugglers, and drug dealers? Do you think he would be in favor of the death penalty for people who kill or order the killing of others involved with drug trafficking?
4. For what reasons does Buckley reverse his previous opposition to the legalization of heroin?
5. Twice in the essay Buckley refers to our "free society." How does he mean the term? How does he relate the concept of a free society with the use of drugs in America?
6. In Buckley's scheme to fight drugs, what role would civic organizations and television play? Do such suggestions seem feasible to you?
7. How does Buckley address the ethical problems of addiction, that is, how legalization would send the message that drugs are socially acceptable?
8. What do you think of Buckley's overall idea? Do you, in other words, think illegal drugs should be legalized? Do you think both the drug problem and the crime problem would be solved or at least mitigated? Has Buckley changed your attitude any on the subject?
9. Consider some of the potential problems of legalizing drugs. What effect would cheap, available drugs have on addiction? What would be the effect on health costs? What about the message to children that legalization makes drugs socially acceptable? What about the potential market for synthetic drugs or derivatives such as crack, whose effects are potentially deadly?

▼ RHETORICAL CONSIDERATIONS

1. How does Buckley's opening paragraph prepare for the arguments that follow?
2. In paragraph 3, Buckley likens "a vivid [radar] image" of plains flying cocaine into America to "a swarm of locusts" headed our way. Evaluate this simile. How appropriate is it? What biblical references are conjured up?
3. What does Buckley think of columnist William Safire's suggestions for curbing the drug trade? What indirect ways does he make clear his opinion of Safire's ideas?
4. Buckley ends his essay by suggesting that drugs could be sold "at the same price as rat poison." Evaluate the impact of this closing line. What does it say about Buckley's attitude toward drugs? What does it say about his attitude towards those who use them and towards those who would sell them legally?

▼ WRITING ASSIGNMENTS

1. Write a letter to Mr. Buckley telling him what you think of his suggestion to legalize drugs.

2. If drugs were legalized, would you take them? Write a paper in which you answer this question specifying the particular reasons.
3. A recent survey by the University of Michigan revealed that over 10 percent of the high school students and 14 percent of college students interviewed admitted to having tried cocaine. From your own observations, why do you think young people use cocaine? Write a paper in which you try to examine the various forces—from family, society, peers—that turn young people onto coke.
4. Buckley brings up the subject of educating people about drug abuse. How much media education have you noticed in recent months? Consider the extent of the "Just Say No!" campaigns and any antidrug programs or messages aired on television and radio. Do you think enough has been done to discourage use? Do you think that other measures need to be taken? Do you think the "education" is paying off? In short, are young people recognizing the great risk of cocaine and other drugs?
5. Write a paper in which you argue against the legalization of drugs. What stronger methods to curb the import and use do you recommend?
6. Write a paper in which you call for the strongest penalties for drug pushers and users. Use the library to cite some data to support your arguments.
7. Write a paper in which you consider the decriminalization of drug abuse, that is, the elimination of criminal penalties for use rather than sale. Do you think that treating addicts as sick people instead of criminals is more ethical? Do you think that such decriminalization would discourage kids from using drugs?

▼ LEGALIZE DRUGS? NOT ON YOUR LIFE

Charles B. Rangel

Despite the frustration over failed policy, soaring drug-crime, and rising profits to drug-lords, there are many who loudly oppose the idea of making drugs legal. One such opponent is Democratic Congressman Charles B. Rangel, who represents a drug-infested district in New York's Harlem and who chairs the House Committee on Narcotics Abuse and Control. Voicing the opinion that legalization would be a dangerous experiment, Rangel poses a long list of tough questions for those who would legalize drugs. This piece was first printed in the *New York Times* in May 1988.

1 The escalating drug crisis is beginning to take its toll on many Americans. And now growing numbers of well-intentioned officials and other opinion leaders are saying that the best way to fight drugs is to legalize them. But what they're really admitting is that they're willing to abandon a war that we have not even begun to fight.

2 For example, the newly elected and promising Mayor of Baltimore, Kurt Schmoke, at a meeting of the United States Conference of Mayors, called for a full-scale study of the feasibility of legalization. His comments could not have come at a worse time, for we are in the throes of the worst drug epidemic in our history.

3 Here we are talking about legalization, and we have yet to come up with any formal national strategy or any commitment from the Administration on fighting drugs beyond mere words. We have never fought the war on drugs like we have fought other legitimate wars—with all the forces at our command.

4 Just the thought of legalization brings up more problems and concerns than already exist.

5 Advocates of legalization should be reminded, for example, that it's not as simple as opening up a chain of friendly neighborhood pharmacies. Press them about some of the issues and questions surrounding this proposed legalization, and they never seem to have any answers. At least not any logical, well thought out ones.

6 Those who tout legalization remind me of fans sitting in the cheap seats at the ballpark. They may have played the game, and they may think they know all the rules, but from where they're sitting they can't judge the action.

7 Has anybody ever considered which narcotic and psychotropic drugs would be legalized?

8 Would we allow all drugs to become legally sold and used, or would we select the most abused few, such as cocaine, heroin and marijuana?

Who would administer the dosages—the state or the individual? 9

What quantity of drugs would each individual be allowed to get? 10

What about addicts: Would we not have to give them more in order to satisfy 11 their craving, or would we give them enough to just whet their appetites?

What do we do about those who are experimenting? Do we sell them the 12 drugs, too, and encourage them to pick up the habit?

Furthermore, will the Government establish tax-supported facilities to sell 13 these drugs?

Would we get the supply from the same foreign countries that support 14 our habit now, or would we create our own internal sources and "dope fac-tories," paying people the minimum wage to churn out mounds of cocaine and bales of marijuana?

Would there be an age limit on who can purchase drugs, as exists with 15 alcohol? What would the market price be and who would set it? Would private industry be allowed to have a stake in any of this?

What are we going to do about underage youngsters—the age group hardest 16 hit by the crack crisis? Are we going to give them identification cards? How can we prevent adults from purchasing drugs for them?

How many people are projected to become addicts as a result of the introduc- 17 tion of cheaper, more available drugs sanctioned by government?

Since marijuana remains in a person's system for weeks, what would we do 18 about pilots, railroad engineers, surgeons, police, cross-country truckers and nuclear plant employees who want to use it during off-duty hours? And what would be the effect on the health insurance industry?

Many of the problems associated with drug abuse will not go away just 19 because of legalization. For too long we have ignored the root cause, failing to see the connection between drugs and hopelessness, helplessness and despair.

We often hear that legalization would bring an end to the bloodshed and 20 violence that has often been associated with the illegal narcotics trade. The profit will be taken out of it, so to speak, as will be the urge to commit crime to get money to buy drugs. But what gives anybody the impression that legalization would deter many jobless and economically deprived people from resorting to crime to pay for their habits?

Even in a decriminalized atmosphere, money would still be needed to support 21 habits. Because drugs would be cheaper and more available, people would want more and would commit more crime. Does anybody really think the black market would disappear? There would always be opportunities for those who saw profit in peddling larger quantities, or improved versions, of products that are forbidden or restricted.

Legalization would completely undermine any educational effort we under- 22 take to persuade kids about the harmful effects of drugs. Today's kids have not yet been totally lost to the drug menace, but if we legalize these substances they'll surely get the message that drugs are O.K.

Not only would our young people realize that the threat of jail and punish- 23 ment no longer exists. They would pick up the far more damaging message that the use of illegal narcotics does not pose a significant enough health threat for the Government to ban its use.

If we really want to do something about drug abuse, let's end this nonsensical talk about legalization right now. 24

Let's put the pressure on our leaders to first make the drug problem a priority issue on the national agenda, then let's see if we can get a coordinated national battle plan that would include the deployment of military personnel and equipment to wipe out this foreign-based national security threat. Votes by the House and more recently the Senate to involve the armed forces in the war on drugs are steps in the right direction. 25

Finally, let's take this legalization issue and put it where it belongs—amid idle chit-chat as cocktail glasses knock together at social events. 26

▼ TOPICAL CONSIDERATIONS

1. Rangel complains that people who call for the legalization of drugs leave too many questions unanswered. Which of the questions he raises seem the most problematic from an administrative point of view? Which questions seem to be the least problematic? How about from a moral point of view? Do you agree that more problems would be created rather than solved?
2. Can you think of any problems of legalization that Rangel has not addressed?
3. Why does Rangel feel that decriminalization will not solve the addiction problem? The crime problem?
4. Rangel says that for "too long we have ignored the root cause" of our drug problems. What are those causes and how does he address them? Do you agree that such causes have been ignored?
5. Do you think the black market on drugs would disappear under a system of legalization?
6. How would legalization adversely affect children according to Rangel? Do you agree with his assessment?
7. What specific measures does Rangel call for in dealing with the drug problem in America? Do his suggestions seem viable? Do you foresee any problems these measures might create?

▼ RHETORICAL CONSIDERATIONS

1. How do the first three paragraphs prepare the arguments against the legalization of drugs?
2. What would you say is the thesis statement of this essay?
3. The core of this piece consists of more than a dozen questions about the legalization of drugs. Do you detect any logic or plan to the sequencing? Are the questions just randomly listed?
4. In the last paragraph Rangel says that legalization should be confined to

"idle chit-chat as cocktail glasses knock together at social events." What does he mean by this? What sarcastic statement is he making?

▼ WRITING ASSIGNMENTS

1. Try to imagine how William F. Buckley, Jr. might answer some of the questions Rangel brings up (paragraphs 7 through 18) about administering drugs were they legalized.
2. Some people have pointed out that it is hypocritical to ban narcotics while allowing the sale of alcohol and tobacco. In a paper express your own views on this apparent hypocrisy. Do you think the government has a right telling people what they may or may not put into their bodies? Do you think that use of tobacco and alcohol should be made criminal?
3. Consider the argument that the continued war on drugs by law enforcement agencies threatens individual freedom posed by drug searches, demands for testing, and the use of the military to enforce narcotics laws. Write a paper in which you weigh the encroachment on freedom against the problems Rangel foresees under legalization.
4. Some people opposed to full-scale legalization opt for decriminalization of drug use. What do you think of this half-way solution? Write a paper in which you explore such an alternative to full legalization. Do you think current problems would be diminished or increased?

▼ DEATH AND JUSTICE: HOW CAPITAL PUNISHMENT AFFIRMS LIFE

Edward I. Koch

There are more murders committed in New York than in any other American city. Since 1978, Edward Koch, a long active Democrat, has served as mayor of New York City. In those years he established a reputation as a hard-driving, no-nonsense, and feisty leader. In the piece below, originally published in *The New Republic* in March 1985, Koch argues that the death penalty is the only just recourse we have to "heinous crimes of murder." In building his case, he examines the arguments most frequently voiced by opponents to capital punishment. Koch is the author of *Mayor: an Autobiography* (1984) written with William Rauch.

Last December a man named Robert Lee Willie, who had been convicted of raping and murdering an 18-year-old woman, was executed in the Louisiana state prison. In a statement issued several minutes before his death, Mr. Willie said: "Killing people is wrong. . . . It makes no difference whether it's citizens, countries, or governments. Killing is wrong." Two weeks later in South Carolina, an admitted killer named Joseph Carl Shaw was put to death for murdering two teenagers. In an appeal to the governor for clemency, Mr. Shaw wrote: "Killing is wrong when I did it. Killing is wrong when you do it. I hope you have the courage and moral strength to stop the killing."

It is a curiosity of modern life that we find ourselves being lectured on morality by cold-blooded killers. Mr. Willie previously had been convicted of aggravated rape, aggravated kidnapping, and the murders of a Louisiana deputy and a man from Missouri. Mr. Shaw committed another murder a week before the two for which he was executed, and admitted mutilating the body of the 14-year-old girl he killed. I can't help wondering what prompted these murderers to speak out against killing as they entered the deathhouse door. Did their newfound reverence for life stem from the realization that they were about to lose their own?

Life is indeed precious, and I believe the death penalty helps to affirm this fact. Had the death penalty been a real possibility in the minds of these murderers, they might well have stayed their hand. They might have shown moral awareness before their victims died, and not after. Consider the tragic death of Rosa Velez, who happened to be home when a man named Luis Vera burglarized her apartment in Brooklyn. "Yeah, I shot her," Vera admitted. "She knew me, and I knew I wouldn't go to the chair."

1

2

3

During my twenty-two years in public service, I have heard the pros and cons   4
of capital punishment expressed with special intensity. As a district leader,
councilman, congressman, and mayor, I have represented constituencies generally thought of as liberal. Because I support the death penalty for heinous crimes
of murder, I have sometimes been the subject of emotional and outraged attacks
by voters who find my position reprehensible or worse. I have listened to their
ideas. I have weighed their objections carefully. I still support the death penalty.
The reasons I maintain my position can be best understood by examining the
arguments most frequently heard in opposition.

1. The death penalty is "barbaric." Sometimes opponents of capital punish-   5
ment horrify with tales of lingering death on the gallows, of faulty electric chairs,
or of agony in the gas chamber. Partly in response to such protests, several states
such as North Carolina and Texas switched to execution by lethal injection. The
condemned person is put to death painlessly, without ropes, voltage, bullets, or
gas. Did this answer the objections of death penalty opponents? Of course not. On
June 22, 1984, the *New York Times* published an editorial that sarcastically
attacked the new "hygienic" method of death by injection, and stated that "execution
can never be made humane through science." So it's not the method that really
troubles opponents. It's the death itself they consider barbaric.

Admittedly, capital punishment is not a pleasant topic. However, one does not   6
have to like the death penalty in order to support it any more than one must like
radical surgery, radiation, or chemotherapy in order to find necessary these
attempts at curing cancer. Ultimately we may learn how to cure cancer with a
simple pill. Unfortunately, that day has not yet arrived. Today we are faced with
the choice of letting the cancer spread or trying to cure it with the methods
available, methods that one day will almost certainly be considered barbaric. But
to give up and do nothing would be far more barbaric and would certainly delay
the discovery of an eventual cure. The analogy between cancer and murder is
imperfect, because murder is not the "disease" we are trying to cure. The disease
is injustice. We may not like the death penalty, but it must be available to punish
crimes of cold-blooded murder, cases in which any other form of punishment
would be inadequate and, therefore, unjust. If we create a society in which
injustice is not tolerated, incidents of murder—the most flagrant form of injustice—
will diminish.

2. No other major democracy uses the death penalty. No other major   7
democracy—in fact, few other countries of any description—are plagued by a
murder rate such as that in the United States. Fewer and fewer Americans can
remember the days when unlocked doors were the norm and murder was a rare
and terrible offense. In America the murder rate climbed 122 percent between
1963 and 1980. During that same period, the murder rate in New York City
increased by almost 400 percent, and the statistics are even worse in many other
cities. A study at M.I.T. showed that based on 1970 homicide rates a person who
lived in a large American city ran a greater risk of being murdered than an
American soldier in World War II ran of being killed in combat. It is not surprising
that the laws of each country differ according to differing conditions and traditions.

If other countries had our murder problem, the cry for capital punishment would be just as loud as it is here. And I daresay that any other major democracy where 75 percent of the people supported the death penalty would soon enact it into law.

3. An innocent person might be executed by mistake. Consider the work of   8
Hugo Adam Bedau, one of the most implacable foes of capital punishment in this country. According to Mr. Bedau, it is "false sentimentality to argue that the death penalty should be abolished because of the abstract possibility that an innocent person might be executed." He cites a study of the 7,000 executions in this country from 1893 to 1971, and concludes that the record fails to show that such cases occur. The main point, however, is this. If government functioned only when the possibility of error didn't exist, government wouldn't function at all. Human life deserves special protection, and one of the best ways to guarantee that protection is to assure that convicted murderers do not kill again. Only the death penalty can accomplish this end. In a recent case in New Jersey, a man named Richard Biegenwald was freed from prison after serving 18 years for murder; since his release he has been convicted of committing four murders. A prisoner named Lemuel Smith, who, while serving four life sentences for murder (plus two life sentences for kidnapping and robbery) in New York's Green Haven Prison, lured a woman corrections officer into the chaplain's office and strangled her. He then mutilated and dismembered her body. An additional life sentence for Smith is meaningless. Because New York has no death penalty statute, Smith has effectively been given a license to kill.

But the problem of multiple murder is not confined to the nation's peniten-   9
tiaries. In 1981, 91 police officers were killed in the line of duty in this country. Seven percent of those arrested in the cases that have been solved had a previous arrest for murder. In New York City in 1976 and 1977, 85 persons arrested for homicide had a previous arrest for murder. Six of these individuals had two previous arrests for murder, and one had four previous murder arrests. During those two years the New York police were arresting for murder persons with a previous arrest for murder on the average of one every 8.5 days. This is not surprising when we learn that in 1975, for example, the median time served in Massachusetts for homicide was less than two and a half years. In 1976 a study sponsored by the Twentieth Century Fund found that the average time served in the United States for first-degree murder is ten years. The median time served may be considerably lower.

4. Capital punishment cheapens the value of human life. On the contrary, it   10
can be easily demonstrated that the death penalty strengthens the value of human life. If the penalty for rape were lowered, clearly it would signal a lessened regard for the victims' suffering, humiliation, and personal integrity. It would cheapen their horrible experience, and expose them to an increased danger of recurrence. When we lower the penalty for murder, it signals a lessened regard for the value of the victim's life. Some critics of capital punishment, such as columnist Jimmy Breslin, have suggested that a life sentence is actually a harsher penalty for murder than death. This is sophistic nonsense. A few killers may decide not to

appeal a death sentence, but the overwhelming majority make every effort to stay alive. It is by exacting the highest penalty for the taking of human life that we affirm the highest value of human life.

5. *The death penalty is applied in a discriminatory manner.* This factor no 11 longer seems to be the problem it once was. The appeals process for a condemned prisoner is lengthy and painstaking. Every effort is made to see that the verdict and sentence were fairly arrived at. However, assertions of discrimination are not an argument for ending the death penalty but for extending it. It is not justice to exclude everyone from the penalty of the law if a few are found to be so favored. Justice requires that the law be applied equally to all.

6. *Thou Shalt Not Kill.* The Bible is our greatest source of moral inspiration. 12 Opponents of the death penalty frequently cite the sixth of the Ten Command- ments in an attempt to prove that capital punishment is divinely proscribed. In the original Hebrew, however, the Sixth Commandment reads "Thou Shalt Not Com- mit Murder," and the Torah specifies capital punishment for a variety of offenses. The biblical viewpoint has been upheld by philosophers throughout history. The greatest thinkers of the 19th century—Kant, Locke, Hobbes, Rousseau, Montesquieu, and Mill—agreed that natural law properly authorizes the sovereign to take life in order to vindicate justice. Only Jeremy Bentham was ambivalent. Washington, Jefferson, and Franklin endorsed it. Abraham Lincoln authorized executions for deserters in wartime. Alexis de Tocqueville, who expressed profound respect for American institutions, believed that the death penalty was indispensable to the support of social order. The United States Constitution, widely admired as one of the seminal achievements in the history of humanity, condemns cruel and inhu- man punishment, but does not condemn capital punishment.

7. *The death penalty is state-sanctioned murder.* This is the defense with 13 which Messrs. Willie and Shaw hoped to soften the resolve of those who sen- tenced them to death. By saying in effect, "You're no better than I am," the murderer seeks to bring his accusers down to his own level. It is also a popular argument among opponents of capital punishment, but a transparently false one. Simply put, the state has rights that the private individual does not. In a democracy, those rights are given to the state by the electorate. The execution of a lawfully condemned killer is no more an act of murder than is legal imprisonment an act of kidnapping. If an individual forces a neighbor to pay him money under threat of punishment, it's called extortion. If the state does it, it's called taxation. Rights and responsibilities surrendered by the individual are what give the state its power to govern. This contract is the foundation of civilization itself.

Everyone wants his or her rights, and will defend them jealously. Not everyone, 14 however, wants responsibilities, especially the painful responsibilities that come with law enforcement. Twenty-one years ago a woman named Kitty Genovese was assaulted and murdered on a street in New York. Dozens of neighbors heard her cries for help but did nothing to assist her. They didn't even call the police. In such a climate the criminal understandably grows bolder. In the presence of moral cowardice, he lectures us on our supposed failings and tries to equate his crimes with our quest for justice.

The death of anyone—even a convicted killer—diminishes us all. But we are 15
diminished even more by a justice system that fails to function. It is an illusion to
let ourselves believe that doing away with capital punishment removes the murderer's
deed from our conscience. The rights of society are paramount. When we protect
guilty lives, we give up innocent lives in exchange. When opponents of capital
punishment say to the state, "I will not let you kill in my name," they are also
saying to murderers: "You can kill in your *own* name as long as I have an excuse
for not getting involved."

It is hard to imagine anything worse than being murdered while neighbors do 16
nothing. But something worse exists. When those same neighbors shrink back
from justly punishing the murderer, the victim dies twice.

▼ TOPICAL CONSIDERATIONS

1. What would you say is Koch's key reason for supporting the death penalty? Does his argument seem convincing? Has it changed your attitude on the issue?
2. In the debates over capital punishment Koch distinguishes two issues: punishment and deterrence. Which of the arguments against his opposition are rooted in punishment? Which are rooted in deterrence?
3. What is Koch's argument against opponents' claim that the death penalty makes great the risk of putting to death innocent people? How sound is his stand?
4. In paragraph 4, Koch says that he supports capital punishment for "heinous crimes of murder." Do you think he is distinguishing different kinds of murder? In other words, do you think he is arguing capital punishment for special cases of murder? If so, what might be the criteria Koch suggests? Which criteria would you consider?
5. Of the seven opposition arguments Koch counters, which do you find the strongest? Which do you find the weakest? Why? Which of Koch's counter-arguments did you find to be the most convincing? Which did you find the least convincing? Why?
6. Can you think of any arguments against the death penalty that Koch fails to address? Can you think of any arguments for the death penalty that Koch may have missed?

▼ RHETORICAL CONSIDERATIONS

1. Where exactly does Koch make his thesis statement in this essay?
2. In paragraph 6, Koch likens murder to cancer and the death penalty to cancer treatment. How apt is this analogy?
3. Koch has built his case against the abolition of capital punishment by appeals to logic, emotions, and ethics. Reread the essay and find examples

of each of these different appeals. Which were the most effective? Which were the least effective? Explain your answers.

4. How would you describe the tone of Koch's writing?

▼ WRITING ASSIGNMENTS

1. Suppose that your state legislature is considering a bill to abolish capital punishment. Write a letter to your state representative urging him or her to oppose the bill. Use the arguments from Koch's essay that you feel will be most convincing.

2. There are many opponents of capital punishment who say that the death penalty is "cruel and unusual punishment" and argue that the government should not be in the business of taking human lives. What is your feeling about this particular argument? Do you think the government has the right to take lives? Do you think that capital punishment reduces the government to the level of those who murder?

▼ THE DEATH PENALTY

David Bruck

In April 1985, a month after *The National Review* published Mayor Koch's defense of capital punishment, it published the following response by David Bruck. Questioning the basis of Koch's defense argument and finding it morally dangerous, Bruck goes on to suggest that Koch has made the electric chair a campaign platform. Frustrated and enraged by violent crime and the inability of government to stop it, the public, of course, supports the call for blood, says Bruck—even if the measure doesn't work. Bruck is a lawyer in the South Carolina Office of Appellate Defense. Many of his defendants are prisoners under the death sentence.

1   Mayor Ed Koch contends that the death penalty "affirms life." By failing to execute murderers, he says, we "signal a lessened regard for the value of the victim's life." Koch suggests that people who oppose the death penalty are like Kitty Genovese's neighbors, who heard her cries for help but did nothing while an attacker stabbed her to death.

2   This is the standard "moral" defense of death as punishment: even if executions don't deter violent crime any more effectively than imprisonment, they are still required as the only means we have of doing justice in response to the worst of crimes.

3   Until recently, this "moral" argument had to be considered in the abstract, since no one was being executed in the United States. But the death penalty is back now, at least in the southern states, where every one of the more than 30 executions carried out over the last two years has taken place. Those of us who live in those states are getting to see the difference between the death penalty in theory, and what happens when you actually try to use it.

4   South Carolina resumed executing prisoners in January with the electrocution of Joseph Carl Shaw. Shaw was condemned to death for helping to murder two teenagers while he was serving as a military policeman at Fort Jackson, South Carolina. His crime, propelled by mental illness and PCP, was one of terrible brutality. It is Shaw's last words ("Killing was wrong when I did it. It is wrong when you do it. . . . ") that so outraged Mayor Koch: he finds it "a curiosity of modern life that we are being lectured on morality by cold-blooded killers." And so it is.

5   But it was not "modern life" that brought this curiosity into being. It was capital punishment. The electric chair was J. C. Shaw's platform. (The mayor mistakenly writes that Shaw's statement came in the form of a plea to the governor for clemency: actually Shaw made it only seconds before his death, as he waited, shaved and strapped into the chair, for the switch to be thrown.) It was the chair

that provided Shaw with celebrity and an opportunity to lecture us on right and wrong. What made this weird moral reversal even worse is that J. C. Shaw faced his own death with undeniable dignity and courage. And while Shaw died, the TV crews recorded another "curiosity" of the death penalty—the crowd gathered outside the deathhouse to cheer on the executioner. Whoops of elation greeted the announcement of Shaw's death. Waiting at the penitentiary gates for the appearance of the hearse bearing Shaw's remains, one demonstrator started yelling, "Where's the beef?"

For those who had to see the execution of J. C. Shaw, it wasn't easy to keep in mind that the purpose of the whole spectacle was to affirm life. It will be harder still when Florida executes a cop-killer named Alvin Ford. Ford has lost his mind during his years of death-row confinement, and now spends his days trembling, rocking back and forth, and muttering unintelligible prayers. This has led to litigation over whether Ford meets a centuries-old legal standard for mental competency. Since the Middle Ages, the Anglo-American legal system has generally prohibited the execution of anyone who is too mentally ill to understand what is about to be done to him and why. If Florida wins its case, it will have earned the right to electrocute Ford in his present condition. If it loses, he will not be executed until the state has first nursed him back to some semblance of mental health.* 6

We can at least be thankful that this demoralizing spectacle involves a prisoner who is actually guilty of murder. But this may not always be so. The ordeal of Lenell Jeter—the young black engineer who recently served more than a year of a life sentence for a Texas armed robbery that he didn't commit—should remind us that the system is quite capable of making the very worst sort of mistake. That Jeter was eventually cleared is a fluke. If the robbery had occurred at 7 P.M. rather than 3 P.M, he'd have had no alibi, and would still be in prison today. And if someone had been killed in that robbery, Jeter probably would have been sentenced to death. We'd have seen the usual execution-day interviews with state officials and the victim's relatives, all complaining that Jeter's appeals took too long. And Jeter's last words from the gurney would have taken their place among the growing literature of death-house oration that so irritates the mayor. 7

Koch quotes Hugo Adam Bedau, a prominent abolitionist, to the effect that the record fails to establish that innocent defendants have been executed in the past. But this doesn't mean, as Koch implies, that it hasn't happened. All Bedau was saying was that doubts concerning executed prisoner's guilt are almost never resolved. Bedau is at work now on an effort to determine how many wrongful death sentences may have been imposed: his list of murder convictions since 1900 in which the state eventually *admitted* error is some 400 cases long. Of course, very few of these cases involved actual executions: the mistakes that Bedau documents were uncovered precisely because the prisoner was alive and able to 8

---

*Florida lost its case to execute Ford. On 26 June 1986 the Supreme Court barred execution of convicted murderers who have become so insane that they do not know they are about to be executed nor the reason for it. If Ford regains his sanity, however, he can be executed. (Editor's note)

fight for his vindication. The cases where someone is executed are the very cases in which we're least likely to learn that we got the wrong man.

I don't claim that executions of entirely innocent people will occur very often. 9
But they will occur. And other sorts of mistakes already have. Roosevelt Green was executed in Georgia two days before J. C. Shaw. Green and an accomplice kidnapped a young woman. Green swore that his companion shot her to death after Green had left, and that he knew nothing about the murder. Green's claim was supported by a statement that his accomplice made to a witness after the crime. The jury never resolved whether Green was telling the truth, and when he tried to take a polygraph examination a few days before his scheduled execution, the state of Georgia refused to allow the examiner into the prison. As the pressure for symbolic retribution mounts, the courts, like the public, are losing patience with such details. Green was electrocuted on January 9, while members of the Ku Klux Klan rallied outside the prison.

Then there is another sort of arbitrariness that happens all the time. Last 10
October, Louisiana executed a man named Ernest Knighton. Knighton had killed a gas station owner during a robbery. Like any murder, this was a terrible crime. But it was not premeditated, and is the sort of crime that very rarely results in a death sentence. Why was Knighton electrocuted when almost everyone else who committed the same offense was not? Was it because he was black? Was it because his victim and all 12 members of the jury that sentenced him were white? Was it because Knighton's court-appointed lawyer presented no evidence on his behalf at his sentencing hearing? Or maybe there's no reason except bad luck. One thing is clear: Ernest Knighton was picked out to die the way a fisherman takes a cricket out of a bait jar. No one cares which cricket gets impaled on the hook.

Not every prisoner executed recently was chosen that randomly. But many 11
were. And having selected these men so casually, so blindly, the death penalty system asks us to accept that the purpose of killing each of them is to affirm the sanctity of human life.

The death penalty states are also learning that the death penalty is easier 12
to advocate than it is to administer. In Florida, where executions have become almost routine, the governor reports that nearly a third of his time is spent reviewing the clemency requests of condemned prisoners. The Florida Supreme Court is hopelessly backlogged with death cases. Some have taken five years to decide, and the rest of the Court's work waits in line behind the death appeals. Florida's death row currently holds more than 230 prisoners. State officials are reportedly considering building a special "death prison" devoted entirely to the isolation and electrocution of the condemned. The state is also considering the creation of a special public defender unit that will do nothing else but handle death penalty appeals. The death penalty, in short, is spawning death agencies.

And what is Florida getting for all of this? The state went through almost all of 13
1983 without executing anyone: its rate of intentional homicide declined by 17 percent. Last year Florida executed eight people—the most of any state, and the sixth highest total for any year since Florida started electrocuting people back in

1924. Elsewhere in the U.S. last year, the homicide rate continued to decline. But in Florida, it actually rose by 5.1 percent.

But these are just the tiresome facts. The electric chair has been a centerpiece 14 of each of Koch's recent political campaigns, and he knows better than anyone how little the facts have to do with the public's support for capital punishment. What really fuels the death penalty is the justifiable frustration and rage of people who see that the government is not coping with violent crime. So what if the death penalty doesn't work? At least it gives us the satisfaction of knowing that we got one or two of the sons of bitches.

Perhaps we want retribution on the flesh and bone of a handful of convicted 15 murderers so badly that we're willing to close our eyes to all of the demoralization and danger that come with it. A lot of politicians think so, and they may be right. But if they are, then let's at least look honestly at what we're doing. This lottery of death both comes from and encourages an attitude toward human life that is not reverent, but reckless.

And that is why the mayor is dead wrong when he confuses such fury with 16 justice. He suggests that we trivialize murder unless we kill murderers. By that logic, we also trivialize rape unless we sodomize rapists. The sin of Kitty Genovese's neighbors wasn't that they failed to stab her attacker to death. Justice does demand that murderers be punished. And common sense demands that society be protected from them. But neither justice nor self-preservation demands that we kill men whom we have already imprisoned.

The electric chair in which J. C. Shaw died earlier this year was built in 1912 17 at the suggestion of South Carolina's governor at the time, Cole Blease. Governor Blease's other criminal justice initiative was an impassioned crusade in favor of lynch law. Any lesser response, the governor insisted, trivialized the loathsome crimes of interracial rape and murder. In 1912 a lot of people agreed with Governor Blease that a proper regard for justice required both lynching and the electric chair. Eventually we are going to learn that justice requires neither.

▼ TOPICAL CONSIDERATIONS

1. Compare Bruck's account of J. C. Shaw's crime with that of Koch's account. Does knowing the circumstances—that is, the crime being "propelled by mental illness and PCP"—strengthen Bruck's argument against capital punishment? Do these details weaken Koch's argument? How about the fact that Shaw's words, coming moments before his execution, were not, as Koch suggests, an appeal for clemency? Do these details change your stand on capital punishment?

2. What would you say form the basis of Bruck's opposition to the death penalty? How does it compare with the basis of Koch's advocacy for the death penalty?

3. What is the heart of Bruck's counter-argument against Edward Koch? Do you agree or disagree with Bruck's view?

4. How does Bruck use the Lenell Jeter case? In your estimation, is this a convincing argument for the abolition of the death penalty? Why, or why not?

5. How does Bruck make use of the research of abolitionist Hugo Adam Bedau who is cited as support in Koch's essay? Do you think Bruck is successful in undermining Koch's own use of Bedau?

6. If not capital punishment, what form of justice do you think Bruck would see fit for "heinous crimes of murder"? What punishment(s) do you see fit?

7. In paragraph 10, Bruck brings up the case of Ernest Knighton executed for a murder that was not premeditated. What do you think Koch would say about this case?

8. In paragraph 14, Bruck says that the public's support of capital punishment is fueled by the "frustration and rage of people who see that government is not coping with violent crime." Do you agree with this claim? Do you agree with the rationalization that even "if the death penalty doesn't work," at least "we got one or two of the sons of bitches."

▼ RHETORICAL CONSIDERATIONS

1. Where exactly does Bruck state his thesis?

2. What is the point of letting the reader know about the crowd's reaction to the execution of J. C. Shaw? How do these details add to the arguments the author is making?

3. In the previous essay, Mayor Koch says that the Bible, "our greatest source of moral inspiration," takes the eye-for-an-eye view of justice: The punishment for murder is death. How does Bruck counter this stand and how effective is his argument against it?

▼ WRITING ASSIGNMENTS

1. Adopt the point of view of a supporter of capital punishment who has just read Bruck's essay. Write a letter to the author in which you offer a rebuttal to his argument. Include some emotional appeals and try to show some fallacies in Bruck's reasoning.

2. Suppose that your state legislature is considering a bill to abolish capital punishment. Write a letter to your state representative asking that he or she support the bill. Include the arguments in Bruck's essay that you feel will be most convincing.

3. Suppose you were on a panel of judges presiding over a debate between Edward Koch and David Bruck. Having heard their arguments in these essays, who would you decide had won the debate? Write an essay in which you defend your decision.

THE NATURAL WORLD

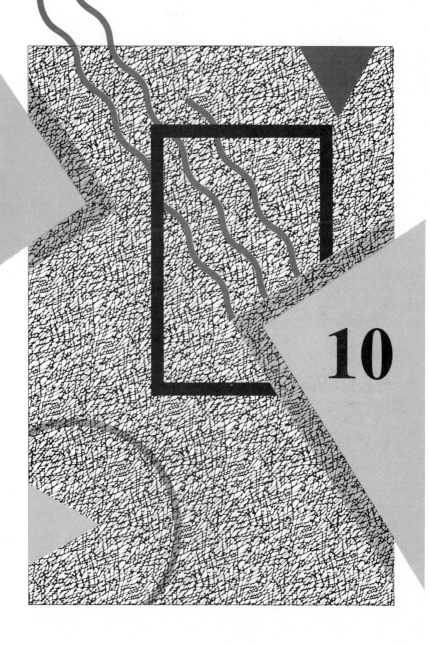

10

▼ WHAT ON EARTH ARE WE DOING?

Thomas A. Sancton

Our magnificent planet has endured for 4.5 billion years, but its future is clouded by humankind's reckless ways: overpopulation, pollution, waste of resources, and wanton destruction of natural habitats. What follows is the opening essay of *Time* magazine's analysis of the looming ecological crisis—an analysis that had its origins in the environmental disasters that dominated the news in 1988. To underscore the magnitude of the crisis and the need for urgent action, the editors made the unorthodox choice of "Endangered Earth" as Planet of the Year in lieu of the usual Man or Woman of the Year. This essay was first published on January 2, 1989.

One generation passeth away, and another generation cometh: but the earth abideth forever.

—*Ecclesiastes*

1　No, not forever. At the outside limit, the earth will probably last another 4 billion to 5 billion years. By that time, scientists predict, the sun will have burned up so much of its own hydrogen fuel that it will expand and incinerate the surrounding planets, including the earth. A nuclear cataclysm, on the other hand, could destroy the earth tomorrow. Somewhere within those extremes lies the life expectancy of this wondrous, swirling globe. How long it endures and the quality of life it can support do not depend alone on the immutable laws of physics. For man has reached a point in his evolution where he has the power to affect, for better or worse, the present and future state of the planet.

2　Through most of his 2 million years or so of existence, man has thrived in earth's environment—perhaps too well. By 1800 there were 1 billion human beings bestriding the planet. That number had doubled by 1930 and doubled again by 1975. If current birthrates hold, the world's present population of 5.1 billion will double again in 40 more years. The frightening irony is that this exponential growth in the human population—the very sign of homo sapiens' success as an organism—could doom the earth as a human habitat.

3　The reason is not so much the sheer numbers, though 40,000 babies die of starvation each day in Third World countries, but the reckless way in which humanity has treated its planetary host. Like the evil genies that flew from Pandora's box, technological advances have provided the means of upsetting nature's equilibrium, that intricate set of biological, physical and chemical interactions that make up the web of life. Starting at the dawn of the Industrial Revolution,

323

smokestacks have disgorged noxious gases into the atmosphere, factories have dumped toxic wastes into rivers and streams, automobiles have guzzled irreplaceable fossil fuels and fouled the air with their detritus. In the name of progress, forests have been denuded, lakes poisoned with pesticides, underground aquifers pumped dry. For decades, scientists have warned of the possible consequences of all this profligacy. No one paid much attention.

This year the earth spoke, like God warning Noah of the deluge. Its message 4 was loud and clear, and suddenly people began to listen, to ponder what portents the message held. In the U.S., a three-month drought baked the soil from California to Georgia, reducing the country's grain harvest by 31% and killing thousands of head of livestock. A stubborn seven-week heat wave drove temperatures above 100° F across much of the country, raising fears that the dreaded "greenhouse effect"—global warming as a result of the buildup of carbon dioxide and other gases in the atmosphere—might already be under way. Parched by the lack of rain, the Western forests of the U.S., including Yellowstone National Park, went up in flames, also igniting a bitter conservationist controversy. And on many of the country's beaches, garbage, raw sewage and medical wastes washed up to spoil the fun of bathers and confront them personally with the growing despoliation of the oceans.

Similar pollution closed beaches on the Mediterranean, the North Sea and the 5 English Channel. Killer hurricanes ripped through the Caribbean and floods devastated Bangladesh, reminders of nature's raw power. In Soviet Armenia a monstrous earthquake killed some 55,000 people. That too was a natural disaster, but its high casualty count, owing largely to the construction of cheap high-rise apartment blocks over a well-known fault area, illustrated the carelessness that has become humanity's habit in dealing with nature.

There were other forebodings of environmental disaster. In the U.S. it was 6 revealed that federal weapons-making plants had recklessly and secretly littered large areas with radioactive waste. The further depletion of the atmosphere's ozone layer, which helps block cancer-causing ultraviolet rays, testified to the continued overuse of atmosphere-destroying chlorofluorocarbons emanating from such sources as spray cans and air-conditioners. Perhaps most ominous of all, the destruction of the tropical forests, home to at least half the earth's plant and animal species, continued at a rate equal to one football field a second.

Most of these evils had been going on for a long time, and some of the worst 7 disasters apparently had nothing to do with human behavior. Yet this year's bout of freakish weather and environmental horror stories seemed to act as a powerful catalyst for worldwide public opinion. Everyone suddenly sensed that this gyrating globe, this precious repository of all the life that we know of, was in danger. No single individual, no event, no movement captured imaginations or dominated headlines more than the clump of rock and soil and water and air that is our common home. Thus in a rare but not unprecedented departure from its tradition of naming a Man of the Year, TIME has designated Endangered Earth as Planet of the Year for 1988. . . .

What would happen if nothing were done about the earth's imperiled state? 8

According to computer projections, the accumulation of CO_2 in the atmosphere could drive up the planet's average temperature 3° F to 9° F by the middle of the next century. That could cause the oceans to rise by several feet, flooding coastal areas and ruining huge tracts of farmland through salinization. Changing weather patterns could make huge areas infertile or uninhabitable, touching off refugee movements unprecedented in history.

Toxic waste and radioactive contamination could lead to shortages of safe   9
drinking water, the sine qua non of human existence. And in a world that could house between 8 billion and 14 billion people by the mid-21st century, there is a strong likelihood of mass starvation. It is even possible to envision the world so wryly and chillingly prophesied by the typewriting cockroach in Donald Marquis' *archy and mehitabel:* "man is making deserts of the earth / it wont be long now / before man will have it used up / so that nothing but ants / and centipedes and scorpions / can find a living on it."

There are those who believe the worst scenarios are alarmist and ill founded.   10
Some scientists contest the global-warming theory or predict that natural processes will counter its effects. Kenneth E.F. Watt, professor of environmental studies at the University of California at Davis, has gone so far as to call the greenhouse effect "the laugh of the century." S. Fred Singer, a geophysicist working for the U.S. Department of Transportation, predicts that any greenhouse warming will be balanced by an increase in heat-reflecting clouds. The skeptics could be right, but it is far too risky to do nothing while awaiting absolute proof of disaster.

Whatever the validity of this or that theory, the earth will not remain as it is   11
now. From its beginnings as a chunk of molten rock and gas some 4.5 billion years ago, the planet has seen continents form, move together and drift apart like jigsaw-puzzle pieces. Successive ice ages have sent glaciers creeping down from the polar caps. Mountain ranges have jutted up from ocean beds, and landmasses have disappeared beneath the waves.

Previous shifts in the earth's climate or topology have been accompanied by   12
waves of extinctions. The most spectacular example is the dying off of the great dinosaurs during the Cretaceous period (136 million to 65 million years ago). No one knows exactly what killed the dinosaurs, although a radical change in environmental conditions seems a likely answer. One popular theory is that a huge meteor crashed to earth and kicked up such vast clouds of dust that sunlight was obscured and plants destroyed. Result: the dinosaurs starved to death.

Whether or not that theory is correct, an event of no less magnitude is taking   13
place at this very moment, but this time its agent is man. The wholesale burning and cutting of forests in Brazil and other countries, as one major example, are destroying irreplaceable species every day. Says Harvard biologist E.O. Wilson: "The extinctions ongoing worldwide promise to be at least as great as the mass extinction that occurred at the end of the age of dinosaurs."

Humanity's current predatory relationship with nature reflects a man-centered   14
world view that has evolved over the ages. Almost every society has had its myths about the earth and its origins. The ancient Chinese depicted Chaos as an enormous egg whose parts separated into earth and sky, yin and yang. The Greeks

believed Gaia, the earth, was created immediately after Chaos and gave birth to the gods. In many pagan societies, the earth was seen as a mother, a fertile giver of life. Nature—the soil, forest, sea—was endowed with divinity, and mortals were subordinate to it.

The Judeo-Christian tradition introduced a radically different concept. The   15
earth was the creation of a monotheistic God, who, after shaping it, ordered its inhabitants, in the words of *Genesis:* "Be fruitful and multiply, and replenish the earth and subdue it: and have dominion over the fish of the sea and over the fowl of the air and over every living thing that moveth upon the earth." The idea of dominion could be interpreted as an invitation to use nature as a convenience. Thus the spread of Christianity, which is generally considered to have paved the way for the development of technology, may at the same time have carried the seeds of the wanton exploitation of nature that often accompanied technical progress.

Those tendencies were compounded by the Enlightenment notion of a mecha-   16
nistic universe that man could shape to his own ends through science. The exuberant optimism of that world view was behind some of the greatest achievements of modern times: the invention of laborsaving machines, the discovery of anesthetics and vaccines, the development of efficient transportation and communication systems. But, increasingly, technology has come up against the law of unexpected consequences. Advances in health care have lengthened life-spans, lowered infant-mortality rates and, thus, aggravated the population problem. The use of pesticides has increased crop yields but polluted water supplies. The invention of automobiles and jet planes has revolutionized travel but sullied the atmosphere.

Yet the advance of technology has never destroyed man's wonder and awe at   17
the beauty of the earth. The coming of England's Industrial Revolution, with its "dark Satanic mills," coincided with the extraordinary flowering of Romantic poetry, much of it about the glory of nature. Many people in this century voiced the same tender feelings on seeing the first images of the earth as viewed from the moon. The sight of that shimmering, luminescent ball set against the black void inspired even normally prosaic astronauts to flights of eloquence. Edgar Mitchell, who flew to the moon aboard Apollo 14 in 1971, described the planet as "a sparkling blue-and-white jewel . . . laced with slowly swirling veils of white . . . like a small pearl in a thick sea of black mystery." Photos of the earth from space prompted geologist Preston Cloud to write, "Mother Earth will never seem the same again. No more can thinking people take this little planet . . . as an infinite theater of action and provider of resources for man, yielding new largesse to every demand without limit." That conclusion seems all the more imperative in the wake of the environmental shocks of 1988.

Let there be no illusions. Taking effective action to halt the massive injury to   18
the earth's environment will require a mobilization of political will, international cooperation and sacrifice unknown except in wartime. Yet humanity is in a war right now, and it is not too Draconian to call it a war for survival. It is a war in which all nations must be allies. Both the causes and effects of the problems that

threaten the earth are global, and they must be attacked globally. "All nations are tied together as to their common fate," observes Peter Raven, director of the Missouri Botanical Garden. "We are all facing a common problem, which is, How are we going to keep this single resource we have, namely the world, viable?"

As man heads into the last decade of the 20th century, he finds himself at a   19
crucial turning point: the actions of those now living will determine the future, and possibly the very survival, of the species. "We do not have generations, we only have years, in which to attempt to turn things around," warns Lester Brown, president of the Washington-based Worldwatch Institute. Every individual on the planet must be made aware of its vulnerability and of the urgent need to preserve it. No attempt to protect the environment will be successful in the long run unless ordinary people—the California housewife, the Mexican peasant, the Soviet factory worker, the Chinese farmer—are willing to adjust their life-styles. Our wasteful, careless ways must become a thing of the past. We must recycle more, procreate less, turn off lights, use mass transit, do a thousand things differently in our everyday lives. We owe this not only to ourselves and our children but also to the unborn generations who will one day inherit the earth.

Mobilizing that sort of mass commitment will take extraordinary leadership,   20
of the kind that has appeared before in times of crisis: Churchill's eloquence galvanizing his embattled countrymen to live "their finest hour," F.D.R.'s pragmatic idealism giving hope and jobs to Depression-ridden Americans. Now, more than ever, the world needs leaders who can inspire their fellow citizens with a fiery sense of mission, not a nationalistic or military campaign but a universal crusade to save the planet. Unless mankind embraces that cause totally, and without delay, it may have no alternative to the bang of nuclear holocaust or the whimper of slow extinction.

▼ TOPICAL CONSIDERATIONS

1. What does Sancton name as the historical genesis of our planet's demise?
2. How did nature in 1988 strike back? According to the author, what might be some human contributions to the portentous extremes in nature that year? Has this year produced any such warnings from nature? If so, what were they?
3. In paragraph 8, Sancton asks, "What would happen if nothing were done about the earth's imperiled state?" What are some possible consequences if nothing is done to reverse environmental demise?
4. Sancton says that some scientists believe the ecological disaster scenarios are "alarmist and ill founded." What consolation do these skeptics offer to the environmental changes? How seriously does the author take their counter theories? What about you?
5. Sancton says that humankind's "current predatory relationship with nature" mirrors an anthropocentric world view. How, according to the author, did the spread of Christianity contribute to the "wanton exploitation of nature"?

6. What must be the future agenda if we are to stop the enormous damage done to the environment?

7. "We must recycle more, procreate less, turn off lights, use mass transit, do a thousand things differently in our everyday lives," says Sancton, if we are to reverse the destruction of our planet. Do you think most people could be so committed? Do you think laws should be passed to force people to be more conservative? What about laws restricting the use of the family car, the use of electricity, or the number of babies couples could have?

8. Since this story was published, what efforts to avoid ecological disasters have you seen on the local level and on the national level? Have you witnessed the rise of "extraordinary leadership"? Has the fate of the environment become more of a social and political issue than it had been? If so, in what ways?

▼ RHETORICAL CONSIDERATIONS

1. How well does the title of this essay convey both the subject and the attitude toward it?

2. Most well-written essays present a "big picture" in the introductory paragraph. How does the opening paragraph of this essay forecast what is to come? How does the opening paragraph state the principle idea of the essay?

3. Discuss the organization of this essay. Do you find a clear organizational pattern? If so, attempt to trace the progress of the author's thoughts. Do you find a clear beginning, middle, and end? Which paragraphs make up these parts? Do you find clear transitions between paragraphs and parts? If possible, construct a formal outline of this essay.

4. Select a sample paragraph and determine what its topic sentence is. How well does this topic statement relate that paragraph to the thesis of the essay?

5. Did you find the use of specific details adequate? Did you find the essay too abstract, too lacking in supporting details?

6. Discuss the tone of the essay. Did you find Sancton balanced and reasonable? Did you find him an alarmist? Explain your answer.

7. Do you recognize the literary allusion in the last line of this essay? What is it? How effective is it?

▼ WRITING ASSIGNMENTS

1. One of the major causes of environmental decline is the burning of fossil fuels. Raising the gasoline tax from the current nine cents per gallon to fifty-nine cents per gallon over the next five years would spur conservation of fuel. Would you be willing to pay an extra fifty cents for a gallon of gasoline if it would help save the environment? Write an essay in which you answer this question and explore the reasons.

2. Some communities require residents to sort their garbage so that bottles, cans, and paper can be recycled. Would you spend the effort of sorting your garbage into separate categories in order to help save natural resources? Write an essay in which you answer this question and explore the reasons.

3. Write a letter to your congressman (or to the president) in which you call for increased funding for research on alternate energy sources, including solar power and safe designs for nuclear reactors.

4. As Sancton points out, one of the most devastating assaults on the environment is the wholesale burning of the world's rain forests, particularly in Brazil's Rondonia state, once an unspoiled showcase for life's diversity. Write a paper in which you try to impress upon people the need to value the genetic diversity and the irreversible damage that occurs when species are wiped out.

5. In the name of conservation, of curbing the problem at its source, what do you think of the idea of charging households according to the amount of garbage they produce? Would you be willing to accept a sliding price for garbage collection? Write out your thoughts in an essay.

6. Write a paper in which you argue for or against laws requiring households to sort garbage into recyclable and non-recyclable items.

7. Write a paper in which you argue for or against tax laws penalizing married couples who have more than two children.

▼ "BUT A WATCH IN THE NIGHT": A SCIENTIFIC FABLE

James C. Rettie

> What follows is a highly imaginative analogy that reads like a science fiction story. An employee of the National Forest Service in Upper Darby, Pennsylvania, Rettie intended this piece to be a conservationist's lament over the loss of forests and the resultant erosion of soil in the blind rush of modern development. Given the ingenious narrative strategy he picked, however, his "scientific fable" also enables us to witness the evolution of the Earth and the life on it. What Rettie helps us realize is both the enormous amount of time spanned by the history of our planet and the mere moment that has elapsed since the origin of humankind. This article first appeared in *Forever the Land* (1950) edited by Russell and Kate Lord.

Out beyond our solar system there is a planet called Copernicus. It came into existence some four or five billion years before the birth of our Earth. In due course of time it became inhabited by a race of intelligent men. 1

About 750 million years ago the Copernicans had developed the motion picture machine to a point well in advance of the stage that we have reached. Most of the cameras that we now use in motion picture work are geared to take twenty-four pictures per second on a continuous strip of film. When such film is run through a projector, it throws a series of images on the screen and these change with a rapidity that gives the visual impression of normal movement. If a motion is too swift for the human eye to see it in detail, it can be captured and artificially slowed down by means of the slow-motion camera. This one is geared to take many more shots per second—ninety-six or even more than that. When the slow motion film is projected at the normal speed of twenty-four pictures per second, we can see just how the jumping horse goes over a hurdle. 2

What about motion that is too slow to be seen by the human eye? That problem has been solved by the use of the time-lapse camera. In this one, the shutter is geared to take only one shot per second, or one per minute, or even one per hour—depending upon the kind of movement that is being photographed. When the time-lapse film is projected at the normal speed of twenty-four pictures per second, it is possible to see a bean sprout growing up out of the ground. Time-lapse films are useful in the study of many types of motion too slow to be observed by the unaided human eye. 3

The Copernicans, it seems, had time-lapse cameras some 757 million years ago and they also had superpowered telescopes that gave them a clear view of 4 what was happening upon this Earth. They decided to make a film record of the life history of Earth and to make it on the scale of one picture per year. The photography has been in progress during the last 757 million years.

In the near future, a Copernican interstellar expedition will arrive upon our Earth and bring with it a copy of the time-lapse film. Arrangements will be made for showing the entire film in one continuous run. This will begin at midnight of New Year's eve and continue day and night without a single stop until midnight of December 31. The rate of projection will be twenty-four pictures per second. Time on the screen will thus seem to move at the rate of twenty-four years per second; 1440 years per minute; 86,400 years per hour; approximately two million years per day; and sixty-two million years per month. The normal life-span of individual man will occupy about three seconds. The full period of Earth history that will be unfolded on the screen (some 757 million years) will extend from what the geologists call Pre-Cambrian times up to the present. This will, by no means, cover the full time-span of the Earth's geological history but it will embrace the period since the advent of living organisms.

During the months of January, February, and March the picture will be desolate and dreary. The shape of the land masses and the oceans will bear little or no resemblance to those that we know. The violence of geological erosion will be much in evidence. Rains will pour down on the land and promptly go booming down to the seas. There will be no clear streams anywhere except where the rains fall upon hard rock. Everywhere on the steeper ground the stream channels will be filled with boulders hurled down by rushing waters. Raging torrents and dry stream beds will keep alternating in quick succession. High mountains will seem to melt like so much butter in the sun. The shifting of land into the seas, later to be thrust up as new mountains, will be going on at a grand scale.

Early in April there will be some indication of the presence of single-celled living organisms in some of the warmer and sheltered coastal waters. By the end of the month it will be noticed that some of these organisms have become multicellular. A few of them, including the Trilobites, will be encased in hard shells.

Toward the end of May, the first vertebrates will appear, but they will still be aquatic creatures. In June about 60 per cent of the land area that we know as North America will be under water. One broad channel will occupy the space where the Rocky Mountains now stand. Great deposits of limestone will be forming under some of the shallow seas. Oil and gas deposits will be in process of formation—also under shallow seas. On land there will still be no sign of vegetation. Erosion will be rampant, tearing loose particles and chunks of rock and grinding them into sand and silt to be spewed out by the streams into bays and estuaries.

About the middle of July the first land plants will appear and take up the tremendous job of soil building. Slowly, very slowly, the mat of vegetation will spread, always battling for its life against the power of erosion. Almost foot by foot, the plant life will advance, lacing down with its root structures whatever pulverized rock material it can find. Leaves and stems will be giving added protection against the loss of the soil foothold. The increasing vegetation will pave the way for the land animals that will live upon it.

Early in August the seas will be teeming with fish. This will be what geologists   10
call the Devonian period. Some of the races of these fish will be breathing by
means of lung tissue instead of through gill tissues. Before the month is over, some
of the lung fish will go ashore and take on a crude lizard-like appearance. Here are
the first amphibians.

In early September the insects will put in their appearance. Some will look   11
like huge dragonflies and will have a wing spread of 24 inches. Large portions of
the land masses will now be covered with heavy vegetation that will include the
primitive spore-propagating trees. Layer upon layer of this plant growth will build
up, later to appear as the coal deposits. About the middle of this month, there will
be evidence of the first seed-bearing plants and the first reptiles. Heretofore, the
land animals will have been amphibians that could reproduce their kind only by
depositing a soft egg mass in quiet waters. The reptiles will be shown to be freed
from the aquatic bond because they can reproduce by means of a shelled egg in
which the embryo and its nurturing liquids are sealed and thus protected from
destructive evaporation. Before September is over, the first dinosaurs will be
seen—creatures destined to dominate the animal realm for about 140 million
years and then to disappear.

In October there will be series of mountain uplifts along what is now the   12
eastern coast of the United States. A creature with feathered limbs—half bird and
half reptile in appearance—will take itself into the air. Some small and rather
unpretentious animals will be seen to bring forth their young in a form that is a
miniature replica of the parents and to feed these young on milk secreted by
mammary glands in the female parent. The emergence of this mammalian form of
animal life will be recognized as one of the great events in geologic time. October
will also witness the high water mark of the dinosaurs—creatures ranging in size
from that of the modern goat to monsters like Brontosaurus that weighed some 40
tons. Most of them will be placid vegetarians, but a few will be hideous-looking
carnivores, like Allosaurus and Tyrannosaurus. Some of the herbivorous dinosaurs will be clad in bony armor for protection against their flesh-eating comrades.

November will bring pictures of a sea extending from the Gulf of Mexico to   13
the Arctic in space now occupied by the Rocky Mountains. A few of the reptiles
will take to the air on bat-like wings. One of these, called Pteranodon, will have a
wingspread of 15 feet. There will be a rapid development of the modern flowering
plants, modern trees, and modern insects. The dinosaurs will disappear. Toward
the end of the month there will be a tremendous land disturbance in which the
Rocky Mountains will rise out of the sea to assume a dominating place in the
North American landscape.

As the picture runs on into December it will show the mammals in command   14
of the animal life. Seed-bearing trees and grasses will have covered most of the
land with a heavy mantle of vegetation. Only the areas newly thrust up from the
sea will be barren. Most of the streams will be crystal clear. The turmoil of
geologic erosion will be confined to localized areas. About December 25 will
begin the cutting of the Grand Canyon of the Colorado River. Grinding down
through layer after layer of sedimentary strata, this stream will finally expose

deposits laid down in Pre-Cambrian times. Thus in the walls of that canyon will appear geological formations dating from recent times to the period when the Earth had no living organisms upon it.

The picture will run on through the latter days of December and even up to its final day with still no sign of mankind. The spectators will become alarmed in the fear that man has somehow been left out. But not so; sometime about noon on December 31 (one million years ago) will appear a stooped, massive creature of man-like proportions. This will be Pithecanthropus, the Java ape man. For tools and weapons he will have nothing but crude stone and wooden clubs. His children will live a precarious existence threatened on the one side by hostile animals and on the other by tremendous climatic changes. Ice sheets—in places 4000 feet deep—will form in the northern parts of North America and Eurasia. Four times this glacial ice will push southward to cover half the continents. With each advance the plant and animal life will be swept under or pushed southward. With each recession of the ice, life will struggle to reestablish itself in the wake of the retreating glaciers. The woolly mammoth, the musk ox, and the caribou all will fight to maintain themselves near the ice line. Sometimes they will be caught and put into cold storage—skin, flesh, blood, bones and all.

The picture will run on through supper time with still very little evidence of man's presence on the Earth. It will be about 11 o'clock when Neanderthal man appears. Another half hour will go by before the appearance of Cro-Magnon man living in caves and painting crude animal pictures on the walls of his dwelling. Fifteen minutes more will bring Neolithic man, knowing how to chip stone and thus produce sharp cutting edges for spears and tools. In a few minutes more it will appear that man has domesticated the dog, the sheep and, possibly, other animals. He will then begin the use of milk. He will also learn the arts of basket weaving and the making of pottery and dugout canoes.

The dawn of civilization will not come until about five or six minutes before the end of the picture. The story of the Egyptians, the Babylonians, the Greeks, and the Romans will unroll during the fourth, the third and the second minute before the end. At 58 minutes and 43 seconds past 11:00 P.M. (just 1 minute and 17 seconds before the end) will come the beginning of the Christian era. Columbus will discover the new world 20 seconds before the end. The Declaration of Independence will be signed just 7 seconds before the final curtain comes down.

In those few moments of geologic time will be the story of all that has happened since we became a nation. And what a story it will be! A human swarm will sweep across the face of the continent and take it away from the . . . red men. They will change it far more radically than it has ever been changed before in a comparable time. The great virgin forests will be seen going down before ax and fire. The soil, covered for eons by its protective mantle of trees and grasses, will be laid bare to the ravages of water and wind erosion. Streams that had been flowing clear will, once again, take up a load of silt and push it toward the seas. Humus and mineral salts, both vital elements of productive soil, will be seen to vanish at a terrifying rate. The railroads and highways and cities that will spring up may divert attention, but they cannot cover up the blight of man's recent activities. In great sections of Asia, it will be seen that man must utilize cow dung and every scrap of available straw or grass for fuel to cook his food. The forests that once provided wood for this purpose will be gone without a trace. The use of these agricultural wastes for fuel, in place of returning them to the land, will be leading to increasing soil impoverishment. Here and there will be seen a dust storm darkening the landscape over an area a thousand miles across. Man-creatures will be shown counting their wealth in terms of bits of printed paper representing other bits of a scarce but comparatively useless yellow metal that is kept buried in strong vaults. Meanwhile, the soil, the only real wealth that can keep mankind alive on the face of this Earth is savagely being cut loose from its ancient moorings and washed into the seven seas.

We have just arrived upon this Earth. How long will we stay?   19

▼ TOPICAL CONSIDERATIONS

1. What would you say Rettie's purpose was in writing this essay? What was he trying to demonstrate?
2. Explain Rettie's extensive analogy. Does it work for you? How does it dramatize the various geological developments in earth's history? The evolution of different life forms? The emergence of humankind?
3. How does Rettie's strategy of using the year-long time-lapse movie of Earth's history as an analogy mirror his interests in soil conservation?

▼ RHETORICAL CONSIDERATIONS

1. Do you think Rettie spends too much time at the beginning of his essay explaining how the camera works? Explain your answer.
2. Why do you think Rettie chose to create alien observers?
3. At what point in this essay did you suspect that Rettie was giving more than a simple narrative of the development of life on Earth? Where does he begin to sound critical? Where is there a tone change?
4. Explain the effectiveness of the rhetorical question that concludes the piece.
5. Rettie took the title of his essay from Psalm 90 in the King James version of the Bible: "For a thousand years in Thy sight are but as yesterday when it is past, and as a watch in the night." How does this passage help you understand Rettie's title choice?

▼ WRITING ASSIGNMENT

1. This essay was written some 40 years ago. Try to splice more recent environmental problems onto the end of the piece. In other words, pick

up from where Rettie left off in an essay of your own, using the same camera-eye technique. You might want to end at the present or extend the narrative to some future time.

▼ HOW NATURAL IS NATURAL?

Loren Eiseley

Loren Eiseley had the remarkable ability to make the natural world come alive and to draw profound insights from the most common scenes. Eiseley (1907–77) was an anthropologist, educator, poet, and essayist. His works include *The Immense Journey* (1957), *The Unexpected Universe* (1969), and *The Night Country* (1971). Here Eiseley pays a visit to a favorite New England lake. His visit brings him face to face with a busy little lakeside creature from an ancient world that is sadly fading into the shadows of a brave, new world. This essay was taken from Eiseley's *Firmament of Time* (1960).

In the more obscure scientific circles which I frequent there is a legend circulating   1
about a late distinguished scientist who, in his declining years, persisted in wearing enormous padded boots much too large for him. He had developed, it seems, what to his fellows was a wholly irrational fear of falling through the interstices of that largely empty molecular space which common men in their folly speak of as the world. A stroll across his living-room floor had become, for him, something as dizzily horrendous as the activities of a window washer on the Empire State Building. Indeed, with equal reason he could have passed a ghostly hand through his own ribs.

The quivering network of his nerves, the awe-inspiring movement of his   2
thought had become a vague cloud of electrons interspersed with the light-year distances that obtain between us and the farther galaxies. This was the natural world which he had helped to create, and in which, at last, he had found himself a lonely and imprisoned occupant. All around him the ignorant rushed on their way over the illusion of substantial floors, leaping, though they did not see it, from particle to particle, over a bottomless abyss. There was even a question as to the reality of the particles which bore them up. It did not, however, keep insubstantial newspapers from being sold, or insubstantial love from being made.

Not long ago I became aware of another world perhaps equally natural and   3
real, which man is beginning to forget. My thinking began in New England under a boat dock. The lake I speak of has been pre-empted and civilized by man. All day long in the vacation season high-speed motorboats, driven with the reckless abandon common to the young Apollos of our society, speed back and forth, carrying loads of equally attractive girls. The shores echo to the roar of powerful motors and the delighted screams of young Americans with uncounted horse-power surging under their hands. In truth, as I sat there under the boat dock, I had some desire to swim or to canoe in the older ways of the great forest which once

lay about this region. Either notion would have been folly. I would have been gaily chopped to ribbons by teen-age youngsters whose eyes were always immutably fixed on the far horizons of space, or upon the dials which indicated the speed of their passing. There was another world, I was to discover, along the lake shallows and under the boat dock, where the motors could not come.

As I sat there one sunny morning when the water was peculiarly translucent, I   4 saw a dark shadow moving swiftly over the bottom. It was the first sign of life I had seen in this lake, whose shores seemed to yield little but washed-in beer cans. By and by the gliding shadow ceased to scurry from stone to stone over the bottom. Unexpectedly, it headed almost directly for me. A furry nose with gray whiskers broke the surface. Below the whiskers green water foliage trailed out in an inverted V as long as his body. A muskrat still lived in the lake. He was bringing in his breakfast.

I sat very still in the strips of sunlight under the pier. To my surprise the   5 muskrat came almost to my feet with his little breakfast of greens. He was young, and it rapidly became obvious to me that he was laboring under an illusion of his own, and that he thought animals and men were still living in the Garden of Eden. He gave me a friendly glance from time to time as he nibbled his greens. Once, even, he went out into the lake again and returned to my feet with more greens. He had not, it seemed, heard very much about men. I shuddered. Only the evening before I had heard a man describe with triumphant enthusiasm how he had killed a rat in the garden because the creature had dared to nibble his petunias. He had even showed me the murder weapon, a sharp-edged brick.

On this pleasant shore a war existed and would go on until nothing remained   6 but man. Yet this creature with the gray, appealing face wanted very little: a strip of shore to coast up and down, sunlight and moonlight, some weeds from the deep water. He was an edge-of-the-world dweller, caught between a vanishing forest and a deep lake preempted by unpredictable machines full of chopping blades. He eyed me nearsightedly, a green leaf poised in his mouth. Plainly he had come with some poorly instructed memory about the lion and the lamb.

"You had better run away now," I said softly, making no movement in the   7 shafts of light. "You are in the wrong universe and must not make this mistake again. I am really a very terrible and cunning beast. I can throw stones." With this I dropped a little pebble at his feet.

He looked at me half blindly, with eyes much better adjusted to the wavering   8 shadows of his lake bottom than to sight in the open air. He made almost as if to take the pebble up into his forepaws. Then a thought seemed to cross his mind—a thought perhaps telepathically received, as Freud once hinted, in the dark world below and before man, a whisper of ancient disaster heard in the depths of a burrow. Perhaps after all this was not Eden. His nose twitched carefully; he edged toward the water.

As he vanished in an oncoming wave, there went with him a natural world,   9 distinct from the world of girls and motorboats, distinct from the world of the professor holding to reality by some great snowshoe effort in his study. My muskrat's shore-line universe was edged with the dark wall of hills on one side and the waspish drone of motors farther out, but it was a world of sunlight he had taken down into the water weeds. It hovered there, waiting for my disappearance. I walked away, obscurely pleased that darkness had not gained on life by any act of mine. In so many worlds, I thought, how natural is "natural"—and is there anything we can call a natural world at all?

▼ TOPICAL CONSIDERATIONS

1. Eiseley mentions three separate "worlds" in this essay. What are they?
2. Both E. B. White in "Once More to the Lake" (p. 103) and Loren Eiseley became acutely aware of changing worlds after visiting favorite lakes. What similar changes do they note in the natural world? In society? In the relationship between people and nature?
3. In paragraph 5, why is the author surprised to find a muskrat living in the lake? Given what he notes about the lake, why would he feel so? What details suggest that the muskrat's world is being threatened?
4. Explain what illusion the muskrat appears to be living under. (See paragraph 5.)
5. In his reference to Eden, what is Eiseley saying about how far humans have progressed?
6. What do you make of the author's warning to the muskrat in paragraph 7? How does he mean the statement, "I can throw stones"?
7. Cite some examples of Eiseley's use of descriptive details. How effective are they in evoking a sense of the lake and the encounter with the muskrat?
8. This essay is more than just a simple reflection on a muskrat's watery world. What is Eiseley really despairing about here? How appropriate is the title?

▼ RHETORICAL CONSIDERATIONS

1. How is the introductory discussion of the scientist in the enormous padded boots relevant to the rest of the essay?
2. In paragraph 3, Eiseley says that the lake had been "pre-empted and civilized by man." What do "pre-empted" and "civilized" mean? Explain how Eiseley uses these terms.
3. Explain the allusion to "young Apollos of our society" (paragraph 3). What is the effect of this allusion?
4. In general, what is Eiseley's attitude toward the teenagers on the lake? Explain the allusion and the rhetorical effect of the Garden of Eden, cited in paragraph 5. Explain the allusion to "the lion and the lamb" in paragraph 6.
5. In the last paragraph, Eiseley refers both to "a world of sunlight" and to the approaching darkness. How does he use these images symbolically? How do they project his feelings and attitudes here?

▼ WRITING ASSIGNMENTS

1. Eiseley contrasts aspects of the natural world with those of modern society. Write an essay in which you use specific details that do the same. Consider an experience of your own where you tried to escape to the woods, the mountains, the desert, or the seashore but found that you were constantly reminded of the "other" civilized world.

2. Write an essay about an encounter you once had with some animal whose world you felt was threatened.

3. Write an essay in which you debate the need to protect the wilderness, even at the expense of industrial and economic growth.

4. The muskrat in this essay is threatened by the encroachment of civilization, although it is not one of an endangered species. Write an essay arguing the need to protect species that are endangered, such as the California condor, the snail darter, and the cougar.

5. Extinction is an irrefutable law of nature, as evidenced by the thousands of different species preserved only in fossils. Write an essay arguing that attempts to protect endangered species are costly and vain efforts to reverse a natural process.

▼ MAN'S ROLE ON EARTH

Lewis Thomas

Human beings are still in the learning stage and may discover they are meant to be a set of eyes for the creature known as Earth. So says Dr. Lewis Thomas, president emeritus of Memorial Sloan-Kettering Cancer Center and best-selling author of several books of essays, including *The Lives of a Cell* (1974) and *The Medusa and the Snail* (1979). He has also written a memoir of his life as a doctor, *The Young Scientist* (1983). In the following essay, Thomas says that we wrongly treat the Earth as a kind of household pet, living in an environment we invented. For Dr. Thomas, human beings are part of the Earth's life and inseparable from the living planet. This essay was first published in the *New York Times* in April 1984.

Human beings have never before had such a bad press. By all reports, we are 1 unable to get anything right these days, and there seems to be almost nothing good to say for ourselves. In just the past century we have increased our population threefold and will double it before the next has run out. We have swarmed over the open face of the earth, occupied every available acre of livable space, displaced numberless other creatures from their accustomed niches, caused one extinction after another—with more to come—and polluted all our waterways and even parts of the oceans. Now, in our efforts to make energy and keep warm, we appear to be witlessly altering the earth's climate by inserting too much carbon dioxide into the atmosphere; if we do not pull up short, we will produce a new greenhouse around the planet, melting the Antarctic ice shelf and swamping all coastlines.

Not to mention what we are doing to each other, and what we are thinking 2 seriously of doing in the years just ahead with the most remarkable toy ever made by man, the thermonuclear bomb.

Our capacity for folly has never been matched by any other species. The long 3 record of evolution instructs us that the way other creatures get along in nature is to accommodate, to fit in, to give a little whenever they take a little. The rest of life does this all the time, setting up symbiotic arrangements whenever the possibility comes into view. Except for us, the life of the planet conducts itself as though it were an immense, coherent body of connected life, an intricate system, even, as I see it, an organism. An embryo maybe, conceived, as each one of us was first brought to life, as a single successful cell.

I have no memory of ever having been a single cell, 70 years ago. But I was, 4 and whenever I think of it I tremble at the sheer luck. But the thought that the whole biosphere—all that conjoined life, all 10 million or whatever the number is (a still incalculable number) of what we call species of living things—had its collective beginning as a single, solitary cell, 3.5 or so billion years ago, sweeps me off my feet.

Our deepest folly is the notion that we are in charge of the place, that we own 5 it and can somehow run it. We are beginning to treat the earth as a sort of domesticated household pet, living in an environment invented by us, part kitchen garden, part park, part zoo. It is an idea we must rid ourselves of soon, for it is not so. It is the other way around. We are not separate beings. We are a living part of the earth's life, owned and operated by the earth, probably specialized for functions on its behalf that we have not yet glimpsed. Conceivably, and this is the best thought I have about us, we might turn out to be a sort of sense-organ for the whole creature, a set of eyes, even a storage place for thought. Perhaps, if we continue our own embryologic development as a species, it will be our privilege to carry seeds of life to other parts of the galaxy.

But right now, we have a lot to learn. One of our troubles may be that we are 6 still so new and so young. In the way evolution clocks time, we arrived on the scene only a moment ago, down from the trees and puzzling over our opposing thumbs, wondering what we are supposed to do with the flabbergasting gift of language and metaphor. Our very juvenility could account for the ways in which we fumble, drop things, get things wrong.

I like this thought, even though the historians might prefer to put it otherwise. 7 They might say, some of them *do* say, that we have been at it thousands of years, trying out one failed culture after another, folly after folly, and now we are about to run out our string. As a biologist, I do not agree. I say that a few thousand years is hardly enough time for a brand-new species to draw breath.

Now, with that thought, for the moment anyway, I feel better about us. We 8 have the making of exceedingly useful working parts. We are just new to the task, that's our trouble. Indeed, we are not yet clear in our minds what the task is, beyond the imperative to learn.

We have all the habits of a social species, more compulsively social than any 9 other, even bees and ants. Our nest, or hive, is language; we are held together by speech, *at* each other all day long. Our great advantage over all other social animals is that we possess the kind of brain that permits us to change our minds. We are not obliged, as the ants are, to follow genetic blueprints for every last detail of our behavior. Our genes are more cryptic and ambiguous in their instructions: get along, says our DNA, talk to each other, figure out the world, be useful, and above all keep an eye out for affection.

One important thing we have already learned. We are a novel species, but 10 we are constructed out of the living parts of very ancient organisms. We go back a long way.

Sometime around a billion years ago, the bacterial cells that had been the sole 11 occupants of the earth for the preceding two-and-a-half-billion years began joining up to form much larger cells, with nuclei like ours. Certain lines of bacteria had learned earlier on to make use of oxygen for getting their energy. Somehow or other, these swam into the new cells and turned into the mitochondria of "higher" nucleated cells. The creatures are still with us, thank goodness, packed inside every cell in our bodies. Were it not for their presence and hard work, we could never make a move or even a song.

The chemical messages exchanged among all the cells in our bodies, regulat-   12
ing us, are also antique legacies. Sophisticated hormones like insulin, growth hormones and the sex steroids, a multitude of peptides, including the endorphins, which modulate the functions of our brains, were invented long ago by the bacteria and their immediate progeny, the protozoans. They still make them, for purposes entirely obscure. We almost certainly inherited the genes needed for things like these from our ancestors in the mud. We may be the greatest and brainiest of all biological opportunities on the planet, but we owe debts of long standing to the beings that came before us, and to those that now surround us and will help us along into the future.

▼ TOPICAL CONSIDERATIONS

1. According to Thomas, how are humans a misfit species on the planet Earth?
2. What does Thomas mean by the statement, "Our deepest folly is the notion that we are in charge of the place, that we own it and can somehow run it" (paragraph 5)? How is this notion dangerous?
3. What might be humankind's special functions on behalf of the Earth? What might be our privilege?
4. In paragraph 6 Thomas speaks of our "flabbergasting gift of language and metaphor." What does he mean by "metaphor," and how is it a "gift"?
5. How do Thomas's views of human history differ from those of historians? What does he say is our main trouble?
6. According to Thomas, what is our "great advantage over all other social animals"?

▼ RHETORICAL CONSIDERATIONS

1. In most fine essays, there is a controlling metaphor that unifies the writing and generates the themes. What would you say is the controlling metaphor of this essay? How are the themes generated from it?
2. Thomas speaks about how the human animal is "a living part of the Earth's life, owned and operated by the Earth." Where does he actually demonstrate our biological connectedness to the Earth and all other organisms?
3. In the last sentence Thomas refers to us as possibly "the greatest and brainiest of all biological opportunities on the planet." Given Thomas's particular slant in the essay, how apt is the word "opportunities" in describing us as a species?

4. How would you describe the writing tone in this piece? Does Thomas come across as too intellectual or abstract? Do you find him hostile? Condescending? Naive or wise? Do you think Thomas is optimistic or pessimistic about our future?

▼ WRITING ASSIGNMENTS

1. In paragraph 7, the author stands in mild opposition to the pessimistic view of biologists regarding the future of humankind. How do you feel on this issue? Do you think "we are about to run out our string," as do some historians? Do you think we can eventually learn "what the task is" and save ourselves from ourselves?

2. In paragraph 1, Thomas catalogs reasons why "there seems to be almost nothing good to say for ourselves." Take one of the follies he cites and write a paper in which you discuss the specific dangers. You might consider overpopulation, the pollution of our natural environment, the threat to other species, or the threat to ourselves. Select a topic you have particularly strong feelings about, and use specifics to back up your arguments.

▼ CATERPILLAR AFTERNOON

Sue Hubbell

One need not travel to exotic locales to discover the wonders and magic of the natural world. They are about us in infinite variety—in wild things both great and small. What follows is a personal narrative from naturalist Sue Hubbell, who has a remarkable talent for looking at the natural world around her and making it fascinating. Here she records her chance encounter with a procession of maggoty-like caterpillars. It is a fine illustration of how we might see our own environment in very different ways if we just take the time to look. Sue Hubbell (born 1936) is a commercial bee keeper who lives in the Ozark Mountains. She is author of the book, *A Country Year* (1986), from which this essay was taken.

A year ago, on an afternoon late in springtime, I was walking on the dirt road that 1 cuts across the field to the beehives. I noticed a light-colored, brownish dappled something-or-other stretched across the roadway ahead of me, and decided that it was a snakeskin. I often find them, crumpled husks shed by snakes as they grow. They are fragile and delicate, perfect but empty replicas of the snakes that once inhabited them. I started to turn it over with the toe of my boot, but stopped suddenly, toe in air, for the flecked, crumpled-looking empty snakeskin was moving.

It gave me quite a start and I was amused at my own reaction, remembering 2 that Ronald Firbank wrote somewhere that the essence of evil was the ordinary become unnatural, the stone in the garden path that suddenly begins to move.

I squatted down to see what queer thing I had here, and found that my 3 supposed snake skin was a mass of maggoty-like caterpillars, each one no more than half an inch long. They were hairless, with creamy white smooth skin, black heads and brown stripes along their backs. They were piled thickly in the center, with fewer caterpillars at the head and rear end of the line, which was perhaps eighteen inches long. They moved slowly, each caterpillar in smooth synchrony with its fellows, so that a wave of motion undulated down the entire length of the line.

They seemed so intensely social that I wondered what they would do on their 4 own. I gently picked up half a dozen or so, and isolated them a few inches from the column. Their smooth, easy movements changed to frantic, rapid ones, and they wriggled along the ground quickly until they rejoined the group. They certainly were good followers. How did they ever decide where to go? The single caterpillar in the lead twisted the forepart of his body from side to side as though taking his bearings; he appeared to be the only one in the lot capable of going in a new direction, of making a decision to avoid a tuft of grass here, of turning there. Was he some special, super-caterpillar? I removed him from the lead position and put him off to the side, where he became as frantic as had the others, wriggling to rejoin the group somewhere in the middle, where he was soon lost to view, having turned into just another follower. At the head, the next caterpillar in line had simply assumed leadership duties and was bending his body from side to side, making the decision about the direction the column was to take. I removed three leaders in a row with the same result: each time, the next caterpillar in line made an instant switch from loyal and will-less follower to leader.

What were they doing? Were they looking for food? If so, what kind? What manner of creature were they? The beework that I had set out to do could wait no longer, so I went back to the hives. When I returned along the road, the caterpillars, if that is what they were, had disappeared. 5

Back in my cabin, none of the books on my shelves were much help explaining what I had seen, except one by Henri Fabre, the nineteenth-century French entomologist who had conducted one of his famous experiments with pine processionaries, one of the Thaumatopoeidae. Fabre's caterpillars were *Thaumatopoea processionea,* "the wonder maker that parades"; eventually they become rather undistinguished-looking moths. 6

The pine processionaries are a European species, but their behavior was similar to that of my caterpillars, although not identical. Pine processionaries travel to feed in single file, not massed and bunched, but they do touch head to rear and have only one leader at a time. Fabre found them so sheeplike that he wondered what they would do if he could somehow manage to make them leaderless. In a brilliant experiment, he arranged them on the upper rim of a large vase a yard and a half in circumference, and waited until the head end of the procession joined the tail end, so that the entire group was without a leader. All were followers. For seven days, the caterpillars paraded around the rim of the vase in a circle. Their pace slowed after a while, for they were weary and had not been able to feed, but they continued to circle, each caterpillar unquestioningly taking his direction from the rear of the one in front, until they dropped from exhaustion. However, even Fabre never discovered what it was that could turn one caterpillar into a leader as soon as he was at the head of the line. 7

It was not until several months later, when I was talking to Asher, that I was able to find out anything about the caterpillars I had found in the roadway. He said that I probably had seen one species or another of sawfly larvae. They are gregarious, he told me, and some are whitish with brown stripes. Sure identification could only be made by counting the pairs of their prolegs, and of course I had not known enough to look at them that closely. Asher said that they were a rare sight and that I would probably never see them again, but if I did I should gather up a few and put them in a solution of 70 percent alcohol; then he would help me identify them. He had read about Fabre's experiment too, but knew nothing more about their behavior. 8

He added, "If you ever find out what makes processionary caterpillars prosesh, 9 please enlighten me. Maybe it's the same thing that makes people drive in Sunday traffic or watch TV or vote Republican."

It is springtime again. I would like to count the caterpillars' prolegs and am   10 prepared to pickle a few to satisfy my curiosity, but mostly I should just like to watch them again. This time I should let the beework go. I should like to know where these caterpillars go, and what it is they are looking for. I wonder if I could divide them up into several small columns that would move along independently side by side. I have more questions about them than when I first saw them.

This spring I often walk along, eyes to the ground, looking for them. There   11 may have been nobler quests—white whales and Holy Grails—and although the Ahabs and Percivals of my acquaintance are some of my most entertaining friends, I am cut of other stuff and amuse myself in other ways. The search for what may or may not be sawfly larvae seems quite a good one this springtime.

▼ TOPICAL CONSIDERATIONS

1. Lewis Thomas once commented that Sue Hubbell's writings remind us how "enchanting and engrossing" the world of nature is. After reading this essay, do you agree? How does Hubbell demonstrate her own enchantment and engrossment?
2. In paragraph 2, Hubbell recalls Ronald Firbank's definition of evil: "the ordinary become unnatural." In your estimation, how adequate a definition of evil is this? Why is it appropriate here? Why is Hubbell amused by her own reaction to the caterpillars?
3. Hubbell describes Henri Fabre's "brilliant experiment" with processionary caterpillars. What did Fabre's experiment show, and what, in Hubbell's estimation, was "brilliant" about it?
4. How has the passage of the year affected Hubbell's regard toward the caterpillars?
5. How does Hubbell distinguish herself from "the Ahabs and Percivals" of her acquaintances? Is she saying that her own quests are less noble?

▼ RHETORICAL CONSIDERATIONS

1. Hubbell waits until paragraph 3 to make clear what she came upon in the road. Why this strategy instead of just opening with a description of the caterpillars?
2. How would you describe Hubbell's attitude toward the caterpillars? What words or expressions convey that attitude?
3. Essential to good descriptive writing is the use of specific details. Comment on the descriptive details Hubbell employs to make vivid the procession of caterpillars. What descriptions do you find particularly effective, and why? What examples of personification can you find?

4. Does a thesis unify Hubbell's essay? If so, where is it stated?
5. Paragraph 5 opens with four questions. What is the point of all the questioning? Does Hubbell come up with any answers to the questions?

▼ WRITING ASSIGNMENTS

1. Write an account of a natural sighting, either accidental or intentional, you once had in the wild. Use Hubbell's piece as a model, and include facts, details, and information about the habits and characteristics of the animal(s) you observed.
2. In the fashion of Sue Hubbell, play nature sleuth. Find a place where you might observe some small ritual of the natural world. Patiently watch and record the details of creatures in action whether they be ducks in a pond, squirrels in a tree, ants in a mound, or grubs under a rock. Then, like Hubbell, put on paper your observations with a mind to "enchanting and engrossing" your reader.
3. Write an observation of the wild, but reverse the point of view. That is, write your observation through the eyes of an animal. You might describe yourself through the eyes of a fox, owl, deer, or sawfly larva observing you.
4. Write an essay in which you discuss the joys and rewards of nature exploration. Pick a particular experience you had and discuss it.

▼ A CRUEL UNIVERSE, BUT THE ONLY ONE WHERE HUMANS COULD EXIST

Gwynne Dyer

Most of us have wondered at times why the natural universe seems so cruel and unjust a place. Just look at some of the brutal headlines over the past few years—the thousands of innocents lost to famine, earthquakes, volcanic eruptions, and diseases. Or consider the death of a child. As Gwynne Dyer says, even nonbelievers often wish the universe were a kinder, more forgiving environment. But, as he explains, it can't be and still be natural. Mr. Dyer is a columnist specializing in foreign affairs and creator of the 1985 PBS television series *War*. This article first appeared in *The Boston Globe* in November 1985.

Why do babies die? Why do people starve to death in famines? Why is the universe so cruel, taking some people's lives away before they even had a chance to enjoy life, while others have long, happy lives and die peacefully in bed?

Religious people call it "the problem of evil." If God is all-powerful, why does he allow such horror and pain in his universe? A god who deliberately allowed Auschwitz and the killing fields of Cambodia to happen would not deserve our love, or even our respect—and if he couldn't prevent them, then he isn't all-powerful.

Cardinal Basil Hume, an English clergyman, was recently asked why God permitted such things by a journalist as they both stood in the middle of an Ethiopian refugee camp. Hume had the honesty to answer that he had "no idea." More sophisticated men of religion, whether Christian, Muslim or Jewish, might give longer answers that sounded plausible—but they are all answers that go round in circles.

If you don't believe in God, of course, then there is no philosophical problem. The universe is impersonal, human beings are on their own, and terrible things happen to them for the same reason they happen to fruit flies: no reason at all, except blind chance. But even non-believers often wish the universe were a kinder, more forgiving environment. And the answer is: it can't be.

It is an answer that applies equally to a universe created by a loving God and to a Godless universe which doesn't care about people at all. Any universe which could conceivably be a habitat for human beings must be one in which events have predictable consequences—even if those consequences include terrible tragedies for human beings.

348

Imagine, for a moment, a universe in which tragedies didn't happen. When the   6
engines of a jet airliner fail on takeoff, it does not crash at the end of the runway
and burn 150 people to death. Instead, it just wafts gently to the ground, because
God loved the passengers and chose to save them.

But if that were all that happened when aircraft engines failed, there   7
would be no need for aircraft maintenance. Indeed, there would be no need for
engines, or even wings—and people could safely step off the edge of cliffs and
walk on air. The law of gravity would be suspended whenever it endangered
human lives.

So would all the other laws of nature. Whenever children's lives were at risk   8
from disease, biochemistry would change its rules to save them. If an earthquake
were going to kill thousands of people, continental drift would simply have to
stop: so much for geology. And if someone tried to kill somebody else, the gun
wouldn't work, or the bullet wouldn't fly straight, or it would turn into a marshmal-
low before it struck the victim.

In such a universe, there could be no science or technology, because there   9
would be no fixed natural laws on which we could base them. The strength of steel
and the temperature of boiling water would vary depending on whether human
lives were threatened by a given value. There could not even be logic, since the
same causes would not invariably have the same effects. It would be an entirely
magical universe.

It is all a package, and quite indivisible. Either you have a magical Garden   10
of Eden where non-human creatures closely resembling angels, with no hard
choices to make and no penalties to pay, browse idly on lotus leaves. Or else you
get the remorselessly logical universe we live in, where actions have consequences
and you pay dearly for your own mistakes (and those of others).

I know there is little consolation in all this for those who have had to watch   11
helplessly while their child died, or for the millions whose loves and hopes lie 40
years buried with the last world war. It is a cruel universe, and knowing why does
not make it less cruel. But even God could not have made it any different if he
wanted it to be an appropriate home for human beings.

It's cold comfort, but maybe there is some consolation to be had in the fact   12
that we're extremely fortunate to have been able to visit the universe even briefly.
At the instant of your conception and mine, a million other potential men and
women lost their only chance to see the place at all.

▼ TOPICAL CONSIDERATIONS

1. The author writes: "Any universe which could conceivably be a habitat for
   human beings must be one in which events have predictable consequences."
   In your own words explain what he means by this.
2. Why does Dyer say that "Hume had the honesty to answer that he had 'no
   idea'" when asked why God permits bad things to happen? What answer
   would you give?

3. If God prevented tragedies from happening in the universe, why would that mean there could be no science or technology?
4. According to Dyer, what consolation can we derive from recognizing that we live in a cruel universe?

▼ RHETORICAL CONSIDERATIONS

1. What rhetorical strategy is Dyer using when he begins his essay with questions?
2. How well does Dyer illustrate his argument that the universe by necessity must be a cruel place for human habitation?
3. How does the final paragraph encourage appreciation of the universe as we know it? How does it reflect back on the opening paragraph?

▼ WRITING ASSIGNMENTS

1. Write an essay supporting Dyer's thesis, using three examples from your own experience.
2. In paragraph 3, we are told that Cardinal Basil Hume, an English clergyman, said he had no idea why God permitted terrible things to occur. In a well-documented essay, write your own answer to the journalist's question.

▼ WERE DINOSAURS DUMB?

Stephen Jay Gould

Ever since their bones were discovered in the nineteenth century, dinosaurs have gotten bad press. They were the biggest land creatures; surely they must have been the clumsiest and the dumbest. In fact, didn't some of the giants of these giants have brains the size of walnuts? Maybe so, but as scientist and writer Stephen Jay Gould says, any creature that held sway for some 100 million years couldn't have been all that stupid. What follows is a reevaluation of the intelligence of dinosaurs by a man who is highly qualified to speak for them. Stephen Jay Gould teaches biology and the history of science at Harvard University. He also writes the award-winning column "This View of Life" for *Natural History* magazine, and he is author of the widely acclaimed books, *Ever Since Darwin* (1977), *The Panda's Thumb* (1980), from which this piece comes, *The Mismeasurement of Man* (1981), *Hen's Teeth and Horse's Toes* (1983), and *The Flamingo's Smile* (1985).

When Muhammad Ali flunked his army intelligence test, he quipped (with a wit 1 that belied his performance on the exam): "I only said I was the greatest; I never said I was the smartest." In our metaphors and fairy tales, size and power are almost always balanced by a want of intelligence. Cunning is the refuge of the little guy. Think of Br'er Rabbit and Br'er Bear; David smiting Goliath with a slingshot; Jack chopping down the beanstalk. Slow wit is the tragic flaw of a giant.

The discovery of dinosaurs in the nineteenth century provided, or so it 2 appeared, a quintessential case for the negative correlation of size and smarts. With their pea brains and giant bodies, dinosaurs became a symbol of lumbering stupidity. Their extinction seemed only to confirm their flawed design.

Dinosaurs were not even granted the usual solace of a giant—great physical 3 prowess. God maintained a discreet silence about the brains of behemoth, but he certainly marveled at its strength: "Lo, now, his strength is in his loins, and his force is in the navel of his belly. He moveth his tail like a cedar. . . . His bones are as strong pieces of brass; his bones are like bars of iron [Job 40:16–18]." Dinosaurs, on the other hand, have usually been reconstructed as slow and clumsy. In the standard illustration, *Brontosaurus* wades in a murky pond because he cannot hold up his own weight on land.

Popularizations for grade school curricula provide a good illustration of 4 prevailing orthodoxy. I still have my third grade copy (1948 edition) of Bertha Morris Parker's *Animals of Yesterday,* stolen, I am forced to suppose, from P.S. 26,

351

Queens (sorry Mrs. McInerney). In it, boy (teleported back to the Jurassic) meets brontosaur:

> It is huge, and you can tell from the size of its head that it must be stupid. ... This giant animal moves about very slowly as it eats. No wonder it moves slowly! Its huge feet are very heavy, and its great tail is not easy to pull around. You are not surprised that the thunder lizard likes to stay in the water so that the water will help it hold up its huge body. ... Giant dinosaurs were once the lords of the earth. Why did they disappear? You can probably guess part of the answer—their bodies were too large for their brains. If their bodies had been smaller, and their brains larger, they might have lived on.

Dinosaurs have been making a strong comeback of late, in this age of "I'm OK, you're OK." Most paleontologists are now willing to view them as energetic, active, and capable animals. The *Brontosaurus* that wallowed in its pond a generation ago is now running on land, while pairs of males have been seen twining their necks about each other in elaborate sexual combat for access to females (much like the neck wrestling of giraffes). Modern anatomical reconstructions indicate strength and agility, and many paleontologists now believe that dinosaurs were warmblooded. ...

The idea of warmblooded dinosaurs has captured the public imagination and received a torrent of press coverage. Yet another vindication of dinosaurian capability has received very little attention, although I regard it as equally significant. I refer to the issue of stupidity and its correlation with size. The revisionist interpretation, which I support in this column, does not enshrine dinosaurs as paragons of intellect, but it does maintain that they were not small brained after all. They had the "right-sized" brains for reptiles of their body size.

I don't wish to deny that the flattened, minuscule head of largebodied *Stegosaurus* houses little brain from our subjective, top-heavy perspective, but I do wish to assert that we should not expect more of the beast. First of all, large animals have relatively smaller brains than related, small animals. The correlation of brain size with body size among kindred animals (all reptiles, all mammals, for example) is remarkably regular. As we move from small to large animals, from mice to elephants or small lizards to Komodo dragons, brain size increases, but not so fast as body size. In other words, bodies grow faster than brains, and large animals have low ratios of brain weight to body weight. In fact, brains grow only about two-thirds as fast as bodies. Since we have no reason to believe that large animals are consistently stupider than their smaller relatives, we must conclude that large animals require relatively less brain to do as well as smaller animals. If we do not recognize this relationship, we are likely to underestimate the mental power of very large animals, dinosaurs in particular.

Second, the relationship between brain and body size is not identical in all groups of vertebrates. All share the same rate of relative decrease in brain size, but small mammals have much larger brains than small reptiles of the same body weight. This discrepancy is maintained at all larger body weights, since brain size increases at the same rate in both groups—two-thirds as fast as body size.

Put these two facts together—all large animals have relatively small brains, and reptiles have much smaller brains than mammals at any common body weight—and what should we expect from a normal, large reptile? The answer, of course, is a brain of very modest size. No living reptile even approaches a middle-sized dinosaur in bulk, so we have no modern standard to serve as a model for dinosaurs. 9

Fortunately, our imperfect fossil record has, for once, not severely disappointed us in providing data about fossil brains. Superbly preserved skulls have been found for many species of dinosaurs, and cranial capacities can be measured. (Since brains do not fill craniums in reptiles, some creative, although not unreasonable, manipulation must be applied to estimate brain size from the hole within a skull.) With these data, we have a clear test for the conventional hypothesis of dinosaurian stupidity. We should agree, at the outset, that a reptilian standard is the only proper one—it is surely irrelevant that dinosaurs had smaller brains than people or whales. We have abundant data on the relationship of brain and body size in modern reptiles. Since we know that brains increase two-thirds as fast as bodies as we move from small to large living species, we can extrapolate this rate to dinosaurian sizes and ask whether dinosaur brains match what we would expect of living reptiles if they grew so large. 10

Harry Jerison studied the brain sizes of ten dinosaurs and found that they fell right on the extrapolated reptilian curve. Dinosaurs did not have small brains; they maintained just the right-sized brains for reptiles of their dimensions. So much for Ms. Parker's explanation of their demise. 11

Jerison made no attempt to distinguish among various kinds of dinosaurs; ten species distributed over six major groups scarcely provide a proper basis for comparison. Recently, James A. Hopson of the University of Chicago gathered more data and made a remarkable and satisfying discovery. 12

Hopson needed a common scale for all dinosaurs. He therefore compared each dinosaur brain with the average reptilian brain we would expect at its body weight. If the dinosaur falls on the standard reptilian curve, its brain receives a value of 1.0 (called an encephalization quotient, or EQ—the ratio of actual brain to expected brain for a standard reptile of the same body weight). Dinosaurs lying above the curve (more brain than expected in a standard reptile of the same body weight) receive values in excess of 1.0, while those below the curve measure less than 1.0. 13

Hopson found that the major groups of dinosaurs can be ranked by increasing values of average EQ. This ranking corresponds perfectly with inferred speed, agility and behavioral complexity in feeding (or avoiding the prospect of becoming a meal). The giant sauropods, *Brontosaurus* and its allies, have the lowest EQ's—0.20 to 0.35. They must have moved fairly slowly and without great maneuverability. They probably escaped predation by virtue of their bulk alone, much as elephants do today. The armored ankylosaurs and stegosaurs come next with EQ's of 0.52 to 0.56. These animals, with their heavy armor, probably relied largely upon passive defense, but the clubbed tail of ankylosaurs and the spiked tail of stegosaurs imply some active fighting and increased behavioral complexity. 14

The ceratopsians rank next at about 0.7 to 0.9. Hopson remarks: "The larger   15
ceratopsians, with their great horned heads, relied on active defensive strategies
and presumably required somewhat greater agility than the tail-weaponed forms,
both in fending off predators and in intraspecific combat bouts. The smaller ceratopsians, lacking true horns, would have relied on sensory acuity and speed to escape
from predators." The ornithopods (duckbills and their allies) were the brainiest
herbivores, with EQ's from 0.85 to 1.5. They relied upon "acute senses and relatively
fast speeds" to elude carnivores. Flight seems to require more acuity and agility
than standing defense. Among ceratopsians, small, hornless, and presumably
fleeing *Protoceratops* had a higher EQ than great three-horned *Triceratops*.

Carnivores have higher EQ's than herbivores, as in modern vertebrates.   16
Catching a rapidly moving or stoutly fighting prey demands a good deal more
upstairs than plucking the right kind of plant. The giant theropods (*Tyrannosaurus*
and its allies) vary from 1.0 to nearly 2.0. Atop the heap, quite appropriately
at its small size, rests the little coelurosaur *Stenonychosaurus* with an EQ well
above 5.0. Its actively moving quarry, small mammals and birds perhaps, probably
posed a greater challenge in discovery and capture than *Triceratops* afforded
Tyrannosaurus.

I do not wish to make a naive claim that brain size equals intelligence or, in   17
this case, behavioral range and agility (I don't know what intelligence means in
humans, much less in a group of extinct reptiles). Variation in brain size within a
species has precious little to do with brain power (humans do equally well with 900
or 2,500 cubic centimeters of brain). But comparison across species, when the
differences are large, seems reasonable. I do not regard it as irrelevant to our
achievements that we so greatly exceed koala bears—much as I love them—in
EQ. The sensible ordering among dinosaurs also indicates that even so coarse a
measure as brain size counts for something.

If behavioral complexity is one consequence of mental power, then we might   18
expect to uncover among dinosaurs some signs of social behavior that demand
coordination, cohesiveness, and recognition. Indeed we do, and it cannot be
accidental that these signs were overlooked when dinosaurs labored under the
burden of a falsely imposed obtuseness. Multiple trackways have been uncovered,
with evidence for more than twenty animals traveling together in parallel movement.
Did some dinosaurs live in herds? At the Davenport Ranch sauropod trackway,
small footprints lie in the center and larger ones at the periphery. Could it be that
some dinosaurs traveled much as some advanced herbivorous mammals do today,
with large adults at the borders sheltering juveniles in the center?

In addition, the very structures that seemed most bizarre and useless to older   19
paleontologists—the elaborate crests of hadrosaurs, the frills and horns of ceratopsians, and the nine inches of solid bone above the brain of *Pachycephalosaurus*
—now appear to gain a coordinated explanation as devices for sexual display and
combat. Pachycephalosaurs may have engaged in head-butting contests much as
mountain sheep do today. The crests of some hadrosaurs are well designed as
resonating chambers; did they engage in bellowing matches? The ceratopsian
horn and frill may have acted as sword and shield in the battle for mates. Since

such behavior is not only intrinsically complex, but also implies an elaborate social system, we would scarcely expect to find it in a group of animals barely muddling through at a moronic level.

But the best illustration of dinosaurian capability may well be the fact most often cited against them—their demise. Extinction, for most people, carries many of the connotations attributed to sex not so long ago—a rather disreputable business, frequent in occurrence, but not to anyone's credit, and certainly not to be discussed in proper circles. But, like sex, extinction is an ineluctable part of life. It is the ultimate fate of all species, not the lot of unfortunate and ill-designed creatures. It is no sign of failure. 20

The remarkable thing about dinosaurs is not that they became extinct, but that they dominated the earth for so long. Dinosaurs held sway for 100 million years while mammals, all the while, lived as small animals in the interstices of their world. After 70 million years on top, we mammals have an excellent track record and good prospects for the future, but we have yet to display the staying power of dinosaurs. 21

People, on this criterion, are scarcely worth mentioning—5 million years perhaps since *Australopithecus,* a mere 50,000 for our own species, *Homo sapiens.* Try the ultimate test within our system of values: Do you know anyone who would wager a substantial sum, even at favorable odds, on the proposition that *Homo sapiens* will last longer than *Brontosaurus?* 22

▼ TOPICAL CONSIDERATIONS

1. According to Gould, dinosaurs have long suffered from the big-is-dumb-and-clumsy stereotype. What are some of the sources of that stereotype that Gould cites?
2. Why have attitudes toward dinosaurs recently been turned around?
3. On what basic grounds does Gould argue his defense of dinosaurs? Explain his reasoning regarding brain and body size ratios.
4. Explain "encephalization quotient" or EQ. Why didn't the brontosaurus and other less brainy beasts need higher EQs?
5. Why did carnivores necessarily have higher EQs? Which had the highest? Why was a higher EQ necessary for them?
6. How does Gould's interpretation of some of the bizarre head structures of some dinosaurs counter interpretations of earlier paleontologists?

▼ RHETORICAL CONSIDERATIONS

1. How well does the Muhammad Ali anecdote that opens the essay illustrate Gould's stand? Was it appropriate and convincing?
2. Find examples of Gould's use of humor. How does it add to or detract from his argument?

3. Gould refers to scientists and scientific studies in his essay. How well does he use their evidence to support his arguments? Be specific.
4. A good conclusion to an essay should wrap up some of the major points made and leave some impact. Evaluate Gould's concluding paragraph.

▼ WRITING ASSIGNMENT

1. Gould's essay is a defense against the popularly held attitude that dinosaurs were dumb. Try your own hand at writing a defense of animals against popularly held beliefs—for example, that cats are sneaky, pigeons are stupid, pigs are dirty, and so on. If you cannot find some scientific evidence to back you up, at least use reasoned arguments and your own observations.

WAR AND PEACE IN THE NUCLEAR AGE

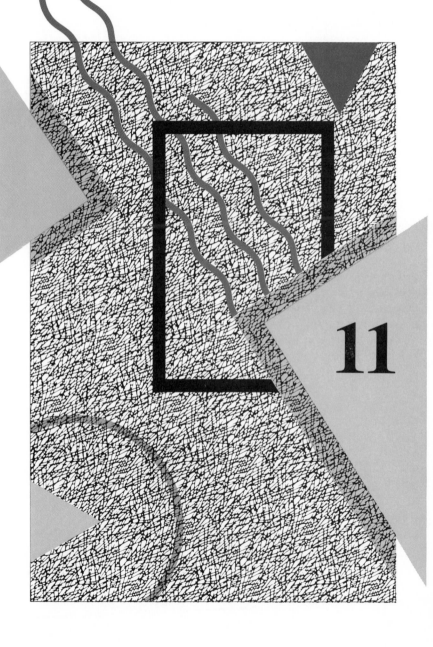

11

▼ THE EFFECTS OF A NUCLEAR EXPLOSION

Jonathan Schell

On August 6, 1945, America dropped the first atomic bomb in warfare on Hiroshima, Japan. Three days later, a second atomic bomb fell on Nagasaki. A quarter of a million people died, and the nuclear age was born. Since then, America and the Soviet Union have created vast nuclear arsenals in the name of defense. In recent years the super-powers have signed treaties to eliminate certain classes of warheads, however, geopolitical rivalry and suspicions still exist. So do most machines of destruction. Furthermore, the big-power monopoly on nuclear weapons is ending. Four other countries have reportedly built nuclear warheads—and developed means to deliver them—and others are not far behind. Some people argue that if we had a realistic sense of the actual consequences of a nuclear war, our leaders would be more hasty to disarm. The following essay was written with just that intent. Cast in a coldly objective tone, this piece details the effects a thermonuclear bomb would have on New York City. This piece was taken from the widely read *The Fate of the Earth* (1982) in which Schell considers the theories and effects of the arms race and the consequences of nuclear war.

What happened at Hiroshima was less than a millionth part of a holocaust at present levels of world nuclear armament. The more than millionfold difference amounts to more than a difference in magnitude; it is also a difference in kind. The authors of "Hiroshima and Nagasaki"* observe that "an atomic bomb's massive destruction and indiscriminate slaughter involves the sweeping break-down of all order and existence—in a word, the collapse of society itself," and that therefore "the essence of atomic destruction lies in the totality of its impact on man and society." This is true also of a holocaust, of course, except that the totalities in question are now not single cities but nations, ecosystems, and the earth's ecosphere. Yet with the exception of fallout, which was relatively light at Hiroshima and Nagasaki (because both the bombs were air-burst), the immediate devastation caused by today's bombs would be of a sort similar to the devastation in those cities. The immediate effects of a twenty-megaton bomb are not different in kind from those of a twelve-and-a-half-kiloton bomb; they are only more extensive.... In bursts of both weapons, for instance, there is a radius within

1

*A comprehensive study, carried out by a group of distinguished Japanese scientists, of the consequences of the bombing of those two cities.—Ed.

which the thermal pulse can ignite newspapers: for the twelve-and-a-half-kiloton weapon, it is a little over two miles; for the twenty-megaton weapon, it is twenty-five miles. (Since there is no inherent limit on the size of a nuclear weapon, these figures can be increased indefinitely, subject only to the limitations imposed by the technical capacities of the bomb builder—and of the earth's capacity to absorb the blast. The Soviet Union, which has shown a liking for sheer size in so many of its undertakings, once detonated a sixty-megaton bomb.) Therefore, while the total effect of a holocaust is qualitatively different from the total effect of a single bomb, the experience of individual people in a holocaust would be, in the short term (and again excepting the presence of lethal fallout wherever the bombs were ground-burst), very much like the experience of individual people in Hiroshima. The Hiroshima people's experience, accordingly, is of much more than historical interest. It is a picture of what our whole world is always poised to become—a backdrop of scarcely imaginable horror lying just behind the surface of our normal life, and capable of breaking through into that normal life at any second. Whether we choose to think about it or not, it is an omnipresent, inescapable truth about our lives today that at every single moment each one of us may suddenly become the deranged mother looking for her burned child; the professor with the ball of rice in his hand whose wife has just told him "Run away, dear!" and died in the fires; Mr. Fukai running back into the firestorm; the naked man standing on the blasted plain that was his city, holding his eyeball in his hand; or, more likely, one of millions of corpses. For whatever our "modest hopes" as human beings may be, every one of them can be nullified by a nuclear holocaust.

One way to begin to grasp the destructive power of present-day nuclear weapons is to describe the consequences of the detonation of a one-megaton bomb, which possesses eighty times the explosive power of the Hiroshima bomb, on a large city, such as New York. Burst some eighty-five hundred feet above the Empire State Building, a one-megaton bomb would gut or flatten almost every building between Battery Park and 125th Street, or within a radius of four and four-tenths miles, or in an area of sixty-one square miles, and would heavily damage buildings between the northern tip of Staten Island and the George Washington Bridge, or within a radius of about eight miles, or in an area of about two hundred square miles. A conventional explosive delivers a swift shock, like a slap, to whatever it hits, but the blast wave of a sizable nuclear weapon endures for several seconds and "can surround and destroy whole buildings" (Glasstone). People, of course, would be picked up and hurled away from the blast along with the rest of the debris. Within the sixty-one square miles, the walls, roofs, and floors of any buildings that had not been flattened would be collapsed, and the people and furniture inside would be swept down onto the street. (Technically, this zone would be hit by various overpressures of at least five pounds per square inch. Overpressure is defined as the pressure in excess of normal atmospheric pressure.) As far away as ten miles from ground zero, pieces of glass and other sharp objects would be hurled about by the blast wave at lethal velocities. In Hiroshima, where buildings were low and, outside the center of the city, were often constructed of light materials, injuries from falling buildings were often minor. But in New York, where the buildings are tall and are constructed of heavy materials, the physical collapse of the city would certainly kill millions of people. The streets of New York are narrow ravines running between the high walls of the city's buildings. In a nuclear attack, the walls would fall and the ravines would fill up. The people in the buildings would fall to the street with the debris of the buildings, and the people in the street would be crushed by this avalanche of people and buildings. At a distance of two miles or so from ground zero, winds would reach four hundred miles an hour, and another two miles away they would reach a hundred and eighty miles an hour. Meanwhile, the fireball would be growing, until it was more than a mile wide, and rocketing upward, to a height of over six miles. For ten seconds, it would broil the city below. Anyone caught in the open within nine miles of ground zero would receive third-degree burns and would probably be killed; closer to the explosion, people would be charred and killed instantly. From Greenwich Village up to Central Park, the heat would be great enough to melt metal and glass. Readily inflammable materials, such as newspapers and dry leaves, would ignite in all five boroughs (though in only a small part of Staten Island) and west to the Passaic River, in New Jersey, within a radius of about nine and a half miles from ground zero, thereby creating an area of more than two hundred and eighty square miles in which mass fires were likely to break out.

If it were possible (as it would not be) for someone to stand at Fifth Avenue and Seventy-second Street (about two miles from ground zero) without being instantly killed, he would see the following sequence of events. A dazzling white light from the fireball would illumine the scene, continuing for perhaps thirty seconds. Simultaneously, searing heat would ignite everything flammable and start to melt windows, cars, buses, lampposts, and everything else made of metal or glass. People in the street would immediately catch fire, and would shortly be reduced to heavily charred corpses. About five seconds after the light appeared, the blast wave would strike, laden with the debris of a now nonexistent midtown. Some buildings might be crushed, as though a giant fist had squeezed them on all sides, and others might be picked up off their foundations and whirled uptown with the other debris. On the far side of Central Park, the West Side skyline would fall from south to north. The four-hundred-mile-an-hour wind would blow from south to north, die down after a few seconds, and then blow in the reverse direction with diminished intensity. While these things were happening, the fire-ball would be burning in the sky for the ten seconds of the thermal pulse. Soon huge, thick clouds of dust and smoke would envelop the scene, and as the mushroom cloud rushed overhead (it would have a diameter of about twelve miles) the light from the sun would be blotted out, and day would turn to night. Within minutes, fires, ignited both by the thermal pulse and by broken gas mains, tanks of gas and oil, and the like, would begin to spread in the darkness, and a strong, steady wind would begin to blow in the direction of the blast. As at Hiroshima, a whirlwind might be produced, which would sweep through the ruins, and radioactive rain, generated under the meteorological conditions created by the blast, might fall. Before long, the individual fires would coalesce into a mass fire, which, depending largely on the winds, would become either a conflagration

3

or a firestorm. In a conflagration, prevailing winds spread a wall of fire as far as there is any combustible material to sustain it; in a firestorm, a vertical updraft caused by the fire itself sucks the surrounding air in toward a central point, and the fires therefore converge in a single fire of extreme heat. A mass fire of either kind renders shelters useless by burning up all the oxygen in the air and creating toxic gases, so that anyone inside the shelters is asphyxiated, and also by heating the ground to such high temperatures that the shelters turn, in effect, into ovens, cremating the people inside them. In Dresden, several days after the firestorm raised there by Allied conventional bombing, the interiors of some bomb shelters were still so hot that when they were opened the inrushing air caused the contents to burst into flame. Only those who had fled their shelters when the bombing started had any chance of surviving. (It is difficult to predict in a particular situation which form the fires will take. In actual experience, Hiroshima suffered a firestorm and Nagasaki suffered a conflagration.)

In this vast theatre of physical effects, all the scenes of agony and death that 4 took place at Hiroshima would again take place, but now involving millions of people rather than hundreds of thousands. Like the people of Hiroshima, the people of New York would be burned, battered, crushed, and irradiated in every conceivable way. The city and its people would be mingled in a smoldering heap. And then, as the fires started, the survivors (most of whom would be on the periphery of the explosion) would be driven to abandon to the flames those family members and other people who were unable to flee, or else to die with them. Before long, while the ruins burned, the processions of injured, mute people would begin their slow progress out of the outskirts of the devastated zone. However, this time a much smaller proportion of the population than at Hiroshima would have a chance of escaping. In general, as the size of the area of devastation increases, the possibilities for escape decrease. When the devastated area is relatively small, as it was at Hiroshima, people who are not incapacitated will have a good chance of escaping to safety before the fires coalesce into a mass fire. But when the devastated area is great, as it would be after the detonation of a megaton bomb, and fires are springing up at a distance of nine and a half miles from ground zero, and when what used to be the streets are piled high with burning rubble, and the day (if the attack occurs in the daytime) has grown impenetrably dark, there is little chance that anyone who is not on the very edge of the devastated area will be able to make his way to safety. In New York, most people would die wherever the blast found them, or not very far from there.

If instead of being burst in the air the bomb were burst on or near the ground 5 in the vicinity of the Empire State Building, the overpressure would be very much greater near the center of the blast area but the range hit by a minimum of five pounds per square inch of overpressure would be less. The range of the thermal pulse would be about the same as that of the air burst. The fireball would be almost two miles across, and would engulf midtown Manhattan from Greenwich Village nearly to Central Park. Very little is known about what would happen to a city that was inside a fireball, but one would expect a good deal of what was there to be first pulverized and then melted or vaporized. Any human beings in the area would be reduced to smoke and ashes; they would simply disappear. A crater roughly three blocks in diameter and two hundred feet deep would open up. In addition, heavy radioactive fallout would be created as dust and debris from the city rose with the mushroom cloud and then fell back to the ground. Fallout would begin to drop almost immediately, contaminating the ground beneath the cloud with levels of radiation many times lethal doses, and quickly killing anyone who might have survived the blast wave and the thermal pulse and might now be attempting an escape; it is difficult to believe that there would be appreciable survival of the people of the city after a megaton ground burst. And for the next twenty-four hours or so more fallout would descend downwind from the blast, in a plume whose direction and length would depend on the speed and the direction of the wind that happened to be blowing at the time of the attack. If the wind was blowing at fifteen miles an hour, fallout of lethal intensity would descend in a plume about a hundred and fifty miles long and as much as fifteen miles wide. Fallout that was sublethal but could still cause serious illness would extend another hundred and fifty miles downwind. Exposure to radioactivity in human beings is measured in units called rems—an acronym for "roentgen equivalent in man." The roentgen is a standard measurement of gamma- and X-ray radiation, and the expression "equivalent in man" indicates that an adjustment has been made to take into account the differences in the degree of biological damage that is caused by radiation of different types. Many of the kinds of harm done to human beings by radiation—for example, the incidence of cancer and of genetic damage—depend on the dose accumulated over many years; but radiation sickness, capable of causing death, results from an "acute" dose, received in a period of anything from a few seconds to several days. Because almost ninety per cent of the so-called "infinite-time dose" of radiation from fallout—that is, the dose from a given quantity of fallout that one would receive if one lived for many thousands of years—is emitted in the first week, the one-week accumulated dose is often used as a convenient measure for calculating the immediate harm from fallout. Doses in the thousands of rems, which could be expected throughout the city, would attack the central nervous system and would bring about death within a few hours. Doses of around a thousand rems, which would be delivered some tens of miles downwind from the blast, would kill within two weeks everyone who was exposed to them. Doses of around five hundred rems, which would be delivered as far as a hundred and fifty miles downwind (given a wind speed of fifteen miles per hour), would kill half of all exposed able-bodied young adults. At this level of exposure, radiation sickness proceeds in the three stages observed at Hiroshima. The plume of lethal fallout could descend, depending on the direction of the wind, on other parts of New York State and parts of New Jersey, Pennsylvania, Delaware, Maryland, Connecticut, Massachusetts, Rhode Island, Vermont, and New Hampshire, killing additional millions of people. The circumstances in heavily contaminated areas, in which millions of people were all declining together, over a period of weeks, toward painful deaths, are ones that, like so many of the consequences of nuclear explosions, have never been experienced.

    A description of the effects of a one-megaton bomb on New York City gives   6 some notion of the meaning in human terms of a megaton of nuclear explosive power, but a weapon that is more likely to be used against New York is the twenty-megaton bomb, which has one thousand six hundred times the yield of the Hiroshima bomb. The Soviet Union is estimated to have at least a hundred and thirteen twenty-megaton bombs in its nuclear arsenal, carried by Bear intercontinental bombers. In addition, some of the Soviet SS-18 missiles are capable of carrying bombs of this size, although the actual yields are not known. Since the explosive power of the twenty-megaton bombs greatly exceeds the amount necessary to destroy most military targets, it is reasonable to suppose that they are meant for use against large cities. If a twenty-megaton bomb were air-burst over the Empire State Building at an altitude of thirty thousand feet, the zone gutted or flattened by the blast wave would have a radius of twelve miles and an area of more than four hundred and fifty square miles, reaching from the middle of Staten Island to the northern edge of the Bronx, the eastern edge of Queens, and well into New Jersey, and the zone of heavy damage from the blast wave (the zone hit by a minimum of two pounds of overpressure per square inch) would have a radius of twenty-one and a half miles, or an area of one thousand four hundred and fifty square miles, reaching to the southernmost tip of Staten Island, north as far as southern Rockland County, east into Nassau County, and west to Morris County, New Jersey. The fireball would be about four and a half miles in diameter and would radiate the thermal pulse for some twenty seconds. People caught in the open twenty-three miles away from ground zero, in Long Island, New Jersey, and southern New York State, would be burned to death. People hundreds of miles away who looked at the burst would be temporarily blinded and would risk permanent eye injury. (After the test of a fifteen-megaton bomb on Bikini Atoll, in the South Pacific, in March of 1954, small animals were found to have suffered retinal burns at a distance of three hundred and forty-five miles.) The mushroom cloud would be seventy miles in diameter. New York City and its suburbs would be transformed into a lifeless, flat, scorched desert in a few seconds.

If a twenty-megaton bomb were ground-burst on the Empire State Building, the range of severe blast damage would, as with the one-megaton ground blast, be reduced, but the fireball, which would be almost six miles in diameter, would cover Manhattan from Wall Street to northern Central Park and also parts of New Jersey, Brooklyn, and Queens, and everyone within it would be instantly killed, with most of them physically disappearing. Fallout would again be generated, this time covering thousands of square miles with lethal intensities of radiation. A fair portion of New York City and its incinerated population, now radioactive dust, would have risen into the mushroom cloud and would now be descending on the surrounding territory. On one of the few occasions when local fallout was generated by a test explosion in the multi-megaton range, the fifteen-megaton bomb tested on Bikini Atoll, which was exploded seven feet above the surface of a coral reef, "caused substantial contamination over an area of more than seven thousand square miles," according to Glasstone. If, as seems likely, a twenty-megaton bomb ground-burst on New York would produce at least a comparable amount of fallout, and if the wind carried the fallout onto populated areas, then this one

7

bomb would probably doom upward of twenty million people, or almost ten per cent of the population of the United States.

▼ TOPICAL CONSIDERATIONS

1. What similarities would there be between the destruction incurred by the bombs dropped on Hiroshima and Nagasaki and that caused by a nuclear holocaust? What differences would there be?
2. In describing the devastation caused by a one-megaton bomb exploded over New York City, Schell subdivides the effects and moves from one to another. What is the first effect he discusses? What is the second? What is the third?
3. What is there about New York City that would make escape or refuge from death virtually impossible?
4. What differences in effects would there be if the bomb were detonated at ground level instead of 8,500 feet above the city?
5. What does Schell say about the effects of radiation and their range?
6. Why does Schell say in paragraph 6 that a twenty-megaton bomb would most likely be used against New York? What different effects would this bomb have from those of a one-megaton device?

▼ RHETORICAL CONSIDERATIONS

1. Schell gives us grim and thorough details of what nuclear weapons could do to a city. How well does he back up his speculations with factual information?
2. What is Schell's point in giving us so many details at so many different stages of a bomb's destruction? Do all these details clutter the essay or make it more persuasive? Explain.
3. What is the advantage of beginning the piece with details of the destruction of Hiroshima and Nagasaki?
4. This essay is a horribly frightening scenario that details how millions of people could die. How would you define Schell's tone throughout? Does he ever display emotions or reveal his own fears and feelings? Is his tone here an effective one? Does his style fit his subject and purpose?
5. At the end of paragraph 3, Schell makes some comments in parentheses about the difficulty in predicting "which form the fires will take," and he goes on to specify the forms of the fires in Hiroshima and Nagasaki. Why would Schell even bother considering such a difficulty, when it really doesn't make any difference given the consequences? Is there some higher rhetorical purpose behind this?
6. Do you think Schell has written this essay for the general reader or for one with more technical knowledge? Explain your answer.

7. Schell writes in very long paragraphs. Would breaking them up into shorter paragraphs weaken or strengthen their effects?

▼ WRITING ASSIGNMENTS

1. If this essay had any effects on you, write a paper describing them. Did it change your mind about war, nuclear arms, or the future?
2. Nuclear bombs were introduced for use in wars, for military purposes. As Schell points out, however, the destructive power of these weapons has far exceeded military needs and intent. Write a paper in which you argue that today's nuclear weapons are not military weapons.
3. Write a letter to the president of the United States (and/or the premier of the Soviet Union) and attempt to convince him of the need to support nuclear disarmament.
4. Write a letter to the president of the United States urging him to support development of bigger and newer weapons to ensure the safety of the United States.

▼ NUCLEAR HOLOCAUST IN PERSPECTIVE

Michael Kinsley

Immediately following its publication, Jonathan Schell's *Fate of the Earth* was adopted by the American antinuclear movement as its manifesto. There were other reactions as well, however, including the following essay, reprinted from *Harper's Magazine* in May 1982. Michael Kinsley's statement not only is in opposition to the antinuclear movement, it is a point-for-point attack on Jonathan Schell's arguments—what Kinsley calls his "hothouse reasoning" and his "pretentious" style. Kinsley says that there is more bad poetry than good policy in Schell and the antinuclear movement. He specifically criticizes the strategy, style, and intention of the Schell essay.

It would be very sad if the world were destroyed in a nuclear holocaust. Jonathan Schell may well feel this sadness more profoundly than I do. His acclaimed three-part series in *The New Yorker,* "The Fate of the Earth," now rushed into book form by Knopf, is mostly a meditation on how sad it would be. He demands "the full emotional, intellectual, spiritual, and visceral understanding of the meaning of extinction." He asserts that even now "The peril of extinction surrounds . . . love with doubt." And "Politics, as it now exists, is . . . thoroughly compromised." And "Works of art, history, and thought . . . are undermined at their foundations. . . . " Schell cites scientific evidence against any complaisant hope that human life, once destroyed in a nuclear war, might evolve again in a few million years. And don't suppose that humanity might escape nuclear war by fleeing the earth in a spaceship. Schell points out that this would be not only "an injustice to our birthplace and habitat," but futile: "[T]he fact is that wherever human beings went, there also would go the knowledge of how to build nuclear weapons, and, with it, the peril of extinction." I confess that this spaceship business had never occurred to me. But, really, I think a nuclear holocaust would be very, very sad. 1

That said, where do we stand? 2

We stand where we've stood for three decades, with East and West in a nuclear stalemate that could turn at any moment into mutual annihilation. In addition, we stand with nuclear weapons as the only genuine deterrent to a Soviet invasion of Europe (and of the Middle East, a threat implicitly invoked in the Carter Doctrine). Third, we stand at the edge of a large expansion of the nuclear club, with unpredictable consequences. 3

Over the past few months a mass political movement—the first in years—has 4 sprouted in the United States and Europe, demanding that something be done about this. Something, but what? On this, the movement is vaguer, because it's hard to think what the Western governments can do to prevent a nuclear war. On the third point, they might stop competing with one another to sell nuclear equipment to the third world, but it's already a little late for that. On the first point, they might show a bit more enthusiasm for a strategic arms limitation treaty. But this would be primarily a matter of saving money and reducing the risk of a disastrous accident. The basic balance of terror cannot be dismantled without perfect trust between the world's greatest enemies—an unlikely development.

The West really could do something about problem number two, the depend- 5 ence on nuclear weapons to protect Europe. That something would be to replace nuclear arms with conventional defense. . . . But a conventional defense strong enough to justify forswearing first use of nuclear weapons would require massively increased military spending for the other NATO countries, and probably a draft for the United States.

The thought of increasing conventional military strength to replace nuclear 6 bombs (like the thought that a successful nuclear ban would increase the chance of conventional warfare) is utterly alien to the mentality of most antinuclear activists. Is the horror of nuclear weapons sui generis, or is the goal abolition of all weapons and war? Are there practical steps that can be taken, or must we await a transformation of human nature? Jonathan Schell's essay well illustrates the confusion of the antinuclear movement.

Perhaps it is lèse majesté to call a major three-part series in *The New Yorker* 7 "pretentious," but "The Fate of the Earth" is one of the most pretentious things I've ever read, from the title through the grand finale (which begins, "Four and a half billion years ago, the earth was formed"). "Gosh, is this profound," is about all that many sonorous passages convey:

> [T]he limitless complexity [of nuclear war] sometimes seems to be as great as that of life itself. But if these effects should lead to human extinction, then all the complexity will give way to the utmost simplicity— the simplicity of nothingness.

> Like the thought "I do not exist," the thought "Humanity is now extinct" is an impossible one for a rational person, because as soon as it is, we are not.

Even funnier are the pompous generalities that come attached to *New Yorker*-style cautionary notes:

> Human beings have a worth—a worth that is sacred. But it is for human beings that they have that sacred worth, and for them that the other things in the creation have their worth (although it is a reminder of our indissoluble connection with the rest of life that many of our needs and desires are also felt by animals).

Hannah Arendt "never addressed the issue of nuclear arms," Schell tells us, 8 but of course she is dragged in. "I have discovered her thinking to be an indispensable foundation for reflection on this question." Evil, you know. What is really indispensable is her graphic descriptions of Nazi death camps. They pop up here to illustrate the point (both unenlightening and untrue, on recent evidence) that you can't deny horrors that have already happened. Himmler appears a little later, expressing his desire to make Europe "Jew-free." Schell observes, "His remark applies equally well to a nuclear holocaust, which might render the earth 'human-free.' " In fact, Hannah and Himmler are here for aesthetic rather than pedagogical purposes. This is simply how you decorate apocalyptic bigthink.

Despite a lot of wacky judiciousness ("From the foregoing, it follows that   9
there can be no justification for extinguishing mankind"), Schell's method is basically bullying rather than argument. The pomp is intended to intimidate, and the moral solemnity is a form of blackmail. Unless you feel as anguished about nuclear war as Jonathan Schell, unless you worry about it *all the time* like him (allegedly), your complacency disqualifies you from objecting. In fact, you are suffering "a kind of sickness" or "a sort of mass insanity." So shut up.

Much of Schell's essay does take the form of argument, but it tends to be   10
hothouse reasoning: huge and exotic blossoms of ratiocination that could grow only in an environment protected from the slightest chill of common sense. For example, here he is arguing that we should not have an experimental nuclear war in order to see what would happen:

> We cannot run experiments with the earth, because we have only one
> earth, on which we depend for our survival; we are not in possession of
> any spare earths that we might blow up in some universal laboratory in
> order to discover their tolerance of nuclear holocausts. Hence, our knowl-
> edge of the resiliency of the earth in the face of nuclear attack is limited
> by our fear of bringing about just the event—human extinction—whose
> likelihood we are chiefly interested in finding out.

Now welcome please "The famous uncertainty principle, formulated by the German physicist Werner Heisenberg," which makes a brief star turn at this point in the argument. Its role is to escort "an opposite but [not very] related uncertainty principle: our knowledge of extinction is limited because the experiments with which we would carry out our observations interfere with us, the observers, and, in fact, might put an end to us."

The argument is crowned with a portentous aphorism: "the demand for   11
certainty is the path toward death." Then, just to show that he's thought of everything, Schell considers and rejects the idea of holding an experimental nuclear war on another planet, " . . . for if we have no extra, dispensable earths to experiment with, neither are we in possession of any planets bearing life of some different sort." The reader is left convinced that an experimental nuclear war is a bad idea, and that Jonathan Schell possesses either an absurdly swelled head, or a "philosophical synthesis" that is "profoundly new" (—Eliot Fremont-Smith, the *Village Voice*).

Schell prefaces his discussion of the consequences of nuclear war with a   12
discussion of the difficulty of imagining it. Some of the alleged obstacles are of

this sort: "when we strain to picture what the scene would be like after a holocaust we tend to forget that for most people, and perhaps for all, it wouldn't be *like* anything, because they would be dead."

But the main set of obstacles involves a supposed reluctance of people to hear   13
about it. Schell pleads with his readers to make this sacrifice: "it may be only by descending into this hell in imagination now that we can hope to escape descending into it in reality at some later time." He promises to protect their delicate sensibilities: "I hope in this article to proceed with the utmost possible respect for all forms of refusal to accept the unnatural and horrifying prospect of a nuclear holocaust." He flatters their "investigative modesty" as "itself . . . a token of our reluctance to extinguish ourselves." And thence to pages of the usual gruesome description. The horror is lightened only by some *New Yorkery* punctiliousness, as when having killed off millions in a one-megaton bomb over Manhattan, he adds that newspapers and dry leaves would ignite "in all five boroughs (though in only a small part of Staten Island)."

Schell's posture of reluctant scientific inquiry will be familiar to aficionados of   14
pornographic movies. And there *is* something pornographic about the emphasis on grisly details that is the distinguishing feature of the antinuclear movement in its latest manifestation. Perhaps Jonathan Schell is so sensitive that he really does find these disaster scenarios painful to contemplate, and probably we all do withhold true visceral understanding of what it would be like. But others will find such disaster scenarios grimly fascinating (certainly the most interesting part of Schell's book). Is that sick? If so, it is a sickness that is widespread, and one that the antinuclear movement both shares and exploits. So the coy posture is annoying.

But destruction of civilization, or even the agonizing death of everybody in   15
the whole world, would be, to Schell, just a minor aspect of the tragedy of a nuclear holocaust. The greatest crime would be against "the helpless, speechless unborn." Schell brandishes this notion of the unborn as his trump card, in case anyone still thinks nuclear war is a good idea. By "the unborn," he does not merely mean fetuses (though by his analysis—liberals please note—abortion is unthinkably immoral). Nor does he mean the future human race as an entity. He does not even mean future people who might inherit a nuclear-wrecked civilization and environment. He means individual people who will *never be born* if there is no one left to conceive them. "While we can launch a first strike against them," Schell inimitably points out, "they have no forces with which to retaliate."

Schell concedes "the metaphysical-seeming perplexities involved in pondering   16
the possible cancellation of people who do not yet exist—an apparently extreme effort of the imagination, which seems to require one first to summon before the mind's eye the countless possible people of the future generations and then to consign these incorporeal multitudes to a more profound nothingness. . . ." But he's up to the challenge:

> Death cuts off life; extinction cuts off birth. Death dispatches into the nothingness after life each person who has been born; extinction in one stroke locks up in the nothingness before life all the people who have not

yet been born. For we are finite beings at both ends of our existence—natal as well as mortal—and it is the natality of our kind that extinction threatens. We have always been able to send people to their death, but only now has it become possible to prevent all birth and so doom all future human beings to uncreation.

And so on and on. Schell is *very strict* about what might be called "aliveism." Having waxed eloquent for pages about the unborn as repositories for our hopes and dreams, he stops to warn that we should not treat them merely "as auxiliaries to *our* needs," because "no human being, living or unborn, should be regarded as an auxiliary." The unborn, he scolds, "are not to be seen as beasts of burden. . . . "

Well, my goodness. Do we really have a moral obligation not to deny birth to 17 everyone who, with a bit of help, might enjoy the "opportunity to be glad that they were born instead of having been prenatally severed from existence by us"? I shudder to think how I've failed. For that matter, I shudder for Jonathan Schell—for every moment he's spent banging away on his typewriter, instead of banging away elsewhere.

In solving the problem of nuclear war, Schell cautions, we must "act with the 18 circumspection and modesty of a small minority," since "even if every person in the world were to enlist, the endeavor would include only an infinitesimal fraction of the people of the dead and unborn generations." Yes, the dead count too. So he proposes "a worldwide program of action," involving an "organization for the preservation of mankind." We must "delve to the bottom of the world" and then "take the world on our shoulders." He writes, "Our present system and the institutions that make it up are the debris of history. They have become inimical to life, and must be swept away." What he proposes, in short, is that the nations of the world abjure all further violence—nuclear *and* conventional warfare—and give up their sovereignty to some central organization.

This idea will win no prizes for circumspection and modesty. Other problems 19 come to mind, too. Like, how shall we arrange all this? Schell writes:

> I have not sought to define a political solution to the nuclear predicament—either to embark on the full-scale examination of the foundations of political thought which must be undertaken . . . or to work out the practical steps. . . . I have left to others those awesome, urgent tasks.

Good heavens. This sudden abandonment, on page 219, puts Schell's hyperventilated rhetoric in an odd light. Is he just going to head off on a book tour and leave us stranded?

Schell is convinced, though, like the rest of the antinuclear movement, that 20 the main task is education—convincing people of how bad a nuclear war would be. "If we did acknowledge the full dimension of the peril . . . extinction would at that moment become not only 'unthinkable' but also undoable." The key word here is "we." But there is no "we." There are individual actors who cannot completely know or trust one another. That's life. Even if everyone in the world shared Schell's overwrought feelings about nuclear war, the basic dilemma would not disappear: the best defense against an enemy's use or threat to use nuclear weapons is the threat to use them back.

Schell correctly points out the weakness in deterrence theory: since nuclear   21
wars are unwinnable, it's hard to make a potential aggressor believe you would actually strike back once your country was in ruins. "[O]ne cannot credibly deter a first strike with a second strike whose raison d'être dissolves the moment the first strike arrives." This may be "a monumental logical mistake," as Schell asserts, but it has prevented anyone from using a nuclear weapon, or even overtly threatening to use one first, for thirty-five years. And in any event, pending his proposed outburst of "love, a spiritual energy that the human heart can pit against the physical energy released from the heart of matter," it's all we've got.

So the first problem with Schell's solution is that you can't get there from here.   22
The second problem is what "there" could be like. Speaking, if I may, for the unborn, I wonder if they might not prefer the risk of not being born at all to the certainty of being born into the world Schell is prepared to will them.

The supreme silliness of "The Fate of the Earth," and of much of the   23
antinuclear movement, is the insistence that any kind of perspective on nuclear war is immoral. Schell complains, "It is as though life itself were one huge distraction, diverting our attention from the peril to life." And to Schell, apparently, all considerations apart from the danger of nuclear war *are* mere distractions. He repeatedly asks, What could be worse than the total annihilation of the earth and everything and everyone on it forever and ever? He demands that "this possibility must be dealt with morally and politically as though it were a certainty." We can opt for "human survival," or for "our transient aims and fallible convictions" and "our political and military traditions."

> On the one side stand human life and the terrestrial creation. On the other side stands a particular organization of human life—the system of independent, sovereign nation-states.

Gee, I just can't decide. Can you?

If the choice were "survival" versus "distractions," it would be easy, and   24
Schell wants to make it seem easy (though I have to wonder whether he really lives his own life at the peak of obsessive hysteria posited in his writing). In fact, that's not the choice. The choice is between the chance, not the certainty, of a disaster of uncertain magnitude, versus institutional and social arrangements that have some real charm.

Schell suggests at one point that "say, liberty" and other "benefits of life" are   25
relatively unimportant in his scheme of things, because

> to speak of sacrificing the species for the sake of one of these benefits involves one in the absurdity of wanting to destroy something in order to preserve one of its parts.

But it's clear that he imagines his postnuclear world as a delightful lion-and-lamb affair, no nation-states, no war, free hors d'oeuvres at the Algonquin bar, a place anyone would prefer even apart from the nuclear dilemma. Some of his admirers know better. In a recent column, Eliot Fremont-Smith of the *Village Voice* expressed the general dazzlement "The Fate of the Earth" has induced in the New York literary scene. He called on Knopf to cancel the rest of its spring list in deference to Schell's vital message. But Fremont-Smith did indicate some passing regret for what might have to be given up when Schell's world organization replaces national sovereignty. His list includes "freedom, liberties, social justice"— but he is willing to kiss these trinkets away in the name of "a higher and longer-viewed morality." Others may demur.

Actually, if Schell and his admirers really believe that the nuclear peril outweighs all other considerations, they are making unnecessary work for themselves by proposing to convince all the leaders of the world to lay down their weapons. Schell concedes that the people of the Soviet Union don't have much influence over their government, and suggests, rather lamely, that "public opinion in the free countries would have to . . . bring its pressure to bear, as best it could, on all governments." But why not avoid this problem by concentrating on our own governments? Schell is right: the doctrine of deterrence is only necessary for nation-states that wish to preserve themselves as political entities. Nothing would reduce the peril of nuclear war more quickly and dramatically than for the free and open societies of the West to renounce the use of nuclear weapons unilaterally. That would solve the flaw Schell sees in deterrence theory by making the Soviet threat to use them thoroughly credible, and therefore making their use unnecessary. More creatively, we might offer the Soviets a deal: you forswear nuclear weapons, and we'll forswear *all* weapons, nuclear and conventional. They might find this very tempting. So, by his own logic ("the nuclear powers put a higher value on national sovereignty than they do on human survival"), would Jonathan Schell. 26

In practice, the antinuclear movement *is* concentrating on the free governments of the West, for the obvious reason that these are the only governments susceptible to being influenced. I do not think most antinuclear protesters want unilateral disarmament. But the suspicion that they do is widespread among the political leaders they must attempt to persuade, and is hampering their basically worthy efforts. The glorious muddle of their thinking is hampering those efforts even more. What *do* they want? 27

▼ TOPICAL CONSIDERATIONS

1. What does Kinsley say is fundamental to the "dismantling" of the nuclear terror between enemies? What hope does he see for this possibility?
2. On what issues is the antinuclear movement vague and confused, according to Kinsley?
3. Throughout the essay, Kinsley refers to Jonathan Schell's "Fate of the Earth" essay. Why does he say the piece is "pretentious"? Is his evidence convincing?
4. What is Kinsley's central argument against Schell—his style? His arguments? His politics? What is Kinsley's argument on some of each?

5. What does Kinsley mean when he accuses Schell of "hothouse reasoning" (paragraph 10)?
6. At the end of paragraph 13, Kinsley specifically refers to that portion of "Fate of the Earth" reprinted in the preceding essay. Kinsley refers to these as "pages of the usual gruesome description," then goes on to say that there is something "pornographic" about such emphasis. How does he mean this term? Looking back over Schell's piece, do you agree? Do you agree with Kinsley's assessment of the "sickness" of the antinuclear movement?
7. According to Kinsley, what is Schell's proposal for avoiding nuclear war? What does he think of Schell's idea? What is Kinsley's proposal?

▼ RHETORICAL CONSIDERATIONS

1. Much of Kinsley's attack on Jonathan Schell centers on his style and writing tone. How would you characterize Kinsley's style and tone? Would you say he is cynical? Despairing? Fatalistic? Ironical? Cite passages for evidence.
2. Occasionally, Kinsley slips from attacking Schell's writing to attacking him personally. Cite some of these passages. Do these personal insults weaken or strengthen Kinsley's case? Explain.
3. What do you make of the sentence at the end of paragraph 1: "But, really, I think a nuclear holocaust would be very, very sad"? Is Kinsley being serious and sincere? Do you think he is being cynical? Sarcastic? Understated?
4. Find some examples of Kinsley's humor in this essay. How were the humorous effects created?
5. The author quotes from Schell's essay. How well does he use the sample passages? Do his commentaries seem accurate and fair?

▼ WRITING ASSIGNMENTS

1. If you have read the Schell piece in this book, how has Kinsley's essay affected your view of it? Write an essay detailing how your attitudes have been changed.
2. Did this essay put nuclear holocaust in perspective for you? Did it affect your attitudes about nuclear war, the future, nuclear disarmament, or the antinuclear movement? If so, describe these effects in an essay.
3. Kinsley says that Schell and other antinuclear supporters are fooling themselves when they think they can "convince all the leaders of the world to lay down their weapons" (paragraph 26). Write an essay in which you argue either for or against this position.

▼ STAR WARS: THE LEAKY SHIELD

Carl Sagan

Carl Sagan is famous on many fronts—as a scientist, a writer, and a television personality. He is director of the Laboratory for Planetary Studies and the David Duncan Professor of Astronomy and Space Science at Cornell University. He is also author of *The Cosmic Connection* (1972), the Pulitzer Prize-winning *Dragons of Eden* (1977), *Broca's Brain* (1981), and the best-selling science fiction novel *Contact* (1985). He is probably most widely recognized as creator and narrator of the PBS TV series *Cosmos.* In this article, Dr. Sagan evaluates Star Wars, the current Strategic Defense Initiative offered by the Reagan Administration as a new disincentive to nuclear war. The problems with Star Wars, says Sagan, are not political, but technical. The shield would leak, no matter what. And America would be destroyed despite the trillion-dollar effort. This article originally appeared in *Parade* magazine in December 1985.

1   After World War II, the United States was invulnerable. Bounded east and west by great oceans and north and south by weak and friendly neighbors, we had no reason to fear an attack by any other nation.

2   All that has now changed. We invented the hydrogen bomb, having a destructive power up to 1000 times that of the weapons that destroyed Hiroshima and Nagasaki, and a succession of other bright ideas and brilliant inventions insinuated themselves into the American and (often soon afterward) Soviet arsenals.

3   In the late 1950s, the nuclear arms race really got going. The United States had a vast lead in numbers of nuclear weapons and intercontinental bombers. But the bombers, slow and lumbering, would take 10 hours or more to reach their targets in the Soviet Union. Now both sides were pursuing another "delivery system"—the first intercontinental ballistic missiles (ICBMs). Here—unlike most other strategic systems—the Soviets were slightly ahead. ICBMs could not carry as large a payload as a bomber, but even a single hydrogen bomb can destroy a city. And they had distinct advantages: They took only half an hour or less to reach their targets, and they moved so fast that, unlike bombers, they would be almost impossible to shoot down. Propelled well above the Earth's atmosphere into the blackness of nearby space, the warheads would follow long, arcing trajectories, inertially guided to their distant targets.

4   At a meeting at the White House in 1960, the Defense Department asked President Dwight D. Eisenhower to authorize a U.S. contingent of 400 interconti-

nental missiles a year, each tipped by a hydrogen bomb. Eisenhower, who had commanded the Allied forces in the victory over Nazi Germany and who knew something about arms races, was uneasy. "Why don't we go completely crazy," he asked, "and plan on a force of 10,000?" Well, 10,000 missile-delivered strategic warheads is roughly what we now have. The Soviets have a similar number. And a case can be made that we—Americans and Soviets together—*have* gone completely crazy.

The more missile silos, strategic airfields, ballistic missile submarine ports,   5 command and control facilities, weapons storage depots and the like on one side, the more nuclear weapons and delivery systems are needed to destroy them by the other side. The U.S. and the USSR became locked in a deadly embrace. And so, from 1945 to the present, the two nations together have steadily increased the number of strategic nuclear weapons in the world, every year upping the ante. The ability of the United States to destroy the Soviet Union as a functioning society was reached in the 1960s, according to then Secretary of Defense Robert S. McNamara. A few years later, the Soviets achieved a comparable ability to destroy the United States.

But the arsenals kept on growing. Most citizens of the two nations were   6 unconcerned. Ever more weapons of mass destruction were necessary, we were told, to protect us. We believed it. The agencies of national propaganda inculcated fear and hatred of the potential adversary, and many people felt, despite their misgivings, that the issues were too technical and accountability too remote for the nation's leaders to be influenced much by public opinion. So we put it out of our minds. We hoped for the best. Psychiatrists call this "denial."

But eventually the weapons became so numerous, their accuracy so high,   7 their delivery times so short and the consequences of nuclear war finally perceived to be so appalling that public unease reached unprecedented heights. Public education was aided when physicians, first in the United States and then in other nations, began making clear what they had long known but what government officials had apparently chosen not to think about—that the supply of intensive-care units, burn beds, blood, physicians and hospitals was utterly inadequate to care for the survivors of even a small nuclear war. Most of the victims would receive no medical treatment at all. Gradually, physicians and scientists became openly skeptical of bland official reassurances about the consequences of nuclear war, and a range of new and devastating findings emerged. Lately, they seem to be discovered at the rate of one or two a year.

In September 1985, a symposium on the medical implications of nuclear war   8 was held at the National Academy of Sciences in Washington, D.C. It was sponsored by the Institute of Medicine, the nation's most distinguished body of medical experts. At this meeting, scientists from Stanford and Princeton universities estimated that the immediate civilian casualties in a nuclear war would be several times more than the number estimated by official sources, partly because of previously neglected superfires and firestorms. Such fires would pollute the lower atmosphere with toxic chemicals and, according to University of Colorado researchers, would work—together with the rising fireballs and smoke from multiple nuclear explosions—to deplete the thin layer of ozone that protects life on Earth from dangerous solar ultraviolet radiation.

A detailed study by scientists at the University of London of the causes of 9 death at Hiroshima suggests that, under realistic conditions, the amount of radiation necessary to kill a human being might be half that in previous official estimates. According to a Brown University study, the combined effects of radiation, burns, malnutrition, stress and depression would compromise the immune systems of large numbers of survivors, attacking the human T-cells and inducing something rather like a global epidemic of AIDS.

Also reported at the Washington symposium were a number of recent studies 10 on Nuclear Winter (described in PARADE Oct. 30, 1983), including a three-year investigation by 200 scientists from 30 nations. Their report states that the cold and the dark that would follow nuclear war would, by destroying agriculture and halting exports from northern midlatitudes, lead to the starvation of billions of people, including those far from the target zones. The report concludes: "As representatives of the world scientific community drawn together in this study, we conclude that many of the serious global environmental effects are sufficiently probable to require widespread concern. Because of the possibility of a tragedy of an unprecedented dimension, any disposition to minimize or ignore the widespread environmental effects of a nuclear war would be a fundamental disservice to the future of global civilization."

There were, in addition, a number of studies on the psychological and 11 psychiatric aspects of nuclear war. It is evident that, by frightening children and adults and by suggesting that it is foolish to work hard now to ensure a better future later, the prospect of nuclear war already has claimed many casualties.

Scientific findings such as these make it clear that the United States and the 12 Soviet Union have gone too far. They have placed in jeopardy our global civilization and possibly even the human species.

There seem to be only two ways out: to make massive reductions in the 13 nuclear arsenals on both sides, or to erect shields to protect us from each other's strategic weapons. At least until the Geneva summit meeting between President Ronald Reagan and Communist Party Secretary Mikhail Gorbachev, the United States has opted for strategic defense, with massive arms reductions to occur only at some far distant date—after the defenses are in place. The hoped-for system is called the Strategic Defense Initiative (SDI) or Star Wars. The central concept is a multi-tiered defense that will shoot down some Soviet missiles as they leave their launch pads, destroy some warheads in space and mop up some fraction of the residue as they career down on their designated targets. To accomplish this goal, a profusion of new technologies is proposed, many of which could not be fully deployed for decades, even under the most optimistic circumstances—including X-ray and chemical lasers, particle-beam weapons, electromagnetic rail guns and kinetic energy kill vehicles. Also proposed are orbiting mirrors that would reflect lasers beamed up from the United States down to incoming warheads.

If the number of weapons available to the Soviet Union were small, as it was 14 in the 1950s, a vast Star Wars shield might make some sense. But as it is, there are now some 10,000 Soviet strategic warheads (and more U.S. warheads), and if the United States were to go ahead with Star Wars, that number would doubtless increase in compensation. In addition, the Soviets would have powerful incentives to deploy huge numbers of decoys and so-called penetration aids, so that, in a full attack, a "threat cloud" of hundreds of thousands of objects—some warheads, most not—would be streaming, mainly over the Arctic Circle, from the Soviet Union to the United States.

Confronted with such numbers, competent observers—including Lt. Gen.   15
James A. Abrahamson, director of SDI—agree that even after decades of dedicated work (and the expenditure, according to some experts, of $1 trillion), the shield will still be leaky. The overwhelming consensus of computer experts is that writing reliable "battle management" software is hopelessly beyond our abilities for the foreseeable future—although here, as in many other areas of SDI technology, the U.S. is far ahead of the USSR.

Advocates of Star Wars often talk about 50 percent to 80 percent effectiveness.   16
But let us suppose a shield that is 90 percent effective. We imagine that 90 percent of all incoming Soviet warheads are successfully picked out of the threat cloud and made to explode relatively harmlessly far from their American targets. The remaining 10 percent would penetrate the shield and explode in the United States. But a 10 percent leakage of 10,000 warheads corresponds to 1000 nuclear explosions on American territory—more than enough to destroy the United States.

Many experts think that 90 percent is wildly optimistic, but even if we accept   17
higher efficiencies than projected by SDI's advocates, it is entirely clear that Star Wars would be unable to protect the civilian population of the United States—the goal of Star Wars, according to President Reagan's speech on March 23, 1983, and many later official pronouncements. After enormous expenditures of national treasure and the deflection of large numbers of first-rate scientists and engineers from useful research, the shield would not work. A contraceptive shield that deters 90 percent of 200 million sperm cells is generally considered worthless—20 million sperm cells penetrating the shield are more than enough. Such a shield is *not* better than nothing; it is worse than nothing, because it might well engender a false sense of security, bringing on the very event it was designed to prevent. The same is true for the leaky shield of Star Wars.

There are some in the United States who argue that, while a completely   18
leakproof shield is impossible to imagine with present technology, perhaps startling future developments will occur to change all that. "After all," this argument goes, "they said we couldn't send a man to the Moon, didn't they?" But the Moon was unconcerned about U.S. efforts in space. The Moon did not fight back. The circumstances here are different. The Soviets—by increasing their offensive forces, developing decoys and deploying orbiting mines to attack the space-based component of our Star Wars system—can hopelessly complicate the American SDI. The Soviets have caught up with the U.S. in every aspect of the nuclear arms race. No new weapons system has ever given the U.S. a decisive edge. And even with a tiny fraction of its present forces, each side retains an invulnerable capability to destroy the other.

So if Star Wars can't protect the people of America, why does the Soviet   19
Union profess to be afraid of it? Among other things, the Soviets are concerned
that there is a hidden agenda for Star Wars—that its real purpose is not defense
but offense. In Russian nightmares, the United States launches a massive attack
on the Soviet Union, destroying much of its retaliatory force. Then Star Wars is
used to take care of the much smaller number of Soviet warheads that are
launched in retribution. It is no good arguing that the U.S., when it had a nuclear
monopoly, did not attack the Soviet Union. The Soviet military, like our own,
must worry about even remote contingencies. If the situation were reversed, we
would worry also—as we did when, in the negotiations leading to the 1972 ABM
treaty, we successfully urged the Soviets to abandon *their* (feeble) strategic
defense plans, in part by threatening massive buildups of our offensive weapons.

So Soviet military leaders might one day argue that a preemptive nuclear   20
attack on the United States should be made to prevent Star Wars deployment.
And if the Soviets would contemplate such a policy, U.S. leaders might contemplate an earlier, *pre*-preemptive attack.

These are some of the reasons Star Wars has become a key point in the   21
strategic negotiations between the United States and the Soviet Union. The
difficulties with Star Wars are not a matter of different political perceptions or
ideologies. They are intrinsic. They follow directly from the nature of the beast.

If there are no technological "fixes" to the nuclear arms race forthcoming,   22
then it seems that we should consider agreement on equitable, bilateral, verifiable
and massive cuts in the nuclear arsenals. If properly devised, such a treaty might be
one of those endeavors in which both parties, and everyone around them, win big.

▼ TOPICAL CONSIDERATIONS

1. Sagan traces the development stages of our nuclear defense from the end
   of World War II to the present. What are the key stages of development?
   When did the United States reach its ability to destroy Soviet society?
   When did the Soviet Union catch up?
2. According to Sagan, why in the past did public opinion have little effect on
   the leaders of our nation? What are some of the reasons nuclear weaponry
   has surfaced as a major public issue? In particular, what role did scientists
   and physicians play?
3. What is the concept of "Nuclear Winter" that Carl Sagan talks about?
4. What psychological effects does the prospect of nuclear war have on
   children according to other studies?
5. Sagan describes the concept of Strategic Defense Initiative (SDI) or Star
   Wars. What would be the purpose of Star Wars? For what specific reasons
   is Sagan opposed to its implementation?
6. Why does the Soviet Union profess to be afraid of Star Wars?
7. What is Sagan's suggestion for ending the nuclear impasse between the
   United States and the Soviet Union?

8. What are your own feelings about Star Wars? Would you like to see it implemented or not? Explain your position. Did Sagan's article strengthen or change your position?

▼ RHETORICAL CONSIDERATIONS

1. Exactly where is the thesis statement in Carl Sagan's essay? Comment on the strategy of its location in the essay. Demonstrate how he constructs his argument through deductive reasoning.
2. Sagan says that in the past the public, despite its "misgivings" over nuclear arms, was not informed enough to influence political leaders. How "informed" does Carl Sagan sound in the essay? How effective is his use of supporting material? Was he convincing? Could he have used more?
3. How appropriate and convincing is the sperm/contraceptive shield analogy in paragraph 17?
4. If you had not known, could you have guessed from the essay that Carl Sagan is an astronomer? What clues can you find?

▼ WRITING ASSIGNMENTS

1. Write a letter to Carl Sagan in which you clearly explain why you agree or disagree with his stand on Star Wars.
2. Do you think the leaders of the world are capable of rising above their ideological and political differences and their fears and suspicions to eliminate nuclear weapons? Write a paper in which you attempt to answer this question.
3. Sagan says studies show that the prospect of nuclear war has discouraged some people from working hard "to ensure a better future." What about you? Has fear or the feeling of inevitability made it seem foolish to work for a nuclear-free future?

▼ THE PEACE MOVEMENT

Charlton Heston

> Charlton Heston is best known as an actor. He has appeared in some Hollywood classics including *The Ten Commandments* and *Ben Hur*, for which he won an Oscar. Heston is also known as a voice of political conservatism. In the following speech made in 1983 and first published in *Vital Speeches*, he articulates his opposition to the Nuclear Freeze movement by arguing that only through nuclear superiority can America maintain peace with the Soviet Union.

I was in Los Alamos a few weeks ago, doing a minor chore for the Atomic 1
Testing Laboratory the University of California maintains there. As I was leaving, they presented me with a sample of a rare mineral . . . trinitite. It was formed instantaneously, thirty-eight years ago, from the sand of the New Mexican desert in the atomic test, code-named "Trinity," that validated the atomic bombs that ended World War II.

I took it home and gave it to my son, Fraser, a fine young man of twenty-seven, 2
because it occurred to me that it was, in a very real sense, his birthstone. In the summer of 1945, when the blast that coalesced the sands of Los Alamos into trinitite was set off, Fraser was unconceived and his mother was still in school. I was in the Aleutian Islands in the 11th Air Force, preparing to invade the main islands of Japan.

If the trinity test had failed, no atomic bombs would have fallen on Hiroshima 3
and Nagasaki, and the hundred and fifty thousand Japanese who died there would have been spared. Some of them, at least. Many, surely, would have been included in the four million Japanese it was estimated would die in the invasion of Japan. "Operation Coronet" it was called. U.S. losses were expected to be one million men. One million men who would not come home, whose children would not be born. I don't know if I would have been among them or not, of course . . . but I'm glad I didn't have to find out. The creation of that lump of trinitite saved the lives of five million people and allowed the creation of ten million more. Perhaps my son lives because we bombed Hiroshima, ten years before he was born.

In the generation of his lifetime, since those stirring days, much has changed. 4
We thought we had defeated tyranny forever and democracy was the bright wave of the future. We were wrong. It is tyranny that floats on a rising tide, and freedom lives only on islands of democracy scattered in a sullen sea. The climate of the blood is chill. . . . It has turned to dark November in the American soul.

"Peace" is the cry on every hand. From politicians sniffing a breeze bearing 5
votes, from scholars and bishops, and earnest journalists, from anxious mothers

and frightened school children taught to draw crayola mushroom clouds instead of Easter bunnies, we hear it. "Peace. God, give us peace." Amen to that, surely.

The curious thing is, we *have* peace. Since Hiroshima, there has been no global war. Peace has been preserved for almost thirty-eight years by the nuclear deterrent maintained by the United States and her NATO allies. This force has restrained the only conceivable enemy in such a conflict: the Soviet Union.   6

Nevertheless, throughout the Western democracies in the last two years, thousands of decent people, chilled by the fear of nuclear war, have concluded that the way to avoid it is to toss away the shield that has protected us from it. War is a terrible thing, to fear it is reasonable, and common to us all. But fear is not a reasonable guide for human actions.   7

History is. Less than forty-five years ago, we saw the same phenomenon in Europe we see now. The enemy was Hitler then, but the fear of war was just as real. Then, as now, this fear led many to propose the most irrational compromises, the most cringing accommodations. Winston Churchill, out of office and vilified as a war-monger, fought to stem the tide. A rich lady labourite chided him once at dinner. "Tell me, Mr. Churchill," she said. "Why do you try so hard to persuade us that Hitler is a bad man?" "If I do not succeed, Madam," said Churchill, "I'm afraid you will find out." They did.   8

We may well find out in our time. Meanwhile, many of my countrymen propose as a solution a nuclear freeze, to be negotiated bilaterally between the United States and the Soviet Union. This has been the subject of intense debate in the West, to which we are even now contributing. There has of course been no such debate in the Soviet Union, because there *is* no debate in the Soviet Union. This is not to say that the Soviets have not contributed to the debate. They have, very effectively, but their efforts have been confined to the Western democracies, where a highly sophisticated and well-planned KGB disinformation program has functioned most effectively in the freeze movement in the West. This fact does not reflect on the sincerity of the thousands of people in the West who support a nuclear freeze out of a conviction that it will somehow bring us the peace of the world we all seek. I've heard several of them. There is no doubting the passion they bring to their belief in the freeze as a panacea for peace. I'm very pleased to have been asked to speak on this issue tonight, but I'll try to do so without passion. A few months ago, I heard a man . . . another actor, I'm afraid . . . support the freeze by saying, "No, I haven't *read* anything about it. I don't need to. This is a gut issue." Indeed it is. But you can't think with your guts. You can, of course, think of the search for peace as a moral obligation incumbent on every human being. Let us do that, by all means. A great philosopher . . . Hegel, I think . . . put that best. He said, "The most important of all moral obligations is to think clearly." My hope . . . my passionate hope, if you like . . . is that all of us will do that on this subject.   9

Without passion, then, and with as much reason as we can muster, let us consider the nuclear freeze. Reason tells us a freeze will not preserve the peace; worse than that, it threatens the peace we enjoy, because it is unnegotiable, unverifiable, and unequal. Let's examine those three negatives in order.   10

To attempt to negotiate a bilateral freeze treaty with the Soviet Union would, in the first place, derail the American efforts now in progress in Geneva not merely to freeze nuclear arms, but reduce them. It would also fragment the popular support crucial to those negotiations. Indeed, the freeze debate has already done that, a fact not lost on the Soviets. They are unlikely to move in any negotiation until they see how far the debate in this country brings us toward accommodation with the Soviet position. Ignorant as they are of the open function of the democratic process in a free society, and truly unable to comprehend the power of the American media, the Soviets take our debate on this issue merely as a sign of weakness of will and commitment in the American people. That message is false, but it nonetheless echoes in the Kremlin. To a lesser degree, the same message is marked in the NATO countries to whose security we have been committed for two generations, all of them democracies who depend on us for that security. 11

The difficulties of negotiating with the Soviets are compounded not only by their ignorance of our system, but by our ignorance of theirs. David Satter, a journalist of long experience in Russia, wrote recently on this point. "We are not only different countries," he said, "but different mentalities. The Soviet Union is based on an ideology which claims to be a system of universal explanation. Soviet leaders operate on the assumption that they are infallible. Soviet citizens defer to this authority. In order to fulfill their ideology, the Soviets must *create* reality. Instead, they have created a whole series of mirages imitating democratic institutions . . . trade unions without power, newspapers without information, courts to which there is no recourse, and a parliament without function." 12

If we cannot penetrate the Soviet mind, nor comprehend Soviet ideology, we still have a valuable guide in considering negotiations with them. We're all familiar with Santayana's dictum, "He who will not study history is doomed to repeat it." If we fail to study the lessons history provides us on the Soviet Union, we face a very unpleasant doom indeed. The nuclear freeze proposal, as even its supporters concede, requires the adherence of the Soviets to the terms of any treaty that might be negotiated. Lenin, the founding father and patron saint of the Soviet state, set Soviet policy on treaties. "Promises are like pie crust," he said. "Made to be broken." They have followed his advice. 13

To put it succinctly, the Soviets have violated nearly every treaty they have signed since the founding of the Soviet state in 1922, from the League of Nations and the Geneva Convention, through the Atlantic Charter, Yalta, Potsdam, the Four-Power Agreement on Berlin, the United Nations Charter, the Nuclear Test-Ban Treaty, and the Helsinki Human-Rights Agreement, as well as Salt I and II. The several treaties they broke in their brutal invasions of Finland, Hungary, Czechoslovakia, and Afghanistan, and their use of poison gas there, as well as in Laos and Cambodia, revolted the world. This has deterred neither the Soviets nor those eager to undertake yet another treaty with them. The rising evidence linking them to the attempted assassination of the Pope indicates so horrendous a violation of the code by which civilized nations coexist in the world that Western governments can hardly bring themselves to contemplate the consequences. 14

The Soviets did adhere scrupulously to one treaty: their secret pact with   15
Hitler to invade Poland in 1939. Of course, this treaty violated a previous nonag-
gression pact with Poland, so perhaps we can call that a wash.

A nuclear freeze observed by us and broken by the Soviets would be suicidal,   16
I think most would agree. Therefore, on the historical record, it is unnegotiable.

All right, what about verification? An ABC/*Washington Post* poll last year   17
indicated that 80 percent of those polled felt the Soviets would try to cheat on a
freeze treaty, and 87 percent opposed such a treaty if they *could* cheat. Yet freeze
initiatives passed in several states. So much for reason over emotion.

Since almost no one will seriously defend the idea that the Soviets can be   18
trusted to keep an agreement on their own, a freeze treaty *depends* on verification.
Indeed, most freeze proposals specify a verifiable ban on "the testing and/or
production of nuclear weapons or carriers," meaning aircraft. Despite what you
may have heard about the uncanny surveillance capacities of our space satellites,
they are useless in cloudy weather, or over areas not covered by their orbits. Since
those orbits are well known to Soviet intelligence, both as to track and timing, the
movement and storage of vehicles, supplies, and equipment, even in open country,
can be scheduled to the absence of the satellite. The Soviets routinely exploit
these shortfalls in our satellite capacity. Furthermore, design and testing operations are routinely and can entirely be conducted indoors or underground. Satellite surveillance is useless in these circumstances. Lastly, our satellites are vulnerable
in ways I will not specify to attacks from an increasingly effective Soviet anti-
satellite technology. I've attended classified briefings in recent weeks, both by the
Strategic Air Command and at Los Alamos. These briefings specify that our
satellites are not adequate to verify Soviet compliance with the terms of a nuclear
freeze treaty as outlined here.

That leaves on-site inspection. The answer is simple: "No." The Soviets   19
have never permitted it, have never even been willing to discuss it. Indeed, they
cannot. In a country that does not allow freedom of movement to its own citizens,
it is politically and ideologically impossible to allow foreign access to strategic
installations.

I recognize that neither negotiability nor verification concerns many freeze   20
proponents very much. What electrifies them is the need to *do* it. "The arms
race!" . . . or, more often, "the *insane* arms race!" is the rallying cry. The fact is,
there *is* no arms race. The Soviets are the only runners at this point. Since 1946,
when espionage on their side and traitors on ours gave them a start, they have
never *stopped* running. No one worried about nuclear war when we were the only
ones who could launch a preemptive first strike, nor even when a balance of
power was achieved. Indeed, for the past fifteen years, we've been trying to leave
it at that. We have offered and undertaken both bilateral and unilateral bans and
moratoriums on the testing and production of nuclear arms. They have without
exception been either ignored or broken by the Soviet Union.

Since 1967 we have reduced by some thousands the number of our warheads,   21
while the Soviets have added more than six thousand. Meanwhile, they aid
campaigns to prevent the replacement of our aging nuclear armaments with more

effective and cleaner weapons systems . . . systems desperately needed. They did this with spectacular success with the enhanced radiation warhead President Carter intended to install at the urging of all his security and defense advisors, as well as the NATO countries it was designed to protect. All this, while they relentlessly build what can only be defined as an offensive war machine.

True, Soviet leaders periodically announce their desire for peace. I point out   22 that Lenin once said, "Ultimately, peace simply means communist world control." I know, it's old-fashioned to quote Lenin now. It's what resourceful editorialists have called "pre-nuclear thinking." Perhaps Leonid Brezhnev is sufficiently up to date for quotation. In Prague, in 1973, he said, "Trust us, comrades. By 1985, we will have achieved our objectives in Western Europe. A decisive shift in the balance of forces will enable us to exert our will." Conversely, Prime Minister Thatcher said last year, "The last war sprang not from an arms race, but from a tyrant's belief that his neighbors lacked the means and the will to resist him."

Ladies and gentlemen, I am not offering you an apocalyptic forecast. I believe   23 in the capacity of mankind and the love of God. Yet, I share the concerns and fears of every person here. We live . . . God knows we always have . . . in an infinitely dangerous world. We'll never get out of it alive. But while we are here, surely reason must tell us to put the infinite treasure of the peace of the world in the hands of those we love, not those we fear.

▼ TOPICAL CONSIDERATIONS

1. Heston writes, "Perhaps my son lives because we bombed Hiroshima, ten years before he was born." Explain the statistics Heston uses to make this provocative implication. Do you agree with his assessment? Do you agree with his justification for the use of atomic weapons on Japan?

2. In paragraph 5, Heston refers to a wide sampling of the American population fearful of nuclear war and crying out for "peace." In the next paragraph he bluntly states, "The curious thing is, we *have* peace." How can you explain two such contradictory views of our present-day situation?

3. For what reasons is Charlton Heston opposed to a nuclear freeze? Which, in your opinion, seems the strongest argument? Which seems to be the weakest?

4. According to Heston, how does Soviet society differ from American society? Do you agree with his distinctions? Have there been significant changes since Mikhail Gorbachev's policy of "glastnost" (openness) and perestroika (restructuring)?

5. Consider the question of reason versus emotions in the nuclear debate. Is it possible to discuss the issue of nuclear disarmament without emotions? Is it, do you think, desirable to do so?

▼ RHETORICAL CONSIDERATIONS

1. List some quotations from historical figures that Heston employs to support his point of view. In your opinion, do these quotations help or hinder his argument? Would you say Heston is guilty of "pre-nuclear thinking"?
2. Note Heston's word choice in paragraph 5 as he describes those seeking peace. What does his word choice say about his attitude toward these people? Explain how these words "color" those described.

▼ WRITING ASSIGNMENTS

1. If Charlton Heston presented you with a sample of the rare mineral trinitite, how would you respond to him?
2. Take the position of a proponent of the nuclear freeze movement and respond to Heston's argument.

▼ EVACUATING THE CAPITAL? NO NEED TO HURRY NOW

Art Buchwald

Nuclear warfare is not a laughing matter, but if anybody could find something funny to say about it, it would be Art Buchwald. He is one of America's best-known journalists and humorists. Since 1962, Buchwald has written a syndicated column for nearly 400 newspapers. Many of his essays have been published in collections, such as *Son of The Great Society* (1966) and *The Buchwald Stops Here* (1978). What characterizes Buchwald is his good-natured mockery of American politics and social trends. In this typical piece, he goes after a grand evacuation plan dreamed up by the Office of Civil Defense. According to the plan, in the event of a nuclear alert, residents of major cities would jump into their cars and speed off to rural "host" towns, where residents would welcome the evacuees. As Buchwald suggests, however, things don't always go according to plan—especially the government's plan. This essay first appeared in *The Boston Globe* in May 1982.

Unlike most people, I take Civil Defense very seriously. While the evacuation plan for Washington hasn't been fully worked out, I know what we're supposed to do. When the sirens go off, we're all to get in our automobiles, grab our credit cards and head for Lickety Split, West Virginia. 1

The other evening around five o'clock I decided to take a dry run. I came home and told my wife, who was in her housecoat and curlers. 2

"Get in the car, we're going to have a practice evacuation drill." 3

"Let me get dressed first." 4

"You don't have time. Do you think when the real thing happens, the Russians are going to wait for you to get all gussied up? Grab the credit cards and let's go." 5

"Do you have gas in the car?" she wanted to know. 6

"I have half a tank." 7

"That won't get us to Lickety Split." 8

"I'm sure if the real thing happens, the Civil Defense people will have emergency gasoline trucks all along the highway. After all, they can't expect us to evacuate Washington during an atomic bomb attack and not supply the petrol. Now stop talking and get in the car. We have to pretend this is not a drill." 9

As soon as we got near Key Bridge, we found cars bumper to bumper. We moved 10 feet every five minutes. 10

"What's going on?" my wife wanted to know. 11

"It's normal rush-hour traffic," I explained. 12

We made it over the Key Bridge in 45 minutes and moved smoothly along the 13
George Washington Parkway at 25 miles an hour until we hit the Beltway and were
slowed down to 15.

"I guess you didn't get out of town as fast as you had hoped," my wife said. 14

"That's because this is just a drill. When people know they're racing against a 15
Soviet ICBM, they'll be doing 80 miles an hour."

"How do we get to Lickety Split?" my wife asked. 16

"I guess the Civil Defense people haven't put up their signs yet." 17

My wife started to cry. "Let's go back." 18

"We can't go back until the Civil Defense people tell us it's safe. Washington, 19
as far as this drill is concerned, has been completely vaporized."

By asking directions from 40 people, we finally got to Lickety Split six hours 20
later.

It was dark, and no one was on the streets. We knocked on the door of a 21
farmhouse. A man carrying a shotgun answered it.

"Hi," I said, "we're from Washington and we were told to come to Lickety Split 22
in case of an atomic attack. We thought we'd arrive early and look the place over
just to see where we'd be the most comfortable."

"You got one minute to get off my farm." 23

"Don't shoot. Haven't you heard from the federal Civil Defense people? 24
You're supposed to open your homes to us until they can rebuild the capital."

"Thirty seconds." 25

"We'll sleep in the barn," I pleaded. "We're not proud." 26

"Fifteen seconds." 27

My wife pulled me away from the door towards the car. 28

"I'm reporting you to the Federal Emergency Management Administration," I 29
yelled at him. "You're making their atomic war evacuation plan into a farce."

▼ TOPICAL CONSIDERATIONS

1. If you hadn't known Buchwald was a humorist, where in the essay would
   you have caught on?
2. What typically American characteristics and attitudes does he satirize?
3. What assumptions about the Civil Defense people does Buchwald poke fun
   at?
4. If it were a real attack, what kinds of conditions would the Buchwalds
   probably face as they tried to leave Washington?
5. What is Buchwald's point in this piece? Who is the real target of his satire?
   Where is this best dramatized in the piece?

▼ RHETORICAL CONSIDERATIONS

1. What humorous effects does Buchwald intend by naming his assigned evacuation destination Lickety Split, West Virginia?
2. How does Buchwald characterize his wife in this little scenario? How does he characterize himself?
3. The farmer in Lickety Split says only a few words. How well does what he says underscore the problem Buchwald is criticizing?

▼ WRITING ASSIGNMENTS

1. Do what Buchwald does here—imagine making a practice evacuation drill from your home town to some fictitious destination assigned by the Civil Defense Department. Try to imagine the kinds of funny things that could go wrong, including the kind of reception you might get.
2. The real issue of evacuating the Capital or any city during a nuclear emergency is not so funny. Write a paper in which you suggest to the Civil Defense people an alternative to their "host town" plan.

SPORTS

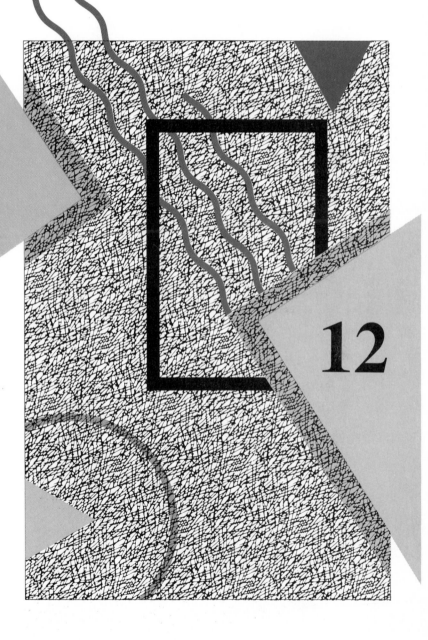

12

▼ SPORT AND THE AMERICAN DREAM

Jeffrey Schrank

> For nearly a century, Americans have had a love affair with sports. It
> has had something to do with the belief that competitive games are
> healthy—not only for the body, but for the national psyche. In this
> section, we will examine different sports and the ways they influence
> our lives inside and outside the fields of play. We begin with an
> explanation of how three American sports—football, baseball, and
> golf—are ritualistic enactments of national values and myths. Jeffrey
> Schrank has written widely on communications and popular culture.
> He is the author of several books, including *Snap, Crackle, and
> Popular Taste: The Illusion of Free Choice in America* (1977) from
> which this was taken.

Sport is a ritual, an acting out of a myth or series of myths. A sport that can be   1
considered a national pastime can be expected to reflect national values and
wishes. Sports that capture the national fancy are ritualistic enactments of the
American Dream. Baseball is still called our national pastime but is rapidly being
replaced by American football. That football should become our "national pastime"
is understandable to those who can see sports as reflections of national character.

American football is passionately concerned with the gain and loss of land, of   2
territory. The football field is measured and marked with all the care of a surveyor
and the ball's progress noted to the nearest inch. Football is a precise game and its
players are often trained like a military unit on a mission to gain territory for the
mother country. The players are the popular heroes but the coaches and owners
run the game, using the players to carry out their plans—there is comparatively
little room for individual initiative. A score comes as the result of a strategic series
of well-executed maneuvers and is bought on the installment plan, yard by yard.

The regulation and almost military precision of American football is a reflec-   3
tion of national psychology. Even the words we use to describe the game include
throwing the bomb, marching downfield, game plan (which has become nearly a
national phrase for any field, from selling toothpaste to covering up political
scandals), guards, executions, blitz, zone, platoon, squad, drills, attack, drives,
marching bands for entertainment, stars on helmets, lines that can be blasted
through and even war paint. Much of the verbal similarity comes from the fact
that war was originally the ultimate game played within the confines of certain
rules agreed upon by both "teams."

Football, more than any other sport, is a game for spectators to watch   4 superhuman, mythical heroes. Football is a sport that more people watch than play. The game requires too many people, too much space and is simply too dangerous for the weekend athlete. The size and speed of professional players and their uniforms make them into heroic figures capable of feats that invite admiration but not imitation. The football spectator is in awe of the armored monsters. The viewer of a golf match or even baseball or tennis dreams of going out the next day and doing likewise, but football is played only by the gods who can run the 100 yard dash in ten seconds, stand six feet three and weigh 260 pounds.

The demise of baseball as our national pastime reflects a change in national 5
character. The change does not mean the disappearance of baseball, merely its relocation to a position as just another game rather than *the* game. Professor John Finlay of the University of Manitoba, writing in *Queen's Quarterlay,* compares baseball to an acting out of the robber baron stage of capitalism, whereas football more clearly reflects a more mature capitalism into which we are now moving. Hence, the rise in popularity of football and apparent decline in baseball. He notes that Japan, still in the early stages of capitalism, has taken avidly to baseball but not to football. It is not a question of Japanese physique serving as a determinant since rugby has a large Asian following. He predicts that when their capitalism moves into a higher stage, the Japanese will move on to football as have Americans.

Baseball is a game of a quieter age when less action was needed to hold 6
interest, when going to the park was enjoyable (baseball is still played in ball parks while football is played in stadiums), when aggression was subservient to finesse. Baseball players did not need exposure as college players to succeed as football players do; they play a relatively calm game almost daily instead of a bruising gladiatorial contest weekly. Baseball has room for unique and colorful characters, while football stresses the more anonymous but effective team member. Baseball is a game in which any team can win at any given contest and there are no favorites; only football has real "upsets." Football's careful concern with time adds a tension to the game that is lacking in the more leisurely world of baseball.

Football has replaced baseball as the favorite American spectator sport largely 7
because of television. A comparison between a telecast of a football game on one channel and a baseball game on another could reveal baseball as a game with people standing around seemingly with little to do but watch two men play catch. Football would appear as twenty-two men engaged in almost constant, frenzied action. To watch baseball requires identification with the home team; to watch football requires only a need for action or a week of few thrills and the need for a touch of vicarious excitement.

Baseball is a pastoral game, timeless and highly ritualized; its appeal is to 8
nostalgia and so might enjoy periods of revitalization in comparison to football. But for now, the myth of football suits the nation better.

According to a 1974 Harris survey, baseball has already been statistically 9
dethroned. In a sports survey a cross section of nearly fourteen hundred fans was asked, "Which of these sports do you follow?"

The decision to play or "follow" a certain sport is also the decision to live a 10 certain myth. The team violence of football, the craftiness of basketball, the mechanistic precision of bowling, the auto racer's devotion to machinery are all subworlds within the universe of sport.

Golf, for example, is a unique subworld, one of the few left as a sport (unlike 11 hunting which does not involve scoring or teams) in which the game is played between man and nature. The winner of a match is one who has beaten the opponent, but the game itself is a person versus the environment. To understand the appeal of golf it is again necessary to consider the game as a ritual reenactment of an appealing myth.

Golf, perhaps more than any other sport, has to be played to be appreciated. 12 Millions who never played football can enjoy the game on TV, but only a dedicated participant can sit through two hours of televised golf. Golf is growing in participation but still has the stigma of an upper-class game. Eighty percent of the nation's golfers must play on 20 percent of the nation's courses that are open to the public. The ratio of public to private facilities hurts public participation in the game but mirrors the inequities of society and provides a convenient status symbol for those who can afford club membership. Its TV audience is not the largest of any sport but it is the most well heeled.

Golf is a reenactment of the pioneer spirit. It is man versus a hostile environment 13 in search of an oasis. The goal is a series of lush "greens," each protected by natural hazards such as water, sand and unmanageably long grass. The hazards are no threat to physical life but they are to the achievement of success. Golf is a journey game with a constantly changing field. Golfers start the eighteen-hole journey, can rest at a halfway point and then resume until they return to near the point of origination.

The winner of the match is one who has fallen victim to the fewest hazards 14 and overcome the terrain. Many golf courses have Indian names as if to remind the golfer of the frontier ethos. A local course called Indian Lakes invites golfers to use either one of two courses—the Iroquois trail or the Sioux trail.

Golf, like baseball, is a pastoral sport—with a high degree of tensions and 15 drama but relatively little action. It is a game in which players are constantly in awe of the magic flight of the golf ball. To hit any kind of ball 100 or 200 or more yards with accuracy or to hit a small target from 150 yards is an amazing feat to be appreciated only by those who have at least tried the game. Golf is very likely the most difficult game to master, yet one in which the average player occasionally hits a shot as good as the best of any professional. It is this dream of magic results that keeps the golfer on course.

▼ TOPICAL CONSIDERATIONS

1. Why is watching a football, baseball, or golf game a ritualistic act? What myths are Americans acting out when they participate in this way?
2. How is football a reflection of the American character? In other words, what does the game of football reveal about ourselves, our life styles, and our values as Americans?

3. What does "pastoral" mean? How are baseball and golf pastoral sports? Can you think of other sports that would fit this category? How is golf's television audience "well-heeled"?
4. Do you have a favorite sport? How does this preference reflect your personality?
5. According to Schrank, a 1974 Harris survey revealed that baseball has been "dethroned." How have we as Americans changed to cause the national pastime to shift from baseball to football?
6. What is a "robber baron"? How was the "robber baron stage of capitalism" a less mature capitalism than we have now? Why does Schrank feel that the Japanese, too, will eventually prefer football to baseball?

▼ RHETORICAL CONSIDERATIONS

1. What underlying idea links the descriptions of football, baseball, and golf together? Where in the essay is it introduced? Is this the thesis? Where else in the essay does Schrank rephrase, restate, or touch on this idea?
2. Outline the essay. Identify its major sections. Show how Schrank orders his ideas within each section. Cite the transitional words and phrases Schrank uses to move from one section to another.
3. Does Schrank use topic sentences effectively? Cite specific paragraphs to prove your answer.
4. Schrank begins four of his last five paragraphs with the word *golf*. Why does he do this? What effect does it have on the development of the essay?

▼ WRITING ASSIGNMENTS

1. What is your favorite sport? Write an essay showing how this sport is a reflection of your own personality.
2. Identify another leisure time activity that a majority of Americans like to either watch or participate in. In an essay, explain how it is a reflection of the American character.
3. Television programs and motion pictures also often portray ritualistic enactments of the American dream. Choose a television program or motion picture that does this and write about it. Show how it is "an acting out of a myth or series of myths."

▼ PLAYING TO WIN

Margaret A. Whitney

There was a time when sports were all-male experiences. But over the last several years, a rush of women into athletic competition has taken place on every level—secondary schools, college, Olympic games, and professional sports. What follows is an assessment of one such female, a high school basketball player who overcame family and social forces to sit still and be pretty. It is told by her mother who finds in the message of sports inspiration for her own mid-life quest. Margaret A. Whitney is a writer and a doctoral candidate in technical communications at Rensselaer Polytechnic Institute. This article was first published in the *New York Times Magazine* in July 1988.

1   My daughter is an athlete. Nowadays, this statement won't strike many parents as unusual, but it does me. Until her freshman year in high school, Ann was only marginally interested in sport of any kind. When she played, she didn't swing hard, often dropped the ball, and had an annoying habit of tittering on field or court.

2   Indifference combined with another factor that did not bode well for a sports career. Ann was growing up to be beautiful. By the eighth grade, nature and orthodontics had produced a 5-foot-8-inch, 125-pound, brown-eyed beauty with a wonderful smile. People told her, too. And, as many young women know, it is considered a satisfactory accomplishment to be pretty and stay pretty. Then you can simply sit still and enjoy the unconditional positive regard. Ann loved the attention too, and didn't consider it demeaning when she was awarded "Best Hair," female category, in the eighth-grade yearbook.

3   So it came as a surprise when she became a jock. The first indication that athletic indifference had ended came when she joined the high-school cross-country team. She signed up in early September and ran third for the team within three days. Not only that. After one of those 3.1-mile races up hill and down dale on a rainy November afternoon, Ann came home muddy and bedraggled. Her hair was plastered to her head, and the mascara she had applied so carefully that morning ran in dark circles under her eyes. This is it, I thought. Wait until Lady Astor sees herself. But the kid with the best eighth-grade hair went on to finish the season and subsequently letter in cross-country, soccer, basketball and softball.

4   I love sports, she tells anyone who will listen. So do I, though my midlife quest for a doctorate leaves me little time for either playing or watching. My love of sports is bound up with the goals in my life and my hopes for my three daughters. I have begun to hear the message of sports. It is very different from many messages that women receive about living, and I think it is good.

My husband, for example, talked to Ann differently when he realized that she   5
was a serious competitor and not just someone who wanted to get in shape so
she'd look good in a prom dress. Be aggressive, he'd advise. Go for the ball. Be
intense.

Be intense. She came in for some of the most scathing criticism from her dad,   6
when, during basketball season, her intensity waned. You're pretending to play
hard, he said. You like it on the bench? Do you like to watch while your
teammates play?

I would think, how is this kid reacting to such advice? For years, she'd been   7
told at home, at school, by countless advertisements, "Be quiet, Be good, Be still."
When teachers reported that Ann was too talkative, not obedient enough, too
flighty. When I dressed her up in frilly dresses and admonished her not to get dirty.
When ideals of femininity are still, quiet, cool females in ads whose vacantness
passes for sophistication. How can any adolescent girl know what she's up against?
Have you ever really noticed intensity? It is neither quiet nor good. And it's
definitely not pretty.

In the end, her intensity revived. At half time, she'd look for her father, and he   8
would come out of the bleachers to discuss tough defense, finding the open player,
squaring up on her jump shot. I'd watch them at the edge of the court, a tall man
and a tall girl, talking about how to play.

Of course I'm particularly sensitive at this point in my life to messages about   9
trying hard, being active, getting better through individual and team effort. Ann,
you could barely handle a basketball two years ago. Now you're bringing the ball
up against the press. Two defenders are after you. You must dribble, stop, pass.
We're depending on you. We need you to help us. I wonder if my own paroxysms
of uncertainty would be eased had more people urged me — be active, go for it!

Not that dangers don't lurk for the females of her generation. I occasionally   10
run this horror show in my own mental movie theater: an unctuous but handsome
lawyer-like drone of a young man spies my Ann. Hmmm, he says unconsciously to
himself, good gene pool, and wouldn't she go well with my BMW and the condo?
Then I see Ann with a great new hairdo kissing the drone goodbyehoney and
setting off to the nearest mall with splendid-looking children to spend money.

But the other night she came home from softball tryouts at 6 in the evening.   11
The dark circles under her eyes were from exhaustion, not makeup. I tried too
hard today, she says. I feel like I'm going to puke.

After she has revived, she explains. She wants to play a particular position.   12
There is competition for it. I can't let anybody else get my spot, she says, I've got
to prove that I can do it. Later we find out that she has not gotten the much-
wanted third-base position, but she will start with the varsity team. My husband
talks about the machinations of coaches and tells her to keep trying. You're doing
fine, he says. She gets that I-am-going-to-keep-trying look on her face. The
horror-show vision of Ann-as-Stepford-Wife fades.

Of course, Ann doesn't realize the changes she has wrought, the power of her   13
self-definition. I'm an athlete, Ma, she tells me when I suggest participation in the
school play or the yearbook. But she has really caused us all to rethink our views

of existence: her younger sisters who consider sports a natural activity for females, her father whose advocacy of women has increased, and me. Because when I doubt my own abilities, I say to myself, Get intense, Margaret. Do you like to sit on the bench?

And my intensity revives.   14

I am not suggesting that participation in sports is the answer for all young   15
women. It is not easy—the losing, jealousy, raw competition and intense personal criticism of performance.

And I don't wish to imply that the sports scene is a morality play either. Girls'   16
sports can be funny. You can't forget that out on that field are a bunch of people who know the meaning of the word cute. During one game, I noticed that Ann had a blue ribbon tied on her ponytail, and it dawned on me that every girl on the team had an identical bow. Somehow I can't picture the Celtics gathered in the locker room of the Boston Garden agreeing to wear the same color sweatbands.

No, what has struck me, amazed me and made me hold my breath in wonder   17
and in hope is both the ideal of sport and the reality of a young girl not afraid to do her best.

I watch her bringing the ball up the court. We yell encouragement from the   18
stands, though I know she doesn't hear us. Her face is red with exertion, and her body is concentrated on the task. She dribbles, draws the defense to her, passes, runs. A teammate passes the ball back to her. They've beaten the press. She heads toward the hoop. Her father watches her, her sisters watch her, I watch her. And I think, drive, Ann, drive.

▼ TOPICAL CONSIDERATIONS

1. How did Ann Whitney's beauty at first work against her sports career in high school?
2. Why did it come as a surprise to the author that her daughter became a jock?
3. What does the author mean by the statement, "I have begun to hear the message of sports." What is the "message of sports"? Do you agree the message "is good"?
4. What social forces were at work against Ann becoming a serious athlete? Do you see these forces working still? Have you ever had to confront such forces?
5. In paragraph 7, Whitney says that advertisements promote "quiet and cool" images of females "whose vacantness passes for sophistication." Do you find this observation to be generally true? Find some ads in magazines to support your answer. Can you find many ads in which such traditional female "ideals" are not projected—ads of active, competitive women?
6. Reread the essay *Officer and a Feminist* by James Dubik earlier in this text. How would Dubik regard Ann Whitney's athletic style?
7. The author says that she wishes when she was young she had been encouraged to be more active, to "go for it!" Why does she say this?

8. What "dangers" to her daughter's athletic career does Whitney fear? How does Ann allay her mother's fears?
9. This essay is more than just a celebration of the author's daughter. In your own words, what higher matters are celebrated?

▼ RHETORICAL CONSIDERATIONS

1. How do the opening two lines forecast the central conflicts of the essay?
2. In paragraph 4, the author relates her daughter's athletic drive to her own "midlife quest" for a doctorate. How well does the author weave this issue into her essay? Does it ever take away from the story of her daughter? Does it add to it?
3. What is the rhetorical purpose and effect of the sudden switch to a direct address of Ann in the present tense in paragraph 9? Where else does this switch in perspective appear?
4. Explain the "Lady Astor" allusion in paragraph 3. Explain the "Ann-as-Stepford-Wife" allusion in paragraph 12.

▼ WRITING ASSIGNMENTS

1. The author makes the point that female beauty works against female drive. Do you find this to be true? Do you think that women who are attractive are encouraged to be passive? Write an essay in which you explore this question. In it, address the same forces of school, family, and advertising.
2. Do you think females in sports receive the same quality of training as do males? Do they receive the same kind of encouragement? Write an essay examining any differences you have observed.
3. Do you see any difference in the athletic training females of your generation received and that of your parents? Talk to your parents about this, or someone from an older generation. Write an essay in which you compare the training of today's women with that of women from the past. Include personal experiences to illustrate the differences.
4. Write your own essay about "playing to win." Speak from either your own experience as an athlete or from the observation of athletes—male or female—you know or admire. Try to capture a sense of the drive and determination to excel in your essay.

▼ ATTITUDE

Garrison Keillor

> Garrison Keillor did a remarkable thing in this television age. In 1974, he managed to pull two-million Americans to their radio sets each Saturday night. He has been doing that since he created and began hosting the live variety show *Prairie Home Companion,* from Minneapolis. What made Keillor's National Public Radio production so popular is just the kind of warm wit and wisdom that characterizes the following article. In the essay he gives some thoughts about playing softball—particularly about attitude and how it might be the most important part of the game. This essay is taken from a collection of Keillor's pieces—most published in *The New Yorker*—*Happy to Be Here* (1982). Keillor is also the author of the best-selling novels *Lake Wobegon Days* (1985) and *Leaving Home* (1987).

Long ago I passed the point in life when major-league ballplayers begin to be   1
younger than yourself. Now all of them are, except for a few aging trigenarians and a couple of quadros who don't get around on the fastball as well as they used to and who sit out the second games of double-headers. However, despite my age (thirty-nine), I am still active and have a lot of interests. One of them is slow-pitch softball, a game that lets me go through the motions of baseball without getting beaned or having to run too hard. I play on a pretty casual team, one that drinks beer on the bench and substitutes freely. If a player's wife or girlfriend wants to play, we give her a glove and send her out to right field, no questions asked, and if she lets a pop fly drop six feet in front of her, nobody agonizes over it.

Except me. This year. For the first time in my life, just as I am entering the   2
dark twilight of my slow-pitch career, I find myself taking the game seriously. It isn't the bonehead play that bothers me especially—the pop fly that drops untouched, the slow roller juggled and the ball then heaved ten feet over the first baseman's head and into the next diamond, the routine singles that go through outfielder's legs for doubles and triples with gloves flung after them. No, it isn't our stone-glove fielding or pussyfoot base-running or limp-wristed hitting that gives me fits, though these have put us on the short end of some mighty ridiculous scores this summer. It's our attitude.

Bottom of the ninth, down 18-3, two outs, a man on first and a woman on   3
third, and our third baseman strikes out. *Strikes out!* In slow-pitch, not even your grandmother strikes out, but this guy does, and after his third strike—a wild swing at a ball that bounces on the plate—he topples over in the dirt and lies flat on his back, laughing. *Laughing!*

Same game, earlier. They have the bases loaded. A weak grounder is hit   4
toward our second baseperson. The runners are running. She picks up the ball,
and she looks at them. She looks at first, at second, at home. We yell, "Throw it!
Throw it!" and she throws it, underhand, at the pitcher, who has turned and run to
back up the catcher. The ball rolls across the third-base line and under the bench.
Three runs score. The batter, a fatso, chugs into second. The other team hoots
and hollers, and what does she do? She shrugs and smiles ("Oh, silly me"); after
all, it's only a game. Like the aforementioned strikeout artist, she treats her error
as a joke. They have forgiven themselves instantly, which is unforgivable. It is *we*
who should forgive them, who can say, "It's all right, it's only a game." They are
supposed to throw up their hands and kick the dirt and hang their heads, as if this
boner, even if it is their sixteenth of the afternoon—*this* is the one that really and
truly breaks their hearts.

That attitude sweetens the game for everyone. The sinner feels sweet remorse.   5
The fatso feels some sense of accomplishment; this is no bunch of rumdums he
forced into an error but a team with some class. We, the sinner's teammates, feel
momentary anger at her—dumb! dumb play!—but then, seeing her grief, we
sympathize with her in our hearts (any one of us might have made that mistake or
one worse), and we yell encouragement, including the shortstop, who, moments
before, dropped an easy throw for a force at second. "That's all right! Come on!
We got 'em!" we yell. "Shake it off! These turkeys can't hit!" This makes us all feel
good, even though the turkeys now lead us by ten runs. We're getting clobbered,
but we have a winning attitude.

Let me say this about attitude: Each player is responsible for his or her own   6
attitude, and to a considerable degree you can *create* a good attitude by doing
certain little things on the field. These are certain little things that ballplayers do
in the Bigs, and we ought to be doing them in the Slows.

7

1. When going up to bat, don't step right into the batter's box as if it were an
   elevator. The box is your turf, your stage. Take possession of it slowly and
   deliberately, starting with a lot of back-bending, knee-stretching, and torso-
   revolving in the on-deck circle. Then, approaching the box, stop outside it
   and tap the dirt off your spikes with your bat. You don't have spikes, you have
   sneakers, of course, but the significance of the tapping is the same. Then,
   upon entering the box, spit on the ground. It's a way of saying, "This here is
   mine. This is where I get my hits."

2. Spit frequently. Spit at all crucial moments. Spit correctly. Spit should be   8
   blown, not ptuied weakly with the lips, which often results in dribble. Spitting
   should convey forcefulness of purpose, concentration, pride. Spit down, not
   in the direction of others. Spit in the glove and on the fingers, especially after
   making a real knucklehead play; it's a way of saying, "I dropped the ball
   because my glove was dry."

3. At the bat and in the field, pick up dirt. Rub dirt in the fingers (especially after   9
   spitting on them). Toss dirt, as if testing the wind for velocity and direction.
   Smooth the dirt. Be involved with dirt. If no dirt is available (e.g., in the

outfield), pluck tufts of grass. Fielders should be grooming their areas constantly between plays, flicking away tiny sticks and bits of gravel.

4. Take your time. Tie your laces. Confer with your teammates about possible situations that may arise and conceivable options in dealing with them. Extend the game. Three errors on three consecutive plays can be humiliating if the plays occur within the space of a couple of minutes, but if each error is separated from the next by extensive conferences on the mound, lace-tying, glove adjustments, and arguing close calls (if any), the effect on morale is minimized.   10

5. Talk. Not just an occasional "Let's get a hit now" but continuous rhythmic chatter, a flow of syllables: "Hey babe hey babe c'mon babe good stick now hey babe long tater take him downtown babe . . . hey good eye good eye."   11

    Infield chatter is harder to maintain. Since the slow-pitch is required to be a soft underhand lob, infielders hesitate to say, "Smoke him babe hey low heat hey throw it on the black babe chuck it in there back him up babe no hit no hit." Say it anyway.   12

6. One final rule, perhaps the most important of all: When your team is up and has made the third out, the batter and the players who were left on base do not come back to the bench for their gloves. *They remain on the field, and their teammates bring their gloves out to them.* This requires some organization and discipline, but it pays off big in morale. It says, "Although we're getting our pants knocked off, still we must conserve our energy."   13

    Imagine that you have bobbled two fly balls in this rout and now you have just tried to stretch a single into a double and have been easily thrown out sliding into second base, where the base runner ahead of you had stopped. It was the third out and a dumb play, and your opponents smirk at you as they run off the field. You are the goat, a lonely and tragic figure sitting in the dirt. You curse yourself, jerking your head sharply forward. You stand up and kick the base. How miserable! How degrading! Your utter shame, though brief, bears silent testimony to the worthiness of your teammates, whom you have let down, and they appreciate it. They call out to you now as they take the field, and as the second baseman runs to his position he says, "Let's get 'em now," and tosses you your glove. Lowering your head, you trot slowly out to right. There you do some deep knee bends. You pick grass. You find a pebble and fling it into foul territory. As the first batter comes to the plate, you check the sun. You get set in your stance, poised to fly. Feet spread, hands on hips, you bend slightly at the waist and spit the expert spit of a veteran ballplayer—a player who has known the agony of defeat but who always bounces back, a player who has lost a stride on the base paths but can still make the big play.   14

    This is *ball,* ladies and gentlemen. This is what it's all about.   15

▼ TOPICAL CONSIDERATIONS

1. What does Keillor believe is the wrong attitude to have toward playing softball? What does he believe is the right attitude? If it's just a game, why is attitude so important?

2. Why does Keillor encourage his teammates to tap the dirt off their spikes when they are only wearing tennis shoes without spiked soles? What other apparently unnecessary acts does he insist they perform? Why does he feel these acts are so essential to the way the game is played?

3. How could Keillor's thesis and his comments about how to approach a game of softball be related to other activities? How could it help a student pass a course? Earn a promotion on a job? Get along better with a girlfriend or boyfriend?

4. How familiar is Keillor with professional baseball practices? Is he writing from firsthand or little, if any, experience? Cite specific passages to prove your point.

5. In comparing football to baseball, Jeffery Schrank, in "Sport and the American Dream" (p. 393), remarks that baseball has more "finesse." If Schrank were to happen by one afternoon while Keillor and his team were playing a casual game of slow-pitch softball, do you think Keillor would be likely to invite him to play? Why or why not? While sitting on the bench with Schrank, what comments might Keillor make about baseball as a reflection of American character?

▼ RHETORICAL CONSIDERATIONS

1. Keillor introduces his thesis in installments. Where does he actually state it? Identify each of the stages that leads up to it.

2. Writers strive to use specifics to show their readers what they mean and to avoid speaking in vague generalities. Is Keillor successful in this? Cite specific passages that prove your point.

3. Keillor refers to the "Bigs" and the "Slows." He describes a member of the opposite team as "a fatso" and his team as "no bunch of rumdums." Given these examples, how would you characterize the diction of this essay? Can you cite other examples?

4. Keillor often uses verbs that create a vivid word picture. In paragraph 4 he states: "The batter, a fatso, chugs into second." What image does "chugs" convey? What other interesting verbs does Keillor use?

5. Reread Keillor's list of things to do to create a proper attitude toward playing softball. What kind of sentence does he use here? What effect does it have on the reading of the essay?

6. What does Keillor's last sentence remind you of? Why is this a good concluding line?

▼ WRITING ASSIGNMENTS

1. Write an essay in which you explain your own views on the proper attitude to take toward some other sport. Draw on ideas from Keillor's essay that you agree with. Select incidents and examples that illustrate the points you want to make.
2. Attitude is important for professional athletes, musicians, singers, actors, and other performers. Write an essay about the effect the right attitude has on a nonathletic activity such as playing a musical instrument, singing, or writing.

▼ ON THE BALL

Roger Angell

> The name Roger Angell is synonymous with baseball. No, he doesn't
> play professional ball. He just writes about it better than most people.
> He is the author of *The Summer Game* (1972), *Five Seasons: A
> Baseball Companion* (1977) from which this was taken, *Late Innings*
> (1982), and *Season Ticket* (1988). He is also an editor and sports-
> writer for *The New Yorker.* In the following brief piece, Angell describes
> the essential ingredient in the game—the baseball. Notice how he
> moves from near-scientific objectivity to some strong feelings about
> the ball and the game.

It weighs just over five ounces and measures between 2.86 and 2.94 inches in   1
diameter. It is made of a composition-cork nucleus encased in two thin layers of
rubber, one black and one red, surrounded by 121 yards of tightly wrapped
blue-gray wool yarn, 45 yards of white wool yarn, 53 more yards of blue-gray wool
yarn, 150 yards of fine cotton yarn, a coat of rubber cement, and a cowhide
(formerly horsehide) exterior, which is held together with 216 slightly raised red
cotton stitches. Printed certifications, endorsements, and outdoor advertising
spherically attest to its authenticity. Like most institutions, it is considered inferior
in its present form to its ancient archetypes, and in this case the complaint is
probably justified; on occasion in recent years it has actually been known to come
apart under the demands of its brief but rigorous active career. Baseballs are
assembled and hand-stitched in Taiwan (before this year the work was done in
Haiti, and before 1973 in Chicopee, Massachusetts), and contemporary pitchers
claim that there is a tangible variation in the size and feel of the balls that now
come into play in a single game; a true peewee is treasured by hurlers, and its
departure from the premises, by fair means or foul, is secretly mourned. But never
mind: any baseball is beautiful. No other small package comes as close to the ideal
in design and utility. It is a perfect object for a man's hand. Pick it up and it
instantly suggests its purpose; it is meant to be thrown a considerable distance—
thrown hard and with precision. Its feel and heft are the beginning of the sport's
critical dimensions; if it were a fraction of an inch larger or smaller, a few
centigrams heavier or lighter, the game of baseball would be utterly different.
Hold a baseball in your hand. As it happens, this one is not brand-new. Here, just
to one side of the curved surgical welt of stitches, there is a pale-green grass
smudge, darkening on one edge almost to black—the mark of an old infield play, a
tough grounder now lost in memory. Feel the ball, turn it over in your hand; hold it
across the seam or the other way, with the seam just to the side of your middle

finger. Speculation stirs. You want to get outdoors and throw this spare and sensual object to somebody or, at the very least, watch somebody else throw it. The game has begun.

▼ TOPICAL CONSIDERATIONS

1. Why do you think Angell wrote this essay?
2. Do Angell's feelings about the baseball reflect your own?
3. Angell points to a "pale-green grass smudge" on his baseball, which he explains is "the mark of an old infield play, a tough grounder now lost in memory." What does this remark suggest about Angell's past association with the game of baseball? What associations does it have for you?
4. Is there any other sports equipment that might evoke the same response in an avid sports fan like Angell?
5. Why does Angell say that the baseball is a *sensual* object? What connotations does the word have within the context of his essay?

▼ RHETORICAL CONSIDERATIONS

1. What is Angell's attitude toward his subject? Cite specific phrases to illustrate your point.
2. Identify the primary rhetorical pattern used to develop this essay.
3. Why are there no paragraphs in this essay? Does it need these divisions? Explain.
4. Angell moves from an objective to a subjective description of a baseball. How does one relate to the other? Where and how does he make the transition? What can you point out about the way he orders his ideas in each section?

▼ WRITING ASSIGNMENT

1. Write an essay about an object that has fond associations for you. Adopt Angell's method of organization, moving from an objective to a subjective description. Include numerous details in your essay.

▼ ON THE BENCH

Robert B. Parker

There was a time when men who pumped iron were regarded as densely wadded muscle-freaks whose manhood was questionable. Over the last dozen years, however, weightlifting—and body building—not only has become popular, it is positively *au courant.* In nearly every city and suburb across America, you can find big, flossy health clubs full of physical-fitness-minded men and women on the benches of fancy weight machines, pumping chrome. What follows is a humorous and insightful confession of a man who has been on the bench before it was fashionable. In his characteristic style, Robert B. Parker tells how he got interested in weightlifting, why he continued for thirty years, and what it has done for his body and psyche. Since 1974, when he wrote his *Sports Illustrated Training with Weights* (with John R. Marsh), Parker has written sixteen novels about a tough, wisecracking private eye named Spenser—the most notable of which include the best-selling novels *Early Autumn* (1981), *Ceremony* (1982), and *Crimson Joy* (1988). (Like Parker, Spenser is occasionally on the bench.) Parker is also the author of several non-Spenser books including the thriller *Wilderness* (1979)—which has been contracted for a movie—and *Love and Glory* (1983). His latest Spenser novel is *Playmates* (1989). *Spenser for Hire* was an American Broadcasting Corporation television series based on Parker's novels. This article first appeared in *Sportscope* in 1981, and the author has updated it for this edition.

When I came home from Korea in the early '50s I weighed 148 pounds. While   1
I was cat-quick and a trained killer, I did have to hold onto my wife's arm in a strong wind, and the only reason people couldn't kick sand on me was that I stood sideways and they missed. Judicious management of food and drink helped me get up to 160 by the time my first son was born. But neither Pabst Blue Ribbon nor meatloaf sandwiches has much positive effect on biceps or pectoral muscle, and I remember thinking in the first rush of parenthood, a boy needs a strong father. So, at age 26 I got my first set of weights.

It was a big step, because when I was a boy, weightlifting was not fashionable.   2
Only muscle-bound freaks lifted weights, and, while one would hesitate to actually tell a weightlifter that he was a muscle-bound freak, one knew it to be true. His manhood was open to speculation as well.

When I got my first set of weights I had my wife buy them for me. I hid in the   3
bedroom when they were delivered and she signed for them. After the delivery

man left, I scurried out and assembled the weights and began to do the exercises described in the accompanying pamphlet. That was 30 years ago and I am still shoving away at the irons. The results have been mixed, but now when it's windy Joan holds onto *my* arm.

My first set of weights allowed me to lift a maximum of 110 pounds, if I put all 4
the weights on the bar. I especially wanted to do bench presses. So I made a bench out of two-by-fours and plywood and added a rack for the barbell. I put the bar on the rack, put all the weights on the bar, lay on the bench on my back, feet on the ground, hands comfortably apart, grasped the bar firmly near each end, tested the balance, hoisted it off the bar and lowered it to my chest: step one of the bench press. Step two is to press the barbell back up to arm's length. Ah, there's the rub. The bar, resting with nice balance on my chest, would not move. After a manful struggle I faced the hopelessness of my situation and called for Joan. She arrived, helped me tip the barbell off my chest, smiled her Mona Lisa smile, and went away without comment.

I tried again with less weight until I could do one bench press, then 5
several, then ten, and then three sets of ten. The muscles in my chest and arms got stronger. I added a little more weight and started the same routine again.

When I got too powerful for my 110-pound barbells, I graduated to the big 6
York barbells at the local Y. York barbells are the kind they use in the Olympics. The poundage plates slide onto a 45-pound bar easily and needn't be locked in place. The 100-pound weight plates for a York set look like spare wheels for a McCormick reaper.

The trick to weight training is simple: you isolate one muscle, or muscle 7
group, and exercise it repeatedly; then you exercise another, and another, *voilà* —Arnold Schwarzenegger. A good deal of ingenuity is required to find positions that will isolate, say, the upper abdominals, or the trapezius muscles.

After some regular congress with the Yorks (though I tended to eschew the 8
100-pound plates), I was presentable enough to go public at the Universal Trainer in the weight room at Northeastern University. During my Babylonian captivity, when I had access to the Universal, I more than doubled my earliest bench pressing efforts and was able to mingle with the weight room crowd undetected. No one suspected me of being an English teacher (this was, unfortunately, also true in the English Department).

One of the charms of the Universal is that it is a weight lifting machine with 9
several lifting stations. The weights are fixed on pulleys or runners, and poundage can be adjusted by simply moving a pin. Now that I am no longer at Northeastern, the Universal is denied me. But, ever venturesome, I signed up to try the new Nautilus system at the Colonial in Lynnfield. Remember Yaz in '67? Next summer I tore up the Lynnfield Men's Softball League.

I didn't devote myself exclusively to the irons all this time. Joan and I had 10
another son. Further motivated, I built up to 190 pounds of bone and sinew. At this writing there are still 190 pounds of bone and sinew. It is, however, almost entirely disguised by about 30 pounds of what could generously be called tissue. If

you think weightlifting is sure to trim you down you haven't been watching the Russian weightlifters.

Why have I spent several hours each week for 30 years, straining to exercise, with weights, at the outer limits of my strength, and trying to do it again and again at the outer limits of my endurance? In 30 years I've had to thrash no bullies on behalf of my sons. I have occasionally glared at someone who got uppity with Joan. But she needs my protection about as much as Mike Tyson does. I am good at picking up one end of something. Over the last twenty years my friend, John Marsh, and I have picked up and carried about an impressive assortment of refrigerators, pianos, sofas, washing machines, boulders, bags of Portland cement, stoves, timbers and beer kegs. But that seems small recompense for 30 years of Ben-Gay.   11

There *are* drawbacks to all that lifting. I'm probably heavier (though not fatter) than I would have been if I hadn't started lifting. I have distorted my upper body so that I am nearly impossible to fit off the rack. Clothing salesmen blanch when I enter. At 5'10" I take a size 50 suit. The pants have to be shortened so much that the cuffs catch in the zipper.   12

You are also brought face-to-face with the validity of an old truth: never a horse that couldn't be rode; never a rider that couldn't be throw'd. If you can bench press 300 pounds you're certain to have a friend who can do 350, and he knows someone who can do 450. I'm fairly strong for a 56-year-old fat man. But in any weight room in the country there are twenty people (mostly men) who are stronger than I am and maybe one that's better looking. Weightlifting is very useful in understanding the inequality of nature's dispensation.   13

Of course it is embarrassing at first when you go into the weight room with your little potbelly and your skinny white arms wearing the brand new gym suit your spouse bought you at K–Mart; and there are a lot of people who look like the Great Blue Hill pumping iron with their sleeves cut off. But progress is rapid, and you can learn from watching others. Most of them will be preoccupied with the wall mirrors and won't notice you anyway.   14

For a man who makes his living sitting down, alone, all day, weightlifting has much to offer. It pays off promptly, it fits conveniently into my schedule, it provides exercise that my profession does not (helping to offset typists' hump), and, perhaps more to the point, it makes me sweat. I *like* to sweat. Inelegant, but true. I like the feeling of effort, of tension followed by release (Arnold Schwarzenegger has already pointed out the sexual parallels; I try to write only of what I know). I like the sense of work carried through to resolution, and I like the sense of near endless possibility in goals accomplished and new goals set.   15

But most simply I lift weights for the reason with which I began. I want to be strong. I want to be strong the way I want to be smart. So I study to be smart and lift to be strong. (Joan says I'm oh-for-two, but she's never admitted my resemblance to the young Olivier either.) In the case of strong, as in the case of smart, there are limits to what can be made of the raw material. Like study, exercise can only improve on the basics. It can't supply them.   16

But within the limits of how you start, it seems to me that the renaissance ideal   17 of the warrior poet (Sir Philip Sidney, say) isn't a bad one. It needn't, of course, be weights. One of my sons is a dancer and he can do things with his body that no one else I know can do. It could be running. It could be gymnastics. Physical accomplishment doesn't have to include the ability to pick up the front end of a Buick. To be physically accomplished would seem as much a fulfillment of one's humanity as to be intellectually accomplished. To be both would seem most fully human.

▼ TOPICAL CONSIDERATIONS

1. What were Parker's original reasons for buying a set of weights? Back then, what was the general attitude toward men who were weightlifters, according to Parker?
2. What has 30 years of pumping iron done for Parker? How has it physically changed him? What has it done for his self-image? What drawbacks has he had to face as a result? How has it helped him?
3. What reasons does the author give for continuing to lift weights after 30 years? Is it for physical accomplishments alone?

▼ RHETORICAL CONSIDERATIONS

1. What is the organizing principle of this essay?
2. What is there about the first paragraph that makes you want to read on?
3. What kind of humor does Parker use in this piece? What is the source of his humor? How does his wife Joan serve his humorous effects?
4. Could you tell from this essay that Parker was once a professor of English? What literary allusions does he make directly and indirectly?
5. Could you tell from this essay that Parker is a successful novelist? If so, how?
6. Explain the following allusions and how they sustain the humorous tone of this essay: Mona Lisa, Mike Tyson, Ben-Gay, Arnold Schwarzenegger, Sir Philip Sidney.

▼ WRITING ASSIGNMENTS

1. Parker says that 30 years ago the attitude toward men who were weightlifters was not complimentary. What is the current attitude toward people who lift weights? Write a paper about how the general attitude toward weightlifters has changed.
2. If you lift weights regularly, write a report on how you got started. Try to capture the experience and explain how it has affected your physical development as well as your attitude.

3. If you are not a weightlifter but play a sport regularly, write a paper in which you tell how you first got interested in that sport, why you enjoy it, and what it has done for you physically and mentally.

▼ BLOOD SPORT

Edward Abbey

Hunting was an important part of Edward Abbey's childhood. Born and raised on a farm in the Allegheny Mountains, he remembers how his father had no choice but to hunt if the family of seven was to eat. Even under those conditions, they hunted according to a private code. They always preferred to get their deer the day before the season opened. "We liked our venison poached," writes Abbey. He offers some down-home reasons that have less to do with the taste of meat than with the appeal of breaking the law. As he explains, it is a higher law that eventually puts an end to his hunting days. Abbey was a naturalist, a novelist, an essayist, and a social gadfly. Abbey wrote, he said, to make a difference: "to oppose injustice, to defy the powerful, to speak for the voiceless." Taken from *One Life at a Time, Please* (1988), this essay does all of that. Other collections include *Slumgullion Stew: an Edward Abbey Reader* (1984) and *Down the River* (1982). Abbey also published seven novels. He died in March 1989 at the age of 62.

What can I say about hunting that hasn't been said before? Hunting is one of the 1 hardest things even to think about. Such a storm of conflicting emotions!

I was born, bred, and raised on a farm in the Allegheny Mountains of 2 Pennsylvania. A little sidehill farm in hardscrabble country, a land of marginal general farms, of submarginal specialized farms—our specialty was finding enough to eat without the shame of going on "The Relief," as we called it during the Great Depression of the 1930s. We lived in the hills, surrounded by scrubby third-growth forests, little coal-mining towns down in the valleys, and sulfur-colored creeks meandering among the corn patches. Few people could make a living from farming alone: my father, for example, supplemented what little we produced on the farm by occasional work in the mines, by driving a school bus, by a one-man logging business, by peddling subscriptions to a farmer's magazine, and by attending every private and public shooting match within fifty miles of home—he was an expert small-bore rifleman and a member, for several years running, of the Pennsylvania state rifle team; he still has a sashful of medals to show for those years. He almost always brought back from the matches a couple of chickens, sometimes a turkey, once a yearling pig.

None of this was quite enough, all together, to keep a family of seven in meat, 3 all the time, through the frozen Appalachian winters. So he hunted. We all hunted. All of our neighbors hunted. Nearly every boy I knew had his own rifle, and maybe a shotgun too, by the time he was twelve years old. As I did myself.

What did we hunt? Cottontail rabbit, first and foremost; we'd kill them, clean   4
them, skin them, cut them up; my mother deep-fried them in bread crumbs and
cooked and canned the surplus in Mason jars, as she did tomatoes, stringbeans,
succotash, pork sausage, peaches, pears, sweet corn, everything else that would
keep. We had no deep-freeze; in fact, we had no electricity until the Rural
Electrification Administration reached our neck of the woods in 1940.

So rabbit was almost a staple of our diet; fencerow chicken, we called it, as   5
good and familiar to us as henyard chicken. My father seldom bothered with
squirrel, but my brothers and I potted a few with our little Sears Roebuck
single-shot .22s, out among the great ancient white oaks and red oaks that were
still standing in our woodlot. Squirrel meat can be good, but not so good as rabbit,
and a squirrel is much harder to kill; we missed about ten for every one we hit.

There were no wild ducks or other waterfowl in the hills; our only gamebird   6
was the ringneck pheasant, rising with a thrilling rush from the corn stubble. My
father bagged a few of those with his old taped-together double-barrel shotgun.
Not many. He didn't like to hunt with a shotgun. Wasteful, he thought, and the
shells were too expensive, and besides, he disliked chewing on lead pellets. The
shotgun was primarily a weapon (though never needed) for home defense. Most of
the time he shot rabbits with his target rifle, a massive magazine-loaded .22 with a
peep sight. Shot them sitting.

Was that legal? Probably. I don't remember. But he had a good eye. And he   7
was a hunter—not a sportsman. He hunted for a purpose: to put meat on the table.

We kept a couple of beagle hounds on the place, but their job was to lie under   8
the front porch and bark at strangers. Only when our Uncle Jack came out from
town, with his sleek gleaming 16-gauge pumpgun (as we called it), and the red
bandana and hunting license pinned to the back of his hunting coat, only then
would our old man load his own shotgun and turn loose the dogs for some sport
hunting through the fields and along the edge of the woods. What my father really
liked about those occasions was not the shooting but the talk, the wild stories—
Uncle Jack was a great storyteller.

And then there were the deer. The woods of Pennsylvania swarmed with deer,   9
though not so many then as now, when many small farms, abandoned, have gone
back to brush, thicket, trees. There were even a few black bear still wandering the
woods, rarely seen. But deer was the principal game.

My father usually bought a license for deer, when he could afford it, but only   10
because the penalty for getting caught with an untagged deer would have been a
small financial catastrophe. In any case, with or without a license, he always killed
his deer on the evening before opening day, while those red-coated fellows from
the towns and cities were busy setting up their elaborate camps along the back
roads, stirring the deer into movement. Our father was not a stickler for strict
legality, and he believed, as most country men did, that fear tainted the meat and
therefore it was better to get your deer before the chase, the gunnery—The
Terror—began. We liked our venison poached. (As a result I find that after these
many years I retain more admiration and respect for the honest serious poacher
than I do or ever could for the so-called "gentleman hunter.")

My old man practiced what we called "still hunting." On the day before   11
opening, about noon, when the deer were bedded down for their midday siesta,
he'd go out with his gun, his cornfodder-tan canvas coat with its many big pockets,
and his coal miner's oval-shaped lunch bucket full of hot coffee and sandwiches
and Mother's stewed-raisin cookies, and he'd pick a familiar spot along one of the
half-dozen game paths in our neighborhood, settle down in the brush with his
back to a comfortable tree, and wait. And keep on waiting, sometimes into the
long autumn twilight, until at last the first somewhat nervous, always uneasy deer
appeared. Doe or buck, he always shot whatever came first. You can't eat antlers,
he pointed out.

Usually he shot his deer with a "punkin ball" from the battered, dangerous,   12
taped-up shotgun. But at least once, as I recall, he dropped a doe with his target
rifle, like a rabbit. Drilled her right between the eyes with a neat little .22-caliber
long-rifle bullet. Those deer slugs for the shotgun were expensive.

Then he'd drag the deer into the brush, out of sight, and wait some more, to   13
see if anyone had noticed the shot. When nothing happened, he hung the deer to
the nearest tree limb, dressed it out, ate the liver for supper. If it was a legal kill he
would wait through the night, tag it, and take it home by wheel first thing in the
morning. If not, he slung the carcass over his shoulders and toted it home through
the woods and over the hills in the dark. He was a strong, large, and resolute sort
of man then, back in the thirties and early forties, with a wife and five children to
feed. Nowadays, getting on a bit—he was born in 1901—he is still oversize, for an
old man, but not so strong physically. Nor so resolute. He works only four or five
hours a day, alone, out in the woods, cutting down trees, and then quits. He gave
up deer hunting thirty years ago.

Why? "Well," he explains, "we don't need the meat any more."   14

Now that was how my brothers and I learned about hunting. My brothers still   15
like to go out for deer now and then, but it's road hunting, with good companions,
not "still hunting." I wonder if anybody hunts in that fashion these days. I did a lot
of deer hunting in New Mexico from 1947 through the 1950s, during my student
years and later, when I was living on seasonal jobs with the Park Service and
Forest Service, often married, trying to write books. As my father had taught me, I
usually went out on the day before opening. Much safer then, for one thing, before
those orange-vested hordes were turned loose over the landscape, shooting at
everything that moves.

Gradually, from year to year, my interest in hunting, as a sport, waned away to   16
nothing. I began to realize that what I liked best about hunting was the companionship of a few good old trusted male buddies in the out-of-doors. Anything, any
excuse, to get out into the hills, away from the crowds, to live, if only for a few
days, beyond the wall. That was the point of hunting.

So why lug a ten-pound gun along? I began leaving my rifle in the truck. Then   17
I left it at home. The last time I looked down the bore of that old piece there was a
spider living there.

"We don't need the meat any more," says my old man. And I say, Let the   18
mountain lions have those deer; they need the meat more than I do. Let the

Indians have it, or hungry college students, or unpublished writers, or anyone else trying to get by on welfare, food stamps, and hope. When the money began arriving from New York by airmail, those checks with my name on them, like manna from heaven, I gave up hunting deer. I had no need. Every time you eat a cow, I tell myself, you are saving the life of an elk, or two mule deer, or about two dozen javelina. Let those wild creatures live. Let being be, said Martin Heidegger. Of course, they're going to perish anyway, I know, whether by lion or wolf or starvation or disease—but so are we. We are all going to perish, and most of us miserably, by war or in a hospital, unless we are very lucky. Or very resolute. I am aware of that fact and of our fate, and furthermore, I have no objections to it, none whatsoever. I fear pain, suffering, the likely humiliations of old age (unless I am lucky or resolute), but I do not fear death. Death is simply and obviously a part of the process; the old, sooner or later, have got to get out of the way and make room for the young.

The subject remains: death. Blood sport. The instinct to hunt. The desire to   19
kill. Henry David Thoreau, notorious nature lover, was also a hunter and fisherman, on occasion. And among the many things that Thoreau wrote on the matter was this, from *Walden:*

> There is a period in the history of the individual, as of the race, when the hunters are the "best men," as the Algonquins called them. We cannot but pity the boy who has never fired a gun; he is no more humane, while his education has been sadly neglected.

But he adds:

> No humane being, past the thoughtless age of boyhood, will wantonly murder any creature which holds its life by the same tenure he does. The hare in its extremity cries like a child. I warn you, mothers, that my sympathies do not make the usual *philanthropic* distinctions.

And concludes:

> But I see that if I were to live in a wilderness, I should become . . . a fisher and hunter in earnest.

In earnest. There lies the key to the ethical issue. Earnestness. Purpose. That sly sophist Ortega y Gasset wrote, somewhere, that "one kills in order to have hunted." Not good enough. Thoreau would say, one kills in order to eat. The killing is justified by the need and must be done in a spirit of respect, reverence, gratitude. Otherwise hunting sinks to the level of mere fun, "harvesting animals," *divertissement,* sadism, or sport. *Sport!*

Where did the ugly term "harvesting" come from? To speak of "harvesting"   20
other living creatures, whether deer or elk or birds or cottontail rabbits, as if they were no more than a crop, exposes the meanest, cruelest, most narrow and homocentric of possible human attitudes toward the life that surrounds us. The word reveals the pervasive influence of utilitarian economics in the modern mindset; and of all the sciences, economics is the most crude and obtuse as well as

dismal. Such doctrine insults and violates both humanity and life; and humanity will be, already is, the victim of it.

Now I have railed against the sportsman hunter long enough. I wished only to explain why first my father and then I have given up hunting, for the time being. When times get hard again, as they surely will, when my family and kin need meat on the table, I shall not hesitate to take that old carbine down from the wall and ramrod that spider out of the barrel and wander back once more into the hills. 21

"Paw," says my little brother, as the old man loads the shotgun, "let me shoot the deer this time." 22

"You shut up," I say. 23

Our father smiles. "Quiet," he whispers, "both of you. Maybe next year." He peers down the dim path in the woods, into the gathering evening. "Be real still now. They're a-comin'. And Ned—" He squeezes my shoulder. "You hold that light on 'em good and steady this time." 24

"Yes, sir," I whisper back. "Sure will, Paw." 25

▼ TOPICAL CONSIDERATIONS

1. Abbey says that hunting is a subject surrounded by "a storm of conflicting emotions." What conflicts about hunting does the author bring up? Any others that you can think of?

2. Why according to Abbey did his family and his neighbors do so much hunting in the past? How does sport hunting differ from the kind of hunting his father practiced?

3. Abbey says his father, with or without a license, would always hunt his deer the night before the season officially opened. What reasons does Abbey offer?

4. Why do you suppose Abbey has "more admiration and respect for the honest serious poacher" than he does for the " 'gentleman hunter' " (paragraph 10)? In fact, what would you say is Abbey's attitude toward the latter?

5. Abbey says that he gave up hunting in stages? What were the stages and why did he finally give it up for good?

6. In paragraph 19, Abbey refers to Ortega y Gasset as a "sly sophist." What is a sophist? Why does Abbey consider Ortega y Gasset's words "sophistical" and "sly"?

7. Abbey opens his essay with the question, "What can I say about hunting that hasn't been said before?" Does he say anything about the subject that you haven't heard before? If so, what? If not, did you still get something out of the piece? Explain.

▼ RHETORICAL CONSIDERATIONS

1. Why do you suppose Abbey chose the title he did for this essay? Why not something like "On Hunting"? Consider the connotations and denotations of the words "blood" and "sport."

2. In paragraph 6, Abbey says his father thought shooting with a shotgun wasteful. How is this attitude consistent with the image Abbey paints of his father? How else is the older man characterized?

3. Toward the end of the essay Abbey quotes three separate passages from Henry David Thoreau. Summarize Thoreau's points in your own words. What is the rhetorical advantage of the Thoreau passages? How do they support Abbey's arguments?

4. Toward the end, the essay turns from an autobiographical account of hunting to an argument about the ethics of hunting. Where exactly is the turning point in the essay? Is the transition smooth, or abrupt? Do you think Abbey strays too far from his subject, or merely adds greater support? Do you think Abbey's arguments appeal more to reason or emotion?

5. What is the point of the flashback in the last four paragraphs? How effective is it? Do you think the essay would be better off without it?

▼ WRITING ASSIGNMENTS

1. Even though this piece is primarily about hunting, Abbey sketches a portrait of his father through a few actions and words. Try to do the same, that is, write a character sketch of somebody through small actions, gestures, and words.

2. What are your own feelings about hunting? Do you think "killing is justified by the need" alone? Do you feel otherwise about the sport? Use specific arguments to support your stand.

3. If you have ever gone hunting, try to capture the experience in an essay. Following Abbey's example, make use of physical details of the environment, the clothing worn, the weapons, the prey, the kill, etc. Also, try to capture the emotions of the hunt making use of interior monologue and if the case, dialogue with your hunting partner(s).

▼ THE JOGGER'S CODE

Frederic Morton

Anyone who jogs will agree that something special takes place once the Nikes are laced and running. No, not just the stitch in the side or the burning of the lungs or the sweat lubricating the joints. Something special on the inside. Something that sets the jogger apart from the common leather-shod walker. It has to do with a whole different code of behavior. Perhaps even a code of honor nothing short of Pilgrim's pride and Galahad's determination. At least that's how writer Frederic Morton perceives his jogs in the park in this amusing, mock-heroic reflection. Morton is the author of *The Rothchilds* (1983), *A Nervous Splendor* (1980), and *The Forever Street* (1985). His most recent novel is *The Crosstown Sabbath*. This essay first appeared in the *New York Times* in January 1985.

---

1 Every day except Sunday I'm a multiple personality. (I don't jog on Sundays.) The change in roles starts around noon, with my stretching exercises. By the time I lace on my Nikes, a protocol has taken hold of me which has no meaning to my leather-shod self. A certain signal will trigger one response when I amble along at 3 miles per hour; but when I'm running at 13 . . . well, here are a few examples:

2 Footsteps dog me while I am walking. They are persistent. They are gaining. I glance back. It's not a mugger but the mailman in a hurry. I smile at him, entirely unembarrassed. The look-behind-thee tic is just normal urban survival procedure. I'm walking on upper Broadway.

3 Similar footsteps dog me while I'm sneakered, footsteps emerging quite possibly from the underbrush. They are persistent. They are gaining. My face remains stalwartly turned forward. Those sounds at my back may be malevolence about to pounce. But they may also be a fellow sportsman's. I will not lapse into an unduly competitive gesture. I will show no nervousness about someone else's being faster. I will not look back. I'm jogging in Riverside Park.

4 Or: a woman is walking toward me, a woman in her sumptuous 30's—without a bra. I indulge in an appreciative glance that might be mistaken for a crass stare. So what? We are all swingers, we *boulevardiers* of Broadway. Yet, let that same woman run toward me while I'm running, and my eyes, as well as my smile, chastely focus on her forehead. I will not mar with lust the comradeship of athletes. I am jogging in Riverside Park.

5 Or: I'm taking a "work walk" up West 83d Street, one of my neighborhood's quieter streets. I'm trying to think of a couple of transitions that will give the embryonic chaos of the chapter I'm writing a veneer of coherence. I pass the

garage near Amsterdam Avenue, and—blessed moment!—the transition comes to me. I pronounce it out loud, because the sound of the words will fix them in my memory. "All of which informed Edna that summer was here," I say to the driver of the Pontiac backing into the street. He nods from behind the wheel. What vibrant Upper West Sider doesn't talk to himself when out for a stroll?

An hour later, my brain lights up, unexpectedly, with a second and more 6
difficult transition: "That was the month Edna discovered how good she was at cultivating people she didn't like." It's a serviceable phrase, but it must remain unspoken, because it was born during my jog in Riverside Park. Silently I lope on, obeying decorum—and a sense of civic duty. You see, the world will be out of joint once even runners start blathering into the thin air. Runners set up expectancies that have become rare and precious in our time.

The public contours of the jogger suggest someone disciplined, dedicated, 7
responsible, quasi-heroic, a veritable emblem of muscular rectitude. He is very different from other high-profile characters of our street theater. How meritorious the contrast between him and the drug heads, winos and exhibitionists! The jogger looks undebauchable. Consider the steely steadiness of his stride, the elevated fanaticism tautening his features, the hardy skimpiness of his athletic shirt in the cold gusts. Like the aristocrat on horseback, he is more prominent in his locomotion, faster and nobler than the pedestrians in his wake. He looms on a pinnacle where machismo and morality meet.

Indeed, the jogger encompasses the hallmarks of two august models: Pilgrim 8
Father (upright, admirably goal-directed, pleasure-deferring, ascetic) and Arthurian Knight (borne along by his mission, lonely and yet undeterred). True, the errand of this knight-errant is narcissistic. He pursues only the fitness of his own body. On the other hand, Sir Galahad wasn't so very different, being rather vain about his soul. Holy Grail or five-minute mile: both are targets of a perfectionism that will brook no indulgence before the end of the quest. Anyone worried that society is falling apart ought to find reassurance on the track around the Central Park Reservoir. Here the moral fibers of the Occident are regrouping from the rot, warming up and vibrating. Too bad William Butler Yeats did not live to see the spectacle. Would he still feel that "the center cannot hold"? Hundreds of joggers seem to be rushing in to steady the damn thing.

Of course, I stick to Riverside Park, where running addicts diffuse among 9
jugglers, mothers on roller skates pushing prams, winter suntanners, and midgets tossing Frisbees to their Schnauzers. Amid all that, I attempt to do justice to the specialness of my habit, to the obligations of its noblesse oblige. In other words, I must live up to a code capable of admirable subtleties.

If I overtake a man, I will never rub in my superiority by looking at him or 10
even looking haughtily ahead as I pass. No, I will glance up a tree, interested in the twitter of that blue jay and in nothing else. If I pass a woman, the ethics of the situation are a bit more arduous. I will make an elaborate detour around her, insuring that my higher speed gets lost in the space between us.

And if I'm the one who's overtaken? It happens, and it's always a little hairy. 11
As long as the hustler is still behind me, I will not—as you know already—turn

around to see who's doing all that huffing and stomping. When he passes me and turns out to be a gray-haired fellow who gives me hope for my own later years, I'll be a complacent sluggard. I'll let him pull away in glory. If he's young and brash, however, I'll whistle a few bars of "It's a Long Way to Tipperary" while the punk is still in earshot, just to let him know how much unused wind there's left in the old boy.

If he who overtakes me is a she ... ah, then you'll find me severely tested. .12 Then I'll try very hard not to try to stay ahead with my last reserves. I'll try very hard not to swerve down the side road to the 79th Street marina that will take me away from defeat. I'll try very hard not to develop a suddenly sprained ankle forcing me to stop and thus fudge the outcome of what should never have been a contest. And if I defy all these temptations, if I succeed in just simply, frankly falling behind her, why then I console myself with self-congratulation. I have paid my final dues to running gallantry. I am the jogger *sans peur et sans reproche.*

▼ TOPICAL CONSIDERATIONS

1. Why does Morton refer to himself as a "multiple personality"? What does he mean when he says that "a protocol takes hold of" him when he puts on his running shoes?
2. What are some of the items of his jogger's code? How does jogging change his behavior? Cite some of his examples. If you are a jogger, does your behavior change as Morton's does? Do you have any jogger's codes?
3. How does public opinion affect Morton as a jogger? Why can he speak to himself while walking but not while jogging?
4. How does Morton's behavior toward women differ with his change from walker to runner?
5. Morton says that the jogger "encompasses the hallmarks of two august models: Pilgrim Father . . . and Arthurian Knight." What does he mean by this statement? Do you think he is being serious, or just humorously exaggerating? Explain.

▼ RHETORICAL CONSIDERATIONS

1. What is the function of the parenthetical second sentence in paragraph 1?
2. How well does Morton illustrate his code? Are his examples convincing?
3. Do you find this essay humorous at all? If so, what did you find funny about it? How does Morton create some of the humorous effects? Cite examples of exaggeration, irony, satire, bathos.
4. How would you define the tone of this essay? What role does Morton's language play in creating the tone?

▼ WRITING ASSIGNMENTS

1. If you are a jogger, do you share any of Morton's "code" of behavior? If so, write an essay in which you describe them.
2. This essay is written in a mock-heroic style—that is, the author treats something as common as jogging in lofty, exaggerated terms. Try your own hand at writing mock-heroically. Choose a trivial event or experience and give it a lofty treatment.
3. Write an essay entitled "Why I hate Joggers" or "Why I Hate Jogging."
4. Write an essay entitled "Why I love Joggers" or "Why I Love Jogging."

ON
CONTEMPORARY
LANGUAGE

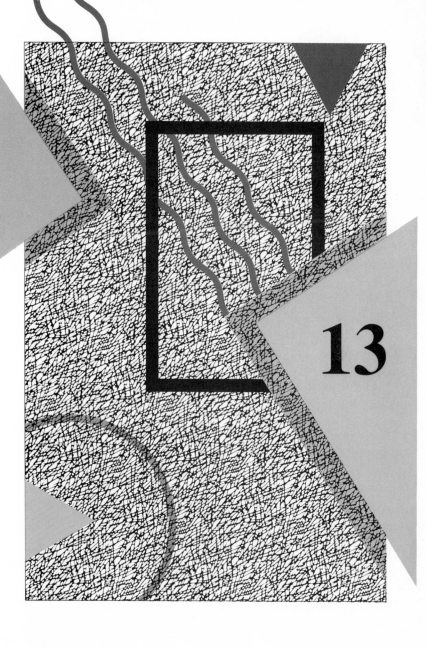

13

▼ IF SLANG IS NOT A SIN

Lance Morrow

> Slang is as contemporary as today. Everybody uses it, but few people ever consider where it comes from, how it functions for social subgroups, and the way it passes in and out of standard speech. What follows is an amusing discourse on contemporary slang—its variety, its origins, its rise, and its fall. Yes, fall, for as Lance Morrow, a senior writer for *Time* magazine, sees it, today's slang has lost some of its past renegade charm. This essay first appeared in *Time* magazine in November 1982.

The classic slang of the '60s is almost a dead language now. In unadulterated form   1
it survives only under the protection of certain purists with long memories, heirs
to the medieval tradition of monastic scribes. Their honorary abbot is Phil
Donahue.

The '60s-bred clergyman, especially the Episcopalian, is for some reason a   2
wondrous curator of the lingo. He ascends his pulpit. "God doesn't want you on a
guilt trip," he begins, inspired. "God's not *into* guilt. *Bad vibes!* He knows *where
you're coming from.* God says. 'Guilt, that's a *bummer.* The Lord can be pretty *far
out* about these things, you know." He goes into a wild fugue of nostalgia: *"Sock it
to me! Outasight! Right on!"*

But slang cannot live forever on the past, no matter how magnificent it may   3
have been. Slang needs to be new. Its life is brief, intense and slightly disreputable,
like adolescence. Soon it either settles down and goes into the family business of
the language (like *taxi* and *cello* and *hi*), or, more likely, slips off into oblivion,
dead as Oscan and Manx. The evening news should probably broadcast brief
obituaries of slang words that have passed on. The practice would prevent people
from embarrassing themselves by saying things like *swell* or *super.* "*Groovy,*
descendant of *cool* and *hip,* vanished from the language today."

Where is the next generation of slang to come from? Not from Valley Girl, the   4
argot made famous lately by singer Frank Zappa and his daughter, who is named
Moon Unit Zappa. "Val" is really a sort of satire of slang, a goof on language and
on the dreamily dumb and self-regarding suburban kids who may actually talk like
that. It would come out all wrong if a minister were to compose his sermon in Val.
"The Lord is awesome," he would have to begin. "He knows that life can sometimes be, like, *grody—grody to the max! Fer shirr!*"

Still, slang has deep resources. The French resist barbaric intrusions into   5
the language of Voltaire and Descartes. But American English has traditionally
welcomed any bright word that sailed in, no matter how ragged it may have looked

on arrival. That Whitmanesque hospitality has given America the richest slang in the world.

An inventory of American slang now, however, can be somewhat disappointing. 6 Slang today seems to lack the playful energy and defiant self-confidence that can send language darting out to make raffish back-alley metaphorical connections and shrewdly teasing inductive games of synonym.

Examine one fairly new item: *airhead.* It means, of course, a brainless person, 7 someone given to stupid behavior and opinions. But it is a vacuous, dispiriting little effort. The word has no invective force or metaphorical charm. When slang settles for the wearily literal (*airhead* equals empty head), it is too tired to keep up with the good stuff.

Much new slang originates with people who have to be in by 8. Junior high 8 and even grade school are unexpectedly productive sources. Sometimes children simply take ordinary words and hold them up to the light at a slightly different angle, an old trick of slang. The ten-year-old will pronounce something *"excellent"* in the brisk, earnest manner of an Army colonel who has just inspected his regiment. (*Primo* means the same thing.) The movie E.T. has contributed *penis breath,* an aggressively weird phrase in perfect harmony with the aggressively weird psyche of the eight-year-old. In Minnesota, they say, *for weird. Bogus* is an ordinary, though slightly out-of-the-way word that has been recommissioned as youth slang that means fraudulent or simply second-rate or silly. *Bogus* is a different shading of *lame.* Something that is easy is *cinchy.* Overexcited? One is *blowing a hype.*

The young, as always, use slang as an instrument to define status, to wave to 9 peers and even to discipline reality. A real jerk may be a *nerkey,* a combination of *nerd* and *turkey.* Is something *gnarly?* That may be good or bad. But if it is *mega-gnarly,* that is excellent. One may leave a sorority house at U.C.L.A. to *mow a burger.* Slang has less ideological content now than it had in the '60s. Still, it sometimes arises, like humor, from apprehension. High school students say, "That English test really *nuked* me." On the other hand, in black neighborhoods of Washington, D.C., if you had a good time at a party, you *dropped the bomb.*

The old '50s frat-house leer is evident in today's collegiate slang. To *get naked* 10 means to have a good time, whether or not sex is involved. (That is a new shortened form of the *get-drunk-and-get-naked party,* which collegians fantasized about 20 years ago.) At Michigan State University, one who is vomiting is *driving the bus,* a reference to the toilet seat and the wretch's need to hang on to it. *Sckacks* means ugly. A *two-bagger* is a girl who requires exactly that to cover her ugliness. Young women, of course, retaliate. At breakfast in Bates Hall at Wellesley, they wonder, "Why bother with a guy if he doesn't *make your teeth fall out?*" *Time to book* means time to leave, which can also be *time to bail.* None of this is exactly brilliant. Slang is sometimes merely a conspiracy of airheads.

American slang is fed by many tributaries. Feminists are busy *networking* 11 —the liberated version of using the old-boy network. Cops, as sardonic with language as criminals are, refer to a gunshot wound in the head as a *serious headache.* Drug users have their codes, but they seem to have lost some of their glamour. Certain drugs have a fatality about them that cannot be concealed in jaunty language. The comedian Richard Pryor introduced the outer world to *freebasing* a couple of years ago, and John Belushi died after he *speed-balled* (mixed heroin and cocaine). Punk language has made a couple of its disarmingly nasty contributions: *sleaze* (as in, "There was a lot of sleaze at the party," meaning much of the transcendentally rotten) has passed from the homosexual vocabulary into punk, and is headed for mainstream English.

The Pentagon speaks of *the power curve,* meaning the direction in which   12
things are tending. Employees at McDonald's describe their specialized burnout as being *burgered-out.* Homosexuals possess a decadently rich special vocabulary that is on the whole inaccessible to *breeders* (heterosexuals).

Television has developed an elaborate jargon that has possibilities as slang.   13
Voice-over, segue, intro and *out of sync* have been part of the more general language for a long time. Now there is the *out-tro,* the stand-up spiel at the end of a news reporter's segment. A vividly cynical new item of TV news jargon is *bang-bang,* meaning the kind of film coverage that TV reporters must have in order to get their reports from El Salvador or the Middle East onto the evening news.

Black slang may not be quite as strong as it was in the '60s. That may mean   14
either that black slang is less productive than before or that it is more successful at remaining exclusive and secret. Two expressions that have popped up . . . (recently): *serious as a heart attack* and *that's Kool and the Gang.* The second is a reference to a popular musical group and a little flourish added to the ancient *that's cool.*

The richest new territory for slang is computer technology. That is unexpected.   15
Slang is usually thought of as a kind of casual conversation in the street, not as a dialogue between the human brain and a machine. Those who go mountaineering up the interface, however, are developing a wonderfully recondite vocabulary. *Hackers* (computer fanatics) at M.I.T. and Stanford maintain a Hacker's Diction-ary to keep their common working language accessible to one another. *Input* and *output* have long since entered the wider language. So have *software* and *hardware.* The human brain in some circles is now referred to as *wetware.* When a computer *goes down,* of course, it *crashes. Menu,* meaning a computer's directory of functions, is turning up now as noun and verb, as in "Let me *menu* my schedule and I'll get back to you about lunch."

In the Hacker's Dictionary, one finds *gronk* (a verb that means to become   16
unusable, as in "the monitor *gronked*"), *gweep* (one who spends unusually long periods of time hacking), *cuspy* (anything that is exceptionally good or performs its functions exceptionally well), *dink* (to modify in some small way so as to produce large or catastrophic results), *bagbiter* (equipment or program that fails, usually intermittently) and *deadlock* (a situation wherein two or more processes are unable to proceed because each is waiting for the other to do something. This is the electronic equivalent of *gridlock,* a lovely, virtually perfect word that describes automobile traffic paralyzed both ways through an intersection). The hacker's lexicon is endless and weirdly witty, and inspiring in a peculiar way; the human language is caught there precisely in the act of improvisation as it moves

through a strange new country. The mind is making itself at home in the mysteries and possibilities of the machines.

A word, Justice Oliver Wendell Holmes wrote, "is the skin of a living thought." The flesh of slang is a little weaker than usual now. Why? For several reasons. Perhaps slang follows the economy and now finds itself a bit recessed. 17

Tribes make slang, and the old tribes are dissolving. Slang has always been the decoration and camouflage of nervous subgroups: youth, blacks, homosexuals, minorities, pickpockets, small tribes using language as solidarity against the big tribes. Slang proclaims one's specialness and conceals one's secrets. Perhaps the slang of today seems a bid faded because we still live in an aftermath of the '60s, the great revolt of the tribes. The special-interest slangs generated then were interminably publicized. Like the beads and the Afros and gestures and costumes and theatrical rages, slang became an ingredient of the national mixed-media pageant. Now, with more depressingly important things to do (earn a living, for example), Americans may feel a sense of cultural lull. 18

As the University of Cincinnati's William Lasher remarks, "Slang doesn't get written down, so it doesn't endure. If you do write it down, it gets into the language, and stops being slang." In a maniacally open electronic society, the news and entertainment industries sift hungrily through the culture searching for color, anecdote, personality, uniqueness and, of course, slang. All these items instantly become part of the show. Slang is wonderful entertainment. But its half-life is shorter now. Good slang gets commercial in a hurry, like certain country-music singers. 19

There may be a deeper reason for the relative decline of slang. Standard English is losing prestige and even legitimacy. Therefore, deviations from the "correct" also lose some of their force. Slang forfeits a little of its renegade quality, its outlaw savor. If slang is no longer a kind of sin, it cannot be as much fun as it once was. 20

▼ TOPICAL CONSIDERATIONS

1. Morrow says that slang either settles down into standard language or slips off into oblivion. Can you think of some slang that has become standard and some that has died out? Investigate some of the slang from the sixties.
2. Morrow says in paragraph 4 that "Val" could never be the source of the next generation of slang. Why not? Has his prophecy proven true?
3. What is Morrow's complaint against the slang of today? What fault does he find with the term *airhead?*
4. Why would much of our slang be the creation of junior high and even grade school children? When you were younger did you and your peers have a slang of your own?
5. The author mentions collegians as a source of fresh slang. Do you use any slang that seems exclusively collegiate?
6. "The richest new territory for slang is computer technology," writes Morrow.

Why might that be so? Are you familiar with some of the computer jargon he gives? Can you think of other terms?

7. Why does slang seem to be suffering a "recession" today, according to Morrow? Why is it less "fun" than it used to be?

▼ RHETORICAL CONSIDERATIONS

1. Explain the transitional link between paragraphs 1 and 2.
2. How apt is Morrow's analogy in paragraph 3 of slang to adolescence?
3. In paragraph 7 Morrow analyzes the weak slang-value of the term *airhead*. How convincing is his explanation?
4. Did you find a sense of humor in this piece? If so, point to passages that struck you as funny. Try to explain what you found funny about them.

▼ WRITING ASSIGNMENTS

1. Morrow makes the point that there is a tribal quality about slang: It gives a group status and identity; it separates the group from the rest of society in an almost renegade fashion while sustaining a sense of privacy and solidarity and ethnicity. Write a paper on the function and use of slang, especially by young people today.
2. Morrow says that slang has suffered a recession today. Write a paper in which you look into his claim. Do you see a decline in vitality and imaginativeness, or not?
3. Select a short editorial from the newspaper and rewrite it in slang. (Consult a dictionary of slang from your library for assistance.) What differences have you made in the tone, effect, and communicability? Which version do you prefer, and why?
4. Morrow suggests that the slang of the 1960s was "magnificent." See how many slang items from this era you can come up with. In a paper, analyze the imaginativeness of that lingo. Have some of these items survived that era and become part of the language?
5. Morrow says that computer technology is the newest and richest source of slang today. Write a paper—or a dialogue between two people—using as much computer slang as you can. Have some fun with this.

▼ NUCLEAR LANGUAGE AND HOW WE LEARNED TO PAT THE BOMB

Carol Cohn

One fact of language is that it colors the way we think about things. All things, even the unthinkable—nuclear war. After spending a year immersed in the world of nuclear strategists, Carol Cohn learned nuclear language and something about its numbing, sexy power. Nukespeak is an "emphatically male discourse. But learning the language shows how thinking can become abstract, focusing on the survival of weapons rather than the survival of human beings." Cohn is a senior research fellow at the Center for Psychological Studies in the Nuclear Age in Cambridge, Massachusetts. This article first appeared in the journal *Signs* in 1987.

My close encounter with nuclear strategic analysis started in the summer of 1984. I was one of 48 college teachers attending a summer workshop on nuclear weapons, strategic doctrine, and arms control that was held at a university containing one of the nation's foremost centers of nuclear strategic studies, and that was co-sponsored by another institution. It was taught by some of the most distinguished experts in the field, who have spent decades moving back and forth between academia and governmental positions in Washington. When at the end of the program I was afforded the chance to be a visiting scholar at one of the universities' defense studies center, I jumped at the opportunity.

I spent the next year immersed in the world of defense intellectuals—men (and indeed, they are virtually all men) who, in Thomas Powers's words, "use the concept of deterrence to explain why it is safe to have weapons of a kind and number it is not safe to use." Moving in and out of government, working sometimes as administrative officials or consultants, sometimes in universities and think tanks, they create the theory that underlies U.S. nuclear strategic practice.

My reason for wanting to spend a year among these men was simple, even if the resulting experiences were not. The current nuclear situation is so dangerous and irrational that one is tempted to explain it by positing either insanity or evil in our decision makers. That explanation is, of course, inadequate. My goal was to gain a better understanding of how sane men of goodwill could think and act in ways that lead to what appear to be extremely irrational and immoral results.

I attended lectures, listened to arguments, conversed with defense analysts, interviewed graduate students throughout their training, obsessed by the question,

430

"How *can* they think this way?" But as I learned the language, as I became more and more engaged with their information and their arguments, I found that my own thinking was changing, and I had to confront a new question: How can *I* think this way? Thus, my own experience becomes part of the data that I analyze in attempting to understand not only how "they" can think that way, but how any of us can.

This article is the beginning of an analysis of the nature of nuclear strategic thinking, with emphasis on the role of a specialized language that I call "techno-strategic." I have come to believe that this language both reflects and shapes the American nuclear strategic project, and that all who are concerned about nuclear weaponry and nuclear war must give careful attention to language—with whom it allows us to communicate and what it allows us to think as well as say. 5

I had previously encountered in my reading the extraordinary language used to discuss nuclear war, but somehow it was different to hear it spoken. What hits first is the elaborate use of abstraction and euphemism, which allows infinite talk about nuclear holocaust without ever forcing the speaker or enabling the listener to touch the reality behind the words. 6

Anyone who has seen pictures of Hiroshima burn victims may find it perverse to hear a class of nuclear devices matter-of-factly referred to as "clean bombs." These are weapons which are largely fusion rather than fission; they release a somewhat higher proportion of their energy as prompt radiation, but produce less radioactive fallout than fission bombs of the same yield. Clean bombs may provide the perfect metaphor for the language of defense analysts and arms controllers. This language has enormous destructive power, but without the emotional fallout that would result if it were clear one was talking about plans for mass murder, mangled bodies, human suffering. Defense analysts talk about "countervalue attacks" rather than about incinerating cities. Human death, in nuclear parlance, is most often referred to as "collateral damage." While Reagan's renaming the MX missile "the Peacekeeper" was the object of considerable scorn in the community of defense analysts, the same analysts refer to the missile as a "damage limitation weapon." 7

These phrases, only a few of the hundreds that could be chosen, exemplify the astounding chasm between image and reality that characterizes technostrategic language. They also hint at the terrifying way the existence of nuclear devices has distorted our perceptions and redefined the world. "Clean bombs" as a phrase tells us that radioactivity is the only "dirty" part of killing people. 8

It is hard not to feel that one function of this sanitized abstraction is to deny the uncontrolled messiness of the situations one contemplates creating. So that we not only have clean bombs but also "surgically clean strikes": "counterforce" attacks that can purportedly "take out"—that is, accurately destroy—an opponent's weapons or command centers, without causing significant injury to anything else. The image is unspeakably ludicrous when the surgical tool is not a delicately controlled scalpel but a nuclear warhead. 9

Feminists have often suggested that an important aspect of the arms race is phallic worship; that "missile envy," to borrow Helen Caldicott's phrase, is a significant motivating force in the nuclear buildup. I have always found this an 10 uncomfortably reductionist explanation and hoped that observing at the center would yield a more complex analysis. Still, I was curious about the extent to which I might find a sexual subtext in the defense professionals' discourse. I was not prepared for what I found.

I think I had naively imagined that I would need to sneak around and 11 eavesdrop on what men said in unguarded moments, using all my cunning to unearth sexual imagery. I had believed that these men would have cleaned up their acts, or that at least at some point in a long talk about "penetration aids," someone would suddenly look up, slightly embarrassed to be caught in such blatant confirmation of feminist analyses.

I was wrong. There was no evidence that such critiques had ever reached the 12 ears, much less the minds, of these men. American military dependence on nuclear weapons was explained as "irresistible, because you get more bang for the buck." Another lecturer solemnly and scientifically announced, "To disarm is to get rid of all your stuff." A professor's explanation of why the MX missile is to be placed in the silos of the newest Minuteman missiles, instead of replacing the older, less accurate missiles, was "because they're in the nicest hole—you're not going to take the nicest missile you have and put it in a crummy hole." Other lectures were filled with discussion of vertical erector launchers, thrust-to-weight ratios, soft lay downs, deep penetration, and the comparative advantages of protracted versus spasm attacks—or what one military adviser to the National Security Council has called "releasing 70 to 80 percent of our megatonnage in one orgasmic whump."*

But if the imagery is transparent, its significance may be less so. I do *not* want 13 to assert that it somehow reveals what defense intellectuals are really talking about, or their motivations; individual motives cannot necessarily be read directly from imagery, which originates in a broader cultural context. The history of the atomic bomb project itself is rife with overt images of competitive male sexuality, as is the discourse of the early nuclear physicists, strategists, and members of the Strategic Air Command.† Both the military itself and the arms manufacturers are constantly exploiting the phallic imagery and promise of sexual domination that their weapons so conveniently suggest. Consider the following, from the June 1985 issue of *Air Force Magazine:* Emblazoned in bold letters across the top of a two-page advertisement for the AV-8B Harrier II—"Speak Softly and Carry a Big Stick." The copy below boasts "an exceptional thrust-to-weight ratio," and "vectored thrust capability that makes the . . . unique rapid response possible."

Another vivid source of phallic imagery is to be found in descriptions of 14 nuclear blasts themselves. Here, for example, is one by journalist William Laurence, who was brought by the Army Air Corps to witness the Nagasaki bombing.

---

*Gen. William Odom, "C³I and Telecommunications at the Policy Level," incidental paper from a seminar, *Command, Control, Communications and Intelligence* (Cambridge, Mass., Harvard University Center for Information Policy Research, Spring 1980), p. 5.
†See Brian Easlea, *Fathering the Unthinkable: Masculinity, Scientists and the Nuclear Arms Race* (London: Pluto Press, 1983).

Then, just when it appeared as though the thing had settled down into a state of permanence, there came shooting out of the top a giant mushroom that increased the size of the pillar to a total of 45,000 feet. The mushroom top was even more alive than the pillar, seething and boiling in a white fury of creamy foam, sizzling upward and then descending earthward, a thousand geysers rolled into one. It kept struggling in an elemental fury, like a creature in the act of breaking the bonds that held it down.*

Given the degree to which it suffuses their world, the fact that defense intellectuals use a lot of sexual imagery is not especially surprising. Nor does it, by itself, constitute grounds for imputing motivation. The interesting issue is not so much the imagery's possible psychodynamic origins as how it functions—its role in making the work world of defense intellectuals feel tenable. Several stories illustrate the complexity. 15

At one point a group of us took a field trip to the New London Navy base where nuclear submarines are home-ported, and to the General Dynamics Electric Boat yards where a new Trident submarine was being constructed. The high point of the trip was a tour of a nuclear-powered submarine. A few at a time, we descended into the long, dark, sleek tube in which men and a nuclear reactor are encased underwater for months at a time. We squeezed through hatches, along neon-lit passages so narrow that we had to turn and press our backs to the walls for anyone to get by. We passed the cramped racks where men sleep, and the red and white signs warning of radioactive materials. When we finally reached the part of the sub where the missiles are housed, the officer accompanying us turned with a grin and asked if we wanted to stick our hands through a hole to "pat the missile." *Pat the missile?* 16

The image reappeared the next week, when a lecturer scornfully declared that the only real reason for deploying cruise and Pershing II missiles in Western Europe was "so that our allies can pat them." Some months later, another group of us went to be briefed at NORAD (the North American Aerospace Defense Command). On the way back, the Air National Guard plane we were on went to refuel at Offut Air Force Base, the Strategic Air Command headquarters near Omaha, Nebraska. When word leaked out that our landing would be delayed because the new B-1 bomber was in the area, the plane became charged with a tangible excitement that built as we flew in our holding pattern, people craning their necks to try to catch a glimpse of the B-1 in the skies, and climaxed as we touched down on the runway and hurtled past it. Later, when I returned to the center I encountered a man who, unable to go on the trip, said to me enviously, "I hear you got to pat a B-1." 17

What is all this patting? Patting is an assertion of intimacy, sexual possession, affectionate domination. The thrill and pleasure of "patting the missile" is the proximity of all that phallic power, the possibility of vicariously appropriating it as one's own. But patting is not only an act of sexual intimacy. It is also 18

*William L. Laurence, *Dawn Over Zero: The Study of the Atomic Bomb* (London: Museum Press, 1974), pp. 198–99.

what one does to babies, small children, the pet dog. The creatures one pats are small, cute, harmless—not terrifyingly destructive. Pat it, and its lethality disappears.

Much of the sexual imagery I heard was rife with the sort of ambiguity 19 suggested by "patting the missiles." The imagery can be construed as a deadly serious display of the connections between masculine sexuality and the arms race. But at the same time, it can also be heard as a way of minimizing the seriousness of militarist endeavors, of denying their deadly consequences. A former Pentagon target analyst, in telling me why he thought plans for "limited nuclear war" were ridiculous, said, "Look, you gotta understand that it's a pissing contest—you gotta expect them to use everything they've got." This image says, most obviously, that this is about competition for manhood, and thus there is tremendous danger. But at the same time it says that the whole thing is not very serious—it is just what little boys or drunk men do.

Sanitized abstraction and sexual imagery, even if disturbing, seemed to fit 20 easily into the masculine world of nuclear war planning. What did not fit was another set of words that evoked images that can only be called domestic.

Nuclear missiles are based in "silos." On a Trident submarine, which carries 24 21 multiple-warhead nuclear missiles, crew members call the part of the sub where the missiles are lined up in their silos ready for launching "the Christmas tree farm." In the friendly, romantic world of nuclear weaponry, enemies "exchange" warheads; weapons systems can "marry up." "Coupling" is sometimes used to refer to the wiring between mechanisms of warning and response, or to the psychopolitical links between strategic and theater weapons. The patterns in which a MIRVed missile's nuclear warheads land is known as a "footprint." These nuclear explosives are not dropped; a "bus" "delivers" them. These devices are called "reentry vehicles," or "RVs" for short, a term not only totally removed from the reality of a bomb but also resonant with the image of the recreational vehicle of the ideal family vacation.

These domestic images are more than simply one more way to remove oneself 22 from the grisly reality behind the words; ordinary abstraction is adequate to that task. Calling the pattern in which bombs fall a "footprint" almost seems a willful distorting process, a playful, perverse refusal of accountability—because to be accountable to reality is to be unable to do this work.

The images evoked by these words may also be a way to tame the uncontrol- 23 lable forces of nuclear destruction. Take the fire-breathing dragon under the bed, the one who threatens to incinerate your family, your town, your planet, and turn it into a pet you can pat. Or domestic imagery may simply serve to make everyone more comfortable with what they're doing. "PAL" (permissive action links) is the carefully constructed, friendly acronym for the electronic system designed to prevent the unauthorized firing of nuclear warheads. The president's annual nuclear weapons stockpile memorandum, which outlines both short- and long-range plans for production of new nuclear weapons, is benignly referred to as "the shopping list." The "cookie cutter" is a phrase used to describe a particular model of nuclear attack.

The imagery that domesticates, that humanizes insentient weapons, may also 24
serve, paradoxically, to make it all right to ignore sentient human beings. Perhaps
it is possible to spend one's time dreaming up scenarios for the use of massively
destructive technology, and to exclude human beings from that technological
world, because that world itself now includes the domestic, the human, the warm
and playful—the Christmas trees, the RVs, the things one pats affectionately. It is
a world that is in some sense complete in itself; it even includes death and loss.
The problem is that all things that get "killed" happen to be weapons, not humans.
If one of your warheads "kills" another of your warheads, it is "fratricide." There
is much concern about "vulnerability" and "survivability," but it is about the
vulnerability and survival of weapons systems, rather than people.

Another set of images suggests men's desire to appropriate from women the 25
power of giving life. At Los Alamos, the atomic bomb was referred to as
"Oppenheimer's baby"; at Lawrence Livermore, the hydrogen bomb was "Teller's
baby," although those who wanted to disparage Teller's contribution claimed he
was not the bomb's father but its mother. In this context, the extraordinary names
given to the bombs that reduced Hiroshima and Nagasaki to ash and rubble—
"Little Boy" and "Fat Man"—may perhaps become intelligible. These ultimate
destroyers were the male progeny of the atomic scientists.

The entire history of the bomb project, in fact, seems permeated with imagery 26
that confounds humanity's overwhelming technological power to destroy nature
with the power to create: imagery that converts men's destruction into their
rebirth. Laurence wrote of the Trinity test of the first atomic bomb: "One felt as
though he had been privileged to witness the Birth of the World." In a 1985
interview, General Bruce K. Holloway, the commander in chief of the Strategic
Air Command from 1968 to 1972, described a nuclear war as involving "a big
bang, like the start of the universe."

Finally, the last thing one might expect to find in a subculture of hard-nosed 27
realism and hyper-rationality is the repeated invocation of religious imagery. And
yet, the first atomic bomb test was called Trinity. Seeing it, Robert Oppenheimer
thought of Krishna's words to Arjuna in the *Bhagavad Gita:* "I am become death,
destroyer of worlds." Defense intellectuals, when challenged on a particular
assumption, will often duck out with a casual, "Now you're talking about matters
of theology." Perhaps most astonishing of all, the creators of strategic doctrine
actually refer to their community as "the nuclear priesthood." It is hard to decide
what is most extraordinary about this: the arrogance of the claim, the tacit
admission that they really are creators of dogma; or the extraordinary implicit
statement about who, or rather what, has become god.

Although I was startled by the combination of dry abstraction and odd 28
imagery that characterizes the language of defense intellectuals, my attention was
quickly focused on decoding and learning to speak it. The first task was training
the tongue in the articulation of acronyms.

Several years of reading the literature of nuclear weaponry and strategy had 29
not prepared me for the degree to which acronyms littered all conversations, nor
for the way in which they are used. Formerly, I had thought of them mainly as

utilitarian. They allow you to write or speak faster. They act as a form of abstraction, removing you from the reality behind the words. They restrict communication to the initiated, leaving the rest both uncomprehending and voiceless in the debate.

But being at the center revealed some additional, unexpected dimensions. 30 First, in speaking and hearing, a lot of these terms are very sexy. A small supersonic rocket "designed to penetrate any Soviet air defense" is called a SRAM (for short-range attack missile). Submarine-launched cruise missiles are referred to as "slick'ems" and ground-launched cruise missiles are "glick'ems." Air-launched cruise missiles are magical "alchems."

Other acronyms serve in different ways. The plane in which the president will 31 supposedly be flying around above a nuclear holocaust, receiving intelligence and issuing commands for where to bomb next, is referred to as "Kneecap" (for NEACP—National Emergency Airborne Command Post). Few believe that the president would really have the time to get into it, or that the communications systems would be working if he were in it—hence the edge of derision. But the very ability to make fun of a concept makes it possible to work with it rather than reject it outright.

In other words, what I learned at the program is that talking about nuclear 32 weapons is fun. The words are quick, clean, light; they trip off the tongue. You can reel off dozens of them in seconds, forgetting about how one might interfere with the next, not to mention with the lives beneath them. Nearly everyone I observed—lecturers, students, hawks, doves, men, and women—took pleasure in using the words; some of us spoke with a self-consciously ironic edge, but the pleasure was there nonetheless. Part of the appeal was the thrill of being able to manipulate an arcane language, the power of entering the secret kingdom. But perhaps more important, learning the language gives a sense of control, a feeling of mastery over technology that is finally not controllable but powerful beyond human comprehension. The longer I stayed, the more conversations I participated in, the less I was frightened of nuclear war.

How can learning to speak a language have such a powerful effect? One 33 answer, discussed earlier, is that the language is abstract and sanitized, never giving access to the images of war. But there is more to it than that. The learning process itself removed me from the reality of nuclear war. My energy was focused on the challenge of decoding acronyms, learning new terms, developing competence in the language—not on the weapons and wars behind the words. By the time I was through, I had learned far more than an alternate, if abstract, set of words. The content of what I could talk about was monumentally different.

Consider the following descriptions, in each of which the subject is the 34 aftermath of a nuclear attack:

Everything was black, had vanished into the black dust, was destroyed. Only the flames that were beginning to lick their way up had any color. From the dust that was like a fog, figures began to loom up, black, hairless, faceless. They screamed with voices that were no longer human.

Their screams drowned out the groans rising everywhere from the rubble, groans that seemed to rise from the very earth itself.*

[You have to have ways to maintain communications in a] nuclear environment, a situation bound to include EMP blackout, brute force damage to systems, a heavy jamming environment, and so on.†

There is no way to describe the phenomena represented in the first with the language of the second. The passages differ not only in the vividness of their words, but in their content: the first describes the effects of a nuclear blast on human beings; the second describes the impact of a nuclear blast on technical systems designed to secure the "command and control" of nuclear weapons. Both of these differences stem from the difference of perspective: the speaker in the first is a victim of nuclear weapons, the speaker in the second is a user. The speaker in the first is using words to try to name and contain the horror of human suffering all around her; the speaker in the second is using words to insure the possibility of launching the next nuclear attack. 35

Technostrategic language articulates only the perspective of the users of nuclear weapons, not the victims. Speaking the expert language not only offers distance, a feeling of control, and an alternative focus for one's energies; it also offers escape from thinking of oneself as a victim of nuclear war. No matter what one deeply knows or believes about the likelihood of nuclear war, and no matter what sort of terror or despair the knowledge of nuclear war's reality might inspire, the speakers of technostrategic language are allowed, even forced, to escape that awareness, to escape viewing nuclear war from the position of the victim, by virtue of their linguistic stance. 36

I suspect that much of the reduced anxiety about nuclear war commonly experienced by both new speakers of the language and longtime experts comes from characteristics of the language itself: the distance afforded by its abstraction, the sense of control afforded by mastering it, and the fact that its content and concerns are those of the users rather than the victims. In learning the language, one goes from being the passive, powerless victim to being the competent, wily, powerful purveyor of nuclear threats and nuclear explosive power. The enormous destructive effects of nuclear weapons systems become extensions of the self, rather than threats to it. 37

It did not take long to learn the language of nuclear war and much of the specialized information it contained. My focus quickly changed from mastering technical information and doctrinal arcana, to an attempt to understand more about how the dogma I was learning was rationalized. Since underlying rationales are rarely discussed in the everyday business of defense planning, I had to start asking more questions. At first, although I was tempted to use my newly acquired proficiency in technostrategic jargon, I vowed to speak English. What I found, 38

---

*Hisako Matsubara, *Cranes at Dusk* (Garden City, New York: Dial Press, 1985).
†Gen. Robert Rosenberg, "The Influence of Policy Making on C³I," speaking at the Harvard seminar, *Command, Control, Communications and Intelligence,* p. 59.

however, was that no matter how well informed my questions were, no matter how complex an understanding they were based upon, if I was speaking English rather than expert jargon, the men responded to me as though I were ignorant or simpleminded, or both. A strong distaste for being patronized and a pragmatic streak made my experiment in English short-lived. I adopted the vocabulary, speaking of "escalation dominance," "preemptive strikes," and one of my favorites, "sub-holocaust engagements." This opened my way into long, elaborate discussions that taught me a lot about technostrategic reasoning and how to manipulate it.

But the better I became at this discourse, the more difficult it became to express my own ideas and values. While the language included things I had never been able to speak about before, it radically excluded others. To pick a bald example: the word "peace" is not a part of this discourse. As close as one can come is "strategic stability," a term that refers to a balance of numbers and types of weapons systems—not the political, social, economic, and psychological conditions that "peace" implies. Moreover, to speak the word is to immediately brand oneself as a soft-headed activist instead of a professional to be taken seriously. 39

If I was unable to speak my concerns in this language, more disturbing still was that I also began to find it harder even to keep them in my own head. No matter how firm my commitment to staying aware of the bloody reality behind the words, over and over I found that I could not keep human lives as my reference point. I found I could go for days speaking about nuclear weapons, without once thinking about the people who would be incinerated by them. 40

It is tempting to attribute this problem to the words themselves—the abstractness, the euphemisms, the sanitized, friendly, sexy acronyms. Then one would only need to change the words: get the military planners to say "mass murder" instead of "collateral damage," and their thinking would change. The problem, however, is not simply that defense intellectuals use abstract terminology that removes them from the realities of which they speak. There *is* no reality behind the words. Or, rather, the "reality" they speak of is itself a world of abstractions. Deterrence theory, and much of strategic doctrine, was invented to hold together abstractly, its validity judged by internal logic. These abstract systems were developed as a way to make it possible to, in Herman Kahn's phrase, "think about the unthinkable"—not as a way to describe or codify relations on the ground. 41

So the problem with the idea of "limited nuclear war," for example, is not only that it is a travesty to refer to the death and suffering caused by *any* use of nuclear weapons as "limited," or that "limited nuclear war" is an abstraction that obfuscates the human reality beneath any use of nuclear weapons. It is also that limited nuclear war is itself an abstract conceptual system, designed, embodied, and achieved by computer modeling. In this abstract world, hypothetical, calm, rational actors have sufficient information to know exactly what size nuclear weapon the opponent has used against which targets, and adequate command and control to make sure that their response is precisely equilibrated to the attack. No field commander would use the tactical nuclear weapons at his disposal at the height of a losing battle. Our rational actors would have absolute freedom from emotional response to being attacked, from political pressures from the populace. They 42 would act solely on the basis of a perfectly informed mathematical calculus of megatonnage. To refer to limited nuclear war is to enter a system that is de facto abstract and grotesquely removed from reality. The abstractness of the entire conceptual system makes descriptive language utterly beside the point.

This realization helped make sense of my difficulty in staying connected to 43 concrete lives as well as of some of the bizarre and surreal quality of what people said. But there was still a piece missing. How is it possible, for example, to make sense of the following:

> The strategic stability of regime A is based on the fact that both sides are deprived of any incentive ever to strike first. Since it takes roughly two warheads to destroy one enemy silo, an attacker must expend two of his missiles to destroy one of the enemy's. A first strike disarms the attacker. The aggressor ends up worse off than the aggressed.*

The homeland of "the aggressed" has just been devastated by the explosions of, 44 say, a thousand nuclear bombs, each likely to be at least 10 to 100 times more powerful than the bomb dropped on Hiroshima, and the aggressor, whose home-land is still untouched, "ends up worse off"?

I was only able to make sense of this kind of thinking when I finally asked 45 myself: Who—or what—is the subject? In technostrategic discourse, the refer-ence point is not human beings but the weapons themselves. The aggressor ends up worse off than the aggressed because he has fewer weapons left; any other factors, such as what happened where the weapons landed, are irrelevant to the calculus of gain and loss.

The fact that the subjects of strategic paradigms are weapons has several 46 important implications. First, and perhaps most critically, there is no real way to talk about human death or human societies when you are using a language designed to talk about weapons. Human death simply *is* collateral damage— collateral to the real subject, which is the weapons themselves.

Understanding this also helps explain what was at first so surprising to me: 47 most people who do this work are on the whole nice, even good, men, many with liberal inclinations. While they often identify their motivations as being concern about humans, in their work they enter a language and paradigm that precludes people. Thus, the nature and outcome of their work can utterly contradict their genuine motives for doing it.

In addition, if weapons are the reference point, it becomes in some sense 48 illegitimate to ask the paradigm to reflect human concerns. Questions that break through the numbing language of strategic analysis and raise issues in human terms can be easily dismissed. No one will claim that they are unimportant. But they are inexpert, unprofessional, irrelevant to the business at hand. The dis-course among the experts remains hermetically sealed. One can talk about the weapons that are supposed to protect particular peoples and their way of life without actually asking if they are able to do it, or if they are the best way to do it,

*Charles Krauthammer, "Will Star Wars Kill Arms Control?" *New Republic* (Jan. 21, 1985), pp. 12–16.

or whether they may even damage the entities they are supposedly protecting. These are separate questions.

This discourse has become virtually the only response to the question of how 49 to achieve security that is recognized as legitimate. If the discussion of weapons was one competing voice in the discussion, or one that was integrated with others, the fact that the referents of strategic paradigms are only weapons might be of less note. But when we realize that the only language and expertise offered to those interested in pursuing peace refers to nothing but weapons, its limits become staggering. And its entrapping qualities—the way it becomes so hard, once you adopt the language, to stay connected to human concerns—become more comprehensible.

Within a few weeks, what had once been remarkable became unnoticeable. 50 As I learned to speak, my perspective changed. I no longer stood outside the impenetrable wall of technostrategic language and once inside, I could no longer see it. I had not only learned to speak a language: I had started to think in it. Its questions became my questions, its concepts shaped my responses to new ideas. Like the White Queen, I began to believe six impossible things before breakfast— not because I consciously believed, for instance, that a "surgically clean counter-force strike" was really possible, but because some elaborate piece of doctrinal reasoning I used was already predicated on the possibility of those strikes as well as on a host of other impossible things.

My grasp on what I knew as reality seemed to slip. I might get very excited, for 51 example, about a new strategic justification for a no-first-use policy and spend time discussing the ways in which its implications for the U.S. force structure in Western Europe were superior to the older version. After a day or two I would suddenly step back, aghast that I was so involved with the *military* justifications for not using nuclear weapons—as though the moral ones were not enough. What I was actually talking about—the mass incineration of a nuclear attack—was no longer in my head.

Or I might hear some proposals that seemed to me infinitely superior to the 52 usual arms control fare. First I would work out how and why these proposals were better and then ways to counter the arguments against them. Then it might dawn on me that even though these two proposals sounded different, they still shared a host of assumptions that I was not willing to make. I would first feel as though I had achieved a new insight. And then all of a sudden, I would realize that these were things I actually knew before I ever entered this community and had since forgotten. I began to feel that I had fallen down the rabbit hole.

The language issues do not disappear. The seductions of learning and using it 53 remain great, and as the pleasures deepen, so do the dangers. The activity of trying to out-reason nuclear strategists in their own games gets you thinking inside their rules, tacitly accepting the unspoken assumptions of their paradigms.

Yet, the issues of language have now become somewhat less central to me, 54 and my new questions, while still not precisely the questions of an insider, are questions I could not have had without being inside. Many of them are more practical: Which individuals and institutions are actually responsible for the endless "modernization" and proliferation of nuclear weaponry, and what do they gain from it? What role does technostrategic rationality play in their thinking? What would a reasonable, genuinely defensive policy look like? Others are more philosophical, having to do with the nature of the "realism" claimed for the defense intellectuals' mode of thinking and the grounds upon which it can be shown to be spurious. What would an alternative rationality look like?

My own move away from a focus on the language is quite typical. Other recent   55
entrants into this world have commented that while the cold-blooded, abstract discussions are most striking at first, within a short time you get past them and come to see that the language itself is not the problem.

I think it would be a mistake, however, to dismiss these early impressions.   56
While I believe that the language is not the whole problem, it is a significant component and clue. What it reveals is a whole series of culturally grounded and culturally acceptable mechanisms that make it possible to work in institutions that foster the proliferation of nuclear weapons, to plan mass incinerations of millions of human beings for a living. Language that is abstract, sanitized, full of euphemisms; language that is sexy and fun to use; paradigms whose referent is weapons; imagery that domesticates and deflates the forces of mass destruction; imagery that reverses sentient and nonsentient matter, that conflates birth and death, destruction and creation—all of these are part of what makes it possible to be radically removed from the reality of what one is talking about, and from the realities one is creating through the discourse.

Close attention to the language itself also reveals a tantalizing basis on which   57
to challenge the legitimacy of the defense intellectuals' dominance of the discourse on nuclear issues. When defense intellectuals are criticized for the cold-blooded inhumanity of the scenarios they plan, their response is to claim the high ground of rationality. They portray those who are radically opposed to the nuclear status quo as irrational, unrealistic, too emotional—"idealistic activists." But if the smooth, shiny surface of their discourse—its abstraction and technical jargon—appears at first to support these claims, a look below the surface does not. Instead we find strong currents of homoerotic excitement, heterosexual domination, the drive toward competence and mastery, the pleasures of membership in an elite and privileged group, of the ultimate importance and meaning of membership in the priesthood. How is it possible to point to the pursuers of these values, these experiences, as paragons of cool-headed objectivity?

While listening to the language reveals the mechanisms of distancing and   58
denial and the emotional currents embodied in this emphatically male discourse, attention to the experience of learning the language reveals something about how thinking can become more abstract, more focused on parts disembedded from their context, more attentive to the survival of weapons than the survival of human beings.

Because this professional language sets the terms for public debate, many who   59
oppose current nuclear policies choose to learn it. Even if they do not believe that the technical information is very important, some believe it is necessary to master the language simply because it is too difficult to attain public legitimacy without

it. But learning the language is a transformative process. You are not simply adding new information, new vocabulary, but entering a mode of thinking not only about nuclear weapons but also about military and political power, and about the relationship between human ends and technological means.

The language and the mode of thinking are not neutral containers of information. 60 They were developed by a specific group of men, trained largely in abstract theoretical mathematics and economics, specifically to make it possible to think rationally about the use of nuclear weapons. That the language is not well suited to do anything but make it possible to think about using nuclear weapons should not be surprising.

Those who find U.S. nuclear policy desperately misguided face a serious 61 quandary. If we refuse to learn the language, we condemn ourselves to being jesters on the sidelines. If we learn and use it, we not only severely limit what we can say but also invite the transformation, the militarization, of our own thinking.

I have no solutions to this dilemma, but I would like to offer a couple of 62 thoughts in an effort to push it a little further—or perhaps even to reformulate its terms. It is important to recognize an assumption implicit in adopting the strategy of learning the language. When we outsiders assume that learning and speaking the language will give us a voice recognized as legitimate and will give us greater political influence, we assume that the language itself actually articulates the criteria and reasoning strategies upon which nuclear weapons development and deployment decisions are made. This is largely an illusion. I suggest that technostrategic discourse functions more as a gloss, as an ideological patina that hides the actual reasons these decisions are made. Rather than informing and shaping decisions, it far more often legitimizes political outcomes that have occurred for utterly different reasons. If this is true, it raises serious questions about the extent of the political returns we might get from using it, and whether they can ever balance out the potential problems and inherent costs.

I believe that those who seek a more just and peaceful world have a dual task 63 before them—a deconstructive project and a reconstructive project that are intimately linked. Deconstruction requires close attention to, and the dismantling of, technostrategic discourse. The dominant voice of militarized masculinity and decontextualized rationality speaks so loudly in our culture that it will remain difficult for any other voices to be heard until that voice loses some of its power to define what we hear and how we name the world.

The reconstructive task is to create compelling alternative visions of possible 64 futures, to recognize and develop alternative conceptions of rationality, to create rich and imaginative alternative voices—diverse voices whose conversations with each other will invent those futures.

▼ TOPICAL CONSIDERATIONS

1. According to the author, why did she decide to spend a year as visiting scholar at the university "defense studies center"?

2. What essential lesson did Cohn learn about the powers of language? What did she learn about the habitual use of abstractions and euphemisms?
3. How does nuclear language tend to absolve its users of moral guilt?
4. Why was Cohn initially skeptical about feminists' claims regarding the sexual coloration of nuclear language? How do defense analysts prove her naive?
5. In paragraph 15, Cohn says it's not the "psychodynamic origins" of all the phallic imagery in nuclear language that is "interesting," but how it affects defense intellectuals. How does such language affect them? Do you agree with her analysis?
6. In her discussion of the phrase "patting the bomb," how does Cohn explain that more than just male-sexual competitiveness is at work in the language?
7. Sexual imagery in nuclear parlance, although disturbing, seems "to fit easily into the masculine world of nuclear war planning" Cohn says in paragraph 20. But what doesn't fit is the "domestic" images. Why are these more disturbing to the author? Do you agree?
8. In paragraph 32, Cohn says that nuclear jargon is "fun." How does she mean this? What effect did all this "fun" talk have on her?
9. What dilemma did Cohn discover when she tried to speak straight English to defense experts? Why did she have difficulty expressing her own ideas and values?
10. The author says that her experience with nuclear language and thinking has taught her that American nuclear policy is "misguided." What recommendations does she make to change it?

▼ RHETORICAL CONSIDERATIONS

1. What allusion is Cohn making in the opening sentence when she refers to her "close encounter with nuclear strategic analysis"?
2. Where exactly is the thesis statement of this essay?
3. In paragraph 7, the author says that the expression "clean bombs" might serve as the "perfect metaphor" for the nuclear language of defense intellectuals. From all the expressions she cites, do you agree that this is the most effective example?
4. How effective was the author's personal account of her immersion in the world of nuclear strategists?
5. In paragraph 34, the author cites two descriptions of the aftermath of a nuclear attack. How effective are these examples? Do they serve the author's purpose well, or not? How convincing is her discussion of them?

▼ WRITING ASSIGNMENTS

1. Do you think the vocabulary of nuclear technology colors the way you think about nuclear issues? Write an essay in which you explore your own thoughts on this question.
2. Select some specific terms of nuclear jargon and analyze them from the point of view of euphemisms. How do they abstract reality? What images come to mind? How are real horrors avoided, abstracted, and sanitized?
3. Write an essay in which you argue in favor of nuclear jargon, that is, defend it as necessary to dealing rationally with hard issues.
4. Pretend you are the manufacturer of nuclear missiles. Employing nuclear terminology, write advertising copy for a missile brochure to be sent to the Department of Defense.

▼ ROCK LYRICS AND VIOLENCE AGAINST WOMEN

Caryl Rivers

> Popular music has always been both voice and echo of its own time. In the fifties, rock 'n roll was born and with it the teen culture whose innocent sexiness and mild rebelliousness was celebrated in song. But over the last few years some people have objected to the kinds of musical messages climbing the charts—songs whose lyrics are full of Satanism, Nazism, drugs, sex, and sadistic violence. Songs whose impact on young listeners is damaging. In response, the multimillion-dollar music industry has cried "censorship." The short essay that follows is not so much a call for censorship as it is a protest against the kinds of rock lyrics that describe—maybe even incite—violence against women. Caryl Rivers is a professor of journalism at Boston University and the author of several popular novels including *Virgins* (1984) and *Intimate Enemies* (1987). This essay first appeared in the *Boston Globe* in 1984.

After a grisly series of murders in California, possibly inspired by the lyrics of a rock song, we are hearing a familiar chorus: Don't blame rock and roll. Kids will be kids. They love to rebel, and the more shocking the stuff, the better they like it. 1

There's some truth in this, of course. I loved to watch Elvis shake his torso when I was a teen-ager, and it was even more fun when Ed Sullivan wouldn't let the cameras show him below the waist. I snickered at the forbidden "Rock with Me, Annie" lyrics by a black Rhythm and Blues group, which were deliciously naughty. But I am sorry, rock fans, that is not the same thing as hearing lyrics about how a man is going to force a woman to perform oral sex on him at gunpoint in a little number called "Eat Me Alive." It is not in the same league with a song about the delights of slipping into a woman's room while she is sleeping and murdering her, the theme of an AC/DC ballad that allegedly inspired the California slayer. 2

Make no mistake, it is not sex we are talking about here, but violence. Violence against women. Most rock songs are not violent—they are funky, sexy, rebellious, and sometimes witty. Please do not mistake me for a Mrs. Grundy. If Prince wants to leap about wearing only a purple jock strap, fine. Let Mick Jagger unzip his fly as he gyrates, if he wants to. But when either one of them starts garroting, beating, or sodomizing a woman in their number, that is another story. 3

I always find myself annoyed when "intellectual" men dismiss violence against women with a yawn, as if it were beneath their dignity to notice. I wonder if 4

445

the reaction would be the same if the violence were directed against someone other than women. How many people would yawn and say, "Oh, kids will be kids," if a rock group did a nifty little number called "Lynchin," in which stringing up and stomping on black people were set to music? Who would chuckle and say, "Oh, just a little adolescent rebellion" if a group of rockers went on MTV dressed as Nazis, desecrating synagogues and beating up Jews to the beat of twanging guitars?

I'll tell you what would happen. Prestigious dailies would thunder on edi-   5
torial pages; senators would fall over each other to get denunciations into the Congressional Record. The president would appoint a commission to clean up the music business.

But violence against women is greeted by silence. It shouldn't be.   6

This does not mean censorship, or book (or record) burning. In a society that   7
protects free expression, we understand a lot of stuff will float up out of the sewer. Usually, we recognize the ugly stuff that advocates violence against any group as the garbage it is, and we consider its purveyors as moral lepers. We hold our nose and tolerate it, but we speak out against the values it proffers.

But images of violence against women are not staying on the fringes of society.   8
No longer are they found only in tattered, paper-covered books or in movie houses where winos snooze and the scent of urine fills the air. They are entering the mainstream at a rapid rate. This is happening at a time when the media, more and more, set the agenda for the public debate. It is a powerful legitimizing force—especially television. Many people regard what they see on TV as the truth; Walter Cronkite once topped a poll as the most trusted man in America.

Now, with the advent of rock videos and all-music channels, rock music has   9
grabbed a big chunk of legitimacy. American teen-agers have instant access, in their living rooms, to the messages of rock, on the same vehicle that brought them Sesame Street. Who can blame them if they believe that the images they see are accurate reflections of adult reality, approved by adults? After all, Big Bird used to give them lessons on the same little box. Adults, by their silence, sanction the images. Do we really want our kids to think that rape and violence are what sexuality is all about?

This is not a trivial issue. Violence against women is a major social problem,   10
one that's more than a cerebral issue to me. I teach at Boston University, and one of my most promising young journalism students was raped and murdered. Two others told me of being raped. Recently, one female student was assaulted and beaten so badly she had $5,000 worth of medical bills and permanent damage to her back and eyes.

It's nearly impossible, of course, to make a cause-and-effect link between   11
lyrics and images and acts of violence. But images have a tremendous power to create an atmosphere in which violence against certain people is sanctioned. Nazi propagandists knew that full well when they portrayed Jews as ugly, greedy, and powerful.

The outcry over violence against women, particularly in a sexual context, is   12
being legitimized in two ways: by the increasing movement of these images into

the mainstream of the media in TV, films, magazines, albums, videos, and by the silence about it.

Violence, of course, is rampant in the media. But it is usually set in some kind   13
of moral context. It's usually only the bad guys who commit violent acts against the innocent. When the good guys get violent, it's against those who deserve it. Dirty Harry blows away the scum, he doesn't walk up to a toddler and say, "Make my day." The A Team does not shoot up suburban shopping malls.

But in some rock songs, it's the "heroes" who commit the acts. The people we   14
are programmed to identify with are the ones being violent, with women on the receiving end. In a society where rape and assaults on women are endemic, this is no small problem, with millions of young boys watching on their TV screens and listening on their Walkmans.

I think something needs to be done. I'd like to see people in the industry   15
respond to the problem. I'd love to see some women rock stars speak out against violence against women. I would like to see disc jockeys refuse air play to records and videos that contain such violence. At the very least, I want to see the end of the silence. I want journalists and parents and critics and performing artists to keep this issue alive in the public forum. I don't want people who are concerned about this issue labeled as bluenoses and bookburners and ignored.

And I wish it wasn't always just women who were speaking out. Men have as   16
large a stake in the quality of our civilization as women do in the long run. Violence is a contagion that infects at random. Let's hear something, please, from the men.

▼ TOPICAL CONSIDERATIONS

1. What characteristic of rock music does Rivers say she enjoyed as a teenager? Can you think of any current or recent rock songs that support her complaints about some of today's rock lyrics?
2. Do you agree with Rivers' argument? Do you think she is making too much of a few examples? What about her comments on the power of rock video images?
3. How does rampant violence in the media differ from what Rivers finds in rock lyrics and rock videos?
4. Rivers' condemnation of some rock lyrics brings up a sensitive question: censorship. Do you think Rivers is advocating censorship? Do you think there should be some censorship exercised? Do you think records and compact discs should be clearly rated as are movies so consumers are warned that lyrical material might be objectionable?
5. Do you think it is feasible that record industries would exercise self-censorship? Do you think it is feasible that journalists, disc jockeys, and rock stars—particularly female—would protest music that expresses violence against women?

▼ RHETORICAL CONSIDERATIONS

1. A well-fashioned argument should contain solid examples to support itself. Does Rivers use solid enough examples to back up her argument?
2. How would you characterize the tone of this essay?
3. What rhetorical use does Rivers make of her reference to Big Bird in paragraph 9?
4. Comment on the effectiveness of Rivers' plea in the concluding sentence.

▼ WRITING ASSIGNMENTS

1. Rivers opens her essay with statements about the comparatively mild shock-effect and sexiness of early rock lyrics. In a paper, compare sample lyrics of old rock songs with those of today particularly with regard to attitudes toward women. What differences do you find? Are today's songs more or less sexist than yesterday's? Are they more or less violent to women?
2. Select a particular song (or songs) by an artist and analyze it for its sanctioning of violence against women.
3. Many people claim that today's rock lyrics are full of sex. Do you agree? Do you think there is too much celebration of sexuality in current rock music? Citing specific examples, write your thoughts on these questions.
4. Study a few rock videos in which women are victims of violence. Write a paper in which you analyze the messages. How might such images and words affect a twelve-year-old boy? How might they affect a twelve-year-old girl?
5. Rivers' essay brings up the question of censorship. What are your thoughts about the subject? Using examples and clear reasons, write a paper in which you either advocate or reject the censorship of rock music.

▼ FOUR-LETTER WORDS CAN HURT

Barbara Lawrence

Whether we like it or not, obscene language has always been part of our culture and will probably continue to be. In fact, it is fashionable to some. The reasons people use such language are varied and complex. But what about the effects of obscene language? Are some of us subtly victimized by dirty words? In this essay Barbara Lawrence, associate professor of humanities at the State University of New York at Old Westbury, argues that much of the "rich, liberating" sexual language currently fashionable is "implicitly sadistic or degrading to women." It is language intended to reduce women to sex objects, she explains. This article first appeared in the *New York Times* in October 1973.

Why should any words be called obscene? Don't they all describe natural human 1 functions? Am I trying to tell them, my students demand, that the "strong, earthy, gut-honest"—or, if they are fans of Norman Mailer, the "rich, liberating, existential"—language they use to describe sexual activity isn't preferable to "phony-sounding, middle-class words like 'intercourse' and 'copulate' "? "Cop You Late!" they say with fancy inflections and gagging grimaces. "Now, what is *that* supposed to mean?"

Well, what is it supposed to mean? And why indeed should one group of words 2 describing human functions and human organs be acceptable in ordinary conversation and another, describing presumably the same organs and functions, be tabooed—so much so, in fact, that some of these words still cannot appear in print in many parts of the English-speaking world?

The argument that these taboos exist only because of "sexual hang-ups" 3 (middle-class, middle-age, feminist), or even that they are a result of class oppression (the contempt of the Norman conquerors for the language of their Anglo-Saxon serfs), ignores a much more likely explanation, it seems to me, and that is the sources and functions of the words themselves.

The best known of the tabooed sexual verbs, for example, comes from the 4 German *ficken,* meaning "to strike"; combined, according to Partridge's etymological dictionary *Origins,* with the Latin sexual verb *futuere;* associated in turn with the Latin *fustis,* "a staff or cudgel"; the Celtic *buc,* "a point, hence to pierce"; the Irish *bot,* "the male member"; the Latin *battuere,* "to beat"; the Gaelic *batair,* "a cudgeller"; the Early Irish *bualaim,* "I strike"; and so forth. It is one of what etymologists sometimes call "the sadistic group of words for the man's part in copulation."

The brutality of this word, then, and its equivalents ("screw," "bang," etc.), is   5
not an illusion of the middle class or a crotchet of Women's Liberation. In their
origins and imagery these words carry undeniably painful, if not sadistic, implications,
the object of which is almost always female. Consider, for example, what a
"screw" actually does to the wood it penetrates; what a painful, even mutilating,
activity this kind of analogy suggests. "Screw" is particularly interesting in this
context, since the noun, according to Partridge, comes from words meaning
"groove," "nut," "ditch," "breeding sow," "scrofula," and "swelling," while the
verb, besides its explicit imagery, has antecedent associations to "write on,"
"scratch," "scarify," and so forth—a revealing fusion of a mechanical or painful
action with an obviously denigrated object.

Not all obscene words, of course, are as implicitly sadistic or denigrating to   6
women as these, but all that I know seem to serve a similar purpose: to reduce the
human organism (especially the female organism) and human functions (especially
sexual and procreative) to their least organic, most mechanical dimension; to
substitute a trivializing or deforming resemblance for the complex human reality
of what is being described.

Tabooed male descriptives, when they are not openly denigrating to women,   7
often serve to divorce a male organ or function from any significant interaction
with the female. Take the word "testes," for example, suggesting "witnesses" (from
the Latin *testis*) to the sexual and procreative strengths of the male organ; and the
obscene counterpart of this word, which suggests little more than a mechanical
shape. Or compare almost any of the "rich," "liberating" sexual verbs, so fashionable today among male writers, with that much-derided Latin word "copulate"
("to bind or join together") or even that Anglo-Saxon phrase (which seems to have
had no trouble surviving the Norman Conquest) "make love."

How arrogantly self-involved the tabooed words seem in comparison to either   8
of the other terms, and how contemptuous of the female partner. Understandably
so, of course, if she is only a "skirt," a "broad," a "chick," a "pussycat," or a
"piece." If she is, in other words, no more than her skirt, or what her skirt
conceals; no more than a breeder, or the broadest part of her; no more than a
piece of a human being, or a "piece of tail."

The most severely tabooed of all the female descriptives, incidentally, are   9
those like a "piece of tail," which suggest (either explicitly or through antecedents)
that there is no significant difference between the female channel through which
we are all conceived and born and the anal outlet common to both sexes—a
distinction that pornographers have always enjoyed obscuring.

This effort to deny women their biological identity, their individuality, their   10
humanness, is such an important aspect of obscene language that one can only
marvel at how seldom, in an era preoccupied with definitions of obscenity, this
fact is brought to our attention. One problem, of course, is that many of the
people in the best position to do this (critics, teachers, writers) are so reluctant
today to admit that they are angered or shocked by obscenity. Bored, maybe,
unimpressed, aesthetically displeased, but—no matter how brutal or denigrating
the material—never angered, never shocked.

And yet how eloquently angered, how piously shocked many of these same 11
people become if denigrating language is used about any minority group other
than women; if the obscenities are racial or ethnic, that is, rather than sexual.
Words like "coon," "kike," "spic," "wop," after all, deform identity, deny individuality and humanness in almost exactly the same way that sexual vulgarisms and
obscenities do.

No one that I know, least of all my students, would fail to question the values 12
of a society whose literature and entertainment rested heavily on racial or ethnic
pejoratives. Are the values of a society whose literature and entertainment rest as
heavily as ours on sexual pejoratives any less questionable?

▼ TOPICAL CONSIDERATIONS

1. What is Lawrence's central thesis?
2. Is the view of obscenity in this essay strictly feminist? Explain your answer.

▼ RHETORICAL CONSIDERATIONS

1. Does the series of questions in the first paragraph prepare the reader for
   the rest of the essay? Are the questions rhetorical, or does Lawrence
   answer them? What does the last sentence suggest to you?
2. What methods does Lawrence use in her extended definition of that "best
   known of the tabooed sexual verbs" (paragraph 4)? Are they convincing?
3. Does this essay have a clearly defined beginning, middle, and end? Where?
   Are the lines of argument clearly defined?
4. Why does the author avoid using the obscene words she discusses? Does
   this support or weaken her position?
5. Select a paragraph and analyze the way the author proceeds from the
   general to the specific. Is this the basic paragraph structure in this essay?
6. How does Lawrence illustrate the difference between *denotation* and
   connotation? Cite examples.

▼ WRITING ASSIGNMENTS

1. Do liberated women who use "liberated" language defeat their own cause?
   Explain your answer.
2. List synonyms of a common sexual obscenity. How are they sadistic,
   mechanical, or dehumanizing? Do they demean women more than men?
   Defend your position.
3. From your experience, do people react more negatively to racial slurs than
   to obscenities?

▼ WHAT'S WRONG WITH BLACK ENGLISH

Rachel L. Jones

Is it elitist or racist to suggest that black English is an unacceptable medium of communication in American society at large, or that it is a handicap to its users? Rachel Jones does not think so, and she is black. Hers might be an unpopular position with some fellow students, but through a mixture of personal experience and cogent insights she defends it well. In 1982, when she wrote this essay, which appeared in the "My Turn" column of *Newsweek,* Jones was a sophomore at Southern Illinois University.

William Labov, a noted linguist, once said about the use of black English, "It 1
is the goal of most black Americans to acquire full control of the standard language without giving up their own culture." He also suggested that there are certain advantages to having two ways to express one's feelings. I wonder if the good doctor might also consider the goals of those black Americans who have full control of standard English but who are every now and then troubled by that colorful, grammar-to-the-winds patois that is black English. Case in point—me.

I'm a 21-year-old black born to a family that would probably be considered 2
lower-middle class—which in my mind is a polite way of describing a condition only slightly better than poverty. Let's just say we rarely if ever did the winter-vacation thing in the Caribbean. I've often had to defend my humble beginnings to a most unlikely group of people for an even less likely reason. Because of the way I talk, some of my black peers look at me sideways and ask, "Why do you talk like you're white?"

The first time it happened to me I was nine years old. Cornered in the school 3
bathroom by the class bully and her sidekick, I was offered the opportunity to swallow a few of my teeth unless I satisfactorily explained why I always got good grades, why I talked "proper" or "white." I had no ready answer for her, save the fact that my mother had from the time I was old enough to talk stressed the importance of reading and learning, or that L. Frank Baum and Ray Bradbury were my closest companions. I read all my older brothers' and sisters' literature textbooks more faithfully than they did, and even lightweights like the Bobbsey Twins and Trixie Belden were allowed into my bookish inner circle. I don't remember exactly what I told those girls, but I somehow talked my way out of a beating.

I was reminded once again of my "white pipes" problem while apartment 4 hunting in Evanston, Illinois, last winter. I doggedly made out lists of available places and called all around. I would immediately be invited over—and immediately turned down. The thinly concealed looks of shock when the front door opened clued me in, along with the flustered instances of "just getting off the phone with the girl who was ahead of you and she wants the rooms." When I finally found a place to live, my roommate stirred up old memories when she remarked a few months later, "You know, I was surprised when I first saw you. You sounded white over the phone." Tell me another one, sister.

I should've asked her a question I've wanted an answer to for years: how does   5
one "talk white"? The silly side of me pictures a rabid white foam spewing forth when I speak. I don't use Valley Girl jargon, so that's not what's meant in my case. Actually, I've pretty much deduced what people mean when they say that to me, and the implications are really frightening.

It means that I'm articulate and well-versed. It means that I can talk as freely   6
about John Steinbeck as I can about Rick James. It means that "ain't" and "he be" are not staples of my vocabulary and are only used around family and friends. (It is almost Jekyll and Hyde-ish the way I can slip out of academic abstractions into a long, lean, double-negative-filled dialogue, but I've come to terms with that aspect of my personality.) As a child, I found it hard to believe that's what people meant by "talking proper"; that would've meant that good grades and standard English were equated with white skin, and that went against everything I'd ever been taught. Running into the same type of mentality as an adult has confirmed the depressing reality that for many blacks, standard English is not only unfamiliar, it is socially unacceptable.

James Baldwin once defended black English by saying it had added "vitality to   7
the language," and even went so far as to label it a language in its own right, saying, "Language [i.e., black English] is a political instrument" and a "vivid and crucial key to identity." But did Malcolm X urge blacks to take power in this country "any way y'all can"? Did Martin Luther King Jr. say to blacks, "I has been to the mountaintop, and I done seed the Promised Land"? Toni Morrison, Alice Walker and James Baldwin did not achieve their eloquence, grace and stature by using only black English in their writing. Andrew Young, Tom Bradley and Barbara Jordan did not acquire political power by saying, "Y'all crazy if you ain't gon vote for me." They all have full command of standard English, and I don't think that knowledge takes away from their blackness or commitment to black people.

I know from experience that it's important for black people, stripped of   8
culture and heritage, to have something they can point to and say, "This is ours, *we* can comprehend it, *we* alone can speak it with a soulful flourish," I'd be lying if I said that the rhythms of my people caught up in "some serious rap" don't sound natural and right to me sometimes. But how heartwarming is it for those same brothers when they hit the pavement searching for employment? Studies have proven that the use of ethnic dialects decreases power in the marketplace. "I be" is acceptable on the corner, but not with the boss.

Am I letting capitalistic, European-oriented thinking fog the issue? Am   9

I selling out blacks to an ideal of assimilating, being as much like whites as possible? I have not formed a personal political ideology, but I do know this: it hurts me to hear black children use black English, knowing that they will be at yet another disadvantage in an educational system already full of stumbling blocks. It hurts me to sit in lecture halls and hear fellow black students complain that the professor "be tripping dem out using big words dey can't understand." And what hurts most is to be stripped of my own blackness simply because I know my way around the English language.

I would have to disagree with Labov in one respect. My goal is not so much to   10
acquire full control of both standard and black English, but to one day see more black people less dependent on a dialect that excludes them from full participation in the world we live in. I don't think I talk white, I think I talk right.

▼ TOPICAL CONSIDERATIONS

1. What is Jones's argument against linguist William Labov?
2. What does Jones mean by "talking white"? Does the expression mean the same as talking "standard English"? And what is so "frightening" about the implications of that charge?
3. Does the author like anything about black English? What does she find wrong with the practice of it?
4. What does Jones feel about James Baldwin's opinion of black English? What is the point of her references in paragraph 7 to Malcolm X, Martin Luther King, Jr., and other notable black political figures and writers?
5. What is the thrust of the concluding comments of Jones in her essay?

▼ RHETORICAL CONSIDERATIONS

1. Does the title of this essay clearly indicate the author's position?
2. Where in her essay does the author give a clear thesis statement?
3. What is the advantage of opening the essay with a statement by William Labov? How does Jones use the statement? Where else in the essay does she refer to Labov and for what effect?
4. What audience would not like this essay? How does she address that disapproval?

▼ WRITING ASSIGNMENTS

1. Jones remarks that studies have shown "that the use of ethnic dialects decreases power in the marketplace." If you were a recruiter for a business would an applicant's speaking in an ethnic dialect influence your decision to hire? In a paper explain your answer.

2. Do students have a right to their own nonstandard language? Does any group? What would happen if different segments of our society spoke "private" languages?

▼ LITTLE RED RIDING HOOD REVISITED

Russell Baker

For years Russell Baker has been writing an entertaining column for the *New York Times.* His popularity is based partly on his satiric, sometimes biting reviews of social issues, American politics, and current jargon. In this characteristically humorous piece Baker takes a familiar folk tale and translates it into modern American double-talk just to illustrate how silly and obfuscating it is. This article was first published in the *New York Times* in January 1980.

In an effort to make the classics accessible to contemporary readers, I am 1 translating them into the modern American language. Here is the translation of "Little Red Riding Hood":

Once upon a point in time, a small person named Little Red Riding Hood 2 initiated plans for the preparation, delivery and transportation of foodstuffs to her grandmother, a senior citizen residing at a place of residence in a forest of indeterminate dimension.

In the process of implementing this program, her incursion into the forest was 3 in midtransportation process when it attained interface with an alleged perpetrator. This individual, a wolf, made inquiry as to the whereabouts of Little Red Riding Hood's goal as well as inferring that he was desirous of ascertaining the contents of Little Red Riding Hood's foodstuffs basket, and all that.

"It would be inappropriate to lie to me," the wolf said, displaying his huge jaw 4 capability. Sensing that he was a mass of repressed hostility intertwined with acute alienation, she indicated.

"I see you indicating," the wolf said, "but what I don't see is whatever it is 5 you're indicating at, you dig?"

Little Red Riding Hood indicated more fully, making one thing perfectly 6 clear—to wit, that it was to her grandmother's residence and with a consignment of foodstuffs that her mission consisted of taking her to and with.

At this point in time the wolf moderated his rhetoric and proceeded to 7 grandmother's residence. The elderly person was then subjected to the disadvantages of total consumption and transferred to residence in the perpetrator's stomach.

"That will raise the old woman's consciousness," the wolf said to himself. He 8 was not a bad wolf, but only a victim of an oppressive society, a society that not only denied wolves' rights, but actually boasted of its capacity for keeping the wolf from the door. An interior malaise made itself manifest inside the wolf.

"Is that the national malaise I sense within my digestive tract?" wondered the wolf. "Or is it the old person seeking to retaliate for her consumption by telling wolf jokes to my duodenum?" It was time to make a judgment. The time was now, the hour had struck, the body lupine cried out for decision. The wolf was up to the challenge. He took two stomach powders right away and got into bed.

The wolf had adopted the abdominal-distress recovery posture when Little Red Riding Hood achieved his presence.

"Grandmother," she said, "your ocular implements are of an extraordinary order of magnitude."

"The purpose of this enlarged viewing capability," said the wolf, "is to enable your image to register a more precise impression upon my sight systems."

"In reference to your ears," said Little Red Riding Hood, "it is noted with the deepest respect that far from being underprivileged, their elongation and enlargement appear to qualify you for unparalleled distinction."

"I hear you loud and clear, kid," said the wolf, "but what about these new choppers?"

"If it is not inappropriate," said Little Red Riding Hood, "it might be observed that with your new miracle masticating products you may even be able to chew taffy again."

This observation was followed by the adoption of an aggressive posture on the part of the wolf and the assertion that it was also possible for him, due to the high efficiency ratio of his jaw, to consume little persons, plus, as he stated, his firm determination to do so at once without delay and with all due process and propriety, notwithstanding the fact that the ingestion of one entire grandmother had already provided twice his daily recommended cholesterol intake.

There ensued flight by Little Red Riding Hood accompanied by pursuit in respect to the wolf and a subsequent intervention on the part of a third party, heretofore unnoted in the record.

Due to the firmness of the intervention, the wolf's stomach underwent ax-assisted aperture with the result that Red Riding Hood's grandmother was enabled to be removed with only minor discomfort.

The wolf's indigestion was immediately alleviated with such effectiveness that he signed a contract with the intervening third party to perform with grandmother in a television commercial demonstrating the swiftness of this dramatic relief for stomach discontent.

"I'm going to be on television," cried grandmother.

And they all joined her happily in crying, "What a phenomena!"

▼ TOPICAL CONSIDERATIONS

1. Baker uses many examples of jargon. Select some and try to determine what professions they are drawn from.
2. Cite some examples of repetition and excessive Latinisms.

3. Can you find any political allusions in this rewrite of Little Red Riding Hood?
4. In your own words, state Baker's thesis.
5. The ending of this version is different from that of the original. In what ways is it different? Why did Baker make the changes?

▼ RHETORICAL CONSIDERATIONS

1. Discuss the tone of this essay. Does Baker capture the flavor of officialdom?
2. Discuss the satiric import of the first line. For what purpose did Baker select the words "small person," "senior citizen," "delivery and transportation," "a place of residence," and "forest of indeterminate dimension"? What is he poking fun at?

▼ WRITING ASSIGNMENTS

1. Choose another story—for example, Jack and the Beanstalk, Hansel and Gretel, Cinderella—and rewrite it using Baker's satiric approach.
2. Find a particularly flagrant example of bad jargon in Baker's piece and write an essay on its failure to communicate.
3. Write a letter to Russell Baker in full-blown jargon telling him how much you liked his modernized version and how much more you got out of it than the traditional version.

▼ TWO-HEADED MONSTERS

From the *Columbia Journalism Review*

Words are the business of journalism, and accuracy of usage is undoubtedly the pride of any newspaper. Occasionally, however, words may turn against the meaning intended, as is the case when printer's devils plague the presses. The result is news gone askew. Such was the case in the real headlines that follow, in which unforeseen misprints, double entendres, and grammatical goofs turned into news that did not fit the print. The *Columbia Journalism Review*, a watchdog magazine of the media, has a department called "The Lower Case" that gathers such gaffes; these examples were originally reprinted there.

Vatican Unveils
Procreation Position

Cortland, N.Y., *Standard* 3/10/87

Professor attached to chair

UAA Voice (Anchorage, Alaska) 4/11/88

Downtown hogs grant cash

Chicago Tribune 2/25/87

Royal Bank of Scotland Considers Buying Citizens

American Banker 3/22/88

Hemorrhoid victim turns to ice

Milwaukee Sentinel 12/10/85

JAIL GUARD
PROBED
IN INMATE SEX

Chicago Tribune 6/20/86

Reader requests tanning procedure for hunter's wife

Express-News (San Antonio, Tex.) 8/1/87

Ground broken for grain suppository

The Aberdeen (Ida.) *Times* 8/12/87

Third Reich field goal nips Hawks

The Daily Iowan 8/31/87

BEE SMOKING BLAMED IN FIRE: 40 ACRES BURN

The Daily Report, (Ontario, Calif.) 9/8/87

Rock star hit with sick child

Mansfield, O., *News Journal* 8/4/87

Officials to monitor games for mosquitoes

Journal and Courier (Lafayette, Ind.) 5/15/87

Pentagon urged to keep personnel exposed to AIDS

Yuba-Sutter Appeal-Democrat (Marysville, Calif.) 12/17/86

Police Discover Crack in Australia

International Herald Tribune 9/10/86

French offer terrorist reward
The Denver Post 11/20/86

Tulsan Arrested With Explosive, Baby Sentenced
Tulsa World 10/18/86

DR. RUTH TALKS ABOUT SEX WITH NEWSPAPER EDITORS
Rutland (Vt.) *Herald* 4/14/86

Fire Suspected as Arson Guts Three Haddam Structures
The Middletown (Conn.) *Press* 3/13/86

Jerk Injures Neck, Wins Award
The Buffalo News 4/6/83

U's food service feeds thousands, grosses millions
The Minnesota Daily 5/6/83

Safe driver hits 1 million
The Sentinel-Echo (London, Ky.) 8/8/85

Utah Girl Does Well in Dog Shows
Salt Lake Tribune 12/30/81

ON DEATH
AND DYING

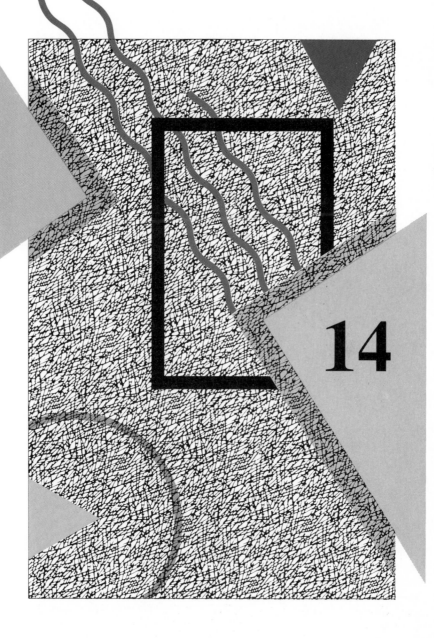

14

▼ ON NATURAL DEATH

Lewis Thomas

In his second essay reprinted here, Dr. Lewis Thomas reflects on the subject of death from the viewpoint of a physician and biologist. When regarded in so grand a context as the natural world, dying might not seem the cruel and extraordinary phenomenon we have made of it. As he points out, dying is as "natural" as living. Thomas, who has served as chair of the Departments of Medicine and Pathology at New York University and Bellevue Medical Center and dean of Yale Medical School, has also distinguished himself as a writer. His articles have appeared in both scientific and popular journals. The following originally appeared in his column, "Notes of a Biology Watcher," for the *New England Journal of Medicine* in 1979. His many books include *The Lives of the Cell* (1974), *Late Night Thoughts on Listening to Mahler's Ninth Symphony* (1983), and his most recent work, *The Lasker Awards: Four Decades of Scientific Medical Progress* (1986).

1 There are so many new books about dying that there are now special shelves set aside for them in bookshops, along with the health-diet and home-repair paperbacks and the sex manuals. Some of them are so packed with detailed information and step-by-step instructions for performing the function that you'd think this was a new sort of skill which all of us are now required to learn. The strongest impression the casual reader gets, leafing through, is that proper dying has become an extraordinary, even an exotic experience, something only the specially trained get to do.

2 Also, you could be led to believe that we are the only creatures capable of the awareness of death, that when all the rest of nature is being cycled through dying, one generation after another, it is a different kind of process, done automatically and trivially, more "natural," as we say.

3 An elm in our backyard caught the blight this summer and dropped stone dead, leafless, almost overnight. One weekend it was a normal-looking elm, maybe a little bare in spots but nothing alarming, and the next weekend it was gone, passed over, departed, taken. Taken is right, for the tree surgeon came by yesterday with his crew of young helpers and their cherry picker, and took it down branch by branch and carted it off in the back of a red truck, everyone singing.

4 The dying of a field mouse, at the jaws of an amiable household cat, is a spectacle I have beheld many times. It used to make me wince. Early in life I gave up throwing sticks at the cat to make him drop the mouse, because the dropped mouse regularly went ahead and died anyway, but I always shouted unaffections at

the cat to let him know the sort of animal he had become. Nature, I thought, was an abomination.

Recently I've done some thinking about that mouse, and I wonder if his dying is necessarily all that different from the passing of our elm. The main difference, if there is one, would be in the matter of pain. I do not believe that an elm tree has pain receptors, and even so, the blight seems to me a relatively painless way to go even if there were nerve endings in a tree, which there are not. But the mouse dangling tail-down from the teeth of a gray cat is something else again, with pain beyond bearing, you'd think, all over his small body.

There are now some plausible reasons for thinking it is not like that at all, and you can make up an entirely different story about the mouse and his dying if you like. At the instant of being trapped and penetrated by teeth, peptide hormones are released by cells in the hypothalamus and the pituitary gland; instantly these substances, called endorphins, are attached to the surfaces of other cells responsible for pain perception; the hormones have the pharmacologic properties of opium; there is no pain. Thus it is that the mouse seems always to dangle so languidly from the jaws, lies there so quietly when dropped, dies of his injuries without a struggle. If a mouse could shrug, he'd shrug.

I do not know if this is true or not, nor do I know how to prove it if it is true. Maybe if you could get in there quickly enough and administer naloxone, a specific morphine antagonist, you could turn off the endorphins and observe the restoration of pain, but this is not something I would care to do or see. I think I will leave it there, as a good guess about the dying of a cat-chewed mouse, perhaps about dying in general.

Montaigne had a hunch about dying, based on his own close call in a riding accident. He was so badly injured as to be believed dead by his companions, and was carried home with lamentations, "all bloody, stained all over with the blood I had thrown up." He remembers the entire episode, despite having been "dead, for two full hours," with wonderment:

> It seemed to me that my life was hanging only by the tip of my lips. I closed my eyes in order, it seemed to me, to help push it out, and took pleasure in growing languid and letting myself go. It was an idea that was only floating on the surface of my soul, as delicate and feeble as all the rest, but in truth not only free from distress but mingled with that sweet feeling that people have who have let themselves slide into sleep. I believe that this is the same state in which people find themselves whom we see fainting in the agony of death, and I maintain that we pity them without cause. . . . In order to get used to the idea of death, I find there is nothing like coming close to it.

Later, in another essay, Montaigne returns to it:

> If you know not how to die, never trouble yourself; Nature will in a moment fully and sufficiently instruct you; she will exactly do that business for you; take you no care for it.

The worst accident I've ever seen was on Okinawa, in the early days of the 10 invasion, when a jeep ran into a troop carrier and was crushed nearly flat. Inside were two young MPs, trapped in bent steel, both mortally hurt, with only their heads and shoulders visible. We had a conversation while people with the right tools were prying them free. Sorry about the accident, they said. No, they said, they felt fine. Is everyone else okay, one of them said. Well, the other one said, no hurry now. And then they died.

Pain is useful for avoidance, for getting away when there's time to get away, 11 but when it is end game, and no way back, pain is likely to be turned off, and the mechanisms for this are wonderfully precise and quick. If I had to design an ecosystem in which creatures had to live off each other and in which dying was an indispensable part of living, I could not think of a better way to manage.

▼ TOPICAL CONSIDERATIONS

1. Thomas remarks on all the new literature about death and dying in the bookstores. How does he seem to regard this current fascination?
2. What exactly does Thomas mean by "natural" death? How, by implication, might death be "unnatural"?
3. What is the point of Thomas's anecdote about his elm tree dying? How does it connect to the central idea of the essay?
4. Observing the fate of the field mouse, Thomas decided that nature "was an abomination." Why might he have drawn this conclusion? Why, after reflecting upon the mouse's death, did Thomas change his view of nature?
5. What observations about dying does Montaigne make? How do they support Thomas's thesis?

▼ RHETORICAL CONSIDERATIONS

1. This essay is a fine example of building a central thesis through the use of anecdotes. Explain how each of the anecdotes Thomas chose helps develop his thesis. What purpose does each serve? How are they thematically connected to each other?
2. Evaluate the tone of this essay. In your analysis, consider the use of language, in particular his mixture of colloquial expressions (for example, "Montaigne had a hunch about dying") and scientific terminology (see paragraph 6).
3. Where exactly does Thomas offer his thesis statement in the essay? What is the strategy for placing it here?

▼ WRITING ASSIGNMENTS

1. Having read Lewis Thomas's reflections on death, have your own feelings about the subject changed any? Does death seem more "natural" to you now? In an essay, write your own reflections on the topic incorporating your response to Dr. Thomas's essay.

2. Have you ever had an experience with death? If so, write an essay on the loss of that person. Try to capture the feelings you experienced—anger, grief, and fear. Does Thomas's essay on the "naturalness" of death help you to come to terms with the experience?

▼ ON THE FEAR OF DEATH

Elizabeth Kübler-Ross

Elizabeth Kübler-Ross, a Swiss-born American psychiatrist, is considered one of the world's foremost experts on the treatment of the terminally ill. She has conducted seminars and written widely about death and dying in order to help people better understand and cope with the process. Her most famous book is *On Death and Dying* (1969), from which this essay is taken. In 1988 she published *AIDS: The Ultimate Challenge* which describes her interaction with victims of this devastating disease.

*Let me not pray to be sheltered from
dangers but to be fearless in facing
them.
Let me not beg for the stilling of
my pain but for the heart to conquer it.
Let me not look for allies in life's
battlefield but to my own strength.
Let me not crave in anxious fear to
be saved but hope for the patience to
win my freedom.
Grant me that I may not be a
coward, feeling your mercy in my
success alone; but let me find the grasp
of your hand in my failure.*

Rabindranath Tagore, *Fruit-Gathering*

Epidemics have taken a great toll of lives in past generations. Death in infancy and   1
early childhood was frequent and there were few families who didn't lose a member of the family at an early age. Medicine has changed greatly in the last decades. Widespread vaccinations have practically eradicated many illnesses, at least in western Europe and the United States. The use of chemotherapy, especially the antibiotics, has contributed to an ever-decreasing number of fatalities in infectious diseases. Better child care and education has effected a low morbidity and mortality among children. The many diseases that have taken an impressive toll among the young and middle-aged have been conquered. The number of old people is on the rise, and with this fact come the number of people with malignancies and chronic diseases associated more with old age.

Pediatricians have less work with acute and life-threatening situations as they   2
have an ever-increasing number of patients with psychosomatic disturbances and

adjustment and behavior problems. Physicians have more people in their waiting rooms with emotional problems than they have ever had before, but they also have more elderly patients who not only try to live with their decreased physical abilities and limitations but who also face loneliness and isolation with all its pains and anguish. The majority of these people are not seen by a psychiatrist. Their needs have to be elicited and gratified by other professional people, for instance, chaplains and social workers. It is for them that I am trying to outline the changes that have taken place in the last few decades, changes that are ultimately responsible for the increased fear of death, the rising number of emotional problems, and the greater need for understanding of and coping with the problems of death and dying.

When we look back in time and study old cultures and people, we are 3
impressed that death has always been distasteful to man and will probably always be. From a psychiatrist's point of view this is very understandable and can perhaps best be explained by our basic knowledge that, in our unconscious, death is never possible in regard to ourselves. It is inconceivable for our unconscious to imagine an actual ending of our own life here on earth, and if this life of ours has to end, the ending is always attributed to a malicious intervention from the outside by someone else. In simple terms, in our unconscious mind we can only be killed; it is inconceivable to die of a natural cause or of old age. Therefore death in itself is associated with a bad act, a frightening happening, something that in itself calls for retribution and punishment.

One is wise to remember these fundamental facts as they are essential in 4
understanding some of the most important, otherwise unintelligible communications of our patients.

The second fact that we have to comprehend is that in our unconscious mind 5
we cannot distinguish between a wish and a deed. We are all aware of some of our illogical dreams in which two completely opposite statements can exist side by side—very acceptable in our dreams but unthinkable and illogical in our wakening state. Just as our unconscious mind cannot differentiate between the wish to kill somebody in anger and the act of having done so, the young child is unable to make this distinction. The child who angrily wishes his mother to drop dead for not having gratified his needs will be traumatized greatly by the actual death of his mother—even if this event is not linked closely in time with his destructive wishes. He will always take part or the whole blame for the loss of his mother. He will always say to himself—rarely to others—"I did it, I am responsible, I was bad, therefore Mommy left me." It is well to remember that the child will react in the same manner if he loses a parent by divorce, separation, or desertion. Death is often seen by a child as an impermanent thing and has therefore little distinction from a divorce in which he may have an opportunity to see a parent again.

Many a parent will remember remarks of their children such as, "I will bury 6
my doggy now and next spring when the flowers come up again, he will get up." Maybe it was the same wish that motivated the ancient Egyptians to supply their dead with food and goods to keep them happy and the old American Indians to bury their relatives with their belongings.

When we grow older and begin to realize that our omnipotence is really not so 7 omnipotent, that our strongest wishes are not powerful enough to make the impossible possible, the fear that we have contributed to the death of a loved one diminishes—and with it the guilt. The fear remains diminished, however, only so long as it is not challenged too strongly. Its vestiges can be seen daily in hospital corridors and in people associated with the bereaved.

A husband and wife may have been fighting for years, but when the partner dies, the survivor will pull his hair, whine and cry louder and beat his chest in regret, fear and anguish, and will hence fear his own death more than before, still believing in the law of talion—an eye for an eye, a tooth for a tooth—"I am responsible for her death, I will have to die a pitiful death in retribution." 8

Maybe this knowledge will help us understand many of the old customs and rituals which have lasted over the centuries and whose purpose is to diminish the anger of the gods or the people as the case may be, thus decreasing the anticipated punishment. I am thinking of the ashes, the torn clothes, the veil, the *Klage Weiber* of the old days*—they are all means to ask you to take pity on them, the mourners, and are expressions of sorrow, grief, and shame. If someone grieves, beats his chest, tears his hair, or refuses to eat, it is an attempt at self-punishment to avoid or reduce the anticipated punishment for the blame that he takes on the death of a loved one. 9

This grief, shame, and guilt are not very far removed from feelings of anger and rage. The process of grief always includes some qualities of anger. Since none of us likes to admit anger at a deceased person, these emotions are often disguised or repressed and prolong the period of grief or show up in other ways. It is well to remember that it is not up to us to judge such feelings as bad or shameful but to understand their true meaning and origin as something very human. In order to illustrate this I will again use the example of the child—and the child in us. The five-year-old who loses his mother is both blaming himself for her disappearance and being angry at her for having deserted him and for no longer gratifying his needs. The dead person then turns into something the child loves and wants very much but also hates with equal intensity for this severe deprivation. 10

The ancient Hebrews regarded the body of a dead person as something unclean and not to be touched. The early American Indians talked about the evil spirits and shot arrows in the air to drive the spirits away. Many other cultures have rituals to take care of the "bad" dead person, and they all originate in this feeling of anger which still exists in all of us, though we dislike admitting it. The tradition of the tombstone may originate in the wish to keep the bad spirits deep down in the ground, and the pebbles that many mourners put on the grave are leftover symbols of the same wish. Though we call the firing of guns at military funerals a last salute, it is the same symbolic ritual as the Indian used when he shot his spears and arrows into the skies. 11

I give these examples to emphasize that man has not basically changed. Death is still a fearful, frightening happening, and the fear of death is a universal fear even if we think we have mastered it on many levels. 12

Klage Weiber: wailing wives. [Eds.]

What has changed is our way of coping and dealing with death and dying and our dying patients. 13

Having been raised in a country in Europe where science is not so advanced, where modern techniques have just started to find their way into medicine, and where people still live as they did in this country half a century ago, I may have had an opportunity to study a part of the evolution of mankind in a shorter period. 14

I remember as a child the death of a farmer. He fell from a tree and was not expected to live. He asked simply to die at home, a wish that was granted without question. He called his daughters into the bedroom and spoke with each one of them alone for a few moments. He arranged his affairs quietly, though he was in great pain, and distributed his belongings and his land, none of which was to be split until his wife should follow him in death. He also asked each of his children to share in the work, duties, and tasks that he had carried on until the time of the accident. He asked his friends to visit him once more, to bid goodbye to them. Although I was a small child at the time, he did not exclude me or my siblings. We were allowed to share in the preparations of the family just as we were permitted to grieve with them until he died. When he did die, he was left at home, in his own beloved home which he had built, and among his friends and neighbors who went to take a last look at him where he lay in the midst of flowers in the place he had lived in and loved so much. In that country today there is still no make-believe slumber room, no embalming, no false makeup to pretend sleep. Only the signs of very disfiguring illnesses are covered up with bandages and only infectious cases are removed from the home prior to the burial. 15

Why do I describe such "old-fashioned" customs? I think they are an indication of our acceptance of a fatal outcome, and they help the dying patient as well as his family to accept the loss of a loved one. If a patient is allowed to terminate his life in the familiar and beloved environment, it requires less adjustment for him. His own family knows him well enough to replace a sedative with a glass of his favorite wine; or the smell of a home-cooked soup may give him the appetite to sip a few spoons of fluid which, I think, is still more enjoyable than an infusion. I will not minimize the need for sedatives and infusions and realize full well from my own experience as a country doctor that they are sometimes life-saving and often unavoidable. But I also know that patience and familiar people and foods could replace many a bottle of intravenous fluids given for the simple reason that it fulfills the physiological need without involving too many people and/or individual nursing care. 16

The fact that children are allowed to stay at home where a fatality has struck and are included in the talk, discussions, and fears gives them the feeling that they are not alone in their grief and gives them the comfort of shared responsibility and shared mourning. It prepares them gradually and helps them view death as part of life, an experience which may help them grow and mature. 17

This is in great contrast to a society in which death is viewed as taboo, discussion of it is regarded as morbid, and children are excluded with the presumption and pretext that it would be "too much" for them. They are then sent off to relatives, often accompanied by some unconvincing lies of "Mother has gone on a 18 long trip" or other unbelievable stories. The child senses that something is wrong, and his distrust in adults will only multiply if other relatives add new variations of the story, avoid his questions or suspicions, shower him with gifts as a meager substitute for a loss he is not permitted to deal with. Sooner or later the child will become aware of the changed family situation and, depending on the age and personality of the child, will have an unresolved grief and regard this incident as a frightening, mysterious, in any case very traumatic experience with untrustworthy grownups, which he has no way to cope with.

It is equally unwise to tell a little child who lost her brother that God loved little boys so much that he took little Johnny to heaven. When this little girl grew up to be a woman she never solved her anger at God, which resulted in a psychotic depression when she lost her own little son three decades later. 19

We would think that our great emancipation, our knowledge of science and of man, has given us better ways and means to prepare ourselves and our families for this inevitable happening. Instead the days are gone when a man was allowed to die in peace and dignity in his own home. 20

The more we are making advancements in science, the more we seem to fear and deny the reality of death. How is this possible? 21

We use euphemisms, we make the dead look as if they were asleep, we ship the children off to protect them from the anxiety and turmoil around the house if the patient is fortunate enough to die at home, we don't allow children to visit their dying parents in the hospitals, we have long and controversial discussions about whether patients should be told the truth—a question that rarely arises when the dying person is tended by the family physician who has known him from delivery to death and who knows the weaknesses and strengths of each member of the family. 22

I think there are many reasons for this flight away from facing death calmly. One of the most important facts is that dying nowadays is more gruesome in many ways, namely, more lonely, mechanical, and dehumanized; at times it is even difficult to determine technically when the time of death has occurred. 23

Dying becomes lonely and impersonal because the patient is often taken out of his familiar environment and rushed to an emergency room. Whoever has been very sick and has required rest and comfort especially may recall his experience of being put on a stretcher and enduring the noise of the ambulance siren and hectic rush until the hospital gates open. Only those who have lived through this may appreciate the discomfort and cold necessity of such transportation which is only the beginning of a long ordeal—hard to endure when you are well, difficult to express in words when noise, light, pumps, and voices are all too much to put up with. It may well be that we might consider more the patient under the sheets and blankets and perhaps stop our well-meant efficiency and rush in order to hold the patient's hand, to smile, or to listen to a question. I include the trip to the hospital as the first episode in dying, as it is for many. I am putting it exaggeratedly in contrast to the sick man who is left at home—not to say that lives should not be saved if they can be saved by a hospitalization but to keep the focus on the patient's experience, his needs and his reactions. 24

When a patient is severely ill, he is often treated like a person with no right to   25
an opinion. It is often someone else who makes the decision if and when and
where a patient should be hospitalized. It would take so little to remember that the
sick person too has feelings, has wishes and opinions, and has—most important of
all—the right to be heard.

Well, our presumed patient has now reached the emergency room. He will be   26
surrounded by busy nurses, orderlies, interns, residents, a lab technician perhaps
who will take some blood, an electrocardiogram technician who takes the
cardiogram. He may be moved to X-ray and he will overhear opinions of his
condition and discussions and questions to members of the family. He slowly but
surely is beginning to be treated like a thing. He is no longer a person. Decisions
are made often without his opinion. If he tries to rebel he will be sedated and after
hours of waiting and wondering whether he has the strength, he will be wheeled
into the operating room or intensive treatment unit and become an object of great
concern and great financial investment.

He may cry for rest, peace, and dignity, but he will get infusions, transfusions,   27
a heart machine, or tracheotomy if necessary. He may want one single person to
stop for one single minute so that he can ask one single question—but he will get a
dozen people around the clock, all busily preoccupied with his heart rate, pulse,
electrocardiogram or pulmonary functions, his secretions or excretions but not
with him as a human being. He may wish to fight it all but it is going to be a useless
fight since all this is done in the fight for his life, and if they can save his life they
can consider the person afterwards. Those who consider the person first may lose
precious time to save his life! At least this seems to be the rationale or justification
behind all this—or is it? Is the reason for this increasingly mechanical, depersonalized
approach our own defensiveness? Is this approach our own way to cope with and
repress the anxieties that a terminally or critically ill patient evokes in us? Is our
concentration on equipment, on blood pressure, our desperate attempt to deny
the impending death which is so frightening and discomforting to us that we
displace all our knowledge onto machines, since they are less close to us than the
suffering face of another human being which would remind us once more of our
lack of omnipotence, our own limits and failures, and last but not least perhaps
our own mortality?

Maybe the question has to be raised: Are we becoming less human or more   28
human? . . . it is clear that whatever the answer may be, the patient is suffering
more—not physically, perhaps, but emotionally. And his needs have not changed
over the centuries, only our ability to gratify them.

▼ TOPICAL CONSIDERATIONS

1. To what does Kübler-Ross attribute the increased fear of death and related
   emotional problems in our society?
2. What point is Kübler-Ross illustrating in her anecdote of the farmer? How
   does the farmer's dying differ from the way most people die today?

3. According to the author, what are the potential dangers of excluding children from the experience of another's death?
4. What is the thrust of Kübler-Ross's argument regarding the treatment of terminally-ill patients? Do you agree with her view? Do you think that there is some justification for this kind of treatment?
5. To what does the author attribute the "depersonalized approach" to a patient's dying?

▼ RHETORICAL CONSIDERATIONS

1. Where in the essay does Kübler-Ross move from explanation to argument?
2. Where does the author give the thesis statement in this piece?
3. Divide this essay into three parts. Which paragraphs constitute the beginning? Which constitute the middle? Which constitute the end? Briefly explain how each of the parts are logically connected to each other.

▼ WRITING ASSIGNMENTS

1. The author opens her essay with a quotation. Write a paper in which you discuss the appropriateness of this quotation to the essay.
2. Do you recall your fear of death as a child? If so, try to describe it and any experiences that might have contributed to it.
3. Has anyone close to you ever died? If so, in a paper try to describe how you dealt with that person's death. In the process of grief did you feel conflicting emotions of shame, guilt, and anger?
4. Kübler-Ross recalls the memory of a farmer who took charge of his own dying. What would you do if you were so critically wounded?
5. The author criticizes the impersonal treatment of emergency-room patients. Did you ever find yourself in an emergency room? Did you think the treatment you received was "lonely, mechanical, and dehumanized"? Try to recapture the experience, whether you were the patient or someone you accompanied.
6. In a paper, try to explain what it means to "die with dignity." You may choose to refer to the Kübler-Ross essay or other readings. (You might first read the essay "It's Over, Debbie" and the editorial responses.) If possible, try to make your discussion concrete, even personal if possible.
7. Toward the end of this essay Kübler-Ross criticizes the "well-meant efficiency" of medical people. Do you think that cool efficiency of medical care is sometimes needed in order to save lives? Explore this question in a paper.

▼ AIDS: BEARING WITNESS

George Whitmore

It has been called the most devastating disease of the century. Since the first cases appeared in 1981, nearly 60,000 victims of "acquired immune deficiency syndrome" have been reported in America, and over half have resulted in death. The very name of AIDS produces responses of fear and uncertainty—and sometimes hysteria. Dozens of books have been written about the disease. One of the most gripping accounts is George Whitmore's *Someone Was Here: Profiles in the AIDS Epidemic* (1988), from which the following was adapted. Whitmore, a free-lance journalist who wrote about the brutal effects of AIDS on others, describes the impact of the disease upon himself. This article first appeared in the *New York Times Magazine* in 1988. Whitmore died of the disease in April 1989 at the age of 43.

> *And we go,*
> *And we drop like the fruits of*
> *the tree,*
> > *Even we,*
> > *Even so.*

— George Meredith
"Dirge in Woods"

Three years ago, when I suggested an article to the editors of this magazine on   1
"the human cost of AIDS," most reporting on the epidemic was scientific in nature and people with AIDS were often portrayed as faceless victims. By profiling a man with AIDS and his volunteer counselor from Gay Men's Health Crisis, I proposed to show the devastating impact AIDS was having on a few individual lives. It had certainly had an impact on mine. I suspected that I was carrying the virus and I was terrified.

Plainly, some of my reasons for wanting to write about AIDS were altruistic,   2
others selfish. AIDS was decimating the community around me; there was a need to bear witness. AIDS had turned me and others like me into walking time bombs; there was a need to strike back, not just wait to die. What I didn't fully appreciate then, however, was the extent to which I was trying to bargain with AIDS: If I wrote about it, maybe I wouldn't get it.

My article ran in May 1985. But AIDS didn't keep its part of the bargain. Less   3
than a year later, after discovering a small strawberry-colored spot on my calf, I was diagnosed with Kaposi's sarcoma, a rare skin cancer that is one of the primary indicators of acquired immune deficiency syndrome.

Ironically, I'd just agreed to write a book on AIDS. The prospect suddenly   4
seemed absurd, but "Write it," my doctor urged without hesitation. And on
reflection, I had to agree. I don't believe in anything like fate. And yet clearly,
along with what looked like a losing hand, I'd just been dealt the assignment of
a lifetime.

That I was able to take it on isn't as remarkable as some might think. Kaposi's   5
sarcoma alone, in the absence of the severe opportunistic infections that usually
accompany AIDS, can constitute a fortunate diagnosis. Many Kaposi's sarcoma
patients have lived five years and beyond. Although my own disease has steadily
accelerated, I'm one of the very lucky ones. Although increasingly disabled,
I haven't even been hospitalized yet.

I'm also hopeful—though it gives me pause to write that, since I value realism   6
and pragmatism over the ill-defined "positive attitude" I'm often counseled to
cultivate. Last summer, I began taking the antiviral drug AZT in an experiment to
test how it works in people with Kaposi's sarcoma. Partly because testing has been
completed on so few other drugs in this country, AZT or something like it is our
best hope for an AIDS treatment and, in spite of possible severe side effects, it has
already been shown to benefit other categories of people with AIDS. I have no
doubt that, administered in combination with drugs that boost the immune
system, antiviral drugs like AZT will eventually prolong the lives of countless
people like me.

But I don't want to give the impression that I'm patiently waiting, hands   7
folded, for that day to come.

When I began taking AZT, I bought a pill box with a beeper that reminds me   8
to take the medication every four hours. The beeper has a loud and insistent tone,
like the shrill pips you hear when a truck is backing up on the street. Ask anybody
who carries one—these devices insidiously change your life. You're always on the
alert, anticipating that chirp, scheming to turn off the timer before it can detonate.
It's relentless. It's like having AIDS. At regular intervals your body fails to perform
in some perhaps subtle, perhaps not new, but always alarming way. The clock is
always ticking. Every walk in the park might be your last. Every rent check is a
lease on another month's life. The beeper is a reminder that with chronic illness,
there is no real peace and quiet and no satisfaction, not without the sure prospect
of complete health. Paradoxically, this same sense of urgency and unrest enabled
me to write my book.

Needless to say, reporting on the AIDS epidemic from my particular point of   9
view has had its advantages and handicaps. My book includes my original article
on Jim Sharp, then 35, a New Yorker with AIDS, and Edward Dunn, 43, his
counselor from Gay Men's Health Crisis, both white gay men, like myself. But it
also profiles men, women and children, black and brown, in all walks of life, who
have been touched profoundly by AIDS, too. We are more alike than not. If I felt a
special affinity for Manuella Rocha, a Chicano woman in rural Colorado who
defied her family and community to nurse her son at home until his death in 1986,
it was in no small part because I recognized in her eyes the same thing I saw in my
own mother's eyes the day I gave her the news about myself. If I was scared sitting

for hours in an airless room in the South Bronx with a bunch of junkies with AIDS, it wasn't because I was scared of *them.* It was because their confusion and rage were precisely what I was feeling myself. The journalist's vaunted shield of objectivity was of little use at times like those. On the contrary, what often counted most wasn't my ability to function as a disinterested observer, but my ability to identify with my subjects.

Although some reporters might, I didn't need to be told what it feels like to   10
wait a week for biopsy results or to be briefed on the unresponsiveness of governments and institutions. Nor did I need to go out of my way to research issues of AIDS discrimination—not after I was informed at my neighborhood dental clinic, where I'd been treated for years, that they would no longer clean my teeth.

So, there's much to be said for subjective truth. Nevertheless, I worried for a   11
long time about the morality, even the feasibility, of producing a documentary-style piece of reportage like the one I'd contracted for—that is, without literally putting myself into it, in the first person. It wasn't until I found myself alone in a cabin in the woods, poised to write, that I began to confront just who that "first person" had become.

The Macdowell colony in Peterborough, N.H., is a collection of quaint artists'   12
studios, each isolated from the others on 450 acres of dense woodland. Since 1907, the colony has served as a retreat and a safe haven for generations of writers, composers and other artists, and it surely did for me. But it would be a lie to say that people who go there can escape; up there, in the woods, the world is very much with you. Up there, away from my constant lover and loving friends, at a certain remove from the Catherine wheel of death and mourning that my life in New York had become, off the treadmill of interviews and deadlines, I came face to face with everything I'd successfully evaded about AIDS.

Having it, for instance. Before I went to New Hampshire, it was still possible,   13
even necessary, to pretend that in some essential way I didn't have AIDS in order to keep working. As far as I know, no one I interviewed during the course of researching my book knew that I had AIDS. And the telltale marks hadn't spread to my face.

My body. I hadn't looked at it much.   14

Before I left for New Hampshire, at the Passover seder with my lover Michael's   15
family, we took turns reading the Haggadah in booklets illustrated with line drawings. When we reached the page with the plagues God brought down on the Egyptians, there was a locust, there was a dead fish with X's for eyes, there was the outline of a man with dots all over him, signifying boils. I stared at the cartoon of the man with the boils. I knew Michael, sitting next to me, was thinking the same thing. My body was like that now. I'd had three lesions 12 months before. Now there were three dozen.

One day in New Hampshire, in the shower, I looked at my body. It was as if I'd   16
never seen it before.

A transformation had taken place and it was written on my skin. When I met   17
Jim Sharp three years ago, I have to confess, I could only see a dying man. A

chasm had separated me from him and the other men with AIDS I interviewed for The Times. Even though they were gay, even though most of them were my own age, each one of them remained safely at arm's length. But now that chasm was breached and there was no safety.

Grief, despair, terror—these feelings easily come to mind when AIDS does. They threatened to engulf me when I began writing my book. But what about anger? 18

When you have AIDS, the fear and loathing, the black paranoia, the everlasting, excruciating uncertainty of AIDS colors everything. When you walk down the street with AIDS, everything in your path is an aggravation, an impediment, a threat—for what in your life isn't now? A cab overshoots the crosswalk. Someone at the head of the line is arguing with the bank teller. All the petty frustrations of urban life get magnified to the limit of tolerance. Not even the infirm old man counting out his pennies at the newsstand is exempt from your fury—or perhaps especially not him, for in the prime of life aren't you becoming just that: elderly and infirm? 19

It wasn't until I returned to the transcripts of my original interviews with Jim that I realized that he—a voluble ad man with a wicked sense of humor, a short fuse and an iron will to live—had a special gift for anger, and Jim was now speaking for me, too. 20

Anger, life-affirming anger was the lesson Jim, Manuella Rocha and that room full of addicts taught me. Without it, I couldn't have written about the ocean of pain and loss that surrounds us without drowning in it. 21

My article about Jim Sharp and Edward Dunn was a portrait of two strangers united in adversity. In 1984, after his lover died of AIDS, Edward felt compelled to volunteer at Gay Men's Health Crisis. He couldn't, he said, sit passively on the sidelines while the epidemic raged on. Jim's case was the first one assigned to Edward when he finished his training as a crisis counselor. It was Edward's job to help Jim negotiate the labyrinth of problems—medical, financial, legal—that an AIDS diagnosis entails. In time, they became remarkably good friends as well. 22

An intensely private person, Edward was willing to expose himself in a series of grueling interviews because he was, I think, desperate to make a difference. The sole stipulation he attached to our work together was that his lover be given a pseudonym. Edward wanted to spare "Robert's" family—who had never been able to acknowledge their son's homosexuality, even unto death—any possible hurt. 23

Soon after the article came out, Edward brought me a gift. It was a little teddy bear—a nice ginger-colored bear with a gingham ribbon tied around its neck—and I didn't know quite what to make of it. But Edward explained to me that he often gave teddy bears to friends, as they represented warmth and gentleness to him. Later, he asked me what I was going to name mine. 24

"I hadn't thought of naming it ... " 25

"Oh, you have to name him," Edward said. 26

"I don't know, what do you think?" 27

"I thought you might call him Robert." 28

That summer, Jim, a transplanted Texan, moved back to Houston from New York. Then, Edward moved to Los Angeles, saying it was time to begin a new life. Perhaps grandiosely, I wondered if our interviews hadn't played a part in Edward's decision to leave the city—that perhaps they'd served as something of a catharsis or a watershed. 29

Over the next year and a half, Robert the bear sat on the bookshelf in the hall and only came down when the cat knocked him down. Every once in a while, I'd find Robert on the floor, dust him off and put him back on the shelf. I felt vaguely guilty about Robert. I was no longer in touch with Edward. 30

It has been called "the second wave" of the AIDS epidemic. Its casualties include, in ever-increasing numbers, drug abusers, their wives and lovers, and their babies. I knew one of those babies. 31

I first saw Frederico—this is not his real name—one gloomy day last March, in the pediatrics ward at Lincoln Hospital in the South Bronx. Room 219, where Frederico was kept out of the way, is down the hall from the nurses' station. Not many people pass by its safety-glass windows. I doubt that I would have known Frederico even existed had I not been told about him by Sister Fran Whelan, a Catholic chaplain at the hospital. 32

Sister Fran, a petite woman with a neat cap of salt-and-pepper hair, was instrumental in getting me permission to visit Lincoln to observe its "AIDS team." For a few months, I sat in on meetings, went on rounds with its members, interviewed patients and health-care workers, and attended the weekly support group for people with AIDS. 33

In the early years of the epidemic, when Sister Fran, a member of the Dominican Sisters of the Sick Poor, began working at Lincoln, there were no more than one or two people with AIDS in the hospital at any given time. By last winter, there were always more than two dozen, with dozens more on the outpatient rolls. Virtually all of the AIDS patients at Lincoln, a huge municipal hospital, were heterosexual, virtually all were black or Hispanic. Although blacks and Hispanics account for some 20 percent of the United States population, they now represent, nationwide, 39 percent of those with AIDS. In the Bronx, rates of AIDS infection are believed to be among the highest in the nation. Currently, one out of 43 newborn babies there carries antibodies to the HIV virus, indicating that their mothers were infected. 34

When I first saw him, Frederico was 2½ years old and had been living at Lincoln for nine months. His mother, an alcoholic and former drug addict, had apparently transmitted the AIDS virus to him in the womb. The summer before, a few weeks before Frederico's father died from AIDS, his mother had left him in the hospital. Then she died of AIDS, too. From then on, Frederico was a "boarder baby," one of about 300 children living in New York City hospitals last March because accredited foster homes couldn't be found for them. Frederico happened to be disabled—he was born with cerebral palsy in addition to his HIV, or human immunodeficiency virus, infection—but lots of other children who were no longer ill and had no handicaps remained in hospital wards indefinitely. 35

Frederico's only visitor from the outside was a distant relation, a Parks 36

Department worker named Alfred Schult who came to the hospital religiously, on Tuesdays and Sundays. Frederico's mother had been, Mr. Schult later told me, "the daughter I never had." When she died, Mr. Schult sent a telegram to her widowed father in Florida. The telegram wasn't returned but it wasn't answered, either. Frederico's father's mother, who lived in the Bronx, visited him in the hospital once, I was told. She had custody of Frederico's 5-year-old brother, whom she'd sent to Puerto Rico to live with relatives. But no one in Frederico's father's family was willing to take Frederico. Nor was Mr. Schult, ailing himself, able to.

At 2½, Frederico couldn't talk. He couldn't sit up or stand. He couldn't hold a 37
bottle. Since he'd never had any of the cancers or opportunistic infections that spell AIDS, his official diagnosis was AIDS-related complex, or ARC. He had not, however, escaped the stigma of AIDS. Sister Marie Barletta, his patient advocate at the hospital, had to argue long and vigorously with authorities and submit reams of paperwork to get Frederico into a rehabilitation day-care program elsewhere. Unfortunately, just when he was about to go to day care, Frederico got a temperature, so day care was postponed.

The hospital personnel and the volunteers who held and fed Frederico did the 38
best they could.

The day Sister Fran took me to see Frederico, he was sleeping. We stood side 39
by side, peering into his crib.

That day, he was wearing mitts made of stretch-knit bandage material knotted 40
at one end and fastened around his wrists with adhesive tape. These were to keep him from scratching himself or pulling out tubes; sometimes Frederico had to be fed formula through a nasal-gastric tube taped to his cheek and nose, and sometimes he had to be given antibiotics intravenously.

The nurses on Frederico's floor noticed that he picked up everything, every 41
little fungus, every little infection.

Stuffed animals were lined up at the head of Frederico's crib. A musical 42
mobile of circus animals in primary colors was fastened to the headboard. A heart-shaped balloon with the words "I Love You" was tethered to the rail. Frederico was propped up in an infant carrier in the crib, facing a blank wall with a bed-lamp on it and a red sign that said No Smoking/No Fumar.

I stood next to Sister Fran, looking at Frederico. I heard a ringing in my ears. I 43
almost bolted out of the room. Somehow, I kept my feet planted where they were on the floor.

I'd seen eyes unblinking from lesions. I'd spoken into deaf ears. I'd held the 44
hand of a dying man. But nothing prepared me for this.

Frederico was beautiful. In his sleep, he expelled little sighs. His eyelids 45
twitched. He was very fair, with light brown curly hair. His skin was translucent. You could see violet veins through the skin of his eyelids.

I wanted to snatch him out of his crib, snatch him up and run away with him. 46
It was all at once horribly, cruelly clear that I wanted for Frederico what I wanted for myself, and I was powerless.

Later, walking down the hall beside Sister Fran, I struggled to retain my 47
composure.

"It's good the nurses saw you with me," Sister Fran was saying. "Now you can   48
come visit him lots, whenever you like, and there'll be no questions." Sister Fran
has her ways. She knew I'd come back.

And I did, more than once. I held Frederico in my arms. He smelled like urine   49
and baby powder, and he was quite a handful. He squirmed in my arms. I was a
stranger. He didn't know me. He wanted to be put down.

The day I first saw Frederico, when Sister Fran was distracted for a moment, I   50
took Robert the bear out of the plastic bag I was carrying and set him down
among the other stuffed animals in the crib. I had felt I shouldn't come empty-
handed. I knew Edward would approve. What I didn't know was that Edward had
AIDS and would die before the year was out.

Irony of ironies, Jim outlived Edward, the counselor sent to aid him in his   51
affliction.

Today, Jim lives in a modest bungalow house on a tree-lined street in   52
Houston, where I visited him last June. He's something of a celebrity and has
served on the board of the local AIDS foundation. He spends lots of time every
day on the phone, dispensing comfort and advice to other people with AIDS.
Among his other distinctions, Jim is probably the only man with AIDS in Texas
who has lived through the mandatory two-year waiting period there to collect
Medicare.

As we sat talking in Jim's living room, I noticed, on the mantelpiece, the   53
stuffed piranha Edward once brought back from Brazil and gave to him, joking
that, "This is what you look like when you don't get your way."

I remember vividly my reaction to the piranha, when I first interviewed Jim in   54
New York three years ago—with its slimy hide and repulsive grin, it was the
perfect image of AIDS to me. Now it seemed strange to see it in a living room in
Texas, alongside all the ordinary things people accumulate. Still fearsome, still
bristling with malevolence, the piranha had nevertheless somehow grown familiar,
almost domesticated, like the gnawing terror Jim and I and thousands like us have
had to learn to accommodate. Every time he has to go to the hospital, Jim told me,
he takes along the piranha. It's a kind of talisman.

A week after I got back from Texas, Mr. Schult called to tell me Frederico   55
was dead.

Things had been looking up for Frederico. Sister Barletta had finally gotten   56
him into day care. The agency had placed him in a foster home. But on his second
night outside the hospital, inexplicably, Frederico turned blue. By the time the
ambulance arrived, he was dead. And for some reason, I was told, the emergency
medical service didn't even try to revive him.

I went to the funeral parlor. The long, low, dim basement room in East   57
Harlem seemed full to overflowing with grieving women—Sister Barletta, the
women from Frederico's day-care center, nurses and volunteers who'd taken care
of Frederico in the hospital—all of them asking why.

Frederico's body lay up front in a little coffin lined with swagged white satin.   58
He was dressed in a blue playsuit with speedboats on it.

"You dressed him in a playsuit," I said to Mr. Schult, at my side.   59

"And now he's at play," Mr. Schult sobbed. "He's romping in heaven now with   60
Jesus like he never was able to down here."

I held Mr. Schult's arm tightly until the sobbing passed. I couldn't help but   61
notice, the coffin was too small for the top of the catafalque. You could see gouges
and scrapes and scars in the wood in the parts the coffin didn't cover. I looked
down into the coffin, at the body beyond help. I agreed aloud with Mr. Schult that
Frederico was in heaven now, because it seemed to make him feel a little better.

I don't know why, but I always thought Frederico would live.   62

▼ TOPICAL CONSIDERATIONS

1. Whitmore says that for awhile he felt that if he wrote about AIDS, maybe
   he wouldn't get it. What was the emotional "logic" behind this feeling?
2. How did Whitmore bear witness to AIDS discrimination?
3. When did Whitmore finally confront the fact that he had AIDS? How had
   he previously evaded the truth?
4. In her essay "On the Fear of Death," Elizabeth Kübler-Ross says that a
   universal reaction to death is anger. How does Whitmore characterize his
   own anger at having AIDS? How did anger help him cope?
5. How did Jim Sharp cope with his AIDS in Houston? Do you see a parallel
   between his life and Whitmore's own life? Why does Jim keep the stuffed
   piranha on his mantlepiece?
6. How has this article affected your own understanding of AIDS and AIDS
   victims?

▼ RHETORICAL CONSIDERATIONS

1. Consider George Whitmore's choice of titles. How appropriate is it? How
   does it connote the essential irony of Whitmore's plight?
2. In paragraph 8, Whitmore says his beeper is "like having AIDS." How does
   Whitmore specifically liken the two? How apt is the analogy?
3. How does "Robert" help link the story of Edward with that of Frederico?
   How else are they connected?
4. In his description of Frederico in his crib, Whitmore uses descriptive
   details to evoke in the reader strong emotions of pity and sorrow. What are
   some of the specific details and how do they create their effect?
5. Whitmore says that the piranha on Jim's mantlepiece was "the perfect
   image of AIDS." How effective a metaphor is this?
6. At the end of the essay, Whitmore says he couldn't help but notice that
   Frederico's "coffin was too small for the top of the catafalque. You could
   see gouges and scrapes and scars in the wood in the parts the coffin didn't
   cover." Why would Whitmore record these seemingly insignificant details?
   How do they symbolically comment on the child's life and death?

7. Evaluate the impact of the last sentence of the essay. Why is it rendered in a paragraph all its own? How does it connect to a theme early on in the essay?

▼ WRITING ASSIGNMENTS

1. As some have pointed out, AIDS is really two epidemics: that of a disease and that of fear. Fear not only manifests itself in irrational behavior— needless discrimination against victims of the disease—but it stirs up already built-in prejudices against homosexuals, minorities, and drug addicts. In a paper, explore your own attitudes towards AIDS victims. How has this article affected your attitudes?
2. Do you know anybody with AIDS or an AIDS-related condition? If so, write a paper about that person and how he or she has coped.
3. Many books and articles have been written on the subject of AIDS. Using some of these materials from the library, write a paper on how concerned individuals are working to slow the course of the disease and ease the suffering of its victims. Consider the work done at home, in schools, at churches and synagogues, at the workplace, on campus, in the arts and media, etc.

▼ A WAY TO SAY FAREWELL

Dr. Benjamin Spock

The subject of human death does not readily lend itself to upbeat reflections. However, we have found one that at least regards the matter in a positive spirit. Appropriately, it was written by America's most famous baby doctor who reflects on the end of a life—his own. "I don't want tiptoers around me. I want cheerful people who will look me in the eye." Dr. Spock, who was born in 1904 and who still actively writes on children, is the author of *Baby and Child Care,* which has sold more than 32 million copies. This article originally appeared in *Parade Magazine* in 1985.

Being in good health and of sound mind, except for absentmindedness and a poor memory for names, I'm not expecting to die for a long time—not if I can help it. But, at 81, I'd like to give some guidelines to my relatives. As far as I know, and one never knows for sure until his time comes, I don't fear the dying as long as it's not very painful or lonely or lacking in dignity.

I say "one never knows" because I've been surprised by the behavior of some physicians as they've died; by my own behavior when a patient died; and by the behavior of an old friend during a fatal illness.

It is a fairly common occurrence for a physician, who should know better, to ignore obvious symptoms of cancer in himself until it is too late for treatment, apparently preferring to hope against hope that his suspicion is not correct.

The mother of a patient of mine long ago called me in dismay at 7 a.m. to say that she had just found her infant son dead in his crib. I told her to rush him to a hospital that was close to their home, much closer than I was. If he was dead, I suggested she ask for an autopsy that would reassure her and her husband that there had been no neglect on their part. It was clear to me that they wanted me to meet with them—sooner or later—but I could not face them. I gave excuses. Years later, when I read that some staff people in hospitals tend to avoid, and thereby neglect, a patient who is dying, I understood. The fear of facing death is truly powerful.

A close, wise friend and colleague of mine (not a physician) died slowly and painfully of inoperable cancer. She was the sole support of three young children and should have been making careful plans for their future and discussing this with them. But she never asked anyone about her diagnosis. And, respecting her apparent wish to remain in ignorance, nobody ever volunteered the information. Each time I visited, I expected her finally to ask, and each time I was flabbergasted that she did not. Now, years later, I realize that she might have preferred a frank discussion with her doctor but had been put off by his reluctance to raise the issue. Perhaps she only was following his cue.

I'm reminded of an episode in Elisabeth Kübler-Ross's book *On Death and Dying,* in which she was asked by a physician to talk with his patient, whom he confidently believed did not know his diagnosis. She didn't want to shock the patient; on the other hand, she wanted to make it easy for him to communicate with her. So she simply asked, "How sick are you?" and he replied, "I am full of cancer." 6

This case made me realize that I would want a physician and a spouse who were, on the one hand, cheerful but who would not pretend that everything was lovely. I don't want around me solemn, whispering tiptoers. But I also don't want hearty, loud-voiced types who keep asking me, in a routine way, how I feel or whether there is anything I want. I want people, preferably attractive ones, who will look me in the eye in a friendly or even loving manner, discuss openly any of my concerns and ask only those questions that apply to my actual situation. 7

I would want my doctor to give any treatment available if it had a chance of curing me or keeping me alive and lively for a number of years. But I would not want to be kept alive with antibiotics, infusions, transfusions, anticancer drugs or radiation if they were just to postpone my death for a few months—especially if I had lost my marbles. 8

Having been brought up with a strong emphasis on the importance of appearances, I have a real dread of going visibly senile without realizing it. 9

I remember my distress when, some years ago, I happened to descend in a Plaza Hotel elevator with a famous architect. Though he was old, he still maintained a dashing appearance: a broad-brimmed but flat-topped cowboy hat such as Gary Cooper wore in *High Noon,* an expensive-looking suit and a flowing silk bow tie. His jacket, however, was dotted with food spots. He seemed carefree, but I felt deeply embarrassed for him. Since then, I've inspected my jacket carefully each morning, though I realized at that time that, if senility sets in, I will have forgotten this precaution. 10

Of course, the reason that physicians often will go to such extremes to keep a hopelessly ill patient alive is because their job, their training and their ethics direct them to do so. Besides, they can be sued by a disgruntled relative for not having done everything conceivable. 11

When I wonder what directions to leave, I realize that, in addition to my own wishes, there will be my wife's feelings and my doctor's ethics to consider. For instance, even though I've decided in advance that I want to be put out of my misery if the pain proves unbearable, will my doctor be willing to give the necessary dose of medication—or to leave it handy—and will Mary have the nerve to jab the needle? 12

The omission of artificial life-support systems is only one aspect of being allowed to die naturally. I would want to be at home, if that wasn't too burdensome, or in a hospice, rather than in a hospital. I have been a frequent patient in hospitals, and I am grateful for having had excellent doctors and nurses. But hospitals are nothing like home. They are more like factories—clean, modern factories to produce diagnoses and treatments. A stream of staffers barges in, as if 13 from outer space: history taker, physical examiners, temperature and pulse takers, meal servers, bath givers, stretcher pushers, X-ray technicians, bed makers, pill pushers, specimen takers. Not one of them is primarily interested in the person, of course.

In recent years, the hospice movement, which began in England, has spread over the U.S. The aim is to let the person die as pleasantly as possible in a homelike setting, surrounded by family and some familiar possessions and spared pain by regular, heavy medication—without any fussing that is not provided solely for comfort. That's the departure for me.   14

I'd also like to have something to say about my memorial service, though I don't expect to be looking down from heaven at the time of the event. I don't like to think of myself as being unceremoniously buried or burned up without some kind of service to mark my passage from person to memory.   15

I dislike intensely the atmosphere of the conventional funeral: the darkened room, the solemn people, silent or whispering or sniffling, the funeral director's assistants pretending to feel mournful. My ideal would be the New Orleans black funeral, in which friends snake-dance through the streets to the music of a jazz band. But a satisfactory compromise would be a church service for my friends to think of me together for an hour and say farewell.   16

I would like the people to be normally noisy and cheerful. The music might consist of the ragtime and jazz to which I love to dance in order to liberate myself from my puritanical upbringing, lively hymns, and such tunes as "The Battle Hymn of the Republic" and "America the Beautiful," which always choke me up, not with sorrow but with exultation. I like the service for the dead delivered in the rich cadences that have come down to us through the centuries. I'd like the minister, preferably William Sloane Coffin Jr., who enjoys life and with whom I was put on trial for our opposition to the Vietnam war, to speak of our hope that the peacemakers really will prevail. And some child-development person or parent could speak of my belief in the infinite perfectibility of children and of my agreement with Jesus' words: "Suffer little children, and forbid them not, to come unto me: for of such is the kingdom of heaven."   17

Then there could be a cheerful cocktail party somewhere nearby.   18

▼ TOPICAL CONSIDERATIONS

1. What three examples does Spock give to show that one never knows what his own reaction to death will be?
2. Spock says that he doesn't want "solemn, whispering tiptoers" at his deathbed. What type of person does he want?
3. Why would Spock prefer hospice care to hospital care in the event of a long terminal illness?
4. What kind of memorial service does Spock say he would like for himself? What kind of service would you design for yourself? Consider your choice of place, guests, music, speakers, and readings.

▼ RHETORICAL CONSIDERATIONS

1. What single detail makes Dr. Spock's description of the aging architect poignant?
2. Find examples where Spock concludes a very serious, potentially grim series of sentences with a short, clipped, and cheerful remark. Why does he do this?
3. Why does Spock begin the piece with the phrase, "being in good health and of sound mind"? What is the effect?

▼ WRITING ASSIGNMENTS

1. Write an essay describing the way someone you know dealt with death.
2. Read Elizabeth Kübler-Ross's essay, "On the Fear of Death" on page 469 in this text, then write an essay expressing your reaction to her ideas.
3. Write a mock will in which you lay down the guidelines for your own funeral. Design the kind of service you would like to have specifying the guests, location, music, readings, etc.

ACKNOWLEDGMENTS

▼ ACKNOWLEDGMENTS

TO THE STUDENT

If we are to make THE CONTEMPORARY READER a better book next time, we must know what students think of what we've already done. Please help us by filling out this questionnaire and returning it to English Editor, Scott, Foresman/Little, Brown Higher Education, 1900 East Lake Avenue, Glenview, IL 60025.

School: _____ Course title: _____

Instructor's name: _____

Other required texts: _____

Tell us what you think about the readings.

	Liked best				Liked least	Did not read
Gregory, "Shame"	5	4	3	2	1	_____
Staples, "Black Men and Public Space"	5	4	3	2	1	_____
Francke, "The Ambivalence of Abortion"	5	4	3	2	1	_____
Angelou, "Graduation"	5	4	3	2	1	_____
Ephron, "A Few Words About Breasts"	5	4	3	2	1	_____
Hughes, "Salvation"	5	4	3	2	1	_____
Wakefield, "Returning to Church"	5	4	3	2	1	_____
Barry, "It's In the Genes"	5	4	3	2	1	_____
Neal, "My Grandmother, the Bag Lady"	5	4	3	2	1	_____
Kozol, "Rachel and Her Children"	5	4	3	2	1	_____
Fasel, "A Son on His Own"	5	4	3	2	1	_____
Reese/Abramson, "Homosexuality: One Family's Affair"	5	4	3	2	1	_____
Williams, "Daddy Tucked the Blanket"	5	4	3	2	1	_____
Baker, "In My Day . . ."	5	4	3	2	1	_____
Bombeck, "Technology's Coming . . . Technology's Coming"	5	4	3	2	1	_____
Weltner, "Stripping Down to Bare Happiness"	5	4	3	2	1	_____
Anscombe, "Stranger Than Fiction"	5	4	3	2	1	_____
Ward, "They Also Wait Who Stand and Serve Themselves"	5	4	3	2	1	_____
White, "Once More to the Lake"	5	4	3	2	1	_____
Thurber, "Courtship Through the Ages"	5	4	3	2	1	_____
Mackintosh, "Masculine/Feminine"	5	4	3	2	1	_____
Dubik, "An Officer and a Feminist"	5	4	3	2	1	_____
Raspberry, "Homemaking"	5	4	3	2	1	_____
Syfers, "I Want a Wife"	5	4	3	2	1	_____
Perrin, "The Androgynous Male"	5	4	3	2	1	_____
Trillin, "Success"	5	4	3	2	1	_____
Boggs, "Finding the Fury"	5	4	3	2	1	_____
Quinn, "The Jeaning of America—and the World"	5	4	3	2	1	_____
Britt, "That Lean and Hungry Look"	5	4	3	2	1	_____
Royko, "Farewell to Fitness"	5	4	3	2	1	_____
McManus, "The Backpacker"	5	4	3	2	1	_____
Kratcoski, "What Did Kids Do Before Television Was Invented?"	5	4	3	2	1	_____
Winn, "The Plug-In Drug"	5	4	3	2	1	_____
Goodman, "The Violence Is Fake, the Impact Is Real"	5	4	3	2	1	_____
Boyd, "Packaged News"	5	4	3	2	1	_____
Newsweek, "MTV's Message"	5	4	3	2	1	_____
O'Rourke, "Why I Quit Watching Television"	5	4	3	2	1	_____
Greenfield, "Don't Blame TV"	5	4	3	2	1	_____
Ciardi, "Is Everybody Happy?"	5	4	3	2	1	_____
Rooney, "Advertising"	5	4	3	2	1	_____
O'Neill, "The Language of Advertising"	5	4	3	2	1	_____

Will, "Printed Noise"	5	4	3	2	1	_____
White, "Resisting Those Awful Commercials"	5	4	3	2	1	_____
King, Jr., "Pilgrimage to Nonviolence"	5	4	3	2	1	_____
Gansberg, "38 Who Saw Murder Didn't Call the Police"	5	4	3	2	1	_____
Will, "A West Coast Story"	5	4	3	2	1	_____
Buchalter, "Why I Bought a Gun"	5	4	3	2	1	_____
Morrow, "It's Time to Ban Handguns"	5	4	3	2	1	_____
Goldwater, "Why Gun Control Laws Don't Work"	5	4	3	2	1	_____
Anonymous, "It's Over, Debbie"	5	4	3	2	1	_____
Letters to the editors in response to "It's Over, Debbie"	5	4	3	2	1	_____
Buckley, Jr., "It Isn't Working"	5	4	3	2	1	_____
Rangel, "Legalize Drugs? Not on Your Life"	5	4	3	2	1	_____
Koch, "Death and Justice: How Capital Punishment Affirms Life"	5	4	3	2	1	_____
Bruck, "The Death Penalty"	5	4	3	2	1	_____
Sancton, "What On Earth Are We Doing?"	5	4	3	2	1	_____
Rettie, "But a Watch in the Night: A Scientific Fable"	5	4	3	2	1	_____
Eiseley, "How Natural is Natural?"	5	4	3	2	1	_____
Thomas, "Man's Role on Earth"	5	4	3	2	1	_____
Hubbell, "Caterpillar Afternoon"	5	4	3	2	1	_____
Dyer, "A Cruel Universe, but the Only One Where Humans Could Exist"	5	4	3	2	1	_____
Gould, "Were Dinosaurs Dumb?"	5	4	3	2	1	_____
Schell, "The Effects of a Nuclear Explosion"	5	4	3	2	1	_____
Kinsley, "Nuclear Holocaust in Perspective"	5	4	3	2	1	_____
Sagan, "Star Wars: The Leaky Shield"	5	4	3	2	1	_____
Heston, "The Peace Movement"	5	4	3	2	1	_____
Buchwald, "Evacuating the Capital? No Need to Hurry Now!"	5	4	3	2	1	_____
Schrank, "Sport and the American Dream"	5	4	3	2	1	_____
Whitney, "Playing to Win"	5	4	3	2	1	_____
Keillor, "Attitude"	5	4	3	2	1	_____
Angell, "On the Ball"	5	4	3	2	1	_____
Parker, "On the Bench"	5	4	3	2	1	_____
Abbey, "Blood Sport"	5	4	3	2	1	_____
Morton, "The Jogger's Code"	5	4	3	2	1	_____
Morrow, "If Slang is Not a Sin"	5	4	3	2	1	_____
Cohn, "Nuclear Language and How We Learned to Pat the Bomb"	5	4	3	2	1	_____
Rivers, "Rock Lyrics and Violence Against Women"	5	4	3	2	1	_____
Lawrence, "Four Letter Words Can Hurt"	5	4	3	2	1	_____
Jones, "What's Wrong with Black English"	5	4	3	2	1	_____
Baker, "Little Red Riding Hood Revisited"	5	4	3	2	1	_____
From the Columbia Journalism Review, "Two-Headed Monsters"	5	4	3	2	1	_____
Thomas, "On Natural Death"	5	4	3	2	1	_____
Kübler-Ross, "On the Fear of Death"	5	4	3	2	1	_____
Whitmore, "AIDS: Bearing Witness"	5	4	3	2	1	_____
Spock, "A Way to Say Farewell"	5	4	3	2	1	_____

1. Are there any contemporary topics not covered that you would like to see included? _____

_____

2. What magazines do you read regularly? _____

_____

3. May we quote you in our promotional efforts for this book? _____

_____

Date   Signature

THE CONTEMPORARY READER

INSTRUCTOR'S MANUAL

THIRD EDITION

▼CONTENTS

THE CONTEMPORARY READER

INSTRUCTOR'S MANUAL

THIRD EDITION

▼PREFACE

This instructor's manual provides answers to the questions asked after each selection in THE CONTEMPORARY READER, Third Edition. Such answers do not presume to do the work for the instructor; they are just meant to help. Certainly these answers are not exhaustive or the only ones appropriate, and I hope that students and instructors will conspire to provide others.

Gary Goshgarian

▼PART 1   PERSONAL DISCOVERIES

Dick Gregory SHAME

TOPICAL CONSIDERATIONS

1. This is really up to the students. They need to draw on their own insights and experiences.
2. Gregory describes Helene as light-complexioned, clean, well-mannered, popular, and smart in school. His choice of adjectives suggests that success to him means being socially acceptable. It seems fairly obvious that he felt this way because of the extreme poverty of his home. Students can answer the rest of the questions on their own.
3. The first question is more for students to consider based on what they perceive happened with Gregory as a child. It is possible to argue that Gregory's own actions prompted the teacher to make a scene, but outward circumstances deserve, perhaps, a larger share of the blame. The teacher's lack of sensitivity intensified Gregory's embarrassment instead of easing or removing it. On a deeper level, his home environment was perhaps the real culprit. Your students can discuss whether any of us *need* to feel shame when the circumstances are beyond our control. Shame to Gregory meant not being clean, having to wipe his nose on his hand because he didn't have a handkerchief, wearing clothes that didn't fit, being on relief, not having a Daddy—all of which added up to not "belonging," being different, being an outcast. Gregory's refusal to go to school after this incident, of course, is not the only way he could have handled the situation. But returning to school might have demanded more courage and been more difficult than could be expected of a seven-year-old.
4. Helene Tucker symbolized all that Gregory lacked in order to be socially acceptable. His attempt to impress her that day in the classroom was motivated by his desire to hide or overcome this lack. When he failed, his shame was intensified. Achieving goals that would be impressive enough to win Helene's approval would mean erasing the sense of failure this incident had created.

Although this was obviously a successful motivational device, students can no doubt suggest others from their own experience.

5. Gregory doesn't tell us exactly how he was finally able to get Helene Tucker out of his system, but that he was married and making money are significant clues. Obviously, once he had become successful and socially acceptable, he no longer felt the need to prove himself to anyone. He had passed the test.

6. From Gregory's account, the teacher appears to have been extremely insensitive. It might be useful to have students consider whether they feel his point of view is biased or objective. They might discuss how the teacher would have described the incident. It is up to the students to decide how else the teacher might have handled the situation. One answer might be that she could have allowed Gregory to pledge an amount of money and then spoken to him about it afterward.

7. This is really up to the students.

RHETORICAL CONSIDERATIONS

1. In the first two sentences, it is a succinct, attention-getting opening that leads logically into the narrative.

2. Light-complexioned, clean, smart. These are useful adjectives. They give clues as to why Gregory was in love with Helene and, more importantly, why he felt inferior. It's a good number of adjectives—more would overdo it. It might be useful to point out to students that adjectives should be used sparingly and with a distinct purpose.

3. NARRATIVE: Several of the paragraphs are developed by example. The last paragraph is a good sample passage.

4. The first paragraph is a good example of how Gregory tells and shows how he feels about Helene. He tells us he was in love with her. He then gives several narrative examples of how he acted, which shows that he was in love with her. He explains that he brushed his hair before going to school, got a handkerchief so that he wouldn't have to wipe his nose on his hand, and washed his only shirt and socks out every night so that he could be clean. He mentions that the latter often made him sick because they were sometimes wet when he put them on for school.

5. The tone is more straightforward, sincere, plain-talking. He isn't being funny. There is no verbal irony in his narrative.

6. Gregory introduces his narrative by telling us that school taught him what shame is. But it isn't until his conclusion that he fully *explains* what shame meant to him. Yes, this is effective. Because of the narrative incident that precedes this explanation, the reader understands better what Gregory means. The conclusion gives a perspective on the incident while avoiding any redundancy or unnecessary repetition. The last sentence is a succinct reminder of the crux of the problem.

Brent Staples **BLACK MEN AND PUBLIC SPACE**

TOPICAL CONSIDERATIONS

1. The encounter with the fleeing woman, which happened when he was ten years younger, made Staples realize how as a black man he could "alter public space in ugly ways." In particular, how at night he was indistinguishable from one of the muggers who "occasionally seeped into the area ¡from the surrounding ghetto." The realization, says Staples, "surprised, embarrassed, and dismayed" him "all at once." He adds, "Her flight made me feel like an accomplice in tyranny."
2. In paragraph 2, Staples says that were he to stumble upon somebody armed and threatened he could easily be shot just for being black. Farther on he mentions how he was once mistaken for a burglar in the office of the magazine for which he wrote. Also, how a jewelry store proprietor feeling the same apprehension brought out her Doberman pinscher only because he was black.
3. Part of his explanation is that he was one of the few "good boys" growing up in a neighborhood of gang warfare, knifings, and murder. He says he chose to be noncombatant and timid as the result of having seen too many young men killed including family members and friends.
4. After his story about another black journalist being mistaken for a murderer, Staples' own smothering of rage seems wise. In paragraph 11, he explains that not doing so "would surely have led to madness."
5. He lists several strategies: giving "wide berth to nervous people on subway platforms," trying not to appear as if he's following people, remaining "calm and extremely congenial" when questioned by police. He also says he has taken to whistling classical tunes to reduce tension of nighttime pedestrians.
6. FOR THE STUDENT: This question might generate some lively discussion since some students might argue that Staples goes too far not to intimidate—for example, why should a nonviolent black man have to go out of his way to make others feel at ease with his presence? Others might find his strategies socially responsible. There are still others who might be able to identify with the threat Staples poses, whether they are black or white. A large male, no matter what his race, is aware of the threat he poses to a lone woman walking on a deserted street. Of course, the key issue here is race, and black men are aware of the burden of the urban mugger stereotype.

RHETORICAL CONSIDERATIONS

1. The opening line is provocative. It makes the reader want to go on. Victim is a charged word, yet the woman is simply a victim of Staples' blackness.
2. Staples is trying to delineate the image from which the woman fled—a large, young black man with "a beard and billowing hair" and wearing a military jacket with his hands shoved into the pockets. The image in context of the deserted night streets of affluent, predominantly white Hyde Park at the edge of

a black ghetto is menacing particularly, as Staples sadly learns, because he is black.

3. There are some mildly humorous places, mostly ironic in intent. For instance, in paragraph 2 the author says how he is "scarcely able to take a knife to a raw chicken—let alone hold one to a person's throat." Most of the humor resides in the final paragraph in images of him whistling Beethoven and Vivaldi. In particular, the final two lines are amusing in a darkly ironic way.

Linda Bird Francke THE AMBIVALENCE OF ABORTION

TOPICAL CONSIDERATIONS

1. A new baby would preclude her husband's option of changing his career at the same time as it would put the author "right back in the nursery," just when her youngest child was finally in school and when she had taken on a full-time job after so many years of part-time freelancing.

2. They are nervous, ill at ease. None of the men speak to each other, knowing that they "had to be there, wishing they weren't." She notices a depressed embarrassment for being at the clinic.

3. Francke says that shame links the rather disparate group of women. Those pregnant women were "losing life that day, not giving it."

4. She panicked because of a crisis of conscience. There she was, a woman who cherished life, now in an abortion clinic. Her political convictions about a woman's right to have an abortion are stripped away as she suddenly faces the reality of what she is about to do. She adds that she would still defend a woman's right to have an abortion, but for her there is a moral crisis.

5. She had always supported a woman's right to have an abortion. I do not think she experienced any change of heart.

6. By "modern" she means "liberated," "enlightened" by the principles espoused by the women's movements of the last decade, particularly that right "to exercise the option of motherhood." But "modern" also carries the kind of political cold-mindedness that comes from adherence to abstractions, which crumble for her when she herself faces the termination of the fetus growing inside her.

7. This might suggest female conventionality—a stereotypical need to be saved from a bad decision by a man. But I think her fantasy goes beyond rigid sexual roles of heroic rescuer and helpless damsel in distress. She is close to the edge of turning back, and she seems to want her husband—whom she treats as an equal throughout—to convince her by bursting into the operating room and pulling her back.

8. She will be haunted for a long time by that little ghost of the last paragraph.

RHETORICAL CONSIDERATIONS

1. Ambivalence is the state of having contradictory thoughts or feelings about a particular matter. In this case, the contradiction that besets the author is both

wanting to have an abortion and not wanting to have one. The ambivalence is illustrated immediately when the pregnancy is "heralded" with "shocked silence and Scotch" instead of with "champagne and hope." She begins to discuss her ambivalence directly in paragraph 13.

2. The repetition signals that they are trying to convince themselves that there was no room in their lives for another baby. She repeats herself twice in paragraph 27: the first occasion, like that in paragraph 3, shows how much they are trying to convince themselves that "it certainly does make more sense not to be having a baby right now"; the second emphasizes the persistent ambivalence, "Of course, we have room," "Of course, we do," which perhaps comes closer to the truth.

3. She is never sentimental, which is why this is so powerful a piece of writing.

4. The change, a euphemistic one, conceals the fact that abortions are performed there—a change that reflects a conflict with antiabortion attitudes of the community.

5. Her seemingly neutral stance is a way of highlighting the irony that the procedure of abortion is so simple and easy in contrast with the anxiety she suffers.

6. She is fairly neutral in describing the other women in the clinic, although her description of the youngest Puerto Rican girl with head lowered in shame while refusing birth control options is a pathetic one.

7. The smiling aide is responding to the woman's fear of physical pain. The image of the woman doing a jig later on that day counters the potentially crippling effect of the operation on the spirit—one the author experiences.

8. She is being sardonic here. Women suffer most during abortion.

9. The image is a powerful metaphor of the aborted baby as a flower wrapped in a wet towel like a diaper, with the plastic bag functioning as both the placental sac and a suffocation chamber. The image captures the ambivalence at once.

10. The switch to the present tense demonstrates how even now—years later—she has not gotten over the emotional anguish of her decision and perhaps never will. The paragraph will always be in the present tense.

Maya Angelou **GRADUATION**

TOPICAL CONSIDERATIONS

1. Angelou remarks that all the children had "graduation epidemic" and "trembled visibly with anticipation." She remembers that graduating students frequently forgot their books, tablets, and pencils; the younger children fell all over themselves to loan them theirs. Everyone was involved in the preparations: Small children rehearsed their songs. Older girls prepared refreshments and older boys made sets and stage scenery. Parents ordered new shoes and clothes from Sears and Roebuck or Montgomery Ward. Seamstresses were hired to make graduation dresses and alter secondhand pants. Even the subject for the minister's sermon on the preceding Sunday was graduation. Apparently Stamps

did not have many important occasions. The people were poor, and many of their children did not continue on to college. Graduation was the high point of their educational career.

2. Booker T. Washington was a black leader who discouraged political dissent or rebellion and promoted the idea that the blacks' interests could be better served by improving their education than by political agitation. Black political activists have criticized Washington's views as promoting an attitude of subservience. Such an attitude seemed inherent in the response of the principal and assembly to Mr. Donleavy's speech. In his introduction, the principal mumbled something about "the friendship of kindly people to those less fortunate than themselves" and spoke of gratitude for Mr. Donleavy's being able to make time in his busy schedule to speak at the graduation ceremony. Angelou comments, too, that during the speech, "Amens and Yes sir's began to fall around the room like rain through a ragged umbrella."

3. Angelou remarks that she felt something unrehearsed and unpleasant was about to occur when the choir director and principal unexpectedly signaled for everyone to be seated for the prayer after the singing of the American National Anthem and the Pledge of Allegiance. She noticed, too, that the principal's voice had changed when he returned to the dais following the prayer. Angelou comments that the Amens and Yes sir's became fewer and fewer as Mr. Donleavy's speech progressed. Those which could be heard "lay dully in the air with the heaviness of habit." Later, she comments that "the man's dead words fell like bricks around the auditorium." Mr. Donleavy's speech implied that black children could aspire only to be maids and farmers, handymen and washerwomen. He praised the nearby white school graduates for the academic achievements but held up black athletes as the only models for the black students. As Angelou points out, "The white kids were going to have a chance to become Galileos and Madame Curies and Edisons and Gauguins, and our boys (the girls weren't even in on it) would try to be Jesse Owenses and Joe Louises."

4. Angelou resents the condescension in Mr. Donleavy's remarks. Numerous historical and literary allusions suggest that there was more academic excellence than Mr. Donleavy was aware of. Angelou could say the preamble to the Constitution faster than her brother, Bailey, and knew the names of the presidents in chronological and alphabetical order. The title of Henry Reed's valedictory speech quoted Hamlet's famous line: "To Be or Not to Be." Bailey gave Angelou a book of poems by Edgar Allen Poe, and they both walked through the rows of dirt in the garden reciting "Annabel Lee." The daughter of the Baptist minister recited "Invictus" at the graduation exercises. Historical allusions include Galileo, Madame Curie, Edison, and Gauguin. Angelou mentions, too, that students had drawn "meticulous maps," learned how to spell decasyllabic words, and memorized "The Rape of Lucrece."

5. Just as the assembly was about to sing the Negro National Anthem, the graduation ceremony was interrupted so that Mr. Donleavy could be introduced to give his speech. Questions 3 and 4 illustrate what happened after this.

Mr. Donleavy's speech left everyone feeling despondent and defeated. Very few could appreciate the idealistic philosophizing about future aspirations in Henry Reed's speech "To Be or Not to Be." It wasn't until Henry Reed, sensing the despondency, abruptly stopped speaking and began leading the graduating class in the singing of the Negro National Anthem that Angelou and the rest of the assembly were able to regain their pride and confidence in themselves. The Anthem inspired them to forge ahead in spite of the implications in Mr. Donleavy's remarks. If they had sung the anthem earlier, it would not have meant as much and would have been lost in Mr. Donleavy's talk.

6. Gregory, too, as a child had felt the shame of being considered not good enough or smart enough. He, too, had been made to feel that he was inferior and must take a back seat to those with more money and better advantages. He could have told them about his moment of shame and how he had overcome it. He could have inspired them to become not just athletes but Galileos, Madame Curies, Edisons, or Gauguins, if that was what they chose to be.

7. Given Angelou's later achievements, you could say that she began her life that day when the entire graduating class sang the Negro National Anthem and gained renewed inspiration to forge ahead in response to Henry Reed's challenging speech "To Be or Not to Be."

RHETORICAL CONSIDERATIONS

1. Children "trembled with anticipation" and adults were "excited." They all had "graduation epidemic." Junior students were "anxious" to help. Graduating students were "travelers with exotic destinations" who "strutted" around school like "nobility." Younger students "fell all over themselves" to loan them forgotten school supplies. Angelou's word choices emphasize the excitement everyone felt in preparing for graduation. Such an emphasis, in turn, accentuates the heaviness of the atmosphere when Mr. Donleavy gave his speech.

2. Angelou describes the incident from the point of view of a graduating eighth grader much involved in the preparation and ceremony. Her immediate, first-hand account creates for the reader a sense of closeness to the events and promotes empathy for the black students and their families. Although Angelou writes from a distinct point of view, her account seems fairly accurate. Bailey, being older and no longer directly involved with graduation, might have told the incident with more detachment. He might have compared his own graduation to Angelou's or discussed what could be expected to take place after graduation. The minister, too, would have brought a more detached point of view to the occasion. He might have offered a philosophical discussion of the moral implications of the event. Mr. Donleavy might have remarked on the respectful sobriety of the audience, emphasized the problems involved with his even being able to attend the ceremony, and continued the essay with a discussion of more significant items on his agenda for that day.

3. Rain falling through a ragged umbrella suggests a dejected, defenseless, neglected condition. Angelou uses numerous figures of speech: In preparing for graduation,

former years of isolation were left behind as "hanging ropes of parasitic moss." The morning of graduation was like young childhood, whereas the hours that followed resembled the maturity of an adult. Children dressed in crepe-paper dresses and butterfly wings dashed about on the evening of graduation "like fireflies." The principal's voice introducing Mr. Donleavy was "like a river diminishing to a stream and then to a trickle." Mr. Donleavy's "dead words fell like bricks." Professor Parsons sat like a "sculptor's reject." At the end of the ceremony, the echoes of the Negro National Anthem "shivered" in the air. The assembly had been in "icy," "dark" waters but had risen to the surface to a "bright sun" that "spoke to our souls."

4. Angelou uses numerous specific, concrete details. This is a good opportunity to point out to students that specific words are more effective than general ones. Instead of saying that it never hurt younger students to call older students nicknames, Angelou remarks: "It never hurt a sixth grader to have a play sister in the eighth grade, or a tenth-year student to be able to call a twelfth grader Bubba." Instead of stating generally that a nearby Negro school trained students for agricultural and mechanical jobs, Angelou refers to "South's A & M (Agricultural and Mechanical) schools, which trained Negro youths to be carpenters, farmers, handymen, masons, maids, cooks, and baby nurses." She doesn't say simply that parents ordered new clothes from a mail-order store but instead: "Parents . . . had ordered new shoes and ready-made clothes for themselves from Sears and Roebuck and Montgomery Ward." The younger children weren't just rehearsing their skit. They were "practicing their hops and their little songs that sounded like silver bells."

Nora Ephron A FEW WORDS
ABOUT BREASTS

TOPICAL CONSIDERATIONS

1. This is up to the students. It might be interesting to ask students if they think today's views of what makes a woman attractive are the same as in the fifties and sixties. If the fashion world or movie industry are accurate barometers, large breasts aren't worshiped as much as they once were. If they are not, would fewer women identify with Ephron's dilemma?

2. Ephron apparently believes that the heart-to-heart conversation with the wife of a Lutheran minister who was the mother of one of her boyfriends was a significant cause. This incident was the beginning of "a never-ending string of women" remarking to her about breast size. On a deeper level, Ephron's obsession reflects a typical teenager's feelings about her physical appearance. Such feelings seem natural enough because the teenage years are a self-conscious age when young people fix their attention on what they look like. Adults can have the same or similar hangups. They often worry about not being tall enough, being too tall, being overweight, underweight, wearing glasses, having an unattractive nose, eyes that are too close together. The list can go on and on.

3. Ephron claims that she is stuck with her obsession. But she admits that she has grown up enough to understand that "my feelings have very little to do with the reality of my shape." It does seem that, as teenagers grow up and become adults, they gain enough poise and confidence that they can turn their thoughts away from too much stress on physical appearance.

4. A woman traditionally stayed home to raise the children while her husband pursued a career outside the home. The husband was expected to be stronger and more capable and more intelligent than his wife and to assume a superior role. His wife was supposed to submit passively to her husband's views. Women faced economic and legal discrimination. Men's and women's roles don't appear to be as rigid as they once were. There is more flexibility and equality in the relationships between them. Women's legal and economic status have improved. Often both husband and wife have careers outside the home. Women are able to pursue careers that in previous years were open only to men (law, construction, the military), and are recognized for their strength and intelligence. Men, too, are freer to express gentleness and sensitivity and to demonstrate "mothering" qualities. Both parents in the family are encouraged to share the responsibility for caring for the children. Economic conditions requiring that both spouses work, larger numbers of women entering the work force and becoming financially independent, and support for ERA have had much influence on the changing attitudes toward the sex roles of men and women.

5. Motion picture sex symbols of the fifties included Spencer Tracy, Cary Grant, James Dean, Rock Hudson, Marilyn Monroe, Jayne Mansfield, Brigitte Bardot, Lauren Bacall, and Jane Russell. The men were usually tall, dark, and handsome, and the women were sultry and beautiful. This question is designed to encourage the students to consider whether motion picture or television idols of today fit the same stereotype. Dustin Hoffman is perhaps a good example of a star who doesn't fit this mold. Likewise, Woody Allen characters are self-conscious parodies of the traditional cinematic heroes. Today we have Mel Gibson, Sylvester Stallone, and Richard Gere as well as Kim Basinger, Sigourney Weaver and Kate Capshaw—all of whom are promoted for their sex-symbol qualities, among others. We'll leave this one for the students.

RHETORICAL CONSIDERATIONS

1. Angry. Gregory's essay also expresses some anger. But it is more serious and thoughtful. Angelou's essay is serious and thoughtful as well.

2. Ephron varies the length of her sentences. She often positions short ones at the beginning or end of a paragraph (the first sentence in paragraph 8, the only sentence in paragraph 9, the last two sentences in paragraph 10, and the last sentence in the essay), which gives them added emphasis and helps create the forceful, angry tone.

3. Yes. A woman's breasts are ordinarily a taboo subject.

4. Ephron's thesis is developed in stages. After describing two conversations with women about breast size, Ephron introduces her thesis with a question: "Why

do women say these things to me?" Later, she rephrases the question: "Why do I deserve it?" Her answer to these questions fully states the thesis. Implicit in it is the view that women who make such remarks are motivated by a competitive impulse and that, regardless of how much they belie the point, they believe, as much as she does, that having large breasts is important. It's possible to argue that the last sentence in the essay is the final stage in establishing Ephron's thesis.

Langston Hughes SALVATION

TOPICAL CONSIDERATIONS

1. The first sentence refers to his having gone through the motions of being saved—how he is regarded by the rest of the congregation. However, from inside—from where Hughes narrates this piece—he felt no salvation; he felt and saw no Jesus come.

2. Hughes' motivation was nearly all group pressure—his aunt, the preacher, his friend Westley, and the rest of the congregation. Ironically, the very promise of his elders—that Jesus would enter his life—prevents him from going forth until the very end. Hughes says that he sat there dutifully waiting for Jesus to come as expected. It was only out of pressure, the tearful pleading of his aunt in particular and his shame for holding things up, that moved him to his feet. Westley, on the other hand, is much more practical, less gullible than young Hughes. " 'God damn!' " he whispers (his words ringing with irony). " 'I'm tired o' sitting here. Let's get up and be saved.' " Westley is more realistic about "salvation." It has more to do with getting the ceremony over with than saving his soul.

3. Hughes says that he cried for three reasons: that he had lied to his aunt about seeing Jesus, that he "had deceived everybody in church," and that he "didn't believe there was a Jesus any more, since he didn't come." His aunt says that it was because the Holy Ghost had come into his life, and because he had seen Jesus. In reality, just the opposite is true for the boy. Neither Jesus nor the Holy Ghost entered his life. What young Hughes learns is that he has been deceived by the adult world and the promise of "salvation." Also, that "faith is the substance of things hoped for, the evidence of things not seen." It might be said that the only "salvation" he experiences is that from religious conformity.

4. I suppose I would tell the young boy that some people believe that there is a God and a Jesus, and that salvation comes to those who practice their belief. Also that there are others who don't believe, that life on earth is it, that there is nothing beyond the grave. I would say that belief should and could not be based on "proof" or miracles, that just because Hughes did not see Jesus, that does not mean Jesus didn't exist or that there was no God or afterlife as promised in the scriptures.

5. See above. In many ways this essay describes not simply a rite of passage, a coming of age experience for Hughes. It represents the dilemma of modern

man and woman—religious belief in our highly rational world. Religious teachings, particularly Judeo-Christian, hold up ancient miracles as evidence of the supernatural, of the existence of God. That miracles apparently don't occur today points to the necessity of religious faith to come from within, to rise above the need for scientific evidence and the empirical world. No doubt, this question should raise some interesting responses among the students. It would be interesting to see which students have been made cynical by a society so lacking in myths and mysticism and which have sustained their faith.

RHETORICAL CONSIDERATIONS

1. Hughes wisely chose to recreate the flashback rather than simply tell the reader about the events in church. A writer's best hope of achieving the truth is not talking about emotions, but the things that cause them. If the writer gets it "right" the reader will reduplicate the writer's emotions, therefore experiencing what the writer experienced. Of course, the things that matter greatly to a writer are often intangible—love, fear, disappointment, hatred, pride, and passion—and they cannot be described well. One cannot successfully describe love or fear; one must describe a person in love or a frightening event. In other words, one must embody the indescribable in the describable, the abstract in the concrete. Hughes cannot exactly articulate the feelings he had about not finding Jesus, about doubt and the sense of shame sitting there in the church. However, Hughes can recreate the circumstances that helped produce such feelings—feelings that the reader can perhaps experience reading about the event. One can explain ideas, but emotions have to be illustrated. Hughes does it very well here.

2. In a short time, Hughes creates a vivid scene in the church and uses words that help to create a boy's perspective. Paragraph 4 is particularly descriptive as is paragraph 7, where an anxious congregation "in mighty wail of moans and voices" surround the boy all alone with his doubts.

3. Hughes' choice of words are accurately chosen to create a twelve-year-old's perspective. Occasionally, the language sounds more sophisticated than that of a child. In paragraph 4, "old men with work-gnarled hands" is a phrase beyond most boys of twelve. But in most of the other places the language is in line with the boy's point of view. The last line in particular has the breathless catalog of a child, especially "and that now I didn't believe there was a Jesus any more, since he didn't come to help me." Even the self-centered logic has the ring of a child's mind.

Dan Wakefield RETURNING TO CHURCH

TOPICAL CONSIDERATIONS

1. Wakefield's decision to go to church was not the result of long-range planning, nor a product of reflection and deliberation. As he reports, he was sitting in a bar when a housepainter named Tony remarked that he wanted to find a place

to attend mass on Christmas Eve. Suddenly and unexpectedly Wakefield found himself thinking that he'd like to do that, too.

2. Wakefield was undergoing several major life crises: the seven-year relationship with the woman he expected to spend his life with ended; he went broke; he left the work, home, and city he had lived in; and in that same year both his parents died. At this time he turned to the 23rd Psalm. This poem comforted him; and although he felt no belief in God, he did experience a sense of relief and comfort.

3. Wakefield talks about a sense of emotional refreshment and relief he feels as he recites psalms and sings hymns with the congregation. On an aesthetic level he enjoys the "calm reassurance in the stately language of the litanies and chants of the Book of Common Prayer." Finally, he says he enjoys the sense of unity when praying with the congregation.

4. Wakefield found that the study of scripture written thousands of years ago illuminated his own life. A passage from Luke about a man who cleans his house of demons only to discover seven new ones had special significance for the author. A parallel, in fact: he had recently given up alcohol only to turn to marijuana, all the while feeling good and self-righteous about abandoning the booze. The shock of this recognition made him realize how much more house-cleaning he had to do.

5. At one time Wakefield wasn't certain if he had kicked his addictions because of diet and physical exercise, mental therapy, or the church. After considerable fretting, he concluded that it was not possible to "compartmentalize and isolate the influence of God, like some kind of vitamin." He could not answer the question. He did suspect, however, that at some level "grace" was at work lifting him above his addictions. He found that he no longer needed an iron will to curb his habits. Rather, "it simply felt better not to have to do them." A nice distinction.

6. To the author, "conversion" suggests being "born again," a phrase he dislikes because of its melodramatic overtones and political associations—for example, the conservatism of Jerry Falwell. Wakefield says he learned that the root of "conversion" is not "rebirth" but "turning." He feels that "turned" more aptly describes his own spiritual journey: "that's what this has felt like—as if I were walking in one direction and then, in response to some inner pull, I turned—not even all the way around, but only at what seemed a slightly different angle."

7. A noted Dutch Roman Catholic clergyman, Father Henri J. Nouwen is author of *Cry for Mercy: Prayers from the Genesee,* which deals with the anguish and confusion he has experienced in his relationship with God. Wakefield, who read the book, was disturbed that someone as spiritually advanced as Nouwen could suffer such pain in his pursuit of God. Wakefield asked the priest how he, a spiritual neophyte, could possibly attain any spiritual knowledge. Angrily, Father Nouwen replied, "Christianity is not for getting your own life together." In other words, Nouwen meant that the goal of religion is not necessarily happiness and fulfillment in a wordly sense. As stated in his book *Reaching Out,* "it would be just another illusion to believe that reaching out to God will

free us of pain and suffering. Often, indeed, it will take us where we would rather not go. But we know that without going there we will not find our life."

RHETORICAL CONSIDERATIONS

1. The bar suggests Wakefield's lifestyle before his "conversion"—a life in which he tried to solve problems through drink, promiscuity, and drugs. At this time Wakefield apparently was content to seek escape or relief through what he later called "life-numbing addictions." He posed for a book-jacket photo in his living room bar, flanked by "bottles of favorite vodkas, bourbons and burgundies." It was to drugs and alcohol that he later turned in order to cope with the end of his seven-year romance, his financial problems, and the death of both parents. Opening the essay in a bar congeals the image of a dissolute life. On the other hand, the monastery suggests a life focused on spiritual pursuits, a life in control, a life striving for peace through reflection. Where the bar offered escape from turmoil, the monastery offers an oasis, a place to find strength to deal with confusion and turmoil. The two contradictory loci also reflect the underlying biblical theme in the essay: that of the Prodigal Son who leaves a degenerate life to return to a forgiving father. In this case, the church or God is the forgiving father to Wakefield.

2. In paragraph 2, Wakefield discusses his choice of Christmas Eve service at Boston's King's Chapel. He concludes with the humorous statement, "I assumed 'Candlelight Service' meant nothing more religiously challenging than carol singing." And in paragraph 3 he describes his flu with the "suspicion that church was a very dangerous place, at least if you weren't used to it." Later in that paragraph he explains the flu by saying "Perhaps my flesh was rebelling against this unaccustomed intrusion of spirit." See also comments in paragraphs 7 and 8. These humorous touches help humanize the narrator while making him accessible and friendly. They also help us identify and sympathize with the author in his moments of doubt and uncertainty about his new role as churchgoer. The humor helps create the engaging tone of the piece.

3. The word reminds Wakefield of the "sanctuary" movement in New England churches to offer shelter to Central American political refugees. He sees a parallel to his own relationship to the church, which offers him "a kind of private refuge . . . from the daily assaults of business and personal pressures and worries." In paragraph 9 the term "sanctuary" is related to the metaphor in which he describes life's daily stresses as "the psychic guerilla warfare of everyday life." In the next paragraph the term connects to the sanctuary movement for Central American refugees in expressions such as "sense of safety," "refuge," "passport," and "fleeing to a powerful embassy."

4. Each meeting offered a new and enriching experience for the author. The first meeting was a sensuous and emotional experience rather than an intellectual exercise. In recalling Christ's words, Wakefield says that he felt "an interior glow" and a sense of belonging and community. But what stands out from the evening's discussion was not the text but the sensuous details

from it. He writes "I can still smell the rain and coffee and feel the aura of light and warmth."

The second meeting led by the minister for a group of twenty was a potent reminder of the awesome power of faith. The discussion of the story of Abraham and Isaac was a reminder of such potency. And he uses the word "power" to describe the meeting.

The third and final meeting describes yet another dimension—that of self-exploration and discovery. Wakefield says it was like "holding up a mirror to my own life, a mirror in which I sometimes saw things I was trying to keep hidden, even from myself." Luke's story of the man and his demons reminds the author of his own giving up of alcohol only to take up marijuana. Each illustration reveals a different layer of experience for him.

▼PART 2 FAMILY MATTERS

Dave Barry IT'S IN THE GENES

TOPICAL CONSIDERATIONS

1. Not much. They had electricians move the light fixture from one side of the dining room to the other.
2. He actually gives three reasons, the most important being genetic—that he and his wife are missing the brain part that controls decorating their home. As Barry says, he lacks the Mr. Goodwrench gland and his wife, the Betty Crocker gland—a very funny concept. But he also suggests that they are incapable of change, particularly getting rid of anything such as the light fixture and their pathetic furniture. Finally, he explains, were they to bring into their living room tasteful furniture, the old stuff would ridicule and infect it with "shabbiness germs."
3. In contrast, their friends have tasteful Danish furniture they just went out and bought—something Barry just cannot comprehend.
4. He cannot get rid of the plastic models of his teeth for three reasons, one more ridiculous than the other. First is his habitual problem with throwing things away. Second, he says he fears that his dentist will get angry with him and make him come in for an appointment. Third, his house is already suffering from a lack of taste, so why add the teeth.
5. Barry is a very funny man who is famous for exposing life's little insanities. Here he has fun ridiculing his own idiosyncrasies and foibles. No doubt for the sake of humor most of this is exaggeration. However, he does delineate a few familiar syndromes. One is the inability some people have to make changes in their home environments. Another is ambivalence. Haven't we all held onto some ugly, useless item for reasons that escape rationality? A third human failing is simply bad taste—not knowing what looks good. And don't we all know people who lack this discriminatory power? Students should be able to relate to these tendencies.

RHETORICAL CONSIDERATIONS

1. ALLUSION: "Elk on the walls" alludes to the 30,000 year-old paintings found on caves in southern France and Spain, such as at Altamira. Other allusions: South Bronx, Betty Crocker, Mr. Goodwrench, Fisher-Price, and Nancy Reagan.

   IRONY: "This is not one of those chairs that are sold for a song but turn out to be tasteful antiques worth thousands of dollars." No such luck, for their chair is a genuine piece of junk.

   SATIRE: "Snotty interior design magazines" and "wealthy people who eat out and keep their children in Switzerland."

   OVERSTATEMENT: That there is a brain part for decorating the home. That were his old, hideous chair left in the tasteful living room of his friends' home it would turn into a sleek Danish piece in a few days.

   UNDERSTATEMENT: How his friends "just went out and got it [their furniture] somehow."

   PRETENSE TO IGNORANCE: How unsightly all the black plastic is.

   SURPRISE: "None of my friends . . . have plastic models of their teeth in their cars."

   ABSURD ANALOGY: Their shabby old furniture infecting any new pieces.
2. The opening sentence is a direct statement of the thesis.
3. Very effective, very funny.
4. The key word here is "keep" which equates children with prize horses. The notion is that wealthy people have children but really don't want them, so they send them to Switzerland to be educated and do their growing up so the parents can eat out and do other leisure-life things.

Patsy Neal MY GRANDMOTHER, THE BAG LADY

TOPICAL CONSIDERATIONS

1. The transformation of Neal's grandmother to bag lady was gradual, not sudden. Once moved to a nursing home, she visited her own home less frequently as she became more infirm. Much of each visit was spent walking about the house touching beloved objects and browsing through closets and drawers. As periods of confinement in the nursing home lengthened, she took to hiding her few possessions under mattresses and chair cushions while complaining that her things were being stolen. Finally, she placed her things in a bag attached to her walker. As Neal eventually comes to realize, "that walker and her purse . . . [became] her home."
2. For the family, security meant meeting physical needs: a safe environment, regular medication, bodily warmth and well-rounded meals. For the grandmother, on the other hand, security was tied to her possessions, to things she could call her own. Over the years she lost possessions—her car, dogs,

and, finally, her home—and with these her security and sense of control over life.

3. The note underscores for Neal the traits of quiet dignity, courage, and caring that the grandmother still possesses. Though lonely the grandmother does not wake her family, but takes pleasure in their comfort and rest.

4. The grandmother controls her few material possessions by keeping them by her side, tucked in bags, and in her purse. In a greater sense, she still exerts great control over her character. The tiny note reveals how she subordinates her own need for companionship to her daughter's and granddaughter's need for rest. It also reveals what pleasure and comfort she takes in this protectiveness.

RHETORICAL CONSIDERATIONS

1. In the first paragraph the author describes the bag ladies found on today's city streets. When she confirms that her own grandmother "had become one of them," the reader is shocked, immediately curious, and involved. We associate bag ladies with poverty and abandonment while grandmothers conjure up Norman Rockwell images of white-haired old women making cookies and telling children stories. The conjunction of the two is at once provocative and disturbing.

2. The author writes, "over the years my grandmother's space for living had diminished *like melting butter...*" And later, "... over the years those possessions had dwindled away *like sand dropping through an hourglass...*" Both similes are quite effective. Each underscores the notion of a slow, almost imperceptible diminishing of space and possessions. The second simile has the added poignancy of time running out for the old woman. Though not highly original these figures of speech are in keeping with the straightforward account.

3. To be sentimental, something must evoke an excess of emotion. It must elicit a reaction out of proportion to the subject discussed. I found this conclusion touching. It does evoke a strong reaction of pity and sorrow. However, it underscores a theme established early in the piece, namely that of loss—loss of place, possessions, and independence. This last sentence is a hope that on some level Neal's elderly grandmother can have back what she has lost.

Jonathan Kozol **RACHEL AND HER CHILDREN**

TOPICAL CONSIDERATIONS

1. Rachel alludes to the famine in Africa, specifically Ethiopia, which prompted British and American rock artists in 1985 to unite in concert and to record "We Are the World." Proceeds from this highly popular recording went to fight famine in drought and war ravished Africa. The success of this effort and its accompanying publicity provided a cruelly ironic insight to Rachel. While the

public at large lamented the plight of starving Africans, the homeless and, in many cases, starving Americans were ignored. While Rachel and her family suffer the ignominy of poverty, hunger, and dislocation, the western world opens its heart not to them but to others of foreign lands. Her complaint is a sad commentary on how disenfranchised groups are pitted against each other.

2. Rachel's children have little time for play. Instead, their daily life is a struggle to survive both physically and emotionally. They endure overheated or cold rooms. Their diet is inadequate: bologna, Kool-Aid, peanut butter and jelly. But worse are the threats to their safety posed by an environment rife with drugs and people willing to prey on their innocence. Angie tells of being chased home one night and injuring her eye on a door that wouldn't open. Raisen tells of a rat biting her baby sister. All children are exposed to drug users: "One day she asks us do we want a puff. So we said, 'No. My mother doesn't let us do it.' " In addition, child abuse is something they have witnessed. Raisen describes a little boy about two years old beaten by his father with a bat. The work of their childhood is survival.

3. Rachel loves her children. She agonizes over their predicament. She worries about their diet, their education, their exposure to sex and drugs. But most of all she worries about preserving their innocence. In her efforts to protect and nurture them, Rachel has relied on welfare and suffered some humiliation. " 'Cause they sittin' on the other side of this here desk, they think we're stupid and we do not understand when we're insulted.' 'Oh you had another baby?' 'Yeah! I had another baby! What about it?' " On one occasion when she was out of food and money and found herself turned away by a crisis center, Rachel sent her children out to panhandle. " 'That's right. Whole night long they was in Herald Square panhandlin'. Made five dollars.' " Her guilt over this torments her. ("Letting them panhandle made me cry.") She entertains fantasies of selling parts of her body for the money to support her children. "I would do it. I would do it for my children. I would give my life if I could get a thousand dollars. What would I lose?" Rachel's love for her children leads her to desperate measures, and she tells of prostituting herself for twenty dollars to buy diapers and food. In short, her willingness to sacrifice body and soul underscores the "authenticity" of her love.

4. For the students.

5. The future holds the answer to these questions, of course. Nonetheless, the future does not bode well for them given their constant exposure to the menace of drugs, alcohol, violence, and poverty. Should these influences triumph, the children as well as society will suffer. The children lose their opportunity for full and rewarding lives; and society's social fabric is further damaged.

6. Rachel's children have a simple unquestioning faith in God who they turn to in fear. The night Angie hurt her eye being chased, she tells of praying all night for help. Rachel's faith, on the other hand, has been battered by experience. She wants to believe, but her hardships contradict a belief in a caring God. " 'I don't pray! Pray for what? I been prayin' all my life and I'm still here.' " She goes on to say that she eventually lost all her faith. " 'Ain't nobody—no God, no Jesus—

gonna help us in no way.'" Though disillusioned, Rachel feels guilt and confusion for expressing her doubts. She says, "'I do believe God forgive me. I believe He's there. But when He sees us like this, I am wonderin' where is He?'" Tenaciously she clings to some faith; she wants to believe but can't find the evidence in her own life that God hears her pleas or cares. And, yet, her final description of God is of one who provides escape from daily torments—a white-haired, white-bearded man in a place with "'. . . no more sickness, no more hunger for nobody. No panhandlin'. No prostitution. No drugs. I had a dream like that.'"

RHETORICAL CONSIDERATIONS

1. The dialogue, unembellished, conveys Rachel's situation in a direct and blunt way. Her remarks and those of her children are chillingly honest and authentic. Their plight is so disturbing that commentary and stylistic flairs by a journalist might blunt the impact. Also, it is clear that Kozol wants his characters to speak for themselves, to reveal their humanity and dignity as he saw it.

2. Kozol's introductory remarks create a framework for the essay and reveal his purpose. "If we listen to these parents carefully we may be no less concerned by their impaired abilities, but we may be less judgmental or, if we remain compelled to judge, we may redirect our energies in more appropriate directions." Kozol creates a vivid picture of Rachel and her children at the opening of the piece. His depiction of her is shocking: "They stare at her as I do, as her arms reach out—for what? They snap like snakes and coil back. Her hair is gray—a stiff and bushlike Afro." In the course of the piece we learn that this Medusa-like figure has a heart, love, and sorrows. Later it is clear that Kozol feels the pain of his subjects' tormented faith: "The room is like a chilled cathedral in which people who do not believe in God ask God's forgiveness."

3. The poem is a poignant note to close on. It underscores the humanity and creative drive of the woman. It also points out that even in squalor beauty tries to grow. Its simplicity, its childlike quality, and its insights express her limits as well as her reach.

George Fasel A SON ON HIS OWN

TOPICAL CONSIDERATIONS

1. For the son, military service will take four years of his life, provide travel, professional training as an air-traffic controller, two years of college credit, and two years college tuition. For the father thirty years ago, the military service meant being pushed to one's physical limits, a physical regimen under the auspices of a dictatorial, possibly irrational, drill sergeant. As the son sees it, the military provides much more—training, education, and fringe benefits. As the father reflects, the military when he was young provided abusive experience which would deter rather than promote personal growth.

2. As the essay progresses, the father's reaction to his son's decision is what unfolds as does his attempt to understand his own feelings and reservations. He first says he fears the military might send his son to one of the world's military hot spots. He also admits to a prejudice against the military stemming not just from his youth when the draft was a great dread, but from family tradition. In fact, the father upheld the family tradition of going to college instead. But behind these lesser concerns is the realization that his son is making decisions on his own. "My son is ready—so quickly, it now seems—to make his own choices, by himself on his own, and to take the consequences for them." In short, that his son has grown up.

3. The half-empty bottle suggests the father's view of the future. He is worried and anxious about what may go wrong. He focuses on negative possibilities. The half-full bottle suggests the son's optimistic view of tomorrow. He signed up for the navy with solid, pragmatic reasons. Seeing the best in a situation, he tells his father, "The worst that can happen is I'll hate the service and be out at 22, with college paid for and money in the bank."

4. So often we see the role of the parent as guide or mentor—the experienced adult whose values and views a child should emulate. But in this instance the father excels in his role as parent not by forcing his will on his son, but by allowing his son his own choice and control over his own future. Since the son already signed up, the decision is irreversible. Nonetheless, had Fasel imposed his attitudes on his son, had he protested for all the reasons he gives, he would have risked alienating the young man. The author is still a father, but a father to a man not a boy anymore.

5. For the student.

RHETORICAL CONSIDERATIONS

1. Baseball, an all-American sport, is usually something shared by father and son in childhood. The father-son bond is strengthened by games of catch, excursions to baseball games, and the general enthusiasm for favorite teams. That this essay takes place in the Baseball Hall of Fame evokes these father-son associations. The setting is also ironic. Though the father looks forward to sharing baseball anecdotes from his past with his son, he ends up "pumping him for information about what he has done, what he's going to do." In other words, the knowledge and wisdom Fasel hoped to pass on isn't sought out. Instead, the reverse occurs—the father seeks information about the boy's future.

2. The irony of the setting is reinforced when the father and son discuss Ted Williams' batting average. Whereas the father bemoans it—"Imagine what he would have done if he hadn't spent five years flying for the Marines"—the boy celebrates it—"I don't know, Dad. Five-hundred-twenty-one homers is pretty good, anyway." In other words, while the father cynically points to lost opportunities, the son says that Williams did both—served his country and made it to the Hall of Fame.

3. Though uncertain and anxious about his son's decision, the father poses his

questions in a direct and tactful way. The son's answers are straightforward, uncomplicated, and optimistic. Therefore, the dialogue while reflective of the open, trusting father-son relationship reveals the anxiety of a father and the confidence of a son.

Michael Reese and **HOMOSEXUALITY: ONE**
Pamela Abramson **FAMILY'S AFFAIR**

TOPICAL CONSIDERATIONS

1. The authors explain that by being a teacher's pet, a hustler in football practice, and a member of many social groups, Kelly managed "to mask his insecurities." In a way his demanding self-standards, like his highly competitive spirit, might have been Kelly's way of compensating for what he perceived as a fundamental imperfection in himself. As the authors say in the article, for years he feared that he was an outsider and different from his peers; he also feared rejection.

2. The article says Kelly came to realize that he was gay through "vague sexual feelings" as early as age seven, "when he would linger in the boys' shower room after swimming lessons." By the time he was a teenager, his sexual feelings had "blossomed," as had his realization. He knew when he looked through his father's girlie magazines that he was hunting for shots of men. His reaction to the discovery was confusion and anxiety because he was forced to hide his true identity, to make cover excuses for his disinterest in girls, even to join in with "faggot jokes." What is sad is how alone he was with his secret. He had feelings that confused and scared him, yet nobody to talk them out with, no frame of reference. When he saw a pornographic picture of a man putting on nylons, his reaction was confused denial: "That isn't me."

3. His cover-ups were "elaborate" the article says. He refused to ask his parents for a new coat and tie for his yearbook photo session out of fear they would expect him to date. He gave the excuse that he had nothing to wear when asked about going to his senior prom. He had managed to convince his parents that he was shy, and thus not interested in girls.

4. Kelly found little more than despair in college. Eastern Washington University back then had no gay student organizations or union as it has now. There was no place to seek counseling. As the article says, Kelly's sexual contact was restricted to one relationship. The only relief from anxiety was the energy spent in studies and long bicycle rides. He "timidly continued his sexual education" by reading gay psychology texts and flirting with the idea of visiting gay bars.

5. Kelly announced his gayness when he brought home his friend David, who was "loud, flamboyant and sissified in dress." As the article says, one look and Joan Chronister knew David was gay. Needing proof, she searched his drawers and steamed open his mail. When she found the book *Young, Gay and Proud,* her fears were confirmed.

6. Kelly's father Paul felt anger, sadness, and confusion upon learning his son was gay. He did not want to place blame, yet it occurred to him that his wife "was more domineering" than he was. Joan, on the other hand, having sought out gay parent support groups, realized that no one was to blame. Yet, she blamed Paul for not being more understanding now that the truth was out.

7. Paul still struggles with his son's homosexuality. He feels "inner anguish" and embarrassment still; he also feels anger over having been cheated out of "all the things that a father wants to have," including grandchildren. Joan, on the other hand, having benefited from parent support groups, is more open and accepting. She had taken part in gay functions, including rallies and parades, hoping to achieve acceptance. She seems to be better off than her husband.

RHETORICAL CONSIDERATIONS

1. In paragraph 2 we find the thesis statement: "What the Chronisters have learned is that there is no easy way for an American family to confront homosexuality." The essay never strays from the elaboration and illustration of this fact in the Chronister family.

2. There is an almost mathematical balance in the treatment of each of the three Chronisters' struggles.

3. The authors seem to have taken pains to avoid judgment of the people involved. In fact, the article is commendably sensitive and unsensational and free of prejudices.

4. This article was written for *Newsweek* magazine—for the general readership of that magazine, which is ideologically "liberal." It is not the "enlightened" readership that, say, would subscribe to gay publications. Although the article was written with sensitivity and no sensationalism, some might feel that it lacked the enlightenment the gay community would hope to see. The article is focused on Kelly Chronister, who is not the limp-wrist effeminate but, in fact, a young man of "preppy good looks, athletic prowess and all-American demeanor." He looks like the archetypal American male, just as the reader addressed is the archetypal or average intelligent American reader. Also, the article is focused on parents who needed support groups to handle the discovery, which might suggest that is the only alternative. Yet, of course, many "enlightened" parents would give support and love to their children no matter what their sexual orientation.

Randall Williams **DADDY TUCKED THE BLANKET**

TOPICAL CONSIDERATIONS

1. He says that he found his freedom and "was getting out." His escape was from the poverty and the humiliation of it. Throughout the essay, Williams stresses how painful poverty is, particularly for young people who want to be accepted

by peers, who want to have the things other kids have, things they see on television. Thus his breaking out, his escape, is a way of looking for more. At the same time, it is an escape from the humiliation of being poor—the same humiliation that kept him from bringing a friend to his house while in high school.

2. The house was apparently not large enough to comfortably sleep the Williams family, which, the author says, was large. Several young people slept in one room. The house was old, hot in summer and cold in winter, and in disrepair. Plaster kept falling from the ceiling above his bed and the walls also crumbled when they tried to paint them. The kitchen had no counter space and no hot water; also, the house had no closets. The windows were broken, the hallway was dirty, and the wallpaper was peeling.

3. He characterizes his parents as hardworking, caring, unselfish, kind, and frustrated by their impoverished status. His father worked hard at a full-time job outside the home as his mother did inside the home. But no matter how much his father made, they never got out of their economic rut. Williams says he got out because of scholarships to college.

4. According to Williams the anger between his parents was really displaced from the economic "trap their lives were in. It ruined their marriage because they had no one to yell at but each other."

5. He is grateful for that moment of humiliation, probably because it made him determine not to be poor when he grew up. Perhaps it helped him decide to go after scholarships so that he could go to college and thus into a profession that would afford him escape from the poverty of his past.

RHETORICAL CONSIDERATIONS

1. The first sentence of paragraph 5 serves as Williams's thesis statement.

2. All the details pointing to the uncomfortable and ruinous conditions of the houses they lived in certainly illustrate their plight. In particular, his reference to the plaster falling on his face at night; trying to paint a crumbling wall; how bright paint emphasized the holes in the walls; the reference to the dirty hallway, broken windows, and cracked ceiling that would greet a prospective date for his sisters. The most moving detail is his illustration of his father's using wire to tie his boots in winter because any money he had went for the kids' clothes.

3. He talks about his parents' frustrations and anger. He first introduces the potential ruin in paragraph 12, where he says his father used to yell at his mother because she couldn't keep the house clean. Williams observes that his father probably knew his yelling was an outlet for his rage at being poor. He mentions that again in paragraph 16. Then in the following paragraph Williams says that the anger climaxed in a "particularly violent argument" about the washing machine that broke down. In an aside we learn that the only water faucet was outside on the porch; we also learn that his mother had to do their school clothes in a washtub.

4. He uses illustrative details through the essay, although it is not particularly

descriptive. Paragraphs 11 and 15 are the most descriptive. I would have liked more descriptive details.

5. The style of Williams's essay probably is closer to that of most composition students than to the style of many essays in the text. It is simple and direct, achieved by simple vocabulary and short declarative sentences with few modifiers. Many of Williams's sentences, particularly at the beginning, open with "I" or "we" followed by a simple verb. He even opts for clichés instead of fresh expressions: "We lived like hell," "my father worked his head off." And, as indicated by the brief paragraphs, he does not go into much detail or analysis but keeps on the surface or impression level pretty much throughout.

6. The title carries a touching suggestion of how, despite the awful conditions of their lives, the home had love and caring. The specific reference is in paragraph 18, where the author describes his father's tucking the blanket around his sleeping mother on the night they had a violent argument. Again, the message is that there was loving and caring in the family; however, even that broke down under the stress of poverty.

7. "Sentimental" implies exploitation of the reader's emotions. I do not find the essay sentimental, although it is touching in places. In fact, I sense Williams holding back, consciously avoiding the sound of sentimentality, even in describing his father's tucking in his mother while tears fell from his eyes. He applies the same control at the end when he describes the classroom humiliation. He could have exaggerated the scene or dramatized it for greater emotional appeal, but he chose not to.

Russell Baker "IN MY DAY . . ."

TOPICAL CONSIDERATIONS

1. Baker wishes he hadn't "thrown off [his] own past so carelessly" and yearns to know more about his mother's life as a child and young adult. Now that she is no longer able to share this past with him, he is beginning to sense that something of value in life is lost when children don't know about their parents' lives and the people they knew.

2. Baker wants his children to know about the family members who came before them and what their lives and the world was like in previous years. The rest of the questions are up to the students.

3. Students can answer these questions from their own experience.

4. Children assume that their parents are invulnerable. This seems to be a fairly common attitude, but the answer is up to the students. Once after a visit to his mother when she was seventy-eight, Baker wrote a letter chastising her for not being more cheerful. Later, when he read her answer to his letter, he realized that he had been insensitive to her needs and had hurt her feelings. Three years later, after a bad fall, she began retreating into the past.

RHETORICAL CONSIDERATIONS

1. There is much to like about his opening. It's a touching portraiture that conjures up familiar family scenes. Baker's references to his mother traveling through space and time with a "speech and ease beyond the gift of physical science" has an amusing, ironic twist.
2. The dialogue makes the scene more real and brings the reader closer to what is happening.
3. Paragraph 10: Baker's physical description of his mother as "short, light-boned, delicately structured," tiny against a white hospital sheet, suggests a fragile vulnerability. His comparison of her to a doll with fierce eyes adds to this impression. But it hints, too, at her formidable, fighting spirit. Paragraph 15: The narrative incidents in this paragraph *show* what a fierce, formidable woman she was.
4. Baker remarks that his mother "*hurled* herself at life" and was always *running*. Such verbs reflect her forcefulness, energy, and determination.

▼PART 3 CHANGING TIMES

Erma Bombeck TECHNOLOGY'S COMING . . .
TECHNOLOGY'S COMING

TOPICAL CONSIDERATIONS

1. Bombeck mentions several modern electronic devices that threaten her: the digital watch, VCR, signal finder devices (for her keys and/or glasses), home computer, photocopier, memory phones, and microwave ovens. Bombeck admits that she cannot figure out how her German-made digital watch works. She also says that she and her husband waited six months before using their VCR because of the complicated directions. Once the VCR directions were mastered, Bombeck is presented with new problems—how to keep up with all the movies and self-help tapes, and shows she and her husband feel compelled to follow. Instead of making life easier for her, the VCR—and other technological wonders—have made life more complicated, less leisurely.
2. Her major reason for resisting the 21st century technology is lack of need. Her resistance is evident in the way she let the VCR sit unused for half a year. Also as she directly confronts her son and daughter telling them that she has no use for a personal computer or a photocopier. But she adds that her resistance to automation had something to do with not wanting to be replaced by machines. "I was important. All the slick magazines said so," she adds ironically. With the coming of technology, she finds that she has "been replaced by ouchless adhesive bandages, typewriters that correct their [her children's] spelling, color-coded wardrobes, and computers that praise them when they get the right answers."
3. This issue of replacement lies at the heart of Bombeck's rebellion against

efficiency-minded technology. There was a time when Bombeck taught her children things as they grew up. But technology has come along and displaced her in some of those roles. Once she would teach her kids how to tie their shoes, but Velcro tabs have put an end to that. Likewise, Bombeck's motherly roles as story-reader, spelling corrector, cook, nurse, and general guardian have been replaced by electronic analogs.

4. It sounds as if the Bombecks watch a lot of television. Bombeck seems to be making a statement about the fallout of our brave new high-tech world: the nearly pathological compulsion to keep up with what's happening in television and video. That she spends 6 hours and 44 minutes a day—the exactness itself reflecting her time-neuroses—underscores some problems more directly addressed in the essays in the television section of the text. In particular, Bombeck confesses to an addiction to television and the VCR, an addiction that some view as deadly to human creativity. Bombeck is no doubt exaggerating her addiction; nonetheless, she dramatizes the syndrome in paragraphs 33 through 39 in which she humorously admits to cutting corners: "We've got *60 Minutes* down to 30, *20/20* to 10/10, and anything on World War II we fast-forward because we know the ending."

5. About society, Bombeck laments that the high-tech world is too much with us. She seems to suggest that there is neither the need for such efficiency-minded machines nor benefits reaped. All the gizmos are designed in part to save time, but Bombeck and her husband spend their hours saved in front of the television screens crazily switching channels to keep up with the world, or to feel caught up like everybody else. About her family, the complaint is that modern technology has widened the generation gap while it has altered family roles and threatened unity. Bombeck says her role as cook has been displaced by microwave ovens which her kids know how to use. Presumably, dinners are eaten on the run and separately. She also complains about the lack of time to be a family. On herself, Bombeck satirically confesses to a television addiction created in part by her yielding to cable television and VCRs. Machines are made to be used and once cable and the cassette player are in the home, one is hard put not to use them. By the end of the piece Bombeck characterizes herself as half crazed in her slavish dependence on the devices. The effect is amusing, but with a dark comment about what we have let the modern electronic world do to us and how much we have lost—in particular, self-sufficiency, creative leisure time, and family closeness.

6. Past life is characterized by people doing things themselves and interacting more. This comes through in Bombeck's remembrance of the way things used to be including sitting her kids on her lap and reading to them. Contemporary life is characterized right off in paragraph one as being fast and time-neurotic. Her kids represent today, and she and her husband the past.

7. I think some modern devices have made life easier and better. I do, however, think that some are useless gizmos that function more to impress others than save time. Timesaving machines have become symbols of status, a declaration

that one has more money than time. Consider such efficiency-minded machines as car telephones, ice-cream makers, elaborate food processors that not only knead bread dough, but allow for rising time and do the baking. Even the home computer seems superfluous since the machine's usefulness is greater in work-related areas than in home economics, data storage, and balancing one's checkbook. I also think television and VCRs have taken their toll on people especially the young. Kids would rather watch the flashing pictures than read a book. Also, it has been demonstrated that television threatens the learning process itself.

RHETORICAL CONSIDERATIONS

1. From the opening passages, Bombeck's persona takes the shape of a woman beleaguered by a generation gap and high-tech world that is too much for her. The gap is made evident by the opening reference to "the younger son" who is never named. In fact, none of the family members are named. Her daughter is referred to as "our daughter" and in paragraph 36 she speaks of "a son" without distinguishing him as the older or younger. At the end, she refers to her younger son by the put-down title of "Mr. Technology." The immediate effect is a kind of humorous tension, for here is a mother-persona who regards her offspring with some impersonal distance. This distance, of course, adds to the ironic tone of the essay. No doubt, the author behind the persona adores her children and refers to them by name when recounting family stories to personal friends. But this is Erma Bombeck, a writer famous for her irreverent wit and humor addressing an audience that is both familiar with the crazy crises of family life and that wants to laugh at them.

   Her response in paragraph 4 immediately captures a woman face-to-face with a brave new technology. She's pathetically lost. So is her husband who can't set the controls of their VCR. Their distance from the high-tech world in part explains the gap between the Bombecks and their children. We can safely assume that the depiction of them as helpless victims of the electronic world is not the real Mr. and Mrs. Erma Bombeck, but a humorous exaggeration for the sake of the essay. Her somewhat neurotic and victimized persona succeeds in illustrating symptoms many of us feel in today's world, in particular parents used to less efficient ways.

2. Students might not recognize the reference to the early 1960s comedy, *The Russians Are Coming, The Russians Are Coming.* The title is particularly appropriate since Bombeck parallels modern technology with our traditional enemy and warns of a possible conquest.

3. Bombeck's decision to show instead of tell is a wise one. Reduplicating the scene in words helps us identify with the humor, the emotions, and the issues more so than straight exposition could. Opening with dialogue between Bombeck and her children creates some funny effects, mostly in Bombeck's comebacks. Also, conflict is created as well as a little of the chaos on the home front. Telling us that she doesn't quite understand how digital watches or VCR clocks

work is not the same as dramatizing the circumstances. In so doing, the reader can identify with the issues and the emotions involved.

4. The final paragraph is a nice rounding off of the piece which begins with her son's declaration that he needs his laundry done or he'll be late. The issue is time again. Ironically, however, the same young man who teaches his father how to fix his digital watch and who insists the author come up to the 21st century can't figure out how the washing machine works. Some things don't change. Mother Bombeck hasn't been completely displaced. And there are a few machines she can run. So the final paragraphs end on an upbeat note characteristic of Erma Bombeck.

Linda Weltner STRIPPING DOWN TO BARE HAPPINESS

TOPICAL CONSIDERATIONS

1. Sara and Michael stripped down their lives with the birth of their daughter. They decided that what was most meaningful for them was being a family; and that meant cutting their full-time jobs in half while cutting some of the clutter out of their lives, including luxuries which once interested them but which they now viewed as "wasteful and unsatisfying."
2. I do not think such simplification was a terrible sacrifice. They still have their own home, car, and boat, which they share with another couple. And life without television is probably a blessing. I would miss the convenience of a dishwasher, but could adjust to not having one. Theirs sounds like an enviable life, free of consumer cravings that media have helped train into people. Their lives point out the irony of our own susceptibility to the pressures of advertising, which teaches us to equate security with buying.
3. When the urge to buy is greater than the need for what is bought, then we suffer from a neurotic consumer mentality that, in fact, characterizes many Americans today. This essay illustrates how we have been conditioned toward consumption and materialism, and how we have become convinced that we cannot live happily without some conveniences and excesses.
4. L. L. Bean is a very old mail-order manufacturer whose apparel once appealed solely to country people from New England. The styles are rugged, functional, conservative in a classic way. Today, the L. L. Bean look is popular with many college students because of the rugged, outdoor-chic image. Sara and Michael have not stripped themselves of all identity. Despite their renunciation of consumer frills and excesses, they have maintained an identity commensurate with their new life-style.
5. See above. Students' answers might be very interesting here.
6. They have more time for themselves as a family. And their child is not bombarded with "images of new toys, new things, and new temptations." I could live without television, although I would miss some things such as

the news, news specials and reports, movies, and PBS science and culture programs.

RHETORICAL CONSIDERATIONS

1. This opening quotation makes the topic immediate and personal. Background information opening the essay might be dull material that might not invite us to read on.
2. For the most part Weltner answers each of these questions, which, of course, are foremost in the reader's mind.
3. I think the personal conclusion is very effective. Weltner steps out of her role as reporter; she confesses her own consumer habits. She also says indirectly how impressed she is with Michael and Sara. In a way, the author is speaking for most of us who admire Sara and Michael for stripping down their lives but probably cannot do so ourselves.
4. This short paragraphing is characteristic of journalists. Certainly a few of her paragraphs could be combined—paragraphs 6 and 7, and 8 and 9, for example. But the short paragraph blocks add to the quick pace while highlighting rather than probing aspects of the main topic.

Roderick Anscombe **STRANGER THAN FICTION**

TOPICAL CONSIDERATIONS

1. Television shows of the past, says Anscombe, centered around themes of "patriotism, chivalry, loyalty or special endeavor." These were also the motivations of characters. Such shows represented a far more mild menu than today's airings which try to out-Herod Herod in their "taboo-busting." The problem, as Anscombe says, is that the real world is so brutal script writers are hard put trying to entertain an audience inured to horrors, jaded by reality. We have become unshockable.
2. Reality has become so darkly fantastical and the gap "between news and amusement" so ominously small that docudramas are on the rise. Fiction writers need not tax their imaginations for new shockers for reality provides both substance and plots. No doubt there are recent docudramas that illustrate the author's point. Some of the more sensational news stories of the 1980s have been turned into television movies, such as "The Burning Bed" (starring Farrah Fawcett) based on the life of an abused wife who murders her husband by setting fire to his bed and "Adam" based on the kidnapping and brutal murder of a young boy.
3. This one is for the students. One hopes they are still shockable. I am. I agree with the author that television competes with the news "to scare, shock or intrigue a sated audience." I also think most made-for-television movies and the crime shows are riddled with cliches, full of gratuitous violence, and simplify people to two or three raw instincts. There are, of course, exceptions, but too

few. These represent "quality television" which, unfortunately, are the exception not the norm.

4. I think Anscombe is right about the audience being a "sated" "monster." But I also think that such, unfortunately, is the perception of those who script and produce television shows. As Anscombe says, scriptwriters feel they have to "compete with each other to scare, shock or intrigue a sated audience that has already seen it on the news." We have been conditioned, but not just by the news. The entertainers seem driven to feed us more of the same in more lurid form. Yet there are a few adult "quality" shows that make up for the taboo-busters: "Family Ties," "Cheers," "LA Law," "Thirtysomething," and "The Cosby Show."

5. As Anscombe says in paragraph 5, "Increasing desperation, movies and television series compete with each other to scare, shock or intrigue a sated audience that has already seen it on the news." The challenge is to outdo both reality and each other. Students can supply their own examples from the tube as well as the contradictions. One hopes that the television audience will become super-saturated on hard reality to the point that it prefers quality shows that center on higher themes, on dramas of character—that make us feel good about being human rather than the opposite. Perhaps an examination of those shows that have won recent Emmy Awards (or movies earning Oscars for best picture) might substantiate this point. Yes, such awards are voted by the respective entertainment industries, but they also create audiences.

6. They "touch up reality" making characters bigger than life—"prettier, wittier and simpler than the real people ever were." Or, they do what Hollywood is wont to do, rely on special effects rather than good scripts, characterization, or acting to move their audiences.

7. As Anscombe says, a "secret can be revealed only once." After that, there is only repetition of the same lurid reality. This can be illustrated in movies of violence which out of desperation go one step beyond the last one to stimulate the audience and by so doing leave little to the imagination. In past years, when the bad guys got shot blood was almost never shown. Today's movies spill buckets of pig's blood in the name of verisimilitude. Ultimately the trend is self-defeating since art is reduced to sensation and spectacle.

8. Pornography is the "ultimate docudrama" because it "stages real events" in pretense to drama. There is scant plot and almost no acting in porn movies which graphically depict the mechanics of sex. There is neither art nor room for the audience's imagination so crucial to the success of art. It is self-defeating, perhaps not in terms of financial profits, but in terms of aesthetics which is probably not an issue most pornographers lose sleep over. In terms of the audience, the toll is heavier since people who make porn a steady diet lose more than they gain. Pornography is love-making de-romanticized, de-mythicized, and reduced to mechanics. Though the actors pant and sweat, private acts are made coldly graphic. Likewise, the curiosity and intrigue regarding those mysteries, even purely sexual ones, are diminished.

RHETORICAL CONSIDERATIONS

1. As teachers of writing we always encourage students to substantiate generalities with specifics. That might be said of Anscombe's piece, however, he does in the first paragraph specify the movie cliches—"a suitcase full of cocaine or the body of a dead lover in the trunk of a car." These are such stock scenarios that the author felt no compulsion to name shows or movies. He might also have felt that to do so would be offering free publicity. Furthermore, by not naming shows or films he avoids dating his essay. No doubt that what Anscombe says about today's movies and television will be true a dozen years from now.

2. Although the essay offered some compelling insights, I thought none of them the special preview of psychiatry. An intelligent, educated person from outside the medical profession could have come up with the same observations including those about psychiatry exploring "the gap between reality and what is imagined." But the fact that Anscombe is a practicing psychiatrist adds some weight to his argument.

3. I think this is one of the most forceful sentences in the essay. In fact, it can serve as the thesis statement of the piece. In other contexts, reality might not be a bad thing to be left with. But as characterized here, reality is terrorism, incest, child abuse, preteen prostitution, etc.—the dark underside of reality that has gone public. This sentence is also the only clear statement of solution to the reality-syndrome Anscombe decries.

Andrew Ward THEY ALSO WAIT WHO STAND AND SERVE THEMSELVES

TOPICAL CONSIDERATIONS

1. One of the outstanding qualities of this essay is Andrew Ward's fine eye for detail. His descriptions of Sal and his station are vivid. For instance, Sal is described as dressed in "undersized, popped-button shirts, sagging trousers, and oil-spattered work shoes with broken laces." His "nameless, walleyed assistant" is dressed in a "studded denim jacket." He describes other familiar features at gas stations, the "fume-crazed, patchy German shepherd" and the "gauntlet of hangers-on." The description of the inside of the station in paragraph 6 is, like the others, fresh and vivid.

2. Ward's attitude toward Sal's station and Sal comes through as an affection for the grubby charm of the man and his place. By comparison to the slick, cold, glassed replacement, Sal and his station have character, as reflected in the attention to the texture, color, and tabulation of details. Some details also humanize the rather ornery proprietor—the hangers-on who suggest important values, such as friendships and family; the Sons of Garibaldi peanut dispenser that says Sal is the kind of guy who does favors for people, while suggesting ethnic identity and pride; and the brass plaque from the oil company, a symbol of personal pride.

3. He is clearly hostile to it. He conveys that attitude by what he says directly and by his choice of words and details. In paragraph 11, he says that he does not like

having to pump his own gas. The "mongrel rain" is a choice description that sets a grim atmosphere for his first encounter with the Self-Serve replacement. The sudden and impersonal "Hey, buddy" from the speaker and the command to "flick the switch" three times further characterizes the place as impersonal and dehumanizing. There are also the details of the glob of grease on his glove and the impatience and rudeness of the attendant, and the concluding image of Ward waiting for his change in the rain, wiping the smudge of grease off the glass partition.

4. He is talking about replacement of a little bit of old America, the kind of places that make neighborhoods special—the corner gas station, the corner grocery store, the soda fountain, the cobbler shop. He is talking about how America has become a country full of big, depersonalizing institutions such as department stores, supermarkets, and Self-Serve gas stations.

5. With Sal there was human contact, a human quality, character. With the new place, there is no human contact, and any communication happens across electrical wires or a glass wall. It is appropriate that the Self-Serve station attendant is a rude, irritating kid with no other function than to watch over the machines from a glass booth. Even if Sal did not care about Ward's car, he at least pretended to. The Wild Bill doesn't seem to care about anything except not being disturbed.

6. The scene in the last paragraph perfectly captures the colossal irony of what progress has brought—the customer wiping the windshield of the super oil corporation. The question that the scene asks is, who is serving whom?

RHETORICAL CONSIDERATIONS

1. All the details from paragraph 1 through paragraph 2 characterize so many gas stations. Students should cite such familiar features as the dog, hangers-on, soda machine, battered windshield-wiper case, calendar, brass plaque, even the peanut machine.

2. The description of Sal's clothes, "his walleyed assistant"; the "fume-crazed German shepherd"; Sal's reluctance to give out the rest room key; his reaction to Ward's car problems—these are only a few of the details that students might find humorous.

3. The effect of leaving the plaque of recognition to the end of the paragraph is climactic in an ironic way because what precedes it are descriptions of clutter and disrepair and a grumpy proprietor unhappy with his business.

4. These are not real car problems; at least, there is no such car ailment as "spalding" or any gadget such as a "dexadrometer," or a part called a "flushing drum." This is Ward's fanciful way of confessing his ignorance of auto maintenance.

5. The word "mongrel" connotes a breed impure, inferior, mixed. In this case, the "mongrel rain" is a crude, mean rain, not a steady downpour. The expression sheds some light on Ward's evaluation of the Self-Serve, which is a bastardized version of the old kind of place—a cross between high-efficiency technology and a service station.

6. One good example of irony is the award for Sal's "ten-year business association" from the oil company he no longer likes to work for. Also, the plaque is not an award for outstanding merit, but for longevity. The very end of the essay is the most ironic element in the essay, Ward standing in the mongrel rain washing the windshield of the oil company.

E. B. White ONCE MORE TO THE LAKE

TOPICAL CONSIDERATIONS

1. White records only minor changes at the lake. For one, the middle track where horses used to walk is missing (paragraph 7); also, the waitresses, although still fifteen, had washed hair—the result of having seen pretty girls with clean hair in movies. In paragraph 9 White mentions that today he arrived by car, not train and wagon, and it was less exciting. In paragraph 10 he comments that the only disturbing change "was the sound of the place, an unfamiliar nervous sound of the outboard motors."

2. Except for those minor changes, the lake is nearly unchanged. As a result, he begins to sustain the illusion that his son was himself as a boy and he was his father. He says that this sensation (paragraph 4) kept occurring all the time they were there. It is creepy because he senses that he was living a "dual existence," that he was living in two generations simultaneously.

3. Until now in his return, nothing seems to have changed from the way it was when he visited the place as a child. Thus, such a change as the missing track is momentarily jarring to the man who experiences the strange sensation of reliving his boyhood memories. The missing track happens to be that the horses used to make—a track from an older world and time, before cars and motorboats. The missing track thus takes on a higher meaning, suggesting his own mortality. One might even interpret the middle track as middle life, leaving on one side the path of his youth, on the other the one he is heading down, that of an aged father who will eventually die, as the chill of the wet bathing suit reminds him.

4. The most obvious way in which White creates a sense of the lake's eternal nature is through his memory, which creates the illusory sense that he is at once himself and his father, as well as his recording the minimal changes at the lake. He also makes statements to this effect: in paragraph 6 he refers to the lake as the "utterly enchanted sea," which you leave for a few hours and return to only to find that "it has not stirred," that it is "fade-proof." Something else links the past to the present, creating a timelessness: the little rituals about the lake that White cites, such as campers with the soap, waitresses in the restaurant, "the same country girls," and all the familiar features in paragraph 11.

5. In past summers all motorboats made a "sedative," "sleepy sound." But today's outboards produce a "petulant, irritable sound" shattering the illusion that time has stood still.

6. Already mentioned is the loss of the middle track. Also, the minor changes suggest the passage of time, including references to the arrival by car and the outboards on the lake. There is also the ominous approach of the thunderstorm. But the most striking example is the powerful reminder at the very end of the essay, when White watches his young son pull up his cold, wet bathing suit and, remembering how it once felt, is suddenly aware of his own aging and the chill of death.

RHETORICAL CONSIDERATIONS

1. "Cathedral" suggests a sacredness of the place that has the "stillness" and verticality (the tall pines) of a cathedral as well as a worshipper, White himself. In this same paragraph White refers to the lake as "this holy spot." Other religious references in the essay include the word choice in paragraph 8, sounding like part of a prayer or litany: "juniper forever and ever, summer without end"; and "infinitely precious" and "this cherished body of water" in paragraph 9.
2. Dragonflies have the uncanny ability of hovering on seemingly invisible wings. Here like a mirage they reflect the illusion that no years have passed since White's boyhood. But dragonflies can also flick away as fast as they arrive. The chill of death at the end strikes him with the same suddenness.
3. The turning point occurs in paragraph 4, when he has the "creepy" sensation that his son is himself as a boy and he is his own father.
4. This is a brilliant touch carrying the double effect of time past and time present. Like the minnows actual and minnows shadowed, White sees himself as the father of his son and the son of his father at once.
5. White calls the approaching thunderstorm "the revival of an old melodrama." It is appropriate then that he describes the tumultuous buildup of the approaching event. First the anticipatory "kettle drum," then the louder and shriller "snare" (snare drum), then the even more violent percussion of the bass drum with its booming sound like that of the storm just overhead, and finally the climactic crash of cymbals as lightning and thunder open up the skies.
6. Throughout the essay White says that he confused time because of the timeless quality of the lake and the vivid memories the visit called up. But, of course, time has passed despite the illusion; another generation has come, and another will pass away. The lasting image that reminds him of this passing and finally shatters the illusion of time standing still is the chill of death—the cold of the grave.

▼PART 4 GENDER ROLES

James Thurber COURTSHIP THROUGH THE AGES

TOPICAL CONSIDERATIONS

1. The problems that the peahen and the Empidae fly encounter are two of several good examples he cites: the peahen often falls asleep while the peacock is whisking his beautiful plumes around. And the Empidae female often as not becomes bored with the sweetmeats and tidbits the male fly brings to her. In discussing the courtship habits of peacocks, flies, bowerbirds, fiddler crabs, spiders, and butterflies, Thurber shows that the male of each of these species has to go to absurd lengths to win the female's interest. The rest of the questions are up to the student.

2. Thurber asserts that females dislike the males of their species. He implies that it is part of the courtship ritual for the female to adopt an attitude of indifference. The rest is up to the students. You might ask if they think it is typical for a woman to "play hard to get" or pretend she's not interested when a man is trying to get to know her or ask her for a date.

3. A "love display" is an attempt to attract the attention or affection of a mate. Thurber identifies whiskers and moustaches, somersaults, tilting with lances, parlor tricks, and gifts of candy, flowers, and animal furs as typical love displays. Although most of his examples can be interpreted figuratively, gifts of candy and flowers are typical. Students may think of other examples. In the example Thurber gives, the female could well be pretending indifference as an instinctive part of her courtship behavior; this attitude need not imply that the male's overtures are unsuccessful.

4. As women pursue their own careers and gain a sense of independence and self-reliance, it seems inevitable that they will be on a more nearly equal footing with men and sometimes naturally take the initiative. You might ask the women in the class to consider how they themselves try to win the attention of their male friends and the men to consider how their female friends do so. Some female love displays might include inviting a male friend to dinner, asking him to help move furniture, or even calling him for a date.

5. Students would probably say that they are different. The rest is up to the student.

RHETORICAL CONSIDERATIONS

1. His aim seems to be a little of both. Although his discussion of the antics of peacocks and peahens, fiddler crabs and spiders seems a little absurd, he does show that some of the stereotypical behavior patterns inherent in a real courtship between men and women are laughable.

2. Literally, Thurber says that a man courting a woman is like an actor in a complicated musical comedy trying to make his audience laugh. Figuratively,

he suggests that the male's lighthearted and entertaining attempts to win the female's attention are often clumsy and ineffectual. "Lumber" is a well-chosen word because it means to move heavily or clumsily. Thurber's thesis is that the courtship ritual moves along heavily and clumsily. Nature is personified.

3. The hint of mock seriousness in Thurber's use of these words suggests that he is playing around with his subject and means to be funny. Whiskers and moustaches, instead of attracting the female, make her "nervous and gloomy." The male fly of the Empidae family "can hardly be said to be happy" on his courtship flight. In a complicated musical comedy, a noticeable lack of laughter can verge on gloom when the audience does not respond to the actors' efforts to make them laugh.

4. They have in common a keen sense of wit. Thurber demonstrates by drawing elaborate parallels between the human male's courtship plight and that of males of other species. Allen's wit is given a slightly lunatic, absurdist twist to reflect a world that is not perfect.

5. Thurber establishes the thesis of his essay in the first paragraph and then discusses a different example in each paragraph that follows. Each paragraph reinforces his thesis and shows the reader what he means. An example of good transition is in paragraph 2. Thurber moves from describing the difficulties men encounter in winning a woman's attention to discussing the difficulties that all males share with this statement: "It is rather comforting, then, to discover that the peacock, for all his gorgeous plumage, does not have a particularly easy time in courtship; none of the males do." In paragraph 3, he moves from the peacock to the fly by explaining that when man found that vibrating his whiskers didn't help him any more than vibrating his plumes helped the peacock, the man then went in for a love display that the fly uses: gifts.

Prudence Mackintosh **MASCULINE/FEMININE**

TOPICAL CONSIDERATIONS

1. Seven-year-old Jack comes home singing, "Farrah Fawcett, Farrah Fawcett, I love you" and threatens to give his brother a bloody nose. A friend's daughter hesitates about being a lawyer like Daddy when she learns that no one wears blue tutus in the courtroom. In another friend's family with two sons and a daughter, only the daughter is interested in keeping her room neat and setting the table. A little girl baby sits quietly looking at a blade of grass while Mackintosh's son William uproots the grass by handfuls and eats it. The rest is up to the student.

2. It illustrates Mackintosh's thesis: "Certain inborn traits seem to be immune to parental and cultural tampering." It seems fairly obvious, though, that nurturing qualities do not belong exclusively to girls and aggression is not typical only of boys. You might point to the increase in male nurses and of fathers who seek

and win custody of their children, as well as to the presence of women leaders in Congress, in the military, and in corporations, as evidence.

3. This is up to the student.

4. It seems fair to say that there are qualities that both men and women share. Some of these are intelligence, creativity, strength, dominion, consideration, thoughtfulness. As question 2 implies, even sensitivity, compassion, and aggressiveness cannot be thought of as exclusively belonging to boys or girls.

5. No. Men sometimes choose to be male nurses or secretaries and are good at what they do. Mackintosh simply argues that parents shouldn't try to ignore the fact that there are some innate behavioral differences between boys and girls.

RHETORICAL CONSIDERATIONS

1. Mackintosh's initial sentence implies a question: *Can* the aggressive tendencies in boys be tempered with sensitivity and compassion? She reintroduces this question toward the end of the paragraph: "In such an environment, surely they would grow up free of sex-role stereotypes. At the very least wouldn't they pick up their own socks?" Implicit in this remark is the broader question: *Can* children be raised free of sex-role stereotypes? Mackintosh's answer to the question is explicitly stated in paragraph 14: "Certain inborn traits seem to be immune to parental and cultural tampering."

2. Although Mackintosh's essay is primarily expository, she mixes other rhetorical strategies to develop her exposition. A number of paragraphs (2, 3, 4, and 5) are developed by example. She links paragraphs with a narrative sentence or two. In paragraph 6, Mackintosh begins an analysis of cause and effect that turns out also to be a persuasive strategy that continues to the last paragraph.

3. Any five of Mackintosh's sentences could be cited. One example from paragraph 2: "They know moms and dads do dishes and diapers." A general version might be: "They know parents do household chores." An example from paragraph 3: "These moms looked on Barbie with disdain and bought trucks and science kits." A general version might be: "These mothers shunned feminine toys." The general statements are less colorful and interesting and don't show as vividly what Mackintosh means.

4. The first paragraph explains what she originally intended to do in raising her boys. Throughout the essay she shows what caused her to modify her views. In the last paragraph, she states her new position.

James M. Dubik AN OFFICER AND A FEMINIST

TOPICAL CONSIDERATIONS

1. He would probably define a male chauvinist as a man who thinks women are inferior to men in physical prowess and emotional makeup. In other words, a man who thinks women lacking in aggressiveness, competitive spirit, emotional

control, analytic thinking, physical stamina, and perseverance. In short, a man who thinks women can't be manly. Dubik would probably define a feminist as a woman who regards herself an equal with a man in most areas. His final statement is a concession to biological difference.

2. He met tough women—that is, women who could take what the male cadets could.

3. Not only did he watch his daughters excel at sports once exclusively male, but he saw in them competitive spirit, self-confidence, determination, and ambition.

4. Dubik admits his surprise at meeting women who "took themselves and their futures seriously," who "took charge and seized control of a situation," who "gave orders, . . . were punctual and organized," who "played sports hard . . ." and "survived, even thrived" under real pressure "without folding or giving up." In other words, he was surprised to discover females who could do what male cadets could. No doubt, Dubik is measuring women by male yardsticks, particularly military male yardsticks. He does not sound as liberated as he might think.

5. I can think of a great number of exceptions to Dubik's evaluation of the women of his generation. Students might also as they regard the past generation of women relatives and family friends. One might also invite discussion of this topic in context of middle-aged women visible in politics, the arts, the media, business, entertainment, athletics, and science.

6. Dubik argues that today's women receive "a lot of institutional support not available to women of past generations." Essentially he is saying that today's women have benefited from the feminist movement of the 1960s and 70s and resultant anti-discrimination laws. I agree that there is much greater support for today's women.

7. I think Dubik still suffers some of the old prejudices he suggests he has been liberated from. Throughout the piece he seems to be saying that today's women are extraordinary because they can prove to be as good as men in competitive areas. Again, that is a chauvinistic notion—that is, measuring the worth of women against men. Dubik seems to exercise a prejudice against nonphysical, nonaggressive, noncompetitive women and men. Were one of his daughters passive, he would probably be a disappointed father.

8. I think Dubik is a chauvinist still. I also think his discriminatory attitude is representative of many men from his generation and, to an extent, from the present.

RHETORICAL CONSIDERATIONS

1. I think this first paragraph adumbrates the attitude and organization to follow. Dubik first announces his own roots: "the bastion of male chauvinism." He then defines what he is and the limits of female intrusion: no infantry, no Ranger School, no shooting. There is a concession to those few who become paratroopers and jump out of planes—a statement that looks forward to the women who persevere side-by-side with the male cadets at West Point. His final statement in that paragraph is the pivot point—"All this is as it should be, according

to what I learned while growing up." That final sentence implies a BUT—that is, despite how he once viewed women, experience with female cadets and his daughters have proven wrong or, proven to him that women can work competitively alongside men. And that forecasts the general development of the essay which roughly chronicles his education process—or, more exactly, how women have proven their worth to him, including his daughters.

2. In the past, including Dubik's generation, reading and writing poetry were female endeavors. The implication is that his daughters are not only capable of doing female things, they are also good at traditionally male endeavors.

3. It is possible that Dubik uses "social game" as an extension of athletic games—sports—where his own daughters have excelled. However, the expression seems to trivialize the feminist movement or the efforts to reduce discrimination against women in the workplace. The implication is that women can prove themselves if they kind of fake it by playing male roles.

4. The quotation marks signal euphemism, something less than its name. The implication, therefore, is that Mr. Dubik does not take seriously feminist literature.

5. Dubik's concluding sentence echoes his opening statement while it serves as a kind of QED to the arguments in between. Dubik opens with the admission that he is a member of "a last bastion of male chauvinism." He follows by explaining that there are military operations that are exclusively male—Ranger School, special-operation forces, intelligence operators, "or 'shooters' "—and some almost exclusive—that is, the paratroopers. His argument throughout the rest of the essay is that women have proven themselves capable of making it in a man's military, and he has been witness to the phenomenon. The final sentence toward which the essay builds seems to be Dubik's concession to the liberation of women from traditional roles of passivity. Essentially he concludes that if women are ever discriminated against, it will have to be for reasons of biology alone, not capability. Dubik does not specify, but one can extrapolate that the military will eventually have to yield to women wishing to join the infantry, Ranger School, or " 'shooters.' "

An interesting question to pose to students is whether they feel women should be allowed to partake in the infantry and "special operations" of intelligence. You might remind them that in some militaries, Israel, for instance, women are as much a part of the infantry as are the men. And apparently they are "shooters" in intelligence operations. You might also bring up the controversial subject of women being draftable.

William Raspberry HOMEMAKING

TOPICAL CONSIDERATIONS

1. He argues that husbands, and often wives, don't recognize that homemaking is more than simply doing the chores. He points out that they forget that execu-

tive planning and management are needed to ensure that the chores run smoothly and accomplish what they are supposed to accomplish. Raspberry sees the homemaker's role as analogous to that of the executive in a business. Yes, the analogy is convincing. He points out that executives spend much time doing things that are identical to the homemaker's activity—talking on the phone, holding staff meetings (coffee klatches), having a business lunch (kitchen gathering)—but that the homemaker is accused of wasting time when she does these things.

2. He didn't have to plan the meals, see to the children's nutrition, schedule their activities. In effect, he didn't have to plan, schedule, or fit anything into an overall design. The rest is up to the student.

3. Wives and mothers who do not, and even those who do, have careers outside the home. Also, alert husbands. For those who might not appreciate the article, Raspberry points to "traditional" husbands who don't know anything about homemaking other than that it includes a series of chores. It might inspire her to value more what she is doing. The same could be true for her husband.

4. These questions are up to the student.

5. Raspberry doesn't actually say who should manage the income. But he does argue that it belongs to the family and not solely to the person who happens to bring it home. Worker bees do the work but the honey they produce belongs to the hive. The rest is up to the student.

6. Raspberry thinks women should do whatever their talents, interests, or special needs lead them to do. He points out that some women are better suited to a professional career and others need to pursue one "for reasons ranging from fiscal to psychic." His essay is focused on reversing the tendency to undervalue the homemaker's role so that those who do choose to remain at home can do so without feeling that their talents go unnoticed.

7. See above. Women should have the option to pursue a career or be a homemaker. But if they choose homemaking, or necessity requires that they be homemakers, the responsibility and managerial skills they bring to the task should be valued and appreciated. The value of the work should not depend on whether or not the job receives a salary.

RHETORICAL CONSIDERATIONS

1. Raspberry reveals in his first sentence that he means to present a case for better appreciating the homemaker's role.

2. Raspberry's perceptive analogy is a valid argument for his view that homemakers need to be better appreciated. There is, of course, an obvious bias in favor of the homemaker. Some might argue that it is not entirely objective and balanced because Raspberry fails to discuss any opposing arguments.

3. He begins by talking about something that happened to him and his family last weekend. Yes, this is an effective way to begin. Timely, relevant personal experiences, written in first person, can be attention-getting.

4. It's a persuasive essay that includes narration, description, and exposition.

Judy Syfers I WANT A WIFE

TOPICAL CONSIDERATIONS

1. Syfers wants a wife who will work, take care of the children, take care of guests, be faithful but not expect her to be, quit work and stay home when Syfers has finished school, and allow her to change spouses if and when she should choose to do so.

2. Syfers's ironic account of what she expects a wife to do presents a discriminatory view of the woman's role in marriage that is not flattering to husbands. Her account suggests that from a husband's perspective the wife's feelings, needs, desires, and expectations require little or no consideration. The comment about her friend's ex-wife and her custody of the children is typical of this attitude. The wife is, "of course," expected to take on responsibility for the children regardless of how she feels about it. There are examples throughout the essay: The wife mustn't complain about her tasks but should be ready to listen to her husband's difficulties; she must balance both a job and the home tasks without requiring her husband to take time from his studies; she must quit her job, whether it is fulfilling or not, when her husband wants; she must not object if her husband wants to change spouses.

3. Syfers's portrayal is not complimentary. Self-centered, selfish, and inconsiderate are a few adjectives a student might identify. The rest of the questions are up to the student.

4. If Syfers's wife did all that Syfers expects, she wouldn't have time or energy for an identity of her own. For evidence, students can point to the long list of duties Syfers expects of a wife in addition to holding a job outside the home. Then too, the added requirement that she quit work as soon as Syfers finishes school, implying that the wife's outside job has no significance as a career, reinforces her lack of identity.

5. This is up to the students.

6. Raspberry's description of the executive homemaker accords her the same respect, reward, and consideration for fulfilling her role that her executive husband receives for fulfilling his. In effect, Raspberry's homemaker is on an equal footing with her husband. It seems safe to assume, too, that both the executive homemaker and her husband express thoughtful consideration of the other's needs, desires, and expectations. Syfers's wife clearly does not share these advantages. Subservient to her husband, she is expected to fulfill a series of chores without expecting respect, reward, or consideration in return.

7. Students can suggest their own answers. Some possibilities: The husband must never make unwise financial decisions that would jeopardize his wife's tendency to buy extravagant clothes and plan expensive vacations. He must listen to petty complaints about the children, the house, the bills, but not bore her with complicated business transactions. He should always be ready to go out dining and dancing regardless of whether or not he is tired from work.

RHETORICAL CONSIDERATIONS

1. Syfers announces in her first sentence that she belongs to the "classification of people known as wives." At the end of the second paragraph, she declares that she, too, wants a wife and asks why. In these statements the implication is that, considering her definition of *wife,* she would want one.

2. She is really telling us that she doesn't think highly of husbands who expect all this of their wives; that such an attitude not only encourages self-interest, selfishness, and self-indulgence, but demands so little in return that it would be surprising if anyone didn't want a wife. Every line in the essay is ironic. Syfers does not literally mean that she would like someone to do all these things for her, but that no one should be expected to perform in this way.

3. All three offer a perspective on the relationship between spouses. Thurber humorously characterizes the female as frivolous, pampered, indifferent, and uncooperative in her relationship with her mate. Raspberry sees the wife as capable, intelligent, and responsible without fulfilling her role in the partnership. Syfers defines the wife as a browbeaten, unappreciated second-class citizen in the relationship.

4. Exasperated and critical. The last sentence probably illustrates most vividly Syfers's feelings about her subject. Similar hints are all through the essay: capitalization of "A Wife" in the first paragraph; italicizing of "my" and "good" in paragraph 4; use of "naturally" in paragraph 8. The tone of Thurber's essay is absurd and humorous; Raspberry's is serious and thoughtful; Mackintosh's is friendly and persuasive.

5. Syfers uses it in almost every sentence. It reinforces her point that such demands reveal a selfish, self-centered perspective.

Noel Perrin THE ANDROGYNOUS MALE

TOPICAL CONSIDERATIONS

1. The criteria for determining whether you were "masculine" or "feminine" were rather superficial and silly. If the blots looked like things that caused harm, you were masculine; if you saw "innocent things," you were feminine. Even at age sixteen Perrin was critical of the test, recognizing how limited the criteria were. He says in paragraph 5, "maleness and femaleness are both more complicated than *that.*" Only in later years does Perrin realize that a great number of men and women are essentially androgynous.

2. Perrin says that androgynous men and, by extension, women, are not biologically restricted as are "he-men" or dependent, "feminine" women. Masculine men, attracted to physical power, may be good though overly dominant fathers and husbands, but according to Perrin they could never expand beyond their rigid he-man roles. They would never be found kissing cats or sewing patches in their pants or admitting they can't diagnose minor car problems. Consequently, they are forever hampered by their "single ideal of the dominant male" (paragraph 10).

3. He says being androgynous has freed him as a parent. He says he is a "good natural Mother" insomuch as he enjoys the nurturing role. He says he gets pleasure in seeing his daughter eat and sew her pants. He also feels good about not being self-conscious kissing his daughter's cat.

4. Perrin says that some men — the self-conscious, androgynous ones — owe to the women's movement their liberation from single he-man ideals and roles. He does not say, however, that the true "he-man" is secretly an androgyne or that the world would be a better place if all men came out of the androgyne closet. "It would be [a] duller" place indeed. But for those who are uneasy with not fitting the restrictive roles, women's liberation has also meant freedom for many men.

5. Perrin speaks of the androgynous male as one who enjoys some of the traditional female roles and ideals. By extension, then, the androgynous woman would be one who enjoys some of the traditional male roles and ideals. Students might discuss some of these roles and ideals. They might also consider how androgynous women seek "liberation" from restrictive traditional roles. Consider women who choose traditionally male jobs, such as construction worker or auto mechanic.

6. We'll leave this to the students.

RHETORICAL CONSIDERATIONS

1. Opening the essay with the boyhood anecdote suggests that the author will make the subject personal instead of taking a dry, abstract approach. It also helps establish the friendly, wise tone of the piece. Furthermore, the anecdote is of considerable thematic use because it illustrates the solid yet restricting tradition of male-female stereotyping.

2. Because much of the essay is about the freedom that comes from being androgynous, I would say the opening sentence in paragraph 7 serves as the thesis statement of the essay.

3. They are very convincing, I believe. He gives examples of freedom in the home, with domestic chores and with parenting. He also gives examples of freedom in public — his lack of embarrassment with his car problems and crying in the theater.

4. The final paragraph nicely rounds off the essay by returning to the inkblot test of the opening. Throughout the essay Perrin has convinced us that not only do a great number of androgynes exist, but that they probably enjoy considerable freedom from traditional equating of masculine with "machinery and science" and feminine with "art and nature." His reference to God is wonderfully apt, for the tradition is indisputable that we were made in the image of the Creator — the ultimate mechanic and scientist, artist and naturalist. Though the last line celebrates the possibility that God is in the androgynes' corner, it has, we might think, an androgynous influence — neither too cocky and forceful (the use of the flat, colloquial "nice") nor too meek (a declarative sentence instead of the approval-seeking question "Fellow androgynes, isn't it a nice thought?").

▼PART 5 FADS AND FANCIES

Calvin Trillin SUCCESS

TOPICAL CONSIDERATIONS

1. The very promise of the experiment that is American democracy resides in the promise of the *Declaration of Independence:* " . . . life, liberty and the pursuit of happiness." From this promise has evolved the notion of the "American Dream"—essentially, the rise from humble origins of an individual by virtue of hard work and perseverance. Fundamental to the "dream" is the means not the end, that is, hard, honest work. As illustrated in F. Scott Fitzgerald's *The Great Gatsby* (perhaps the finest illustration of the corruption of the American Dream), pursuit without ethics is corruption, and fortune for its own sake breeds decadence. Like Jay Gatsby, the young man in this parable made his fortunes by underhanded means—"inside-trading violations." His "fortunes"— the 12 million dollars, the limousine, his Fifth Avenue co-op—are ends masking for class. Of course, what's lacking is not measurable in dollars, but years in jail—moral pride. In Trillin's little tale, it is greed that motivates the young man (and, particularly his wife) as well as the yearning to be famous. Ironically, fame seems to be the affirmation of worth in our high-media society. Moral pride does not seem to be enough, Trillin suggests—at least not for some people. The image of importance is what counts. And that is what Trillin is satirizing here—getting one's fortune and face in the papers no matter what the cost in honor. Trillin is no doubt pointing a finger at the wide-spread lack of ethical codes by people high up in the financial industry.
2. The various Wall Street Scandals of the late 1980s certainly have motivated Trillin in this piece. In particular, the famous scandal of billionaire Ivan Boesky who was indicted and jailed for insider trading. He was one of the many financial wizards who was caught in such schemes. As for the image-makers, Trillin also has in mind such super-rich as Donald and Ivana Trump, Kelly and Calvin Klein, Harry and Leona Helmsley (New York real-estate billionaires— they own the Empire State Building and the Helmsley Palace hotel—who in 1988 were indicted for income tax evasion), Harold and Gayfryd Steinberg, and the Kennedys.
3. The young man is impressed with his 12 million dollars, thinking it sufficient to put him in the company of other rich folk. However, his wife considers his fortune insufficient for fame. Sourily she lusts for more: " 'Nobody famous has ever ridden in it [his limousine].' " She wants fabulous wealth and the notoriety that comes with it.
4. For the student.

RHETORICAL CONSIDERATIONS

1. This is a short story in many ways. It has characters, conflict, dialogue, plot, as well as dramatic structure.

2. Nearly everything about the story is exaggeration. The most obvious are the characters and their attitudes—the wife's bitchy craving for fame and the husband's abject eagerness to satisfy her. The husband's suggestions exaggerate the tickets to fame—buying their way onto committees, professional football teams, magazines, etc.

3. These final words are wonderfully ironic since they confirm the utter disregard for moral pride and ethics in the lust for notoriety. They are consistent with the character of the wife who is more impressed with the fame big money buys than the luxuries. Her words also succinctly define what "success" means to many people these days. I found the irony of these words amusing.

Bill Boggs **FINDING THE FURY**

TOPICAL CONSIDERATIONS

1. He discovered the Fury while thumbing through a copy of *Popular Mechanics* magazine as a boy. Boggs says that this particular Fury with the anodized gold trim was a special production model, only 4,485 of which were manufactured.

2. Boggs sounds like a very sentimental man. Not only has he held onto his 30-year-old dream, but he still drives the car he bought back in 1968. But more than a man who simply likes old cars, Boggs seems to cherish the past as evidenced by the special memories attached to the old Parklane convertible—that it drove Hubert Humphrey to the airport, that it was his honeymoon car twice, and that in it he drove his dying dog to the vet. His nostalgic nature is, of course, what motivates him to buy the Fury and fulfill a boyhood passion.

3. Boggs says that for 15 years he had been trying to track down a single Fury. He checked classic car ads and placed some of his own. He says he also alerted service-station attendants, strangers, race-car driver Richard Petty, and his own television viewers of his quest—all to no avail. It was in *Hemmings Motor News* that he spotted the ad that eventually led him to his Fury.

4. Paragraph 14 describes a wonderful little epiphany for Boggs. In the moment of a laugh he realizes how his whole life has been patterned by postponements—postponements of making good relationships, of terminating bad ones, of having a child, of buying a home, of taking vacations. He suddenly realizes that he has put off important things "as if I expected to live two lives instead of one." It's as if a voice inside screamed "carpe diem!" (or carpe dream!).

5. Boggs sounds like a practical kind of person. Even as a boy he managed to squeeze in ten minutes of *Popular Mechanics* before a baseball game. His work schedule is always full and he always has had excuses to put off taking vacations. Characteristically, his reasons for not buying the Fury are soundly pragmatic ones. He rationalizes (1) that he has no garage to put the car in; (2) that he has "no mechanical ability and would have to depend on others to track down out-of-stock parts and fix the car"; and (3) that his rare dream car might get

scratched or, worse, vandalized. Wouldn't that drive him "into a rage"? What all his rationalizing boils down to is that he really does not "need to own the Fury." But man does not live by need alone.

6. What moves him to buy the car, to put aside all the sound reasoning, to make the move is the antithesis of middle-aged practicality: the 14-year-old boy still perking within.

RHETORICAL CONSIDERATIONS

1. The title is a pun, of course. Fury is the name of the car which is the object of young Boggs' passion. Also, it refers to the passion itself, that boyish excitement that motivates Boggs to live out his dream. He buys the car and a little of the old thrill.

2. The first "Hmmmm" is his father's "admiration" when for the first time Boggs and the man lay eyes on the '56 Fury (paragraph 5). The father's reaction is markedly more reserved than young Boggs who yelled "That's it, Dad!" Boggs' "Hmmmm" (paragraph 15) of admiration when he sees the reconditioned Fury thirty years later is appropriate and meaningful for several reasons. Rhetorically speaking, Boggs' own response tightens the essay as it links the first third to the final third. Secondly, it links the thirty years since he's been searching to fulfill a boyhood dream. His response is also reflective of the reserve of his father, for Boggs is now middle-aged and has mellowed since that day with his father. (Had he blurted out "That's it, Bob," he would have sounded a little flaky.) That mellowed response helps create some of the suspense in the essay, because Boggs' practical-mindedness nearly succeeds in talking himself out of flying to Seattle. And, not all of the "fury" in him is gone; for the "Hmmmm," though a quiet, reflective response also hides the boyish urges inside.

3. The movie *Back to the Future* was a very popular nostalgic comedy made in 1986. It is about a teenage boy (played by Michael J. Fox) who goes back to the 1950s and matches up the boy and girl who will become his parents. The allusion is appropriate not just because of the 1950's ambience of the movie, but because the excitement of the teenagers reflects his own early excitement over the car. The fury is still there.

4. The direct dialogue brings immediacy to the conflict within him. Paraphrasing would keep at a distance the struggle he is experiencing—the struggle between his middle-aged pragmatic side and the 14-year-old within who refused to grow up.

5. I found the concluding paragraph rather moving, especially the last sentence.

6. I thought Boggs maintained the suspense to the very end. The first third of the essay (paragraphs 1 through 7) establish his passion for the car and his subsequent quest for it. The middle third (paragraphs 8 through 17) describes how he locates one and drives it. The final third dramatizes how he nearly talks himself out of buying it. When in paragraph 18 Boggs says that following the test drive his "fantasy seemed fulfilled," I felt myself tense with frustration and a little fury. How could he have come so far and not buy it? But, of course, that is

Boggs' clever strategy. So is the articulated ambivalence that follows right to the final paragraph. I thought Boggs did a fine job teasing the reader.

Carin C. Quinn THE JEANING OF AMERICA— AND THE WORLD

TOPICAL CONSIDERATIONS

1. Jeans are probably popular for at least some of the same reasons that they were originally. Quinn explains that they first became popular because they were sturdy and durable. The same is true today. Jeans are worn today by men, women, and children of all ages and social classes because, as Quinn points out, they have become a tradition and because they are comfortable, casual, "smart-looking," and easy to take care of.

2. As Quinn tells it, Strauss immigrated to America to become a door-to-door salesman in New York. When he went to San Francisco with a bolt of tent canvas, he stumbled on an opportunity to use his canvas to make a miner a badly needed pair of work pants. This led to a prosperous business that made Strauss prominent in California.

3. Strauss's running into a miner who needed a pair of pants and happening to have a bolt of material that could be used to make a particularly durable pair of pants was certainly a lucky circumstance. But it seems apparent that Strauss's good business sense, ingenuity, and hard work also were essential factors in his success. Two good examples: In his initial encounter with the miner, Strauss demonstrated promptness and ingenuity in using a bolt of canvas to supply the miner's need for a pair of pants. The incident involving the tailor, Jacob W. Davis, and his idea for using rivets, is another good example (paragraph 5).

4. All can be effective in today's economy. Of the three, marketing, with its far-reaching advertising campaigns, is probably the most effective means for securing the success of a product, simply because it reaches more people.

5. It symbolizes America's respect for the common person and her comparative lack of social distinctions. Other American symbols: baseball, Coca-Cola, Ronald McDonald, Cadillac, running shoes, and television.

RHETORICAL CONSIDERATIONS

1. The essay does have a beginning, middle, and end. In the beginning section, Quinn first reveals that the focus of the essay is on "the story of a sturdy American symbol" and then defines this symbol. The middle section continues with the history of how jeans came to be an American symbol (paragraphs 3 through 6). In the conclusion, Quinn illustrates how jeans are now a tradition.

2. One possible version: This is the story of an American symbol that has now spread throughout the world. The symbol is a simple pair of pants called blue jeans. Blue jeans are favored equally by all classes of people. They draw no distinctions and recognize no classes; they are merely American. Yet they are

sought after almost everywhere in the world. They have been around for a long time, and it seems likely that they will outlive other symbols. The more specific version is more interesting. The specific details give the passage concreteness and make it more vivid for the reader. Also, they show why jeans are an American symbol and who thinks so.

3. Quinn points out that jeans are "sturdy"; they illustrate Alexis de Tocqueville's quotation, "a manly and legitimate passion for equality"; and they "draw no distinctions and recognize no classes" but are "merely American." Quinn's word choices and quotation imply that she has a solid respect for jeans.

4. Because Quinn's essay recounts the history of how jeans came to be an American symbol and tradition and concludes with present illustrations, it seems appropriate to end with an illustration that is particularly dramatic.

Suzanne Britt **THAT LEAN AND HUNGRY LOOK**

TOPICAL CONSIDERATIONS

1. Jordan's amusing caricatures suggest that she is playing around with her subject and means to be funny. But her jibes are also quite perceptive and hint at some telling truths about thin people.

2. This line alludes to the introduction of a poem by Robert Browning called "Pippa Passes." The exact quote is "God's in his heaven—All's right with the world." The title of Jordan's essay is taken from a line in Shakespeare's *Julius Caesar.* The line reads: "Yon Cassius has a lean and hungry look." The opening sentences also allude to lines from this play.

3. This question is up to the student.

4. This question, too, is up to the student.

5. Thin persons could use these same two statements if they wanted to illustrate that fat people are lazy loafers who eat too much. In fact, Jordan's remarks in defense of fat people actually indict them.

RHETORICAL CONSIDERATIONS

1. Jordan establishes her thesis in the opening paragraph. Implicit in her complaint about thin people is the recognition that Jordan is going to point out what it is about thin people that she doesn't like, and therefore why she thinks they are dangerous. Each paragraph in the body of her essay (exception: paragraphs 5 through 8 and 11 and 12 discuss one complaint) points out a complaint she has about them: they aren't fun (paragraph 2); they make her tired (paragraph 3); thin people are not nice (paragraph 4); they believe in logic (paragraphs 5 through 8); thin people don't like to depend on luck or "play it by ear" (paragraph 9); thin people oppress (paragraph 10); they are downers (paragraphs 11 and 12).

2. Thin people: "mechanical," "menacing," "condescending," "efficiency-expert." Fat people: "easygoing," "convivial," "goodly and great."

3. A picture of thin people sitting around discussing rutabagas suggests a boring, intellectual discourse. This is what she seeks to imply about thin people. They aren't comfortable to talk to. The student can point to other apt word choices.
4. Paragraph 12 is a good example of Jordan's use of alliteration. She begins five sentences with "fat." This repetition emphasizes her point that fat people, not thin people, are the ones to like.
5. Jordan uses several clichés in paragraph 12: "writing the great American novel"; "crying in your beer"; "putting your name in the pot"; "letting you off the hook." Why the use of clichés? What is the source of their humorousness? Because they reflect a positive and familiar quality of fat people whose generosity is as universal as the clichés. She also uses a number of words beginning with the letter "g" in this paragraph. Again the alliteration emphasizes one final time how much better fat people are. And in a string, these words create a lightheartedness reflective of fat people.
6. Short, declarative sentences are clear, attention-getting, and conversational. Many of Jordan's sentences are like this.

Mike Royko FAREWELL TO FITNESS

TOPICAL CONSIDERATIONS
1. They are fattening and he loves to eat them. Pork shanks represent all that he has to give up when he is obsessed with keeping physically fit. Conversely, broiled skinless chicken stands for all that is good for your health, nonfattening, and not much fun to eat.
2. Royko would fail miserably on any diet because, as he confesses, he loves to eat fatty foods, and apparently in great quantities.
3. This is up to the student.
4. How students answer this question depends on their own experience. Most, though, can probably think of at least one friend who is caught up in the physical-fitness craze and who, even if he doesn't bounce on the balls of his feet and punch people's abdomens, does talk continuously about how far he is running these days and what he is eating.
5. Royko's plan for "ag[ing] gracefully" includes getting fat on pork shanks and Sara Lee cheesecake and avoiding any exercise more strenuous than walking to the corner tavern. He believes it is "ungraceful" to insist on maintaining a diet of skinless chicken and steamed vegetables and to exercise fanatically to keep the waistline trim. He argues that it leads to wearing hairpieces, jumping around on the disco floor, and, in effect, forgetting to act one's age.

RHETORICAL CONSIDERATIONS
1. Royko indicates the direction his essay is taking and thus establishes his thesis in paragraph 5, where he declares that he is "renouncing the physical fitness

craze." He introduces this thesis by narrating a personal experience that shows why he wants to do so.

2. His first three sentences are relatively short. The only unusually long sentence is the one listing all the good things he would have to give up. Short sentences tend to be clear, attention-getting, and conversational. Paragraph 3 is another example of a paragraph that begins with several short sentences and follows with a rather long sentence.

3. Mock-serious, flippant, and funny. There are examples throughout the essay: After recounting his weekly conversation with the office jock, he announces: "But this is it. No more excuses. I made one New Year's resolution, which is that I will tell him the truth. . . . " When asking rhetorically what the result was of all his exercising and dieting, he replies: "I'll tell you what it led to: I stopped eating pork shanks, that's what." In paragraph 3, Royko declares that he doesn't want to do anything "more strenuous than rolling out of bed."

4. One humorous example is Royko's comparison of what he can eat when he's not on a diet (paragraph 7) with what he must eat if he is on one (paragraph 8). Royko also produces a few laughs when he contrasts aging gracefully with aging ungracefully (paragraphs 9 through 21).

Patrick F. McManus THE BACKPACKER

TOPICAL CONSIDERATIONS

1. Lightness characterizes today's camping gear. The backpack itself is constructed of magnesium frame and nylon pack. Tiny campstoves cook up almost weight-less dehydrated packets of food. And sleeping bags, filled with down, and tents made of "waterproof smoke," make today's camper's burden a light one. The gear of the "old days," on the other hand, was heavy and bulky, making for an unwieldy load. Yesteryear's backboards were canvas and plywood; sleeping bags, according to McManus, looked like rolled-up mattresses; and provisions were never dehydrated. Apples came with the water still in them.

2. McManus found it difficult to give up the old ways. Clearly he was attached to some of the most inconvenient and cumbersome aspects of backpacking. His description of the "old-fashioned" equipment is presented with some pride for the old-time self-sufficiency, endurance, and manliness. His old canvas and plywood backpack, he says, was "designed with the idea that a number of them could be hooked to make an emergency bridge for Sherman tanks." And, speaking of provisions, he declares, "If you wanted apples, brother, you carried them with the water still in them." This was backpacking before technology and those who could afford it—as opposed to those who could endure it—came on the scene and made it faddish. It is only the passage of time that forces McManus to reluctantly consider modern gear, although he views it as sissified. Today's sleeping bags are "filled with the down of unborn geese" and today's tents are "made of waterproof smoke."

3. Sleeping in his sleeping bag brought "a distinct hardening of the earth" to the author's attention. He noticed, too, that nights had become much colder than in the past. "The chill could sink its fangs into my bones in the pre-dawn hours and hang on like a terrier until the sun was high" (paragraph 13). He speculates on the coming of a new ice age. Shockingly he remarks last that apparently trails such as one he traveled easily in his youth had "undergone a remarkable transformation": they doubled in length. His older friends theorize that the earth shifts on its axis every once in a while, causing the trails to stretch. These observations explain the difficulties of camping brought on by aging. Strangely, none of McManus's children noticed these startling geophysical changes.

4. A new back frame, sleeping bag weighing nine ounces, and dehydrated food supplies—these are the concessions the author finally makes.

RHETORICAL CONSIDERATIONS

1. Weight is the key word here. Instead of simply saying that a backpack in the old days was very heavy, McManus specifies that the weight of the pack should "equal the weight of yourself and the kitchen range combined." A mere glance at a pack could "give you a double hernia and fuse four vertebrae." Packs were so heavy that hiking boots were not needed "because your feet would sink a foot and a half into hard-packed earth, two inches into solid rock."

2. See paragraph 10 for examples of repetition. For instance, "A typical meal consisted of fried bacon, potatoes and onions fried in bacon grease, a pan of beans heated in bacon grease, bacon grease gravy, some bread fried in bacon grease, and cowboy coffee (made by boiling an old cowboy in bacon grease)."

▼PART 6   TELEVISION

Peter C. Kratcoski WHAT DID KIDS DO BEFORE TELEVISION WAS INVENTED?

TOPICAL CONSIDERATIONS

1. The implication in the title is a sad one: that kids today cannot imagine how people filled their pastime hours without the tube. The question also points out how much of an authority television is in contemporary life.

2. Kratcoski's childhood activities were more creative, imaginative, and physical. He and his friends planned and made their own Halloween costumes instead of buying them; they read more; they took little expeditions into cemeteries, where they speculated about the dead children. In his childhood, kids "acted out their fantasies themselves, rather than depend on film characters to do it for them."

3. Chances are your students' experiences will differ somewhat from Kratcoski's, because the taboo against buying costumes is long gone in most places. One significant change in Halloween tradition is that trick-or-treating has been

banned in many communities because of such tragedies as the 1982 Tylenol poisonings.
4. He answers it adequately. Kids did more creative things in Kratcoski's day. In the next essay, Marie Winn further documents the decline in creativity caused by addiction to television.

RHETORICAL CONSIDERATIONS
1. The illustrations of Norman Rockwell comprise a *vision* of America, rather than a realistic portrait. His was a sweet village ideal of the Republic. Kratcoski's brief portrait is accurate.
2. He is trying to capture the "tough," insensitive—and self-protective—tone of kids talking about death.
3. There is a clear organization here:
   Introduction—paragraph 1
   First example of activities—paragraph 2
   Second example—paragraph 3
   Third example—paragraph 4
   Fourth example—paragraph 5
   Conclusion—paragraph 6
   Kratcoski's method of organization is inductive, because he begins with evidence for his thesis statement and ends the essay with a specific statement of that thesis.
4. The concluding sentence of the essay is his thesis statement. The rhetorical strategy is to logically build his evidence to this only conclusion. Such is the inductive method.

Marie Winn **THE PLUG-IN DRUG**

TOPICAL CONSIDERATIONS
1. Television consumes the time families would otherwise spend together in their special rituals, games, jokes, songs, and other shared activities. What it prevents—and Winn finds this dangerous—is interaction among members of the family.
2. Family closeness and unity are threatened by the presence of television because one-way involvement with it reduces communication and interaction among family members. Television often is a way to avoid confronting family problems.
3. Winn says nothing about the quality of television in her essay. Her worry is simply the powerful presence of television in the household and its adverse effects on the quality of family life.
4. If children turn on television during those hours when they could be inventing little games or drawing or chatting with others, their ability to create, play, and interact might be threatened, says Winn. Games offer a means for a child to learn how to think and socialize.
5. I think Winn presents sufficient evidence. She cites a variety of authors of

television studies, including Urie Bronfenbrenner and Bruno Bettelheim; she also refers to people she has interviewed, such as the Chicago woman in paragraph 22.

6. Because television is a one-way relationship, it lacks eye-contact, response, real interplay, and argument—it means no communication. For children, in particular, that artificial relationship could condition people to inadequate responsiveness to real people. As Bettelheim says (paragraph 27), real people arouse much less feeling than the skilled actor, who creates an illusion of intimacy. And real-life relationships are far more complicated than those among television personalities.

7. Some network documentaries and news specials are exceptions, I think. Most network television falls under Howe's assessment. The PBS channels offer more depth, variety, and culture. I think Howe would favor many of the offerings on PBS television.

RHETORICAL CONSIDERATIONS

1. "Plug-in drug" is an appropriate metaphor for television because it suggests both the electronic nature of the medium and the addictive, mind-numbing effects.

2. Her example in paragraph 13 is a powerfully convincing illustration.

3. I would say that Winn feels American television audiences are vulnerable to the powerful presence of television. See paragraphs 11 and 14.

4. I think she is accurate in her observation about the way some parents demonstrate their love for their kids—supplying them with "material comforts, amusements and educational opportunities."

5. Her evidence is adequate support for her thesis.

Ellen Goodman **THE VIOLENCE IS FAKE, THE IMPACT IS REAL**

TOPICAL CONSIDERATIONS

1. Goodman's criticism is that broadcasters refuse to accept, even protest against, government studies showing that television violence leads to aggressive behavior among children and teenagers who watch television. Like cigarette manufacturers, they fail to admit to the evidence that their products are harmful to people's health.

2. The major problem cited in paragraph 6 is that there is no regularly scheduled program for children between 7 A.M. and 6 P.M. "A full 80 percent of the programs that kids watch are adult television," which includes "endless sagas of terror, chase, murder, rescue."

3. It is not that the violence on television is just too graphic. The depiction is unrealistic, in that violence is shown without its consequences: the pain and the suffering. Television violence is "sanitized" and "packaged"—violence without consequences—and the message is that violence is right, "that nobody gets hurt."

4. The Japanese television treatment of violence is a lot more disturbing, because when the violence is shown, the results are, too. On American television, says Goodman, the stars just "brush themselves and return same time, same station, next week without a single bruise." And the dead are hauled off camera and forgotten.
5. In the last line of her essay, Ellen Goodman asks broadcasters for some "truth and consequences" if they must give the audience violence. She asks that the painful consequences of violence be shown so that children will not grow up with unrealistic views of it. I agree with her.

RHETORICAL CONSIDERATIONS

1. The final sentence of the essay is her thesis statement.
2. "Sanitized" fits well because it suggests cleanliness and health. She is being ironic in her description of good clean muggings, rapes, and murders, where people don't bleed when they get shot or don't spit out their teeth when they get mashed in the mouth, and where family and friends of the dead do not suffer grief. It is a good choice of words here, suggesting painless violence.
3. The parallel sentence structure makes for dramatic emphasis.
4. The paragraph presents evidence that violence with painful consequences can be presented on television—and perhaps should: an example that American broadcasters should follow.

Brendan Boyd **PACKAGED NEWS**

TOPICAL CONSIDERATIONS

1. Boyd is making the point that on slow news days networks resort to their package of "canned headlines" in their obligation to fill their allotted time slot and to sell products. Of course, there are no real no-news days, but there are days when current events are, according to network news offices, not so eventful, and so the strain to keep up the illusion comes through in the familiar, predictable categories Boyd give us.
2. Boyd says that television news is a way to sell Efferdent and to allow for corporate America to unwind. To help America do that, the news programs entertain us with stories of disasters, a dying economy, lurid and inspirational features—all done without depth. They are "packaged" in the way they are categorized as "World Update," or "Rational Update," or "Human Interest," or "Business and Finance," and so on. Also, headlines and reporting style are packaged—vocabulary, stock phrases, attitudes—in fact, the items themselves.
3. Ominous news, such as troops massing on somebody's borders, holds more attention in its dark implications than news of impending peace along some border. Movements toward peace are "non-events," whereas assemblages of military hardware and troops or a few shots across boundaries are events. Such news coverage is a subtle way of keeping viewers tuned in day after day.

4. This could be a good exercise for students to do in class.
5. By constantly reminding him of "his shrinking worth," television appeals to the viewer's "primal interest" in money. A similarly dark appeal lies in disaster stories, probably because we view disaster as a kind of terrible celebrity who visits other people. We are at once fascinated and repulsed by such stories—something like the voyeuristic quality of people who drive slowly by the scene of a car accident on a highway, on one level hoping to be horrified, on another not wanting to be.

RHETORICAL CONSIDERATIONS

1. These categories are quite accurate, and to structure his essay he uses them in the same order as news programs do. This is a rather clever device.
2. Boyd satirically criticizes the way in which the news latches on to large Third World disasters, whose volume is "meant to compensate for our physical and emotional distance from the event." He is criticizing the way in which we tend to view life more cheaply in Third World countries than in our own.
3. The message is that we would live a lot longer if we didn't watch the seven o'clock news each night.

Newsweek **MTV'S MESSAGE**

TOPICAL CONSIDERATIONS

1. Stylistically, MTV differs from general programming in its "striking imagery, deft choreography, bright colors, and quick cuts" (paragraph 2). Also, it is more explicit in its violence and sexuality.
2. No doubt part of what attracts children to MTV are the flashiness and music, the rapid movement and colors. But what bothers people is the influence of MTV's frightening "nightmare" images, as well as the blatant sexuality. Some parents are appalled that their young daughters are taking their fashion cues from the provocative attire of MTV's "material girls." Others complain that their young sons are talking about "undressing Madonna and marrying her soon."
3. Paragraphs 10 and 11 relate the studies on videos and young viewers. The study conducted by Professor Barry Sherman of the University of Georgia found "no harmful effects on kids who watched MTV—a result that surprised him," reports the article. Sherman says that they found "no negative effects either in perceiving the world as more violent or sexist than it really is." Other studies related in paragraph 15 found a link between television violence in general and "aggressive behavior," and the suggestion is that MTV's own violent images have dangerous social effects. Dr. Snyder, however (paragraph 12), lists some positive social effects of videos, such as the image of "racial harmony" in some clips. The Sherman follow-up study showed that those who watched MTV most often were generally better students and more socially involved. It was mentioned, however, that the results may have had more to do with the economic status of

the students' parents: they could afford cable television, which provides MTV. Students from wealthier homes out perform others in school.

4. The article cites Ken Walz, a video producer, who admits that the prime purpose of MTV is to "sell records, concert tickets and artists." Morality has little to do with it.

5. As with so much of the controversy about television, the ultimate responsibility falls on parents. Television "is one of the few social scourges that parents can control directly." Although parents complain about the messages of MTV, they are hard put to prevent their kids from watching it. Still, theirs is the power to pull the plug.

RHETORICAL CONSIDERATIONS

1. The article does not support outright charges by parents and critics that MTV's violence and sex are bad for kids. It simply explores the question. Therefore, the thesis statement is made in the third sentence of paragraph 2: "And it may simply be impossible to sort out the effects of music videos from network programming, not to mention other social phenomena."

2. The article does present a balance by reporting the views of outraged parents, professionals in the video industry, and university researchers. It suggests no consensus as to whether MTV is harmful. The article does, however, give fewer claims in favor of MTV (see paragraph 12) than reservations and apprehensions.

3. A scapegoat is one who bears the blame for the mistakes of others. The point is that parents who use television as a babysitter are blaming the medium instead of their own permissiveness. As the article says, if parents don't like what their kids are watching on television, in particular MTV, they can simply turn it off. The issue here is really the lack of parental supervision; for some, the resolution is reevaluating the role of television in the home. By concluding with a reminder of parents' responsibility, the essay reflects back on the prime critics of television cited in the opening paragraph. The effect is to round off the essay and at the same time to conclude with a point made throughout—because nobody seems to agree on the effects of MTV, the only solution may be parental discretion.

P. J. O'Rourke **WHY I QUIT WATCHING TELEVISION**

TOPICAL CONSIDERATIONS

1. O'Rourke says he quit watching television the day he realized his girlfriend was more interested in a *Star Trek* rerun than in him. Undoubtedly, he's exaggerating for humorous effect, although his message is that television has a "plug-in drug" effect, as Marie Winn points out in her essay. Also, he says, television is dumb, violent, and a waste of time; and it keeps you from doing more important things.

2. He is being ironic in his complaints here. In paragraph 4 he says that not watching television turned out to be expensive—$1,500 for ski equipment (not to mention the broken leg) and $12,000 for deciding to fix his apartment in his leisure time. He also complains that his reading turned out to be dumber, more violent, and lewder than television. He also says that conversation in his spare time turned into arguments with his new girlfriend about getting a television set. O'Rourke adds that being off television caused him to get fat and put him out of touch with fashions, sports, and personalities.

3. The major drawback is being out of touch with the world of television—the fashions, the personalities, the shows, the sports events.

4. The medium itself has changed somewhat since cable, MTV, and VCRs were introduced. Yet the substantive changes are minimal—just some new shows with new faces. The violence and dumbness have stayed the same. And it's dumb "how perfect everything is in the television world" O'Rourke says.

5. O'Rourke is satirically poking fun at television and the viewer. But, of course, beneath the irony and exaggeration lie some very real messages. He makes fun of the viewer's addiction to television (his first girlfriend's attention to *Star Trek,* his second girlfriend's craving for shows such as *Family Feud,* his neighbor's cable and "TV room," and his own readdiction at the end); our inability to fill our time with more worthwhile activities; the way television keeps us *au courant* and "cultural"; the bizarreness of MTV videos.

6. Despite the violence on television, O'Rourke observes that "The people are all pretty. The pay phones all work. And all the endings are hopeful." His point is that much of television is not about real people in realistic situations. It might be a good idea for students to discuss a show or series in which "television perfection" is analyzed for the messages. Some critics have complained that relationships among characters, particularly in comedy series, are idealized and romanticized and thus create unrealistic expectations for the viewer. Others complain that some people's behavior is modeled on that of television characters.

RHETORICAL CONSIDERATIONS

1. Some examples of irony: (1) the $11,400 that he had to pay carpenters, painters, and plasterers "to repair the damage" he had done when he decided on the "do-it-yourself remodeling" of his apartment; (2) his feuding with his girlfriend over getting a television set so that they could watch *Family Feud;* (3) his first impression of the MTV song video he saw; the parenthetical last two lines of the essay.

2. Beginning: paragraphs 1 through 3 (his getting rid of television)
   Middle: paragraphs 4 through 10 (what went wrong when he did)
   End: paragraphs 11 to the end (his reassessment of television after ten years and his return to it)

3. The final paragraph humorously stresses his ambivalence. He swears he doesn't like the television he sees; he sounds adamant about not returning to the tube.

Yet, parenthetically, that subversive other impulse suggests that despite his convictions he'll start watching and liking it all again. He sounds like a reformed alcoholic dangerously testing himself—or a drug addict slipping back to his habit.

Jeff Greenfield **DON'T BLAME TV**

TOPICAL CONSIDERATIONS

1. Greenfield says that critics have blamed television for what amounts to the decline of Western civilization, including falling SAT scores, growing sexual promiscuity, lower voter turnout, increasing divorce rates, rising crime, and collapsing family life. The reason for all the blame is that television is the most visible and pervasive medium we have. Nearly every American family has one or more television sets.

2. Greenfield says it seems reasonable to assume that television is behind all our social ills. He argues, however, that "you can't make assumptions about causes." And he brings up the fallacy of *post hoc, ergo propter hoc* reasoning.

3. Greenfield continues his line of argument that the cause is not clear. He says that studies (from the David Owen book) show that the drop in SAT scores can be attributed to "nuclear fallout, junk food, cigarette smoking by pregnant women, cold weather, declining church attendance, the draft, the assasination of President Kennedy and fluoridated water." He also points out that scores since 1982 have been on the rise.

4. Greenfield points out that for the last few years the crime rate has, in fact, dropped. The explanation for the drop, he says, is most likely to be the shift of population away from the "youth bulge" and improved criminal justice methods. He wonders how critics can assume that television, with its crime-does-not-pay morality, still manages to turn young people into criminals.

5. On the question of sexual promiscuity, Greenfield says that television "was the most sexually conservative of all media through the first quarter-century of its existence." While movies and magazines such as *Playboy* became more explicit and literary censorship was all but abolished, television "remained an oasis" of propriety. Greenfield adds that it isn't television that has caused young people to become "sexually precocious"; it is probably the "spread of readily available birth control" that encourages premarital sex.

6. He argues that television did not make divorce more acceptable in American society; it was changes in American society that made divorce more acceptable on television.

7. His argument once again is that television is not a cause of social changes but a mirror of them. On the images of women and blacks, Greenfield says that in the early years television borrowed limiting stereotypical images from movies. But despite these images, he argues, women and blacks brought up with television

forcefully rejected these images and organized successfully for their civil rights. His point is that television is a relatively impotent social force, for a major social revolution such as civil rights took place even though blacks on television were being depicted as second-class citizens.

RHETORICAL CONSIDERATIONS

1. The Ward quotation is essentially the gist of Greenfield's argument. He never strays from the idea that critics base all their criticism of television on unfounded assumptions—"what you know that just ain't so."
2. I think Greenfield's most convincing argument is the way in which the civil rights and women's movements were set in motion even though television aired shows in which women and blacks were negatively portrayed. His weakest argument, I think, is his defense of television on the issue of declining SAT scores. He resorts to "writer David Owen" in a "recent book on educational testing" and lists other causes, but without documentation. I would have liked to see more evidence linking these other culprits to the drop in scores.
3. Throughout the essay Greenfield argues against unfounded assumptions that television is behind the decline in our society. Although statements ordinarily have rhetorically greater potency in making an argument, Greenfield is not trying to get to the root of social problems as much as he is trying to expose fallacies in criticism. Thus, the rhetorical questions effectively put down the assumptions by implying the answers. Also, the reasonable tone of the questions is more ingratiating to the reader than a loud, defensive declaration.

▼PART 7   ADVERTISING

John Ciardi IS EVERYBODY HAPPY?

TOPICAL CONSIDERATIONS

1. Ciardi is saying what so many critics of our consumer society have: that we have been conditioned to believe that happiness lies in the pursuit of purchase; that the act of buying is more important than what is bought. I agree with him. This message is glaringly obvious in television commercials aimed at children. Children who watch an average of twenty-eight hours of television a week, an average of four hours a day, are targeted for advertising messages with particular relentlessness and ruthlessness. The message of "No" does not exist in the world of television commercials—or commercials in any medium. The typical ad shows kids in frenzied pleasures around a particular toy or box of "fun" cereal. There is no denial; grabbing and hooting, they get all they want. The message: both product and consumption are joyous. The result: not only are children conditioned to be consumers, but their parents are coerced into complying for the happiness of their kids. Go to any supermarket and notice where the kid ("fun" and, unfortunately, sugar-coated junk) cereals are shelved—

three feet off the floor at a child's eye level and, ironically, about two feet below all the granolas, wheat germ, and other more healthy products.

2. Ciardi makes the good observation that advertising "exists not to satisfy desires but to create them" and faster than we can afford. We are taught that wanting and possessing is being happy. The obverse side of the message is that not having is unhappiness. Since we can neither buy nor afford every new product, we are rendered unhappy until the urge is fulfilled and, then, only for the moment until something else catches our eye. A vicious cycle, an unending pursuit of (un)happiness.

3. Ciardi observes that both the ads and articles in many women's magazines move from "dreams of beauty" in the front to "pharmacopoeia and orthopedics" at the back. In other words, the fantasies of what women want to be followed by the salves, pills, and devices to make those fantasies come true. Particularly true to this pattern are magazines such as *Redbook, Ladies Home Journal, Parents* magazine, and *McCalls.* Newer more trendy women's magazines to consider are *Savvy, Self, New Woman* magazine, *Elle, Woman Beautiful,* and *Working Woman.* You might also have students look at the health and fitness magazines for both men and women. For magazines aimed at the male market, you might refer students to *M, GQ, Esquire,* and *Playboy.*

4. The holy man's idea of happiness is "in needing nothing from outside himself." Admittedly this is an extreme that Westerners cannot fully identify with. Nonetheless, for the holy man happiness comes from within—a lesson for us all. Between the materialistic urge to buy and the ascetic spiritual fulfillment is the author's formula for happiness: in becoming, not having; in the "meaningful pursuit of what is life-engaging and life-revealing," not buying another dream product.

5. See above.

RHETORICAL CONSIDERATIONS

1. Ciardi offers an extended definition of happiness building through a dialectic of materialistic consumption at one extreme and asceticism at the other. The organizing principle here is ingenious, for it is a synthesis that he seeks—a synthesis that rejects life at the extremes. He even states his strategy in paragraph 7 when he says that the idea of " 'happiness' . . . will not sit still for easy definition: the best one can do is to try to set some extremes to the idea and then work toward the middle." He then proceeds to explain that as Westerners we could never settle for the Indian holy man's renunciation of everything outside himself. Likewise, possession for its own sake is not fundamental to American tradition. By introducing in paragraph 12 the all-American notion of having fun by "winning within the rules," Ciardi introduces something we cannot refute, something that is part of our culture: the need for difficulty. (Buying is not difficult especially in this age living on credit.) Almost syllogistically he concludes that happiness is in the pursuit of becoming something, of spiritual self-betterment. As in any game, some odds are against the fulfillment,

but that is part of the fun. A good example is the student who strives to do his or her best in a sport, artistic endeavor, or academics.

2. This is very effective since the concept of pursuit is what Ciardi builds up to in his definition of "happiness" at the end. Also, it contradicts the message of advertisers that not buying is "un-American." Finally, Ciardi returns to the "Founding Fathers" at the end thereby tightening the organization of the essay.

Andy Rooney ADVERTISING

TOPICAL CONSIDERATIONS

1. Rooney claims that most of the legends on the twenty-seven state license plates that have legends aren't true. Or they exaggerate, like those for Rhode Island, "The Ocean State," which has relatively little coastline, and Florida, "The Sunshine State," which is known to get a lot of rain. He also suggests that some legends are meaningless—for example, those for Connecticut ("The Constitution State"), New Hampshire ("Live Free or Die"), and Idaho ("Famous Potatoes"). License-plate advertising probably does not bother most people, but Rooney in his observations makes some valid points, I think. Perhaps license plates should not advertise. His humorous observations and pokes call attention to some of the silliness of the plate advertising.

2. I agree with Rooney. Some plates should just be free of advertising, including license plates.

3. He thinks they are desperate for recognition. He also suggests that they feel they are original and cute.

4. He is offended by designer labels because, as he says in paragraph 21, advertisers have "conned" people into believing that it is chic to wear apparel with the manufacturer's or designer's name displayed as part of the design. He resents the consumer's being seduced into doing the work for the advertisers. I agree with him. His argument against designer-label chic and pride suggests the arbitrariness of labels as well as the susceptibility of the consumer. Such is the power of advertising, O'Neill points out in his essay.

5. Rooney means that because we are such a consumer society, we have allowed advertising to become a natural part of our environment, until we are no longer capable of escaping it; it's everywhere.

RHETORICAL CONSIDERATIONS

1. When a man quotes his grandfather, usually he is summoning the wisdom and authority of experience and tradition. And yet in the second paragraph, Rooney plays down his grandfather's wisdom, leaving both young Rooney and the wisdom of experience up in the air. The result is ambivalence, with grandfather coming off as a foolish absolutist. Automobiles, therefore, go uphill just as good products need to be advertised. As we go through the essay, grandfather's foolish wisdom doesn't sound so foolish as it did at the beginning. In paragraph

15, grandfather is referred to again, and this reference confirms some truth in the man's pronouncements. At the end we can hear some of grandfather's protests in Rooney's own when he complains about designer labels on everything. In effect, Rooney takes us full circle, back to some verity in the old man's universal proclamation—if a product is good it doesn't need to be advertised so heavily.

2. The thesis statement comes in paragraph 3: "the one thing I'm sure of is that there ought to be some sanctuaries, some places we're safe from being advertised at." Also, the last line of the essay restates this thesis. He sticks to this line of argument throughout his discussion of advertising on license plates, car bumpers, and designer goods.

3. In his complaint about license-plate advertising his tone is more tongue-in-cheek. I think he is less convincing in his criticism of the slogans for Maine, New Mexico, Hawaii, Wisconsin, and Idaho. About the other forms of advertising, he sounds more pointed, more serious, more offended, even though his writing has a whimsical, mock-cranky quality. Most of what he says comes from common sense. Consider paragraph 20 and his statements about the desperation of people who boast on their car bumpers the insurance company that represents them.

4. I think the metaphor is very effective. It creates the image of the individual threatened with total consumption by the advertiser. It also calls to mind the notion of the shrinking wilderness; the all-but-certain destruction of both a rare species and its natural ad-free environment.

Charles A. O'Neill **THE LANGUAGE OF ADVERTISING**

TOPICAL CONSIDERATIONS

1. O'Neill clearly believes that the rules of a language—the underlying principles governing composition—are, to a good degree, determined by the context in which the language is used. From this assumption, it follows that there are countless "languages," or usage levels of language—as many, in fact, as there are applications for language.

   In his essay, O'Neill identifies four distinct languages: the powerful, heavily engineered language of advertising; the informal, conversational language of the television talk show; the formal, edited language of publications; and the unedited, "elliptical" language of casual conversation.

   Further, O'Neill believes "language" is not limited to the spoken or written word; it may be, as in television commercials, a combination of visual images (or symbols) and words.

   Acceptance of these assumptions, whether they are "right" or "wrong," depends on the reader's basic concept of language. People who believe, for example, that the English language is governed by inflexible rules, and that word meanings should not be permitted to change, are likely to disagree with O'Neill's assumptions.

2. According to O'Neill, advertising language has special characteristics that separate it from other languages: it is edited and purposeful, rich and arresting, calculated to involve those exposed to the advertising message, and usually simple in structure.

   In addition to these general characteristics, which O'Neill examines in some detail, he suggests that advertising language is different from other languages because it often carries its own special rules of grammar. In the Marlboro cigarette ad cited in his essay, the lines "But, I also want taste.... And real pleasure" are not complete thoughts and therefore do not meet the requirements of the formal standard English sentence.

3. O'Neill cites six charges that have been made against advertising. He quotes critics who feel that advertising debases English; downgrades or underestimates the intelligence of the public; warps our vision of reality; sells us daydreams—distracting, purposeless visions of life-styles beyond our reach; feeds upon human weaknesses; and encourages our unhealthy habits.

   In support of advertising, O'Neill's primary argument is simply that advertising language is only a reflection of the society around it, that "slaying the messenger . . . would not alter the fact—if it is a fact—that America will be the death of English." Also, on the positive side, he offers the thought that advertising is an acceptable stimulus for the natural evolution of language. Further, he says that advertising does not *force* us to buy anything, but stimulates development of new products in the marketplace while conveying useful information.

4. Any number of symbols may be suggested. O'Neill quotes Toffler's reference to the "tiger in the tank," the well-known slogan of a gasoline company. Other symbols could include the strong-armed man on the Mr. Clean detergent bottle, the giant of "Jolly Green Giant" fame, or the fierce, powerful, and responsive cougar for Mercury cars.

   Are symbols effective? O'Neill believes they are, because with repeated exposure they acquire the power to call up in the consumer's mind a host of ideas and images that could not be communicated as effectively in any other way.

RHETORICAL CONSIDERATIONS

1. The story of Shirley Polykoff provides a view of the creative process behind the development of an eminently successful campaign. The use of the story throughout O'Neill's essay strengthens the essay—first, because the story of a person's experience attracts the reader's interest; second, because it adds credibility to some of the points O'Neill raises, serving as a "testimonial" to such concepts as the importance of product position.

2. O'Neill's style could be described as an "advertising" style. In his own writing, he has made use of some of the techniques he has described. First, he has made his writing personal—added a personal dimension to it—by involving the reader in the communication process. To emphasize his point about the simplic-

ity of advertising language, he supports his narrative with the most effective testimonial available, an invitation to the reader to experiment with the "Fog Index."

A second attribute of advertising language, also found in O'Neill's essay, is the concept that advertising language should be "arresting." He attempts to attract and hold our attention with such expressions as "Suddenly, everybody who made TV commercials and movies wanted to show slim, long-haired girls running in slow motion across sunlit fields."

There is also a "carefully engineered" continuity and flow to O'Neill's writing—another quality he has told us is common in the language of advertising.

3. Although he has made a strenuous effort to maintain objectivity by presenting a thorough review of charges made against the language of advertising by such notable critics as Edwin Newman and S. I. Hayakawa, O'Neill's basic sympathy with the advertising business shines through. The manner in which he relates the story of writer Shirley Polykoff hardly leaves the impression that Polykoff and her colleagues are actively scheming to destroy the English language. Rather, he leaves the impression that she is a professional writer who has drawn upon her personal experience as a source of ideas for her client's ad campaign.

O'Neill also uses some of the devices that he has told us are hallmarks of advertising writing, certainly an indication that his personal viewpoint is somewhat more positive than negative.

The only firm position O'Neill takes, however, is that "advertising is likely to continue to influence our behavior, regardless of what we think of the process."

George F. Will PRINTED NOISE

TOPICAL CONSIDERATIONS

1. Will is bothered by the mindlessness and asphyxiating cuteness of some advertising language. He also complains that we, the public, hear so much of this blather that we fail to notice all the nonsense. He does take a swipe at the tendency to give cute names to hamburgers, "made from portions of the cow that the cow had no reason to boast about" (paragraph 14).

2. I'd be hard put to order a *Chicken McNugget* or an *Egg McMuffin* by name, even in McFebruary. I'm sure your students can find some fanciful menu names in local eating places, perhaps even the student cafeteria or snack bar. McD.L.T. is the latest from McDonald's.

3. When we talk about hamburgers or beefburgers, we are talking about the meat, not the animal from which it came. Steerburger, like cowburger, or sheepburger, or pigburger, call to mind the animal's conversion from hoof to sandwich. "Oven-baked" is redundant. Where else would you bake a meat loaf? "Fried to order" is also redundant. Obviously, if you didn't order fried clams, they wouldn't fry them for you. "Liver with smothered onions" should be "liver smothered with onions," unless the onions were prepared by asphyxiation.

"Hearty" is a trite exaggeration, implying that the sandwich would provide you with abundant nourishment.

4. Will's point is that because we are so dumb and blind to the flurry of menu adjectives, nothing would be missed if they were sacrificed. I agree.

RHETORICAL CONSIDERATIONS

1. His examples should be convincing, even though, for the most part, they are not analyzed.

2. This example is effective for several reasons, not the least of which is that it is funny. First, it illustrates the ludicrous names that appear on American fast-food menus. Second, the anecdote dramatizes what Will claims in his last paragraph, that we "Americans hear the incessant roar of commerce without listening to it, and read the written roar without really noticing it." For a moment the girl behind the counter could not link the cutesie name Yumbo with what it stood for—a simple ham and cheese sandwich. Finally, the anec-dote illustrates how some of us refuse to submit to the asphyxiating cuteness of Yumboness. I found the example very appropriate and funny.

3. Will displays an ironic and cynical sense of humor, and a rather sophisticated one. In paragraph 2 he calls Baskin-Robbins's "Hot Fudge Nutty Buddy" an "unutterable name," following with the mock-fastidious claim: "There are some things a gentleman simply will not do, and one is announce in public a desire for a 'Nutty Buddy.'" (Echoes of Walter Mitty's refusal to utter "Puppy Biscuits" in public?) Also, in paragraph 10, Will introduces the example of the Cam-bridge don, followed by the exaggerated claim in paragraph 15: "In a just society it would be a flogging offense to speak of 'steerburgers.'" Although the persona Will adopts is one with a highly refined and precious sensibility, his stand is appreciated, because this is just the kind of pose needed to point out how absurd all the printed noise is. His adopted role is that of the outside observer, not the casual insider who is somewhat deaf to all the commercial blather.

4. Muzak is the trademarked name for recorded music that is piped into shopping centers, supermarkets, dentist's offices, and elevators, to name a few. It is also found on some radio stations. The music is characterized by unobtrusive blankness, hypnotic rhythm, and limited decibel range. For the most part, it functions as background music in public places to facilitate separation of shoppers from their money. Muzak is carefully selected and orchestrated so as not to be distracting. It is an accurate analogy to the verbal litter of menus, because both are ubiquitous, artificial, and barely noticeable.

Diane White **RESISTING THOSE AWFUL COMMERCIALS**

TOPICAL CONSIDERATIONS

1. She was surprised that people cannot remember the commercials they did not like. Yet she remembers them all too well.
2. She offers four possible explanations: (1) she could not get the jingles out of her head; (2) perhaps part of her subconscious needed to be dominated by "lousy advertising"; (3) she felt guilty for hating the Murphy Oil Soap family; and (4) because she was curious "to find out if the product could be as bad as the commercial." Her second possible explanation might strike students as more valid.
3. She says she hates the Close-Up commercial because of the nauseating image of the two people in love because of what their toothpaste has done for their teeth and breath.
4. It might be interesting to see what the students come up with. I avoid commercials for Mercedes-Benz cars because I can't stomach seeing people celebrating ownership of cars I can't afford.

RHETORICAL CONSIDERATIONS

1. I think White is making a good point here—that commercials work on us in ways we may not fully understand. And yet we may hate the fact that they do.
2. Not in any detail does she analyze her contempt. She does detail the features of the Murphy Oil Soap commercial, but she does not say exactly why she hates it. Regarding the ad for Close-Up, she does specify the nauseating image of the young people mindlessly in love with each other because of their toothpaste. White is least analytical in her references to the Hawaiian Punch commercials featuring Donny and Marie Osmond (paragraph 9). Presumably, if we are familiar with these we will sympathize with her contempt for them.
3. I would say her style is conversational—as if she is sitting across a table having a chat and coffee with the reader. White creates a kind of intimacy through familiarity in her writing style. She is also quite humorous in spots; and a key to her humor is her highlighting things familiar though not often voiced—the obnoxious little features of the commercials she cites and the perverse feelings they may call up in us. For instance, the Preparation H commercial with the man unabashedly hopping on his bicycle and peddling off to demonstrate how the ointment has rectified matters, as if he's powered by happy little hemorrhoids.

▼PART 8   ON VIOLENCE IN AMERICA

Martin Luther King, Jr. **PILGRIMAGE TO NONVIOLENCE**

TOPICAL CONSIDERATIONS

1. King was trained in the ministry. His essay hints that he is intimately acquainted with the Bible. He points out, for example, that in the Greek translation of the New Testament, three words are used for love that have different root meanings. (He builds a major portion of the essay on this fact.) King also refers to Paul and the Samaritan who helped the Jew on the road to Jericho.

2. As a young man, Gandhi studied law in London. This training prepared him first for his fight against legal discrimination in South Africa and later for his leadership in India's struggle for political independence. His success as India's leader resulted mainly from his practice of civil disobedience (a term he borrowed from Henry David Thoreau's essay by that name). This form of social protest demands not only that its advocates actively resist injustice and discrimination, but that they do so without resorting to physical violence and without fleeing. It demands instead that they submit to any violence that may be inflicted upon them because of their resistance. Implicit in such nonviolent resistance is the conviction that it will eventually cause the perpetrators of the injustice and violence to see the lack of common humanity and injustice in their acts and cease doing them voluntarily.

3. The first point in King's explanation of his philosophy indicates that there is a difference. King emphasizes that nonviolent resisters are not passive. They don't run away or avoid facing an issue. Instead, they actively protest against injustice or social wrongs by confronting them and by accepting whatever punishment may result from their refusal to submit. Those who fled to Canada did so not only to avoid and protest against the Vietnam War but also to escape punishment. This is passive nonviolent resistance. Also, by fleeing, they were expressing an attitude that could appear to be cowardice. King explains that cowardice is no part of nonviolent resistance. Because conscientious objectors agree to perform noncombative services in lieu of combat duty, they don't actually protest against or resist war but only their own active involvement in it.

4. King's philosophy requires not just physical courage but moral stamina. The qualities of character needed to express such moral stamina are taught in the Sermon on the Mount: poorness of spirit, sorrow for present wrongs, meekness, mercy, hunger for righteousness, desire to be a peacemaker, and rejoicing in the face of persecution.

5. There are obviously no easy answers to this question. World events reveal that returning evil for evil or hatred for hatred results in escalation of terrorism and violence. It is obvious that nations, court systems, and individuals can't sit back and allow acts of violence and terrorism to go unpunished and unchecked. But perhaps as individuals practice the teachings of the Sermon on the Mount and

King's philosophy of nonviolent resistance, this action can go far toward lessening the tensions that result in terrorism and violence.

6. YMCA and YWCA. Girl and Boy Scouts. Rotary Club. Elks. Masons. Shriners. Eastern Star. Salvation Army. Local charity organizations. United Fund. Good Will. American Red Cross. Human and social service organizations. Government-sponsored welfare programs.

7. This is up to the students.

8. He speaks of redemption and reconciliation and reveals an intelligent, wise, practical love for humanity that can be emotionally as well as intellectually appealing.

RHETORICAL CONSIDERATIONS

1. This is up to the students. Many would probably say yes. The pronoun I and personal experiences can be attention-getting, especially at the beginning of an essay.

2. In paragraph 2, King indicates that his purpose in writing is to discuss the basic points in his philosophy. But also, in his narrative introduction, he mentions that when the Montgomery Movement began, he was reminded of the Sermon on the Mount and Gandhi's method of nonviolent resistance. He seems to imply here that his philosophy is derived from these two earlier sources.

3. King's is an expository essay developed primarily by definition. A narrative pattern opens the essay.

4. Notice the variety of words King chooses to achieve a smooth transition when he explains the six basic points in his philosophy: First, a basic fact, second basic fact, a third characteristic, a fourth point, a fifth point, a sixth basic fact.

5. Because King's essay is short and he clearly delineates the six points of his philosophy, he doesn't need to summarize these points in the end. In fact, to do so would be unnecessarily repetitious. Also, the last point is appropriate for a conclusion because it points to the underlying reason nonviolent resisters are convinced that their efforts will count for something.

Martin Gansberg 38 WHO SAW MURDER DIDN'T CALL THE POLICE

TOPICAL CONSIDERATIONS

1. This, of course, is up to the students. It might be useful for them to reread the essay, looking carefully at Gansberg's description of the witnesses, to see if they can relate to any of them or understand why they acted as they did.

2. The first witness asked a friend on the phone and went to another neighbor's apartment for advice before calling the police. He later explained that he didn't want to get involved. Whether or not this is a justifiable reason is, of course, open to question. Given Gansberg's description of the neighborhood as "staid" and "middle-class," with houses ranging in value from $35,000 to $60,000, it

seems fairly reasonable to assume that its residents were financially comfortable and conservative and therefore easily intimidated and unwilling to take risks. One housewife's comment that she thought it was a lover's quarrel is legitimate. But her unwillingness to investigate further again suggests an unnecessary caution that may or may not be excusable. The same is true for the couple who were afraid, the woman who didn't want her husband to get involved, the husband and wife who didn't know why they failed to do something, and even the man who was too tired.

3. The neighborhood is not a run-down ghetto or an inner-city slum. It is a comfortable, prosperous section of town. Yes, it is surprising. But considering that the murderer had previously committed two similar murders, whether the neighborhood was crime-prone or not seems to have had little to do with the crime.

4. This is up to the students.

5. As the introduction to Gansberg's essay explains, it shocked the nation. The rest is up to the students.

RHETORICAL CONSIDERATIONS

1. Gansberg's article is a news story and should have specific terms, addresses, ages, phone numbers, and so on; it wouldn't read like a credible piece of journalism, nor would it be as interesting, vivid, or shocking in its realism if it lacked specifics.

2. Gansberg appears to have wanted to shock his readers out of any complacency they might be tempted to feel toward this incident. And I think he was very successful.

3. Gansberg's choice of words suggests that the crime could have been avoided if the residents of this prosperous neighborhood had not been so unnecessarily fearful, cautious, and indifferent. There's a hint of irony in his use of the adjectives "respectable" and "law-abiding" in the opening sentence and his reference to "good people" in paragraph 4. "Chatter" in the second paragraph implies that the conversation was trivial, mindless, and unimportant in contrast with the life-and-death events taking place in the street. "Killer" and "stalk" dramatize the horror of the event in contrast to the futile, weak excuses of the witnesses. Gansberg's remark that Catherine Genovese was called Kitty by almost everyone in the neighborhood implies that she was familiar to all of them, a friend, and someone whom they should have felt more interest in protecting.

4. Gansberg's use of dialogue was very effective. The dialogue brings the reader closer to what happened and makes the event more real.

5. Gansberg's conclusion ties in very well with his thesis and purpose. The police detective's comment emphasizes the irony of the situation. Gansberg sees a pathetic irony in a group of people who are too afraid, indifferent, or tired to pick up a phone to save someone's life, but who can come out from hiding when the danger is over and there's a curious sight to see.

George F. Will **A WEST COAST STORY**

TOPICAL CONSIDERATIONS

1. As Will points out the term "juvenile delinquency," born of the 1950s, suggests "sporadic naughtiness" and not the kind of brutality of West Coast urban gangs. Will is being darkly ironic in the euphemistic "gentrification." The tragedy of the Los Angeles phenomenon is that, unlike their predecessors, juveniles don't grow out of the gangs but continue on as adults with automatic weapons and pockets full of bloodstained profits.

2. Sam's reaction, says Will, is "only slight interest and no surprise," a reaction that suggests either how inured Sam is to such news or how insensitive he is. Will's label of "atavistic" suggests a low conscience.

3. In paragraphs 6 and 7 Will discusses the past attitude toward juvenile gangs during the 1950s. A political conservative, Will does not take seriously the romanticizing of social rebels by left-wing intellectuals. Nonetheless, he does name some sources, in particular, a fascination with the sense of alienation from the bourgeois status quo—a fascination that characterized some of that era's literature (for example, Camus and Sartre), music (rock and roll), musicals (for example, *West Side Story*) and movies (for examples, James Dean's *A Rebel Without a Cause* and Marlon Brando's *The Wild One*).

4. Novelist George V. Higgins once defined a conservative as a "liberal who's been mugged." Whether or not Will ever was mugged, he clearly espouses the conservative doctrine on criminality. The classic liberal view is that individuals are products as much as victims of their environment and should be given a chance at rehabilitation even if their offense is murder. The classic conservative view is that individuals who commit crimes are fully responsible for their acts and deserve punishment commensurate with the offense (a concept derived from the Old Testament doctrine of "an eye for an eye, a tooth for a tooth"). Even if this is some students' first exposure to George F. Will, they should recognize the conservative stand on criminal justice—a stand from which to extrapolate Will's advocacy of capital punishment.

    From his interview with Sam, Will sizes up the thousands of "gang bangers" as "semisociopaths, utterly indifferent to social norms or any notion of right and wrong." That summary evaluation coupled with Will's ironic swipes at liberal-minded social sciences and his disinterest in the environmental forces behind the sociopathic behavior point to a hardline attitude summed up in the aside (paragraph 3), "The Lord would have saved the LAPD a lot of trouble by being elsewhere" when Sam was shot.

5. Some students might argue that Will fails to address the environmental forces that produce the vicious behavior, that he is insensitive to the tragic conditions of poverty and violence that many of the young gang bangers are reared in.

6. This one is for the students. For a cogent debate on the subject of capital punishment, you might assign your students two selections from the next

section, Edward Koch's "Death and Justice: How Capital Punishment Affirms Life" and David Bruck's "The Death Penalty."

7. For the students.

RHETORICAL CONSIDERATIONS

1. The title, of course, refers to *West Side Story,* the famous long-running Broadway musical and popular movie of the late 1950s. The reference is darkly ironic, for the West Coast phenomenon is anything but romantic, "light years," as Will says, from the "Romeo-and-Juliet" tale of rebellious, disaffected youth.

2. Will is again being darkly ironic here. Mugging, armed robbery, car theft, and drug dealing are hardly "careers" in the ordinary sense. As with "sabbatical" used to describe Sam's incarceration and the like, "an 'institutional man' " (paragraph 9), Will's irony borders on mock-heroic.

3. Atavism means a reversion to an earlier or primitive form. In short, a throwback. Hardly a liberal perception, the term condemns Sam and his kind to a subhuman classification warranted, as Will would argue, by their vicious behavior, their inability to distinguish right from wrong, and their unreformable nature.

4. Very conservative. See above.

Gail Buchalter WHY I BOUGHT A GUN

TOPICAL CONSIDERATIONS

1. Buchalter's purchase of a gun stands in sharp contrast to her cultured upbringing and liberal-minded ideals. Buchalter says that there was no place for guns in her upper-middle class background. When threatened, her parents "simply put another lock on the door." In high school, Buchalter says she underwent a transformation of values, from cashmere sweaters to black arm band. As with so many young people of the late 1960s and early 70s, the author says she became an active pacifist marching for civil rights and against the Vietnam War.

2. The turning point came one Halloween night in Phoenix when Buchalter was pursued by three men threatening "to rape, cut and kill" her. What saved her, no doubt, was the sight of her two large dogs whose protection helped make her daringly aggressive. "I was so scared that I became aggressive," she writes. The men ran off but not without promising to return to kill her. That awful episode taught Buchalter not only to fear the mindless, random violence in our society, but to consider doing something about it. By the time she moved to Los Angeles she had a 3-year-old son to worry about. What convinced her to purchase her Smith & Wesson .38 was the gradual take over of her neighborhood by drug-dealing street gangs. That and the threat of Richard Ramirez, "the Walk-In Killer" whose "crimes were so brutal and bizarre" that she decided she needed to defend herself despite her pacifism. Reluctantly she concluded that she had to insure her and her son's survival and needed a gun.

3. She was held up at gunpoint years before. This discovery no doubt encourages the author to follow the same path before she too became a victim to violence.

4. Buchalter cites two important features of her experience at the National Rifle Association convention: that lots of ordinary people from grandmas to kids were buying guns; and, from the video seminars for women she learns the function and care of firearms.

5. In paragraph 24 Buchalter says that "knowledge . . . is still our greatest defense," a justification fortified by her belief in educating the young about sex and AIDS. In the next two paragraphs she describes how persistent she was in teaching her son how to handle the gun—how to check that it was unloaded and how not to use it if someone broke into their house.

6. In her situation with a young son and gangs infesting the neighborhood, I think I might have done the same. Student reaction here should be interesting.

RHETORICAL CONSIDERATIONS

1. The opening sentence of paragraph 3 is her thesis statement.

2. This detail does several things. First, sitting next to a contributing editor for a gun magazine puts her next to the kind of people she previously would not have associated with. A onetime pacifist and political liberal, Buchalter would probably have avoided NRA men. Here she's a stranger in a strange land. The man's bitter complaint about the outlawing of elephant hunting says something about the kinds of people the NRA attracts, men who are insensitive to killing animals that are high on the endangered species lists. Also, his comment about elephant legs making "wonderful trash baskets" characterizes him as something short of barbaric. Feeling like Thumper, the rabbit friend of Bambi, on "opening day of the hunting season" suggests how vulnerable she feels next to the man. And her twitching foot confirms her lack of ease.

3. By assigning the final comment to its own paragraph gives it special emphasis and dramatic impact. The line functions as commentary to the author's friends who are dismayed that she owns a gun and who "believe that violence begets violence." Sitting alone, the comment carries a note of sad resignation and inevitability. In other words, her friends are "probably right" that someday that nightmare two paragraphs back might come true. The line also rhetorically rounds out the essay as it sadly reflects on how far from the innocence and idealism Buchalter has come since the reflections in the first two paragraphs.

▼PART 9 CONSCIENCE AND CONTROVERSY

Lance Morrow **IT'S TIME TO BAN HANDGUNS**

TOPICAL CONSIDERATIONS

1. Students need to draw from their own experience to answer this question.

2. Morrow argues that a substantive program of well-enforced federal regulations is needed to control handguns effectively. He points out that a large percentage

of Americans support such a program and that the rest of the world is puzzled that it is not already in effect. Morrow implies, too, that the failure of legislators in Washington to pass such legislation cannot be solely attributed to the powerful lobbying efforts of the National Rifle Association (NRA). It is up to the students whether or not they agree with Morrow.

3. Assassination by handgun of six prominent individuals, five of whom were important political figures, is a startling statistic. Whether or not banning handguns would have prevented these assassinations is up to the students. You might ask them to consider what other means might be available to potential assassins and if they would be as likely to use those.

4. Low murder rates are not necessarily the result of prohibitions on handguns. Society in both Britain and Japan tends to be less volatile. Normally, Britain's police do not themselves carry guns. In Japan a heavy sense of shame can act as an effective deterrent. The criminal's family has been known to influence individuals to turn themselves in if they haven't done so themselves.

5. Fifty-five million pistols in the United States. Highest rate of murder by guns in the world. Low murder rates in Britain and Japan. According to a Gallup poll in 1938, 84 percent of Americans wanted gun controls. In the latest Gallup poll, 62 percent wanted stricter laws. One American every thirteen seconds buys a handgun. Twenty-five thousand inconsistent, ineffectual gun regulations already exist. Yes.

6. As Morrow points out, the NRA is Washington's most effective lobbying organization. The rest of the questions are up to the students. It might be useful to point out that many members of this organization are wealthy sportsmen who have resources to contribute to an organization that promotes their interests.

7. Morrow points out that the "patchwork of some 25,000 regulations" affecting gun control are "preposterously ineffectual." Morrow implies that a social malaise or lethargy among the American public and legislators prevents them from correcting this situation. He remarks that firearms are seen to be inevitable; that often "good" people believe they need a gun to defend themselves from the "bad" guys; and that when an assassination does occur, there is a failure to assign blame and search out what can be done.

8. He would have agreed.

RHETORICAL CONSIDERATIONS

1. Morrow links the license to use handguns with a hand grenade and a beehive.

2. See answer to question 2 under Topical Considerations. Morrow prepares his case in the first six paragraphs and then states explicitly in paragraph 7 that the nation needs new federal laws banning handguns.

3. The nation is a wounded victim "twitching and flinching." The years are "bloody," and the NRA is the "deadliest" lobbying organization in its "targeting" of enemies at election time. Because our nation's frontier heritage is "gun-ridden," "good guys" need guns to defend themselves against the "rising tribes of bad guys." The violence of the frontier West is still "blazing away." Yes, these word choices are effective.

4. Emotional and flag-waving. Gansberg also uses emotional terms designed to get a response from his readers, as when he says that the witnesses watched the "killer stalk and stab" his victim. King's article seems more reasoned and objective.

5. The first part of the question is up to the students. Morrow refers throughout the essay to the nation's "frontier heritage." He compares today's owners of handguns to the "good guys" and "bad guys" from frontier history. His mention of Turner's thesis is particularly appropriate at the end, because with it he sums up what he has been implicitly and explicitly stating throughout the essay, that handguns are an "anachronistic tool" that should have stopped when the frontier closed and not continued "blazing away" into the twentieth century.

Barry Goldwater WHY GUN CONTROL LAWS DON'T WORK

TOPICAL CONSIDERATIONS

1. Morrow disagrees with Goldwater on this issue. Whereas Goldwater cites the ineffectiveness of present laws as an argument *against* passing any new legislation, Morrow points to these same laws as an argument *for* passing such legislation. He argues that these present laws are not effective because they are scattered and unsystematic, and that this confusion could be corrected if a systematic, well-enforced program of federal laws were enacted.

2. Goldwater argues that an individual in the throes of passion won't be stopped by lack of a gun but will use whatever else comes to hand—a knife, an ice pick, or a baseball bat. Morrow would argue that this statement is not necessarily true. He cites statistics suggesting a direct correlation between violent crimes and the ready availability of handguns.

3. Goldwater argues that stronger enforcement of current penalties against killing people would cause an individual to think twice before he used any deadly weapon, including a gun. Yet earlier in his essay he contends that a person angry enough to kill is going to strike out with whatever comes to hand, implying that he wouldn't be giving much thought to what he was doing.

4. Goldwater cites the Second Amendment to the Bill of Rights as protecting the right of the individual to bear arms. Although citation of this amendment is valid, opponents would point out that the amendment refers to a state militia and was originally intended to allow the states to defend themselves against unjust encroachment by the federal government and not necessarily to grant free license to anyone and everyone who wanted to own a handgun.

5. Goldwater argues that the real issue is not how to control guns but how to control crime. Whereas Morrow argues that a more consistent and better-enforced system of federal legislation would reduce the crime rate, Goldwater denies that there is any correlation. Goldwater suggests instead that reversal of

the present trend toward leniency and permissiveness in the courts and stronger enforcement of penalties for laws already written are a better solution.

6. This is, of course, up to the students. You can encourage them to analyze the two essays side by side. Some points the students might consider: Goldwater gives valid examples and statistics to prove that present gun legislation doesn't work. Morrow agrees, but argues that this is an argument for, not against a federal program. Goldwater remarks that an angry individual with an urge to kill will find another weapon if a gun is not available. This is a reasonable point that Morrow does not address. Goldwater offers thoughtful objections to the argument that national registration of handguns is at least worth trying. Nothing in Morrow's essay would satisfy Goldwater's objections. Morrow also offers convincing arguments that are not always fully answered by Goldwater's remarks. For example, Morrow's statistics on the correlation between murder rates and handguns in Japan and Britain and the fact that six prominent Americans in recent years have been killed by handguns raise valid questions that Goldwater's essay does not address.

RHETORICAL CONSIDERATIONS

1. Morrow begins this essay with an intriguing, complex comparison equating handguns in modern society with the reptilian brain that lies hidden in the cortex of a man's brain, commenting that either one, like a beehive or hand grenade, can explode quickly when disturbed or activated. Then, before he moves on to a direct statement of his position on gun control, for several paragraphs Morrow graphically describes the violent effects these handguns continue to have on our society. Goldwater's introduction, on the other hand, is more succinct. In two sentences he establishes that he has considered the call for increased gun-control legislation and is convinced that such regulation will not help solve the problem of the rising crime rate. He moves directly from this brief opening into development of his arguments. Both introductions are attention-getting, for different reasons. Morrow's vivid comparisons and dramatic word choices are startling and thought-provoking. Goldwater's succinct two-line opening and immediate use of the pronoun "I" speaks directly to readers to catch their attention.

2. Goldwater adopts an informal, conversational tone in his essay, speaking directly and straightforwardly to readers, and reasoning through his arguments simply and logically. Because of this approach, his remarks do not demand a thoughtful, careful reading to be understood and could easily be delivered orally as a political speech. Morrow, on the other hand, uses arresting, complex figures of speech and vivid word pictures to appeal to his readers' emotions as well as their intellect. As a result his essay seems more literary than Goldwater's.

3. Yes, he does. Goldwater begins his essay with an answer to the overall question of whether gun control is the answer to the rising murder rate. He then offers a series of rebuttals to well-known arguments proposed in favor of such legislation.

4. Yes. For example, when he argues that gun legislation doesn't work, he points

out the 20,000 existing laws and discusses in detail inadequacies in the Gun Control Act of 1968. He frequently cites specific incidents. When discussing the expense of enforcing gun-control legislation, he points out that at one time it cost New York City $72.87 to process one application for a pistol, and that this was equivalent to $100 in mid-1970. In support of his proposal for gun education, he describes an experiment in Highland Park, Michigan, where the store-robbery rate dropped from 1.5 per day to none in four months. All his arguments seem well supported with specific details and illustrations.

5. Yes, the ideas flow logically. Goldwater frequently moves from one issue to another by posing questions and then suggesting answers. Paragraph 5 is a good example. Then, in paragraphs 6 and 7, he answers these questions, moving from one point to another with these transitional phrases: "The first," "then," "on top of that," and "finally."

6. The questions contribute to the informal, conversational tone of this essay. They also provide useful transitions from one section of the essay to another. Notice the first sentence in paragraphs 8 and 10.

Anonymous IT'S OVER, DEBBIE

TOPICAL CONSIDERATIONS

1. The doctor appears to have experienced both emotions although it is difficult to determine which dominated and determined his or her behavior. Clearly the doctor was annoyed at having been disturbed in the middle of the night: "I had come to detest telephone calls, because invariably I would be up for several hours and would not feel good the next day." Out of a sense of duty the doctor answered the telephone then "trudged" toward 3 North and "grabbed" the chart from the nurses station. The word choice here strongly conveys aggravation; yet, it is clear that the doctor's focus changed when face-to-face with the patient. The detailed description of Debbie's condition suggests awareness of her suffering.

2. Thinking that Debbie's suffering is needless, the doctor focused on relieving her immediately. Evidently the doctor did not consult Debbie's medical records nor was Debbie's family or physician consulted. The doctor's reaction was to the moment—Debbie's condition was terminal and her pain unnecessary. She had suffered long enough.

3. Debbie's last words could have meant a number of things. The doctor determined that she wished her suffering to be alleviated by death. One could also argue that Debbie wished her suffering to be over with, but not her life. Or, that she was tired of vomiting. It's also possible she expected the doctor would administer a painful procedure, such as drawing blood or injecting her with drugs, and wished that it would be over with soon. It is also possible that in her weakened, pained, and sleepless condition Debbie did not understand the import of her own words. She could have been half-delirious, dream-talking.

That several interpretations are possible underscores the ambiguity of the remark.

4. "Debbie looked at the syringe, then laid her head on the pillow with her eyes open, watching what was left of her world." With these words the doctor suggests that Debbie knew her life was to be ended. When Debbie stops breathing the doctor recalls that "the dark-haired woman stood erect and seemed relieved." The suggestion is that Debbie approved, however, there remains the uncertainty that Debbie fully understood.

5. Being emotionally moved by the cruel fate of the young woman slowly and painfully dying, students might first react with approval of the doctor's behavior, however, after reconsidering the ethical implications, they might have second thoughts. Aside from checking Debbie's chart and chatting with the nurse, there is no professional support for the resident's almost impulsive decision to "end it all" without asking Debbie, her doctor, or her family.

6. Were I the doctor I would have given Debbie enough morphine to relieve her pain, but not her life. I also would have consulted her personal physician.

RHETORICAL CONSIDERATIONS

1. The doctor's purpose here was to recreate a realistic medical emergency circumstance. We are introduced to the case as the doctor was—gradually and unexpectedly. To some extent the introductory material backfired. The doctor may have been trying to convey the image of an over-worked resident, but the details could be interpreted as symptomatic of a doctor rushed, aggravated, and more concerned with getting back to bed than the future of a patient. For those critical of the doctor's action, such details are damning of both action and character.

2. The term "gallows scene" makes clear the doctor sees Debbie's suffering as terminal. There is no turning back, no relief available, nothing but futile suffering. The mention of "cruel mockery of her youth" suggests that the doctor comprehends the loss. This statement takes the doctor beyond clinical rendering of medical details to an empathetic grasp of Debbie's humanity and potential. The remark points to a reaction borne out of compassion rather than convenience as some had claimed.

3. There is no overt clue to the doctor's gender. Yet I would guess the resident was a male.

Susan D. Wilson **RESPONSE TO "IT'S OVER, DEBBIE"**

TOPICAL CONSIDERATIONS

1. Such protracted suffering is inhumane.
2. The doctor would most likely react with empathy. I would think that the doctor

would also be willing to terminate the suffering of Wilson's father with a lethal injection.
3. For the students.

RHETORICAL CONSIDERATIONS

1. No. I think her letter creates an emotional empathy with the patient and the anguish of Wilson who can only sit back and watch her father suffer to his end.

Harold Y. Vanderpool RESPONSES TO
and Don C. Shaw   "IT'S OVER, DEBBIE"

TOPICAL CONSIDERATIONS

1. According to Vanderpool the physician's language makes "manslaughter" murder sound heroic in two different ways. First, the physician evokes a compelling and dramatic theme: a caring doctor ends the suffering of a patient "by putting a stop to the cruel, 'gallows'-like technology" that keeps her alive. The theme is heartwarming. One's immediate reaction is to empathize with the patient and see the physician as deliverer. Second, the physician employs euphemistic rhetoric that "masks the act of killing Debbie." Vanderpool points to expressions such as doing one's "job," "rest," and "say good-bye." Vanderpool's own language is just the opposite of euphemistic. He speaks of the anonymous doctor's behavior as the "act of killing Debbie" and "premeditated manslaughter." The physician's rhetoric projects a role as compassionate deliverer while Vanderpool's rhetoric projects murderer.
2. Vanderpool effectively catalogs the information the doctor did not have when he decided to terminate Debbie's life. The only information the doctor did have came from a brief exchange with a nurse and a glance at the patient's chart. An ambiguous statement, "Let's get this over," was interpreted as a plea for euthanasia by a fully competent adult. The doctor made no further consultations with Debbie, her family, or physician. Also, no attempts were made to relieve her pain more effectively. The decision seems to have been made on a cursory and incomplete analysis of the information available, according to Vanderpool. I agree with him.
3. According to the guidelines of the Hemlock Society, no action to end a person's life would be taken rashly or impulsively. Legal documentation filed well in advance and second opinions from qualified physicians would be required. These safeguards are designed to insure that aid-in-dying is what the patient desires and that the patient's condition is, without doubt, terminal.
4. Physicians may abuse the powers to legally end a patient's life. Some might act out of frustration or haste; others out of poor professional judgement, even on a misdiagnosis, acting without consultation of other physicians. Students might also bring up the frightening possibility of doctors terminating a patient out of malice.

RHETORICAL CONSIDERATIONS

1. The final statement is full of anger and antipathy toward the anonymous doctor. Vanderpool strongly feels that the doctor's actions require further analysis, perhaps even legal measures.
2. I think the analogies are sound in legal terms although lacking the moral weight of licensing euthanasia.

William F. Buckley, Jr. IT ISN'T WORKING

TOPICAL CONSIDERATIONS

1. Buckley says that the decline in marijuana smoking has less to do with the law enforcement than with "creeping social perception" that pot is more harmful than previously thought.
2. Buckley offers several reasons. The first is the lack of cooperation from foreign governments. He names Mexico, but by extension, Columbia, Panama, the Bahamas, and Turkey to name a few. Second, the meager success of the Drug Enforcement Agency in apprehending drug shipments. And, third, the staggering profits yielded by cocaine, $200 thousand dollars worth of which "you can stuff into a single pocket of a man's jacket." Finally, there is the huge market for coke and crack in America.
3. By implication, Buckley sounds as if he's opposed to the practice of executing drug users or smugglers. However, a political conservative, Buckley has gone on record in favor of the death penalty for murderers, so he would surely vote for the execution of drug dealers who kill and, perhaps, those who order the killing of others.
4. His change of mind is based on "purely empirical" reasoning: that illegal drug use has created a crime problem and the flow of enormous capital into drug-producing countries. His reasoning is simply pragmatic—a matter of crime and economics—rather than ethical or moral.
5. Buckley uses the term twice. The first when referring to the difficulty of stopping the drug trade in paragraph 5. By contrast, "non-free" (non-democratic) societies simply execute abusers and smugglers. Our Constitution prevents that extreme measure even though the death penalty is employed in some states for crimes of murder. The more subtle implication of "free" in this context is explicit in the second use of the expression in the final paragraph. What is implied here is a society where people are "free" to "kill themselves with tobacco and booze." In essence, Buckley is absolving the government of any moral or legal responsibility to its citizens who might choose to endanger their lives with drugs.
6. Buckley says that civic organizations and television would have the burden of educating the masses on the dangers of drug abuse. There seems to be a clear contradiction here: a government that legalized dangerous drugs while trying to teach people not to use them.
7. He doesn't directly. Indirectly he suggests that if people are dumb enough to

kill themselves with dope, let them. They've been doing it for years with tobacco and alcohol anyway.

8. I don't think much of Buckley's idea. In fact, I think it is dangerously defeatist. Legalization would admit that the law doesn't work. But the fact is that drugs are bad, not the laws against them. Abuse of drugs under legalization would get out of control—an ethical and moral problem Buckley's strictly pragmatic plan never addresses or, at least, dismisses. He does fail to address the fact that cheap, available drugs would increase addiction. Only 10 percent of drinkers become addicted to alcohol, while an estimated 75 percent of regular drug users could become addicted according to *Newsweek* magazine (in 1988). Legalization would constitute a blatant disregard of, if not punishment for, those most plagued with drug addiction: minorities and the economically depressed. Also, legalization could lead to the sale of synthetic substances or derivatives, such as crack whose long-term effects are unknown. The medical costs of drug abuse, estimated at $60 billion dollars in 1988, would soar. Finally, there is the problem of social mores: removing legal strictures sends the message that using drugs is okay. The risk to children is indefensible.

9. For the student.

RHETORICAL CONSIDERATIONS

1. The essay opens with an example of crime, graft, and tacit governmental (in this case Mexican) approval of the flow of illegal substances (here, marijuana) into America. This observation begins to develop Buckley's central argument, the thrust of which is the impossibility of effectively preventing the "insinuating [of illegal drugs] into this country."

2. The comparison is a damningly appropriate one since locusts represent the forces of destruction, a symbolism that can be traced back to the Bible. In the Book of Exodus, Moses calls down on Egypt several plagues including a swarm of locusts in retaliation for the Pharaoh's refusal to set free the Hebrews. The plague of locusts also have a specific apocalyptic association from the Book of Revelation in which the fifth angel opens a bottomless pit out of which swarm locusts who were commanded to torment only those who did not "have the seal of God in their foreheads."

3. Buckley does not take seriously William Safire's suggestions. First his word choice, "a hot bundle of ideas," is clearly sarcastic. Also, his slangy euphemisms, "boys with big sacksful of green" and the pun "scarlet letters" convey a less than serious regard. Most dismissing is the absurd suggestion that we "breed 50 million drug-trained dogs." And in case we missed his point, he concludes "what a great idea!"

4. There is dramatic impact in concluding the piece with "rat poison." Each word has strongly negative associations that affect the punch. More subtle are the associate attitudes here, for Buckley is countering lives saved by decreased drug crimes with those lost to addiction. In effect, he is saying that those who choose to become addicted deserve the fate of poisoned rats. In other words,

dope is equated to poison and addicts to rats. By extension those who sell the dope are no more culpable than the salesperson in the local hardware shop who dispenses pesticides.

Charles B. Rangel **LEGALIZE DRUGS? NOT ON YOUR LIFE**

TOPICAL CONSIDERATIONS

1. Administratively speaking, the greatest problem would be the determination of who gets what drugs. The least of the problems might be deciding where the drugs come from. Most likely drugs would be supplied both from abroad and from home "dope factories." The most weighty moral problem is how legalization would make it easier for drugs to fall into the hands of new users, particularly children. In fact, legalization might encourage addiction.
2. I can't think of any, but no doubt there are more unanswered questions.
3. Rangel feels, and rightfully so, that people already hooked on drugs will continue to need both dope and the money to support their habits. Furthermore, legalization will swell the addicted ranks particularly among the poor and unemployed whose depressed economic conditions will create more crime. Legalization I think is both dangerous and immoral for it would greatly increase the number of addicts and turn America into a "society of zombies," in the words of Senator Alfonse D'Amato, New York Republican Senator.
4. The root causes for our drug problems are "hopelessness and helplessness and despair." I agree. People like William F. Buckley, Jr., Mayor Schmoke, and other conservatives calling for legalization, frustrated by the futility of the drug war, prefer to address the pragmatics of economics and crime prevention rather than the more complex moral and social causes. They call attention to the cost and abject failure of enforcement pointing out the huge profits for drug dealers, the overcrowded jails, and neighborhoods terrorized by dope crazy gangs.
5. No. There will always be opportunists with their ears to the ground.
6. Legalization would carry the following messages to kids: that using drugs won't get you in trouble with the law; and that drugs are not harmful to your health. Kids not yet "lost to the drug menace" would be easy victims under legalization, I think.
7. Rangel calls for an end to the talk about legalization. He says pressure should be put on our leaders to make the drug problem a national priority. Viewing the problem as a "national security threat," Rangel says that we need a "coordinated national battle plan" that would include use of the military. Presumably he means using personnel and equipment to cover the borders against smuggling. Yet, there in his call "to wipe out this foreign-based" menace there is the implication that deployment to foreign lands is not out of the question. Rather than outright invasion of drug-producing shores, Rangel is probably thinking

about a cooperative effort with foreign governments to destroy crops and drug factories.

RHETORICAL CONSIDERATIONS

1. Actually they don't. There is mention of the untimely talk of legalization and, yet, the thrust of these paragraphs is the need for a battle plan in the war on drugs. The reader is led to expect from Rangel some suggested strategies. The real launch point and thesis statement is paragraph 4. And what follows is a itemization of problems inherent in legalization. Only in paragraph 25 does Rangel return to the subject of fighting the drug war and a call for a national "battle plan."
2. Paragraph 4.
3. There seems to be a vague ordering, at least from administrative problems to moral ones.
4. Essentially he is saying that as long as all the questions about legalization cannot be satisfactorily answered, then all discussion about it should be no more than the stuff of party small talk. But Rangel is speaking sarcastically, of course. Underlying his statement is a stab at upper society whose insensitivity to "the root cause" of the drug problems is manifest in its pragmatic solutions— solutions voiced by Buckley in the previous article: legalize drugs and reduce crime, the huge costs of enforcement, and massive profits to drug lords while generating tax revenues.

Edward Koch **DEATH AND JUSTICE:
HOW CAPITAL PUNISHMENT
AFFIRMS LIFE**

TOPICAL CONSIDERATIONS

1. Despite the fact that some of Edward Koch's refutations of the seven arguments against the death penalty appeal to reason and some to emotions, the moral heart of his arguments is contained in the title of the essay: "How Capital Punishment Affirms Life." Koch views life as precious and the taking of life as the most heinous act. Therefore, for such a crime, justice can only be death—a moral stand at least as ancient as the Old Testament's code: "an eye for an eye, a tooth for a tooth." Although he does not make much of this argument, he does point to execution as being a deterrent to murder. His arguments are convincing if one accepts the biblical premise. I am morally opposed to the death penalty on the same grounds that Koch supports it. So, I was impressed though not converted.
2. Most of Koch's own arguments are rooted in justice rather than deterrence. Only in his discussion of the third argument against capital punishment does Koch directly address the subject of deterrence: "...one of the best ways to guarantee that protection is to assure that convicted murderers do not kill again" (paragraph 8).

3. Koch enlists the support of death-penalty foe, Hugo Adam Bedau, whose research has not demonstrated that innocent defendants have been put to death. Koch quotes Bedau's figures—some 7,000 executions from 1893 to 1971. Then Koch goes on to talk about multiple murders. This, I think, is Koch's thinnest and least convincing argument. As Bruck points out in the next essay, Bedau did not say that innocent defendants had not been executed, but that it is very difficult to establish. Koch also changes the subject matter very quickly deflecting attention—and doubt—to ugly details of multiple murderers.

4. It is not clear that Koch is saying some murders are more "heinous" than others, however, the implication is there. He does cite in the essay cases of brutal or multiple killings when he is building his argument. One would presume that Koch would consider "heinous" premeditated murder, multiple murder, and murder that was particularly grisly (mutilation and dismemberment). One would assume that Koch would consider "heinous" drug kingpins who order killings, as well as those who commit the killings. He would also support the death penalty, I assume, for those who kill law-enforcement officers.

5. I think the first ("The death penalty is 'barbaric' ") and the third ("An innocent person might be executed by mistake") are morally the strongest of the seven arguments. The weakest for me is the second ("No other major democracy uses the death penalty").

6. I can think of none.

RHETORICAL CONSIDERATIONS

1. The opening sentence of paragraph 3 serves as Koch's thesis statement: "Life is indeed precious, and I believe the death penalty helps to affirm this fact."

2. I think it is an apt analogy and one that would muster support for his view. Cancer is a pathological equivalent to evil, and one we all fear.

3. ETHICAL: argument 1, 4, 6
   LOGICAL: argument 2, 5, 7
   EMOTIONAL: argument 3, 7

4. Edward Koch is known as a feisty, hard-fisted, no-nonsense kind of man who enjoys the outrage he can create. Yet, little of that offensiveness is visible here, for the essay is composed in a voice of reason and moral purpose. The reader may not agree with Koch's stand on capital punishment, but he or she must respect the measured tone in Koch's presentation. Where necessary, Koch is direct and forceful, never shrill. In paragraph 13 for instance, Koch dismisses "a popular argument among opponents of capital punishment" as "transparently false." Yet, he does show some tooth as when he accuses Jimmy Breslin of "sophistic nonsense."

David Bruck THE DEATH PENALTY

TOPICAL CONSIDERATIONS

1. Two aspects of the J.C. Shaw case are omitted by Koch: (1) that Shaw was suffering mental illness and the effects of PCP; (2) that he made his statement about the wrongness of killing moments before his execution. These are important omissions that may not sway opinion, but in the right court of law could render a different verdict than that which Shaw suffered. The circumstances of mental illness and drug influence may not lessen for readers the awfulness of the crime as much as it might convince them to consider a lighter sentence for cases of mental incompetency. In the next paragraph, Bruck brings up litigation against Alvin Ford by the Florida Supreme Court, which in 1986 lost its case because he was too insane to know he was to be put to death and for what reasons. Should Ford eventually be deemed sane, he can be executed. Koch's omission of the circumstances of the Shaw crime weakens his argument somewhat, I think. So does his railing against Shaw for his lecture on morality. Shaw was, according to Bruck, not condemning the state in the name of clemency, but killing itself.
2. The heart of Bruck's argument is that capital punishment is reckless in practice and "irreverent" in its view of human life. I agree with Bruck. The system is inherently faulty even if one innocent defendant has been executed. And it is a fact that the death penalty has been applied prejudicially for decades.
3. See above.
4. I think the Jeter case is convincing.
5. Koch's own use of Bedau is very selective as he carefully quotes just what he needs for support. However, Bruck makes the point that Bedau was simply saying that questions of guilt can never be completely resolved in some cases. Bruck goes on to say that Bedau is currently working on a compilation of "wrongful deaths," a fact that undermines Koch's argument as it does Bedau's own in the Koch essay.
6. Probably Bruck would call for life sentences without parole for the most "heinous" crimes.
7. Koch says in paragraph 11 of his essay that discriminatory use of the death penalty "no longer seems to be the problem it once was." About the Knighton case, Koch might admit that a life sentence should have been in order and that any signs of prejudice should have been caught in the appeal process.
8. I agree that the public, so frustrated with crime and the seeming inability to stem it, views the death penalty as a compensation.

RHETORICAL CONSIDERATIONS

1. The opening line of paragraph 15 serves as Bruck's thesis statement.
2. This detail about the death-house crowds illustrates just what Bruck is complaining about when he says in paragraph 15 that the death penalty "encourages an attitude toward human life that is not reverent, but reckless." The cry for blood

is ugly, a nasty reminder of the kind of rage that kills. When death is a spectacle, something is lost.

3. Bruck effectively dismisses Koch's Old Testament code of justice with extrapolations from other crimes. In paragraph 16, he says that following the same logic of a-death-for-a-death, perhaps rapists should be sodomized. Also effective and persuasive is Bruck's claim that "neither justice nor self-preservation demands that we kill men whom we have already imprisoned."

▼PART 10   THE NATURAL WORLD

Thomas A. Sancton   **WHAT ON EARTH**
                    ARE WE DOING?

TOPICAL CONSIDERATIONS

1. In paragraph 3, Sancton rightfully points to the Industrial Revolution as the beginning of what might be the end of the natural equilibrium. Beginning in England in the first half of the 19th century and rapidly spreading to other countries, the Industrial Revolution was probably the single-most significant era in human history, as it forever changed the nature and quality of life. In essence, technology was invented and so was the threat to the natural environment. While machines and factories replaced handicraft production the earth's atmosphere, rivers, and oceans began to suffer pollution. The modern reflexes of those early days—still "in the name of progress" as Sancton ironically observes—are the denuding of forests, the poisoning of lakes, and the depletion of underground aquifers. The heart of the irony is that the very technology that was designed to make the planet more habitable for mankind is threatening us with extinction.

2. In 1988, the United States suffered some natural extremes in weather. For three summer months, a searing drought plagued the farmlands from California to Georgia, raising fears that the "dreaded 'greenhouse effect'—global warming as a result of the buildup of carbon dioxide and other gases in the atmosphere—might already be under way" (paragraph 4). (One by-product of the burning of fossil fuel is carbon dioxide.) Meanwhile on the east coast, beaches were plagued by garbage, raw sewage, and medical wastes that washed up—all ugly signs of "the growing despoliation of the oceans." Similar pollution, Sancton reports, closed beaches on the Mediterranean, the English Channel, and the North Sea. Other human contributions to environmental disasters cited were radioactive wastes recklessly disposed by weapon-making plants. Also, the continued depletion of the atmosphere's ozone layer by overuse of chlorofluorocarbons emanating from spray cans, air conditioners, and refrigeration units. "Perhaps most ominous of all . . . [were] the destruction of the tropical forests . . . at a rate equal to one football field a second."

3. One major consequence might be the rise in the earth's average temperature as

the result of the increased CO_2 in the atmosphere. A rise of three or more degrees could cause the ocean level to increase enough causing serious coastal flooding and the ruinous salinization of farmland. Sancton also speculates that changes in weather patterns "could make huge areas infertile or uninhabitable, touching off refugee movements unprecedented in history." If nothing is done about toxic and nuclear contamination of the environment, there could be a shortage of safe drinking water resulting in mass starvation. Another chilling possibility is the conversion of fertile land into deserts.

4. Sancton says that some scientists "contest the global-warming theory or predict that natural processes will counter its effects." Sancton cites Kenneth E. F. Watt, professor of environmental studies of the University of California at Davis, who calls the greenhouse effect " 'the laugh of the century.' " Sancton also cites S. Fred Singer, a geophysicist working for the U.S. Department of Transportation, who predicts that the greenhouse warming will be "balanced by an increase in heat-reflecting clouds." One should note that Singer is in the employ of the Department of Transportation, which has been criticized for its laxity in environmental protection. Sancton does not seem impressed with the dissenters here. For he writes, "The skeptics could be right, but it is far too risky to do nothing while awaiting absolute proof of disaster."

5. As Sancton points out, nearly every culture has its myths about the earth and its origins. And in many of these, the earth is perceived as the progenitor of life, as the mother of all things—an entity "endowed with divinity, and mortals were subordinate to it." With the concept of a monotheistic God, the Judeo-Christian tradition was a radical diversion from all other religions. Nature was viewed as "other," not as divine. In Genesis it is written that God created the earth and then ordered man and woman to "be fruitful and multiply . . . and have dominion over" all living things. The notions of dominion and the free population of the earth carry the invitations to "use nature as a convenience" says Sancton.

6. To halt the "massive injury to the earth's environment" will require global cooperation and sacrifice "unknown except in wartime," says the author. And soon since, in the words of Lester Brown, "We do not have generations, we have only years in which to attempt to turn things around." At stake is the very survival of the species. The efforts of governments are not enough, the author points out. What is needed are the concerted efforts of all ordinary people— "the California housewife, the Mexican peasant, the Soviet factory worker, the Chinese farmer"—in short, each of us willing to change our life-styles.

7. I don't think the majority of people could be so enlightened to make such sacrifices. If we are to survive, perhaps the only salvation is the enactment of laws to force people to live more conservatively. Undoubtedly, such legislation would be met with considerable resistance since for years our culture has encouraged indiscriminate consumption. Cutting back for some would mean fundamental changes in behavior patterns.

8. For the student.

RHETORICAL CONSIDERATIONS

1. The title of the essay is quite apt. Through the grim play on words, it captures the sheer disbelief at our brutal violation of the planet.

2. I think the opening paragraph adequately forecasts what follows. The first paragraph introduces several notions back to back: that the earth does not abide forever; that if left alone, it will be incinerated naturally when the sun goes nova in 5 to 6 billion years; but nuclear technology can do the same tomorrow if man is stupid enough; and that somewhere in between falls the planet's life expectancy. These ideas essentially prepare for the concluding sentence which serves as the article's thesis statement and which thematically controls and, therefore, forecasts all that follows. For in that last statement lies the theme of the essay: that today's technology will, "for better or worse," affect "the present and future state of the planet." Much of what follows is a review of the environmental devastation brought on by recent technology and some grim predictions of what might follow if nothing is done to halt the damage.

3.   I. Man is threatening the future of the planet (paragraphs 1–6)
      A. Human birthrate is dooming the earth as a human habitat
      B. Technology has been upsetting nature's equilibrium since the Industrial Revolution
        1. Pollution of the atmosphere by factories
        2. Pollution of rivers and streams by toxic wastes
        3. Depletion of fossil fuels and fouling of air by automobiles
      C. In 1988 nature responded with warnings
        1. Three-month killer droughts
        2. Widespread forest fires
        3. Befouling of beaches by sewage and medical wastes
        4. Pollution of European beaches
        5. Killer hurricanes in Caribbean and Bangladesh
        6. Monstrous earthquake in Armenia
      D. Further forebodings
        1. Reports of secret nuclear wastes
        2. Further depletion of ozone layer
        3. Continued destruction of tropical forests
  II. Theories of what would happen if nothing is done (paragraphs 8–13)
      A. The "greenhouse effect" causing . . .
        1. Flooding of coastal land and ruination of farmland
        2. Mass migration
      B. Shortage of drinking water by toxic/radioactive contamination causing . . .
        1. Mass starvation
        2. Infertilization of lands
      C. Doom-counter theories: Earth would counter greenhouse effect
        1. Kenneth E.F. Watt

      2. S. Fred Singer
   D. Earth will not remain as it is now
      1. Earth's history is one of great geophysical changes
      2. Accompanying waves of extinction
      3. Worldwide deforestation could cause extinctions at least as great as that of dinosaurs
III. Philosophical backdrops to current man/nature relationship (paragraphs 14–17)
   A. Non-anthropocentric world view
      1. Ancient Chinese view
      2. Ancient Greek
      3. Pagan views
   B. Anthropocentric world view
      1. Judeo-Christian tradition
         a) "Be fruitful and multiply"
         b) "Have dominion" over nature
      2. Spread of Christianity
      3. Scientific enlightenment
         a) Great achievements through technology
            1) Labor-saving machines
            2) Life-saving medicines
            3) Transportation and communication systems
         b) Unexpected consequences
            1) Population problem
            2) Pollution of water supplies by pesticides
            3) Pollution of atmosphere by cars and airplanes
   C. Man's wonder and awe over nature continues despite advance of technology
      1. Flowering of romantic poetry
      2. Loving view of earth from space
         a) Edgar Mitchell's description
         b) Preston Cloud's imperative
IV. How to halt damage to environment (paragraphs 18–20)
   A. Global efforts needed
   B. Each individual must do his/her part to change wasteful ways
   C. Extraordinary leadership needed

4. Consider paragraph 4. The topic sentence is the opening sentence: "This year the earth spoke, like God warning Noah of the deluge." What follows are four specific examples of nature striking back and the "warnings": 1) the three-month drought that reduced the country's grain harvest by 31 percent and that killed off thousands of head of livestock; 2) the seven-week heat wave that raised fears of the dreaded "greenhouse effect"; 3) the drought-induced fires in Western forests; 4) the raw sewage, garbage, and medical wastes that plagued beaches in the East.

5. This essay is very well substantiated as nearly each paragraph demonstrates.

Following any one general observation (or topic sentence) are at least three solid examples.

6. Despite the topic, I found the tone reasonable and sober, never alarmist.

7. Chillingly effective, the allusion here is to the last line of T.S. Eliot's *The Hollow Men* which concludes with the sing-songy, nursery-rhyme refrain,

> *This is the way the world ends*
> *This is the way the world ends*
> *This is the way the world ends*
> *Not with a bang but a whimper.*

The allusion is also grimly appropriate since Eliot's apocalyptic vision underscored his pessimistic view of modern civilization.

James C. Rettie BUT A WATCH IN THE NIGHT: A SCIENTIFIC FABLE

TOPICAL CONSIDERATIONS

1. Rettie appears to have had three basic purposes in writing his essay: first, to render a nonanthropomorphic and nonanthropocentric view of ourselves, a view extraterrestrials would have of earth and the evolution of life; second, to dramatize the enormous stretches of time that make up earth's geological history; third, and most important, to demonstrate by condensation the extraordinary process of evolution to life on earth, ending with a shift from the objective camera eye to an impassioned plea for man to conserve the soil of the earth, his "only real wealth."

2. Rettie likens the geologic history of earth to a year-long motion picture made by the Copernicans, beings of another planet. The analogy works well, I think, because it captures, in time-lapse form, the violent geological forces that forged the primitive earth. In paragraph 6, he describes erosion of the land masses, the rains and raging waters that formed the seas, for instance. Something seems to be missing from his early "footage": scenes of the enormous volcanic activity that forged the continents and mountain ranges. Evolution of life he dramatizes in his description of the spreading "mat of vegetation" across the planet and the "lacing down with its root structures whatever pulverized rock material" plant life found. For the evolution of different life forms he highlights the emergence of major species such as insects, lunged fish, reptiles, birds, and mammals. Then in December, after a fear "that man has somehow been left out," Rettie shows us the appearance of "a stooped, massive creature of man-like proportions" followed by Pithecanthropus. From that creature to Homo sapiens, Rettie heightens the drama of evolution in paragraph 16 with a countdown on the clock.

3. Rettie could have given a straight polemic about the wanton erosion of soil by technological progress. Instead, he chose the brilliant and far more dramatic strategy of the movie analogy, reducing man's tenure on earth to only a few

minutes, during which, in his last few seconds, he manages to invent the means for undoing what Nature took 4.5 billion years to bring about.

RHETORICAL CONSIDERATIONS

1. Students may find Rettie's discussion here a bit dragged out, but they must remember that the essay was written in 1948, when readers were less familiar with cameras and special effects such as time-lapse photography.
2. He created alien life so that he could affect a nonanthropomorphic view of ourselves, not blinded by our own self-importance. The alien's-eye view of earth also creates an objective perspective on our planet, exposing its vulnerability while it at once creates a humbling view of Homo sapiens in the context of the enormous span of geological history. The final effect of this strategy is to help us respect just how precious and special our planet is, and how we should not take heedless advantage of it.
3. In paragraph 18, Rettie's tone shifts from a simple narrative to geological development to a critical statement about how man is ravishing the planet in the name of progress. The third sentence of that paragraph hints at his bias in mentioning the "human swarm" sweeping across the face of America and taking it "away from the red men." From there to the end, Rettie's narrative is a gloomy future history of an impoverished earth extrapolated from the present reduction of the natural world.
4. The question is a most effective conclusion, leaving to the reader the logical, awful conclusion. It exposes blind self-destructiveness.
5. From God's point of view, a thousand years of earth's history is a mere "yesterday," as if God and the Copernicans were keeping a short night-watch as soldiers or guards would.

Loren Eiseley **HOW NATURAL IS NATURAL?**

TOPICAL CONSIDERATIONS

1. The first world is the illusion of the famous scientist who wore oversize padded boots because he feared falling through the enormous molecular interstices of material reality. The second world—also natural—is that of the New England lake now "preempted and civilized by man." The third world is that "along the lake shallows and under the boat dock"—that of the muskrat "caught between a vanishing forest and a deep lake." Each world is natural and illusionary in its own way.
2. They mention the few changes brought to the lake by civilization. White mentions that he now gets to the lake of his youth by car instead of by train and wagon as in the old days. He also remarks on another technological change that bothers Eiseley more, the fast and powerful motorboats. While White focuses on the way time seems to have stood still, Eiseley worries about the way the primitive and seemingly eternal world of nature, exemplified by that of the

muskrat, is threatened with extinction by man. But both White and Eiseley see the carelessness of the modern generation in its disregard for the fragility of the environment.

3. He is surprised because the lake, with its ominous high-speed motorboats, seems to have been completely taken over by modern man and his machines. He is also surprised that the muskrat still lives with an illusion of a Garden of Eden, where man and beast enjoyed harmony and mutual respect. The little creature is unaware that people may in their blindness eventually eliminate him, as the man with the brick eliminated the offending garden rat.

4. The "illusion" refers to the misconception that man and animal live in eternal Edenic harmony. It is like the illusion of reality suffered by the senile scientist, who sees only a precarious world full of threatening gaps within and between molecules and atoms.

5. The reference suggests just how far from innocence and harmony with the natural world we have "progressed." Of course, he refers to the mythic ideal—itself an illusion of man's integration with nature—now threatened by modern progress. He is saying that man is knowledgeable, yet not wise, in his dominion over nature.

6. Here Eiseley is talking not as a man but as Man, a species dangerous to muskrats and other living things. The creature in its nearsightedness mistook him for Adam. Eiseley, recognizing the mistake, warns the muskrat that his time is limited.

7. There are some fine descriptive details in paragraph 3.

8. Eiseley laments the way in which the natural world is shrinking under the onslaught of modern human expansion. The question of the title is a profound and disturbing one. The more man "preempts and civilizes" the world, the more he makes it habitable for himself alone, and the closer we move toward a time when man's world is the only thing that is natural. And here Eiseley uses both meanings of "natural": of nature, and regular.

RHETORICAL CONSIDERATIONS

1. It is relevant because it introduces a maddening fear of the illusory nature of reality. Likewise, the seemingly eternal and invulnerable world of nature is a precarious one.

2. "Preempt" means to take for oneself, to seize upon to the exclusion of others. "Civilized" is used ironically here. It means to technically advance from a primitive state, to refine, to better. The word comes from the Latin *civis,* which means citizen or inhabitant of the city. Thus, the notion to civilize means to build cities, which are for people, not muskrats. To civilize Nature is to preempt it.

3. The reference is sarcastic. Apollo was the Greek god of sunlight—one who supports life, and famous for his harmonizing powers. The reference to the "attractive" young men in their speeding boats and "reckless abandon" is ironic. Lost in their conquest of the waves and the hearts of screaming girls, these brave young Apollos are unaware of the primitive, fragile world their

chopping propeller blades menace. In their hands is the power to darken the sunlit world.

4. He regrets their presence, although he displays no overt hostility toward them. They are part of the greater civilizing process of the lake, part of the greater forces that be. The reference to Eden again suggests the distance between man and the natural world; likewise, the modern Apollos, despite their young, godlike beauty, have lost their mythic life-protecting qualities.

5. The world of darkness suggests imminent death and extinction. They project the dark realization—and, perhaps, despair—of the author, who sees a vanishing world like that vision of the senile scientist in paragraph 1.

Lewis Thomas **MAN'S ROLE ON EARTH**

TOPICAL CONSIDERATIONS

1. In paragraph 3 Thomas says human beings are the only creatures that fail "to accommodate, to fit in, to give a little whenever they take a little" as do other species. We are the one species that has not established "symbiotic arrangements" with other creatures—a system that works for the rest of nature. The problem is that we regard ourselves as separate from the rest of the biosphere, the rest of the "organism" of earth—an attitude that, says Thomas, explains the witless wrongs against the natural world listed in paragraph 1.

2. Although he doesn't say it outright, the basis of the folly is egocentricity or, more exactly, "speciocentricity." Thomas says that by perceiving ourselves as a species separate from and superior to the rest of nature, we have begun to treat the earth as a "domesticated household pet, living in an environment invented by us." The danger here is in forgetting our place in the whole scheme of things and the awful imbalance we have already created—an imbalance that can lead to disaster for us and the planet.

3. If we can learn to regard ourselves as a natural part of the organism that is the planet earth instead of as a separate species, we might discover that we have been designed for special functions—"a sort of sense organ for the whole creature, a set of eyes, even a storage place for thought," Thomas says. He adds that it might be our higher destiny, a privilege, in fact, to seed the stars—that is, if we "continue our own embryologic development as a species" and don't, by implication, terminate it prematurely.

4. He means "metaphor" here as symbolic thought. Many creatures have a "language" of signs, either auditory or physical, which communicate the presence of danger, or food, or mating time, and so on. But only mankind can think and express itself in symbols or metaphors which stand for something, which represent something intellectually. Symbols require the exclusive human capacity of intellection. Without it, our language would be only a system of signs.

5. As a biologist he says that we have a long way to go because we are a "brand-new species." He does not, however, say that we will in fact live out our

tenure. Yet he is not so pessimistic as the historians who see a dark biological imperative operating here, one that leads to inevitable self-termination ("and we are about to run out our string"). Thomas does hold out the possibility of continued existence only *if* we can learn to see ourselves as a new "embryologic species" that is organically and evolutionarily bound to the natural world.

6. The ability to change our minds is our greatest advantage. Thomas means that because we are not genetically restricted to set behavior patterns as are all other creatures, we have the ability to change our perceptions of ourselves in relation to the earth, and thus not to continue the folly.

RHETORICAL CONSIDERATIONS

1. In paragraph 3 Thomas speaks of planet earth as "an organism." Allied with that metaphor is the view of mankind as a new "embryologic" species that is part of that living "organism." Throughout the essay Thomas maintains this metaphorical view of man as a living part of a larger organism.
2. With details, in the final two paragraphs.
3. The author has viewed us biologically as "a brand-new species" still trying to determine our priorities, and so "opportunities" is very appropriate. It suggests that with proper self-examination we can make a better future.
4. Wise and gentle.

Sue Hubbell CATERPILLAR AFTERNOON

TOPICAL CONSIDERATIONS

1. I agree. Hubbell looks through a magnifying glass to discover the secret lives of little wild things. Her own fascination is evidenced by the sheer space devoted to describing the larvae as well as the background research. There is also the confession at the end that she walks "eyes to ground, looking for them."
2. This definition echoes 19th century gothic fiction writer Arthur Machen's definition of evil—"when the roses sing." This and Firbank's variation of the definition goes to the heart of evil—when the natural turns unnatural or, more exactly, supernatural. In gothic or horror fiction, the definition is most clearly applicable, for evil is most often embodied in monsters or the demon things that people and animals are turned into—for example, vampires, ghouls, ghosts, or Stephen King's "Frankencat," Church, from *Pet Sematary.* In the real world evil is defined in terms of natural behavior. Humans commit evil when they commit inhuman acts—acts so terrible that they seem inspired by the devil. By definition then, animals cannot commit "evil" acts. Lions and great white sharks may be killers, but acting out natural predatory or territorial instincts does not constitute unnatural behavior. What amuses Hubbell is that for a split instant she felt in the presence of a living snake skin, which in its violation of the natural order would have constituted an evil. Nature may startle, surprise, and baffle, but all that occurs in it has natural causes and explanations.

3. Fabre's experiment was brilliant in its simplicity for determining what the caterpillars would do without a leader. By setting the creatures up on a wide-rimmed vase, he demonstrated that the creatures were perfectly sheeplike, proceeding endlessly in a head-to-tail fashion until exhaustion stopped them.

4. A year later, Hubbell's curiosity about the creatures has grown. In paragraph 10, she says that she would even let her bee work go just to study the behavior of the creatures, even experiment with them. "I have more questions about them than when I first saw them," she writes. Often she will walk with her "eyes to the ground, looking for them."

5. She humbly admits that she knows people whose quests are much higher than hers—people whose interests might be likened to Ahab's obsession with Moby Dick or Percival's with the Holy Grail. Although she is "cut from other stuff," she seems no less determined in her quest. Hubbell chooses to look closely at the small things that cross her path, to discover the secret lives of bees, frogs, birds, and sawfly larvae. But in sharing with us the generous and endearing details of her discoveries, she performs a mission that is perhaps as noble as any Ahab or Percival.

RHETORICAL CONSIDERATIONS

1. She creates both mystery and suspense by delaying the discovery to the third paragraph. The effect is suggestive of the underlying theme of all her writing— that nature is full of surprises and unknowns.

2. Her attitude is a caring fascination. Although "maggoty" has unpleasant associations, she chooses the word for denotative purposes, conveying the hairless, creamy appearance of the larvae. The attention she gives to the mass movement in paragraph 3 establishes her fascination. In the next paragraph we are told that her wonderment leads her to experiment with the creatures. "I gently picked up a half a dozen or so . . . ," she writes, reassuring us that she is neither revolted nor hostile toward the creatures as others might be. Her fascination comes through in the several questions she asks. So does an endearing sense. "They certainly were good followers," she says, then wonders if the leader was "some special, super-caterpillar." Also, the personifying phrases such as "had simply assumed leadership duties" and "making the decision about the direction the column was to take." Throughout paragraphs 4 and 5 Hubbell describes how she patiently experiments with the procession, all the while her fascination mounts—a fascination that culminates in the last of her four questions (paragraph 5), "What manner of creature were they?"—a remark that echoes Pontius Pilate's wonderment of Jesus Christ.

3. Her details are very vivid, of course. First she describes the individual caterpillar specifying its length, color, smoothness, black head, and brown-striped back. Then she moves to the mass itself, "piled thickly in the center, with fewer caterpillars at the head and rear end of the line, which was perhaps eighteen inches long." Finally, in paragraph 4, she then takes in the overall movement of the mass as if it were some gestalt entity. In the next paragraph,

her descriptions become less objective and more personified and charming. I particularly like her description of the lead caterpillar twisting "the forepart of his body from side to side as though taking his bearings; he appeared to be the only one in the lot capable of going in a new direction, of making a decision to avoid a tuft of grass here, of turning there." Her descriptions, though not highly poetic, are precise and easy to visualize.

4. Hubbell's essay has three distinct parts as your students will discover. The first, from paragraphs 1 through 5, deals with the discovery and description of the sawfly larvae on the road. The middle of the essay, from paragraphs 5 through 7, discusses Henre Fabre's own fascination and experiments with processionary caterpillars. The last third, from paragraph 8 through the end, Hubbell is full of more questions than a year ago and declares her determination to spend this springtime in search of what Asher suggests are sawfly larvae. At first, these three sections may not seem related. However, what holds them together is the theme of fascination—her own, Fabre's, and Asher's—which bridges the year. When she's not observing the creatures directly, she is reading or asking about them so that by the end, her curiosity has peaked.

5. These questions provide the thrust of her quest and link the first third of the essay to the next two. She never really answers the questions; nor are they answerable. Such are the mysteries of nature—eternal and forever engrossing of the wondering mind.

Gwynne Dyer A CRUEL UNIVERSE, BUT THE ONLY ONE WHERE HUMANS COULD EXIST

TOPICAL CONSIDERATIONS

1. Because we are reasoning beings, the only universe we could possibly inhabit would have to be one in which events were predictable. Without predictability all experience would be chaotic and random; likewise, there would be no science or natural laws.

2. Dyer says Hume was honest because he did not offer some long, circular answer that came to the same conclusion: simply, that no one knows why God permits terrible things to occur in our universe.

3. There could be no science in a universe of divine favoritism. The laws of nature and all logic would not exist. And all that occurred would be "magical" and unpredictable. Man could not exist in such a "Garden of Eden."

4. Actually, Dyer offers us two consolations. In paragraph 11, he says that even God could not have made the universe any different than it is if he wanted it to be an appropriate home for human beings. And in the final paragraph he says that we can derive consolation from knowing that we are fortunate to be alive, because at our conception "a million other potential men and women lost their only chance to see the place at all."

RHETORICAL CONSIDERATIONS

1. The questions that open the essay are some of our oldest and hardest. Consequently, they are guaranteed to capture our attention and make us read on in the hope that the author will offer some answers.
2. In the central paragraphs—7 through 9—Dyer briefly illustrates why the universe must be a cruel one, why it must be nonselective. He speculates on a universe that would not allow air crashes, diseases, earthquakes, or murder. The result would be a magical realm in which the laws of nature and logic did not work.
3. Dyer ends his essay with a reminder of the miracle of life and how fortunate we are to have visited the universe, cruel as it is, instead of the "million other potential men and women" who could have been conceived by our parents instead of us. This paragraph rounds off the essay by returning to the theme of the questions in the first paragraph—human life is marked by both impersonal cruelty and luck.

Stephen Jay Gould WERE DINOSAURS DUMB?

TOPICAL CONSIDERATIONS

1. The tradition, an old one, is broad-based: folk tales give us Br'er Rabbit and Br'er Bear; from fairy tales we get stories such as Jack and the Beanstalk; and from the Bible the story of David and Goliath.
2. Attitudes toward dinosaurs have turned around for a couple of reasons. First, paleontologists are now certain that, contrary to original belief, dinosaurs were warm-blooded, which would mean that even the huge *Brontosaurus* was probably an "energetic, active, and capable" land animal and not the big, slow pond-wallowing brute that couldn't make it on land. The second reason is that paleontologists today no longer equate brain size with intelligence; nor do they think dinosaurs were small-brained. Instead they are certain that the brains were the right size for their bodies. As Gould points out, it is wrong to compare dinosaur brains to those of mammals. A "reptilian standard is the only proper one."
3. Gould argues that dinosaurs did not have too-small brains, but organs just the right size for their survival, which, in fact, lasted some 100 million years. The huge sauropods, such as *Brontosaurus,* had the lowest brain-to-body ratios as well as the lowest EQs—the ratio of actual brain size to expected brain size. Even if they were big, slow brutes, there was no need for them to be any cleverer at survival, because their great size was enough to ward off predators. Moving up the scale, there is evidence that the forbidding ceratopsians, though smaller than the sauropods, had elaborate social systems, and that their horns were used for combat and sexual display, two complex behaviors reflected in their higher encephalization quotients.
4. The EQ is "the ratio of actual brain size to expected brain size for a standard reptile of the same body weight."

5. Carnivores display higher EQs because hunting down fast-moving or larger prey was more of a challenge than eating a plant. The highest EQ Gould mentions is that for the "little coelurosaur *Stenonychosaurus.*"

6. Paleontologists of the past interpreted elaborate head structures, such as the crests of the hadrosaurs and the horns and frills of the ceratopsians, as useless ornaments. But today these structures have been interpreted as evidence of complex social behavior such as courtship and combat.

RHETORICAL CONSIDERATIONS

1. One does not expect an essay with this title to open up with a Muhammad Ali anecdote; the allusion immediately catches the reader's interest. Second, the anecdote itself illustrates well the tradition of equating size and power with "want of intelligence." Of course, Gould means that Ali's witty response contradicts the tradition as well as the results of Ali's intelligence test.

2. Gould has an engaging sense of humor, which does not distract or intrude but which humanizes and makes his writing personal. Examples: word choice such as "pea brains" (paragraph 2); asides, such as his confession and apology for stealing his grammar-school book; topical references such as Muhammad Ali, and in paragraph 5 the popular 1970s self-psychotherapy book, *I'm OK, You're OK;* and colloquialisms such as "Catching a rapidly moving or stoutly fighting prey demands a good deal more upstairs than . . . " (paragraph 16); and the irony of his conclusion.

3. He uses references very well, adding sufficient support to his own informed claims.

4. I think Gould's conclusion is a dramatic, amusing, and clever illustration of how he defends the relative intelligence of dinosaurs. And in it is the supreme irony that the most intelligent creature, who for so long gave bad press to the intelligence of the long-surviving dinosaurs, may not survive our own brief tenure on earth.

▼PART 11   WAR AND PEACE IN THE NUCLEAR AGE

Jonathan Schell THE EFFECTS OF A NUCLEAR EXPLOSION

TOPICAL CONSIDERATIONS

1. The difference, says Schell, would be not only in magnitude, but in kind. A nuclear holocaust would be felt by a whole society, not just a city, as with each bombing of Japan in 1945. A huge device set off in New York City would cause the collapse of society in a huge area; and by extension, a holocaust could bring about the collapse of civilization and the ecosphere itself.

2. The first effect (see paragraph 3) would come from the tremendous heat

created; the second, the tremendous winds of the blast wave; the third would be the firestorm that would whip through the rubble. Radioactive rain would be another effect.

3. The huge heaps of rubble from masses of construction materials in New York buildings would make escape or refuge virtually impossible.

4. He calculates that the fireball would be as extensive—two miles across—but that the "overpressures" would be much greater at the center of the blast, although with reduced range.

5. Anybody who was lucky enough to survive the heat and blast would be killed by the radioactive fallout, which would extend some 150 miles in a 15-mile-wide path within 24 hours. Depending on the winds, that would mean most of New England would suffer vast radiation deaths, as would Delaware, New Jersey, Pennsylvania, and Maryland.

6. Schell says that the Soviet Union has in its arsenal at least 113 twenty-megaton bombs, each of which alone has destructive potential far exceeding the amount necessary to destroy most military targets. They have been reserved for the destruction of cities.

RHETORICAL CONSIDERATIONS

1. His speculations were drawn from information about the bombs dropped in Japan and from nuclear tests. I think he supports himself very well; he sounds informed.

2. They make his position very persuasive, I think.

3. He extrapolates from the horrors of history in order to emphasize the dangerous potential of a nuclear holocaust. The suggestion is that we should learn some terrible lessons.

4. Schell has adopted a rather cool, objective tone, which I think is far more effective than if he had decided to be emotionally preachy. The subject is an assault on our emotions as it is. His purpose is to let the bald facts in a hypothetical situation horrify us.

5. Of course, it really makes no difference to the victims what form the fire would take. This parenthetical statement and others like it are part of the rhetorical strategy of the cold, impassioned speculation, all the more ironic because the very same dedication to scientific accuracy led to creation of the first bomb. In many respects the adopted tone of the essay reflects the cold-mindedness of nuclear-weapons designers and strategists.

6. The article was intended for the general reader, someone with at least a high school education. It is not too technical.

7. Most of the individual paragraphs are focused on the terrible details of destruction. Blocking out each as he does maintains attention and intensity. To break up the large paragraphs would fragment the different horrible effects, as if to suggest stages instead of one continuous holocaust of heat, blast, firestorm, debris, and radiation. Thus, he maintains the dramatic flow and denies the relief that short paragraphs would provide.

Michael Kinsley **NUCLEAR HOLOCAUST IN PERSPECTIVE**

TOPICAL CONSIDERATIONS

1. He says "perfect trust" is fundamental to dismantling nuclear terror between enemies, which, he adds, seems "an unlikely development."
2. He says that the antinuclear movement is "vague and confused" about how governments can prevent nuclear war. Also, he says the movement is confused in its goals regarding weapons: does the movement want to abolish all weapons or just nuclear weapons?
3. Kinsley finds Schell's essay pretentious because of the stance, the tone, and the language, which he finds pompous and apocalyptic. I do think some of Schell's writing is heavy-handed, although I would not condemn it as Kinsley does. Some of Kinsley's illustrations are convincing, I think.
4. Kinsley's basic difference with Schell is political, I would say, although he condemns Schell's "sonorous passages," his "wacky judgment," and his "hothouse reasoning." Kinsley is undoubtedly right-of-middle, whereas Schell is to the left in political stand on the nuclear issue.
5. "Hothouse reasoning" is the kind that "could grow only in an environment protected from the slightest chill of common sense." Kinsley means by the metaphor that Schell builds an elaborate argument that is self-contained and artificial, in Kinsley's estimation.
6. "Pornographic" connotes here to Kinsley the antinuclear movement's voyeuristic fascination for lurid, offensive details, grisly, not sexual. I think Kinsley is overstating his criticism here.
7. Schell proposes a "worldwide program of action" to end warfare. Just how he plans to arrange such an international network is not explained. Kinsley criticizes Schell's reasoning by saying that even if everybody in the world shared Schell's feelings about nuclear war, we could not abandon all our weapons, for the basic human dilemma of mutual distrust would remain. Just in case the enemy is not true to his word, it is better that we arm ourselves in order to deter attack. Therefore, Kinsley proposes nuclear superiority.

RHETORICAL CONSIDERATIONS

1. Kinsley is not despairing or fatalistic on the surface. He is cynical about human nature and the dreams of the antinuclear movement. That cynicism and hard-nosed reasoning create a tone of disdain, even hostility, to Schell and the antinuclear movement.
2. See paragraph 19, for example. I do not think such attacks weaken Kinsley's strategy, because they serve only as aside comments.
3. I would say that in such an understatement Kinsley creates an ironic effect to cut what Kinsley sees as the sonorous gloom of the Schell work.
4. Some of Kinsley's sarcastic asides and direct comments may strike us as humorous. See the final comment in paragraph 9—"liberals please note." Also,

the opening line of paragraph 17, as well as the "banging-away" references at the end of that paragraph; and the last three sentences of paragraph 19. Kinsley's humorous sarcasm presumably is aimed at reducing the "portentous" stand of Schell.

5. Kinsley is obviously biased; and I think his criticism is heavy-handed. The passages he does cite, however, are not distorted by removal from context, nor are they misread. It might be argued, though, that Kinsley does twist the logic of Schell's argument in paragraph 17 about our obligation to provide a safe world for generations yet unborn. Kinsley has decided to interpret this statement as a moral obligation "not to deny birth to everyone" possible. Schell did not mean that.

Carl Sagan STAR WARS: THE LEAKY SHIELD

TOPICAL CONSIDERATIONS

1. Before the war the United States was invulnerable because of the vast Atlantic and Pacific oceans. But in the 1950s things rapidly changed: nuclear weapons became far more deadly than those we dropped on Japan; intercontinental bombers were developed; then ICBMs cut delivery time to a fraction of that required by bombers; finally, in the early 1960s, with presidential approval, the nuclear arsenal and delivery systems expanded crazily. In the mid-1960s the United States achieved the ability to destroy Soviet society; a few years later the Soviets caught up.

2. Several reasons Sagan cites. First, the propaganda: we were told and convinced that the more weapons we had the more we were protected; we were also made to fear and hate the Soviets or "the potential adversary." Another reason was the technical aspect, which, people convinced themselves, was beyond them, and the accountability factor was "too remote" for our leaders to be influenced. In short, it was fear and ignorance that kept public resistance low and powerless.

   The pressure that turned things around was growing unease about the deadly development of nuclear defense both here and in the Soviet Union—weapons becoming more numerous and accurate, their delivery times ever shorter, their consequences more appalling. The public's education was advanced by scientists and physicians, who made us aware of horrors that "government officials had apparently chosen not to think about," in particular the inadequacy of the natural environment and the medical profession to cope with the consequences of a nuclear war.

3. As mentioned in paragraph 10, the concept of Nuclear Winter arose out of studies reported on during the 1983 Washington symposium on the environmental effects of a large-scale nuclear war. Many scientists concluded that the consequences would be a global catastrophe. Not only would it bring the

obvious mass destruction of life, but so much smoke and debris sent into the atmosphere would plunge the world into long, deadly periods of sunless dark and cold. Sagan reports that because of the "unprecedented dimension" of such a disaster, "any disposition to minimize or ignore" such widespread effects would be "a fundamental disservice to the future of global civilization."

4. Tantamount to the fears of nuclear war is the helplessness and hopelessness that many adults and children feel. The result is grim acceptance of the inevitable, and the feeling that nothing can be done to better the future. Sagan says that these people too might be counted as "casualties" of our nuclear age.

5. The purpose of Star Wars is to set up shields in space to protect us from incoming nuclear missiles by blasting them in their trajectory with laser beams, particle beams, and electromagnetic guns and projectiles. Sagan sees several problems in Star Wars: enormous expenditure of money (estimated at $1 trillion); deployment of the project would take decades; and, most important, the system would leak, letting enough Soviet warheads through the shield to destroy the United States anyway. It is possible too that, threatened by the offensive potential of Star Wars, the Soviet Union will be tempted to make a preemptive strike to prevent its deployment.

6. The Soviets say they fear a "hidden agenda" for Star Wars—that it would be used offensively instead of defensively.

7. His suggestion is the second option listed in paragraph 13: "to make massive reductions in the nuclear arsenals on both sides."

8. This is left for the students.

RHETORICAL CONSIDERATIONS

1. As the title of the essay announces, Sagan writes mostly about the overwhelming problem with Star Wars: it would be a leaky shield. The thesis statement, then, comes in paragraph 16, where Sagan writes, "After enormous expenditures of national treasure and the deflection of large numbers of first-rate scientists and engineers from useful research, the shield would not work." Rhetorically speaking, the statement is strategically located. Here, two-thirds of the way into the article, is a climactic point in his argument, skillfully and logically constructed with historical facts, available options, and scientific and statistical evidence. In other words, the thesis statement functions as an inevitable conclusion from deductive examination of the evidence.

2. Sagan is well informed. He quotes historical facts; he cites several studies and experts, quoting where necessary; and he brings in scientific, economic, and medical evidence to support his stand. His supporting details are more than adequate to make his argument convincing.

3. This is a clever analogy. He expresses in familiar language the uselessness of a leaky shield. Sagan says that contraceptive shields—and, by analogy, Star Wars—"engender a false sense of security." And we can feel a grimly ironic bite in paralleling life-preventing shields to death-preventing shields. It might be

Sagan's subtle way of reminding us of our biological universality—perhaps to humble us as we consider the prospect of self-destruction.

4. Nothing in the essay would give away Sagan's profession as an astronomer. Some readers might suspect, however, from the logical presentation of the arguments, from the deductive logic he applies, and from the comfortable reporting of scientific details and use of technical language, that the author was either a professional scientist or a science writer.

Charlton Heston **THE PEACE MOVEMENT**

TOPICAL CONSIDERATIONS

1. Heston tells us that 150 thousand Japanese died when Hiroshima and Nagasaki were bombed in 1945. However, had Japan been invaded, he estimates that 4 million Japanese and 1 million Americans would have died. He further speculates that 10 million people would not have been born. These figures lead Heston to imply that the taking of 150 thousand lives led to the saving of 15 million others. One might question his statistics since Japan claims that 300 thousand lives were lost in Hiroshima alone. Also, the number of lives that would be lost in conventional warfare is speculation, not fact. Nonetheless, the basic premise that the loss of life rendered by the atomic bombs saved many more is a powerful one.

2. Heston is thinking in terms of outright global war, the annihilating conflict between the superpowers. Therefore, he concludes that peace is here. Confident in a peace "preserved for almost thirty-eight years by nuclear deterrent by the United States and . . . NATO," Heston feels confident in the nuclear shield that protects him. Those who cry "peace," on the other hand, apparently do so because they perceive the world as an uncertain and dangerous place where tyranny "floats on a rising tide, and freedom lives only on islands of democracy scattered in a sullen sea." Heston reflects on the past and feels confident in the forces protecting us. Others look to the future and fear the unleashing of these same weapons.

3. Heston offers three reasons for opposing a nuclear freeze. First, he argues that it is unnegotiable because, in his opinion, the Soviets cannot be counted on to adhere to a signed treaty. For support, he quotes Lenin who said, "Promises are like pie crust . . . made to be broken." He then refers to numerous treaties the Soviets have broken culminating in the "brutal invasions of Finland, Hungary, Czechoslovakia, and Afghanistan. . . . " Heston concludes, "A nuclear freeze observed by us and broken by the Soviets would be suicidal. . . . " Therefore, he concludes, such a treaty is unnegotiable. Second, a freeze depends on verification and Heston sees verification as almost impossible. He says our surveillance systems are useless in cloudy weather or over areas not covered by their orbits. Furthermore, since testing and design usually are conducted underground, satellite surveillance would be useless. And on-sight inspection is not yet

permitted. Third, Heston says that a freeze would be unequal since negotiation and verification cannot be relied upon.

4. Heston views Soviet society as one where debate among its citizenry is impossible or useless since by definition it defers to the authority of its leaders. He says the Soviet system is an imitation of democracy where trade unions, newspapers, courts, and parliament function with no real power.

5. For the students to debate.

RHETORICAL CONSIDERATIONS

1. Twice in the essay Heston quotes Lenin, in paragraph 13 and in paragraph 22. He also quotes Leonid Brezhnev saying that by 1985 "we will have achieved our objectives in Western Europe. A decisive shift in the balance of forces will enable us to exert our will." These quotations support Heston's point of view because they convey the notion that the Soviet Union ruthlessly wishes to bend other nations to its will and dominate the free world. His key argument, that the Soviets are untrustworthy, is augmented. One could, however, question the applicability of quotations made by such Soviet leaders who have been dead for decades. In a sense, Heston is guilty of pre-nuclear thinking, that is, attitudes based on objectives stated in the past. Since 1985 and the appointment of Mikhail Gorbachev as general secretary of the Soviet Communist Party, the Soviet political and economic system has undergone some radical reforms under the policies of "glastnost" and "perestroika." One fortunate by-product was a renewed interest in lessening nuclear tensions with the West. In December 1987, then President Reagan and Gorbachev met in Washington and signed an historic arms-control agreement eliminating intermediate-ranged nuclear forces (INF). In June of 1988, the two men held a second summit meeting in Moscow that continued the dialogue which still looks forward to an agreement on a 50 percent reduction in long-range nuclear arms. At publication, an agreement on a strategic arms reduction treaty (START) was not reached as Gorbachev insisted that the agreement must restrict America's Strategic Defense Initiative (SDI, or "Star Wars") which the Soviets regard as an offensive threat from space. In short, the differences and tensions still exist, but they are not as great as they were when Heston delivered his speech against the Nuclear Freeze movement. On the other hand, the Nuclear Freeze movement, as of late 1988, remains as strong as ever.

Art Buchwald EVACUATING THE CAPITAL? NO NEED TO HURRY NOW!

TOPICAL CONSIDERATIONS

1. Buchwald's humor surfaces quickly in the essay—in fact, in the last sentence of the first paragraph. The humor is clearly satirical.

2. Buchwald pokes fun at many typically American characteristics and attitudes, including some of these:
   — consumer mentality and credit-card dependency
   — our vanity, having to look good even during an air raid drill
   — trust in government bureaucracy, including the Department of Civil Defense
   — some of the nastier aspects of urban living, such as daily rush-hour traffic jams
   — the Civil Defense Department's romantic view of people during crisis—that is, that host towns will welcome evacuees with open arms
3. He makes fun of the supposition that host-town evacuation plans would work during an actual nuclear attack.
4. If there were a real attack, the conditions would be horrible—panic, destruction, and violence.
5. As usual, Buchwald is satirically attacking some aspect of government, in this case the notion that people could easily escape a nuclear attack on their city. The last line dramatically points out the absurdity—the voice of bureaucratic theory, that of the narrator, scolding reality (the farmer) for not complying with the plan. It looked so good on paper!

RHETORICAL CONSIDERATIONS

1. Lickety Split is humorous for a few reasons, not the least of which is the silliness of the name. The name satirizes the backwoods folksiness and rural friendliness belied by the farmer. Lickety Split also, ironically, means at great speed, which is not how the Buchwalds' evacuation drill went.
2. She perhaps typifies disbelief and doubt and lack of seriousness about the Civil Defense plan. She wants to get dressed; she also wants to turn back, though Art dutifully wants to go through with the drill. The wife also is the sensible one who pulls her husband back 15 seconds before the farmer opens fire on him. She is at once the skeptic and the voice of experience.
3. The farmer typifies the survivalist mentality that might prevail, especially in the rural areas into which millions of American evacuees would supposedly head. The farmer's reaction of distrust and hostility is probably a lot closer to the dark truth should bombs fall than the one the Civil Defense folks assume will happen.

▼PART 12   SPORTS

Jeffrey Schrank SPORT AND THE
AMERICAN DREAM

TOPICAL CONSIDERATIONS

1. Schrank describes our national sports as "ritualistic enactments of the American Dream." He points out that football mirrors modern America's preoccupa-

tion with the gain and loss of political territory and the strategies and maneuverings of war. He sees it, too, as an enactment of a mature stage of capitalism, whereas baseball, which has been replaced by football as the national pastime, he sees as a reenactment of the robber stage of capitalism. Schrank recognizes golfing as a reflection of the American pioneering spirit, in which the golfer seeks to journey through and overcome the obstacles of a hostile natural environment.

2. This question is closely linked to the first. Schrank believes football has become the national pastime because most Americans value a sport that exhibits aggression and tension; that they enjoy worshiping without necessarily imitating "superhuman, mythical heroes; and that they admire it when successes are won, as is yardage in a football game, on the instalment plan." He contends that the former popularity of baseball reveals Americans' interest in the individual, as well as their pastoral yearnings, their love for going to the park and observing in a quiet, leisurely way the finesse of an individual play. He explains that Americans' passion for golf demonstrates their admiration for a pioneering spirit.

3. "Pastoral" can be defined as portraying life in the country in an idealized, conventionalized manner. Schrank points out that baseball games are held in parks (as opposed to stadiums), suggesting that baseball evokes an idyllic country scene on a hot, lazy summer afternoon. Golf conjures up scenes of grass, trees, and the rolling hills of the country. Tennis. Marathons. Golf spectators need to play the game themselves to appreciate it. But because only 20 percent of the nation's courses are open to the public and membership in private clubs is expensive, public participation is still limited. Those who watch the game on television, then, are those who can afford to play it.

4. This is up to the students.

5. The aggression, tension, "upsets," vicarious thrills, and "bruising gladiatorial contests" that result from the clash of bodies on the football field have become more compelling to many Americans than the calm, leisurely pace of baseball, with its quiet focus on the individual players. See question 1 for more on this subject.

6. Robber barons were American capitalists in the late nineteenth century who were able, because of the government's laissez-faire attitude toward the growth of big business, to become extremely powerful and wealthy. The economy was in the hands of these few individuals, who were free to exploit natural resources, government influence, and labor to further their own economic interest. Business today is more controlled and regulated, depending on the cooperation of opposing interest groups (that is, labor and management) to function smoothly. Schrank believes that the Japanese are in the robber-baron stage of capitalism now, which explains their love for baseball. He argues that when they advance to a more mature capitalism, they will prefer football.

RHETORICAL CONSIDERATIONS

1. The first sentence introduces the idea that links Schrank's description of football, baseball, and golf. This sentence also functions as his thesis. In the same paragraph, he points out that national sports express American values, reenact the American dream, and reflect the national character.
2. At the same time as Schrank establishes his thesis in the first paragraph, he introduces a contrast between football and baseball as present and former representatives of the national pastime. This tactic allows for a transition to paragraphs 2 through 4, where Schrank ties in the thesis with a discussion of football, showing why football is becoming the American national pastime and how it reflects the American character. It also allows a transition to paragraph 5 when Schrank moves from a discussion of football as the present national pastime to an explanation of why baseball no longer is. He achieves this move in paragraphs 5 through 8 by comparing and contrasting football and baseball. In paragraph 9, Schrank moves to a discussion of how the decision to play or follow sports other than football or baseball is also part of the ritual of acting out myths. This paragraph serves as a further transition to the description of how one of these other sports fits into this category: golf. Paragraphs 11 through 15 show how golf expresses American values, reenacts the American dream, and reflects the national character.
3. Paragraphs 2, 3, 4, and 7 are possibilities.
4. Repetition of a word is an effective transitional device. It also illustrates an effective use of parallelism.

Margaret A. Whitney **PLAYING TO WIN**

TOPICAL CONSIDERATIONS

1. Ann's statuesque beauty summoned traditional attitudes toward female pulchritude. If you're pretty, you don't have to be active to win approval.
2. Having been voted "Best Hair" in her eighth-grade yearbook, Ann was expected to succumb to the passive beauty syndrome. However, the young woman found that athletic competition was far more rewarding than merely being good looking.
3. The message of sports is to be aggressive and intense. Whitney recognizes in her daughter's drive a reflection of her own determination in winning her doctorate despite the demands of home and parenting. Self-definition is the message and goal of sports. Yes, it is good.
4. In paragraph 7 Whitney says that at home and school her daughter had been told to be still, be quiet, be good. The message: female passivity was a virtue. The same is true in "countless advertisements," complains the author. Many ads promote women as nurturers, passive, and noncompetitive.
5. The majority of ads with women in them project the very cool, passive "ideals" Whitney speaks of.
6. Dubik is a man who measures women according to how "male" they behave. He would applaud Whitney's athletic drive.

7. She says her own "paroxysms of uncertainty [regarding her pursuit of a doctorate] would be eased." She is from an older generation that did not encourage women to aim high and play to win.

8. Whitney says she fears that her daughter—and other females of her generation—might be lured off course by the enticements of men. In her dark fantasies, she imagines a predatory young lawyer trapping her in marriage, motherhood, and a material world.

9. More than just a celebration of Ann's drive and accomplishments, the essay is applause for today's young women who "are not afraid to do . . . [their] best." It celebrates the liberation of women on fields and courts of play—a liberation that comes with "paroxysms of uncertainty" for Whitney and other women of her generation.

RHETORICAL CONSIDERATIONS

1. The central issues in this essay have to do with how today's women have broken out of yesterday's molds. The first sentence bespeaks the case. And although the second sentence underscores how common the situation is, it ends with an expression of the author's dismay—a dismay which unifies the essay. Throughout the piece, Whitney measures her daughter's accomplishments and determination against the forces of tradition.

2. Whitney's discussion of Ann's playing to win is not a springboard to her own self-examination. On the contrary, her daughter's story is a central inspiration, occasionally serving to remind the author of the handicaps she must overcome in pursuing her goal as a doctoral student.

3. The sudden switch to a direct, interior dialogue with Ann has the effect of putting the author in the stands of a game and the reader in the head of a proud mother. A sense of immediacy is created—as if the rest of the piece is a reflection made while at a game. This perspective is returned to at the end as Whitney cheers her daughter on. I think the effect is wonderful, even moving at the end.

4. Lady Astor (1879–1964), or Viscountess Astor, an American born Nancy Langhorne, was the first woman member of the British House of Commons. Extremely wealthy, Lady Astor's name became synonymous with elegance and sophistication. *The Stepford Wives,* named after the Ira Levin novel, is a sardonic science fiction movie about men whose ideals of female beauty, submissiveness, and subservience lead to the forced transformation of women into android wives.

Garrison Keillor **ATTITUDE**

TOPICAL CONSIDERATIONS

1. Keillor believes that the wrong attitude is to laugh off mistakes as if they were only a joke. It's his view that even amateur ballplayers should act like professionals and take themselves and the game seriously.

2. He believes it is important for them to signal to each other and to anyone who may be watching their game that they can conduct themselves as professionally as any ballplayers in the Bigs. Spit correctly, frequently, and at all crucial moments. Pick up dirt, rub it in the fingers, toss it, smooth it, be involved with it. If no dirt is available, pluck grass. Maintain a continuous, rhythmic chatter. Keillor apparently believes such behavior builds morale and encourages team members to play a better and more enjoyable game.

3. Although Keillor points to some of the more absurd mannerisms of professional players, his remarks drive home a valid point. Taking a serious professional attitude toward any worthwhile endeavor would certainly ensure greater success for an individual than if he were to laugh at the challenge and shrug his shoulders at his mistakes.

4. Keillor's close observation of some of the more laughable idiosyncracies of ballplayers suggests that he has been a frequent spectator.

5. Given Keillor's dissatisfaction with his team's lack of professionalism and Schrank's appreciation of the finer points of baseball, it is unlikely that he would invite Schrank to play. If they were on a bench together, Keillor might lean back and reminisce about the time when baseball was the national pastime, when people were less in a hurry, less eager for aggressive, tension-filled clashes on the football field, and more interested in a quiet visit to the ballpark, where they could watch individual players exhibit their talents on the ballfield. See also answers to questions 1, 2, and 5 under Topical Considerations for Schrank's essay.

RHETORICAL CONSIDERATIONS

1. In the first paragraph, Keillor describes his own and his teammates' freewheeling approach to the game, explains that no one agonizes over mistakes, and then remarks: "Except me. This year." At the end of this paragraph, he identifies the problem: attitude. In paragraphs 3 through 5, he contrasts what he feels is the right and wrong attitude toward playing the game. Then, in paragraph 6, he establishes his thesis: he proposes to map out the steps even amateur ballplayers should follow in order to adopt a professional attitude toward the game.

2. Yes. Keillor is very successful in his use of specifics. The first paragraph is a good example to cite. Keillor doesn't just talk about older players who can't play very well any more. He refers to "aging trigenarians and quadros who don't get around on the fastball as well as they used to and who sit out the second games of double-headers." Instead of simply remarking that slow-pitch baseball lets him play baseball without getting hurt, he states specifically that he can play "without getting beaned or having to run too hard." He doesn't stop with a vague reference to a "pretty casual team," but specifies that they are a team that "drinks beer on the bench and substitutes freely," a team that watches a wife or girlfriend let a "pop fly drop six feet in front of her," without agonizing over it.

3. For the most part, his diction is informal and conversational. The other team members are "turkeys." One of Keillor's teammates makes a "dumb! dumb play!" A batter is "this guy." The opposing team "hoots and hollers." His team gets "clobbered."

4. "Chugs" suggests a slow-moving locomotive pulling a heavy weight into second base. A player "*topples* over in the dirt." The right attitude "*sweetens* the game." Their team gets "*clobbered.*" Fielders should "*groom* their areas" and "*flick away* tiny sticks and bits of gravel." A player might have "*bobbled* two fly balls."

5. Keillor uses the imperative mood to speak more directly to his reader.

6. This last sentence sounds like a broadcaster's comment over the loudspeaker during a professional major league ballgame. In effect, Keillor is saying: "Now that we have the proper professional attitude, let's play ball." It's a way to bring the essay to an end while suggesting a new beginning.

Roger Angell **ON THE BALL**

TOPICAL CONSIDERATIONS

1. By closely scrutinizing the baseball, a small object that plays such a pivotal role in the game of baseball, he is able to show instead of simply telling how he feels about this sport. Why Angell wrote this essay seems a more revealing question to ask than the more obvious question: What is he saying?

2. This is up to the student.

3. Baseball is like an old friend to Angell. He has fond memories of the times they've spent together. The last question is up to the student.

4. Probably no other item of sports equipment evokes exactly the same response, because the baseball is the focal point of the game. But other less pivotal equipment might still produce a similar response: a favorite bat, an old glove, home plate, the catcher's mask.

5. The baseball evokes in him not just an intellectual or aesthetic appreciation but a strong, passionate love for the game.

RHETORICAL CONSIDERATIONS

1. He reveals an obvious bias toward it. His apparent sympathy with those who treasure "a true peewee" and mourn its departure is one of the first clues. His perspective becomes more obvious when he refers to the baseball as "ideal" and "perfect" and declares: "Any baseball is beautiful."

2. Descriptive.

3. Angell is developing one main idea: his love for the baseball and the game in which it is used. Divisions would detract from the unity and cohesiveness of his idea.

4. Angell's objective description is attention-getting and intriguing. The subjective analysis that follows it reveals why Angell scrutinizes the physical traits of a

baseball as closely as he does. The transition comes when he says: "But never mind: any baseball is beautiful." There is an orderly progression of ideas in both the objective and subjective sections of this essay: In the objective section, Angell gives the weight and measurement of the baseball; describes a typical ball, starting with the nucleus and moving to the other layers; moves into a comparison of the present version to earlier archetypes; and finishes the section by explaining how a baseball is made and discussing the controversy over the size and feel of the baseballs used in any given game. He switches to the subjective section by stating that any baseball is beautiful, follows with his reasons for thinking so, and concludes with a sentimental description of a favorite baseball.

Robert B. Parker ON THE BENCH

TOPICAL CONSIDERATIONS

1. He bought the weights so that he could build up his muscles and be stronger. He says that when he returned from Korea, he weighed only 148 pounds and that he had to hang on to his wife's arm so that he wouldn't get blown away in a strong wind. Back in the 1950s, weightlifters were looked upon as "muscle-bound freaks" whose manhood was in question.

2. The physical result of Parker's thirty years of pumping was his increase in body weight from 160 to 220—although, he explains, some thirty pounds is excess "tissue." He has also gotten stronger; as evidence, he says that over the years he has lifted one end of practically everything. The psychological effects are shown in his confidence that he can do things with his body that many other people cannot. Although he had "to thrash no bullies" or fight off men who might have made passes at his wife, lifting has made him feel better about his capacity to do both. Pumping iron has also served as a form of exercise for a man who makes his living at the typewriter. Parker does admit some drawbacks; namely, the distortion to his upper body, so much that he cannot be fitted for a suit off the racks. He is also heavier than he would have been had he not started lifting. Finally, there is the constant reminder of "the inequality of nature's dispensation"—that there is always someone stronger and more muscular than you.

3. Parker says he continues to lift weights to maintain his strength. He sees weightlifting as a form of physical improvement, just as study is a form of intellectual improvement. "To be physically accomplished would seem as much a fulfillment of one's humanity as to be intellectually accomplished."

RHETORICAL CONSIDERATIONS

1. The essay is chronologically structured. Parker moves from the early 1950s, when he received his first set of weights (paragraphs 1-4) to the present in paragraph 11. After that, Parker analyzes the effects that thirty years of weight

lifting have had on him, and he concludes with the statements about why at age fifty-six he continues to pump iron.

2. Parker's sharp wit and easy style make an interesting subject even more inviting for the reader.

3. Much of Parker's humor is self-deprecating and ironic. He makes fun of himself by creating cartoon images of himself—the skinny 148-pounder who could easily get blown away; hiding in the bedroom while his wife signs for the delivered weights; calling for help from his wife to lift the barbell off his chest; the man at fifty-six topheavy with muscle in a size 50 suit whose pants are so taken up that the cuffs get caught in the zipper. Irony is the heart of Parker's humor. Likewise, his wife Joan serves in the article as an ironic foil for the man who wants to be big and strong and capable—her Mona Lisa smile as she lifts the weights off him; her need for help in the way Mike Tyson needs help; her telling him in paragraph 16 that he is "oh-for-two" in intelligence and strength. In Parker's popular Spenser novels, the character Susan Silverman, Spenser's lover, is modeled on Parker's wife, Joan, to some extent; she plays a similar role in her relation to Spenser.

4. Probably the students could tell Parker once was an academic, not just from the intelligence of the writing and the vocabulary, but from a couple of clear literary allusions: Hamlet's line, "Ah, there's the rub," and the reference to Philip Sidney's "warrior poet."

5. One may not be able to tell from the essay that Parker is a successful novelist, but knowing that, the reader gets some idea why he might be so—style, wit, sense of story line, delineation of character, and issues of manhood, accomplishment, and honor.

6. Mona Lisa's smile evokes a nearly mystical serenity. Here it is humorously alluded to so as to capture the look of serene, ironic satisfaction of Joan, who is called by Parker to help him out of his predicament—being caught under a barbell intended to make him strong and tough. Arnold Schwartzenegger as a world-class body builder before becoming a movie actor. The allusion is, again, humor by exaggeration—like that to the Mona Lisa smile: just exercise one muscle repeatedly, then another, and soon you'll look like the top pros. Tyson is another exaggeration and a succinct way of demonstrating Parker's point in the extreme. Ben-Gay finds its humorous source in the allusion to the ordinary. Also a witty way of saying he has earned thirty years of aches and pains. The Russian weightlifters is another succinct and witty way of saying a lot. They are famous for their strength and enormous dimensions, including 26-inch necks, 19-inch biceps and guts that looks like a sack of cement. Arnold Schwartzenegger and Philip Sidney function in similar ways. These allusions amplify the dichotomy of body and intellect Parker addresses at the end of his essay in his reference to the warrior poet.

Edward Abbey **BLOOD SPORT**

TOPICAL CONSIDERATIONS

1. Throughout the essay Abbey is steadfast in his opinion that people should hunt only out of the need to eat. The actual ethics of hunting are not addressed until the last third of the essay, and then instead of weighing both sides of the debate, he simply repudiates sport hunting as sadistic, cruel, and the "most narrow and homocentric . . . attitudes" toward animal life.

2. The Abbeys (a family of seven) and other farming families of that era and locale could not subsist by what they cultivated or supplementary earnings from odd jobs. They were too poor and too proud for Relief, so, by necessity, they turned to the forests surrounding them for food.

3. There are two reasons the elder Abbey preferred "poached venison" to legal meat. The stated reason is that "fear tainted the meat"—that is, deer suffering "the terror" of hunter-filled woods didn't taste as good as unscared animals. Whether or not that's true, Abbey's explanation points to a second reason: the old man's contempt for sport hunting. The elder Abbey was a proud man who scorned hunting as a sport; therefore, his poaching just before the season opened was a brazen act of defiance that, no doubt, gave him pleasure. That defiance is also manifest in the way he hunted—"Shot them sitting" instead of on the run.

4. Abbey has learned from his father that one kills animals only out of need. Killing for sport is not just a waste, says Abbey. It shows barbaric disrespect for other life.

5. Abbey says he did a lot of hunting from 1947 through the 1950s when he was a student and, apparently, not well off. He says that as the years passed, his interest in hunting waned, although he continued just as an excuse to head back to nature and get away from the city and crowds—"beyond the wall." Adopting the philosophy of his father, Abbey eventually gave up hunting for meat because his income rose. Like his father, Abbey demonstrates a respect, even a reverence, for wild life. He says that once he put down the gun he reminded himself that with each cow he ate he saved the life of an elk, a couple deer, or two dozen javelina.

6. A sophist is a philosopher or thinker; yet, the term also has the connotation of one who argues fallaciously. Abbey rejects Ortega y Gasset's explanation as specious intellectualization founded on speculations about primitive universal urges. Abbey would argue that such hunting instincts are untestable whereas Thoreau's hunting-out-of-need is demonstrable by history.

7. As with many students, I have heard arguments on both sides of the hunting issue. Nonetheless, I got much from the piece since execution is all. I thought his view of modern hunting mentality as "homocentric" and "utilitarian" particularly insightful. Furthermore, Abbey is a first-rate writer and storyteller whose account of his past and whose ethical stand is impressive. He writes, I think, with an accessible and fine prose voice that one moment raises a smile and the next outrage.

RHETORICAL CONSIDERATIONS

1. "Blood sport" is something of an oxymoron—two contiguous though contradictory terms. "Blood" denotes the vital fluids in all living creatures while it connotes violence and mortality. "Sport" denotes a pastime diversion, game, or outdoor athletic pursuit. The term also denotes one interested in or a participant in sports. With "blood" as modifier of sport, the phrase creates a grim tension since no other official American sport besides fishing involves death. (Bullfighting is Hispanic, and, in most states, cock-fighting and pit bull fighting are illegal.) The title is quite provocative—a good choice.

2. The elder Abbey was a man who could just barely provide for his family of seven. He was a hard-working man who obviously appreciated what little they had, who was loathe to wastefulness, whether expensive ammunition or animal life. Therefore, he held in contempt hunters who killed for sport rather than need. As Abbey portrays him, he was a man of great pride who would rather take on several odd jobs than go on Relief. He was a man of independent means and independent thinking. He hunted with a .22 rather than a shotgun; and he only went sport hunting with Abbey's Uncle Jack on few occasions, and then mostly for "the talk, the wild stories." Consistent with that fierce independence was the old man's code. Neither a joiner nor a man of strict legality, he would kill his deer on his own the night before hunting season officially opened. Also, instead of stalking his quarry à la the "gentleman hunter," he would settle down in the bush against a comfortable tree and wait for an animal to show up—buck or doe. (Presumably killing a doe was illegal.) Abbey also portrays the man as resolute and resourceful as evidenced by the measures he'd go through to bring home his kill. Finally, he was a man who shared Thoreau's own humane respect for and love of nature.

3. Thoreau makes a separate point in each of the three passages. First, hunters are a special breed privileged with special knowledge. How disadvantaged is the boy who has never known the hunt? Second, once past boyhood, any nobody who thinks himself or herself humane will not kill wantonly; for life is precious whether human or hare. Third, if necessary, I would become a hunter and fisherman to survive. Essentially, Thoreau is extolling a hunting ethic: kill only if you have to and only what you need to survive. Abbey enlists the august authority of one of America's greatest writers, greatest proponents of independent thinking, and most famous naturalists. These references add great weight to Abbey's arguments while substantiating the tradition of the author and his father's own philosophy.

4. The turning point from autobiography to philosophy comes in paragraph 17. The turning point is when Abbey says "Let those wild creatures live." From here on the essay becomes more abstract beginning with the next statement: "Let being be, said Martin Heidegger." Even this reference is the first of the three secondary sources Abbey enlists—Thoreau and Ortega y Gasset to follow. I think that the next six sentences are somewhat tangential to the discussion of hunting ethics that runs from paragraph 18 to 20. I would have edited these out since the discussion of the inevitability of death is superfluous. The appeal in

paragraph 18 is mainly to reason as Abbey enlists the sober words of Henry David Thoreau. It may be argued that Thoreau himself appeals in part to emotions when he reminds the reader that " 'The hare in its extremity cries like a child.' " On his own, Abbey sounds very reasonable when, pursuing Thoreau's ethics, says that hunting for "mere fun" is "divertissement, sadism." This is a bald statement rather than a reasoned argument. And in the paragraph that follows, Abbey's discussion is aimed at both the audience's reason and emotions by implication. He argues that " 'harvesting' " is an ugly euphemism and that the economics-mindset of modern hunting "violates both humanity and life." By implication these assertions form an emotional appeal. That is, if readers are stirred by the inhumanity of hunting, their enthusiasm for Abbey's point of view may be larger than otherwise.

5. I like this conclusion. It humanizes the preceding "railing against the sportsman hunter" while bringing us back to the subject of hunting with his father in a creative way. Also, the brief dialogue ends the piece with a touch of warm sentiment and nostalgia. The flashback not only reminds us why the Abbeys hunted, but recreates a little of the ritual, the little-boy excitement, and the guidance provided by the wise old man. As Hemingway pointed out in *Death in the Afternoon,* a writer's best hope of achieving something true was not to talk about emotions, but about the things that cause them. Then, if the writer gets it "right" the reader will reduplicate the writer's emotions, therefore experiencing what the writer experienced. Abbey's conclusion gets it right, I think. Instead of saying he and his brother felt excitement and adventure hunting with their father, he describes a little of the event of hunting. Also, for rhetorical purposes, this conclusion brings us back to early recollections in the essay as well as to the reflections of Thoreau.

Frederic Morton **THE JOGGER'S CODE**

TOPICAL CONSIDERATIONS

1. In the opening paragraph Morton tells us that his behavior when jogging is very different from his behavior when not jogging. He says that when he puts his Nikes on, "rare and precious" "protocol" takes hold of him. He means that with his Nikes come rituals of behavior—"admirable subtleties" that he tries to live up to.

2. In paragraphs 3, 4, and 5 Morton confides in us his codes: he will not lapse into "unduly competitive gesture[s]" when being overtaken by another jogger; he will not show nervousness; he will not look back; he will not lust after female joggers; he will not talk to himself when jogging. In the last three paragraphs he adds that when he overtakes another male jogger, he will never rub in his superiority "by looking at him or even looking haughtily ahead" as he passes. If he overtakes a woman, he will "make an elaborate detour around her." And if he is overtaken by an older jogger, he will act the "complacent sluggard" and

slow down to let the hustler "pull away in glory." If overtaken by a younger one he will whistle to let him know there's a lot of "unused wind" left in him.

3. Morton says that the public views the jogger as someone who is "disciplined, dedicated, responsible and quasi-heroic, a veritable emblem of muscular rectitude." And for the sake of hyperbole, Morton adds that the jogger in comparison to other "high-profile" street people is "meritorious" and "undebauchable," aristocratic and nobler than the pedestrian. "He looms on a pinnacle where machismo and morality meet." Morton is having fun with his mock heroics here.

4. Morton says that as a walker he will "indulge in an appreciative glance" at an attractive woman. "So what? We are all swingers, we *boulevardiers* of Broadway." His point is that he is no different from other men when "leather-shod" on the Great White Way. In his Nikes, he's a different man, a knight—with an inflated sense of himself and his running. Women become degenderized equals, comrades engaged in the self-same noble rituals. And as protocol will have it, when overtaking a woman, he is the gallant knight who cuts "an elaborate detour around her" to spare her the embarrassment of superiority. Yet, when overtaken by a woman, he will try to defy temptations to fake his inferiority and let her pass only to console himself with "self-congratulation" that he has paid his "final dues to running gallantry"—he is a jogger without fear or reproach.

5. This is a clear example of humor by hyperbole. In light of the mock-heroic view of his jogging self, Morton is saying that the jogger combines the righteousness, single-mindedness, and asceticism of the Pilgrim Fathers with the moral responsibility, solitude, and determination of Arthurian knights. Besides the simple fun of high burlesque, there is a subtle side to Morton's satire. By inflating the jogger's self-evaluation he is poking fun at a state of mind. He is also having some fun in suggesting how desperate some of us are for rituals, codes of honor, and noble self-esteem in the anonymity and cement-poured chaos of big-city life—so much so that we need to elevate jogging in the park to allegory.

RHETORICAL CONSIDERATIONS

1. A man's gotta have codes, and this is one of Frederic Morton's. Of course the flat, assertive statement, "I don't jog on Sundays," has a Hemingwayesque ring to it. Although it might be a little subtle for the students, this is where the satirical tone begins working in the piece.

2. He more than adequately illustrates his codes. He also illustrates how his code-behavior as a jogger differs from the more instinctive behavior as a walker. He never looks behind him when he runs yet "the look-behind-thee tic is just normal urban survival procedure." Throughout the essay he distinguishes his code behavior with reference to himself and other joggers, including men and women moving faster and slower than he.

3. I think the essay is quite humorous, though it might be a little sophisticated for some students. Some of its effect is created by the high burlesque, the mock-

heroic style, such as his equating the jogger with the ideals of Pilgrim Father and Arthurian knight. As with all mock-heroic writing, the comic effect is created in the disparity between the subject matter and its lofty treatment. By its very nature satire makes fun of something by distorting it. Not only is Morton poking fun at his own representative jogger attitude and ego, but ultimately he mocks our desperate need to feel like distinct code-heroes in a codeless and chaotic big-city existence. Morton distorts by exaggeration his own attitude as a jogger—an attitude that might be presumed of other joggers. Much of the exaggeration is created by the choice of language. His resolve not to look back to gaining footsteps is reported as elevated code: "My face remains stalwartly turned forward." Or his resolve not to "mar with lust the comradeship of athletes." There is also the bathetically humorous repetition of "I am jogging in Riverside Park." Some absurd exaggerations appear in paragraph 6 with "the world will be out of joint once even runners start blathering in thin air. Runners set up expectancies that have become rare and precious in our time." And we find irony in the essay's last paragraph, when Morton explains how he manages to turn defeat into self-congratulated "gallantry."

4. As stated above, much of the tone is mock heroic. The lofty language contributes considerably to the tone and effect. Not only does Morton resort to French words for elevating the commonplace (for example, "we *boulevardiers* of Broadway," and the final line that euphemizes the risks of losing to a woman), but some of his vocabulary and images are amusingly bloated. In paragraph 7 he writes that to the public the jogger is "a veritable emblem of muscular rectitude." A few lines later he lapses into the alliterative imperative: "Consider the steely steadiness of his stride," followed by the absurdly contradicting observation, "the hardy skimpiness of his athletic shirt." There are also such pompous clichés as the final line of that paragraph—"He looms on a pinnacle where machismo and morality meet."

▼PART 13   ON CONTEMPORARY LANGUAGE

Lance Morrow IF SLANG IS NOT A SIN

TOPICAL CONSIDERATIONS

1. A considerable number of slang terms have faded into oblivion. Consider the language of the youth cult of the 1960s: *groovy, freak, freak-out, funky, uptight, happening, love-in, blow your mind, free spirit, where it's at, mantra, karma, telling it like it is, pothead, good vibes,* and *heavy.* Only a handful of expressions from that era have hung on, mostly drug terminology such as *grass* and *pot.*

2. As Morrow says, Val is a kind of self-parodying slang that does not take itself seriously enough to be granted general use. His speculation about its limited life

span seems accurate. *Awesome* may be one of its few survivors, if only because of its pre-Val existence.

3. Morrow's complaint is that today's slang lacks the playful, slightly renegade vitality of past slang.

4. This is probably so because adolescents, ever fraught with anxiety over acceptance and rebellion, are constantly undergoing identity crises, and they use language as a means of establishing self-images and barriers.

5. This is for the student.

6. Because of the prevalence of computers in industry, school, and the home. It is nearly impossible to avoid some contact with computers in America today, or to escape computer lingo.

7. Slang is always a by-product of subcultures, and as Morrow suggests, some of our subcultures are disappearing while others are being absorbed by the culture at large. Another problem is that in our immediate-access culture, slang almost instantly passes from subcultural to nationwide use and thus is no longer slang. Finally, Morrow offers the possibility that because standard English is losing its prestige and legitimacy, slang, which represents deviation from the norm—is beginning to lose its force. It is less "sinful" today and consequently a little colorless and flat.

RHETORICAL CONSIDERATIONS

1. The linkage is in the clerical references—for example, "monastic scribes" and "abbot" (paragraph 1) and "clergyman" (paragraph 2).

2. This is a fine analogy. Slang is like adolescence—"brief, intense and slightly disreputable." It is also appropriate, for he later observes that the young are fertile originators of fresh slang because they are tribal and nervous about their identity and status.

3. I think his explanation is reasonable. He says *airhead* lacks invective force and metaphorical charm, and that it is too literal, too close to "empty head."

4. Yes, Morrow displays a good sense of humor. He employs allusion, as in paragraph 1 (the Phil Donahue reference), and hyperbole, as in the slangy mock sermons of paragraphs 2 and 4. He is humorously ironic in paragraph 9 when he says, "But if it is *mega-gnarly,* that is excellent." Several of his examples of slang are also funny.

Carol Cohn **NUCLEAR LANGUAGE AND HOW WE LEARNED TO PAT THE BOMB**

TOPICAL CONSIDERATIONS

1. The author explains in paragraph 3 that she wanted a "better understanding of how sane men of goodwill could think and act in ways that lead to what appear to be extremely irrational and immoral results."

2. Cohn woefully learns that language affects one's view of reality. After exposure for a year to "nukespeak" euphemisms, Cohn found her own thinking altered. "How can I think this way?" she wonders in paragraph 4.
3. By abstracting the realities of mass killing with sanitized language.
4. Initially she was suspect of all the claims of phallic-worshiping images in nuclear language. Such claims she had regarded as "reductionist" explanations. She had thought that men of such high intelligence would have been above blatantly embarrassing sexist language. However, as she explains, lecturer after lecturer resorted to sexual metaphors unabashedly. She traces such phallic imagery back to the birth of the nuclear age in the 1945 excerpt in paragraph 14.
5. In paragraph 15, she says that the role of such language makes "the work world of defense intellectuals feel tenable."
6. She explains that "patting the bomb" has the added association of "small, cute harmless" creatures. Therefore, B-1 bombers and nuclear missiles are equated to pet cats and dogs and, therefore, the "lethality disappears."
7. She explains herself well in paragraph 22: that such domestic euphemisms demonstrate a willful and perverse "refusal of accountability—because to be accountable to reality is to be unable to do this work."
8. It was fun, she explains, talking in "quick, clean, light" jargon that made you forget the horrors of what you were really discussing. She says it was fun manipulating "an arcane language," fun feeling "mastery over technology" beyond human comprehension and control.
9. Whenever Cohn tried to switch to regular English, she partonized (paragraph 38). "Peace" was a term never used; its use implied "soft-headed activist" rather than a professional. The most serious problem was that since the jargon was sanitized from human horrors, Cohn found herself beginning to speak of nuclear weapons without thinking about "the people who would be incinerated by them" (paragraph 40). She was learning to "think the unthinkable." Language had abstracted reality. The core issue—and what concerns defense people—she learns, is weapons, not people.
10. She recommends both a "deconstructive project" and a "reconstructive project." Deconstruct the technostrategic discourse so as to allow voice to outsiders of the defense industry; and reconstruct "alternative conceptions of rationality" and "alternative voices" to invent futures other than the unthinkable ones.

RHETORICAL CONSIDERATIONS

1. Cohn's expression "close encounters" can only refer to the 1977 Steven Spielberg movie, *Close Encounters of the Third Kind,* about an alien visitation to earth. Cohn is being ironic, of course, likening her encounter with nuclear strategic analysts to that of alien minds.
2. The opening sentence of paragraph 5 is Cohn's thesis statement.
3. This is a powerful and cogent example, and perhaps the best metaphor for nukespeak. As she explains in the next paragraph, "clean bombs" suggest the "dirty" destruction is only in the radiation, not the blast itself.

4. Very effective. We follow the author as she experiences disbelief and dismay at the abstractionisms; frustration with trying to speak regular English with defense people; even some of the "fun" in speaking the secret argot. The personal account dramatizes and humanizes the language issues rather than analyze them from a distance.

Caryl Rivers **ROCK LYRICS AND VIOLENCE AGAINST WOMEN**

TOPICAL CONSIDERATIONS

1. She says in the first two paragraphs that she enjoyed the rebellious and "slightly naughty" nature of early rock music. And she cites the sexy implications of "Rock With Me, Annie" and the half-hidden gyrations of Elvis Presley on "The Ed Sullivan Show." However, some of today's music contains lyrics that express sexual violence against women. Students should come up with several examples—for example, the recordings of Prince, Twisted Sister, even Michael Jackson.
2. I agree with Rivers, particularly on the powerfully damaging messages of rock videos which are rife with sadistic views of women. For evidence, you might want to consider some of the explicitly violent imagery in the lyrics of such rock groups as Twisted Sister, Van Halen, and W.A.S.P., an acronym said to stand for "We Are Sexual Perverts."
3. As Rivers points out, in most violent shows the bad guys are caught and punished. There is a moral context. But in rock music and videos it is the "heroes" who are committing assaults and rape on women—the singers themselves. Rivers' point is convincing: to young and impressionistic teenagers violence against women is condoned, even encouraged.
4. I don't think she is asking for censorship in the sense of legislation. She is simply calling for attention to the problem and asking for self-restraint and self-censorship by the music industry. She is also asking for protest by people outside the industry—journalists, critics, and parents.
5. It is feasible, I think, for the music industry to exercise self-restraint. According to *Billboard Magazine,* parental protests against music containing Nazi pagan rituals and satanism caused the industry to restrain itself. By 1987, the recording of such music was nearly eliminated.

RHETORICAL CONSIDERATIONS

1. Rivers gives two examples of violent musical lyrics in paragraph 2. For the length of the essay, I think these are not only powerful, but sufficient.
2. Rivers is direct and angry. Yet, she sounds reasonable in so much as she tempers her outrage by saying that she is not calling for outright censorship, but for awareness.
3. Her reference to "Sesame Street" and Big Bird is clearly ironic. The same kids

who were being taught numbers, letters, and sweetness are the same kids being exposed to rape and violence in the same medium. And silence from parents sanctions the messages of such images.
4. Her plea to men is very effective since it suggests that liberation has no gender just as violence does not discriminate ultimately.

Barbara Lawrence **FOUR-LETTER WORDS CAN HURT**

TOPICAL CONSIDERATIONS

1. Lawrence's central thesis is that taboo language dehumanizes and denigrates women because it reduces them to sexual functions or objects.
2. She certainly expresses feminist aims and attitudes in her exposure of the way four-letter words reduce women and deny them their identity and humanity.

RHETORICAL CONSIDERATIONS

1. Four of the five sentences that make up the first paragraph are questions, each used for rhetorical purposes. The first serves as a thesis statement—what she will attempt to answer in the essay. The fact that it is framed as a question suggests the kind of opposition she is up against, particularly from her allegedly liberated students. The subsequent questions also voice typical objections to finding any word obscene, especially from those who might pride themselves on being free of middle-class revulsions. The reference to Norman Mailer challenges the vogue of finding justification in literary realists. The final question is what her students might ask after hearing Lawrence suggest that *copulate* is preferable to *screw*. The sentence, with its cutesy pun ("Cop You Late"), captures the kind of smug prose of some students who pretend not to know what that phony, prissy, middle-class term might mean.
2. See paragraph 4. Lawrence provides scholarly evidence that the word *fuck* is rooted in sadistic, mechanical meaning by referring to the respected etymological dictionary of Eric Partridge and offering a list of related words, all of which have violent connotations. They convince me.
3. There is a clear division:
   BEGINNING: What are the issues and why consider them? (paragraphs 1 through 3)
   MIDDLE: Taboo words are especially denigrating to women (paragraphs 4 through 9)
   END: How those most qualified to do something don't (paragraph 10 to end)
4. It is not clear why Lawrence does not spell out obscene words, but we can make some educated guesses. First, the article originally appeared in the *New York Times* in 1973, and the editors may have decided that even a thoughtful and often scholarly discussion of obscenities might offend readers if they were spelled out. A second and perhaps more likely reason is that Lawrence doesn't

want to give the words the dignity of print. Her attitude and arguments throughout the essay testify to that.

5. Paragraph 7 is a good example. She proceeds from the topic sentence, a general statement about "tabooed male descriptives," to specific illustrations—for example, "testes." This is the basic paradigm for most of her paragraphs.

6. In paragraphs 4 and 5 Lawrence illustrates the difference between denotation and connotation. In fact, this distinction is the basis of her argument. Synonyms for sexual intercourse denote the act, but the ones she cites connote brutality, pain, sadism, and victimization. (It might be interesting to have your students list sexual synonyms for copulation and discuss the connotations of mechanism and brutality.) The same distinction is made in paragraph 8. *Skirt, broad, chick, pussycat,* and *piece*—these words, argues Lawrence, are never used denotatively when referring to women but rather are used in their demeaning connotations. *Pussycat,* for instance, suggests softness, suppleness, gentleness, warmness, nonaggressiveness, and animal inferiority.

Rachel L. Jones WHAT'S WRONG WITH BLACK ENGLISH

TOPICAL CONSIDERATIONS

1. Labov advocated the bidialectal approach of the 1960s. Essentially this view holds that blacks should maintain their dialects—practice them at home and with peers—but should also develop a standard dialect to use in society at large. Jones is strongly opposed to bidialectalism because the nonstandard grammar and pronunciation of black English often creates yet another obstacle to black success in a predominantly white society.

2. Some of Jones's arguments echo those of opponents to liberal theories of bidialectalism—people who argue that dependence on nonstandard language is a handicap in the outside world. Jones, while recognizing the "colorful" quality of black English, sees little use for it.

3. For Jones, "talking white" means using standard or proper English.

4. In paragraph 8 she admits that at times the rhythms of people caught up in "some serious rap" sounds "natural and right" to her. But she adds that whenever she hears young blacks speaking in a dialect she thinks how handicapped they will be out looking for a job or in school.

5. She counters Baldwin's romantic claim for the linguistic "vitality" of black English with the historical truth that noted black politicians inspired their hearers in eloquent, "proper" English, not dialect. So too did black writers, including Baldwin.

6. The concluding paragraphs are a forceful and convincing culmination of Jones's arguments.

RHETORICAL CONSIDERATIONS

1. The title is ambiguous: it can be read either as a statement—as intended—or, despite the lack of punctuation, as a question—and one that could be considered mildly defiant.
2. The clearest thesis statement is in the next-to-last sentence of the essay. The thesis is implied elsewhere, as in the third sentence of the first paragraph.
3. The piece begins with a famous white linguist's bold assertion about black goals, an assertion that is immediately refuted by the experience of an unknown black student. This strategy cleverly pits theory against experience, white liberalism against black reality, what should be against what is. The theories of bidialectalism were popular in the 1960s; Jones's point is that many blacks in the 1980s view the use of black dialect as an obstacle to success in American society. Her returning to the views of Labov at the very end of the essay rounds off the argument begun in the introduction.
4. Obviously, Mr. Labov would not approve, nor would people sharing his views on bidialectalism. And, certainly, some blacks would not like hearing Jones argue that black English is an ineffective medium of communication in American society. Hers is a conservative position, which may offend liberal sensibilities.

Russell Baker **LITTLE RED RIDING HOOD REVISITED**

TOPICAL CONSIDERATIONS

1. Baker draws much of his jargon from governmental bureaucracy, academia, and law. We can refine these somewhat with these examples from the essay.
   CRIMINAL JUSTICE: "when it attained interface with an alleged perpetrator" (paragraph 3); "aggressive posture" (paragraph 16)
   PSYCHOLOGY: "Sensing that he was a mass of repressed hostility intertwined with acute alienation" (paragraph 4); "An interior malaise made itself manifest" (paragraph 8)
   SOCIOLOGY: most of paragraph 8
   MEDICINE: paragraphs 9, 10, and 15
   SCIENCE: paragraph 11
2. There are several examples of repetition throughout the story. The most obvious is the opening line: "Once upon a point in time. . . . "
3. One clear political allusion is that to Richard Nixon's favorite line, in paragraph 6, "making one thing perfectly clear."
4. Jargon has the power of turning even a fairy tale into mere ink.
5. Nearly every fairy tale ends with the positive assertion that "they lived happily ever after." Instead of being killed, the wolf is here resurrected to the land of television commercials—a final satirical jab at America's love affair with the tube. Baker is also criticizing television for being a prime disseminator of gobbledygook.

RHETORICAL CONSIDERATIONS

1. Yes, the essay accurately reproduces the obfuscating, numbing nature of bureaucratic and academic jargon.
2. Replacing *little girl* with *a small person* might be a satirical swipe at movements to degenderize English with bland but nonprejudicial substitutes. *Senior citizen* is, of course, a euphemism for old person. *Delivery and transportation is* redundant and dehumanizing in that the charitable, loving act is reduced to mere mechanical movement. The poetic *deep woods* is rendered bloodless as *forest of indeterminate dimension,* with the last two words used to demystify *deep.*

▼PART 14 ON DEATH AND DYING

Lewis Thomas ON NATURAL DEATH

TOPICAL CONSIDERATIONS

1. Thomas finds all the current fascination with dying and death remarkable, as if learning how to die properly is reserved for "the specially trained." His point is that even though human beings have been dying since the beginning, people today need to be instructed on how to perceive, prepare for, and cope with the subject. Perhaps because past generations were closer to the natural world, people regarded dying as a phenomenon as natural as living. What Thomas does in this essay is put the experience in context of the natural order of things.
2. Thomas defines "natural" by association here. His reference to the elm tree and the "cat-chewed" field mouse creates a context for the death of the two young MPs and, by association, all of humanity. All dying is "natural." "Unnatural" death refers to an attitude of those who cannot grapple with the subject matter, who regard human death as a higher phenomenon. The author's focusing on the subject of pain makes clear how the body contains natural mechanisms for the preparation of death. Like the elm feeling no pain, both mice and men are suspended painlessly in the jaws of death. In short, as Montaigne says, "Nature will in a moment fully and sufficiently instruct" us on how to die.
3. We see trees dying and being cut down all the time. Therefore, we might regard such deaths as automatic and trivial, more "natural" than our own. But our own dying is part of the same ecological cycles, cruel as they might seem. See above for more.
4. His first reaction to the sight of the mouse dangling from the jaws of the cat was outrage. The creature, no doubt, was suffering "pain beyond bearing." Nature's cruelty was the "abomination" he could not accept. However, after medically reconsidering the event, Thomas deduced that the endorphins released by the creature's hypothalamus and pituitary gland most likely spared it pain. There is no way of knowing for sure that the mouse died without struggle. But Thomas

finds consolation in the speculation. Not unnecessarily cruel, nature rescued the animal's final moments from agony. Likewise, similar mechanisms are natural components of our own bodies as witnessed by Montaigne and the two dying soldiers.

5. Montaigne records the experience of nearly dying. In the first passage Thomas quotes, the philosopher makes death seem like drifting off to sleep. He uses gentle images of floating and "growing languid" and "letting go." His point is that nature adjusts us to our dying by setting us free gently. Although Montaigne does not say this, nor Thomas directly, the dying experience is the wonderful result of millions of years of evolution, a process that favors the organism—a "death right," perhaps.

RHETORICAL CONSIDERATIONS

1. Thomas gives us three anecdotes. The first, the death and removal of his elm tree, illustrates several things: the sudden, unexpected quality of death; the naturalness of the process (it "caught the blight this summer"); and the casual regard of the "natural" process of trees dying, "done automatically and trivially" (the crew "took it down . . . and carted it off . . . , everyone singing"). This anecdote used in paragraph 5 connects to the second anecdote about the mouse specifically on the matter of pain. Just as the elm, lacking "pain receptors," did not suffer its end, so the mouse dying in the cat's teeth went without struggle. The point is that in the "end game," as Thomas calls death, nature spares its creatures. The third anecdote climbs the chain of being to humans at the moment of death. That the mortally wounded MPs could chat casually dramatically illustrates the extraordinary response the body has to its own death—a response that is common to mice and men and as natural as life.

2. The tone of this piece is reflective, lightly philosophical, and friendly. Although the essay was written for the *New England Journal of Medicine,* Thomas writes less for his medical colleagues than he does for the general reader. His profession obviously comes through in paragraphs 6 and 7 with several technical terms that lend credibility to his speculations. However, balancing the scientific terminology are occasional colloquialisms: "dropped stone dead" and "went ahead and died anyway" (paragraph 4), "a hunch about dying" and "close call" (paragraph 8), and "end game" (paragraph 11). The overall tone might be considered "reader-friendly." His language is accessible and his discussion of the subject matter is positive without being frivolous, and insightful without being heavy or moribund.

3. The clearest statement of his thesis is the last sentence in the final paragraph. It is a statement that he builds up to from the first line. And coming where it does following the anecdotes, references to Montaigne and his own reflections, the statement has the impact of QED.

Elizabeth Kübler-Ross **ON THE FEAR OF DEATH**

TOPICAL CONSIDERATIONS

1. The increased attention to the subject of death really has something to do with the increasing population of older people in the country. The median age in America is rising, so more and more people are concerned with the realities of coping with their own mortality and that of peers. But even more important, dying today is more frightening because it has been made "more lone, mechanical, and dehumanized" by increased technology.

2. When the author was a child she, along with others, was invited to visit the dying farmer. By so doing, she shared in the preparations of his death. The anecdote illustrates her point that both the dying and the survivors need to accept the inevitability of death and the eventual loss. It also illustrates how children in particular need to share in death so as to better accept its reality and the fact that they are not alone in their grief. By contrast to dying in a hospital bed hooked up to machines and surrounded by strangers in medical whites, the farmer dying at home is far less lonely and impersonal.

3. Children who are excluded from death sense that "something is wrong" and end up distrusting adults. They will sense the loss and, "depending on the age and personality of the child" (paragraph 18), may develop "an unresolved grief." Kübler-Ross says that these children might also regard the particular death as "frightening, mysterious," and too traumatic to cope with successfully.

4. Toward the end of the essay, Kübler-Ross argues that severely ill patients be regarded as persons not things, that their emotional needs be addressed not just their medical needs. Dying today, she observes, is made all the more lonely and dehumanized because patients are removed from their homes to hospitals where they find themselves surrounded by machines and impersonal technicians more concerned with treatment than the patient as a person. His or her feelings, opinions, or wishes may be disregarded; and when asserted, they are often met with "infusions, transfusions, a heart machine, or tracheotomy if necessary." In short, Kübler-Ross argues for death with dignity.

5. It is clear that the "we" at the end of the essay refers to people in the medical profession—physicians, nurses, and technicians. In paragraph 27, Kübler-Ross wonders if the increased "mechanical, depersonalized approach" might be medics' "defensiveness" against their helplessness in the face of death as well as their own mortality. Instead of taking time to hold a dying patient's hand, they fill their attention with numbers and equipment thereby emotionally detaching themselves from the event of any human identity with the patient.

RHETORICAL CONSIDERATIONS

1. Up to paragraph 18, the essay is essentially "explanatory" in nature—mostly regarding the fear of death and how societies cope with it. Although paragraph 17 is mostly analytical in nature, Kübler-Ross begins her criticism of making death a taboo for children. The first clear statement of an argument comes at

the beginning of the next paragraph where she says "It is equally unwise to tell a little child who lost her brother that God loved little boys so much that he took little Johnny to heaven." From here to the end her argument is loud and clear: that despite all the advancements in medical science, we are moving farther away from the days when people died "in peace and dignity."

2. The last sentence in paragraph 2 serves as a thesis statement for the essay.

3. Paragraphs 1 through 10 serve as a beginning: despite the advancements in medical science, humans suffer a universal fear of death. The middle, paragraphs 11 through 17, deals with older customs of dealing with death. The end of the essay, from paragraph 18, talks about today's fear of death and the way we attempt to deflect the anxiety and turmoil.

George Whitmore AIDS: BEARING WITNESS

TOPICAL CONSIDERATIONS

1. Writing about others with AIDS, Whitmore felt, rendered him a special immunity against the awful disease. Working to "bear witness" against it seemed to make him feel somehow exempt as if it was other people's disease—as if the journalist's objective detachment kept him safe.

2. Whitmore says that he learned of discrimination first hand when his neighborhood dental clinic, where he had been treated for years, informed him that it would no longer clean his teeth.

3. Whitmore says that it was only when he retreated to the woods of Petersborough, New Hampshire that he "came face to face with everything I'd successfully evaded about AIDS." Before that, he managed to pretend that he didn't have the disease so as to keep working. The fact that the telltale lesions had not spread to his face helped the pretense. Apparently maintaining an active social life allowed him to evade the truth. That and, ironically, his interviewing of dying men who "remained safely at arm's length." The realization took place while taking a shower one day in New Hampshire. "A transformation had taken place and it was written on my skin," Whitmore writes in paragraph 17.

4. Just as Kübler-Ross explains, death or in this case the anticipation of it produces feelings of grief, despair, fear, and rage. Whitmore's own anger is first anticipated in the "confusion and rage" of the junkies "in an airless room in the South Bronx" where his research took him (paragraph 9). In paragraph 19, Whitmore talks specifically about his anger. He says that the "petty frustrations of urban life get magnified to the limit of tolerance." He would find himself angered by minor aggravations—cabbies overshooting the crosswalk, a customer at the head of a line arguing with the teller. Even the sight of old men who remind him of his own growing debilitation, ironically "in the prime of life." Yet, it was anger—"life-affirming anger"—that saved him from drowning in "the ocean of pain and loss" and allowed him to write his book.

5. Like Whitmore, Jim Sharp confronted AIDS straight on. Instead of evading his

fate, he became a successful counselor to others stricken with the disease while serving on the board of a Houston AIDS foundation. Whitmore through his writing and Sharp through his community service have chosen to fight AIDS by serving others. In a sense each has helped defeat the popular myth that AIDS is an unstoppable plague that renders helpless any efforts to slow the course and ease the suffering. Like so many other victims, Jim Sharp has chosen to exercise his talents and resources as a counselor just as Whitmore has employed his gift as a writer to help dispel the myth of powerlessness. No doubt their life-affirming efforts help make possible their own will to go on and not succumb to fear, grief, and despair that might otherwise consume them.

6. For the student. If nothing else, the personalizing of the disease may sensitize students to the magnitude of the tragedy of AIDS. This article is very personal and dramatizes the cruel fate of people confronted with the possibility of death in the prime of their life. It is hoped that students will better understand the crisis and that any myths about the disease or prejudices against AIDS victims will be dispelled. As Whitmore illustrates, what is needed is compassion and will. Too often the prejudice against AIDS victims is an excuse for homophobia, racism, and hatred for drug addicts. Homosexuals have been the most common target for scapegoating, and although Whitmore, a homosexual, does not address that issue, his first-person account should evoke empathy in even the least liberal-minded reader.

RHETORICAL CONSIDERATIONS

1. The title is a clever, bitterly ironic one. "Bearing witness" implies one party rendering an account of the circumstances of another. And that is what Whitmore was doing before he contracted the disease: he was writing articles about others with AIDS. "I was trying to bargain with AIDS: If I wrote about it, maybe I wouldn't get it. But AIDS didn't keep its part of the bargain." Ironically, the article is really about his own confrontation with the disease—his bearing witness to the devastating impact of the disease upon himself. Besides denoting "carrying," "bearing" carries the connotation of suffering, enduring, and carrying a heavy burden—which is the fate of people like Whitmore who know they have the disease. However, instead of simply concentrating on his own suffering, Whitmore switches attention to Jim Sharp, Edward Dunn, and Frederico, therefore fulfilling another meaning of "bearing"—that of "conveying" or "disseminating." And in this sense Whitmore is fulfilling his highest obligation as a writer: educating those who haven't borne witness.

2. The analogy is an apt one. Like AIDS itself, the beeper is a shrill reminder of his condition. It never lets him forget he has the disease. It regulates his life. As Whitmore says, his body, like the mindless device, "fails to perform" at regular intervals. And it ticks away as does his life. The mechanism is an objective correlative to the alarm that goes off in his mind when for a while it lets itself forget the awful reality that he might be dying.

3. "Robert" is the name given to the teddy bear Edward Dunn gives to Whitmore.

As Edward explains to the author, the gift represented "warmth and gentleness." It is named after Dunn's lover who dies of AIDS. That Whitmore gives Robert to the dying Frederico links all three AIDS victims in a cruel fate while dramatizing the need for compassion.

4. The cruel and horrible fate of little Frederico in his crib is made harshly vivid through select details. In particular are the specific medical details—the "stretch-knit bandage material knotted at one end and fastened around his wrists with adhesive tape . . . to keep him from scratching himself or pulling out tubes"; the "nasal-gastric tube taped to his cheek and nose" through which he is fed; the intravenous tubes through which he is fed antibiotics; and the infant carrier in which the child is propped up in his crib, facing a "blank wall" sporting a gratuitous "No Smoking/No Fumar" sign. These are contrasting images that remind us of Kubler-Ross's descriptions of how dehumanizing hospitals and medical equipment are for adult patients. In bitter contrast are the impervious "musical mobile" and "heart-shaped balloon that says 'I Love You' "—suggestions of what Frederico's life should be full of: love and happiness. Then there are the descriptions of the child himself—the "little sighs" expelled from his mouth; how his "eyelids twitched"; his fair "translucent" skin and the "violet veins through the skin of his eyelids"—all images of the baby's freshness and his fragility.

5. The piranha is a fitting metaphor for the disease of AIDS—an ugly, mindless, and vicious flesh-eating predator.

6. These details underscore the brutal unfairness of the disease that kills the most innocent victims. First, is a coffin too small for a child too young to be in it. Second, the "gouges and scrapes and scars" in the wood remind us of Frederico's impoverishment even in death. He was parentless and abandoned by his relatives with the exception of Mr. Schult.

7. The last line is isolated for dramatic impact as it reminds us of the bitter irony of Whitmore's onetime feelings of immunity from the disease. The rather bald expression seems stripped of everything, but hardened resignation.

Benjamin Spock A WAY TO SAY FAREWELL

TOPICAL CONSIDERATIONS

1. Dr. Spock cites three examples, all expressing denial and avoidance. The first is that of physicians, who often ignore symptoms of cancer. Instead of seeking treatment, doctors prefer to "hope against hope" that their suspicions are unfounded. They deny signs of their disease until their conditions are inoperable. The second example comes from Spock's own experience—that of the mother who called him to say that she had found her infant son dead in his crib. Clearly she wished Spock's immediate presence. Instead, Spock directed her to rush the child to a hospital. At a later time, Spock says he realized that his directives were his way of avoiding the situation of death. The third example emphasizes

the difficulty of talking about imminent death—the mother of three who was dying of cancer yet who never asked her doctor for a diagnosis. Apparently she wished to remain ignorant, fearing the worst. Similarly, the attending physicians, including Spock, never spoke bluntly to her about her condition. Years later Spock realized that perhaps the patient had wished for a frank discussion but was discouraged by her physicians' reluctance. "Perhaps she was only following his cue." Though Spock begins his essay saying, "I don't fear the dying as long as it's not very painful or lonely or lacking in dignity," these examples give him pause. He knows he cannot predict with certainty what his reaction to death will be.

2. Spock wants cheerful, straightforward types around him, he says—people who would discuss openly any concerns he might have but who would avoid gratuitous inquiries.

3. Spock compares hospitals to clean factories designed to produce diagnoses and treatments. He stresses the impersonality of hospitals in paragraph 13: "A stream of staffers barges in, as if from outer space: history taker, physical examiners, temperature and pulse takers, meal servers, bath givers, stretcher pushers, X-ray technicians, bed makers, pill pushers, specimen takers." The catalogue makes the patient sound like an item on a production line, and reveals the impersonality of the hospital environment.

   On the other hand, Spock feels that a hospice offers a far more humane alternative. The goal of the hospice is to let a person die as comfortably as possible in a homelike setting, surrounded by family and familiar possessions. Medical attention, in the form of heavy medication, is provided only to ease pain and not to prolong life.

4. For the student to discuss.

RHETORICAL CONSIDERATIONS

1. Clearly, the architect is a man of style. His dashing appearance is emphasized by his broad-brimmed hat, expensive suit, and flowing silk bow tie. A single detail destroys his urbane image: "His jacket, however, was dotted with food spots" (paragraph 10). That detail conveys the embarrassing onset of senility.

2. In paragraph 8 Spock discusses his aversion to treatments designed not to cure illness but to postpone death. He writes, "But I would not want to be kept alive with antibiotics, infusions, transfusions, anticancer drugs or radiation if they were just to postpone my death for a few months. . . . " He concludes this solemn reflection with "especially if I had lost my marbles." The colloquial surprise at the end jolts the reader and reduces the solemnity. Similarly, at the end of paragraph 12 he wonders, if he were in unbearable pain, his doctor would be willing to give him a terminal dose of medication. He concludes with "and will Mary have the nerve to jab the needle?" Again the colloquial aside softens the somber subject matter. Spock uses this blunting technique at the end of paragraph 14, where a discussion of death in a hospice is followed by "That's the departure for me." The most effective use of this technique occurs

in the last sentence of the essay. Following a description of his self-designed memorial service and the biblical passage about children, he cannot resist the upbeat conclusion: "Then there could be a cheerful cocktail party somewhere nearby."

3. The opening phrase sounds like the beginning of a will. It alerts us to Spock's intention of addressing the issue of his own death. Instead of giving directives about the dispersal of his worldly goods, he directs people how to say farewell to him.